JOSEPH DE FINANCE, S.J.

AN
ETHICAL INQUIRY

A. Cainth. Sacerd (signature)

Rma 18 JUL 95

EDITRICE PONTIFICIA UNIVERSITÀ GREGORIANA
ROMA 1991

Original title of the work
ÉTHIQUE GÉNÉRALE
© 1988 – E.P.U.G. – ROMA

Translated and adapted by
Michael O'BRIEN S.J.

IMPRIMI POTEST

Romae, die 4 octobris 1990

R. P. GILLES PELLAND, S.J.
Rector Universitatis

IMPRIMATUR

Dal Vicariato di Roma, 5-10-1990

© 1991 - E.P.U.G. - ROMA

ISBN 88-7652-632-3

EDITRICE PONTIFICIA UNIVERSITÀ GREGORIANA
Piazza della Pilotta, 35 - 00187 Roma

AUTHOR'S PREFATORY NOTE TO THE ENGLISH TRANSLATION

In this English edition of *Ethique générale* (Rome, 1967) the author has introduced some very slight improvements and additions, as he did earlier for the Italian edition of the same work.

He wishes to express his deep gratitude to Father Michael O'Brien, S.J., whose translation, faithful but not slavish, is marked by a concrete, figurative style which gives easier access to the ideas. Thus he has achieved his purpose, which is and must be first of all service to the student.

INTRODUCTION

I. DEFINITION.

1. — The word ethics is derived from the Greek "ēthos", which means custom, a habitual way of acting, character[1], a meaning which is also possessed by the Latin "mos", "moris". It is from this latter that the word *mores* and the adjective *moral* are derived. Consequently, from the etymological point of view, *ethical* and *moral* are synonymous, and it is for this reason that, in their substantive form, the two words are often interchanged. People speak indifferently of *ethics* or morality so as to designate what we can provisionally define as: *the science or philosophy of human action*. — Nowadays however, as we shall see, many writers, particularly in the Anglo-Saxon world, make a distinction between the two terms.

One might well believe that in speaking of *ethics*, the substantive "science", or "philosophy", is implied. Historically, this is not so. *Ethics* is linked, through the Latin "ethica", with the Greek neuter plural "ēthica", whose meaning is simply: what concerns human conduct, and which Aristotle (or the person who edited his writings) has used as the title of his two great moral works: the *Eudemian Ethics* and the *Nicomachean Ethics*. The Latin equivalent would be "Moralia" (which was the title given by St Gregory the Great to his wellknown Commentaries on the book of Job). In its Latin usage, the word "ethica", in common with the words "physica", "metaphysica", "politica", at first retained its plural significance (Ethics, Physics, Metaphysics are indeed the forms which we still use in

---

[1] It means also, in the plural: habitual abode, residence, dwelling-place (of men or of animals). A short form, "ethos", also exists and its meaning is: custom, usage. — The Indo-European root appears to be "suedh-", where "sue-" is a reflexive form and "dh-" has the general sense of placing, making... The primary meaning would then be: an action that is one's own (mine, yours etc.) or else: something that has been appropriated, "made one's own" (for example, a house). Compare the Sanskrit *svadha*: "custom, rule, law, accustomed place, home, (wonted state), ease, pleasure...', A. A. Mac Donnell, *A Practical Sanskrit Dictionary*, Oxford — London, 1924, p. 370b.

English); subsequently, it came to be treated as a feminine noun and it is from this usage that the French "éthique" has resulted.

In the above definition (the science... of human action), the word *action* should be understood in the strict sense, as corresponding to the Aristotelian "praxis": as such, it is distinct both from speculation ("theoria") and from making ("tò poiein": artistic and technical activity, the production of goods, the transformation of the milieu etc.) [2]. What is of consequence from the artistic and technical point of view is the successful completion of a particular work: that the statue should be beautiful, that the table should be evenly balanced on its legs, that the aeroplane should be capable of flying... The agent himself and his action are of importance only in relation to the desired effect. But, from the ethical point of view, it is these — and, more precisely, the agent as revealed through his action — that are of primary importance.

If then we restrict ourselves to etymological considerations, the simple description of the mores or patterns of behaviour, whether of mankind in general or of a particular society, deserves to be called (the science of) ethics or morality. Indeed, in the writings of those who are regarded as moralists *par excellence* — Aristotle, his disciple Theophrastus, La Bruyère, a more recent imitator of this latter, etc. — this type of description occupies an important position. — In our own days, phenomenologists, "characteriologists", sociologists etc., have continued to provide such descriptions; their methods are, of course, more highly developed than those of Aristotle etc., and they are at pains to preserve an attitude of neutrality from which all judgments of value are excluded [3].

---

[2] "To make and to act differ since, as is said in Book IX of the Metaphysics, the effect of the former is on matter exterior to the agent, as occurs in building, cutting etc., whereas the latter activity — when he sees and wills etc. — remains interior to him", I-II, 57, 4. — See Aristotle, *Met.*, 8, 1050a 23 at end, and *Nicom. Eth.*, I, 1, 1094 a 4-6; VI, 4, 1140a 1-23. — But note that the distinction between acting and making is not identical with that between immanent and transitive activity. The conclusion of a process of reasoning is undoubtedly immanent; yet it does not directly come under the jurisdiction of ethics. On the other hand, action naturally tends to effect a transformation of the milieu. Accordingly, while both action (understood as distinct from "making") and speculation are immanent, the former, in virtue of the dynamism that is proper to it, tends to shed its immanent character.

[3] See, for example, Ed. Westermarck's lengthy study, *The Origin and Development of Moral Ideas*, 2 vol., London 1906-1908. — As sociological studies

But should ethics be limited to description? There are not lacking those who think so. To be more precise, in place of the former "theoretical" and "normative" ethics which, they maintain, can provide no "scientific" certainty, they would wish to substitute a "science of mores", which would treat the moral factor as simply one of the many factors that are operative in society: the purpose of such a science would be to describe the customs, the moral judgments and sentiments that are prevalent in different societies: to determine the laws which govern their origin, their development, their evolution, their disappearance, in the way that "science" investigates physical phenomena. This is the view of L. Lévy-Bruhl, for example, in *La morale et la science des moeurs*, Paris, 1903.

According to this author, a "normative science" is a contradiction in terms. It is the task of science to pronounce on what is, not on what ought to be. Science, he insists, has by its very definition no other function than to know what is. It is, and cannot but be, the resultant of the methodical study, by the human mind, of a portion or an aspect of the given reality. It tends towards, and issues in, the discovery of the laws which govern phenomena. Examples are provided by mathematics, astronomy, physics, biology, philology etc. The goal which is aimed at in moral theorizing is, on the contrary, essentially different; the purpose here is to lay down the law. While science simply aims at knowing what is, ethics, on the contrary, wishes to prescribe what should be[4]. Since this is the function of ethics, it cannot, Lévy-Bruhl insists, be called a science.

On the other hand, there are many nowadays who, as a result of the influence of "linguistic analysis", equate ethics or moral philosophy with the logic of moral discourse. Its role would thus be limited to the definition of moral terms or

---

of moral facts, the following may be noted: E. Durkheim, *Le Suicide*, Paris, 1897 (English translation: *Suicide*, G. Simpson, New York, 1951); P. Fauconnet, *La Responsabilité*, Paris, 1920. As applications of the phenomenological method to the study of moral facts, we mention in particular M. Scheler, *Ueber Ressentiment und Moralisches Werturteil*, Leipzig, 1912 (French translation: *L'homme de Ressentiment*, Paris, 1933); *Reue und Wiedergeburt*, in *Vom Ewigen im Menschen*, Leipzig, 1921 (French translation: *Repentir et Renaissance* (in *Le sens de la souffrance*, Paris, 1936); P. Ricoeur, *Finitude et Culpabilité*, 2 vol., Paris, 1960 (Vol. I, *Fallible Man*, translated by C. Kelbley, Illinois, 1965). P. Valori, *L'esperienza morale*, Brescia, 1971.

[4] *Op. cit.*, pp. 10-11.

concepts (good, evil, just, unjust, right, duty etc.), to the determination of their relations both with one another and with non-moral terms or concepts, to the drawing up of the rules for their correct usage, through distinguishing instances in which they retain their strict moral significance from those in which they have either a non-moral significance or no significance at all etc. Ethics understood in this sense could never prescribe anything in an absolute fashion: it could do no more than show whether or not a particular requirement is consistent with the basic principles or values which the individual accepts. But it depends on each one to choose this particular system of values rather than some other: concerning this choice, moral philosophy has no guidance to offer.

J. Hartland-Swann provides an example of this approach: "The moral philosopher... is concerned primarily to discover the logical significance of the concepts used, and how sentences, embodying moral problems, are related to or differ from sentences embodying non-moral problems. For him therefore these problems are, if I may put it this way, *problems in morals*. Moreover, any sentence — whether interrogative or not — in which moral or seemingly moral concepts are embedded is equally interesting from his point of view and therefore equally constitutes a problem in morals"[5]. "It has sometimes been held... that the moral philosopher's task is to settle definitively what moral principles are in fact valid, and what ends are really valuable in themselves... We shall see however that the moral philosopher *as such* is in no position to act as a moral arbiter except in a very restricted sense — a sense which will require to be defined very exactly"[6].

2. – The positive science of mores, or the logic of moral discourse: these definitions of ethics are proposed in opposition to the older and common notion. What is contained in that is something quite different: and it is precisely this that the above-mentioned conceptions wish to exclude: the normative, practical (in the full sense of the word) character of its con-

---

[5] *An Analysis of Morals*, London, 1960, pp. 18-19. Concerning ethics conceived as science of language, see especially R. M. Hare, *The Language of Morals*, Oxford, 1952. Hare does not claim in any way, however, that the choice of a supreme principle or of a model of life is arbitrary and irrational.

[6] *Ib.*, p. 21. By these last words the author means that moral philosophy can help to throw light on complex situations and in this way lead to the appropriate solution, pp. 183-184.

clusions. Ethics is *normative*, not in the way that logic is, namely, with regard to the correctness of our thinking, but with regard to the goodness of our living, the right orientation of our existence. It is a *practical* science, not simply because it treats of human *action*, but also because it aims at guiding this [7]. Moralists are not content to describe human conduct: they intend to judge and to rectify it. They propose rules and give warnings; they provide counsels and issue precepts, so as to make clear to men the path of *right living* and to help them to walk upon it.

This can however be understood in two ways:

1) One can have in mind the *art of living*, the technique for acquiring happiness (understood in an individual or in a social sense). This was — to speak in a general way — the conception which the philosophers of antiquity had of moral philosophy; everything was oriented towards the sovereign good, whose possession will bring man happiness.

---

[7] Not, it is true, by indicating what this particular individual in these particular circumstances should do and how he should behave, given his character, his state, his situation etc., — such decisions call for the exercise of the virtue of prudence and, in a certain measure, for the "direction of conscience" — but by enunciating the general rules and formulating the principles which should regulate moral judgments. Consequently, ethics is not a practical science in the sense that it immediately issues in action: it is not "practico-practical" in the way that the prudential judgment is, nor, in the expression of J. Maritain, "practically practical", as is casuistry and as are most writings on religious living. Immediately, it rectifies the intellect; it is speculative and it is as such that it is a science. But it is not purely speculative: it is concerned with action, which it aims at rectifying through the rectification of the intellect. The retrospective judgment of actions already performed is secondary: an action can be judged as right or wrong only if one already has in one's mind the notion, under the form of a practical requirement, of what this rectitude involves, as will be explained later.

On ethics as a practical science, according to St Thomas, see J. Maritain, *Distinguer pour unir*, Paris, 1932, pp. 618-627 and 869-896 (English translation: *The Degrees of Knowledge*, G. Phelan, London, 1959, pp. 311-316 and 451-464); *Science et Sagesse*, Paris, 1935, pp. 227-240 (English translation: *Science and Wisdom*, B. Wall, London, 1940, pp. 137-145); Y. Simon, *Critique de la Connaissance Morale*, Paris, 1934, pp. 79-87 and J. E. Naus, *The Nature of the Practical Intellect according to Saint Thomas Aquinas*, Rome, 1959, esp. pp. 42-68. — It is worth noting the position of John of Saint-Thomas, for whom ethics becomes a practical science only through being perfected by the virtue of prudence; of itself, it would be purely speculative. See *Ars Logica*, p. II, q. 1, a. 4 and q. 27, a. 1 (*Cursus philosophicus*, ed. Reiser, t. I, pp. 276-277 and 826-827). — There is a good exposition in O. Lottin, *Morale fondamentale*, Paris – Tournai, 1954, pp. 4 seq.

As is in no way surprising, even those whose view of moral philosophy is by no means that of the early philosophers have no difficulty in allowing that it indeed provides men with a technique for acquiring happiness. Lévy-Bruhl regards his proposed *science of mores* as the foundation on which can one day be built a *moral art*, that will indicate what has to be done in order that the well-being and betterment of society be assured. In their turn, those who regard ethics as no more than a species of logic are the first to insist on its usefulness for solving the problems which life presents.

2) But the science of *right living* can be also understood as the science which is concerned with what is *worthy of a human being*. To live rightly will not then be the equivalent of: to live happily, but: to live *as one should*. Through living well, a human being is deserving of esteem, praise, approval etc.: through living badly, through acting in ways that are not worthy of a human being, he is deserving of blame. An ethics of this kind will not say: act in this way if you wish to be happy (or: since you wish to be happy), but: act in this way if you wish to live in a way that is worthy of a human being (and you *ought* so to live). — This conception of morality was not unknown to the philosophers of antiquity: Plato, Aristotle, the Stoics often spoke of what was or was not becoming to a human being, of conduct which was in conformity with or contrary to reason, of what should be done or should be avoided etc. The thesis of Brochard, according to which classical Greek thought was ignorant of the notion of moral obligation, is not sustainable [8]. Nevertheless, it has to be acknowledged that the objective necessity which the good imposes, the duty to act in accordance with it, were of less consequence to these thinkers than its attractiveness and desirableness: indeed, so marked was this character of their thought that their ethics could often be more aptly entitled the aesthetics of the moral life — a confusion which was fostered by the close link, in the Hellenic mind, between the notions of the good and the beautiful [9]. It

---

[8] V. Brochard, *La morale ancienne et la morale moderne*, «Revue Philosophique», 1901, I, pp. 1-12 (reproduced in *Etudes de philosophie ancienne et de philosophie moderne*, Paris, 1912, pp. 489-503).

[9] The moral or "noble" good is called in Greek "kalon" rather than "agathon"; the "noble man" (in classical usage), the man who is fully human is "kalos kagathos". The Latin word "honestum" presents a similar ambiguity. — Cf. L. Ollé-Laprune, *Essai sur la Morale d'Aristote*, Paris, 1881, pp. 76-81.

could be said that for them obligation was simply a datum of their ethico-religious experience: they had an appreciation of it through the demands which life made on them, but they did not reflect upon it scientifically. It is a notion which can, in general, be said to be present in the language of the people, or in mythical interpretations, but which scarcely finds a place in the rational systematization of morality. On the contrary, in the theories which have been elaborated under the influence, direct or indirect, of Christianity, this notion holds an important position — particularly in Kantian ethics, where its role is pivotal (nn. 115-116).

These two conceptions of morality are by no means mutually exclusive. There is no *a priori* reason why a life which is in conformity with man's ideal should not also be for him the path, and indeed the sole path, which leads to happiness; in fact, as we shall show — and in so doing endorse the spontaneous moral insight of mankind — this is the truth of the matter, so that, in consequence, neither of these two aspects of ethics can be adequately developed independently of the other. That this is so can be readily verified by reflecting on the more celebrated moral systems. That of the Scholastics, for example, and in particular that of St Thomas, is ordinarily presented as an ethics of happiness; nevertheless, obligation is very definitely included in it[10]. Kantian ethics, in its turn, concludes by reintroducing, as an element of the sovereign good, the notion of happiness (n. 118).

3. — As is plain from what has been said, the definition of ethics, if it is not to be allowed remain in the region of vague generalities, depends, partially at least, on the way in which moral problems are approached and resolved. The definition we propose can, in consequence, be fully justified only through the investigation we are now beginning. At this stage, it has to be to some extent a postulate. With this proviso, our definition of ethics is that it is a normative science of human actions and, in consequence, of human existence. Normative is here under-

---

[10] Unless one prefers to say — as has been maintained apropos of St Thomas — that such an ethics is rather a theology of man's return to God, or, more exactly, of God as directing and guiding man to his end by means of grace, the law, the virtues etc. See in this sense R. Guindon, *Béatitude et théologie morale chez saint Thomas d'Aquin*, Ottawa, 1956.

stood in the second of the two senses mentioned above, namely, not as helping to foster the art of living happily, but as involving rules which are of themselves worthy of a human being's acceptance, duties in the strict sense of the word, obligation that is absolute or categorical. (This does not at all mean that obligation is the essential element of morality). Ethics is the science which is concerned with what man ought to do so as to live as he ought to, so as to be what he ought to become, so as to attain his supreme value, so as to be true to his *raison d'être*, true to that *towards which and for which he exists*. In two words: ethics is a science which is *categorically normative*.

If ethics is understood in this way, the field with which it is concerned is more determined and more restricted than it would be if what were in question were simply a description of mores, or a technique for leading a happy life. In accordance with our definition, human action is considered more under the subjective or, better, personal, aspect: as *free and deliberate*. This character would not be of such great importance if all that were in question were the art of achieving happiness, since it would then be possible to foster or hinder one's happiness through inadvertent actions, actions concerning which no free decision had been made etc. A sleep-walker could injure himself just as he could also, by means of an opportune suggestion, be led to perform some salutary exercises which he could never have brought himself to perform in his waking state, or could be helped to rid himself of a habit which was injurious to his health. An ethics of happiness seems then, at least at first sight, to be reconcilable with the denial of man's freedom, and there is historical evidence to show that this conjunction has, in fact, often been accepted: the ethics of Spinoza provides an example. For the same reason, an ethics of happiness will, at times, show itself lacking in respect for the autonomy of the individual person. It will believe that it renders human beings a service by deciding for them what path they should walk, so as to arrive at happiness, and by exerting pressure on them, if they are silly enough not to want to walk this path of their own accord. — But once obligation is a feature of morality, man's freedom has also to be granted, since if this is lacking, obligation is meaningless (n. 40). In other words, ethics, as it is here understood, is not concerned with any kind of actions that proceed from a human being, actions that are his in any way whatever, but with actions that he performs in the way that is proper to a human being, and by which his activity is distinguished from that of all the other beings of our experience: actions that are performed with advertence and liberty, as we shall soon consider at more length (nn. 13-14), actions that are in the full sense of the word *human* [10bis].

4. – In order that our definition of moral *philosophy* be complete, one further point has to be made.

For most people, moral laws are also endowed with a religious character. They are considered to be divine commands; knowledge of them is often attributed to a divine revelation etc.

As *philosophers*, we have no hesitation in admitting that such a revelation is possible and, even more, that it is highly desirable. As *Christians*, we know and believe that such a revelation has, in fact, been granted. — Nevertheless, philosophical ethics, precisely because it is philosophical, is not concerned with that knowledge of morality which has come to us through revelation: its proper field is the knowledge of morality which the natural light of reason brings to us. In other words, philosophical ethics is concerned with what lies within the range of our reason, with what can be described and interpreted, with the requirements of morality insofar as these can be rationally appreciated and justified. To say this, however, presents us with a problem to which we shall soon turn our attention.

Accordingly, the complete definition of ethics which we propose is that it is the *categorically normative science of human actions, pursued in accordance with the natural light which reason casts.*

This rational character of philosophical ethics does not at all mean that our approach to morality should be rationalist and "secularized", so that we systematically ignore the religious reality and religious values, any more than it means that our investigation has nothing to contribute to the formation of a genuinely Christian attitude to life. On the contrary, ethics, as well as the other branches of philosophy, is incorporated into the Christian synthesis, to the extent to which it studies the structures and the requirements that are

---

[10bis] Nevertheless A. C. Ewing tries to show how determinism can be reconciled with an ethics of duty and responsibility, although these words then do not have the same meaning as they do for a non-determinist, *Second Thoughts in Moral Philosophy*, London, 1959, pp. 156-166. So too Lucius Garvin, *A Modern Introduction to Ethics*, Cambridge, Mass. 1953, pp. 78-100. But if the words do not have the same meaning, one is not speaking of the same thing.

essential to man and which, precisely because they are essential, are preserved in the Christian order, and ground the possibility of an encounter and a dialogue with non-Christians. The more philosophy is genuinely rational, the greater the service it will render to the faith; but reciprocally, all other things being equal, the more a philosopher is a genuine Christian, the more profound will be his appreciation of what acting in accordance with reason requires.

II. THE IMPORTANCE AND LEGITIMACY OF ETHICS

5. – The importance of ethics does not seem to require either proof or elaboration. What question is of greater urgency for a human being than the question of how he is to act? — Without doubt, this question is at first concerned with the problems to which his needy and threatened condition gives rise and, as such, have an immediate urgency: he has to live and, in order to do so, he requires food, clothing, shelter; he has to support those who depend on him, rear his children; he has to help maintain the unity of the group on which the security and prosperity of all are dependent. But once these problems begin to be less pressing, so that he comes to have some time for reflection, he cannot but question himself on how he is actually behaving, and on how he ought to behave so that his life may have meaning. He is confronted, at least in an implicit manner, with the problem of what moral living requires of him. For, as is only too obvious, it is not general and abstract formulas which involve him in this problem: it is in and through extremely particular, extremely concrete, extremely "day-to-day" problems that the question of the meaning of life, of the orientation he is to give to it, presents itself in him and to him.

Since ethics is nothing other than a reflection on this vital problem, it is, obviously, an eminently human science. — Nevertheless, numerous objections have been, and are still, raised concerning the legitimacy of an investigation, defined in the way which we have done so above.

Certain of these objections are based on quite general grounds: their examination and refutation is the task of other branches of philosophy, so that we are, in consequence, here entitled to presume that they have been, in fact, examined and refuted. Examples of such objections are those which proceed from a refusal to recognize the validity of metaphysical and metaphenomenal knowledge, to admit that there is a human nature which is fundamentally the same in all human beings etc. — In particular, the objection of Lévy-Bruhl, which we have already noted, against the notion of a normative science (n. 1), springs from positivist and "scientific" prejudices: no legitimate source of certitude other than "science", in the modern sense of the word (mathematics and the natural sciences), is acknowledged, so that all certain, methodical and systematic knowledge — hence "scientific" in the older sense of the word — of values and norms is thereby excluded. More profoundly, this objection implies that there is a divorce between, on the one hand, what is good, and, on the other, what exists and what is true: even though the existence of such a divorce is frequently asserted nowadays, any sound meta-physics excludes it. The question raised is, however, one to which we shall have occasion to return [11].

Among these quite general objections, the objection made by the logical positivism of an Ayer, for example, or of a Stevenson, can also be listed. Ethical judgments, in common with aesthetical and metaphysical judgments, have, as such, no meaning. The reason for this is that a meaningful proposition, which is not also a tautology, has always to be empirically verifiable. Now an ethical (or an aesthetical, or metaphysical) proposition is not a tautology: if I say: it is evil to lie, I do not repeat myself, as I would if I were to say: to lie is to lie. But, on the other hand, a proposition of this kind is not empirically verifiable. There is nothing given in our experience, nothing observable and verifiable, which corresponds to the apparent predicate "evil". Consequently, propositions of this kind simply express our subjective reaction: aversion, admiration, desire, fear etc. Note carefully that they express this reaction; they do not signify it. In saying: it is evil to lie, I by no means intend to make known my state of conscience: it is of lying that I speak. But I so speak of it that, literally, I say nothing. My

---

[11] The work of L. Lavelle can be here instanced as at one and the time a magnificent affirmation of the ontological character of value and of the value-character of being.

proposition has no more content than a cry of joy or pain. It is a simple emotive reaction.

Since they mean nothing, ethical propositions are neither true nor false. Hence, any investigation concerning them can only be aimed at discovering the subjective, emotional reasons by which they are explained: ethics, as a science, is entirely reduced to psychology and sociology [12].

---

[12] "For in saying that a certain type of action is right or wrong, I am not making any factual statement, not even a statement about my own state of mind. I am merely expressing certain moral sentiments. And the man who is ostensibly contradicting me is merely expressing his moral sentiments. So that there is plainly no sense in asking which of us is in the right. For neither of us is asserting a genuine proposition», A. J. Ayer, *Language, Truth and Logic*, 2nd ed., London, 1951, pp. 107 seq. Consequently: "There cannot be such a thing as ethical science, if by ethical science one means the elaboration of a 'true' system of morals. For we have seen that, as ethical judgments are mere expression of feelings, there can be no way of determining the validity of any ethical system, and indeed, no sense in asking whether any such system is true... It appears, then, that ethics, as a branch of knowledge, is nothing more than a department of psychology and sociology", *ib.*, p. 112.

Charles L. Stevenson (*Ethics and Language*, Yale, 1945) accepts this "emotive" theory. Less radical in a sense than Ayer, he allows that ethical terms contain a descriptive element but maintains that their strictly ethical character is derived from their emotional colouring, in consequence of which they are capable, in their turn, of exciting the emotions of the hearer or reader. More precisely, according to Stevenson, a judgment such as "A is good" can be interpreted in accordance with two patterns: 1. I approve of A. Do likewise. 2. A possesses certain qualities or relations X, Y, Z — but in addition I approve of it and invite my hearer to do the same. (Obviously, this approbation is not signified descriptively but expressed emotionally). — Quite clearly, this approach rules out the possibility of a science of the good, since *approval* cannot be the conclusion of a process of reasoning. Stevenson concedes, however, that it can be supported by reasons, but, in the final analysis, it depends on the subject's own decision.

In this context, the Neo-Positivists of the Vienna — later to become the Chicago — circle can also be cited: Carnap, Reichenbach, by whom Ayer was manifestly inspired. — Previously L. Wittgenstein, in his famous *Tractatus Logico – Philosophicus* (1921) had excluded ethics and metaphysics from the realm of discourse. Not indeed that he denied the reality of their object but because this object, according to him, pertains to the sphere of the "mystical" ("Das Mystische"), so that it remains entirely ineffable and inexpressible, *Tractatus*, 6. 42 (*Schriften*, Frankf. a. M., 1960, p. 80). But, "whereof one cannot speak, thereof one must be silent», 7 (*ib.*, p. 83).

The point of departure for this school of thought, at least where ethics is concerned, is undoubtedly to be sought in G. E. Moore (*Principia Ethica*, Cambridge, 1903). So much does he insist on the singular and irreducible character of the good (which he conceives of as a "non-natural quality") that he

This objection loses its force once it can be shown that there is a true moral experience, an authentic grasp of value (nn. 28-31). In addition, the postulate on which the objection is grounded has at once to be challenged and rejected. To consider every meaningful and non-tautologous proposition as no more than the description of an experience, presupposes a distorted analysis of knowledge, of thought, of language. Indeed, not only is the assumption on which the objection is based, arbitrary: it is also contradictory. The reason for this is that such an assumption is itself evidently neither tautologous nor empirically verifiable, in the sense intended by its proponents; and, nevertheless, they would be very irate if one were to retort that, in that case, it can mean nothing.

6. – What is of greater consequence to us are the objections which are born, so to speak, in the interior of the ethical domain and, in consequence, directly affect it. Of these, we shall here note two, to which attention is frequently drawn nowadays.

On the one hand, not only is there a diversity in moral practice but, what is even more remarkable, there is also a considerable diversity in the moral judgments passed on these practices, among different peoples and in different eras: this undoubted fact seems to exclude the possibility of an ethics whose laws would be universally binding. — On the other hand, in a given society, different moral systems, even though based on different and even opposed principles (reason, human nature, one's own interest, the common interest, sentiment etc.), all arrive at more or less the same practical conclusions, conclusions which, as if by chance, are, more often than not, in accordance with the standards and practices that are accepted in the society in question. One could conclude from this that moral rules are not really dependent on the basic principles: these latter, and the systematic construction for which they

---

ends by almost making all ethical speculation impossible. One cannot say: the good consists in this or in that (for example, in pleasure, utility etc.) but simply: the good is the good. — Nevertheless, ethical propositions have a meaning since the word good *signifies* something. One is here far from Ayer's radicalism.

On this entire school, see, for example, M. J. Charlesworth, *Philosophy and Linguistic Analysis*, Pittsburgh-Louvain, 1959.

provide the foundation, would seem to be an artificial ideology which is foreign to true morality. The practice of morality has no connection with philosophical morality.

These difficulties will be examined in due course. For the moment all we shall say is this:

The diversity of moral conduct and judgments, of which the first objection makes capital, is concerned with the determination of what is to be done or avoided; it leaves intact the universality of the principle that something — what is good — is to be done, and that something — what is evil — is to be avoided. Even more, it supposes this: without a certain fundamental accord concerning the notions of good and of evil, it would be meaningless to say that an action which some people consider to be good, others consider to be evil. "What is true on this side of the Pyrenees, is false on the other": nevertheless, the two sides of the Pyrenees have to agree on the meaning of the words *truth* and *falsity*.

In addition, as we shall see, the moral consciousness of the human race is not restricted to this purely formal consensus. This extends at least to the more general determinations of what is to be done and to be avoided (nn. 185-190). As we shall also see, it is possible to explain why disagreements arise. But whatever about this, and even granting that the lack of agreement is as wide as any one wishes to claim, the objection would by no means prove that ethics is impossible or useless. This conclusion could be arrived at only through a diligent examination of the question, and to commence such an examination is to engage in the study of ethics.

With regard to the convergence of the different systems towards the same conclusions, note that not only is it not as perfect as one may be tempted to maintain, but that also, and more importantly, in the measure in which it is realized it proves only one thing: that prior to all philosophical investigation, human beings have the power to lead lives that are moral. Ethics, no more than the other scientific disciplines, does not start from zero. Man does not create the universe: he interprets and transforms it. The same holds true for that other universe which constitutes the moral world, with its norms and values. The role of philosophy is to elucidate and interpret this primary datum, to decipher its intelligible structure (for example, by defining carefully the notions of the good, of justice, of rights and duties), to discover its basic principle and foundation, to submit to a critical examination the standards and norms of the individual conscience, of society, of tradition etc.: in this examination, the criterion will be the harmony of conscience etc., with the principle that is acknowledged to be primary in morality, and the purpose of the examination will be to make these standards and norms more explicit, to correct them if that should be necessary, or to eliminate those which contradict this principle. In brief, the role of philosophy is to help make the moral world ever more rational.

Moreover, these difficulties will gradually vanish in the course of our investigation. *Solvitur ambulando*. If an ethics is built up and stands firm, it is because it can be built up.

7. – We turn finally to a difficulty of an entirely different order, a difficulty which has been raised by J. Maritain in particular. It is concerned not with the possibility of ethics in general, but with the possibility of an ethics which, even though elaborated by natural reason alone, would also claim to be a practical science in the full sense. The difficulty can be formulated in tjhis way:

It is impossible to determine what man ought to do, without first knowing what he "exists towards", what is his goal or ideal. Now, in the actual historical order — and it is only with this that ethics is concerned — the only end, the only true ideal, that man has ever had is supernatural: but the knowledge of this end and ideal is beyond the range of reason: it is only by the faith which is man's response to God's Revelation that they can be known. Consequently, a purely rational ethics, considered simply as a practical science, is radically insufficient.

Another way of presenting this objection is to stress that a practical science is concerned with human action. (The science aims at providing the required guidance). But human actions occur in the actual historical order, not in some ideal and merely possible one. What the science has to concern itself with, are existing beings — things or persons — not with beings that can be thought of, not with essences. The conclusion follows that a correct judgment concerning human action, and in particular a directive judgment — such as those which ethics aims at formulating — requires a knowledge of reality as it actually is and, in particular, of man as he actually is. But in the historical, existential order, man's destiny has always been supernatural. If knowledge of this is lacking, or is not applied, there will be a divorce between the guidance provided and that which is actually required[13].

All this certainly hits a nail on the head: it also touches on one of the most delicate points in theology, namely, the relation between nature and grace. But, in any event, it remains true that the latter does not destroy the former, but presupposes and perfects it. Natural requirements, requirements which spring from the very essence of man — from that without which he would cease to be man — are present in whatever state this nature may happen to exist, even though, it is true, the way in which they will be satisfied will vary with the different states. Inasmuch, then, as human reason is capable of knowing the essential structure of man, it is also capable of knowing the requirements which form the core of concrete morality. Man's supernatural destiny would render moral philosophy impossible, only if human nature ceased to be human in consequence of its elevation. But, if that were so, the being who is elevated would no longer be man...

The essential and permanent structure of man — his absolute nature — of which we are here speaking, is very different from the "pure nature" of which the theologians speak, and which has never in fact existed. If it had existed, it would have been a particular instance — one could call it the zero point — of man's absolute nature[14].

---

[13] See J. Maritain: De la philosophie chrétienne, Paris - Bruges, 1933, pp. 102 seq.; Science et Sagesse, Paris, 1935 pp. 268-278 (Science and Wisdom, pp. 161-167). Maritain readily admits the possibility of a natural ethics, or of "moral philosophy inadequately considered", but he denies that such a philosophy is a genuine practical science. M.-M. Labourdette writes in the same sense in an article in "Revue Thomiste", 1948, pp. 142-179, Connaissance pratique et savoir moral. — The opposite view is taken by Th. Deman, Sur l'organisation du savoir moral, "Revue des sc. phil. et théol.", 1934, pp. 270-280, and J. M. Ramirez, De philosophia morali christiana, "Divus Thomas", (Frib.)., 1936, pp. 87-122. — Ch. Boyer, Morsale et surnaturel, "Gregorianum", 1948, pp. 527-543.

[14] See J. Fuchs, Lex Naturae, Dusseldorf, 1955, pp. 43-56 (English translation: Natural Law, Dublin, 1965, pp. 41-58); Theologia moralis generalis, Pars prima, Rome, 1960, pp. 66-88.

The essentialist point of view, which sees in man's elevation to the supernatural order and the requirements which flow from this, a way — and indeed a pre-eminent way — in which man's nature is realized and its requirements satisfied, requires to be complemented and corrected by an existentialist and more theological vision. In accordance with this latter, human nature is seen to be willed and created with a view to its elevation, and to the activity which results from this (in the sense that every existing being, every "substance", exists with a view to its activity, St Thomas, *Summa Theol.* I, 105, 5 etc.).

8. – But it is not the truth of this which J. Maritain contests. If he denied, purely and simply, that a philosophical ethics is possible, he would not have undertaken the task of writing a book with the title of *Moral Philosophy* [15]! For our part, we are the first to acknowledge that a philosophical ethics remains imperfect in its own order, since there is in it a *twofold lacuna*.

The first lacuna is concerned with the motivation which it provides for observing moral rules: motives derived from reflection on man's nature, motives which natural reason can provide..., constitute neither the total nor the supreme motivation of a Christian conscience. The Christian acts out of *filial* love for God, out of fidelity to the Spirit of Christ, so as to collaborate in His redemptive work, so as to honour in himself and in others the dignity which is theirs as sons of God, members of Christ etc. Motivations of this kind are not provided by natural reason.

The second lacuna is concerned with the question of what, in the concrete, is to be done and to be avoided: we have already indicated the reasons why this is so.

We readily agree, then, that philosophical ethics is only an *imperfectly practical* science.

Practical sciences are, as such, concerned with concrete reality, with the theatre in which human activity occurs. If there is a hiatus between them and this concrete activity, they remain imperfect in their own order (imperfect, that is, *as practical sciences*). — It is true

---

[15] *La philosophie morale.* I *Examen historique et critique des grands systèmes*, Paris, 1960 (English translation: *Moral Philosophy*. I. *A historical and critical survey of the great systems*, London 1964).

that as *sciences*, they remain on the level of universality: to consider an action in its singularity is the role of prudence (n. 192). But, precisely because they are *practical* sciences, they cannot leave out of consideration the existential conditions in which man lives. An ethics which is complete as a practical science should treat of man in accordance with the conditions in which he actually is: not in accordance with the conditions which are peculiar to this or that man in this or that particular situation, but in accordance with the existential conditions in which, in the world which is ours, in the economy which is ours, every man finds himself necessarily and in fact. — Nevertheless, the lacunae which are present in philosophical ethics do not invalidate the conclusions at which reason can arrive, nor do they make it impossible to establish a corpus of moral truths which are scientifically correlated.

Note, in addition, that here, as in other spheres, Revelation is of great assistance to human reason, in that it enables us to discern, more fully and more surely, the requirements of the moral order. This assistance is twofold: *subjective* — we are inwardly strengthened and enlightened, the "eyes of our heart" are purified etc. — and *objective* — truths and norms which reason, left to itself, could doubtless have discoverred but, in fact, has failed to do so, are made known to us. We should then be in no way surprised if, at times, it appears extraordinarily difficult to provide completely convincing reasons in favour of what Revelation, or the Magisterium which interprets it, presents to us as a requirement of natural morality. The more we descend from the general and abstract to the particular and concrete, the more numerous are the factors which have to be taken into consideration: very often the knowledge of these factors escapes us or remains hidden from us (nn. 188; 189).

A final point that should be noted: man's existence, considered concretely and historically, presents problems which the unaided resources of reason are incapable of resolving in a fully satisfactory manner. (The problem of evil provides a particularly good example). The explanation of this is that man's existential condition cannot be deduced from the consideration of his "absolute nature". Faced with perplexities of this kind, philosophy should recognize its limitations: such an acknowledgement can dispose the philosopher to accept the light which comes from a higher source (n. 313).

III. ETHICS AND THE OTHER BRANCHES OF PHILOSOPHICAL
    KNOWLEDGE.

9. – Since it is a *practical*, or better, *speculativo-practical*,
science, moral philosophy, as regards its purpose and goal, is
clearly distinguished from metaphysics, cosmology, psychology
etc.: all these pertain to the purely speculative part of philosophy and do not, of themselves, command anything. On the
other hand, it has a certain affinity with logic and aesthetics,
which are both normative. Just as ethics provides the rules of
right living, so does logic provide the rules of *right thinking*, and
aesthetics the rules for *judging rightly* where art etc., is concerned. There is however a difference: only ethical rules are
absolutely imperative. Logic does not say: you ought to reason
correctly, but: if you wish to reason correctly, this is how you
should proceed. Similarly, aesthetics does not say: you ought to
judge with taste, or: you ought to produce a work of beauty,
but: if you wish to be a man of taste, if you wish to produce a
work of beauty, be guided by aesthetic canons. Ethics, on the
contrary, says without qualification: you ought to be good and,
to this end, you ought to act in this manner. Consequently,
only ethics can be said to be normative in the strict sense (n. 3).
It is for this reason that its role in this order is supreme. All
other practical or normative sciences (aesthetics, medicine etc.)
are in some way subordinate to it. This is not to deny that
these other sciences have their own proper principles, their
own finality, their own sphere within which they alone are
competent to decide. It is not for the moral philosopher to
decide whether this statue is beautiful and "says something",
whether this remedy will produce the desired effect, whether
this form of government is efficient. But because ethics treats
of an end and value which transcend and judge all other values
and ends, it is the science which in the last resort, is em-
powered to regulate for all human activities, and, in consequence, to pass judgment on the specific norms by which they
are guided. This subordination is all the more strict, all the more
intrinsic, according as the normative science in question is more
concerned with man as such. From this point of view, politics
and medicine have, obviously, more direct and more intimate
links with morality than have architecture or agriculture.

10. – How is the distinction between speculative and practical philosophy, or, more precisely, between metaphysics and ethics, to be understood? Two extreme replies have been given to this question.

On the one hand, there is the reply of absolute intellectualism: this tends to disregard the distinction and to treat ethics as no more than a logical consequence, or even as a mere chapter, of metaphysics. This was the attitude of the Stoics and, in particular, of Spinoza; his *Ethics* is primarily a study of metaphysics developed in a geometrical fashion. It is noteworthy that, in both instances, the approach is pantheistic. — But if this reply were true, the practical character of moral philosophy would disappear; unless some new factor intervenes, nothing will result from theorizing that is not itself theoretical. As Hume has noted, in a phrase which has won undying fame among English moralists, an "ought" can never be derived from an "is" [16]. (This could also be expressed as: an imperative can never result from an indicative). — Another objection to this view is that if the moral life is absorbed into the intellectual life, what will measure the true worth of a man will be the keenness of his intellect — a conclusion which is far from human.

Are we then to swing to the other extreme of absolute moralism and maintain that ethics is entirely independent, so that conscience, or the heart, is completely dissociated from what is speculative? This is the position of Jean-Jacques Rousseau and, more recently, of F. Rauh in *L'expérience morale* (1903), whose influence on French university circles has been so profound [17]. It is however Kant who, more than anyone else, has made this separation: even further, he has reversed the relation between ethics and metaphysics. In his view, it is the latter which, to the extent to which it still remains possible, is dependent on the former (which alone is capable of attaining to

---

[16] *Treatise on human nature*, III,1, 1.

[17] *L'expérience morale*, Paris, 1903. Rauh had first attempted to base morality on metaphysics: *Essai sur le fondement métaphysique de la morale*, Paris, 1890. On Rauh's thought consult G. Gurvitch, *Morale théorique et science des moeurs*, 2nd ed., Paris, 1948, pp. 135-164. — On the general problem of the relation between morality and metaphysics, see R. Le Senne, *Traité de morale générale*, Paris, 1947, pp. 685-734 (conclusion).

the "in itself"). This type of moralism has strongly impregnated the metaphysical speculation of the 19th century.

This approach runs the risk of preparing the way for moral scepticism. Theoretic reason cannot be indefinitely muzzled, forbidden to call morality in question and to seek its intelligibility. Practical and theoretic reason are but one and the same reason, as Kant himself acknowledged; it is impossible that the former should continue to accept what the latter is powerless to justify.

Here, also, the solution can result only from a profound study of morality. For the moment, we content ourselves with saying that while, in our view, ethics has certainly an original datum, one that is irreducible to that of psychology or metaphysics, this datum needs to be subjected to the inquiring light of reason, and can be fully interpreted only by means of metaphysics. The explanation for this is that both ethics and metaphysics are rooted in the same profound activity of the human subject; while they are distinct sciences, they are also so closely linked that one cannot be developed in isolation from the other. Ethics stands in need of metaphysics so that its datum may be correctly interpreted; metaphysics, in its turn, has need of ethics so that the full significance and richness of its affirmations may be revealed — just as, for example, the metaphysical notion of the "transcendental good" is enriched by the consideration of moral value, so that the truths which are centred on this notion take on a new meaning, and are revealed, so to speak, in a new dimension.

Ultimately, what is involved here is the same as what is involved in a question which is debated in metaphysics: is what is good formally identical with what exists (and with what is true), so that in virtue of a *conceptual* analysis, the principle: "every being, as such, is good", can be established; or are these three distinct, and if so, how are they related to one another? — We maintain, with the Thomists, that what exists, what is true, and what is good are *identical in reality, but formally distinct*. The notion of the good presupposes that of being and adds to it a logical element or relation (that of possessing a certain degree of perfection or of meeting a need), which was not explicitly present in the notion of being. But in the very *act* of affirming that something exists, we necessarily affirm that it is good. And if the foundation and intelligibility of the good are to be found in being, this latter, in its turn, can be completely revealed only by means of its transcendental attributes.

IV. Methodology. The various stages of our investigation.

11. – The approach taken to ethics is often synthetic and deductive. Such an approach is favoured not only by those who consider ethics to be a part of metaphysics, but also by all those, such as the great majority of the Scholastics and many of the Neo-Scholastics, who wish to have as their point of departure the *last end* of man. — What this is can be established in different ways: by making use of Revelation, where moral theology is concerned; as the fruit of a metaphysics in which the orientation towards God of all beings and, in particular, of rational beings, is shown; or by means of a reflective analysis of intelligent and free activity, of its radical finality etc. But, once its existence has been established, it is this end which will provide the ground on which the essential notions of morality are founded: the good, obligation, the natural law, conscience, rights, duties... This deductive approach is not, however, pursued with equal rigour by the various authors, in particular as regards the determination of the moral norm and of the very concept of moral good. — Broadly speaking, we can say that this is the method followed by St Thomas in the *Prima Secundae*.

There is no doubt but that an ethical investigation in which this synthetic approach finds no place is incomplete. Nevertheless, as a basic approach it seems, of its very nature, to be more suited to theology; where the Scholastics — who were primarily theologians — were concerned, it was perfectly in place. But one could well query whether it is suited to *philosophical* ethics. "For in the science of philosophy, which is led by the consideration of creatures to a knowledge of God, reflection on creatures precedes reflection on God" [18].

An additional, and even more important, reason for not taking this line of approach is that a person's own conscience, and the society in which he lives, bear testimony to the fact of morality, prior to all philosophical inquiry and elaboration. Human beings did not wait for the speculations of the moral

---

[18] "In philosophical inquiry, which proceeds from the knowledge of creatures to the knowledge of God, the first consideration is that of creatures and the last that of God", St Thomas, *Cont. Gent.*, II,4.

philosophers on the nature, end and condition etc., of man before acknowledging moral value in practice and responding to the demands of obligation, (any more than they waited for a philosophical proof of God's existence before honouring and worshipping Him). The fact of morality is so much a presupposition for all ethical speculation that any notions which could be elaborated, any conclusions which could be arrived at, in isolation from it, would, in consequence, be empty and arid. It is, then, this fact which provides us with our point of departure, so that our method will primarily be *analytic* and *inductive*. It will commence by acknowledging the data of moral consciousness; through seeking to interpret these and to arrive at their ultimate significance, we shall be led to the source which will make a deductive analysis possible.

12. — The distinction between *general* and *special* ethics is fairly generally accepted. The character of the former is more formal: it treats of the nature and general conditions of moral activity, of what is present in every moral act, no matter what its content may be. To it falls the task of examining the nature of the good (or moral value), of obligation, of law, of sanction etc.; the task of inquiring into the foundation of the moral order and of determining man's last end, of studying the structure of the moral act, the conditions which have to be fulfilled in order that a person be responsible for what he does etc.

Special ethics applies these general principles to the various branches of human activity; it makes clear how a human being ought to conduct himself in the various orders (family, nation etc.) of which he forms part, in the various roles he plays in society, in the various relations he has with others etc. In this way, individual ethics, family ethics, social-in the strict sense-ethics (into which the question of professional ethics enters), religious ethics (the list of "duties towards God") etc., are distinguished [19].

Our present investigation is concerned only with general ethics. The following is the order which we shall follow.

---

[19] A religious ethics as regards its object. In another sense, an ethics will be called religious if it draws its principles and motivations from religion.

The first part of our investigation will be concerned with *moral value*. After a brief consideration of human activity in general, we shall examine the data of moral consciousness as these are revealed in the conduct of individuals, in the institutions and customs of society. This examination will bring to light the notions of a good which is to be done and of an evil which is to be avoided, that is, the notion of a moral order, characterized by the value which is proper to it — moral value — and which takes on either a positive (what is "good") or negative (what is "evil") form; another characteristic of this order is the absoluteness of its requirements, an absoluteness which is expressed, where conscience is concerned, under the form of obligation (of "duty"). Our aim will be to arrive at an accurate understanding of these various notions and, in particular, to determine with exactitude the essence of moral value (Book one). After that, we shall try to discover the link between being and the moral order, and the ultimate foundation of this latter; we shall then be in a position to present the synthetic and deductive approach (Book two).

The *second part* of our investigation will be devoted to the study of the *moral order* itself. This order has a double aspect: *objective* and *subjective*. The objective moral order comprises the totality of *what is to be done*: to describe it in detail is the work of special ethics. All we shall do here is to outline its general traits. In doing this, two notions in particular will occupy our attention: those of *law* and of *right*. This latter, it is true, is concerned with only one class of action, but the treatment of it will be at a more general level than that of the various specific "duties" which are studied in special ethics (Book three). — The subjective moral order is concerned with human actions in themselves, with the "doing" of what "is to be done". Our task at this stage of our investigation will be to throw light on the structure of the moral act, on what conditions its performance as well as on what conditions a person's entire moral existence. The study of conscience in its various states, and also of the virtues, will be of particular importance here (Book four).

Finally, in the *third part*, we shall consider the problem of the relation between *happiness* and *morality*. These two seem, at first sight, to be radically distinct, and our inquiry into the essence of moral value will have required of us that we leave on one side the question of happiness. But, surely, matters cannot be allowed to rest there? Between these two, is there not a profound link of some kind?

We are accordingly faced with the problem of moral *sanctions*. Its solution will enable us to have a unified notion of man's ultimate end and will round off our philosophical inquiry into morality, even though it will also present us with new problems, through revealing to us further horizons (Book five).

FIRST PART
MORAL VALUE

BOOK ONE
ESSENCE AND NORM OF MORAL VALUE

CHAPTER ONE
THE DATA OF MORAL CONSCIOUSNESS

I. HUMAN ACTION.

13. – Man does not always act as man; his activity is not always stamped by what distinguishes him from other beings. Very often, his actions, even though they proceed from him, even though they are his, express only that zone of his being which is common to him and other living bodies; just as with the activity of other living beings, his activity is ruled by a natural necessity: it is determined. Actions of this kind are — in addition to activity on the vegetative level (which, in current usage, we do not call "actions") — instinctive, thoughtless movements, mannerisms, reflex actions, what is done under the influence of psychic constraint, hypnotic suggestion or demented frenzy etc. Such actions are rightly called actions *of a human being*, since their source is that bodily and spiritual individual who is called Peter, Paul etc., but they are not *human* actions. They do not express that individual being; they do not proceed from him precisely as human, The only genuinely human action is the one which a human being performs in virtue of what distinguishes him from other beings. Since this is nothing other than reason, or rather, rationality, human actions are the actions which a human being performs when he acts as a rational being.

The conclusion that could be drawn from this is that the domain of human actions is entirely identical with that of spiritual activity. The formation of an idea, or of a judgment, as a result of the impact of some happening, the intellectual appreciation of a piece of evidence, the spontaneous attraction to the good etc., would, in consequence, have to be classed as human actions. But, while rational psychology could indeed speak in this way, ethics — at least in accordance with traditional usage — could not do so.

The reason for this is that ethics does not have the same viewpoint as psychology. This latter is a speculative science; understood in the way that is richest and truest, it is concerned with the *nature* of man, the *nature* of his activity, the degree of being which this reveals him to possess; it studies the structure, the conditions, the various stages of this activity. Ethics, on the other hand, aims at providing guidance for the actions of the *person*, the *spiritual subject* in whom human nature subsists and to whom, in the final analysis, these actions are attributable. It is for this reason that what this science is primarily concerned with, as regards these actions, is the way in which they are performed by the subject, and the way in which he can be responsible for them. The way in which actions are performed is, for ethics (unlike psychology), not simply an aspect of the object with which it is concerned, but conditions the possibility of this object.

It is worth stressing here that, in distinguishing between *spiritual subject* and *nature*, we by no means intend to make of the former a mysterious entity which is situated outside of or above the latter! A spiritual subject is nothing other than an existing spiritual nature, as at one and the same time both *existing* and *spiritual*. Existing: for it is only an existing being who acts and so makes what was merely possible to become actual. Spiritual: for it is this spiritual, "immaterial" character which, through opening him to the Absolute, makes the subject to be "in some sense everything" and so elevates him above the condition of beings which "are only what they are," whose *natures are simply natures*, so that the degree of being which is theirs confines and encloses them. The subject, on the other hand, precisely because he is spiritual, is not confined and enclosed in this way: he is in a certain sense infinite, and it is this infinity which is the source of his liberty, which is, one could say, the ontological and radical liberty.

Now, there are certain actions which, even though they are essentially on the spiritual level, and, in consequence, proper to man, flow rather from his nature (as spiritual) than from the subject himself. The way in which they are performed is not radically different from the way in which infra-spiritual actions are performed: since they flow from his nature they are subject, no less than are infra-spiritual actions, to the law which governs all merely natural activity: the law of determinism. But there are other actions which, even in the way in which they are performed, manifest man's rationality. To speak more exactly, what these actions express and reveal, in the way in which they arise, is not simply the subject's *nature* (human, spiritual), but the *subject* as such, as *this existing individual*. His nature — and by this is meant not only "nature" in the abstract, but "nature" as concretely realized in this individual who is placed in these circumstances — does not suffice to account for their fixity and, above all, to explain why they have been performed in place of never having come to be [1]. Actions of this type are accordingly proper to man, not only as regards their structure and their quality, but also as regards the way in which they depend on the subject, and it is for this reason that they have a singular title to be called *human actions*. As is obvious, the actions of which we are speaking are those which emanate from a person's free will. Hence, from the ethical point of view, the *free act* and the *human act* are identical.

But note that a person's will is not necessarily the immediate source of a free and voluntary action. An action which proceeds immediately from the will is called an "elicited" (from the Latin "elicere" which means to draw out) action: such, for example, is a person's decision to read this book. An action which proceeds mediately from the will, in the sense that this sets in motion some other power, of which the action is the immediate fruit, is called a commanded action: such, for example, is the activity of my fingers in striking the keys of the typewriter. — The domain of freedom also includes actions of the second category, for without them a human action is not complete (n. 224). — In consequence, it is clear that the distinction between actions "of a human being" and "human actions" is by no means identical with the distinction between those which are external (exteriorized in space) and internal,

---

[1] It is for this reason that we have included existence in the definition of the subject. It is only an existing being who is capable of the initiative through which the indetermination "by excess", due to the transcendence of a nature that is spiritual, can be removed.

between the deed and the intention, since the former, to the extent that it is animated by the latter, is part of the one human action [2].

Note too that one act of the will can be commanded by another. So, for example, when I have made a promise, undertaken an obligation, taken a decision concerning the future, the activity of my will which is required in order to keep my promise etc., occurs under the influence of the decision I have already taken. In more general terms, it is one and the same act of will which both desires to achieve some end and chooses the means to that end [3]. So too my decision to do penance can move me to make an interior act of charity. Obviously, as is clear from the last example, this does not prevent the commanded act from having its own motivation and its own end. The act of will which "commands" consists essentially in ensuring that the motives which will initiate the "commanded" act are properly appreciated [4].

This distinction between "actions of a human being" and "human actions" seems to lead necessarily to the surprising conclusion that the summit of human activity — the immediate knowledge and love of God — is not a human action... A possible reply is that this activity is really *superhuman*, since a human being is capable of it only as "deified", as "made a sharer in the divine nature". But would it not be better simply to acknowledge that our definition of human action is one which cannot be divorced from the purpose that ethics seeks to achieve, namely, to provide guidance for human activity *in the conditions of this present life*; in this life, the actions of the spiritual subject, human actions, are *never* subject to necessity: liberty of choice is always operative in them. The reason for this is that the Total Good is never immediately and concretely presented to him, but always by means of signs which manifest it only in a veiled manner. But it is only when confronted with the Total Good, in which the good for which he craves — and

---

[2] St Thomas, *Summa Theol.*, I-II, 17, 5-9.

[3] *Ib.*, I-II, 9, 3; *De Malo*, 6, a. un.

[4] See on the question V. Frins, *De actibus humanis*, Freiburg-im-Br., 1897-1911, t. I, pp. 406-423. — In the three volumes of this work "one hears the entire School', and notably the later Scholastics, but one also hears scarcely anything else — an indication both of the richness and limits of the thought.

which is worthy of his complete commitment — is to be found, that the spiritual subject is overcome by a love that is irresistible and, at the same time, issues from the very centre of his being, from the inmost recesses of the "I" [5].

14. – Specifically human activity is distinguished from the activity observable in the other beings of our experience by the following traits [6]:

1) Before acting, a human being reflects, with greater or less clarity, on what he is going to do: on what he is going to effect and, together with this, on his action (a book, for example, and all the activity which the writing of it will require).

2) A person not only reflects but also, in virtue of a voluntary decision, aims at and intends the effect in question and the activity which will produce it. An intention of this kind is obviously different from that which is involved in speculative thought, where both the subject and what he is thinking about are "at rest". Here, on the contrary, the subject's attitude is one of "movement towards" some object; this latter, correlatively, presents itself as moving from the stage of what could be to that of what is. "To will" can never be anything other than to will that something *be* which was not, or was not under this aspect, or was not as far as I was concerned.

Nonetheless, this is not sufficient, for a desire is also a "movement towards", and aims at the existence of the object in question. The difference between "willing" and "desiring" is that where the latter is concerned the existence of the object is presented as absolutely independent of the act which intends it; the object of an act of willing, on the contrary, is intended as an effect which is to be achieved through the act itself. But, obviously, my "fiat" is not creative: to decide to write a book is one thing, but to have a manuscript ready for the printers is quite another! There are many intermediate stages between the initial decision and the completion of the undertaking — stages which may not be travelled. Obstacles can arise. I can fall ill. I

---

[5] See our *Essai sur l'agir humain* (henceforward cited: *Essai*), n. 114; pp. 275-277. Also *Existence et Liberté*, pp. 355 seq.

[6] See *Essai*, nn. 14-17; pp. 39-45.

can be deprived of the instruments of work which I require. Or I can quite simply change my mind. My will is no more unchangeable than it is all-powerful. All that can be said is, then: *on condition* that the means are not lacking and that my present resolve continues, the effect will, infallibly, be achieved; the book will be written. My decision is only conditionally effective, but it is effective; it is perhaps even by means of it that we come to appreciate what effectiveness is *from the inside*.

3) This intention of the will is always aimed at something which lies beyond its immediate and particular object: human action is motivated by an end. We have here touched on the wellknown principle that "every agent acts for some end". But note that this is a principle which can be understood in two senses. It can simply mean that the intention of the will is directed towards some object, in place of resting in itself as does sentiment: we do not will in order to will; the intention of the will is not empty. Understood in this sense, it teaches us nothing new. But it can also mean — and this is the sense which it here has for us — that the intention of the will does not stop at the object which is expressly aimed at, or, more precisely, that this intention is supported and nourished by one which is more profound and which is directed towards a goal that constitutes the ground, and horizon, of the object's value.

Recall the example we have already used. It can happen that I find pleasure in writing, as happens in moments of inspiration and euphoria. This pleasure can be the motive which at those moments *moves* me to write another page in place of reading a book or writing a letter. It can also happen that I set to work moved by the thought that idleness is shameful, that work is the law of man's life, that each one should develop his talents, achieve something etc. I can regard my work as a service of humanity, of the Church, as a bearing of witness etc. Finally, it can also happen that the writing of this book, even though not of itself very interesting to me, is necessary in order to obtain a degree, to be appointed to a situation which I judge to be desirable... We recognize the classical distinction — at least since the time of Plato and Aristotle[7] — of the three types of good: the pleasant, the noble, the useful.

---

[7] Plato, *Laws*, II, 667, b c; Aristotle, *Nicom. Eth.*, II, 2, 1104 b 31. — Cf. *Essai*, nn. 18-19 and 39; pp, 45-49 and 91-92.

The motive of the will, what initiates and "stimulates" its activity, is the good or the value which the object is revealed as possessing. This is the objective *a priori* form of the will, just as being is of the intellect, a form which does not limit but rather opens out further horizons, and which, far from resulting in the deformation of the object, is the means whereby the harmony between it and the subject is assured. This is what the will pursues in all its strivings. It can choose nothing except under the aspect of good, in view of the good that is revealed to it.

In the above-mentioned division of good, it seems to be necessary to extend the meaning of the word "pleasant" so as to include the cessation of pain, of feelings of sorrow, or the simple fact of escaping these, even if this does not involve pleasure in the strict sense of the word [8]. Or else "useful" has to be understood to refer to what contributes immediately to the satisfaction of a vital necessity (to escape from a burning house, to eat so as not to be hungry any more), even when this satisfaction is not "thematically" intended as an end in view of which the activities in question would be appreciated as useful.

The useful, as such, is essentially relative either to the pleasant or to the noble, which have of themselves a final character, each in its own line. If something is pleasant, there is no point in asking why it is desirable (although one may certainly ask whether it is to be desired). Similarly, what is noble, considered in general terms, presents itself as what we ought to desire, and there is no point in asking why. (To such a question the only reply that could be made is: because it is noble to do what is noble...).

4) As is shown in rational psychology, and as we shall later consider in more detail (nn. 280-283), a human being, in virtue of the natural elan of his will, pursues in everything that he wills, as his (subjective) final end, that perfect completion of himself, that integral satisfaction of his aspirations, which is called "beatitude". This presents itself to us as the ultimate

---

[8] On the question, and in particular on the difference between pleasure and the cessation od pain or the satisfaction of a need, consult P. Ricoeur, *Philosophie de la volonté*, t. I, Paris, 1950, pp. 85-116. — The classic division of the good has been criticised from another point of view by Al. Roldán in his remarkable work *Metafísica del sentimiento*, Madrid, 1955, pp. 266 seq.

horizon of our desire, which explains why we do not ordinarily intend it "thematically". (What is "thematically" intended is a situation, an increase in one's salary, a television set, a motorcar etc.: only rarely does a person explicitly propose the goal of "happiness" to himself).

5) Since the various goods that present themselves as goals which are more immediately attainable cannot bring him this perfect completion, a human being not only aims at an end and a value in his activity, but is also capable of establishing goals for himself[9], through making himself to be moved by this value rather than by some other, through determining which judgment of value is to be operative in his choice. It is for this reason that he is said to possess "liberum arbitrium" (namely, to be capable of free judgment) and to be "master of his actions", in the sense which has earlier been explained.

Free will is not exercised simply in the choice of means, as is often said in the wake of Aristotle[10]: man's most radical choice is concerned with his ultimate end, in that he can choose to strive for this in one way rather than another (the way of pleasure, of virtue, of glory; he can decide to seek his happiness in God or in himself etc.)[11]. — Note very particularly that the will cannot be adequately defined in terms of the tendency towards happiness: in addition to this eudaemonist dimension it possesses another — of which we shall soon speak — without which a moral existence, in the full sense of the word, would be impossible.

6) Liberty involves *responsibility*. This notion is of social origin. To be responsible is to have to *respond*, to render an account of one's actions, to another (an individual or a society) who has confided a thing, a person, a function etc., to us and to whom we are, at least implicitly, committed. (The Latin "re-spondere" means to promise a thing in return for some-

---

[9] St Thomas, *Summa Theol.*, I, 18, 3.

[10] Aristotle, *Nicom. Eth.*, III, 2, 111 b 26-30.

[11] See the *Summa Theol.*, I-II, 89, 6, where St Thomas, writing as a theologian and consequently expressing his full mind, breaks out of the Aristotelian framework: "when a human being begins to have the use of reason ... what first presents itself to him for his reflection is to deliberate concerning himself: and if he orientates himself towards the end which has a claim on him" etc. "To orientate himself towards the end which has a claim on him" is not the same as "to choose what leads to the end".

thing else and, by extension, to fulfil a promise). More particularly, it is to have, should the occasion arise, to bear the consequences of one's action, to make good the damage which it may have caused to others, to undergo the sanction which it calls for on the part of society... But to promise to take care of a thing or a person, to perform some function in an appropriate manner, supposes that this is in my power; and to be subjected to a penalty, at least if it is a grave one, for an action which was not in my power to perform or avoid, cannot but appear clearly iniquitous to a person of reasonably mature conscience. I can be responsible for an action only if it is really *mine*, only if its true cause is to be found in what makes of me a subject who is capable of self-determination. It is this which disengages the notion of responsibility from the social element in which it was wrapped. Before being responsible before others, I am responsible before myself; I need to acknowledge myself — unpleasant though this can be at times — as the true author of my action, as the one whose free "fiat" has alone made it possible. I am responsible: this means that it is useless to seek to justify myself by appealing to human weakness, heredity, temperament, character, the climate, the milieu etc., for these factors would have been powerless if my liberty had not allowed them free scope.

In accordance with this meaning, which is current among contemporary writers, Sartre in particular, responsibility is presented less as a consequence than as an aspect of liberty. These two notions are one at a profound level, so that liberty refers rather to the exclusion of determinism, and responsibility to the attribution of the action to the "I".

If what has been said is kept in mind, one will steer clear of the edifying but over-facile shortcuts which, from the consciousness of responsibility, wish to conclude directly to the existence of Someone before whom we are responsible. There is need of some mediation if we are to pass from what is sociological to what is metaphysical and to what is theological. (Cf. what is written further on concerning obligation, nn. 161-163, and merit, n. 290).

15. — In the *Prima Secundae* (qq. 8-17) St Thomas, making use of the analyses of Aristotle, St Augustine and, in particular, St John Damascene (unfortunately, in a defective translation),

distinguishes in the unity of a human action several elementary acts or stages. Some of these proceed from the will, while
others issue from the intellect or the executive "powers". The
order followed — a logical one which is exterior to the living
genesis of the action — makes his exposition to be somewhat
confusing. He treats successively of acts of the will which are
concerned with the end and acts of the will which are
concerned with the means, or, more exactly, with what is
oriented towards the end. (This latter notion seems to include
more than that of the means). — Among the first, a
distinction is made between those which are concerned with
the end absolutely considered, and those which are concerned
with the end as aimed at through the means. For the end in
the first sense, there will, in consequence, be an act of
"volition" in the strict sense (qq. 8, 9, 10) and of enjoyment
(q. 11), which come respectively at the beginning and the end
of the process; for the end in the second sense, there will be
an act of "intention" by which the subject tends towards it as
something which is to be attained through the means. With
regard to these latter, the central act is that of choice (q. 13);
this presupposes a process of deliberation (q. 14) in order to
determine the most suitable means: with this is linked an act
which St Thomas calls "consent" (q. 15) — the terminology
is Augustinian — and which he understands as the approval
of certain means prior to the choice. (So, for example, in
order to travel from Rome to Paris, I can choose between rail,
road and air; I can also choose between several different
itineraries, several airlines etc. But only certain of these means
really interest me: for example, it may happen that the
aeroplane has at once to be excluded either for financial
reasons or because of an insurmountable fear: I *consent* only to
the journey by road or by rail). — After the choice comes the
execution (q. 16): the will activates the executive "powers":
the arms, the legs and also the intelligence. This stage of the
human action is "commanded" (n. 13) and the following
question (17) treats of it. Note that, in his view, this
command is an act of reason: it is reason, the faculty of order,
which "orders" the will with regard to the execution of the
decision (*ibid.*, a. 3). — The human action, in consequence,
contains the following series of elementary acts arranged in

their natural order: volition – intention – deliberation – consent – choice – command – execution – enjoyment[12].

Billuart afterwards added to this series so that the human action was held to be composed of twelve elementary acts. These are symmetrically arranged in that six proceed from the intelligence (the last of them being concerned with all the executive powers) and six from the will. The twelve "acts" are arranged in this way:

Intelligence (and executive powers)	Will
1. Simple thought of the good.	2. Simple (inefficacious) volition of the good.
3. Judgment by which the end is presented as possible.	4. Efficacious intention of this end.
5. Deliberation.	6. Consent.
7. Practical judgment concerning the most suitable means.	8. Choice of this means.
9. Command of reason.	10. Active execution on the part of the will.
11. Passive execution on the part of the executive powers and the intellect.	12. Enjoyment.

According to Billuart all these acts "form part of the one moral action when a person acts neither precipitately, nor under the sway of his imagination, but prudently and maturely. But since they occur quickly and in rapid succession the person himself scarcely perceives or distinguishes them[13]. — Not

---

[12] On the historical origin of this analysis, see O. Lottin, *La psychologie de l'acte humain chez saint Jean Damascène et les théologiens du XIIe siècle occidental*, in *Psychologie et morale aux XIIe et XIIIe siècles*, t. I, Louvain, 1942, pp. 393-424.

[13] "Accordingly, these twelve acts form part of the one moral operation when a person acts neither precipitately nor under the sway of his imagination, but prudently and maturely. Since, however, they occur in rapid succession, the person himself scarcely perceives or distinguishes them", Billuart, *De actibus humanis*, Dissert. III, *Prologus*, in *Cursus Theologicus*, t. I, 2a p., Brescia, 1837, p. 64b.

everyone, however, even among the Thomists, is prepared to accept Billuart's analysis. Some authors consider that one or other of these acts is superfluous: this is particularly true of "consent". Could it not also be maintained that this analysis mistakes the point of the Thomistic one? Should we not rather see in its so-called "acts", aspects or stages of the one concrete human action, as this arises in the profound interiority of the person's will and so comes, through the various levels of his mind and will, to be expressed in the appropriate exterior action [14]?

16. – Since a free act is one in which the determining factor is the intervention of the spiritual subject as such (that is, as transcending the determinism of nature), it follows that the act will be all the more free and, in consequence, more human, the more the subject is present to himself and knows what he is doing.

Liberty presupposes lucidity; but this can be of two kinds. There is a lucidity which springs from the knowledge of the object and there is a lucidity which springs from the subject's presence to himself. Both one and the other are required in order than an act be fully attributable to the subject as a fruit which is authentically his. — A lesser degree of knowledge of the object makes the act to be less free and less voluntary *as this act which is directed towards this specific object*, even though it can remain free and voluntary under a more general aspect. A child kills his playmate with a bomb which he thought was only a harmless piece of iron: considered as an act of throwing something, the child's act was free; considered as an act of homicide, it was not free. — On the contrary, a lesser degree of presence to himself, an "alienation" of the subject in his natural, non-spiritual determinations (in his passions, his impulses etc.), makes his act to be less free *as a spiritual act in general*. To the extent that its source is to be found in these

---

[14] See S. Pinckaers, *La structure de l'acte humain suivant saint Thomas*, "Revue Thomiste", 1955, pp. 393-412: the Thomistic analysis is structural not psychological; the various stages do not succeed one another temporally but correspond to the different levels of the action. The principal difference centres on the role of the simple volition: for Billuart, this is an inefficacious act, or "velleity", whereas for S. Pinckaers it is efficacious will, which sustains and animates from within all the other "acts" (or stages of the action).

"natural" determinants rather than in the subject himself, the act sinks to the level of determinism and becomes exterior to the subject as such.

Since a free will is characterized by its mastery of the actions which proceed from it, such a will has it in its power either to choose or not to choose, so that not-willing, abstention from willing, is no less attributable to it than a positive decision [15].

How is this to be understood? Our will is never entirely quiescent except when we are in no way present to ourselves: there is, at the very least, an obscure adhesion of the subject to himself, to the extent that he remains present to himself by means of a confused experience of his own body and of the world, even though he is not attending to any particular object. St Thomas teaches that at the origin of a sin of omission there is always some act on the sinner's part [16]. A person does not go to Mass because he dallies over something which he enjoys doing, because he has business to attend to etc. Consequently, one who does not will what he ought to will does so either because he wills something else or because he is unwilling to take a decision which would disturb his cosy repose. (This latter attitude can have an extremely coarsening effect on a person's conscience so that he becomes deaf to all appeals on his generosity). One could say that this willing-of-something-else, this unwillingness to be disturbed, accompanied as they are by a judgment concerning the positive value of not willing the omitted action [17], are virtually equivalent to a decision whereby the choice of this latter is excluded (for example, the accomplishment of some urgent duty).

It is however difficult to understand how the judgment: "it is good not to will", could be made by the subject in the absence of *all* voluntary acts. If this judgment remains speculative, it does not provide motivation. If it becomes practical, this involves the intervention of the will. This intervention will not, it is true, be formal and thematic; it will not stand out clearly in our consciousness,

---

[15] St Thomas, *Summa Theol.*, I-II, 6, 3.

[16] "The fact that someone fails to do what he could either do or omit inevitably results from some simultaneous or preceding cause or occasion", *ib.*, I-II, 71, 5. — On the question, see V. Frins, *De actibus humanis*, t. I, pp. 229-237, who admits the possibility of a "pure omission", while at the same time acknowledging that it could scarcely ever occur.

[17] "Reason can appreciate that it is good not only to will or to act, but also not to will and not to act", St Thomas, *ib.*, I-II, 13, 6.

but will be obscure and difficult to distinguish, just as are the acts which people of great spiritual insight can discern in the profound recesses of mind and heart. The voluntary act is not the same as the psychic resonance which results from an explicit decision such as: "this is what I want". Note, moreover, that the problem of the imputability of not-willing something is always treated in the context of fault. There is never any question of merit except in relation to some positive act. — Elements which are juridical here interfere with those which are properly ethical (n. 219), even though each of these two orders has its own proper domain (n. 218). The common good, the need to preserve public order, can demand that a *civil* responsibility be acknowledged even where there is no *moral* responsibility.

St Thomas classifies as "directly voluntary" whatever results from a decision, while what results from not-willing he calls "indirectly voluntary" [18] — for example, an accident which is due to a person's negligence (he has forgotten to check whether the gas was turned off). — Modern Scholastic writers use these terms in a somewhat different sense. What they call "directly voluntary" is what St Thomas referred to as "voluntary in itself", namely, what is directly willed by a person: for example, to drink a few glasses of wine in company with one's friends. What they call "indirectly voluntary" is what St Thomas classified as "voluntary in its cause": as a result of his drinking about, a person drives badly so that the car carrying himself and his friends finishes up against a tree. Obviously, this effect was not intended, but since it is in no way a surprising result of what has been directly willed, it is imputed to the person who is responsible for its cause. — Later in our investigation (n. 246), we shall discuss the question of the circumstances under which this imputation is legitimate [19].

From what has been said it follows that ignorance — as St Thomas in the wake of Aristotle teaches — makes a person's action considered as this particular action to be purely and simply involuntary, provided that this ignorance is not itself voluntary and results nevertheless in the person's willing what

---

[18] *Ib.*, I-II, 77, 7.
[19] See V. Frins, op. cit., pp. 216-217.

he would not otherwise will[20]. What a person does when he is possessed by fear, is less voluntary than it would be if he acted in cold blood[21], whereas — still according to Aristotle and his disciple — what is done under the influence of a vehement desire is more voluntary (provided, of course, that emotion does not completely interfere with the functioning of reason)[22]. — The captain who orders his cargo to be jettisoned, so as to avoid being shipwrecked, does not do so lightheartedly; he would prefer not to have to incur this loss; he is, in consequence, torn in two directions and lacks that psychic integration which is possessed by the person whose action is fully voluntary. On the other hand, the person who is very much in love (as in the romances of medieval chivalry) and performs deeds of valour for the "object" of his love, does so with a complete spontaneity. His passion for the beloved effects in him that "crystallization" of which Stendhal speaks — a momentary and often illusory unity of his internal forces. It is with "all his soul", or, at least, with what he believes to be all his soul, that he devotes himself to the object of his love.

Voluntary, in the sense in which St Thomas, in dependence on Aristotle, understands it, is accordingly not synonymous with *free*. The former refers to the vigour of a person's will, to the elan with which it is drawn towards its object whereas the latter refers to the way in which the subject's action depends on the subject himself (n. 13).

These two properties function, up to a certain point, as independent variables. An action cannot be free without being voluntary, but the fact that it is more voluntary does not

---

[20] St Thomas, *Summa Theol.*, I-II, 6, 8. — *Concomitant* ignorance (which does not influence one's action: one would still have done the same if one had known) does not make an action to be involuntary, but simply *not voluntary, ib.* (An example of this is the jealous person who, believing that he is killing a particular rival of his, actually kills another, of whom he was no less anxious to rid himself). Consequent or voluntary ignorance makes an action to be in one sense involuntary, that is, less voluntary. See further on, nn. 242-246. In all this matter, St Thomas is greatly dependent on Aristotle, *Nicom. Eth.*, III, 1, 1109 b 30 - 1111 b 3. But the *hekousion* of Aristotle does not correspond exactly to the voluntary, since he attributes it equally to the animals — which would embarrass St Thomas somewhat.

[21] *Ib.*, I-II, 6, 6.

[22] *Ib.*, I-II, 6, 7.

necessarily mean that it is more free. What is done under the influence of strong emotion is more voluntary but less free.

What has been called the elan of the will should not be confused with feeling and emotion: its relation to these is somewhat like the relation of the concept to phantasms. Just as we cannot form concepts independently of phantasms [23], so also our willing cannot be divorced from our feelings and emotions. We need to be on our guard against the dualism which *separates* what is rational from what is sensible. We have not a *double* consciousness but *one only* — which is both rational and sensitive — because the human soul is *one* and the human subject is a *unity*. Consequently, when a person freely accepts the upsurge of his feelings, this does not remain external to his will but unites with it to form *one and the same* drive of the total subject.

Modern writers, it is true, generally attribute all the elan to the feelings and emotions: the only role they allow the will is that of cold decision. But this view distorts, and detracts unduly from, the true role of the will [24].

II. On Value in General.

17. – What moves the will is the good (n. 14, 3). The good now has a double aspect, that of *end* and *value* [25].

As an *end*, towards which the subject moves through the appropriate means, the good is concerned with initiating the subject's activity, so that correlative to it in him are what Anglo-Saxon psychologists call "conations" (the activity by which the person's will is aimed at the end in question, his effort to mobilize his physical or mental forces and to channel them towards the attainment of some object or the realization of some project).

---

[23] *Ib.*, I, 84, 7.

[24] Among the modern, F. Brentano is one of the few to place affectivity and volition in the same class. See his *Psychologie vom empirischen Standpunkt*, Leipzig, 1874, p. I, bk. 2., ch. 8. — The triple division: knowledge, affectivity, volition, which dates from J. N. Tetens (*Philosophische Versuche über die menschliche Natur und ihre Entwickelung*, Leipzig, 1777, pp. 619-627) has been admitted by several modern Scholastics and, quite recently, by Al. Roldán, *op. cit.*

[25] See J. Maritain, *Neuf leçons sur les notions premières de la philosophie morale*, Paris, 1951, pp. 32-33 and especially *La philosophie morale*, pp. 39-41 (*Moral Philosophy*, pp. 23-24). Likewise *Essai*, n. 23; pp. 55-56.

As a *value*, with which the object appears to be endowed in the manner of a quasi-quality and which, in certain instances at least, communicates itself to the action which is aimed at it[26], the good is concerned with "specifying" the subject's activity. (It would perhaps be better to say: with bestowing some quality on it, since in another sense, his action is *this* specific action because of the end which he intends[27]). Correlative to it in the subject are various *affective dispositions* such as love, admiration, joy, disinterested satisfaction etc.

These two aspects are inseparable. Whatever is appreciated as having a value can be intended as an end, while nothing can be intended in this way unless it is acknowledged to have a value. Hence contemporary definitions of value normally include a reference to the end and the tendency towards it.

In the *Vocabulaire technique et critique de la philosophie*, for example, we read: «Value: A) That character of things which consists in their being prized or desired to a greater or lesser extent...; B) in their deserving to be so prized...; C) in their satisfying a certain need...". We read much the same in Eisler's *Wörterbuch der philosophischen Begriffe*: "There can be no value where there is no need to be satisfied, where there is no will tending towards a goal and settling on some end to be achieved". See also *Dictionnaire de la langue philosophique* (Foulquié-Saint-Jean): "Value. E...: Being as desired... 1. In the abstract sense, the property or character of not only being desired but of being desirable... 2. In the concrete sense: the things themselves which are desirable". — On this point, contemporary writers are in line with those early philosophers, praised by Aristotle, who defined the good as that which all desire[28]. But note that desirableness, lovableness etc., express the phenomenon, or better, the "phenomenological essence" of the good, the aspect under which it immediately manifests itself, rather than its *nature*, namely, that which is the foundation in being of this essence. We shall turn in a moment to the consideration of that nature.

---

[26] It is noble to will what is noble and useful to will what is useful, but it is not always pleasant to will what is pleasant. ... But this is because the activity which the pleasant as such is immediately aimed at is enjoyment; and this is of its nature pleasurable.

[27] *Essai*, n. 32; p. 74.

[28] Aristotle, *Nicom. Eth.*, I, 1, 1094 a 1.

Nevertheless, the term "value", as it is currently used, cannot be purely and simply identified with the good as this was understood by the Scholastics. It implies a relation to the spiritual subject, that is, for all practical purposes, to man. The grass that grows in saltmarshes is good for sheep, but it has a value only for their owner. Further, value seems to connote a recognition, a practical appreciation. Water is good for us as material beings, but it does not possess a value unless its scarcity, the difficulty in finding it, the urgent need for it etc., sets it, so to speak, in "axiological" relief, gives it an *importance*. Value forms part of the more general category of the *important*[29], the interesting, where indifference is ruled out; it is essential to it to break away from the zone of neutrality; often also it will stand in contrast with an anti-value (n. 22,4).

If we now consider the *nature* of the good — in so doing we pass from the phenomenological to the ontological point of view — two aspects can again be distinguished in it: the aspect of contributing to the perfection of a subject who tends towards the good in question or rejoices in his possession of it[30], and the aspect of its own perfection or completion, which does not imply a relation to some other subject but simply signifies that the being which is good in this sense is at rest in its own plenitude[31]. To the good in the first sense the response is that of *desire*, of "need-love", which is grounded, St Thomas tells us, on the ontological relation that exists between what is potential and what is actual. (What is perfectible is, by definition, in potency with respect to what contributes to its perfection). To the good in the second sense, the response is love in the strict meaning of the word (the love of friendship), which of itself does not presuppose any need in the one who loves, but only a rejoicing that stems from his appreciation of the good in question; this love — again according to St Thomas — is grounded on the ontological relation or "similitude" that exists between beings, insofar as each of them is actual (and not merely potential). — This distinction should not be pressed too far[32]. The very notion of perfection is intelligible to us only by means of a certain dynamism, at least

---

[29] D. von Hildebrand, *Christian Ethics*, pp. 23-63.
[30] St Thomas, *De Ver.*, 21, 1.
[31] St Thomas, *Summa Theol.*, I, 5, 1 etc.
[32] *Ib.*, I-II, 27, 3.

ideal: what fully satisfies the requirements of its nature or lives up to its definition, what has realized all its potentialities etc., is "perfect". The very word: perfect, that is, completely achieved, suggests the idea of tendency, of striving towards the achievement of a work. We know God as perfect through thinking of Him as the horizon of our thinking and willing, as the one who is ever and always "beyond". It is noteworthy that St Thomas, at the very moment when he identifies "good" and "perfect", speaks of the latter as desirable: "it is clear that each being is desirable to the extent to which it is perfect, since all beings desire their own perfection" [33].

Strictly speaking, however, just as the good can be an *end* for us only if we first appreciate it as a *value*, so also it can *contribute* to our perfection only in virtue of the *perfection* that is its own.

18. – One of the favourite themes of contemporary philosophical thought is that of value. This does not mean that speculation on the good began only recently. But in classical metaphysics, especially where the Scholastics were concerned, the good is considered in relation to being, that is, as its transcendental attribute. This is not the approach which the philosophy of values takes. The perspective in which everything else is viewed is the good itself, or value, or the subject who evaluates; it is from this point of view, not from the point of view of being, that it arranges and systematizes. Just as classical metaphysics, which is before all else an ontology, delineates and describes the universe of being of which the good is a property, "axiology" [34] aims at describing the universe of the good, in accordance with the structure and the principles of interpretation that are proper to it.

Interpreted in a somewhat stricter sense, the philosophy of values — as distinct from a mere "science of values" — is characterized by a tendency to treat the point of view of value as privileged, to regard it as superior to being and indeed as constituting what is truly being, so that, in consequence, metaphysics is subordinated to

---

[33] *Ib.*, I, 5, 1.

[34] Axiology is the science of values (axiomata = *dignitates*). Axiological: what concerns values. — There is a good historical introduction to the philosophy of values in L. Lavelle, *Traité des valeurs*, t. I, Paris, 1951, pp. 3-181; P. Romano, *Ontologia del valore*, Padua, 1949; A. Guzzo and V. Mathieu, art. *Valore*, in the *Enciclopedia Filosofica*, t. IV, col. 1493-1515; L. R. Ward, art. *Value* (Philosophy of), in the *New Catholic Encyclopedia*.

or reduced to "axiology" (n. 10). At times, values are considered to be entirely divorced from being, or even to be opposed to it, so that they cannot, in consequence, be attained without dying (nn. 5; 22, 1).

In this sense, the thinkers who, with Plato and the Neo-Platonists, situate the Good above Being and maintain that the truest knowledge is to be found through regarding things from the point of view of finality and beauty, can be considered to be forerunners of this type of philosophy. Similarly, when an author underlines the difference between the order of being and that of the good, he gives evidence that he has some initial appreciation of this approach and of its link with metaphysics. Note, for example, St Thomas' observation that the distinction between what has and has not "to be qualified", is not applicable in the same way to the two orders: whereas a substance can be said to exist without qualification, it is only in a qualified sense that its accidental perfections can be said to exist; but, on the other hand, since good signifies perfection, a thing cannot be called good without qualification unless it is completely equipped and in action [35]. Malebranche's distinction between *relations of magnitude* and *relations of perfection* can also be noted [36]. Closer still to a philosophy of values are the last two *Critiques* of Kant and the Fichte — inspired philosophy of Sollen, where reality, as in Platonism, is presented as subordinated to morality and beauty.

In fact, well before the rise of the philosophy of values, two types of value had already been made the object of profound study: *moral values* from the time of the earliest philosophers, under the form of a study of the virtues and, more recently, *economic values*. The particular contribution of the philosophy of values has been to initiate the systematic study of the "axiological" order in its entirety and as worthy of investigation in its own right.

19. – For various reasons, this type of philosophy has developed considerably since the middle of the last century:

1) In the first place, a mistrust of speculation, as a result of the critiques to which theoretical reason has been subjected and of the conflict of the various systems, has led many minds — as Socrates was led in times past — to turn away from the problem of reality as it is in itself, so as to concentrate on things in their relation to the subject: on what is important and interesting to him, on what he has to do...

---

[35] St Thomas, *Summa Theol.*, I, 5, 1 ad Ium.
[36] *Traité de morale*, Ie p., c. 1. 6; *Méditations chrétiennes*, IV, nn. 7, 8. — Cf. St. Augustine: "In the class of things which are not great in size, to be better is to be greater", *De Trinitate*, VI, 8; PL. t. 42, col. 929.

2) In the second place, there has been a reaction against the scientific objectivism, predominant towards the middle of the last century, which ignored the subject and recognized no value other than the true (or the "verifiable"). "Science" has not to concern itself with good or evil, with beauty or ugliness; for it, noble and ignoble do not exist: the dry impartiality of figures, and of formulas that can be verified, reduces all its values to the same level. — The philosophy of values vindicates the subject's right to be concerned with his own point of view.

3) In the third place, the tragic character of the contemporary epoch, with its revolutions and its world wars, has called in question, in an acute manner, the meaning and value of human existence. Man feels that his values are being challenged and endangered: in consequence, he is naturally more concerned about them. — The transformations due to technical progress have had the same effect: since they have changed mankind's style of living, they have revealed that certain hitherto accepted values are really transient, so that, in consequence, men have been led to raise questions concerning the very principle of value.

4) A fourth factor has been the development in the last century of the economic sciences, in which the problem of value plays such a great role and which has resulted in the formation of some renowned theories (Ricardo, Marx, Boehm-Bawerk and the "marginalist" school etc.), together with the growing importance accorded to these sciences in the contemporary industrial and mercantile civilization. The attention of philosophers has accordingly been drawn towards the general problem of value.

5) Special mention has to be made of Fr. Nietzsche in this connection.

In virtue of his bitter criticism of traditional values, and particularly of the more specifically Christian ones (kindness, pity, humility etc.), his exaltation of the will, of life as triumphing, and his concentration on the future, Nietzsche must be classed among those who have done most to turn the attention of contemporary thinkers towards the consideration of value (which he himself identifies with life). — To a lesser extent, pragmatism has also helped to bring about this result: to judge truth by the criterion of utility is to substitute for the intellectualist point of view that of value, since the useful is a value. — Finally, the advent of phenomenology has provided a method which, when applied to our consciousness of values, results in a more accurate description of these latter.

20. – Lotze, Brentano and Meinong are usually regarded as the initiators of the philosophy of values in the strict sense. Its unity is, however, extremely loose: in the course of its development, several tendencies and several schools can be distinguished, at times as opposed as possible.

1) Idealist, "transcendentalist", Neo-Kantian (Rickert, Windelband), Neo-Fichtean (Münsterberg) tendencies: value is a category, an ideal, a transcendental norm; it is related to a transcendental subject, to an evaluative consciousness in general.

2) Psychological interpretations: value is grounded on the needs, the tendencies, the desires of the subject: it is, in consequence, entirely relative (Chr. von Ehrenfels, Müller-Freienfels, Ribot).

3) Sociological interpretations: here also value is relative but the centre of reference is society: values are social facts and should be studied in the same way as are other such facts (Durkheim, Lévy-Bruhl, Bouglé). In reality, what the proponents of this theory are speaking of is not values, but rather the evaluations, the moral judgments etc., which are accepted in a particular society. Their genesis, evolution etc., are to be studied, but there is no question of judging them in their turn.

(Marxism obviously can also be included here: the ways in which a society makes its evaluations depend on the social and economic infrastructure; there is, however, a humanistic aspect to this theory which seems to take it beyond relativism: man is the true source of values and a humanity in which there will be no classes seems to be the point of reference for an objective scale of values).

4) Existentialist (Sartre) and "libertarian" (Polin) interpretations. Values are created by man's liberty which is itself the supreme value. It is the inverse of the preceding tendency in that it upholds an absolute subjectivism. Every objective norm is denied (cf. n. 107).

5) At the opposite extreme, there is the phenomenological and Platonist interpretation which attributes to values some type of "existence in themselves" (Ansichsein); since this interpretation considers that value is the object not of an intellectual but of an emotional intuition, it differs from the interpretations which class value as a category. (M. Scheler: *Der Formalismus in der Ethik und die materiale Wertethik*, Halle a. d. S., 1916 (Engl. trans.: Evanston, 1973); N. Hartmann: *Ethik*, Berlin-Leipzig, 1925 (Engl. trans.: 3 vols: New York, 1932); and, in a certain measure, D. von Hildebrand: *Die Idee der sittlichen Handlung*, 1916; *Christian Ethics*, New York, 1952, who perhaps might be better classified with the following group). — Here there is genuine question of a metaphysics of values. Far from being the projection of man's tendencies it is they, on the contrary, which dominate these tendencies.

6) The same observation applies to the spiritual interpretation, which relates values to man's spiritual activity and, through this

to the Absolute, to God: values are a manifestation of the Absolute, a presence of the Absolute, of the Universal in the particular. God is the identity of Being and of Value (R. Le Senne: *Obstacle et Valeur*, Paris, 1934; *Qu'est-ce que la Valeur, Bulletin de la Société française de philosophie*, 1941; L. Lavelle: *Traité des Valeurs*, 2 vol., 1951-1955 — volume two is posthumous).

Contemporary Scholastic philosophers who treat of value can be included in this group.

We shall say nothing of those for whom judgments of value are, as such, quite meaningless (A. J. Ayer and the proponents of neo-logical positivism, n. 5). It is clear that theories of this kind are the radical negation of all philosophy of values.

21. — Love, desire, choice are not possible, it seems, unless the object is revealed as possessing a value: the object of the will is the good which is first "grasped" by the intelligence. — But does not this "grasp" of the good presuppose in the subject an inclination, an appetite? The "phenomenological essence" of the good, as we have said, is the desirable, the lovable: but these words have meaning for us only through our experience of desire and of love [37].

I can know that something is good because others tell me so: it is on this principle that publicity is based. Nevertheless: 1. This presupposes that I have, at the very least, a general notion of value; and I possess such a notion only through my experience of desiring what is desirable. 2. The more the value which I have desired in the past differs from the one that others tell me about, the more does my appreciation of this latter remain inadequate; it can even happen that I completely misunderstand the value in question, so that I aim at it in a way that is out of harmony with it (as when I desire to do what is morally good as a means to my self-exaltation). 3. At the source of judgments of value which are dictated by public opinion, education etc., there has necessarily to be some personal experience which has been, to a greater or lesser extent, favourably interpreted. If many people, trusting in the judgment of others, admire Picasso or Mathieu, this is because these others have really perceived an artistic value in the work of these painters.

The antinomy is only apparent. The grasp of the good undoubtedly presupposes a tendency; but this tendency is a

---

[37] See the *Essai*, nn. 40-43; pp. 92-104. Also Al. Roldán, *op. cit.*, pp. 397-412.

"natural" one which is anterior to all reflective knowledge. The object is grasped as good or evil according as it harmonizes or clashes with this tendency. Clearly, the accord or disaccord in question is not itself directly known. It is part of the subjective conditions: what is known is its projection in the object under the form of value (positive or negative). For this object is good and desirable only in virtue of a certain "harmony" between its nature and that of the subject. He discovers in it what he was already tending towards — without perhaps knowing it — or, at the very least, what could help, in one way or another, to satisfy this tendency.

Once the good is recognized as such — with a knowledge that will, clearly, be concrete and affective — the person's appetite for it takes on a new character: it becomes an "elicited" appetite of which he is clearly conscious. The more precise and thematic his perception of this value becomes, the more the will distinguishes itself from a mere spontaneous and natural tendency towards it: the more rational, if not reasonable, does his action become. — Finally, the satisfaction of the tendency will normally give pleasure, so that the object will become more desirable and, in consequence, more valuable.

Even though this "elicited" desire and love presuppose knowledge they also go beyond it. Hence the possibility of an obscure appreciation and spiritual "penetration" of the object through a love that is illumined by the intelligence, through an intelligence that is attentive to the message of the heart. This message does not, of itself result in any fresh information concerning the structure of the object: in this sense it does not augment in any way a person's knowledge of the object nor make it more intelligible to him. What he does receive is a greater appreciation of its value, and through this, of its existential character. If we are interested in something, it exists for us in a way that is very different from the way in which what does not interest us exists. Certain affective and moral dispositions are required in order to appreciate that others, no less than ourselves, also exist.

Love, and sentiment in general, affects our knowledge in two ways. Because we are interested, our attention is stimulated and this reveals to us, or sets in relief, aspects, nuances, qualities of the object which would otherwise remain hidden, unperceived or indistinct. In addition to this, the role of love is to be the means by which and through which the subject attains to and "experiences" the value, the existential density etc., of the object. That to which we commit ourselves, that which we prize, becomes part of ourselves and comes to share for us in the incommunicable and immediate character of our own existence.

We have then to keep in mind that a value, whatever it may be, reveals itself fully to us only in the activity by which it is effectively loved, prized, desired etc. The end, St Thomas teaches, moves us — as does Aristotle's primary mover — through allowing itself to be desired[38]. To be desired is then, where the end is concerned, to reveal itself as an end; but it is also to reveal itself as a value, for it is through its value that the end is capable of moving us. Through being actually desired and loved — and only in that way — the good exercises the causality which is proper to it, reveals itself and becomes a value for the subject at a new and deeper level.

22. – We turn now to the consideration of several characteristics of value which, in the context of our ethical investigation, are of particular interest.

1) Value is often said to *transcend what is "given"*, in the sense that it cannot be fully embodied in any object or being that comes within our experience. Each of us can testify to the frequency with which the realization of some long-cherished dream has resulted in disillusionment! We want something more, we want, at the very least, something different — and this seems to be a human characteristic[39]. — With this fact as a starting-point, certain philosophers believe that they can make an absolute opposition between reality and value. But this conclusion is not justified by their premises. All that can be said is that the spiritual subject as such transcends the entire order of things which are beyond the world. It is this which is the source of our restlessness and of our progress.

---

[38] "Just as an efficient cause exercises its influence by acting, so does a final cause exercise its influence by being sought and desired", St Thomas, *De Ver.*, 22, 2.

[39] *Essai*, n. 51; pp. 121-124. — On the chacteristics of value, *ib.*, n. 36; pp. 81-84.

2) Even though it transcends what exists, value looks towards this, in some way. Value manifests itself to us as something whose existence is demanded or justified, as possessed of a title to exist (in some object), as what *should be* (Seinsollen). As such, it demands of the subject that he *make it to be* (Tunsollen). Value moves us to make the object which it affects to exist or, at all events, to exist *for us*; to desire that it should be and, if it already exists, to approve of and rejoice in this etc. A perfect work of art appears to us to be justified by its perfection: it "deserves" to be: the impression of a certain necessity can be conveyed at times. At all events, where the artist himself is concerned, this demand becomes imperious and quasi-physical: the poem has to be written and the statue to take shape beneath his hands...

3) Values — or at least the majority of them (cf. n. 23) — are linked in pairs in that each of them has a positive and a negative pole [40]. In this way are opposed: good and evil (evil is not a lesser good or the simple absence of good but its "privation": it signifies a lack, a frustration; this is particularly true of moral evil, cf n. 234); the pleasant and the unpleasant (pain is not a diminished pleasure; an unpleasant sensation is something quite different from one that is only mildly pleasant or neutral); the beautiful and the ugly; the true and the false (information that is false is dangerous in a way that the absence of information is not) etc.

This bipolarity is a trait which distinguishes value from reality, for this latter, as such, has no contrary. Nothingness is the negation of being but not its negative pole. This absence of a contrary had already been pointed out by Aristotle, apropos of substance and of quantity [41]. (The Philosopher did not know of negative quantities which, moreover, are not found in reality but presuppose the activity of the human mind). — Opposition enters into the order of being only by means of dynamism, finality, of what "should be" — which also introduce value, at least in the broad sense — and it is only then that the absence of a perfection becomes a lack. Contrariety, it is true, is found in the category of quality, of which it provides, as Aristotle notes, the distinguishing characteristic; but it has to be noted that

---

[40] See R. Le Senne, *Obstacle et valeur*, pp. 102-184 and L. Lavelle, *Traité des valeurs*, t. I, pp. 233 seq.

[41] *Categ.*, 5, 3b 24-32.

this category is closely linked with value, as is evidenced in ordinary language (a person of quality). As well, values are at times referred to as "tertiary qualities"; in our own presentation, we have called it a "quasi-quality" (n. 19). The reason for this close link is, on the one hand, that an object is not good, is not truly a value, apart from all its properties and powers, which are of the qualitative order (n. 18), and, on the other hand, that a quality is always related, directly or indirectly, to a being's activity.

4) Between each pair of values there is a definite order: the positive pole is superior to the negative and it alone has an intrinsic worth. Strictly speaking, the term "value" applies only to it; the negative pole, the "negative value" is better referred to as an anti-value [42].

5) Finally, the various orders of values are *heterogeneous*. There is no common measure between the value of truth and that of health, the value of a generous deed and that of a pleasure party. (Hence, as we shall see, Bentham's idea of a calculus of values is futile, n. 63). There is not just one value which is found here and there in varying degrees of intensity. The diversity is qualitative and of this we are spontaneously aware. The moral uplift which results from some sacrifice is not of the same order as the satisfactions which have been renounced; these are not recovered in the way that the capital which has been sunk in a lucrative enterprise is recovered. It is for this reason that the sacrifice really is a sacrifice.

6) Heterogeneous though they are, the various orders of values are not purely and simply diverse: there is an order in their diversity: they constitute a *hierarchy*.

23. – The establishment of a scale of values is one of the chief problems that faces a philosophy of values. Before we turn to this problem it will be helpful to consider two extreme positions.

To some philosophers, the hierarchical character seems to be such an exclusive property of the world of values that they consider it necessary to deny that it is present in reality as such. Being, of itself, allows for no order, no gradation. — But this

---

[42] See L. Lavelle, *op. cit.*, p. 233, who rejects, or at least judges to be less satisfactory, the expression "negative value".

attempt to separate being and goodness is not justified (n. 5). Being signifies what is actual and, in consequence, possessed of a perfection; to the degree to which something is actual and in consequence perfect, to that degree is it a being. The notion of participation, without which the unity-in-multiplicity of being would be unintelligible, implies this order, this hierarchy. — What is true is that the idea of perfection is the hinge of ontology and value-philosophy (and also in consequence of metaphysics and ethics), since being, to the extent to which it is perfect, is good.

The other and diametrically opposed view rejects the entire notion of a hierarchy of values. Values cannot be compared one with another; it is solely as a result of a person's exercise of his liberty that a subjective order is introduced. — It is indeed true that it is only my choice which makes a particular value to be *effectively* valuable for me, which makes it, as we have said (n. 21), to be a value at a new and deeper level. As well, it often happens that a person's knowledge of some value will remain quite imperfect until he compares it with other values and prefers it to them. — Nevertheless, the fact remains that when I am comparing a particular value with others, I appreciate that it is a value independently of my choice. It is not in my power to make certain values become higher and others lower, to make values such as the knowledge of the truth, friendship, generosity become inferior to and less worthy than those which are concerned with my sense life (the value, for example, of a dainty dish or of a well-heated office in winter). The same holds good with regard to the corresponding antivalues... The knowledge of such an objective order of values is an essential element of moral consciousness.

24. – Various classifications of values have been proposed. The most rational seems to be the one which arranges them in accordance with the extent to which they concern the spiritual subject as such. As well, a distinction can be made at each level between the subjective and objective aspects of these values. Finally, the anti-values which correspond to values in the strict sense will also have to be taken into consideration. In this way the following table of values will result. (We pass over "general" values such as those of existence, individuality, universality etc. [43] and those of utility which are reducible [44]).

1) *Infra-human values.* (This does not signify that they do not possess a value where man is concerned — there would be no meaning to this — but only that they are not values for him precisely as man). These are the values of the *sensory* order: the agreeable, the pleasant and their opposites, namely, the disagreeable and the unpleasant; subjectively — pleasure and pain; — and the *biological* values: objectively — what favours health or sickness; subjectively — health and sickness (debility, "physiological poverty") etc. — Even though our sensible consciousness, in that interiority has already commenced, is at a higher level than that of mere biological activity, sensory values are, nevertheless, subordinated to those which are biological: a pleasure which affects our health is disordered. Note also that *man's* sensible consciousness is neither solely nor principally concerned with his bodily activity but rather with his intellectual and volitional activity, so that another criterion for evaluating it is thereby introduced. Our sense life and all that is connected with it cannot then be judged simply at its own level.

2) *Human but infra-moral values.* Human, in that they involve the exercise of the powers which are proper to man, so that they are, in consequence, values for him precisely as man. They are not, however, human to such an extent that it is they which, in the last analysis, measure the value of man as man. Two groups of values can here be distinguished:

a) *Economic* values and those which can be called *eudaemonist,* such as the couples prosperity-destitution, success-failure and, in general, everything which moves the majority of

---

[43] It is the property of these values, according to N. Hartmann, *Ethik*, 2nd ed., 1935, pp. 267-305, not to have a contrary; they are all positive. — For an approach which regards these values as aspects of the transcendental good, see the *Essai*, n. 150, pp. 370-372. — On this entire paragraph (n. 24), consult nn. 150-155 of the *Essai*, pp. 370-381.

[44] But D. von Hildebrand, *Christian Ethics*, pp. 64-71, regards the useful as an irreducible value. The value of an action which produces a result has often no common measure with the value of what is produced. But since the useful implies the adaptation of means to an end, there is involved in it an element of rationality which has of itself a value. "There is here a sober reasonability which is connected with the teleological character of means as such", *ib,* p. 68.

mankind to judge themselves (or to judge others) *happy* or *unhappy*. — The objective element here is the value which is present in a certain situation, in certain events (the possession of great wealth, the success of an undertaking etc.); the subjective element is the state, the "hexis" of the subject as affected by that situation: the "being-rich", the personal success of the entrepreneur etc. — It might seem that these values, or at least certain of them, belong rather to the category of the useful. Nonetheless, there is in the possession of wealth and power an affirmation of oneself, a type of extension of one's personality which, in itself, is good and desirable. These values, situated as they are on the border between the vital and the spiritual — for the economic order is primarily concerned with the more elementary needs — can be said to mediate between the values of the preceding stage and those of which we are now going to speak.

b) Values which are more *spiritual*, in that they are not so closely bound up with the satisfaction of biological needs. Such values are: *noetic* values: objectively — the truth or falsity (of a proposition etc.); the depth or superficiality (of a doctrine, a book etc.); subjectively — knowledge of the truth, penetration of mind, soundness of judgment etc., or, on the contrary, error, ignorance, dullness, frivolity of mind etc.; *aesthetic* and *artistic* values: objectively — beauty or ugliness; subjectively — good or bad taste; *social* values: objectively — the harmony and prosperity etc., which a nation or group enjoys, or the anarchy, disorder, decadence etc., by which it is affected; subjectively — the capacity to establish good relations with others, the qualities of leadership and initiative or, on the contrary, the incapacity to have contact with others, an asocial temperament etc.; finally, there are the values which are part of the *natural* structure of a person's will, such as strength of character, constancy in one's undertakings, the power of resilience, or their opposites: weakness, cowardice, inconstancy, the tendency to capitulate. (The corresponding objective value will here be a certain "style", strong or weak, with which a person acts). These last values are much closer to the moral level; indeed, it is not easy to distinguish between them and moral values: is laziness a vice or a natural defect? But, on the other hand, since what is spiritual in man is conditioned by what is organic, these values have a biological basis. Laziness could be the result of the malfunctioning of some process of secretion...

The values of which we have just been speaking should not be underestimated. Nevertheless, it is not in them that the perfection of man as man consists. This is because they still remain *exterior to the subject as such*. They do not affect him in what is most himself. Even intellectual values, which are undeniably internal — is not intellection the very type of *immanent* action? — do not penetrate to and affect the intimate centre of the personality: their source is the person's (spiritual) nature rather than the person himself, the "I". Cognitional activity, as such, effaces, so to speak, the subject before the object. In: "I know", the subject is more acted upon than acting; he does not so much initiate this activity as become conscious of himself as one of the terms of the noetic relationship, and of the object as the other. To be sure, he is revealed as an existing subject, as one who is the ontological condition of the activity by which he is revealed, but not as a subject who is thereby *committed*. — Because of this relative exteriority, the object which is interiorized in the intellect does not affect the subject as the very core of his being. As a knower, the value of the subject is not dependent on the object known: it is he, on the contrary, who evaluates this [45]. In knowing the beautiful, he does not become beautiful; in knowing the good, he does not become good.

The values which have been considered up to the present can be called "natural" in that they are concerned with the nature (sensible or spiritual) of the subject, not with the subject himself as such.

3) Moral value on the contrary — the singular is here preferable for this order is much more strictly unified than those preceding, as will become clear in the course of our inquiry — affects the subject in what is most himself: in the exercise of his *liberty*. This value is proper to the *practical* order, as distinct both from the *speculative* and the "poietic" (the artistic and technical realms). It is concerned with human action itself — and not solely or directly with the work which

---

[45] St Thomas, *Summa Theol.*, I, 82, 3; *De Ver.*, 22, 11.

is the fruit of this action — as proceeding from the free will (nn. 1; 3). It is this value which is the true measure of the human person's worth.

4) Finally, *religious value* — here also, and for the same reason as we have just given, we prefer to use the singular — is concerned with the subject's relationship with the supreme source both of value and of the subject himself. For the moment we shall not discuss this value. Even though it is irreducible to moral value, the two are nevertheless intimately linked. Each order involves the other, so that morality cannot be perfect without religion, just as there can be no authentic religion without morality [46].

---

[46] On the relation between moral and religious value, see B. Häring, *Das Heilige und das Gute*, Krailling b. München, 1950, especially pp. 45-58 (French translation: *Le Sacré et le Bien*, Paris, 1963, pp. 41-50).

Our classification of values resembles that of M. Scheler, who distinguishes, in an ascending order: the value of the pleasant or unpleasant, vital values, spiritual values, religious values. The higher values are richer, more indivisible, more independent of objective qualities and the organism; the satisfaction they bring is more profound. — But note that moral value is outside that hierarchy, since it can never be directly sought (cf. further on, n. 33, 2). — To the consideration of the ascending order of values, N. Hartmann adds that of their urgency or, as he says, of their force (Kraft). He distinguishes: values that are extremely general (allgemeinste), subjective fundamental values (for example, the value of life, of consciousness, of activity, of liberty etc.), objective fundamental values (the values that are to be found in various "goods", Güterwerte, for example, the value of the situation, of power, of happiness etc.), fundamental moral values (goodness, nobility, purity) and those which are special. There is no supreme value.

L. Lavelle (*Traité des valeurs*, t. II) considers the various relations of man with the world. Each of these relations grounds a double order of values, according as it is envisaged from the point of view of the object or of the subject. Since man can be considered as in the world, as confronted with the world, as above the world, there result, successively, the following values: economic and affective values, intellectual and aesthetic values, moral and religious values.

More recently, H. Reiner has proposed another classification. Values are absolute or relative. These latter, in their turn, are either relative to the subject himself (eigenrelativ) or relative to another (or to others: fremdrelativ). The values relative to the subject are, by definition, subjective; the others, as well as the absolute values, are objective, *Das Prinzip von Gut und Böse*, Freiburg-im-Br., 1949, p. 9; *Gut und Böse*, Freiburg-im-Br., 1965, p. 19. Relative values always suppose the presence of a need.

III. Moral Value.

A. *The Phenomenon of Moral Value.*

25. — The ethical world, as we are here concerned with investigating it, is that of moral value. But the first question that presents itself is, obviously, whether this term is anything more than a form of words.

To ask this question is not the same as asking whether the value which can be described as moral is *objectively grounded* and, as a result, valuable *in itself,* so that the subject, according as he accepts or rejects the requirements which it makes on him, not only appears to himself to be good or evil but is so really, from an absolute point of view, so that in consequence, he ought to be so judged by all. The only question that is here being asked is whether or not human beings are conscious of a value which is distinct from all those which we have called infra-moral, irreducible to them as well as being absolutely superior.

Neither are we here concerned to know how this value has arisen for human beings and how they have gradually come to be conscious of it. To discuss the origin of moral ideas, the genesis of moral consciousness, is the task of psychologists, ethnologists, sociologists... What we are here interested in is moral value as it effectively presents itself in consciousness and this consciousness as it is at present structured. — Now the fact that an author believes he can explain the consciousness of moral value in terms of the evolution of other values (eudaemonist values, for example, as is maintained by certain Utilitarian philosophers of whom we shall later speak) does not mean that he is denying the originality and irreducibility of moral value for *mankind's present consciousness. The two questions are distinct* [46bis].

26. — On the contrary, all those who claim that they can reduce the experience of moral value to the experience of other values are to be classed among those who deny that human beings have a moral consciousness. Here it is not any more a question of genesis but of structure: the term "moral value"

[46bis] Cf. G. E. Moore, *Ethics* (1912), London, 1963, pp. 72-74: even if moral judgment originates in feeling, it does not follow that it is only a feeling.

would merely designate eudaemonist and sociological etc., values (to be praised or blamed, esteemed or despised, to foster or hinder the harmony of the social group, to be a success or failure in life etc.). In consequence, to act well would, *even at the level of consciousness* — by this is meant a consciousness which is enlightened concerning its true motivations, beyond the level of superficial appearance — be the same as increasing one's capacity for action, assuring the success of one's enterprises, acting in accordance with the customs and interests of society etc. (Cf. n. 78).

To be classified in the same way are all those who interpret the higher values and the corresponding inclinations or activities (art, morality, religion) as no more than a "sublimation" — in other words a camouflage — of elementary instincts, in particular of the sexual "libido", as a result of the "censorship" exercised by the "superego" (which is itself that fraction of the ego which has been alienated through introjective identification with the Father...), and who, at times, as did Freud himself, identify the "voice of conscience" with the "superego" (so that there is a certain ambiguity in their view of the moral life) [46ter]. — None are stronger in their denial of moral value than those who, with Nietzsche, regard morality as a kind of hypocrisy which enables men to conceal their helplessness, their cowardice, their resentment, their slavish baseness, by bestowing on these a veneer of respectability.

Nietzsche develops his relentless attack, starting from *The Dawn of Day* (*Morgenröte*, 1881), continued in *The gay Science* (*Die fröhliche Wissenschaft*, 1882), *Thus spoke Zarathustra* (*Also sprach Zarathustra*, 1883-1884; the fourth book appeared in 1892), *Beyond Good and Evil* (*Jenseits von Gut und Böse*, 1886), *The Genealogy of Morals* (*Zur Genealogie der Moral*, 1887), *The Twilight of the Idols* (*Götzendämmerung*, 1889). — His distinction between two classes or races of men is wellknown: the "masters" (Herren) in whom Life affirms itself triumphantly and who cultivate the "noble" — and the "slaves" whose vitality is stunted and who are devoted to the "ignoble" values. Morality — and in particular Christian morality — is, according to Nietzsche, nothing more than the attempt of the slaves to take revenge on the

---

[46ter] Freud's moral ideas are set forth especially in *Totem und Tabu* (1913), and *Unbehagen in der Kultur* (*Civilization and its Discontents*), 1929.

masters by exalting the ignoble values (which are baptized as "good") at the expense of those which are noble (but which are branded as "evil". — Nietzsche also denounces "bad conscience" as a morbid state (Erkrankung) which is present only among the slaves and which springs from a misdirection of the "will to power" (Wille zur Macht). This will exists in all men, but where the masters are concerned it is exercised without hindrance and normally, that is, it is directed against others. The slaves on the other hand are unable to exercise it in this way: as a result, it becomes turned in on the subject himself so as to torture him interiorly, *Genealogy*... II, nn. 16-18.

It is evident that the proponents of logical or linguistic positivism, for whom judgments of value are void of meaning (n. 5), cannot acknowledge any content, even phenomenological, in moral value.

The great majority of philosophers and the generality of ordinary men and women — at least when their moral conscience has arrived at a certain degree of evolution — affirm, on the contrary, that the value which is revealed in moral experience is specifically different from all other values. This affirmation could be expanded in the following way:

Among the various values which can motivate a human action there is one which human beings are conscious of — at least in certain instances — as being quite distinct from all others: not simply different from these others in the way that they differ among themselves, not simply irreducible to the others or to their possible combinations, but without any common measure with them, because situated on a higher level. It is this value and this value alone which, in the final analysis, "measures" the human action as human and through it the person as a person. The action will be judged good or evil *as a human action*, the person will be judged good or evil *as a person*, according as their moral value is positive or negative, so that even if the person has in other respects the finest qualities: intelligence, strength, beauty, *savoir faire* etc., he will have to be regarded, if he is morally "negative", as an "evil person", purely and simply. Inversely, a "poor type", only moderately gifted from the intellectual and physical point of view, provided he is a man of "good will", provided he is morally "positive", is "good", purely and simply.

27. — Is this common moral consciousness anything more than an illusion? Is this alleged experience to be regarded as only imaginary or as the result of a false interpretation? On the contrary, it is here submitted that this experience is authentic and that the value which it reveals corresponds to the description already given.

Obviously, a strict demonstration of this point is impossible. A datum of consciousness cannot be demonstrated: all that can be done is to help the reader or hearer to focus his attention on the datum in question — here it is moral value — so that he may grasp it for himself. The following "arguments" have no other aim than this. (Note their growing interiority. All the three begin from the fact that human beings make moral judgments, but in the first the subject and object of these judgments are outside of ourselves; in the second, the object is still external but the subject is ourselves; in the third, we ourselves are subject and object).

1. *Moral judgments as part of the human condition.*

Whatever one's ideas on morality, one cannot blind oneself to the fact that human beings make judgments of value concerning the actions of individuals. Some of these actions win for those who perform them approval, praise, recompense, while others, on the contrary, draw on them reproach, blame, punishment; yet others, apparently, are neutral from the point of view of value. This distinction and, in particular, the opposition between "good" and "evil" actions is not simply confined to one people, one race or one epoch: they are to be found, as history and ethnology testify, among the most primitive as well as among the most developed peoples, with admittedly immense differences concerning what in the concrete is acknowledged as "good" or as "evil".

Abundant evidence on this point can be found, for example, in V. Cathrein, *Die Einheit des sittlichen Bewusstseins*, Freiburg -im- Br., 1914 and R. Mohr, *Die christliche Ethik im Lichte der Ethnologie*, in *Handbuch der Moraltheologie*, Bd. IV, München, 1954. Even those whose interpretation of the "moral sense" has to be classified under the heading of "moral naturalism" (cf. n. 60) do not generally contest its universality. So, for example, Ed. Westermarck in *The Origin and Development of Moral Ideas*, c. 5, shows clearly, with the aid of numerous examples, how people who are apparently uncultured distinguish between good and evil actions, repent of their transgressions, are indignant at those of others etc. (It is not, moreover, strictly necessary that the universality of the "moral sense" be established. One single authentic moral experience is sufficient for our purpose).

It will be worthwhile to reproduce here, at least partially, a note which an ethnologist — Fr. J. Goetz — has kindly provided:

"It is not the statistical comparison of what is objectively contained in the categories of good and evil which different peoples have, that entitles us to conclude to the universal recognition of moral good and evil but rather, the fact that every 'culture', every human community, possesses some such category...

Moreover, it is wellknown that 'primitives' are generally unable to recite, even in a very general form, the series of positive and negative precepts on which they act; but despite this, they know, down to the last detail, what they should do and what they should avoid 'in order that they may act as men'.

Where do they obtain this knowledge? Who has placed them under these laws and bound them to act in this or that particular way? The usefulness of these laws is not immediately obvious to them and they often fail to arrive at any appreciation of it, so that what seems to be of most concern to them is not the good-to-be-obtained or the evil-to-be-avoided, but the law itself. What is 'taboo' is not to be done, simply because it is 'taboo'; the reason they do not break it is because they have been forbidden to do so.

At first sight, a reasonable reply seems to be that laws are inculcated in the primitive mind through myths, which are linked, to a greater or lesser extent, to a cosmogony; or that prohibitions are associated with, and grounded on, a notion of the world as a complex of interacting forces. But laws cannot be derived from myths: the latter are but subsequent justifications or, rather, they are only ways of expressing that these are the laws. There is no escaping the fact that man experiences the need to impose laws on himself: man is a being who cannot but legislate for himself. Since this need is closely linked with the 'social' living of primitive man (the meaning of 'social' is here extended to include all the environmental factors with which he has to cope), it has been maintained that he has no existence as an individual but only in the group and through the group. The community creates the person; it is the community which imposes laws and expresses itself in myths. In consequence, the morality of 'primitive' man is reduced to the level of 'taboos', through which the group exercises collective pressure on him.

But we cannot today rest content with this over-simplified view, since it is far from doing justice to the evidence.... It is quite true that anthropologists will always be able to dispute whether men came together in society because they were men, or whether they became men only through collective life. It is impossible now to have sufficiently 'primitive' facts to resolve the controversy... There is now no way of deciding whether the collective conscience has in fact been anterior to the individual conscience or *vice versa*.

But it has been possible for some centuries to establish the fact that among 'primitive' peoples the collective conscience is questioned and judged by the individual, when something which concerns his own personal life is at stake. When a 'backwoodsman' finds himself the victim of collective pressures which result in his condemnation by local law, even though he is not conscious of having acted badly, or when the community of which he forms part is unable to protect him against the secret machinations of witchdoctors, he will appeal to a higher source for justice and help: 'God sees what I suffer! God protect me!' — Similarly, even myths, which so 'realistically' express the meaning of man, of life, of events, provide an unexpected testimony to a higher order of reality, an order which is free of imperfection and where all the requirements of morality are perfectly satisfied, when they portray the 'hero' as suddenly transformed into a guardian of the morality of which he had hitherto been neglectful, or when they also delineate a faroff order which transcends and yet includes their 'realism'... It is precisely this element of another order.... that, in ethnology is referred to as God. God is the expression of the judgment of the individual conscience on the demands made by the collective conscience. As well as the good and evil which we call relative, there is a good and evil which are absolute, in virtue of their relationship with this 'faroff God' of the primitives.

On what foundation does this authentically primitive attitude rest? — If cosmogonical and sociological myths express man's realization that he is part of the world, that he is in-the-world, then the idea of a faroff God, or of a God who has made the world, can only be explained as a yet more profound (and consequently, less clear-cut) realization of another aspect of his human condition: his existence-in-the-world; his realization that he himself and the world which he inhabits are dependent on an order which rules them both, and from which the possibility and stability of every other particular order are derived. In this order, good and evil are absolute; it is an 'inexorably just' order, in the words of an old local chieftain, translated for me by my interpreter...".

28. – Note well that there is a very marked difference between the praise and blame which people receive on account of their "natural" qualities or deficiencies (abundance or scarcity of external goods, physical strength or weakness, penetration or dullness of mind etc.), and that which they receive because they have done (or have been willing to do) or have not done what is considered as "to-be-done", in accordance with the norms of accepted values. One pities an imbecile and a sickly person; it can happen that they are made fun of and this is odious; but no one would think of blaming them: "it's not their fault", people say. Inversely, one may praise a person's beauty, intelligence, bodily development etc., but in so doing one is admiring his natural "gifts" and felicitating him in the proper sense of the word (that is, acknowledging his good fortune in possessing them) rather than praising the *person himself* — as one would if one considered that he had "merited" these gifts. It is precisely this notion of merit (n. 289) which most easily enables us to recognize the ordinary person's appreciation — as it is expressed in myths and folklore — of the originality of moral value. We have only to recall the many legends and tales in which the hero, after enduring many trials, obtains the *recompense* of his troubles (Hercules, but also Cinderella). The happiness which he achieves is not presented as simply the natural effect of his activity, nor as merely the result of chance. That the good fairy takes an interest in Cinderella, that the despised daughter wins the heart of a prince, is not simply a happy turn of events for her: there is present in her some quality which calls for that interest and that love: neither her beauty nor even her sufferings alone (as if the fact of suffering of itself called for some compensation: an idea which, moreover, expresses a certain sense, already semi-moral, of order, balance, justice), but a value which she has manifested in her trials, a value which has been displayed in the form of patience, obedience, devotion etc., and as a result of which we are led to say of her good fortune: "it is just: she has deserved this": *moral value*.

Reflect also on the *indignation* that people commonly feel when they find evidence of injustice —, whether it is they themselves who suffer or whether others are the victims — and which, particularly in situations of the second kind, as Camus has well noted in *L'homme révolté*, is very different from the mere consciousness of having suffered some loss. (Undoubtedly, we are naturally drawn to regard as unjust whatever is to our own disadvantage; but what is to our disadvantage and what is unjust are by no means the same: the two notions, and the reactions which they provoke, are different. Our self-love makes use of moral value for the attainment of its own ends but it uses this as a value which differs from that which lies in its own gratification). — In the context of ordinary everyday events, how often do we not hear judgments of this kind: "this is not just; that should not be!" — Think finally on the reactions which greet the successes and failures, the good and bad fortune of certain persons. (We are here speaking not about legends but about real life). X did not deserve that misfortune; Z has got what was coming to him. A person of reasonably mature judgment would certainly not make statements of this kind if all that were in question were natural qualities and values.

Examples could be multiplied. But the reader has only to look about him and what he will discover will provide him with examples which will be, for him, the most convincing. The judgments of value which are expressed in the creations of the popular consciousness, in ordinary language and in the spontaneous reactions of a person who is naturally moral, make clear that in the actions which are being considered, and in their subject (real or fictitious), a value is appreciated and acknowledged which awakens an interest in us, and calls for a homage to which natural values have no claim. The reason for this is that the value in question is not simply concerned with particular and utilitarian ends: with what is advantageous, with the life or the welfare of the individual, of his offspring, of his clan — values of which the animals themselves seem to have a rudimentary and concrete perception; this value is concerned with man as man; he is affected by it according as he does or does not do what is expected of a man; it is the most decisive measure of his *humanization*.

29. – It is true that, very often, these same actions are also considered to be commanded or forbidden by the divinity, or at least possessed of some *sacred* character. (Sin, as a religious transgression, has a negatively sacred character). There is nothing more normal, since moral value involves religious, and *vice versa*. But the problem of their distinction is very different from the problem of the distinction between moral and infra-moral values.

It is however a fact that mankind did not all at once clearly distinguish moral value from other values and acknowledge its primacy.

That this is so is clear from philology. The words which express value first referred to physical force, to power, to effectiveness etc. This is true of the word "value" itself (from the Latin *valēre*: to be strong, vigorous, powerful), of the word "virtue" (from *virtus* which has the same root as *vis*, force) and of its Greek equivalent *aretē*; *agathos* seems to have been first applied to noblemen, to those of high position and power... Moreover, it is wellknown how greatly young people, in general, admire physical force: their heroes are often athletes, boxers, runners: men of endurance and steel... It is only gradually that the adolescent — and adolescent humanity — comes to appreciate that true force, true courage, true worth are to be found in that inner strength through which a person controls his passions and instincts, by submitting them to the influence of reason[47].

Similarly, it is only gradually — and for the most part very imperfectly — that mankind has learned to distinguish between the external dimension of a human action and the inner dimension (which, from the moral point of view, is primary). Since man is naturally turned towards what is external, he is prone to judge others — and himself — by what they have done rather than by what they have sincerely wished to do. A purely external violation of a divine command, even though performed in good faith, was, in times past, sufficient in their eyes to render a human being worthy of the anger of the gods. Cf. the legend of Oedipus.

Finally, the distinction between a person's moral and social value[47bis] has dawned on mankind only by slow degrees; indeed, there are still many people such as, for example, the Marxists, who reject this distinction.

---

[47] J. Plaget's investigations show how in the infant there is first a predominance of "moral realism", which measures the gravity of the fault by the damage caused, without taking account of intention, *Le jugement moral chez l'enfant*[3], Paris, 1969, pp. 81-155.

[47bis] What leads an individual to reflect on the problem of morality and really to become conscious of moral value is, very often, a practical contradiction, some conflict which brings his life to a cross-roads: in consequence, he is obliged to take thought and to place in question his obedience — which hitherto

But note carefully that there is a very definite distinction between the *genesis* of a notion and its *validity*. There is great need to separate the genetic from the critical problem. Who would wish to maintain that mathematics is to some extent cheapened because its origins stem from practical necessities (of exchange, of measurement etc.) as well as being associated with magical practices?

In addition, it often happens that one value is, so to speak, *induced* by another, from which it subsequently comes to be distinguished in consciousness. This is particularly evident in the process of education. A mother's caresses gradually "elevate" the child to a recognition and love of the values of which he has, in his mother, the incarnation [48].

Consequently, it is in no way surprising that when a person's moral development is at an early stage, he scarcely distinguishes between morality and obedience to social im-

---

had given rise to no problems — to the laws of the tribe or clan. See, for example, E. Weil, *Philosophie morale*, Paris, 1961, pp. 30-39. — On conflict, in general, as a factor in moral reflection, see R. Le Senne, *Le Devoir*.

In the West, at least in the Greek world, this type of conflict, with the resulting appreciation of the superiority of moral value to values that are merely sociological, has found literary expression (in the 5th century B.C.) in the *Antigone* of Sophocles and, a little later, in the Platonic dialogues: *Gorgias, The Laws,* etc. — But at the same time as the individual conscience was asserting itself in this way, in opposition to the laws of the city, the Sophists were interpreting this affirmation of the individual in terms of a naturalistic exaltation of instinct, so that every moral rule came to be regarded as conventional and artificial (n. 52). — A little later, Aristippus and Anthistenes orientated this same affirmation in the direction of an absolute autarky and independence; in doing this, they laid the remote foundations of an ethics of pure liberty. — It is clear, in consequence, that, from the beginning, the individual conscience found itself confronted with three possibilities which defined three ethical attitudes: an ethics of moral value, of the good, of duty; an ethics of naturalism and of instinct; an ethics of liberty. The problem will be to do justice to the requirements which are expressed through these three attitudes.

On the development of moral consciousness and the passage from exterior constraint to the notion of obligation, consult A. Ponceau, *Initiation Philosophique*, 4th ed., Paris, 1963, t. II, pp. 201-218.

A study of the formation of the individual's moral sense, and particularly of that of the child, would obviously be appropriate here. Among others, consult J. Piaget, *Le jugement moral chez l'enfant*, Paris, 1932 (English translation: *The Moral Judgment of the Child*, M. Gabain, New York, 1932) and G. Cruchon, *Psychologie pédagogique*, I: *Les transformations de l'enfance*, Mulhouse, 1966, pp. 203-214 and 297-335 (bibliog., pp. 346-400).

[48] On the inducement of values, see the *Essai*, n. 148; pp. 363-366.

peratives for which no reason is given. (Think, not only of prohibitions and taboos, but also of the tremendous pressure exercised by custom, fashion, "human respect", particularly in certain milieux, no matter how developed). It is only as he acquires an increasing power of reflection that a person becomes comscious of the value — true or supposed — that justifies these, at the very least the value of the social integration which their observance helps to maintain. — But note well that to appreciate moral value is one thing; to be able to distinguish it from other values and at once objectify it in a definite concept, in a "mental word", is quite another. The conduct and the judgments of men testify to their appreciation of moral value, even if their understanding of the notion is confused (cf. the text quoted in n. 27). Moreover, to reiterate a point already made, what we are here concerned to do is to verify the fact of moral experience, not to establish its universality. (This question will have to be faced later, n. 184).

30. – 2. *Our judgments of others.*

Each of us, if only we examine ourselves, will find plenty of examples of situations in which our judgment has been motivated by the positive or negative moral value that has been manifested in the conduct of others. In order to have a better appreciation of this value, it will be helpful to conjure up a concrete situation. Let us then imagine a person who dives into the sea so as to save his mortal enemy. Even if this person were also an enemy of ours, we could not but approve of and praise him interiorly. Why is this? Because he has displayed courage, decisiveness etc.? But these qualities can also be manifested in actions of which we do not at all approve. How many gangsters display such qualities! Is it then because such a person could be of help to us if we were in danger? If this were so, our reaction of approval should be proportionate to the probability of danger which we acknowledge; yet it is completely independent of this. Without any thought of our own gain, without calculating, our approval is directed to a value which is manifest in the conduct of this magnanimous rescuer; this value is "valuable" in itself, independently of the advantage it brings or could bring to us, so that our response cannot but be: "that is a good action", "that man is good", or, at the very least, "in spite of everything, there is something good in that man!"

Note carefully that the rescuer would be in no way deserving of our admiration — at least not of this kind of admiration — if he had acted under the effect of irresistible physical or psychic constraint; any more than a person would be blamed if, in similar circumstances, he did what would normally be reprehensible.

31. – 3. *Our judgments of ourselves.*

Here again it is sufficient to draw on our own experience; but for the same reason as we have just given, we shall propose a concrete example.

Let us imagine that we are in a position to concoct some method for succeeding in an examination without really trying — in other words, for cheating — through fraudulently procuring the questions in advance etc. Perhaps this fraud would reveal that we possess certain qualities: smartness, daring etc., — and, in fact, there are those who cheat rather for the pleasure of defeating the attempted surveillance, of demonstrating its ineffectiveness etc. Moreover, the success obtained in this way would, probably, be of very appreciable advantage, so that we could rub our hands and say: "I have done well!" — And nevertheless, we would not do "well" if we were to cheat. The adverb has not the same sense in both these instances, for there is now question of another value. In judging that we would *not do well* to cheat we are not thinking of the sanctions, for their probability can be, in certain situations, negligible. Neither are we thinking of the disadvantages that would affect us if the practice of cheating were to become widespread: what weight would this remote, hypothetical consideration have, in comparison with the certain and immediate advantage of the act in question? What we feel, or rather, what we understand is that if we were to cheat, we would diminish ourselves, we would *descend*, in relation to an order of values without common measure with other orders (for example, the order of economic values). We would be *worthy* of blame, *worthy* of punishment: this is quite different from simply being *in danger of* blame or punishment and also quite different from — as it is incomparably worse than — being *in fact* blamed or punished.

But suppose that we reject the tempting idea and refuse to cheat. Perhaps we shall feel a certain sense of regret that we have neglected a golden opportunity — especially if our uprightness results in our failing the examination. But, at the same time, we shall judge that this sentiment is unworthy, that it is not *right*: it reveals that there is an element in us which is in opposition to the value in question. On the contrary, we shall understand that by our honesty we have come to exist in a fuller way and at a higher level. We have become more human, more in harmony with what we really are: in a word, more *ourselves*. The reason for this is that we have overcome what tied us to our individual particularity (insofar as this means the exclusion and, in consequence, the refusal of others); what could not be approved by all, justified in the eyes of all; what is irrational and dark in us and, in consequence, alien to the centre of our being as persons [49]. As a result, we experience a sense of liberation: because the value to which we have submitted is "ab-solute", it "ab-solves" (i.e. frees) us from our particularity and our partiality. — In a word: in responding in this way to the appeal of moral value, of the *good*, we have genuinely acted as *persons* and not simply as *individuals*, since what personality adds to individuality is an "openness" to the Universal. — But to say this is to say that moral value is the value which is proper to the person, the value which is proper to the spiritual subject, the value which is proper to liberty, the value, finally, which is proper to man considered as specifically different.

Our experience of *repentance* is of singular help in enabling us to come to an appreciation of moral value. (The repentance that is here spoken of is that authentic repentance which springs from a person's recognition that he has freely committed a fault). Three elements can be distinguished in this experience:

1. The deed *has been done* and there is nothing I can do about it. I can do something about the consequences but I

---

[49] Cf. Vl. Soloviev, *La justification du bien*, 1897-1898; French translation Paris, 1939, pp. 28-42: the origin of moral consciousness is to be sought in the sentiment of "shame", which expresses man's profound certainty that he transcends the animals.

cannot undo the deed itself. I now have an existential experience of the principle of contradiction.

2. *It is I who have done this deed* — I myself and not someone else, nor something in me which was foreign to me. No matter how great the part which circumstances, temperament, heredity etc., may have played, once the action has been freely performed, and to the extent to which it has been so performed, it is from me that it derives its existential determination. And here also, there is now nothing I can do about it.

3. *I have done what is evil*: I have done what I ought not to have done; I deserve blame etc., and this blame touches *me* at the core of my being, as the unique person that I am. (It does not simply touch me at some surface level, as does the blame which I receive on account of an involuntary blunder or gaffe). I experience that I am judged by myself, or rather by the ideal which I bear within me but which is independent of me. And, once more, there is nothing I can do about this situation.

32. – From what has been said, it should be clear how far the emotive theory of moral judgments (n. 5) has strayed from the phenomenological truth. The person who makes such judgments is perfectly conscious that he does so in response to a value which he appreciates in the object (for example, in the act of cheating), and he is very far from confusing them with the mere expression of his subjective state or with statements concerning this. It is, on the contrary, that state (for example, the feeling of aversion with regard to cheating) which is revealed as dependent on the value which he has appreciated, as *motivated* by it [50].

The psychoanalytic explanation, which at times considers the moral conscience to be but a sublimation of the libido and at other times attributes it to the pressure of the superego, is no more successful in "saving the phenomena". These factors can create no more than a subjective demand; but, as we have seen,

---

[50] Cf. D. von Hildebrand, *Christian Ethics*, pp. 122-128: moral judgments and sentiments are not simply *caused* (as are superficial states: fatigue, depression etc.); they are *motivated* and present themselves in consciousness as a *response* of the subject to the value of the object (value-response).

the demand which moral value creates presents itself as objective; and all the more so, the more the subject comes to be freed from psychic pressures and constraints, the more he comes to be capable of judging and acting in accordance with his true self. The most that such factors can throw light on are certain misunderstandings concerning moral value, which are found, for instance, in scrupulous people. These errors occur more frequently in persons whose moral growth is in a rudimentary, even though not pathological, state; such people are scarcely able to distinguish moral value from the feelings etc., which normally accompany it, but which are also linked with the appreciation of other values (n. 46). Nevertheless, the fact remains: labelling some actions as good or bad differs from an understanding of what is goodness or badness. This latter pertains to a more profound level of the person and is presupposed by the former. It is only a moral being who can have a scruple; what distinguishes this from a mere phobia is its relation with moral value.

This will suffice for the moment. Our appreciation of moral value will become clearer when we have determined its properties more exactly and discovered its ontological foundation. All we are here concerned with are the immediate data of the prephilosophic moral consciousness.

33. – Without going beyond these data, but simply explicating them, we can distinguish several characteristic traits of moral value:

1) Firstly, in common with all other values, it presents an objective and a subjective aspect. It affects the object of a person's action: to help one's neighbour in his need is good in itself; to take what belongs to another is evil. But this value also affects the subject himself by means of his action: to will to help one's neighbour is good and one who has this "good will" is, to the extent to which he has it, a good person; to will to steal is evil and one who has this "evil will" is, to the extent to which he has it, an evil person — Strictly speaking, it is in the subject's action that moral value is primarily and immediately present. It is only because he acts well or badly that the subject is morally good or evil; his moral growth or diminution occurs at that level of existence which he confers

on himself by the exercise of his liberty. Obviously, it is not necessary that this free act be exteriorized: it is the immanent operation of the will that has primarily to be qualified as good or evil. However, as we shall see (nn. 224-232), the external dimension of the action has also to be qualified in this way, as has the object, but analogically. This participation in moral value, evidently, and with all the more reason, extends to the zone of affectivity: there are good and evil sentiments; we shall have occasion to speak of this later in our investigation (n. 276).

To our assertion that moral value is primarily and immediately present in the subject's action — that what this value signifies is a certain rectitude (or disorder) in an action — the objection could be raised that an action is good when it is directed towards what is good and that, consequently, moral value is primarily found in the object (n. 17). The relation between objective and subjective moral value will be treated of later (nn. 224-232), but even at the present stage of our investigation the following point can be made. The moral good is such only because of its relation with the liberty which ought to will it. The way in which it is chosen is far from being a matter of indifference. It matters little whether a mason builds a wall out of love for his work, or desire of gain, or under the constraint of need: all that is required of him is that the wall be solid, straight etc. His intention, his subjective dispositions do not count, as long as he is simply being considered *as a mason*. — It is, on the contrary, of supreme consequence that the moral good be freely chosen — so much so that an action which is exteriorly in harmony with the criteria of morality ceases to be really moral if this liberty is absent. (Cf. the distinction between "making" and "acting", n. 1).

2) Moral value is estimable, lovable, desirable *of itself* and *for itself*: it is not present in the action of a person who does what is morally good *simply* in view of something else. (To do this would be the equivalent of reducing the noble good to the useful). It is for its own sake that the noble good is to be desired[51]. Hence it is that we admire and approve of a person who is just, generous, loyal etc., independently of any

---

[51] St Thomas, *Summa Theol.*, I, 5, 6.

considerations of self-interest (nn. 30 and 71). — This, to be sure, does not at all mean that what is morally good may not *also* be prized and sought in view of something else — I wish to do what is good so that I may be saved — but only that to make of it a mere means, to make of it a relative good, is to destroy it. There is in it something which imposes itself in virtue of its own worth[52].

But, on the other hand, paradoxically, it seems that it is impossible for a person to act morally if he is directly aiming at this. "Moralism" (to seek to be virtuous for the sake of being virtuous) is but a subtle form of self-love ("Pharisaism). According to Max Scheler, for example, moral value appears "on the shoulders" ("auf dem Rücken") of an action which is directed towards something else, namely, the dignity which persons possess[53]. There is a problem here to which we shall later return. We shall see that moral value can be authentically aimed at only on condition that it be transcended, but not, however — and this is in line with the point that has just previously been made — reduced to the condition of a means to an end.

3) As lovable, desirable etc., of itself, moral value does not seem to differ from the values of truth, beauty and, in general, all those values which are called "spiritual" (n. 24,2). The difference is, however, great and it becomes clear if one contrasts the relation of moral value with these other values and the relation of these with each other.

---

[52] "There are some things ... which are both desired for their own sakes — since, even if no other good came to us through them, they would still be good — and are also desirable on account of something else, since they are the means by which we obtain some more perfect good; it is in this way that virtues are to be cultivated (cf. Aristotle, *Nicom. Eth.*, I, 7, 1097a 30-34). This is why Cicero says .. that there are things which have the power to draw us to themselves and are worthy of our choice, such as virtue, truth, knowledge; and this is sufficient to satisfy the definition of the honourable good", St Thomas, *Summa Theol.*, II-II, 145, 1 ad Ium — St Anselm, in his usual style, well expresses this characteristic of moral value by defining moral goodness as: "uprightness of will which is preserved for its own sake", *De Veritate*, c. 12; PL. t. 158, col. 482 B. Cf. his definition of liberty: "The power of preserving uprightness of will for its own sake" *Dial. de libero arbitrio*, c. 3; ib., col. 494 b. — On "rectitudo" in St Anselm, see the thesis of R. Fouchet which bears this title, Paris, 1964.

[53] Max Scheler. *Der Formalismus in der Ethik*, 1921, pp. 522, 527-528. — In a more nuanced manner, N. Hartmann, *Ethik*, 2nd ed., pp. 236-240.

Cultural values (artistic values, for example), since they are spiritual, are undoubtedly on a higher level than biological values. Nevertheless, I would act wrongly if I were to ruin my health by cutting down excessively on sleep in order to listen to Bach or Beethoven. There can then be situations in which moral value demands the temporary sacrifice of a higher value to one that is lower. On the contrary, and it is this which manifests the transcendence of moral value, it could never be good to subordinate this value to some other. This is self-evident and, indeed, almost a tautology, for how could it be good to prefer anything whatever to the good? It is, however, allowable and, at times, inevitable, but only in certain situations, to prefer one way of doing good to another way which is normally better, or even, outside of these situations, necessary.

It will perhaps be replied that this example proves nothing. If it is necessary to take care of one's health, this is because the realization of higher values is conditioned by the possession of good health: their subordination to lower values is, in consequence, only apparent: one keeps the future in store and steps back in order to leap all the further. — But it is precisely here that the unique character of moral value is manifested: once it enters the scene, the line of reasoning just mentioned is ruled out. The demands of morality do not allow for holidays or strategic retreats. While one has to be alive in order to lead a moral life, one is still not allowed to save one's life at the cost of acting immorally. There can be situations — as Aristotle acknowledged — in which the moral ideal requires the sacrifice of what conditions moral activity!

4) The reason for this is that if life is a necessary condition for the realization of moral value, this latter, in its turn, is the *raison d'etre* of life. Even further: it is this value which reveals the meaning of life and the way in which it is to be lived: from this value, the value which is proper to it, liberty derives its meaning, in accordance with the magnificent Anselmian definition of free will: "the power to preserve rectitude of will for its own sake"; and liberty is the highest expression of existence. The finality of things is towards persons, the "order of bodies" towards the "order of spirits", but this latter is internally orientated towards a summit; moral value. Since this is the value of the person as such, the value

which, above all others, measures the growth or diminution of the *person* (n. 31), it is also the value which indicates the pole of being and outlines, in the order of spirits, an image of the "order of charity".

In saying that moral value is the value of the person as such, and that it possesses an "absolute" character, we do not at all wish to maintain that a small lie makes a person to be absolutely evil, or that the least good action renders him perfectly virtuous! All that is here said is that moral value affects him at the centre of his being as a person, so that there is no higher value to which it is merely relative and for whose sake it could be rejected. It is the moral order, in its entirety, which possesses an absolute and transcendent character: our actions do not all share in this character to the same degree: some do so to a greater extent than others. A small lie does not turn a person into a criminal, but nothing can make the liar, as a liar, to be good.

Note, finally, that if moral value is the value of the person as such, it is not the only human value. An upright person is good purely and simply, but this fact alone does not endow him with the plenitude of human perfection. The supreme value is not the total value. One suspects that there will be a problem when the question arises of determining the relations between various values (nn. 277 seq.).

5) Since it concerns the person, moral value presents itself as absolutely singular: no one can take my place in achieving the value which I am called upon to achieve. — But, at the same time, it presents itself as universal and that in a twofold sense:

1. On the one hand, what is morally good (or evil) for me, would be so for anyone else in the same conditions. To lie, to steal, to torture, to assassinate: these are not simply "repugnant" to me; I am in no doubt but that they should be repugnant to everyone. To save a child who is in danger, to help an unfortunate person to rehabilitate himself: not only would *I be happy* to do these things, but I appreciate that it would be *right* for everybody to do so (supposing that such a situation were to arise and that they were in a position to help). — This does not deny the existence of altogether singular vocations, but in these very vocations a universal value is manifested: *fidelity to the ideal by which one is drawn*. Interior to all duties is the duty to do one's duty. It is not a question here of an abstract universal, of an analogical schema (what your duty

is for you, my duty is for me). It is a question of a concrete, existential attitude which is found at the heart of all authentically moral attitudes (and which we shall have to investigate more closely). In brief: Duty is not an abstract of duties; it is, on the contrary, these which particularize Duty and there is no true morality unless fidelity to particular duties (familial, civic etc.) is grounded on the radical decision to be faithful to Duty [54].

2. On the other hand, when I judge that a certain line of conduct is, due account being taken of the circumstances, morally good or evil for me, I realize that everyone else, even those who do not find themselves in the same conditions, and for whom moral value perhaps takes another form, should, if they knew my situation, approve of my judgment. The young man who judges that he is called to the priesthood, or to the religious life, does not claim that all his companions should follow his example, but he is entitled to expect that they should approve of his choice (without thereby condemning themselves).

This double character of moral value is linked with the double charsacter of liberty. On the one hand, as the expression of the unique subject that each one is, it is our liberty that most of all distinguishes us one from another; on the other hand, since it has its roots in reason, it involves a fundamental appreciation of the liberty that others possess, so that reciprocal communication and recognition are possible. In its turn, this double character of liberty manifests the double character of existence: at one and the same time universal and unique; incommunicable in that it is the basic perfection that each individual being possesses as its own, it is also the radical source of their unity.

6) We have mentioned the word "duty"... This leads us to the consideration of a final feature of moral value: its obligatory character. Because of the importance of this subject, it will be worthwhile considering it at some length.

---

[54] As well, as we shall see later, even the most singular vocations never dispense a person from universal laws: there is no "suspension of ethics" (nn. 184-185 and 191-192).

B. *The Phenomenon of Obligation*.

34. – As we have already noted (n. 2), the notion of obligation has played a primary role in the moral philosophy of the past two centuries. It is Kant who, more than anyone else, has set in relief this aspect of the moral life: for him, obligation has become the essential characteristic of the good, so that the good action is the one to which duty calls (n. 115). — On the other hand, this same notion is nowadays frequently challenged or emptied of its content. Challenged: by the defenders of morality "without obligation or sanction" (n. 94); emptied of its content: by those who see in conscience nothing more than the pressure exercised by the group or society (nn. 52; 78) or by the superego (n. 26). — Moreover, has it not even been maintained that Thomistic morality did not find any place for the notion of obligation, or at least allowed it no more than a restricted role, limiting it to certain sectors of the moral life [55]? — There are, finally, others, of whom we shall speak later (n. 160), who, while they strongly defend the existence of obligation, also claim that there can be no authentic consciousness of it unless this is mediated by the explicit knowledge of God as lawgiver.

There is then need to elucidate the phenomenon of obligation in its link with that of moral value. But here also our aim is not to inquire whether, and how, the consciousness of obligation is grounded on reality, any more than it is to explain its genesis, or to establish its universality. It is of little consequence to our investigation whether this notion, in common with some other moral concepts (those of responsibility, for example, or of law), first presents itself to us charged with sociological connotations (one is obliged to someone, in virtue of some benefit or loan that has been received or simply in virtue of one's condition of dependency, subordination etc.), connotations which, if they are accepted uncritically, lead all too often to a rapid but illegitimate ascent from duty to God. — Our sole aim here is this: since, in fact, the notion of obligation is present in human consciousness we wish to throw

---

[55] See, for example, J. Tonneau, *Devoir et morale*, "Revue des sc. phil. et theol.", 1954, pp. 233-252; *Absolu et obligation en morale*, Montreal-Paris, 1965.

more light on it by disengaging it from the accidental elements which ordinarily accompany it. As in our investigation of moral value, our method will be descriptive, not deductive, much less polemical.

35. – That there is a consciousness of obligation, a phenomenon of obligation, *human conduct and human language* make abundantly clear. One has only to open one's eyes in order to appreciate that human beings — or better, in order to prejudge nothing, some human beings — in all forms of culture, are, or claim to be, guided and governed in their practical life by certain norms, rules or laws which impose themselves on them from within (that is, without exterior constraint), with at times an incredible force. It is not a question of the attraction of pleasure, or of the pressure of vital instincts: what these rules demand of them is very often contrary to the desires and satisfaction of their sensible nature. Neither is it a question of a physical necessity. The ability and the means to violate the law are not always missing. What is not possible in violating it is to escape from the hold which it exercises over them; to ensure that it be no longer the law, so that it ceases to condemn those who violate it. It is precisely for this reason that one speaks of *obligation*: man experiences that he is *bound*; he has the power to do what he ought not to do, but if he does so he cannot alter the fact that he is blameworthy or contemptible (and if he is sincere, cannot but acknowledge that he is): he has, out of love for life, or its pleasures, sacrificed what gives point and purpose to life: hence *his* life, such as he has made it by the exercise of his liberty, has lost its point, has become worthless, deprived of what justifies it... Hence the phenomenon of remorse, which we have already analysed (n. 31), and which, at least when a person's conscience has attained a certain maturity, differs completely from the regret that springs from the loss of a good opportunity, from a blunder or a slip. Hence also the notion, which is so wide-spread, of a certain duality in man, a notion which is at times developed and made clear-cut in frankly dualistic systems, where spirit and matter, soul and body, "purusha" and "prakriti" etc., are strongly opposed. Hence, finally, the idea of conscience as *guide* and *judge*; expressions such as: my conscience orders, forbids, rebukes me; the voice of conscience, the eye of conscience ("The eye was in the tomb and was looking at Cain")[56] etc.

36. – Obligation expresses itself under the form of a necessity: how often do we not hear it said: "It is *necessary* to act in this way! This is not as it *should* be". But this necessity is of an altogether different order from physical necessity. Undoubtedly, this difference is scarcely perceived by those whose consciences have as yet developed very little: such people, except perhaps in exceptional cases (see the text quoted in n. 27), do not distinguish moral obligation from the social pressure exercised through prohibitions and taboos. Gradually however, from the mere consciousness of necessity, there emerges the consciousness of the value which justifies that necessity, as well as the consciousness of the liberty which differentiates moral from natural necessity. This development of consciousness is reflected in language: the word "obligatory" exists as well as the word "necessary". In English and in German there are two distinct verbs: I must, I ought; müssen, sollen...

So the autonomy of moral necessity in relation to social pressure comes gradually to be appreciated: there emerges the realization that above the laws, rules and norms which prevail only within the clan, the tribe, the State, are those others which are binding on man as man — those "unwritten" laws which Sophocles, through the mouth of Antigone, has praised[57].

Ordinarily, as has already been noted — and the text of Sophocles provides a good example — obligation is linked with a divine law. Nevertheless, the consciousness of obligation can be found among agnostics and even among atheists. Even further: a

---

[56] Victor Hugo, *La légende des siècles: La Conscience.*

[57] "Creon: and yet you dared to contravene (the order)? — Antigone: Yes. That order did not come from God. Justice, that dwells with the gods below, knows no such law. I did not think your edicts strong enough to overrule the unwritten unalterable laws of God and heaven, you being only a man. They are not of yesterday or today, but everlasting. Though where they came from, none of us can tell. Guilty of their transgression before God I cannot be, for any man on earth", Sophocles, *Antigone*, vv. 449-460, trans. by E. F. Watling, *The Theban Plays*, Penguin Classics, 1947, p. 151.

quasi-moral character can frequently be discerned in the rejection of every form of genuinely moral obligation by materialists, atheistic Existentialists etc.: they give the impression that they experience an obligation to deny obligation out of love for the truth, in order to free men from their prejudices, in order to open to them a richer form of existence etc. Moral value and obligation are assailed only in the name of another moral value, another obligation...

37. – From this objective consideration we now turn, as we did in our previous analysis, to the consideration of our own moral experience[58]. We have all lived through moments in which the necessity of Duty has become more imperious, and even tragic, under a form which has been at times positive and at others — and more frequently perhaps — negative. Such moments can provide excellent material for our analysis. Nevertheless, in addition to the fact that such experiences remain the secret of each one, their strictly moral element is almost always inextricably linked with a social element (the influence of custom, of accepted opinions, the desire to be approved, the fear of being blamed etc.) and, in particular, with a religious element (the fear of offending God). This close link is beneficial: each of these associated elements reinforces the others. It does not, however, facilitate our investigation. A rigorous reflection on our experience would, without doubt, enable us to isolate the ethical factor, but here also it will be of advantage to make use of a suitable example. Suppose then — in order to vary our examples — that we have the opportunity to acquire a large inheritance by altering someone's will. The economic value of such an action is extremely obvious, but it can also have a real social value. The money obtained in this

---

[58] One could, in order to make the parallelism more exact, consider here the way in which we judge how others should act or should have acted. In order to simplify matters, we have omitted this consideration which, moreover, does not seem to throw any fresh light on the question. Nevertheless, it is interesting to note the difference between the moral judgment: "you ought to do that" and the imperative: "do that" (or: "I want you to do that"). We have seen that certain authors such as C. L. Stevenson, explain the former in terms of the latter (see the Introduction, note 11). It is clear, however, that the first judgment expresses a demand which is universal and impersonal (that is, independent of the person who formulates it), even when it is in fact invoked in support of an extremely personal desire.

way will be devoted to good works, to the support of schools and hospitals etc., in place of coming into the hands of a dissipated or debauched heir. (Similarly, the opportune administration of a dose of poison would, at times, have spared humanity the caprices of a despot). There are undoubtedly some less pleasing features to this action: one could be discovered, arrested, condemned; one risks losing the esteem, the confidence of others etc. But can I not imagine a "perfect" crime where these possibilities are practically non-existent?

And nevertheless, all things considered, this *ought not* to be done. That is as clear as day. But what does it mean? What underlies this "ought not"? Let us try to obtain the required light.

38. – The first step is to eliminate the elements which are alien to morality. The troublesome consequences which are foreseen: we have seen the reason for this. There is, however, one such consequence which, it would seem, our hypothesis has not excluded: *remorse*. My fraud, it is granted, will not be discovered; but if I escape from others, I shall not escape from myself: I shall be my own executioner. The fear of having to condemn myself — is not this the essence of obligation?

A distinction has to be made. The sentiment of remorse can be considered under two aspects: materially, as a distressing feeling, and formally (in relation to the exercise of liberty which gives meaning to this psychic fact), as a *deserved* feeling of distress. If I falsify this document I shall suffer for having done what I ought not to have done.

Now, under the first aspect, the remorse which is foreseen has obviously no ethical character. The same feeling of distress can be experienced when there is no question at all of an immoral action, as for example when a person breaks a settled routine, or does something which is out of the ordinary. There are people who cannot sleep unless they have checked three or four times that the door of their room is securely locked, have made sure that there is not a thief under the bed, have arranged their clothes in this or that particular way... It is worth noting here that the intensity of a psychic state does not depend solely on its objective content. A person is, at times, much more upset by a fear which he *knows* to be empty, or because he has failed to observe a custom which he *knows* to be ridiculous than because he has violated a law which he nonetheless *knows* to be just and sacred. So, for example, from the fact that a woman is more upset by the death of her pet dog than she is by the death of some stranger which she reads about in the newspaper, one would be wrong to conclude that she would be ready to sacrifice a human being's life in order to save that of her dog.

Under the second aspect — as a feeling of distress which is motivated and deserved — remorse and, in consequence, the anticipation of it, has certainly a moral character; but this springs entirely from what motivates and merits the distress: the violation of a duty. This means that obligation cannot be explained in terms of remorse: the consciousness of obligation cannot be derived from the anticipation of remorse, since this latter presupposes it. There would be no remorse and, in consequence, no anticipation of it, unless I appreciated that I am *obliged* to do what I shall reproach myself for not having done.

Here also (cf. n. 31) the words are ambiguous. "I *should* not have done that" has not always a moral significance. A candidate in an examination hesitates between two answers and chooses the wrong one. "I should have answered differently" will be his mortified comment; what he means is that he has not fulfilled what was a condition of success. There is nothing more involved here, Kant would say, than a hypothetical imperative, a prudential rule which is orientated towards what is "advantageous". A person whose conscience has developed to any degree at all has no difficulty in grasping the difference between: "I *should* not have given that reply" and I *should* not have cheated". Remorse is something quite different from regret at the loss of a good opportunity.

Moreover, even if, by means of a drug or of a surgical operation such as lobotomy, I could forestall all feelings of guilt, this assurance would in no way change the moral imperative; on the contrary, when faced with this hypothesis, I realize that a new duty arises for me: that of *refusing these means of violating my duty with impunity.*

Nowadays, many wish to eradicate the "consciousness of guilt" on the grounds that it is an unhealthy emotion. It is true that there can be a consciousness of guilt which proceeds from obscure subconscious processes, from suppressed memories or desires etc., or even simply from an erroneous judgment: such a consciousness is obviously to be treated as an illness, or to be disregarded as an illusion. But there is another and genuine consciousness of guilt, which stems from a correct judgment of practical reason, and of which it can be said to be its affective resonance. This latter consciousness is good, healthy and, indeed, indispensable in a human life where moral disorder always occupies a place. What is required is not to eliminate it, but to strive to bring it into ever growing harmony with the judgment of reason, so that one's affective reaction will be proportionate to the objective value (or anti-value).

39. – The fear of *social sanctions* (loss of reputation etc.) can be eliminated in the same way, not only because, in the hypothesis envisaged, they would be avoided but also, and in particular, because their anticipation, while it could constitute an effective motive for avoiding the action in question, could never of itself constitute one that is *moral*. The fear of sanctions, in common with the fear of remorse, becomes moral only whne the sanctions are feared as *deserved* sanctions: if I act in this way, I shall be despised — and justly so — because I shall have done *what ought not to be done*. Here also this "ought not" cannot be explained in terms of what presupposes it. ...

The same holds true even if the sanction is divine. Such a sanction has moral significance only because it is regarded as proceeding from a just God. Even if — to make an absurd hypothesis — evil were to be rewarded and virtue to be punished, the necessity to practice the latter and avoid the former would still remain. So true is this that a person who would aim at observing the moral law *simply* in order to avoid punishment (in a spirit of "servily servile" fear, as the theologians say) would not have crossed the threshold of morality.

But recall what has been said (n. 29) about the way one value can be "induced" by another. Very often, it is through his desire of, and search for, the approval of those whom he admires — parents, teachers, companions — that the child rises to the authentic love of the good.

A final stage in our analysis will be the elimination of the various sentiments, impressions or emotions which ordinarily accompany the consciousness of obligation and without which this would be "disarmed", but which are not identical with it. The same can be said of the pressure exercised by commonly accepted views or by the superego, to which the sociologists, on the one hand, and the psychoanalysts, on the other, claim to have reduced the imperative character of duty. The pressure from society exists, and by no means everything in the concept of the superego is to be rejected. When a human being's conscience is at a rudimentary or infantile stage of development, or has been badly formed, these factors can play a primary role; but in themselves, they remain on the *natural* (as distinct from the moral) level, the physical, in the broad sense, level. They are simply facts. Once a person's conscience is sufficiently developed to appreciate their true character, they are "demythologized", dethroned. They can still exercise their psychic pressure; but they can no longer make any claim on my reason and liberty. — In brief: social pressure has a moral character only in the measure in which I recognize that society has a moral value and that I have a duty to obey its commands. Once again, "ought not" cannot be explained in terms of what presupposes it ...[59].

40. – Now that all these elements have been eliminated, what remains? We can say that everything remains, that the essential remains. I should not alter this will; this *ought not* to be done. I experience a certain necessity, but of a very special kind. It rules me without being present in me in the manner of a subjective determination; that is, it is not a determination which affects the subject in himself, in his concrete reality, and channels his activity from its initial stages. (Because the nerves in my hands etc., have been affected in a certain way as a result

---

[59] This description of the consciousness of obligation is current even among those whose explanation of it differs from the one given here. See, for example, H. Sidgwick, *The Methods of Ethics*, 7th ed., London, 1907, pp. 23-38: the consciousness of study is distinct from the sentiment of pleasure or pain, from the "prudential" judgment (hypothetical imperative), pp. 25-26, from the thought of the judgment of others, pp. 27-28, from the thought of punishment, pp, 28-31, from the thought of the judgment of God, p. 31.

As examples of other descriptions of moral consciousness, the following may be noted: R. Le Senne, *Traité de morale générale*, pp. 307-331 and 525-607 (pp. 568-575: obligation) and G. Gusdorf, *Traité de l'existence morale*, Paris, 1949, pp. 108-131 (pp. 124-131: duty as accomplishment).

of a burn, my consciousness is clouded with pain; because of the effect which the shock of a blow beneath the knee-cap has, my leg suddenly stretches: physical necessity, exclusive of liberty). The necessity which is moral obligation is far from being of this kind. The knowledge that I am obliged, no more than any other kind of knowledge, does not at all change me in what I naturally am. It is for this reason that the necessity which is moral obligation is not a physical necessity, much less metaphysical. (There is no contradiction in the forbidden action being performed, in the obligatory action being omitted). It is a necessity which not only does not exclude liberty, but has meaning only in relation to it: suppress free will and obligation also disappears, or is no more than an empty word. Moral obligation is *the necessity which is proper to liberty*[60].

This necessity is said to be *objective* because it is imposed on us by the object, which presents itself to us as *demanding to be chosen*. The action itself in its ontological reality, as an act of self-determination by the subject, remains contingent: it is possible that it will not be performed. But as an action which our practical reason reflects on, it borrows from the object an ideal and practical necessity: it too demands to be chosen. The value which I appreciate in it "demands' of me that I perform it, even though it depends on me whether or not I do so.

41. — What does this mean? Does not every value present itself, in some measure, as what should be, as issuing an invitation — at times a pressing one — that it be made to exist, as a "demand" thatit be realized (n. 22, 2)? — Yes; but where moral value is concerned this demand is *absolute*. — The demand which other values create is in relation to the different powers or tendencies with which they are concerned, not in

---

[60] This needs to be carefully understood. To say: every free act is necessarily free is indeed to affirm a necessity with regard to liberty; but this necessity is not proper to it, for everything that is, is necessarily what it is. To say, with Sartre; man is "condemned to be free", or, with the Scholastics: in the free act, we necessarily will what is good, is to affirm a necessity of liberty or in liberty, but one which does not genuinely confront it; this type of necessity is present at the level of the conditions — human nature, the will — of liberty, prior to it, one could say. Obligation, on the contrary, is a type of necessity which confronts liberty; it is operative and has meaning only in the field opened by this latter. See the *Essai*, n. 121; pp. 292-294.

relation to liberty itself. This is the way with the creative demand that is made on a poet or a musician. Not to respond to it does not necessarily involve a misuse of liberty.

A poet who is drafted will, at times, if he wishes to do his duty properly, have to deprive his poetic faculty of its normal outlets. Indeed, in order to brighten up the evening of the regiment and to restore a failing morale, he may be led to compose songs that are unworthy of his talent. Is this a bad use of his poetic ability? Certainly, if we consider this in accordance with its own finality. But he has not misused his liberty, if the value in question has been sacrificed for the sake of a higher ideal.

Where moral value, on the contrary, is concerned a demand is made directly on a person's liberty, on the spiritual subject as such. Consequently, if this demand is frustrated, there will be a bad use of liberty itself, a disorder, a disorientation, a perversion of the subject *in his subjectivity*.

The expression: *to use one's liberty* might seem open to criticism: liberty, the possession of the subject as such, is not to be compared to an instrument. However, since there is in a finite spiritual subject an interior duality, a metaphysical "imbalance" — in that he is, in some way, *beyond himself*, transcending his subjective finitude by his objective infinity (at one and the same time limited being and, in a certain sense, all being) — it can be said that he both *disposes* and *is disposed of*, that he *uses himself* (an Augustinian expression). With all the more reason can this be said of liberty, since this is formally a property of human willing, which is itself not identical with the subject himself and "mediates" between him and the object.

The point can be expressed in another way. Where other values (sensory, economic etc.) are concerned, I appreciate that I am totally free: none of them imposes itself on me; I can, in principle, withdraw myself from their hold; if I am in fact unable to do so, the reason for this is to be sought in my psychic dispositions (inclinations, aversions etc.), not in a demand which stems from the object. When moral value is in question, matters are entirely different. I can withdraw myself from its demands, since I have it in my power to reject them; and yet I cannot withdraw myself, for in my very act of rejection I remain under their jurisdiction: the value I have made little of condemns me. There is something in me which continues to say "yes" to it at the very moment when my conduct ays "no". "Now if I do what I do not want, I agree that the law is good" [61]. Further, I appreciate that this is not merely a psychological *fact*, but is *right*: it is what *ought to be so*. I realize that the value which is now imposing itself on me does not depend on my inner reacting, on my desire etc., but is valuable in itself whatever opinion I happen to hold concerning it. Just as I cannot disengage myself from being, so I cannot disengage myself from this value; to cast it from me is impossible and, even if I could, to do so would be evil.

Note well that there is no question at all here of a psychological impossibility. Psychologically, there are a thousand ways of escaping from remorse or the call of obligation: an absorbing task, the giddy pursuit of pleasure, or, if needed, drink, drugs, L S D etc. The impossibility we are here speaking of is dialectic: at the moment when I decide to still in myself the voice of conscience, I necessarily appreciate that to do so is immoral (n. 38). It is evil to assert — and to seek to believe — that there is no evil.

42. – As is clear from what has already been said (nn. 31; 33, 3), we are conscious that, in accordance with our response to moral value, we ascend or descend on a scale of values which, in the final analysis, judges all others [62]. An additional point has here to be made: we are also conscious that we are *not allowed* to descend. This route is forbidden to us. This is precisely why this scale is an absolute one. What is involved is not simply myself, my perfection, the stylishness of my free decisions. If no more were involved, what would prevent me from renouncing them? In the name of what, would I be forbidden to lose myself? But I have not the right to lose myself in losing my *raison d'être*. I do not have this right because something absolute is involved in my action: it is affected — I have a confused consciousness of this — by something that transcends and surrounds me and dominates my existence: the order of values itself.

---

[61] St Paul, *Rom.*, 7, 16.

[62] In fact, very often, the "honourable" act does not seem to involve any ascent; one is content not to have descended. We shall return to this point when treating the problem of "indifferent acts" (ch. XI). For our present purpose, it is sufficient that there are certain obvious instances of an option between "descending" and "ascending".

Consequently, it is obvious that obligation cannot be reduced to a simple disjunctive necessity (either be moral or be unhappy), or to one that is hypothetical (if you wish to be happy, be moral). These formulas are not false ("If you wish to enter into life, keep the commandments"), but of themselves they do not account for the absolute character of obligation and would make of fidelity to duty a mere calculation of utility or, at the most, a concern to preserve consistency with one-self[63]. Nor will matters be improved if, in place of happiness, one substitutes growth in humanity, a life in accordance with reason etc. If one goes no further than this, one implies that it is allowed not to live in a genuinely human way, not to follow reason. ... Bur this is not so. I ought to be moral if I wish to live as befits a human being, but I ought also live as befits a human being: the necessity that is imposed on me is already completely present in this. Not in the alternative or in the condition, but in one of the members of the alternative, in the conditioned.

Nevertheless, it is true that moral obligation unfolds in consciousness under the form of a disjunction or of a condition. To be obliged to act in a particular way is to be in a situation where, if one refuses so to act, one does evil[64]. Consequently, one is bound, not by the fear of sanctions but — in the obligation as such — by the alternative: either do this good — or you *do evil*... Now evil, since it takes away or clashes with what gives meaning to life, since it involves the loss of one's *raison d'être*, immediately presents itself as *to be avoided*: to ask why is pointless. Good, on the contrary, of itself signifies what is inviting, what is attractive: obligation arises only where the

---

[63] In addition, where beatitude in the strict sense is concerned, its connection with an action presupposes the moral value of this latter and the duty to perform or avoid it: nn. 39; 296. "If you act in this way, you will forfeit beatitude, not because of the physical effect of your act, but because you will have done what you ought not to have done". Clearly, the hypothetical necessity presupposes obligation.

[64] Hence the assertion, current among moral theologians that a legitimate superior can oblige his subjects under pain of mortal sin. The Latin words *"obligare ad peccatum mortale"*, wrongly understood, have sometimes been regarded as scandalous by people not acquainted with scholastic language. Actually they mean that the superior's command can present his subjects with the alternative of obeying or of doing evil.

possibility that this invitation will be rejected emerges. (Hence obligation does not affect liberty as such, but only that inferior form of liberty which is the free will of the creature, to whom the Good is manifested only through goods which are partial and relative). Consequently, one could say that in the classical formula, to which we shall shortly return — good is to be done and evil is to be avoided — the first member refers rather to the pure attraction of the value, so that it is only in the second that the urgency which is proper to obligation appears. Nevertheless, it should be borne in mind that the true force of obligation always springs from value. The insistent demand that evil be avoided is but the detour which the pure attraction of the good takes in a frail subject. Moreover, is it not in this indirect way that the necessity which is interior to being manifests itself to us in all its force, that is, through the impossibility of what is contradictory and, in consequence, through the mediation of non-being?

The moral imperative is then a "categorical imperative". Not indeed in the sense that it is blind, irrational, without foundation etc., but in the sense that it is in itself independent of considerations of utility and self-interest, of one's likes and dislikes, of one's particular and contingent inclinations etc., even though it can depend on all these where the subjective conditions required for perceiving it, and acting in accordance with it, are concerned.

Undoubtedly, the advantages involved, one's personal tastes etc., can and, at times, should be taken into consideration when it is a question of determining the right course of action. When, for example, a person is making a choice of a state of life, it is useful for him, and indeed indispensable, to examine his particular dispositions, attractions, repugnances so as to have a better appreciation of the state for which he is most suited and in which he will have more chance of being what he ought to be. Anticipated joys and sorrows can provide us with powerful motivations for doing our duty, motivations which will perhaps be in the forefront of consciousness. All that is here being underlined is that moral value is of another order and that we have to be in some way motivated by it if our actions are to be morally good. How this is to be understood will be discussed later (nn. 238-239).

Note that it would not be sufficient to assert, as some Neo-Thomists seem to be content to do, that the necessity which is obligation is derived from the fact that we necessarily desire to *be*, to be in a deeper and fuller way, to be happy etc. If this desire is simply a factual necessity (my nature is such that I am physically incapable of not desiring to be happy), the imperative that presents itself to us is no more than assertorical, as Kant has pointed out (because you wish to be happy etc., you should act in this way). To fail in my duty would then be to contradict myself, to rend myself: an absurdity, the door to sorrow, a sin against logic; but an inconsistency is not a fault, unless the duty to be consistent is presupposed.

In order that the necessity which is obligation be derived from the necessity of striving for one's ultimate end, so that obligation is revealed as both conditional and categorical, this latter necessity has to be understood as not only a *de facto* but also as a *de iure* one. The end towards which one necessarily tends is, of itself, absolutely deserving of being striven for and attained. It is only this proviso which preserves the moral character of this tendency and of obligation. But to acknowledge this is also to acknowledge that the entire mystery of obligation is already present in the tendency. The ultimate end is then not only what *I cannot but will*, but what *I ought to will*. — At the end of all our analyses, it is clearer than ever that obligation is simply not reducible.

43. – It is worth remarking, in conclusion, that the supremacy of moral value is most often manifested to us through the conflict between our practical reason and the irrational element in us. So it is that the demands of this value are experienced as restricting, suppressing, *binding* the spontaneity of our sense nature: it is precisely for this reason that we feel "obligated", "bound". Moral necessity seems to limit and mortify our liberty, even though the truth of the matter is that it is only through our fidelity to moral value that our liberty is genuinely itself (n. 31).

The conflict in question is neither solely nor primarily, contrary to what one might be inclined to suppose, between the senses and reason: it is interior to the finite will itself, in that this is attracted at one and the same time towards its own good and towards the Good;

the due balance and order between the two tendencies does not already exist, but has to be achieved through the exercise of free will.

44. – Linked though it is with moral value, obligation is not, however, its formal constituent but a property that can be called dynamic. But this truth, in its turn, calls for further clarification. Everything that is good does not present itself as obligatory; moreover, some good ways of acting will necessarily exclude others. A person may hesitate between two ways, equally virtuous, of serving the common good: both courses of action are authentically valuable, but both cannot be a source of obligation — unless one wishes to admit in company with certain authors, such as N. Hartmann, that the inevitable choice between values necessarily involves a fault. Its obligatory character is not, then, a universal property of moral value. On the other hand, as has already been noted (n. 42), a negative necessity ("you ought not...") is inherent in every anti-value. What is evil is, always and everywhere, to be avoided. Consequently, it would seem that the fundamental obligation (the "first principle" of morality) could be formulated in this way: never do what is evil, or again: never oppose yourself to the order of the good.

Nevertheless, the first principle has been traditionally formulated under another form: Good is to be done and evil is to be avoided [65]. The first member of this principle is definitely not simply an alternative form of the second. On the other hand, the balance of the formula would seem to demand that the necessity expressed by "to be done" and "to be avoided" should both be of the same order: in other words, that the obligation of doing good be as strict as that of avoiding evil. If we keep these remarks in mind, three possible ways of understanding the principle emerge:

1. Only what is good is to be done. This presupposes that there cannot be morally neutral human actions; by no means everyone agrees with this, even when what is in question are actions considered in the concrete (n. 236). If morally neutral actions are possible, then, by definition, there is nothing that forbids me to perform them.

---

[65] St Thomas, *Summa Theol.*, I-II, 94, 2.

2. Every good whose omission would be evil is to be done. The truth of this is incontestable, but it seems strange to define the good that is to be done in terms of the evil that is to be avoided: what is evil is, as such, subordinate to what is good (n. 22, 4). Undoubtedly, in a certain fashion, the idea of *evil as to be avoided* is linked with that of obligation. But the reason for this is not, as the above interpretation would lead one to understand, because the evil to be avoided simply *indicates* that a certain good is obligatory, nor even, strictly speaking, because the necessity of doing good stems from the obligation of avoiding evil. ... There is a much more intimate link between the good and the necessity which is obligation (n. 42): the true source of this latter is the good.

3. For these reasons, we propose a third interpretation: some good is to be done, that is, man's proper task, his vocation, is to bring about what ought to be. It would not be allowable for him, supposing that this were possible (on the hypothesis that there are "indifferent" human actions) to settle permanently into a state of moral hibernation, to rest content with "not doing what is evil". His ideal should not be to "preserve himself", but to bear fruit. The Gospel gives little encouragement to a purely defensive ethics, which would limit man's ambition to not falling.

Consequently, obligation is a feature of the sphere of the good considered in its totality, not in each of its elements. Every course of action that is good is not obligatory, but there is an obligation to do what is good.

45. – It follows from all this that ethics is a normative and not a purely speculative science. It cannot be reduced to a mere description of moral judgments and attitudes, to an "art of living", to a technique for acquiring happiness, any more than it can be to the logic of moral discourse (n. 1).

To say this is not at all to deny that moral value can be made the object of a theoretical consideration. Since the good and the true coincide in reality, the good can be an object of thought: there is a truth of values [66]. And because, for the same reason, our intelligence and will are intertwined [67], it is possible

---

[66] *Ib.*, I, 59, 2 ad 3um.
[67] *Ib.*, I, 16, 4.

for us to have an intellectual grasp of the act of willing, of what is involved in it and, in consequence, of moral value. Hence the possibilty of a speculative ethics.

It is likewise clear that an ever more precise definition of moral concepts, the exact determination of their reciprocal connections and of their relations with non-moral concepts etc., play a very important role in morality. The syntax and logic of moral discourse form part of ethics. But this latter is not reducible to them.

Note, in addition, the necessity to be on our guard lest our concepts become isolated from the experience to which they correspond. If concepts of "spiritual" realities (such as the will and moral value) are not vivified by an experience of the "spiritual" order, they fade into mere symbols. Obligation, for example, cannot be genuinely thought of apart from the actual experience of it (n. 163). It is only to the degree to which moral discourse is related to this appreciation and basic experience of value, that it has meaning. Just as the propositions of physical science have to be verified in the appropriate scientific experience, so too with the truths of morality. Moral discourse that is not checked against experience becomes irrelevant to genuine morality.

The knowledge of the different attitudes concerning moral value, or of the way in which different people arrive at their moral convictions (a knowledge which is derived rather from psychology, sociology, ethnology) should be distinguished from the knowledge that is concerned with this value in itself: ethical knowledge. And it is in relation to this value itself, not to its particular determinations, that to doubt is already to have rejected.

But it is impossible to rest content with a purely theoretical consideration of moral value: to do so would be to falsify it. It is the property of this value to demand of us that we acknowledge it and decide in accordance with it: that we make it the norm of our practical value judgments and of our actions (n. 40). To regard it as an illusion, to suspend our resolve to be faithful to it, is already to have repudiated it. Consequently, if the science of ethics wishes to be a true science of moral value, it has to propose its object not merely as *to be known*, but as *to be acknowledged* and *to be translated into action*: to propose it, in consequence, as the norm of our judgments, our decisions, our actions. But a science which proposes its object in this way is a *normative* and *imperative* science. Our initial attribution of this characteristic to ethics is thus found to be justified (n. 2). Ethics is practical, normative, not, be it noted, despite being speculative, but precisely in virtue of its concern — eminently speculative — to respect the condition of its object.

46. – The great importance of arriving at an accurate understanding of the essence of moral value and of its foundation should now be clear.

This is not to say that without an investigation of this kind we would lack an appreciation of moral value. A person does not have to arrive at an understanding of the nature of human knowledge before being entitled to make affirmations about reality, nor to have grasped the fundamental notions of mathematics before having the right to conclude that two plus three equals five! The evidence is immediate; a real doubt is concretely experienced as impossible. The same is true where the moral order is concerned: we experience concretely the impossibility of withdrawing ourselves from it. To desire to do so is to be condemned by it.

Nevertheless, the double question that has been indicated cannot be evaded. What is involved in the answer is not simply the satisfaction of a perfectly legitimate desire to know, but the safeguarding of our fidelity to the moral order.

The reason for this is that unless we arrive at a reasonably accurate notion of this value, our awareness of it may diminish and runs the risk of being confused with our awareness of other values. Such confusion would without doubt be impossible, if we could always preserve a clear and distinct idea of this value. But since our consciousness of it is not "pure", but accompanied by sentiments of admiration, love, fear, sorrow, joy etc., which also accompany our consciousness of other values, the possibility of confusion arises.

In addition, our natural, even though normally implicit, conviction, is that prior to being, above being, outside of being, there is nothing. The order of values (in common with the ideal order in general) is founded on the ontological order. But what being primarily signifies for us is the empirical order of existence, the "world". Consequently, we naturally tend to seek the foundation of the moral order in "the world we live in" (in which humanity is included). If this is revealed as incapable of playing this role, the danger is that the moral order itself will be placed in question and rejected as illusory, despite the primary evidence for it.

But is it possible to reject such evidence? In the present instance, yes: for just as our knowledge of what is morally valuable requires of us that we live in accordance with it, so is the clarity of this knowledge, in its turn, conditioned by the lives we lead (cf. n. 21). "It is what a person is which determines his view of what is good"[68]. Hence the person who refuses to regulate his life in accordance with the light that is in him can grow blind; the "seed" can be choked and smothered by the "weeds" of attractions, sentiments, emotions etc., whose growth has been nourished by the subject's own choices.

---

[68] Aristotle, *Nicom. Eth.*, III, 5, 1114 a 31.

CHAPTER TWO
THE ESSENCE OF MORAL VALUE

47. – Our investigation up to this point has revealed that moral value is the value which lies in the right use of liberty, the value of the person as a person; but this definition while enabling us to situate moral value on the scale of values, does not enlighten us concerning its internal nature. The examination of its characteristics, particularly that of obligation, has not provided this light: these pertain to moral value but do not constitute it. In what, then, does this value essentially consist? This is the question to which we have now to turn our attention: the reasons why the question cannot be avoided have already been indicated.

An objection that may perhaps be raised is that moral value, in common with "good" in general and the other primary notions, cannot be strictly defined [1]. All that is possible is to relate it to other concepts or to describe it through its effects. Nevertheless, just as we have distinguished between the *phenomenological essence* of the good and its *nature,* is it not possible to discover beneath the phenomenon of moral value an intelligible structure on which it is based? It is with answering this question that the present chapter is concerned.

48. – The discussion of this question is linked, in most authors, with that of other questions from which, frequently enough, it is not at all clearly distinguished. These questions are:

1) That of the *norm* or criterion of *morality*. The Latin word "norma" means a "set square": unless a wall is constructed in line with this, it will be out of plumb. Metaphorically, the word means "a line of conduct, a rule, an ideal

---

[1] "... good is numbered among those things which are primary... These, however, cannot be explained by what is prior to them, but only by what is posterior, just as are causes by their proper effects", St Thomas, *In I Met.*, bk. 1; ed. Pirotta, n. 9.

standard in relation to which judgments of value are made"[2]. Consequently, the norm of morality is what measures the rightness of practical judgments and actions, just as the principle of non-contradiction can be called the norm of our theoretical judgments. An action which is in harmony with the moral norm will be good; an action which is contrary to the norm will be evil.

This question is closely connected with our present one, but is not quite identical with it. Even when the *essence* of moral value has been determined, the further question of the *sign* by which its presence can be recognized remains unanswered[3]. Suppose that the essence of moral value lies in the aptitude of an action to make a person happy or to contribute to the glory of God; to know that does not provide one with a criterion of this aptitude: this will be, for example, the harmony of the action with human nature, with reason etc. — In fact, as we shall see, the essence of moral value lies in the conformity of an action with its norm. In reality, therefore, if not formally, these two questions are but one.

2) The question of the *supreme good*. In what does the complete fulfilment of man, his "beatitude", consist? This is the problem with which, as we have seen (n. 2), the ancient philosophers were most commonly concerned.

---

[2] P. Foulquié - R. Saint-Jean, *Dictionnaire de la langue philosophique*, p. 481.

M. Blondel (*L'être et les êtres*, Paris, 1935, pp. 240-241) makes an ingenious distinction between *rule* and *norm*. The rule is extrinsic, and is indifferent with regard to the dynamism of the subject to whom it is applied. The norm, conformably to its etymology, designates the vertical, ascending orientation that is interior to this dynamism. "It is the perpendicular line, precisely as such, which alone and intrinsically goes straight to the goal", p. 241. It is certainly true that the word *norm* ordinarily expresses a certain transcendence, different from mere exteriority. One speaks of a norm only if the action being considered has a certain density from the point of view of value — moral norms, juridical norms; where a game is concerned, one does not dream of applying the term. ... Nevertheless, Blondel's interpretation does not seem to harmonize with the real usage of the word.

[3] Some authors distinguish between a *constitutive norm* and a *manifestative norm*. Ed. Elter rejects this distinction: "Since the norm is nothing other than the principle which directs the activity, it is of its essence to be the sign which makes known the rectitude of the act", *Compendium philosophiae moralis*, Rome, 1950, p. 15. — This is correct, but it leaves intact the distinction between the norm (essentially manifestative) and the essence of moral value.

3) The question of the *ultimate end*. In view of what, is man in the world? Has human life a meaning and, if so, what is it? The advancement of evolution? The development of Humanity? The glory of God? etc. (Objective ultimate end). — Towards what is man effectively tending, through all his activity? What is the wellspring of all his desires? Pleasure? Truth? Rectitude? Liberty? Union with God? etc. (Subjective ultimare end). — The subjective ultimate end is nothing other than complete fulfilment, but as considered from a different point of view and so giving rise to a separate question. The identity between the two notions is not immediate but mediate, in that it supposes as established that man seeks in everything his complete fulfilment.

4) The question of the *origin of moral ideas*. This queston seems, at first sight, to belong rather to psychology, ethnology and sociology than to ethics; in fact, it is of no less importance in this last. It often happens that from the way in which the origin of these ideas is understood, conclusions — which are, moreover, illegitimate (n. 29) — are drawn concerning their content and validity. As a result, moral value will be reduced to what it is not.

The various moral doctrines can be classified in different ways: either in accordance with the answers they give to the questions indicated above (in particular to questions 1, 2, 3 and the question of the essence of moral value), so that each question furnishes a principle of classification; or else in accordance with the subjective principles to which they attribute the central role in moral living: in this way rational or rationalist ethics, voluntarist ethics, affective ethics will be distinguished... These various divisions, founded as they are on different principles, can only very imperfectly be co-ordinated. Every classification, moreover, since what it is concerned with is a complex reality, such as the thought of an author, will necessarily be to some extent artificial. This point should be constantly kept in mind in reading the pages which follow.

49. — In our inquiry into the essence of moral value, we shall inevitably encounter these various questions. For our purpose is not to establish and to discuss the replies to our question that are theoretically possible; it is sufficient to examine those that have in fact been given. But note that each author is concerned with answering a problem he himself has raised and that we have no right to force him into the structure of our own inquiry; this we would do if we attributed to him a reply to a question which he never raised, under the form in which it is here presented. We shall strive, then, to respect the trend of an author's thought, even if this at times distracts us somewhat from the purpose we have in mind. — Note also that this historical inquiry does not at all aim at being exhaustive; our point of view is not that of the historian. It will be quite sufficient for our purpose to present the principal opinions which have a bearing on the fundamental ethical problem, without ever losing sight of the object of the inquiry on which we are engaged. The criticisms which we shall make will have as their aim not only to detect and refute errors but, even more, to discover the "spirit of truth" which is present in each doctrine and which can, at times, make an error so formidable. A critical — in the primary sense of the word — approach of this kind, involving what may well be styled a «dialogue», will enable us to arrive gradually at our own solution and to have a deeper appreciation of the truth.

The primary standard of reference by which we shall evaluate the various interpretations of moral value will be their fidelity to the data of moral consciousness, which the analyses of the preceding chapter have revealed. Every interpretation that contradicts these data and, implicitly at least, proposes as moral value something other than the value described above, is, on this score alone, ruled out of court.

The order of our inquiry will not be historical since, in all the great epochs of thought, differente types of moral doctrines have had their adherents, so that it is not possible to discern a definite line of evolution. Rather shall we follow a dialectical (in the Platonic-Augustinian sense) order. We shall advance from what is external to what is internal and from what is lower to what is higher. The three stages of our inquiry will, accordingly, be:

1. Does moral value consist in something which is intrinsic to a human action or does it spring from the conformity of an action with a purely extrinsic norm, such as positive law, custom etc.?

2. If it consists in something intrinsic, is this esentially related to an object or an end which are exterior to spiritual

activity as such? (We include in this category of objects the subject himself and other subjects, whenever the spiritual dimension of their being is not taken into consideration). — In other words, since moral value is the value of the spiritual subject as such, the question which is here being asked is: can this value be defined in terms of inframoral or "natural" values?

3. Finally, if the reply to the second question turns out to be negative, is the intrinsic character of moral value to be understood in terms of spiritual activity as immanently exercised, or is it necessary to transcend this in some way, by considering the conditions which ultimately ground the possibility of such activity? If the latter, the question of what this involves arises.

I. EXTRINSIC MORALITY.

50. – Does the moral value of an action essentially consist in a property which is intrinsic to it? In other terms, can an action be morally good or evil simply because of what it is, independently of any exterior judgment declaring it to be such, of any law permitting, commanding or prohibiting it?

Some have denied this. An action's moral value, they maintain, springs entirely from the outside, from its conformity with (or from its opposition to) an *exterior* command (of a human authority or of God), so that one and the same action can be either good or evil, according as it is permitted or forbidden, without this permission or prohibition being in any way dependent on the action's material content or internal structure.

This theory is at times referred to as *moral positivism,* since it identifies the entire moral law with *positive* law (nn. 179; 208). — Nevertheless, in order to avoid possible confusion with the positivism of Stuart Mill and Auguste Comte etc., which is not relevant in the present context, we think it preferable to speak here of *extrinsic morality*. This way of speaking has the added advantage of fitting in better with our dialectical method of approach.

51. – There is no lack of reasons which seem to indicate the truth of this theory.

Consider firstly the diversity of customs and judgments where morality is concerned. That human beings are often unfaithful to the rules of moral behaviour which they accept is in no way astonishing: but that they should be in disagreement concerning the rules themselves, to the extent that some consider to be a sacred duty what others hold in abomination (n. 182), seems to be irreconcilable with the notion of an intrinsic morality. If an action is evil simply because of what it is, its malice should be evident to all, just as it is evident to them whether a fire is providing heat.

The analysis of moral consciousness that has been made seems also, and more directly, to lead to the same conclusion. Morality, as we have seen, involves obligation, but there can be obligation only where there is law. Now, since our human way of knowing advances from the exterior to the interior, what we first of all understand by law is positive law, promulgated by a legislator who is not ourselves and who is exterior to us (n. 180). — Moreover, is it not a fact that human beings ordinarily need the stimulus of commands and prohibitions, which come from without, in order to become alive to their obligations? This is particularly noticeable where children are concerned. Their first appreciation of good and evil is of what is in conformity with, or contrary to, the rules laid down by their parents[4].

52. – Sophists such as Callicles, in Plato's *Gorgias* (482 seq.), can be regarded as forerunners of this theory. These set up an opposition between nature (*phusis*) and law (*nomos*); the latter they held to be a conventional and artificial rule in relation to which all moral judgments were made. It is, however, more accurate to number these Sophists among the ethical sceptics.

As time passed — and particularly after Alexander's campaigns — the increased knowledge of the different moral standards of various peoples led some into a quite definite *moral scepticism*. The difference between good and evil actions

---

[4] Read what St Thomas says on the necessity for human laws in order that men may be led to the practice of virtue, *Summa Theol.*, I-II, 95, 1 (cf. Aristotle, *Nicom. Eth.*, X, 9, 1179 b 31 - 1180 a 22). There is also the famous text of St Paul on the knowledge of sin — with the consequent awakening of moral conscience — that comes through the Law of Moses, *Rom.*, 7, 7.

springs entirely from opinion and custom. This view is attributed to Carneades. — In more modern times and for a
similar reason (the discovery of America, new contacts with
India, China, Japan etc.,), the same sceptical tendency has made
itself felt: it is to be found, for example, in Montaigne [5].

More recently, the *sociological school* (Durkheim, Lévy-
Bruhl) has sought to explain the entire order of moral
judgments and attitudes in terms of thr influence of society. It
should, however, be kept in mind that, for the representatives
of this school and above all for Durkheim, society is not simply
the totality of individuals but a unique reality, the most real of
all realities, superior to its members and the very condition of
their humanization. Moral values are those which society
approves of and imposes on individuals. Nevertheless, this
theory cannot really be regarded as championing extrinsic
morality. The reason for this is that the moral rules imposed by
society reflect its *real* requirements: society commands what
will foster its conservation, development etc. Consequently, an
examination of the sociological theory will be reserved until
later (nn. 85-89).

53. – As an example of one who proposes the doctrine of
extrinsic morality, and grounds the distinction between good
and evil solely on the authority of the "prince", Thomas
Hobbes is usually cited. He writes:

"Before pacts and laws, there was neither justice nor
injustice; and the nature of good and of evil was no more
common among men than among the beasts" [6].

"The rules of good and evil, of just and unjust, are civil
laws; and therefore what the lawgiver commands must be
taken for good and what he forbids must be considered evil" [7].

The true thought of Hobbes is not, however, easy to
grasp.

In his view, man, in the *state of nature,* has no limit set on his
liberty: each one has a right to everything (*De Cive,* c. 1, n. 10); in
particular, the right to preserve his life by every possible means, even
to the extent of killing others, since in this state they are always

---

[5] Montaigne, *Essais*, II, 12; *Apologie de Raymond de Sebonde*.
[6] *De Homine*, c. 10; ed. G. Holesworth, London, 1839-1845, t. II, p. 94.
[7] *Leviathan*, c. XXIX, t. III, p. 232.

possible aggressors. It follows that, in the state of nature, "everybody is at war with everybody else", c. 1, n. 12. In order to emerge from such a disadvantageous state, and in order to free themselves from the perpetual fear which it involves, men make *pacts* among themselves as a result of which society comes to exist; thus men are enabled to live in peace, as "right reason" requires. These pacts are entered into in virtue of the *natural law,* of which Hobbes treats at length, *ib.,* cc. 2 and 3. In addition to the fundamental law: "peace is to be pursued wherever possible; where it is not possible, we must resort to warfare", he gives a catalogue of twenty derivative laws, the first of which states the necessity to transfer or abandon certain rights, while the last condemns drunkenness!

Hobbes expressly states that the natural law is a dictate of reason, *ib.,* c. 2, n. 1; c. 3, n. 33. But the reason of which he is here speaking is reason in the utilitarian — one could almost say technological — sense, whereby man appreciates whether a particular means is adapted to the attainment of the end which he naturally seeks, namely, his own preservation, *ib.,* c. 3, n. 31. Hobbes' view here seems to be somewhat similar to that of the Utilitarians, of whom we shall soon speak.

But this natural law is not sufficient to guarantee peace and the union of wills. An *authority* endowed with coercive power and "absolute dominion" is required, *ib.,* c. 6, p. 13. From its control, nothing is exempt; to it belongs the right to determine what is morally good and what is morally evil, *ib.,* c. 14, n. 10.

Further, the pact by which authority is entrusted to the "prince" is irrevocable. In this way, there is effected a transition, which can be called dialectical, from a state of anarchy to that of totalitarianism.

Hobbes is still more radical in *Leviathan*: "Men's passions are not sins, nor are the actions to which they give rise, as long as those who perform them see that they are forbidden by no authority. For a law cannot be known until it is made, nor can it be made until there is agreement upon a legislator", c. XIII; p. 100. Hence, natural law is not a true law unless it is known to have been decreed by God; and it is Scripture alone which reveals this to us. — It is doubtful whether this last reflection expresses the personal thought of the author. Where he is concerned, the only true law seems to be human law. It is for this reason that "there is no ethics other than the science of what is good or evil in human communities and societies", c. XV. p. 122.

Hobbes does not make clear how his theory of the natural law harmonizes with this authoritarian method of determining moral good and evil. He expressly admits that certain natural laws ought to be observed even in war and so, in consequence, even in the "state of nature", *De Cive,* c. 3, n. 27, note; p. 145. Natural laws, he insists, bind in conscience; even though to violate them is not a "crime", but simply a "fault", the person who does so incurs guilt ("animus reus fit"), *Leviathan,* c. XV; p. 121. Hobbes speaks of the duties of rulers; he concedes that subjects may sometimes have the right to resist the state: if they are killed while resisting in such circumstances, those who kill them have the right to do so, but nonetheless sin against the natural law, *De Cive,* c. 6, n. 13.

It seems, then, on the evidence of these texts, that Hobbes admits some distinction, prior to all positive law, between moral good and evil. But do these texts express his true thought, or are they to be attributed rather to a prudent conformance? His authentic position would seem to be that there is no moral value in acting in accordance with reason (as we are commanded by the natural law), unless we are so commanded by positive law.

Somewhat similar ideas are to be found in Nietzsche; he too derives the distinction between good and evil from (positive) law [8]. This is imposed by the "masters", of whose morality it is the expression (see further on, n. 95). — Moreover, as has already been noted (n. 26), Nietzsche regarded traditional morality, and Christian morality in particular, as the product of the slaves' "resentment" and an attempt to justify their own mediocrity.

54. – Another type of extrinsic morality is that which grounds moral value on a positive and arbitrary law of God.

In the middle ages, William of Ockham and his school held that the moral order, as well as the ontological, depends on the divine free will. "God cannot, it is true, act contrary to right reason; but right reason, where His externally directed activity is concerned, is nothing other than His will. ... It is not because an action is right and just that God wills it, but rather that because He wills it, this becomes right and just" [9].

---

[8] "Hence it is only in consequence of the establishment of law that there is right and wrong", *Zur Genealogie der Moral,* n. 11; ed. Kroner, t. 8, p. 368 (Eng. trans.: *The Genealogy of Morals,* in *Collected Works,* New York, 1964).

[9] "God cannot, it is true, act contrary to right reason, but right reason, where what is external to Him is concerned, is nothing other than His will. ... For it is not because something is right or just that God orders it; rather is it right and just because He orders it", G. Biel, *Collectorium circa IV Sent.,* I, d. 17, q. 1,a. 3, corrol. 1, K. — Cf. P. Vignaux, art. *Nominalisme,* in *Dict. de théol. cath.,* col. 764-769.

This is the thesis which Descartes will take up and urge, particularly in his letters to Mersenne, in the spring of 1630[10]. Note that Descartes is not at all denying that moral value lies in fidelity to reason: but, he maintains, what is reasonable and unreasonable depends on a free decree of God. To speak in any other way would be to subject God to Destiny.

But it is Samuel Pufendorf — a jurist rather than a philosopher — who, starting from premises rather similar to those of Descartes, has most fully developed the moral theory of divine voluntarism[11].

According to Pufendorf, the rational order, of itself, is not yet the moral order. Reason (as in Hobbes) enables us to appreciate what is useful but not, of itself, what is moral. Morality commences only when there are laws and there can be no laws until the legislator is known. Consequently, morality presupposes the knowledge of God.

Now, the law which superimposes the moral order on the natural order proceeds from the absolutely free will of God, who gives to each being the nature which He pleases. There is no absolute and intrinsic necessity: everything depends, in the last resort, on the divine good pleasure[12]. The same supreme liberty which disposes of *physical beings* and their natures, disposes likewise of moral beings (settling what is good, what is just etc.). These also are the fruit of His good pleasure.

Pufendorf, if our interpretation of him is correct, is not content to affirm, as do some Scholastics (nn. 151; 160), that moral obligation is immediately based, even where *we* are concerned, on the *hypothetically necessary* will of God (if God wills to create man, He necessarily wills that man act in accordance with the norm of goodness); he grounds obligation, and with it the entire moral order, on a free divine decree. Even if this decree is identical with the one by which God freely gives to man the nature which he has, moral value, Pufendorf maintains, is not grounded on this nature but on the free decision of God. ...

---

[10] Written on April 15, May 6 and 27. In the Adam-Tannery ed., t. I, pp. 145, 149, 151 seq. — Cf. *Respons. ad sextas objectiones*, t. VIII, p. 432; *Lettre au P. Mesland*, t. IV, pp. 118-119. — Descartes explicitly extends his doctrine to the order of values: there is no good or evil prior to the free divine decree. This presents him with the embarrassing problem of how the divine veracity can then be maintained. His solution is simply to appeal to the simplicity of the perfect Being, which prevents Him from contradicting Himself by violating the law He has freely decreed. ...

[11] *De Jure naturae et gentium*, Amsterdam, 1688, bk. I, c. 2, n. 6; pp. 18-19.

[12] *Ib.*, p. 19.

55. − The theory of extrinsic morality is not sustainable.

That certain actions *immediately* receive their moral value (positive or negative) from their conformity with, or opposition to, an exterior rule, is quite evident: this is the situation with regard to all purely positive legislation, all orders given by legitimate authority etc. The boy who smokes, even though he has been forbidden to do so by his parents, acts wrongly, not because smoking is evil in itself but, directly, because he is *disobedient*.

Nevertheless, this is not true of *all* actions: there are those which, independently of all precepts, are manifestly good or evil, simply because of what they are. Even further: if we reflect a little more on the matter, it becomes clear that even when the moral value of an action seems to be derived from a precept, all that this latter really does is to introduce the action into the sphere of moral value; it applies this value to the action, but does not constitute its essence. − In the example given above, it is because of his parents' prohibition that the boy does wrong to smoke, but it is not this prohibition which makes disobedience to be evil. The prohibition introduces the act in question into the category of acts of disobedience which, as such, have a negative value; it applies this negative value to his act, but does not formally constitute it.

56. − The basic weakness of the extrinsic theory is that it begs the question at issue. In order that conformity with or opposition to the law be capable of determining the moral value of an action, it is first necessary that obedience to the law be morally good, and disobedience to it be morally evil. Now this cannot be derived from the law itself, nor from a prior law, since where every such law is concerned the same problem keeps on recurring. The reason, then, why we are required to obey the law is because to do so is in accordance with reason, with human nature, because without this obedience life in society would be impossible, or for some motive of this kind whose exact nature we shall later determine. In other terms: if one seeks to explain the moral value of an action by its conformity with the law, one is still left with the problem of explaining the value of conformity to the law.

Further, obedience to the law has a moral value only if the law is itself just, or, at the very least, not unjust. Consequently, it is the very value of the law which now requires to be explained. Once again, this explanation cannot be derived from the law itself. The criterion, the norm, has to come from some other source, so that the theory of extrinsic morality is not, in consequence, sustainable.

There are three ways in which a human law can be obeyed: out of routine (one obeys because everyone else is obeying, or because one' has been thoroughly conditioned so to act etc.); through fear of sanctions; in virtue of a reasoned conviction, either of the value of t-his law, or of the value of obedience to *the law*. The first type of obedience remains outside the moral sphere; so also does the second, if fear provides the exclusive motivation (n. 39). It is only with the third type that we arrive at the moral level. But this means that an action's moral value does not result simply from conformity to the law or to a precept: its source is anterior to this. It is not human laws which impose on us the basic obligation to seek the common good, to strive to promote order, justice and civic harmony etc.

57. – To this rather dialectical argument, another and more immediate one can be added. It does not require any very prolonged or difficult moral reflection to appreciate that some actions, simply because of what they are, are good, and that others, again simply because of what they are, remain evil, no matter what hypothetical situation is envisaged. To assist one's fellowmen, to will their true good, to strive to submit egoistic and sensual inclinations to those which are noble and generous etc.: in no situation could these become evil. On the contrary, to torture others, to mow them down wantonly, to sow dissension by spreading false reports, to abandon oneself utterly to debauchery etc: all this, even if commanded by a barbarous law, could never be sincerely approved of as worthy of a human being. The theory of extrinsic morality leads logically to consequences which are unacceptable, it would seem, even to Hobbes.

58. – These criticisms are still valid if, in company with Pufendorf, one grounds the moral order, not now on a human law, but on an arbitrary decree of God. This decree can determine the value of an action only because to obey God is already "right and fitting", so that, in consequence, and independently of all precepts, there is an order of justice and injustice, an order of good and evil (nn. 161-163). — Further, it is only because God is the supreme Value and the Source of every moral value that the divine law obliges us. To obey an evil Demiurge, such as the "malevolent genius" of Descartes, would be immoral. In speaking in this way, what we wish to submit to the tribunal of the human conscience is not God, but simply our *idea* of God. A being, no matter how powerful, who was himself in the slightest degree morally evil, *would not be God*.

A point that has already been noted is again relevant here: it is a contradiction in the moral order to maintain that God could have created a world in which deceit, exploitation of the poor, hatred of Himself etc., would be licit. This would involve a contradiction, since one and the same action would, as licit, have a positive moral value as well as an all too apparent negative value. Absolute contingence is no less unthinkable and impossible in the moral order than it is in the metaphysical and logical order.

St Thomas does not hesitate to write: "The wisdom of the divine intellect is the source on which the essence of all justice is primarily dependent. This wisdom constitutes beings in their due relation both to one another and to their cause; and it is in this relation that the essence of created justice consists. To say that justice depends purely and simply on the (divine) will is to say that this will is not guided by the divine wisdom — and this is blasphemy" [13]. Here too, the proponents of extrinsic morality do not dare to draw all the consequences of their doctrine but prudently decline to envisage them.

Note, finally, that at the root of Pufendorf's theory, there seems to be a certain confusion. It is quite true that God freely causes beings other than Himself to exist: but He cannot choose to give them any nature other than the one that is proper to them: the contrary assertion has no meaning. If God, then, creates human beings, the nature He gives them cannot, obviously, be other than human. Consequently, it is impossible to maintain that He gives to beings the nature that it pleases Him to give them. It is where the existence of beings, and

---

[13] *De Ver.*, 23, 6.

not directly their essence, is concerned, that the divine liberty is operative [14].

But it is readily admitted that the *existential conditions* in which these created natures are placed depend — just as does their very existence — on a free divine decree and that these conditions have to be taken into consideration when it is a question of determining the requirements of morality in the concrete (n. 8).

59. — The two opinions which we have here rejected are not equally wide of the mark: that of Pufendorf is less so than that of Hobbes. This is because, as we shall show in nn. 152-157, God is the source and ultimate foundation of the entire moral order: His will, which is essentially holy, provides the norm and exemplar of every upright will [15]. Pufendorf's error seems to have primarily consisted in his failure to distinguish sufficiently between moral value *as deriving its ultimate intelligibility from God* and *as essentially constituted by a relation to the divine will*.

The merit of the first opinion is to have emphasized the important role which authority plays in the development of moral conscience. This role is not limited to that of teaching or of exhortation. In checking and curbing animal spontaneity by means of threats and promises, authority effectively stimulates the child, or the still childish adult, to reflect on himself and see himself more as he really is: it helps to free his thoughts from the swamp of images and instincts, so that he comes to think clearly and decide deliberately. In this way, he is taught to exercise a rational control over his impulses. — As well, if authority knows how to make itself loved, if those who exercise it — parents or teachers — are not only people of high moral worth but are also capable of inspiring affection, the child or pupil, by means of this latter quality, will come to know and appreciate, in the persons on whom he depends, moral value itself (n. 29).

---

[14] Cf. St Thomas, *Cont. Gent.*, II, 30: "How in created things there can be an absolute necessity" and III, 129: "That where human actions are concerned, there are things which are of their nature right and not only because ordained by law".

[15] St Thomas, *De Ver.*, 23, 7; *Summa Theol.*, I-II, 19, 9.

Since the moral value of a human action is not simply derived from an exterior source, it has to consist in an intrinsic property. What is this? That is the question which still occupies us.

II. MORAL NATURALISM

A. *Eudaemonism.*

60. – At first sight, it might well seem that this intrinsic property of a human action, which measures the value proper to it (moral value), is to be found in its *capacity to lead* — directly or indirectly — *to happiness,* to the complete satisfaction of the person who performs it. Is it not happiness that man seeks in all that he strives for and in all that he desires (nn. 14, 4; 280-283)? Is it not for him, in some manner, the supreme value, the "highest good"? Consequently, is it not in function of this that the rectitude of our actions should be judged? It is the degree to which an activity helps to the attainment of the appropriate goal that enables us to judge whether, and to what extent, it has been correctly accomplished. I judge that a watch is going well if it indicates the exact time: this is what it is meant to do. A human life "goes well" — it is good as a human life — if it leads straight to happiness; a person is good as a person, if he does what is necessary to obtain it.

This approach to morality can be called, in general, *Eudaemonism* (from the Greek "eudaimōn", happy) [16]. There are three main versions of it and the difference between each of them is considerable. This springs from the three senses in which happiness is understood: sense satisfaction (Hedonism, from "hēdonē", pleasure); the complete natural human good (in which, consequently, the rational good will primarily be included) insofar as this can be achieved in the present life (rational Eudaemonism); or finally, a good whose full enjoyment is reserved for the next life. This third form can be called eschatological Eudaemonism, from "eschatos" (last) because it is concerned with the "last things". As is only too obvious,

---

[16] On the history of the word *eudaimonia*, see A. J. Festugière, *Contemplation et vie contemplative chez Platon*, Paris, 1936, pp. 268-334 (Summarized in J. Vanier, *Le bonheur, principe et fin de la morale aristotélicienne*, Paris-Bruges, 1965, pp. 180-185).

these different forms of the theory do not merit the same judgment.

The hedonistic doctrines, in particular, do not pose the moral problem in the same fashion as we have done and do not seem even to make a clear distinction between moral and other values; it might appear then, at first sight, that they fall outside our perspective and are without relevance to the inquiry on which we are here engaged. But, in reality, man never completely escapes from the confused appreciation of "something to be done or avoided", of a value to be achieved. In proposing their rule of life, the thinkers in question necessarily present it as suitable for man, as good — purely and simply — for him: and this is precisely the characteristic by which moral value is distinguished.

61. – The most unsophisticated form of Hedonism is that attributed to a disciple of Socrates, Aristippus the Cyrenaic, whose followers, in consequence, have been called *cyrenaics*.

The doctrine of Aristippus is a type of subjectivism. All that we know are the impressions that are made on us, so that the only criterion of truth is the sensation of the moment. Similarly, the sole criterion of value is the pleasure of the moment, which consists in gentle movement.

At first sight, it might appear that such principles could not but lead to the unrestrained pursuit of pleasure. Bur this is far from being so. The reason for this is that, since pleasure is an internal state, it is pointless to seek one's happiness in external objects. The genuinely happy man is he who is content with little and finds his pleasure in the most ordinary things, which are also the easiest to obtain [17].

In practice, then, this morality is rather ascetical. There is nothing surprising in this, once we recall that what Aristippus prizes above all is "autarkeia", independence, self-sufficiency, self-mastery. "I possess: I am not possessed". It could be maintained that, strictly speaking, Aristippus' version of Hedonism is concerned rather with the way in which moral value is to be achieved than with this value in itself (which would be identified more with *autarkeia*).

---

[17] Diog. Laert., *Lives of the Philosophers*, bk. II, ch. 8, or H. Ritter - L. Preller, *Historia phil. graec.*, 8th ed., nn. 263-275. — Likewise consult R. Le Senne, *Traité de morale générale*, Paris, 1947, pp. 381-382, whose interpretation we follow.

62. – The form of Hedonism taught by Epicurus is more refined.

For him also, pleasure is the highest good. But pleasure, as he understands it, does not consist in movement: it is found in *repose,* in the absence of disturbance (*ataraxia*).

Pleasure, for Epicurus, is essentially of the sense, bodily pleasure. "The root of all good is the pleasure that comes from eating and drinking". Bur a distinction has to be made between pleasures which are *neither natural nor necessary* (for example, honours), pleasures which are *natural but not necessary* (such as are provided by exquisite food), and finally, pleasures which are both *natural and necessary* (such as are provided by a very simple meal when one has a good appetite). Those of the first kind are to be avoided, while those of the second are to be availed of in moderation; only those of the third type, which moreover are always readily available, are purely and simply desirable.

Even though the pleasures of the mind surpass those of the body, they nonetheless have their source in the latter, since they consist solely — the epicurean materialism is here in evidence — in the remembrance of past bodily pleasures and in the expectation of future ones. But note that Epicurus and his disciples set great store by friendship — and their friendships are celebrated — even though this seems scarcely consistent with the principles of their school[18].

It seems that for Epicurus also, what was primary was interior liberty, independence.

In more modern times, Epicureanism, as a moral doctrine, has had its defenders, notably in 18th century thinkers such as Helvetius, d'Holbach. The hedonistic morality of Fourier, in the 19th century, has much in common with that of Epicurus.

63. – A form of Hedonism which aimed at being more scientific was developed by Jeremy Bentham (1748-1832), who was really more a jurist than a philosopher. HIs doctrine is often labelled *utilitarian* and, in fact, as we shall soon consider, Stuart Mill's utilitarian ethic (n. 77) stems from Bentham. But

---

[18] Diog. Laert., *op. cit.*, bk. X; Ritter-Preller, *op. cit.*, nn. 470-476. Cf. Le Senne, *op. cit.*, pp. 382-84.

since he aims at helping men to lead lives which are as pleasurable as possible, his teaching can also be classed as Hedonism [19].

According to Bentham, man necessarily seeks to have as much pleasure as he can and to avoid pain at all costs. "Nature has placed mankind under the government of two sovereign masters: *pain* and *pleasure*. — It is for them alone to point out what we ought to do, as well as to determine what we shall do. On the one hand, the standard of right and wrong, on the other, the chain of causes and effects, are fastened to their throne. They govern us in all we do, in all we think: every effort we can make to throw off our subjection will serve but to demonstrate and confirm it. In words a man may pretend to abjure their empire; but in reality he will remain subject to it all the while" [20].

Errors of conduct spring from a false judgment concerning the happy or troublesome consequences of our actions. Hence the necessity for some kind of arithmetic of pleasures and pains [21], by means of which it will be possible to calculate where the maximum of the former and the minimum of the latter lie. Now there are seven different *dimensions* of pleasure: intensity, duration, certainty, proximity, fruitfulness (of new pleasures), purity (a pleasure is pure when it is untainted by displeasure), extension (a pleasure shared with others is more valuable, all other things being equal, than one that is not shared). Similarly, there are seven dimensions of pain or displeasure. All this can be measured and worked out, so that there results a "moral calculus" which provides guidance for our decisions. In this way it is possible, for example, to demonstrate mathematically the superiority of temperance to drunkenness.

Bentham was well aware that pleasures (and pains), since they are heterogeneous, cannot always be directly compared. But just as temperatures which are qualitatively different are measurable by their relation with a quantitative standard (the expansion of a column of mercury etc.), so also pleasures and pain can be indirectly measured

---

[19] Among his writings those of most relevance to us are: *An Introduction to the Principles of Morals and Legislation*, 1789; *Traité de législation civile et pénale*, translated and edited by Et. Dumont, 3 vols, 1802; *Deontology* (posthumous), 1834.

[20] *An Introduction ...*, c. 1; ed. Harrison, Oxford, 1948, p. 125; similarly in *Traité ...*, 2nd ed., Paris, 1820, t. I, pp. 2-3.

[21] Bentham was not the originator of this idea but it was he who elaborated and publicized it. In the *Traité ...*, t. I, pp. 49-51, he gives the rules for putting it into practice. These operations "are the elements of moral calculation and legislation becomes a matter of arithmetic", p. 50.

and compared by their relation to a common point of reference: the amount of money a person is prepared to pay in order to obtain a particular pleasure, or to avoid a particular pain[22]. In this way of speaking, the moral structure of a capitalist and liberalist era is given ingenuous expression[23].

In order to avoid interpreting Bentham in a way that would be both crude and unjust, it has to be added that he sets great store by *benevolence,* source of the most pure pleasures. Consequently his ethics, as regards its content, cannot be said to be egoistic. Even further: he considers that the principle by which the legislator should be inspired is that of the greatest happiness of the greatest number: any action whatever deserves praise or blame in accordance with its tendency to produce pleasure or pain, to augment or diminish the sumtotal of happiness enjoyed by all sentient beings (animals included). At this point, Bentham is very close to the altruistic Utilitarianism which Mill was later to develop.

---

[22] "If I having a crown in my pocket ... hesitate whether I shall buy a bottle of claret with it for my own drinking, or lay it out in providing sustenance for a family I see about to perish for want of any assistance, so much the worse for me at the long run: but it is is plain that, so long as I continued hesitating, the two pleasures of sensuality in one case, of sympathy in the other, were exactly worth to me five shillings, to me they were exactly equal"; an unedited fragment to be found in E. Halevy, *La formation du radicalisme philosophique,* t. I: *La jeunesse de Bentham,* Paris, 1901, app. II, p. 413 (text p. 412).

Cf. what Hobbes had already written: "The value or *worth* of a man is, as of all other things, the *price,* that is to say, so much as would be given for the use of this power", *Leviathan,* c. 10; ed. Molesworth, t. III (from the English workd), p. 76.

[23] Compare the charge which Marx makes against capitalism of lumping together all values, through reducing them to that of money, and of degrading human dignity as a result, *Oekonomisch-philosophische Manuskripte,* in Marx-Engels Gesamtausgabe (MEGA), I, bd. 3, p. 149; *Misère de la Philosophie,* ch. 1, MEGA, I, bd. 5, p. 123. The same reproach is made by Newman in a sermon that has a contemporary ring: *Discourses addressed to Mixed Congregations* (1849), Longmans, Green and Co., 1909, pp. 89-92.

[24] This is the *principle of utility* which Bentham explained in this way: "I act on the *principle of utility* when I measure my approval or disapproval of a private or public action by its tendency to produce pain or pleasure; ... it should be clearly understood that I take the words *pain* and *pleasure* in their ordinary sense, without inventing definitions in order to exclude certain pleasures or to deny the existence of certain pains. Away with subtlety, away with metaphysics; no need to consult Plato or Aristotle. *Pain and pleasure* are what each one experience to be such", *Traité...,* t. I, p. 4. Cf. *An Introduction...,* c. 1, n. 2; p. 126. Later, he preferred to speak of the *greatest happiness (or felicity) principle, ib.,* n. 1; p. 125, in a note written in 1822.

It is important to note that, in all this, Bentham's intention is more practical than speculative. His aim is the reform of behaviour. He desires — in advance of his time — that punishment should be educative. (To this end, he goes so far as to imagine a prison — the "Panoptic" — where the prisoners are constantly under the eyes of an invisible watcher). The question he puts himself is: how is it possible to influence human beings? What chord does one have to strike so as to move them to choose what is good ? He considers that the pleasure-principle provides the desired answer and his ethics is rather the exposition of a method which is capable of effectively leading men to the practice of virtue.

One could say that the pursuit of one's own interest, the obtaining of as much pleasure as possible, is the psychological law by which the conduct of the individual is governed. But what the legislator is seeking is the greatest possible total of pleasure for the community. As legislator, he is obedient to another criterion and seems to be the product of a different approach to morality. To this, Bentham's reply would be that to seek the greatest possible pleasure of the community is to seek, for one's own sake, the maximum extension of pleasure. Consequently, the legislator's attitude is itself governed by his subjective quest for pleasure. The two aims are, however, distinct and Bentham's legislator is better than man as Bentham sees him.

64. — The classical type of rational Eudaemonism is found in Aristotelian ethics.

The object of moral science, according to Aristotle, is the good. Not, however, the Good in itself, the separated Good of Plato, which, even granted its existence, would not be of concern to us, but the *human* good. Now the human good, the achievement of which is man's proper task[25], is happiness (*eudaimonia*), that is, the most perfect exercise of his human activities. This good does not essentially consist in pleasure which is but the sign and consequence of harmonious activity: "pleasure ... supervenes as the bloom of youth does on those in the flower of their age"[26].

---

[25] *Nicom. Eth.*, I, 7, 1097-1098. — On Aristotelian Eudaemonism see L. Ollé-Laprune, *Essai sur la morale d'Aristote*; J. Léonard, *Le bonheur chez Aristote*, Brussels, 1948; R. A. Gauthier, *Ls morale d'Aristote*, Paris, 1958; and the work of J. Vanier already referred to, *Le bonheur, principe et fin de la morale aristotélienne*. Ans, obviously, the *Commentary* by R. A. Gauthier and J. Y. Jolif, Louvain-Paris, 1959, on the *Nicomachean Ethics*.

[26] *Nicom. Eth.*, X, 4, 1174 b 33. — Aristotle is careful, moreover, not to proscribe all seeking after pleasure.

An essential of happiness is *virtue,* which lies in activity that is exercised in accordance with the rule of reason and in which a certain objective balance (the just mean) is achieved: this mean, only the man of practical wisdom is capable of determining[27] (n. 268). — Virtue alone is not, however, sufficient for complete happiness. Certain exterior circumstances are also required: health, sufficient wealth, friends etc.[28]. Man, moreover, becomes fully human only through living in community: the human ideal ist that of the virtuous citizen and, still more, of the *statesman,* who strives to ensure that the laws of the state are just, so that a rational order will prevail.

But the moral virtues, of which Aristotle has made such remarkable analyses (particularly of justice, *Nich. Eth.,* V, and of friendship – which to speak strictly is not a virtue — IX and X) are not the summit of human activity. They yield to the intellectual or "dianoetic" virtues. Man's highest activity, that which most approaches to perfect happiness and to the divine condition, is philosophical contemplation. But this is possible only to a small number and intermittently. Complete happiness is not within man's reach for it is something divine. Virtue merits praise, but one who is happy is not praised: he is honoured as are the immortals... Happiness lies beyond virtue.

An ethics of contemplation, an ethics of moral and civic virtues: there is, in Aristotle's doctrine, a tension and what can be called a "bifocalism". It should also be noted that he nowhere makes allusion to a survival of the soul (except in reporting the views of others) and that, in any event, this idea has no role to play.

Aristotelian ethics is centred on the aspect of morality which preoccupied the ancient philosophers (n. 2). What is of importance is to know what happiness consists in and how it may be attained. Nonetheless the term: "eudaemonism" does not express the entire moral doctrine of Aristotle. The moral value of an action is not, in his view, simply identical with its capacity to lead a person to happiness. To act in conformity with reason[29] has a value in itself. Even if nothing resulted from a virtuous action, it should still be

---

[27] *Ib.,* II, 6, 1106 b 36.
[28] *Ib.,* I, 9, 1099 a 31 - b 8.
[29] "... act according to right reason ...', *ib.,* II, 2, 1103 b 31-32.

performed [30]. The notion of obligation is also present, even though it does not receive anything like the same prominence that it receives in Christian and modern ethics. "Though surely there are some things which a man cannot be compelled to do — which he will rather die than do, however painful the mode of death" [31]. He will rather die: for so to act has a *greater beauty*: so to act is also, and in consequence, more productive of happiness. Eudaemonism is not disowned, but it has not that narrow and utilitarian aspect that is often attributed to it. For Aristotle "a virtuous action... implies a relation to happiness, not, it is true, as means is related to end, but as part is related to whole" [32].

65. – The type of Eudaemonism which we have called "eschatological" is not a doctrine that has been systematically proposed, but rather a tendency and "temptation" of the religious consciousness — or at least of that religious consciousness (such as the Christian one) which maintains that human existence does not end with death.

Since religious people are aiming at "salvation", "beatitude" or, at the least, freedom from evil — winning heaven avoiding hell — they are easily led to measure the value of their actions according as these help towards the attainment of this end, whose importance eclipses all else. Once this utilitarian value is given pride of place, it readily comes to be

---

[30] *Ib.*, I, 6, 1097 b 2-4. See Ollé-Laprune, *Essai sur la morale d'Aristote*, pp. 81-104. Gauthier and Jolif, *op. cit.*, 2 e p., pp. 563-575, bring out well the genuinely moral character of Aristotelian ethics. — Note, however, that in the text cited, Aristotle includes virtue, honours and pleasures in the same category. They all deserve to be willed for their own sakes, but they may also be willed in view of something else; in this they are distinguished from happiness, which has no end beyond itself. It is happiness, in consequence, which si the supreme value.

[31] *Ib.*, III, 1, 1110 a 26-27. Translation of J. Thomson, Penguin Books, 1958, p. 78.

[32] R. A. Gauthier, *Magnanimité*, Paris, 1951, p. 84 (who refers to *Eud. Eth.*, II, 1, 1219 b 12-13).

As a contemporary type of rational Eudaemonism, Eric Weil's *Philosophie morale* may be cited; here, however, the eudaemonist theme is combined with a Kantian one. "First and last, morality is, and remains, the search for one's own happiness (rational and, as such, moral)", p. 131. The happiness that is rational is the satisfaction of reason; even better: "reason, the exercise of reason, reason that has been perfected in man and by man, *is* happiness", p. 49. Nevertheless, what reason requires is that the happiness of the empirical individual, and not simply the satisfaction of reason, be pursued, p. 149.

identified with *moral* value, the value by which the humanness of a human action is measured. A morally good action will then be, *in essence,* one that "leads to heaven".

In fact, the relation between an action and the ultimate end has, at times, been proposed as the norm of morality (n. 128). If this end is understood in the sense of beatitude and of beatitude subjectively considered, such views can be classed as higher forms of Eudaemonism.

It could be objected that, since eschatological beatitude is on the level of knowledge and love, this form of Eudaemonism should not be considered here. But although it is true that authentic beatitude cannot but involve knowledge and love, it is also true that, as long as all we are speaking about is beatitude in the abstract, this spiritual activity is still being considered as the activity of which we are capable because our *nature* is spiritual: the further dimension that this activity possesses, because it expresses us as personal *subjects,* is not considered (n. 278).

It should be carefully noted that Christian beatitude, far from signifying purely subjective happiness, a happiness that is centred on the person himself, involves on the contrary — since it is "joy in the truth", joy in the Joy of God — the recognition and disinterested love of the supreme Value, which is the pre-eminent source and transcendent exemplar of moral value. "In the Christian perspective, a displacement occurs, as a result of which the traditional designation 'ethics of happiness' continues to be justified only on condition that happiness is understood, as not only the total satisfaction of my desires, but also and primarily as transforming union with one who is Other than myself and whom I love more than myself, as the entry into His life for the fuller accomplishment of His will"[33]. It is clear that Eudaemonism in this sense transcends Eudaemonism.

66. – Before we attempt a critical appraisal of these diverse forms of Eudaemonism, what is in question should be carefully noted. We are not here discussing whether the human will in all its activity tends necessarily and implicitly towards "beatitude", that is, towards a fulfilment that is consciously possessed (nn. 14, 4; 280-283). Neither are we concerned with the question of whether activity that is conformed to the moral rule is the sole means of arriving at the desired goal, insofar as

---

[33] J. Maritain, *Neuf leçons...*, p. 22.

this can be obtained by human endeavour (nn. 294-296). Finally, we are far from denying that there is some intrinsic connection between a person's moral value and his human fulfilment: does not each, in its own way, denote a perfection of man as man? The total human achievement embraces both the one and the other, as virtue that is rewarded and as happiness that is deserved (n. 285).

The only point that is here being investigated is this: is an action to be called "good" morally, because, and to the extent that, it leads to happiness — or *vice versa?* In other words: is the relation with happiness the immediate foundation and norm of moral value?

In the discussion which follows, we shall speak of "happiness" or "felicity" in preference to "beatitude". "Beatitude.., in the full sense of the word, is a happiness which is completely satisfyng, a happiness which sets at rest all the aspirations of a human being (n. 278). Now, most of the authors with whom we are here occupied, from the sole fact that the only happiness they envisage is terrestrial, are not at all thinking in terms of this total happiness. It is for this reason that we prefer to employ a more modest term.

We shall begin our inquiry with a discussion of Hedonism, since this is more straightforward. Afterwards, we shall consider the general principle on which Eudaemonism is based.

67. – It is sufficient to know the hedonistic attitude in order to arrive at an appreciation (completely pre-critical) of the way in which it contradicts spontaneous moral judgments. In virtue of these judgments, or, more exactly, by the exercise of practical reason, there results a confused knowledge that to make pleasure the goal and rule of human action is to cheapen and degrade this latter. The sensualist, the lover of his own comfort, the person who is skilled in dodging what makes demands on him, do not inspire much respect in others and often provoke their contempt; the person, on the contrary, who is capable, given a worthy cause, of sacrificing his own wellbeing, and his very life, evokes the approval and admiration even of his enemies [34]. Now all this would be impossible,

---

[34] Bradley has clearly shown the opposition that exists between Hedonism and the data of moral consciousness (even though his criticism often manifests the "idealism" which he professes): see *Ethical Studies*, 2nd ed., Oxford, 1927,

if the value of a human action were measured by pleasure or in relation to pleasure.

It is true that a virtuous person at times finds a delicate pleasure in his very act of self-sacrifice. But this pleasure, which is far from being a matter of feelings, derives all its worth and meaning from the moral value that is inherent in his sacrifice. It is nothing other than the awareness he has of having grown in humanity (n. 71).

68. – But why is it that spontaneous moral judgments of this kind arise? It is not because pleasure, as such, is condemned — the moral sense of mankind is not rigorist — but because a double disorder is revealed in the systematic pursuit of pleasure. 1. The person who acts in this way is making an end out of what is, of itself, the accompaniment, the sanction and the epiphenomenon of a well-executed action, of the achievement of a goal (n. 64): for the meaning and purpose of pleasure is to foster the correct execution of actions. 2. A more profound disorder is that the systematic and calculated search for pleasure involves the subordination to the particular of a capacity for the universal. Pleasure cannot but be subjective and particular; the undustry which the sensualist exercises in order to obtain it, calls into play an intelligence that is open to the universal and the totality. Consequently, a superior value is made subordinate to one that is inferior (which is a very different matter from the merely occasional and temporary preference of an inferior value, n. 33, 3). And the more a person commits his spiritual powers — reason and will — to the quest for pleasure, the more does he aggravate the contrast between the universal character of the means and the particular character of the end. — An analogous disorder is present wherever an individual seeks his own pleasure, exclusively or principally, in activities which, of their nature, are directed

---

ch. 3: "Pleasure for pleasure's sake", especially pp. 85-93. "When moral persons without a theory on the matter are told that the moral end for the individual and the race is the getting a maximum surplusage of pleasurable feeling, and that there is nothing in the whole world which has the smallest moral value except this end and the means to it, there is no gainsaying that they repudiate such a result. They feel that there are things we should choose even if no pleasure come from them", *ib.*, p. 88.

towards the good of the human family, or the community, or whose essential meaning is "other-directed": this is particularly true of sexual activity [35].

From the fact that pleasure stimulates to action and helps towards its correct accomplishment, the conclusion is at times drawn that there is no disorder in seeking it as an end. But this conclusion is valid only if end is understood in a secondary and concomitant sense. Moreover, what is here involved is less a goal that is expressly intended (I desire pleasure ...) than a profound attitude of the will, which is the core of moral activity. The true disorder does not lie in the fact that, at a given moment, the thought of pleasure is uppermost in consciousness, but in living one's life habitually on hedonistic principles and in serenely accepting these as providing the key to the meaning of life.

From what has been said, it might seem that Epicureanism and Bentham's version of Utilitarianism are further from true morality than the unsophisticated approach of Aristippus. Paradoxically, this is not so, for another factor comes into play, or rather the same factor, considered under another aspect. Because of the introduction of calculation into the hedonistic quest, the spontaneity of the senses comes to be restrained and a person learns not to yield to the present attraction but to control his impulses; he looks to the future and knows how to deprive himself of satisfaction today so as to have still greater satisfaction tomorrow. In one respect, this calculating approach, in transforming naive Hedonism into a reflective and scientific Hedonism, tends to aggravate its immorality, as we have seen; but, in another respect, it inserts in human action an element which can later develop into authentic morality, once a person, through reflecting on his activity, comes to appreciate the necessity to provide the powers, which he calls into play, with a goal that is worthy of them, a *rational* goal.

69. – Moreover, Hedonism, as a moral doctrine, makes tacit use of a norm other than pleasure. Why are we urged to search for it, if not because such an effort is judged to be in accordance with human nature, because the deliberate pursuit of what naturally attracts man is considered to be right and reasonable? There is, then, an implicit acknowledgment that the essence of moral value does not lie in pleasure or in what

---

[35] Cf. the study of A. Plé: *La Masturbation*, "Supplément de la Vie Spirituelle", n. 77, May 1966, pp. 258-292.

helps to procure it, but in the harmony of an action with human nature, with reason, or with something along these lines.

An illustration of this is had in Bentham's concern to justify his "principle of utility": he insists that other possible principles (the principle of asceticism, the principle of sympathy and antipathy etc.) result necessarily either in despotism or anarchy [36]. But this supposes that to avoid despotism and anarchy is *morally good*.

70. – In addition to these directly ethical errors, there is another and more serious error involved in the doctrine of Hedonism, an error which forms the presuppositon of the entire theory: namely, that man's happiness consistes in pleasure of the senses. Now the difference between happiness and pleasure is such that, even if the principle of Eudaemonism were sound, the case in favour of Hedonism would be in no way advanced. There is a plenitude and depth to happiness: it is a relatively stable state in which everything combines to satisfy us in the depths of our being. It is substantial and supra-temporal in a way that pleasure is not: hence it is proof against trials which, on the surface level, may be devastating, provided these are not of excessive intensity. Pleasure, on the contrary, and particularly pleasure of the senses, belongs to a superficial zone where the gusts of change blow freely; it has no ontological density; it is purely subjective so that an attempt to justify it rationally can be made only by appealing to some objective motivation ("it is necessary to amuse oneself", "one has a body in order to derive pleasure from it" etc.). — But this error implies, in its turn, that man is really nothing other than a more evolved animal. (The refutation of this error is the task of rational anthropology).

The opposition between the subjectivity of pleasure and the objectivity that is involved in happiness has been clearly noted by Bradley. Moreover, he observes, happiness signifies permanence and harmonious completion; pleasures, on the contrary, come and go as the tide ebbs and flows, so that they cannot all be possessed at one and the same time, nor can they even be systematically classified and arranged etc. It is for this reason that Hedonism is incapable of

---

[36] *Traité*.., I, pp. 6-32; *An Introduction*..., c. 1, n. 14, pp. 129-131.

providing us with any real guidance: in the matter of pleasures, one man's meat is another man's poison; even the experience of others is not a sufficient criterion, for what gives them pleasure will not necessarily give me pleasure; and anyway, why should I be guided by their judgment rather than by my own?[37].

Moreover, the systematic pursuit of pleasure, especially for "round the clock" pleasure, tends to reduce a person to despair, because of the impossibility of achieving the satisfaction he craves and the continual disappearance of the satisfaction he has achieved. Consequently, it is in no way astonishing that a disciple of Aristippus, Hegesias, recommended suicide as the sole remedy; hence the nickname "peisithanatos" (the one who urges death) which was bestowed on him.

71. – We now turn to the examination of the general theory of Eudaemonism. As has already been indicated (n. 49), our primary criterion, in the entire course of the present inquiry, is the harmony between the various theories and what moral experience reveals. Accordingly, the question that has now to be put is whether the eudaemonist interpretation harmonizes with that experience; whether moral value, as conceived of in Eudaemonism in accordance with the limits imposed by its own principles, differs from that value which the analysis of moral consciousness has brought to light.

Now the relation to happiness, in which Eudaemonism places the essence of the good action, can be understood in two ways (and in two ways only, it seems): either as a *teleological* relation (of means to an end, so that an action is good because it leads to happiness), or as a relaton of *participation* (so that virtue is an element of happiness and the joy etc., which an action brings makes this to be morally good). Will one or other of these relations enable us to rediscover the value which our reflection on the data of moral consciousness has revealed?

The first relation cannot do so. What is of moral value presents itself in moral experience as immediately lovable, as valuable in itself and consequently, in this sense, absolute (n. 33,2). But if an action is good, "honourable", because it leads to happiness and to the extent to which it does so, moral

---

[37] *Op. cit.*, pp. 93-103, where, however, certain statements call for reservation.

value becomes relative: it is no longer lovable, estimable for its own sake, but only for the sake of something else; the "honourable" good is reduced to the level of the "useful" good. Or, in other words, moral value loses its transcendence over other values, notably over those which are eudaemonist, since it is from them that its own value is now derived. Eudaemonism understood in this sense is, then, in opposition to the data of moral consciousness.

Moreover, as we shall see more clearly later (nn. 294-296), complete happiness ("beatitude") does not result from good actions by way of physical causality, but by way of "merit"; but since merit is founded on the moral goodness of an action, it cannot constitute this. — This point is particularly applicable where eschatological Eudaemonism is concerned. Good actions merit heaven — but on condition that they are good.

We now consider the second relation (that of participation). Without doubt, a good action is ordinarily accompanied by a certain interior contentment — the "joy of a good conscience" of which the *Imitation of Christ* speaks — a sense of spiritual plenitude, the satisfaction that results from the tranquillity of order, from being what one should be and which, in default of happiness in the full sense, at least provides a foretaste and pledge of it. But note firstly that, very often, this feeling scarcely surfaces in consciousness: it is swamped by sorrows and cares. Secondly and more importantly: in every instance, this joy, far from constituting an action's moral value, presupposes this. It is revealed in consciousness as the fruit and natural recompense of a morally good action, just as pleasure in general is the fruit and sanction of activity which is well-executed in its own order. Hence, while the joy of a good conscience can reveal the presence of moral value, it cannot define this.

The immorality of Eudaemonism becomes strikingly apparent in the manner in which, logically, it should regard duties towards others: namely, as mere means of assuring the subject's own happiness (for example, by giving him a sentimental satisfaction). One will do good because so to act gives one pleasure; one will love others so as to ensure one's own joy, since it is to oneself that one gives in giving oneself to others... But love that is true loves the *other*: it seeks him for his sake and not for one's own.

This deviation can be encountered in eschatological Eudaemonism: in a person, for example, who gives alms and visits the poor, exclusively in order to win heaven (considered under the aspect of subjective felicity).

It is readily conceded that disinterested love is the source of a very pure joy; but if the moral value of love springs from the joy it brings, then the other is loved only because he provides me with an occasion for tasting it: he himself is of no more interest to me than the words which are attached to a melody interest the lover of music. To call a love of this kind "disinterested" is a poor joke, or a serious illusion [38].

These remarks lead us to a fresh considertion.

72. – If the principle of Eudaemonism were true, it would be necessary to maintain that an action has more moral value, the more expressly it is performed in view of the happiness which it promises or actually provides. But this contradicts the evidence that is present in moral consciousness, namely, that actions performed out of pure love of what is good, of what is morally upright, are on a much higher level than those performed out of self-interest [39]. Eudaemonism, in common with Hedonism, renders disinterestedness unintelligible and immoral; it would logically lead to an attitude diametrically opposed to that which an analysis of moral consciousness reveals as the ideal to be striven for.

It is not at all a question, obviously, of condemning the desire of beatitude and of eliminating the virtue of hope. The desire of beatitude, as natural and necessary, remains, of itself, outside the moral sphere: it cannot, in consequence, be condemned (n. 288). Even further: insofar as it is directed not only towards beatitude *in general* but towards authentic beatitude, which consists in a union with God of loving contemplation, so that the blessed rejoice in the joy of God rather than in their own (n. 65), this desire is moral in the extreme: it glorifies God magnificently, just as does Christian hope, since it is an expression of confidence in the divine goodness and fidelity. Now, such a glorification of God is eminently moral, since it

---

[38] J. Maritain, *Philosophie morale*, I, pp. 422-423 (*Moral Philosophy*, p. 339).

[39] The disinterested character of moral value — "uprightness of will which is preserved for its own sake" — as opposed to the search for what is "advantageous", is an essential note of St Anselm's ethics. See R. Pouchet, *La Rectitudo chez saint Anselme*, Paris, 1964.

is directly referred to the source and origin of all value (nn. 152-157). Moral value is here subsumed under religious value (n. 24,4). — In addition, all the great spiritual writers have made it their aim to guide souls towards a pure and disinterested love, so that a person's own beatitude comes to be primarily desired because it provides him with a further motive, and a new capacity, for loving and glorifying God for His own sake.

73. — It is necessary, finally, to come to an agreement about the very notion of happiness or felicity. This can be envisaged from the *subjective* point of view, as the enjoyment of a good that is possessed, or from the *objective* point of view, as the good whose possession provides this enjoyment. In the first instance, the criticism made of hedonism becomes applicable here also (nn. 67-69): for Eudaemonism, in this sense, is but a form of hedonism which can, indeed, be elevated and refined, but still presents the same essential defect as the grosser forms.

In particular, it will be impossible to propose a moral rule which will indicate the true path to happiness. What will please some will not please others; these pleasures or these joys cannot all be tasted at the same time, nor can they be measured on a scale that is universally valid: each has his preferences and no one can judge in my place about what gives me pleasure (n. 70).

Then again, as we know from our own personal experience and as people in general readily appreciate, there is a qualitative difference, a difference of value, between the various types of satisfaction. The pleasure which a good glass of wine gives is different from the joy that is born of a genereous action and the latter, even though it may well be psychologically less intense or practically zero, is of greater value. The felicity of "artificial paradises" is not in the same class as the joy of knowing, the *gaudium de veritate*. — Now, it requires no prolonged moral reflection to appreciate that this gradation is not just a gradation among subjective states, in whose subjectivity it shares, as is the case, for example, with our judgments concerning what is pleasurable and even, to a great extent, with our judgments of taste. this gradation, on the contrary, presents itself as the measure and norm of these states. There are true and counterfeit delights, satisfactions which are authentic and deserve to be desired, as well as false satisfactions which are unworthy of being desired. This the proponents of Eudaemonism do not deny; they even assign to ethics the task of making the required distinctions. But, as we have seen, such a distinction cannot be established, if all that is taken into consideration is subjective felicity or pleasure. The source from which this is derived has also to be considered, that is, happiness has to be envisaged *objectively*[40].

But once this is done, Eudaemonism has been transcended. The criterion of a good action is no longer its relation to happiness but to *true* happiness, to the happiness that is in accord with human nature, with reason etc. Happiness has itself a norm, by which true and counterfeit happiness can be distinguished. But if a norm can exercise its function only in dependence on another norm, it is this latter which is the true one.

We have here touched on a principle which can be expressed as follows: whenever a proposed moral norm itself requires a further norm, it is this latter which is the true one. We have, in fact, already employed this principle when treating of extrinsic morality (n. 56), and we shall have occasion to use it again in the discussions that follow. The point being made can be illustrated by means of very simple examples. If, in order to know the temperature of my room, I have first to check my thermometer with another thermometer, that is, if I trust my own thermometer only because of its accordance with this further standard, it is this latter which provides the true point of reference; whenever it is equally possible for me to use either, this is obviously the one I shall choose. Similarly, when I say: this piece of material measures a yard, I acknowledge that this length is a true yard, in harmony with the primary yard-standard ... It is this ultimate standard which provides the true point of reference. But since it is out of the question for me to compare the measure I actually have (of wood, or oilcloth, or plastic material) with the primary yard-standard, I am content with it and take it to be correct,

---

[40] "If pleasure were the ultimate end, it should be sought for its own sake. But this is not the truth: whether or not a pleasure is to be sought, depends on its source; pleasure that accompanies actions which are good and to-be-done is itself good and to-be-sought; pleasure that accompanies actions which are evil is itself evil and to-be-avoided. The goodness and worthiness of pleasure spring, then, from a source other than itself", St Thomas, *Cont. Gent.*, III, 26. Cf. Aristotle, *Nicom. Eth.*, X, 5, especially 1175 b 24 - 1176 a 3.

until the contrary is proved. — Where the moral norm is concerned, the situation is completely different. The harmony of an action with human nature, or with reason, is easier to establish than its aptitude for ensuring *true* happiness. Even further: I can form a correct notion of this, only by taking into consideraton the requirements of human nature and of reason (n. 284, end). Consequently, it is the norm of the (alleged) norm which here provides the true and directly utilizable norm.

In brief: Eudaemonism is either reduced to the level of a type of Hedonism — as refined as one wishes — which clashes with the data of moral consciousness, or else it transcends itself, by appealing to a criterion other than happiness, to a criterion *of* happiness [40bis].

In order to justify their opinion, the proponents of Eudaemonism sometimes point to the fact that all men seek happiness [41]. But, of itself and independently of all metaphysical interpretation, this fact proves, not that happiness ought to be desired, but simply that it is desirable. Eudaemonism here commits the naturalistic fallacy, so strongly criticised by G. E. Moore [42].

But note that not everything in these theories is to be discarded. Moral philosophy cannot ignore the problems connected with man's natural and necessary desire for happiness. The relation between the satisfactin of this desire and a person's moral value needs to be investigated. Even though situated on two different planes of value, both happiness and moral goodness are revealed as desirable in themselves and, consequently, as ends: the desire in both instances takes on the form of a necessity, physical for the former and moral for the latter. This fact gives grounds for thinking that there must be an intrinsic connection between the two. The problem will be examined later.

74. – In addition to the positive Eudaemonism which has just been treated of, mention should also be made of what can be styled negative Eudaemonism, namely, the doctrines which

---

[40bis] W. G. Maclagan likewise sees in the eudaemonist theories, "a confused compromise between egoistic hedonism on the one hand and, on the other hand, a doctrine of obligation to realize *values*", *The Theological Frontiers of Ethics*, London, 1960, p. 59, n. 2.

[41] See, for example, J. Stuart Mill, *Utilitarianism*, ch. 4; ed. E. Rhys, London, 1931, pp. 32-33.

[42] *Principia ethica*, pp. 66-67 etc.

measure the value of a human action by its power to free a human being from sorrow and from his existence as an individual, which, it is maintained, is the source of all suffering and evil. This attitude is particularly strong in Indian thought and has found its most complete expression in Buddhism. In the West and in more recent times, the theme has been systematically developed by Arthur Schopenhauer, *Die Welt als Wille und Vorstellung* (*The World as Will and Idea*, 1819). — Note, though, that neither Buddhism nor Schopenhauer teaches an egoistic morality: quite the contrary, since what they most of all recommend is pity for the suffering that is so widespread, a pity which, as H. de Lubac has remarked of Buddhism, is not an authentic love, directed to the *person* of the other, since he, in common with myself, is no more than a bundle of appearances [43].

The criticisms that have been here made of Eudaemonism in general retain their validity where this negative form is concerned. — But, in addition, the principle on which this form is grounded has to be rejected absolutely. Our existence as individuals is neither evil nor the source of evil; it simply makes evil possible. But this possibility is not in itself an evil: it simply indicates a limitation on good, without which *this* particular good would not be possible, and for which the term "metaphysical evil" — introduced by Leibniz — is extremely unhappy. — Finally, while the sacrifice of one's life often has a very high moral value, the reason for this is not because one's own existence is rejected but because a higher value is preferred and positively chosen. Moreover, the sacrifice of life is not the same as the renunciation of existence, even though, subjectively, it might well appear to be. To develop these various points is the task of metaphysics and, where the last and vital one is concerned, of rational anthropology.

Since the norm and essence of moral value do not lie in the subject's own particular good or satisfaction, they have to be sought elsewhere. But where?

If we do not wish to go outside the world of concrete realities, of existing beings, the line of approach that immediately presents

---

[43] See H. de Lubac, *Aspects du Bouddhisme*, Paris, 1951 (*Aspects of Buddhism*, New York, 1954).

itself is provided by other human beings and the communities they form: particular societies (nation, state etc.) and the universal society (humanity). It is, then, in this direction that we have now to direct our inquiry.

B. *Altruistic and communitarian theories.*

75. – Several reasons invite us to identify the moral value of our actions with their orientation to the good of others or of society, with their tendency to increase the sumtotal of well-being in the world, to promote social harmony and prosperity etc. And this time, there does not seem to be any clash with the data of moral consciousness.

Is it not — as our criticism of Eudaemonism has served to underline — when a person sacrifices his own private good to the good of others, or of the community, that his moral goodness is most clearly manifest? A "good" man primarily means for us a man who "does good", who encourages and consoles others, who spreads happiness and joy. Is not Christian morality summed up in the command of charity? "He who loves his neighbour has fulfilled the law" [44].

Moreover, so profound is the social dimension of lives that every action we perform, no matter how "private" and secret it may appear, has some effect on others and comes by degrees to concern all humanity. Society, then, seems to be at the horizon of our activity; in it we live and move, without ever having the power to make ourselves free of its influence and of our responsibility towards it. In it we find our completion: without it, what would we be? There is abundant evidence — such as that provided by "children of the wilderness" — that human beings can grow genuinely human only within its womb. Since, then, society is the condition of our full humanization, it appears also and, in consequence, to be the standard in relation to which the value that measures our human uprightness is defined: moral value.

Furthermore, according to many contemporary thinkers, the radical constituent of personality is a relation to others, a capacity to open oneself to them through a generous and

----

[44] *Rom.*, 13, 8-10; *Gal.*, 5, 14 (R S V).

welcoming attitude. "I" am an "I" only through and for a "Thou"[45]. But moral value is the value of the person as a person, the value with which he comes to be endowed when he acts in accordance with his dignity as a person. Consequently, this value, in its turn, will consist in what promotes genuine communication, openness and generosity.

76. — The systems which identify — at least implicitly — the norm of moral goodness with a relation to others (either as individuals or as a community) are of very different kinds, as one might expect.

Some insist primarily on the affective dispositions, the feelings which inspire a person's action: this will be good when his feelings are directed towards others, their happiness and fulfilment, in place of egoistically enfolding himself. Those who write more or less in this vein are: Hutcheson (morality of benevolence), Adam Smith (morality of sympathy), Auguste Comte (altruism etc.[46]. These approaches to morality are often called "moralities of sentiment".

---

[45] Examples of such writers: M. Scheler, *Natur und Formen der Sympathie* (*The Nature of Sympathy*, P. Heath, London, 1954); M. Buber, *Ich und Du* (*I and Thou*, R. Smith, Edinburgh, 1952); M. Nédoncelle, *La réciprocité des consciences*, Paris, 1942; E. Mounier, *Le personnalisme*, Paris, 1950.

[46] Francis Hutcheson (1694-1746): *Inquiry into the Ideas of Beauty and Virtue*, 1725; *System of Moral Philosophy*, 1755 (where the principle of the greatest happiness of the greatest number appears). — Adam Smith (1723-1790), better known as an economist: *Thoery of Moral Sentiments*, 1759, where the morality of sympathy is developed. — Auguste Comte (1798-1857), the founder of Positivism: *Discours sur l'esprit positif*, 1844; *Système de politique positive*, 1851-1854; *Catéchisme positiviste*, 1852. On Comte, consult: J. Maritain, *La philosophie morale*, I, pp. 327-436 (*Moral Philosophy*, pp. 261-350). Also, H. de Lubac, *Le drame de l'humanisme athée*, 3rd ed., Paris, 1945, pp. 135-278 (Eng. trans.: *The Drama of Atheist Humanism*, E. Riley, London, 1949, pp. 75-159). For a more complete study, see H. Gouhier, *La jeunesse d'Auguste Comte et la formation du positivisme*, 3 vols., Paris, 1933-1941.

Anthony Ashley, Earl of Shaftesbury (1671-1713) is often included among the proponents of sentimentalist ethics. It is indeed true that he primarily situates morality in the sentiments, concerning which the "moral sense" ("reflex affection") judges in an instinctive and immediate fashion, somewhat similar to the way in which judgments of taste are formed (*An Inquiry concerning Virtue and Merit*, 1699). But this "sentiment", as described by Shaftesbury, seems to involve the spontaneous exercise of reason, to which there is an affective accompaniment. (Cf. further on, n. 190). Moreover, Shaftesbury does not completely

We shall dwell a little on the thought of Comte. It was only tardily that this author added morality to the six fundamental sciences, ranging from mathematics to sociology, which studied objective reality. The concern of morality is with the subjective, affective life; its role is to foster the tendencies which promote social harmony. In proposing this view, Comte was reacting against revolutionary individualism; in common with the Traditionalists (Bonald, de Maistre) on whom he depends in certain respects, he insists so much on the reality and predominance of society that this becomes for him the true subject, while the individual is regarded as an abstraction. Society is itself a structured body of elementary societies, of which the first is the family; a human being is human only through his insertion into the social body and the only right he has is that of fulfilling his duty towards this.

Social harmony can be achieved thanks to the "altruistic" inclination which man possesses; it is the task of ethics to work systematically for the victory of these inclinations over those which are egoistic. Comte's ethics will have "love for its principle", disinterested love, in accordance with the sentence in the *Imitation of Christ* (a sentence of which Comte was fond)": May I love You more than myself and myself only on account of You" [47].

Comte, who has a great admiration for medieval Catholicism, even though he was absolutely impervious to Christian dogma and to the idea of God, wished, partly under the influence of personal factors, to crown his ethics with a religious and ecclesial institution which would retain, by being provided with a "positive" foundation, all that he judged valuable in the ancient religion: an exterior structure and the cultivation of certain values. This is the *positive religion*, which he devised in the last period of his life and which he zealously strove to organize and to propagate: it essentially involved the cult of the "Great Being" (humanity, in which the dead, who are "subjectively" immortal in the memory of the living, are also included), flanked by the 'great Fetish" (the earth) and the "Great Milieu" (space)... Comte seems to have lived his moral doctrine with an absolute sincerity.

---

identify a person's social inclination and his moral goodness; this consists rather in a harmonious equilibrium between love of self and love of others and, more profoundly, in the smooth adaptation of the individual to the "system" of which he forms part (the society in which he lives, the human race, the universe itself), an adaptation in which the individual finds his true good. It is the "moral sense" which judges of this harmony. So the ethics of Shaftesbury is, in certain respects, an "aesthetic" ethics and even, one could say, "cosmic", in that it identifies the fulfilment of the individual with his integration into the Totality.

[47] *The Imitation of Christ*, bk. III, c. 5; but the love that is here spoken of is the love of the disciple for God.

77. – Among other writers, the objective norm of moral value is rather the advantage an action brings to individuals, without the subject's own advantage being in any way privileged. The good action is that which tends to promote the greatest happiness of the greatest number. This is the doctrine of Utilitarianism, whose chief representative is John Stuart Mill (*Utilitarianism*, 1863), and which has exercised wide influence, particularly in English-speaking countries. (See, for example, the classic work of H. Sidgwick, *Methods of Ethics*, 1875). It has indeed been so generally accepted that many have come to regard it as a doctrine whose truth is so obvious that there is no need to attempt to justify it.

As we have seen (n. 63), among the dimensions of pleasure listed by Bentham was that of *extension*, by which he understood the greater or lesser number of people who would share in the pleasure. But, where Bentham was concerned, the pleasure of others is considered as an element in the subject's own pleasure: it is, finally, in order to increase my own enjoyment that I wish others to enjoy themselves with me. On the contrary, according to Mill and Utilitarians of his way of thinking, what the morally good person *immediately* seeks is the good of the greatest number. Utilitarianism makes its own the golden rule of "Jesus of Nazareth" (as Mill calls Him): "Whatever you would that men should do to you, do you also to them in like manner" [48]. In judging between his own good and that of others, a man should remain "as strictly impartial as a disinterested and benevolent spectator" [49]. What is good and what is evil, advantageous and disadvantageous, should not be measured by subjective impressions but by the judgment of those who are wise and experienced. "It is better to be a human being dissatisfied than a pig satisfied; better to be Socrates dissatisfied than a fool satisfied. And if the fool, or the pig, are of different opinion, it is because they only know their own side of the question. The other party to the comparison knows both sides" [50]. It is clear that Mill's empiricism is not a gross empiricism.

78. – While Utilitarianism is concerned with the good of individuals — the good of humanity simply being the sumtotal

---

[48] *Matt.*, 7, 12.

[49] "As strictly impartial as a disinterested and benevolent spectator", *Utilit.*, ch. 2; p. 16.

[50] *Ib.*, p. 9.

of the good of each of its members — the sociological school (E. Durkheim. L. Lévy-Bruhl, C. Bouglé etc.) under the inspiration of Comte, considers that the source of moral value is society, which imposes on its members, by means of rules and moral judgments, the actions that are useful for its well-being. Now, the well-being of society is not the same as the sumtotal of the well-being of its members, for society is a reality *sui generis*, superior to all individuals who owe to it their dignity, their "sacredness" as human persons; without it, they would be scarcely more than superior animals (nn. 52; 75). Moral progress will be achieved by a more perfect knowledge — thanks to the science of sociology — of the nature of society, of its true good and of the conditions which make possible the attainments of this. Moreover, this science is itself a social fact: as a product of reason, it pertains to the human race and expresses what is true of every society. Consequently, it never ceases to be a social fact.

See, for example, E. Durkheim, *La détermination du fait moral*, "Bulletin de la Société française de philosophie", 11 Feb., 1906: "An inquiry into the contemporary moral consciousness .. reveals that there is agreement on the following points: 1. Never, in fact, is the qualification moral applied to an action which has for its object only the good of the individual, or his perfection understood in a purely egoistical manner; 2. If I as an individual do not constitute an end which *of itself*, has a moral character, the same is necessarily true of the individuals who are similar to me and who differ from me only in degree, whether they are superior or inferior to me. 3. The conclusion to be drawn from this is that *if there is to be any morality*, the only object it can have is the group formed by a plurality of associated individuals, that is, society, *on condition however that this can be considered as a personality qualitatively different from the individual personalities who compose it*. Hence, morality commences at the point at which attachment to some group or other commence", p. 115. (Author's italics). Cf. pp. 127-129. The existence of society, superior to the individual, is a postulate of morality. It alone explains the twofold character of moral good, obligatory and desirable at one and the same time — two aspects which should not be dissociated, p. 114, and by which morality enters the region of the sacred. It is society which, for Durkheim, provides the foundation of religious value: at one and the same time immanent and transcendent, pp. 131-132, it "is to its members what a god is to his faithful" [51]; it "preserves in us a sense of perpetual dependence" [52]; it inspires respect and moves us from within, since it can exist only in the consciousness of individuals... It is a "Reality from which springs everything that counts in our eyes and which, nonetheless, transcends us on every side... It is ourselves and the best part of ourselves, since man is man only in the measure in which he is civilized", p. 131. Thus the two characteristics of moral good "are but two aspects of one and the same reality which is the collective reality", p. 133.

It is, moreover, society which, in Europe, has consecrated the value of the person. "Analyse man in an empirical manner and you will find nothing that implies his sacredness; there is in him nothing that is not transient. But, as a result of causes which we have not to inquire into here, it is to the human person that the social conscious-ness of the peoples of Europe has come to attach itself more than to anything else; now, at last, the person has acquired an incomparable value. It is society which has consecrated him. This halo of Sacredness that surrounds man and protects him against sacrilegious encroachments is not a natural endowment: it is the way in which society thinks of him, it is the high esteem in which it now holds him, projected exteriorly and objectified", p. 135.

What he is speaking about is the ideal society which is seeking itself in the real society; or more exactly, what he is speaking about is the real society, the society that *exists here and now*, but arrived at a more lucid consciousness of itself, such as can be obtained only by the science of sociology, *ib.*, p. 176. It is in the name of this more perfect society that the present state of development can be criticised and reformed, so that moral progress becomes possible.

Even though Comte exercised a certain influence on the socio-logical school, there is a difference between the two approaches. For Comte, morality is concerned with the subjective order; this is what distinguishes it from the system of objective sciences, of which it is the crown. For the sociologists, morality is a social fact which is studied, as are all social facts, in a purely objective manner. (The notion of a normative science is contradictory, insists Lévy-Bruhl, n. 1).

79. – In Marxism, we again meet with this total sub-ordination of the individual to the collectivity, but now linked with a much broader vision of the world.

---

[51] Em. Durkheim, *Les formes élémentaires de la vie religieuse*, Paris, 1912, p. 295 (Eng. trans.: *The Elementary Forms of the Religious Life*, J. Swain, London, 1964).
[52] *Ib.*

What is said here presupposes as already known the general philosophy of Marxism, dialectical materialism and its application to human history, or at least the form under which it primarily presented itself to Marx, historical materialism. According to this doctrine, all thought-forms, all "ideologies", notably those which centre on rights, morality and religion, are entirely conditioned by the social and economic substructure. So, for example, feudal morality, based on honour, differs from capitalist and bourgeois morality, where respectability and respect for property occupy such a prominent position, while proletarian morality differs from both. "The dominant ideas in a particular epoch are those of the dominant class". This is particularly true of moral ideas. The dominant class imposes the rules and dogmas which help to maintain its own supremacy. Thus, a system based on private property will necessarily confer on this a sacred character.

What this theory should lead to is the complete relativization of morality and, in consequence, its disappearance. And, in fact, one finds texts, in Lenin for example, which seem to signify the dismissal of morality along with religion. But the morality of which there is question is bourgeois morality and morality that is grounded on a transcendent source. While Soviet Marxism has undoubtedly neglected the problem of morality up to very recent times, it is today making strenuous efforts to fill this lacuna.

One can say that, for the Marxist, there are authentic moral values: these are already present to the proletarian consciousness in which alone — untained as it is by the sin of exploitation — is preserved a vision of the human reality that is free from distortion. These values will find their full flowering in the future "classless" society where man, reconciled with himself, will enjoy all the richness of his humanity. Once private property, exploitation, class divisions etc., have been abolished, man, become master of nature and of social determinants, will pass definitively from the sphere of necessity to that of liberty (Engels): he will be the new, the total man. Moral value, for the moment, is defined in function of this ideal: whatever prepares for and hastens the arrival of this is morally valuable. To foster the coming of the classless society is morally good; to hinder it is evil. It is this that, for the Marxist, provides the norm of moral goodness. Since one and the same type of action will, in some situations, aid, and in other situations, hinder the revolutionary project, this one action will be at times good and at times evil. In acting on this principle, the Marxist does not consider that he is in any way in bad faith or in contradiction with himself: he has, on the contrary, the conviction of being perfectly consistent, perfectly faithful to his ideal and to the only task that matters. Thus, Marxism provides an example of an entirely teleological morality, of a morality where the value of actions is judged exclusively in accordance with their relation to the end and not at all in accordance with their internal conformity to an ideal[53].

80. – The doctrines that have just been outlined are in agreement that, if a human being is to act morally, he has to advance, in some way, beyond considerations of self-interest and attain to a more universal outlook. On this point, they are closer to the truth than are the doctrines centred on the happiness of the individual. It has also to be acknowledged that, as has already been said (n. 75), our actions are never without some social repercussion, so that we have an inescapable responsibility towards others and towards the community.

But despite this, should we, can we, accept the norm of value which these theories implicitly or explicitly propose to us?

81. – Firstly, as regards the "sentimental" approaches to morality, let us see if — in virtue of the principle that the true norm does not itself require a further norm (n. 73) — "altruistic" feelings are, of themselves, a sufficient, sure, unconditional measure of the rectitude of an action. Such feelings can be considered under two aspects: materially, as a subjective

---

[53] On Marxist ethics, see J. Y. Calvez, *La pensée de Karl Marx*, Paris, 1946, pp. 432-439. — What interests us here is less the true thought of Marx than that of contemporary Marxists. It goes without saying that the subject would need to be treated at much greater length; in particular, a study of Marx's economic doctrine, notably of his theory of value, would be required. See also J. Maritain *La philosophie morale*, I, pp. 261-324 (*Moral Philosophy*, pp. 209-260). On the Soviet version of Marxist ethics, see S. Vagovic, *Etica communista*, 2nd ed., Rome, 1966.

state; formally, in accordance with their altruistic orientation. (Cf. in n. 38, an analogous distiction apropos of remorse).

Now, considered *subjectively*, altruistic feelings are no different from any other feelings. To make of them the norm of goodness, to measure the value of our actions by the satisfaction which they bring us, is to remain within the confines of Hedonism — a rather refined Hedonism, it is true, but which of itself is foreign to morality.

Feelings, no matter of what kind, take on a positive moral value only if channelled by our reason. Otherwise, they quickly become disordered: think of the murders and suicides to which love-affairs give rise! — Moreover, feelings are not, directly at least, dependent on a person's will, whereas an action can be moral or immoral only to the extent that it is free.

Considered formally as *altruistic*, the feelings of which we are speaking have undoubtedly a definite value: they are estimable, praiseworthy etc.; one readily prides oneself on them, whereas egoistic inclinations are concealed, not only from others but from oneself... But such feelings derive their value from the object towards which they are directed. It is, then, in function of this object that the norm of value will have to be explained, a norm which it is the task of reason both to propose and to evaluate.

What is this object? It is, on the one hand, the good that one wills to others, that one *desires* for them and, on the other hand and more profoundly, others "in person", *loved* for what they are, for the value that they possess. If one does go beyond the first aspect, the welfare of others becomes the norm of action: this is the utilitarian thesis which we shall shortly discuss. (The good of others, according to this superficial view, can obviously be only their "empirical good", exterior to the spiritual and personal depths that are theirs). If one considers the second aspect, the perspective is altered: the norm of value is derived from the dignity of the person or of man's rational nature — a possibility that will be discussed in the following section. (It is clear that another, simply as "other", as "not-I", is possessed of no special dignity; to think the contrary would be, according to Scheler, a sign of "resentment") [54]. If one maintains, in

---

[54] M. Scheler, *L'homme du ressentiment*, Paris, 1933, pp. 124-127.

company with Comte and the sociologists, that the value of altruistic sentiments lies in their social utility, the norm will then be the good of society, a theory which will shortly be subjected to examination (nn. 85-89).

It should not, however, is forgotten that:

1. Emotions play an important role in moral living. In order to persevere in doing good, a human being has need of the support which his feelings can provide. It is because of this link that noble sentiments and, in particular, those which are "altruistic", should be carefully fostered. This is a highly important feature of the educative process.

2. There is an affective element in moral virtues. These consist for the most part, as we shall see (nn. 270, 275, 276), in channelling our affectivity (the "sense appetite") in accordance with the requirements of practical reason. A purely rational virtue would not be human.

3. There is a deeply personal, and in that sense, subjective dimension to morality. But an "ethics of sentiment" confuses spiritual and emotional subjectivity; while seeking to transcend the impersonal character of pure reason, it yet fails to penetrate the authentic depths of the person and stops short at an equivocal affectivity, in which one has the satisfaction of tasting the sweetness of one's own benevolence.

82. – Does the moral value of our actions spring from their aptitude for bringing happiness to others, for increasing the sumtotal of happiness in the world?

A point that has first of all to be noted is this: to will the happiness of others is moral, only if this happiness is itself moral. I have not the right to will — and still less to seek to ensure — that others satisfy their desires, no matter what way they choose to do so and no matter what these may happen to be. There is need, then, of a criterion to determine which desires are worthy of satisfaction; or, if one prefers, to distinguish "true" happiness from its counterfeits (which, for the person involved, may bear a strange resemblance to the former). Mill, as we have seen (n. 77), was not unaware of this need. But then, is it not this criterion which will provide the true norm of morality: whenever a ptoposed moral norm itself requires a further norm, will not this latter be the true one (n. 73)? Not happiness as such, but what makes it to be true and worthy of being desired. Thus, empiricism is transcended and the moral norm is sought in the sphere of reason [55].

The process of reasoning employed in n. 73 is again applicable here. For if Hedonism and Eudaemonism are not valid norms where I myself am concerned, they become no more valid where others are concerned. This point has been well made by Durkheim (n. 78).

83. – Moreover, to seek "the greatest happiness of the greatest number" does not mean anything, unless there exists a commonly accepted norm, by means of which agreement is reached as to what will bring happiness. But, as has been shown (n. 73), the desires of each individual cannot provide this norm, since tastes and preferences are so diverse. Hence, there is need for an objective norm: but then, once again, one has turned to reason as the norm and has discarted the pure principle of happiness. Consequently, the very principle which, according to Utilitarianism, measures the moral value of our actions, acquires a definite meaning only through the mediation of a rational norm.

In the absence of such a norm, the most that "the greatest happiness of the greatest number" could mean would be the greatest possible extension of economic advantages, or the maximum of bodily comforts (more or less measurable) for all, or perhaps a state of affairs which allowed each individual the fullest scope for exercising his liberty, with the sole proviso that he not hinder others in the exercise of *their* liberty. But, understood in the first sense, the slogan is open to the same criticisms as were made of Hedonism: the ideal of a humanity saturated with enjoyments — an ideal to which contemporary civilization is so much attracted — cannot provide the required understanding of moral value; rather would it involve the extinction of this value, not through elevating it to a higher level (as happens in Christian beatitude) but through swamping it. Understood in the second sense, the slogan grounds moral value on the value of liberty and of free subjects: this introduces a fresh line of thought which will be considered later. (But, in fact, within the utilitarian frame of reference, "liberty" would mean not so much the inner liberty of the authentically human person, or liberty of choice, as the power to "do what one wishes" and so, in consequence, to

---

[55] Cf. the definition of "good" given by H. Sidgwick: "What a man may reasonably desire", *The Methods of Ethics*, 3rd ed., p. 401.

follow one's caprices, to give free rein to one's instincts. Once again, we are led back to hedonistic pastures).

84. – Finally, Mill and his followers seem to regard it as evident that there is a duty to seek the greatest happiness of the greatest number. But, in doing this, they grant themselves straightoff what is in question. What is the meaning of: *duty*?

According to Mill, a person, noticing that his own good is bound up with that of others, comes gradually, in virtue of the laws of association, to desire and will their good as strongly as, or even more strongly than, he desires and wills his own. There is here operating a psychological law, according to which the means tend to capture the attention and interest that were first directed towards the end: so, for example, all the miser's thoughts come to be centred on money, which, of itself, is but a stepping-stone to enjoyment [56].

But this reply casts no moral light: it is concerned only with a psychological process. It is incapable of explaining how the altruism which has flowered from the seed of egoism can sometimes lead a person to the supreme sacrifice, to the denial of the self. (Mill could, it is true, argue that the miser sacrifices the love of enjoyment to the love of money, a love which has issued from the former love.... But the love of money has other sources: money is power; it is first and foremost, for the miser, security...). — Whatever about this point, what still remains absolutely unexplained is how an inclination, no matter how vehement, can give rise to a duty. There is between the two the chasm that separates the physical from the moral order.

But, in fact, Mill and the Utilitarians do not stop short at this "association" theory. They demand, as we have seen, that a person be impartial in judging between his own good and that of others. But this is to require of him that he transcend subjectivism and rise to a viewpoint that is universal. In other words, it is to require of him that he judge in accordance with reason. Once again, reason is revealed as the true norm.

Consequently, Utilitarianism, too, can justify itself (or rather, can attempt to justify itself) only by invoking reason. It does not, of itself, provide the moral norm.

---

[56] *Utilitarianism*, pp. 33-34.

This ethics reflects rather well the mentality of a "bourgeois" age, characterized by an esteem, hitherto unknown, for material comfort and the pleasures of life. Where such an ethics prevails, social life can be very pleasant and there can be a high degree of culture, but existence remains on a superficial level; there will be neither tragedy nor heroism and the highest values and deepest joys will be unknown. Such an ethics fails to appreciate the values which transcend the entire order of temporal happiness, values for the sake of which this latter should, at times, be sacrificed and without which there can be no authentic happiness. For it is from our capacity to respond to these values that our human dignity derives.

The mentality of which we are speaking is well-expressed by Mill in his judgment on the value of sacrifice: unless it increases the sumtotal of happiness in the world, it is useless. "All honour to those who can abnegate for themselves the personal enjoyment of life, when by such renunciation they contribute worthily to increase the amount of happiness in the world; but he who does it, or professes to do it, for any other purpose, is no more deserving of admiration than the ascetic mounted on his pillar. ... The utilitarian morality does recognise in human beings the power of sacrificing their own greatest good for the good of others. It only refuses to admit that the sacrifice is itself a good. A sacrifice which does not increase, or tend to increase, the sumtotal of happiness, it considers as wasted. The only self-renunciation which it applauds is devotion to the happiness, or to some of the means of happiness, of others" [57]. — The happiness he has in mind is, obviously, temporal, the only happiness with which Utilitarianism concerns itself. Moreover, even happiness in the next life should not be sought if. by an impossible hypothesis, it could be obtained only at the cost of violating the moral order. (Cf. the "impossible suppositions" which some saints have made).

Another objection which can be made to the utilitarian theory is this: once it is admitted that the increase of pleasure or happiness in the world is the moral criterion, the conclusion follows that those in authority are bound to deliver an innocent person to a sadistic mob, when the sumtotal of pleasure which they will experience in torturing him, or the sumtotal of frustration which they are thereby spared, exceeds the sufferings of their victim. In this way, gladatorial combats would be morally justifiable, as would the maiming of buffoons (cf. V. Hugo's *L'homme qui rit*), and other "sports" of this type etc. A reply which might be made to this objection is that pleasure which is *motivated* by the sufferings of others is a false

---

[57] *Ib.*, pp. 15-16. — See the wellgrounded reflections of J. Leclercq on the theory, in *Les grandes lignes de la philosophie morale*, Louvain, 1947, pp. 109-110.

pleasure, of which, Utilitarianism, in virtue of the principle on which it is based, does not have to take account. Without discussing this reply, we simply note that this same principle would be of no less service in justifying the worst exploitation of human beings, once the benefits which come to the exploiters exceed the wretchedness of those who are downtrodden; no consideration of human dignity, no rule other than that of the arithmetic of pains and pleasures need fix a limit to this oppression. — The fact that people, even "civilized" ones, have all too often acted on this principle, does not make it any the more worthy of human beings.

85. — What judgment is to be passed on the sociological school of ethics? Has moral value to be defined in function of the good of society or of humanity?

For the sake of argument, let us accept this hypothesis: society is the supreme good and its interests are the measure, in all circumstances, of the value of our actions.

Now, obviously, these actions have to be human actions (n. 13). If they are fruit of an unreflective impulse — as when a person exposes his hand to the danger of injury so as to protect his head [58] — they remain outside the sphere of morality. The orientation of the "part" to the good of the "whole" is no more than an empirical datum; it is a matter of fact and, as such, is no more capable of being the source of moral value than any other fact.

This value emerges, in the hypothesis envisaged, only if the action which promotes the common good is the fruit of a judgment that this good is *worthy* of being sought before all else [59]. But then the essence of moral value does not consist in the relation of the action to the common good materially considered, but in its relation to what makes this good supremely worthy of being sought and reveals it to be such. It is not sufficient to tell me: to act in this way will help your country; I need to appreciate that my country possesses a value; I have

---

[58] St Thomas, *Summa Theol.*, I, 60, 5 etc.

[59] "The values and the ideas which the collectivity proposes to or imposes on its members are, for the individual, as long as he does not accept them or regard them as legitimate, no more than pressures brought to bear on him. They need to be ratified directly or indirectly, implicitly or explicitly, by a judgment of conscience; and this judgment, which appreciates the moral order as it is, cannot be made", G. Madinier, *Conscience et signification*, Paris, 1953, p. 54.

not only to feel myself naturally drawn to desire its greatness, its prosperity etc., but to judge that these are worthy of being desired. ... And even if I say "my country, right or wrong!", I again acknowledge the need for a rational justification.

Consequently, this school of ethics, no less than Utilitarianism, needs the mediation of practical reason. The good of society should be sought because so to act is right and *reasonable*. The norm is not the social good purely and simply, but this good to the extent that it is in accordance with reason and because it so accords. But what does this mean except that it is the harmony with reason which provides the true norm?

86. – But once the good of society is confronted with the requirements of reason, it ceases to appear as supremely worthy of being sought after and the hypothesis with which we started is revealed as erroneous. Eminent though it be, in the order of empirical values, it is transcended by the spiritual subject.

What immediately follows (under a) should, strictly speaking, have been included in the discussion of extrinsic morality (n. 52). But it seemed preferable to unify our treatment of sociological ethics.

a) First and foremost, it is not true that society is the norm of truths and values. It is not the norm of truths: that two and two equal four is true, not because society says so, but because it is so and because I *understand* that it is so. Admittedly, society has enabled me to arrive at this understanding: without education, I would not know the name and value of the figures; I would perhaps not appreciate the process of addition etc.; but once I have received the instruction which society provides, I myself am capable of appreciating the truth in question. — Nor is society the norm of values. If it were, to reject the accepted standards would be evil. But this is precisely what has been done by most of those who have advanced mankind's moral growth (Socrates etc.). Have these, then, acted immorally?

To this argument the sociologists have a reply. Socrates, they maintain, gave expression to the authentic social conscience, the conscience which was in harmony with the true state of the Athenian society of his time, profoundly transformed as it had been in consequence of the Peloponnesian war. The social conscience which he critised — and which condemned him — was a retarded conscience that reflected the requirements of a former situation, but was unenlightened with regard to those of the present[60]. — But to say this is to acknowledge that the true moral norm is not the social conscience, but something to which this conscience should conform itself: the present state of society and its objective requirements. So the question that now arises is whether these can provide the needed understanding of moral value.

Recall, in this context (cf. n. 29), the distinction between the *historical conditions* in which a value comes to be recognized and this *recognition itself*. The fact that people began to count on account of the necessities of commerce, or for any other reason whatever, in no way affects the validity of methods of calculation. Similarly where values are concerned. Certain historical, economical, sociological etc., conditions were doubtless necessary, in order that people should arrive at a clear appreciation of a value such as justice and, more particularly, of this or that form of it; but once they possess this appreciation, they become conscious of a value-content which transcends these conditions.

b) But society itself — and in consequence its objective requirements — is very far from possessing this transcendent character which the sociologists attribute to it. How could it take the place of the Absolute, when it is itself, in every way, limited by conditions? For its origin, continuance and activity, it is dependent on numerous exterior circumstances (sun, climate etc.), just as is each individual organism. Even further, unlike these latter, it depends on the good will of its members, who alone exist and subsist of themselves, who alone are *persons*, in the true sense of the word. Contingent and dependent as it is, society is incapable of accounting for the absolute character of moral value.

c) In addition, if the good of society were the norm of values, everything which promoted this good would, by that very fact, become morally valuable. In this way, many kinds of activity, whose immorality can be readily appreciated, would be justified: killing those who cannot make a useful contribu-

---

[60] "Bulletin de la soc. fr. de phil.", 1906, p. 173 (a reply of Durkheim to an objection of Parodi, in the discussion on *La détermination du fait moral*).

tion, eliminating the unemployable, the mentally deficient, exterminating a race or a people judged to be dangerous to the public good etc.

The reply that has often been made to this point will undoubtedly be made here also, namely, that actions of this kind, which are apparently to the advantage of society, will always, in the long run, turn to its disadvantage. This outcome is indeed possible, but it is not at all evident[61]; and, in any event, it is not this result which reveals the immorality of the actions in question but rather their intrinsic repugnance to the norm of goodness.

d) A more profound reason: since a spiritual subject is openness towards the Absolute and the Universal, he is a universe in himself and so cannot be considered simply as part of society, nor entirely related to it. He transcends it.

The sociological approach fails to appreciate the true dignity of the person and the true nature of spiritual subjectivity[62].

In this theory, society or humanity takes the place of God. Just as Comte had excogitated his positive religion, with its cult of the Great Being (n. 76), Durkheim, in his turn, at the end of his work: *Les formes élémentaires de la vie religieuse*, looks forward to the establishment of a *secularized religion*, which would consist in the cult of society. (This latter he considers to be the true, though implicit, object of all religion).

87. – Another objection to the sociological theory is that it provides no criterion for distinguishing between the moral value of different societies. In these, the common good is variously understood: are we to renounce any attempt at appraising them? Is a society in which slavery, in the true sense, is practised, to be regarded, all other things being equal, as no less conformed to the moral ideal than a society of free persons?

---

[61] Cf. G. de Broglie, *Réponse à une attaque*, "Rech. de sc. rel.", 1932, pp. 129-150; *Malice intrinsèque du péché et péchés heureux par leurs conséquences*, ib., 1943, pp. 302-343, 578-605; 1935, pp. 5-44. — For a contrary view, see J. Vialatoux, *Morale et politique*, Paris, 1931.

[62] Consult, on this subject, J. Maritain, *La personne et le bien commun*, Paris, 1947 (*The Person and the Common Good*, London, 1957); and John H. Wright, *The Order of the Universe in the Theology of Saint Thomas Aquinas*, Rome, 1957.

The principles of the sociological school do not seem to allow any meaning to this question. But if the testimony of conscience is heeded, the validity of the question, as well as the reply that is called for, will be readily appreciated: the second society is undoubtedly superior to the first. But in virtue of what principle? The social good, as understood by the sociological school, seems incapable of providing the answer.

88. – Finally, the very notion of the social or common good is ambiguous. It can be understood to mean no more than material prosperity, economic, political, military power etc. But to regard these as the supreme rule of action is to disregard the dignity of the person, whom these values affect at a relatively superficial zone, exterior to the centre of his subjectivity (n. 24). Alternatively, the common good can be understood in a more comprehensive fashion, in which moral value is included: the common good will be the just order, the civic virtues and, in general, the various conditions which enable individuals to lead an upright life, conformed to the moral ideal. But then, the common good cannot be really understood unless one has already arrived at an understanding of moral value (which is one of its elements and which it is its function to promote). Since, then, it is from moral value that the worthiness of the common good is chiefly derived, this latter cannot provide the required understanding of the former.

89. – We can now sum up the criticisms that have been made of the sociological thesis: since moral value presents itself as the proper value of the spiritual subject, it cannot be intrinsically related to what is inferior to him in dignity. Since it involves a demand that is absolute, it cannot be grounded on what is dependent and relative.

But society and, in consequence, its well-being, are revealed as inferior in dignity to the spiritual subject, as dependent and conditioned through and through.

Consequently, neither society nor its good can be the ground of moral value; they cannot make this intelligible nor provide the true norm of goodness.

90. – Marxist ethics is open to the same criticisms (with the exception of that made in n. 87, for Marxism has a principle by which various societies can be graded in accordance with the degree to which they approach the Communist ideal). Moreover, since this ethics justifies itself only by the dialectical materialism on which it is based, it has no greater validity than its foundation. But what has to be particularly noted is its continual appeal to values whose foundation it is incapable of providing. The liberty and justice, about which the Marxists continually speak, are of the spiritual order. What meaning have they in a materialist vision of the world? In such a perspective, they are but ideologies, the fruit of a certain social and economic state and, in the last analysis, of a certain stage in the evolution of matter, which will, in due course, be left behind, just as have the preceding stages. But if this is so, then these values lose their pre-eminence; the unrivalled character of moral demands disappears. Hence the contradiction, by which Marxism is rent, between an appreciation of human dignity — a "humanism" on which it prides itself and to which it owes the favour it enjoys, particularly among those of noble and generous disposition — and a conception of man (and of the world) which involves an implicit denial of this dignity. For it is, above all, in his openness to values that are absolute and, through these, to the Absolute which is their ground, that the dignity of man consists.

Marxists strongly insist that they should not be regarded as crude materialists, who value nothing beyond what is tangible, and they claim that their programme will not only result in well-being, prosperity etc., but is also in conformity with reason and will ensure that man's dignity is respected etc. Moreover, even where material prosperity alone is concerned, why should the individual sacrifice himself for society, or the present generation for those that are to come, unless it be something of greater worth than the entire order of temporal advantages? And, in fact, over and above these advantages — whether the beneficiary be their own or a future generation — what very often buoys up sincere Marxists is a sort of naive faith: their conviction that, in acting in this way, they are being true to the direction in which history is moving, true to the direction in which the universe is evolving, true to the requirements of reason. Dialectical materialism is presented as being in accordance with reason. (The Marxist review *La Pensée* has as its sub-title: *Revue du rationalisme moderne*). In consequence, whether or not they wish it, Marxists situate human worth, beyond the sphere of temporal advantage, in a life conformed to reason.

A Marxist will doubtless reply that in all this we are pushing an open door. Dialectical materialism, precisely because it is dialectical and not "metaphysical", does not set up a mutually exclusive opposition (as did the materialists of the eighteenth century) between what is material and what is spiritual. Recently, at the International Congress of Philosophy in Mexico (1963), Prof. Mitin of the University of Moscow strongly defended spiritual values. But, he insisted, these values are entirely grounded on, and conditioned by, what is material. The dialectical aspect of their doctrine allows Marxists to acknowledge that a qualitative difference, a change to a new order, occurs on the various levels of the evolution of matter. — But the question which this leaves us with is whether it is really possible for these differences and changes to occur in a process which, it is emphasized, always remains one of evolving matter. This question, as is obvious, leads us well beyond the limits of the problem which we are at present investigating. It is a question, however, which we sall soon touch on again when we are discussing evolutionary ethics (n. 99).

This further field of investigation is imposed on us by the trend of our inquiry. For, as we have seen, society, even when it is understood as including all mankind, cannot provide the norm of moral value, cannot be the source which accounts for this value; and this for the reason that the value of society is itself a conditioned one. Since, however, the human race does not exist in isolation, but forms part of the universe, and since man's origin and history represent a stage in the history of the world, the question that now suggests itself is: should not the source on which the value of human actions is dependent be sought in the universe, or in the evolutionary process which seems to be its essential law?

C. Cosmic and biological ethics.

91. – The universe — the sumtotal of beings, man included, which constitutes the world — appears to many nowadays as the total reality: it contains all, it sustains all, it is the source and, as it were, the womb from which all beings come into existence; and the phenomenologists have shown how our knowledge and our projects have the "world" as the ground and horizon of their possibility [63]. Since everything is included in the universe, values also, it seems, should be included in it, if

---

[63] See M. Merleau-Ponty, *Phénoménologie de la perception*, Paris, 1944 (Eng. trans.: *Phenomenology of Perception*, C. Smith, London, 1962).

it is true that these are not nothing and that outside of everything there is nothing; hence it is the universe which is their foundation, their condition and their measure. Just as beings exist only by their insertion in the world, so also they have value only through, and in accordance with, their relation to that plenitude which is the ground of everything. In this way, the universe comes to be endowed with a quasi-religious aspect; it becomes the object of respect and veneration, and that not only among the ancient philosophers (more or less tainted by pantheism), but among a good number of modern and contemporary writers, to whom its immensity, complexity and history are much more manifest [64]. One understands then how tempting it can be to seek in the universe the norm of moral goodness.

Another factor which fosters this temptation is the natural tendency of the human mind to seek unity, so that it cannot rest content with the irreducible duality of the physical and the moral. Some people will thus be led, in virtue of their turn of mind and, in particular, of their scientific specialization, to eliminate this duality by making of the moral order a province of the physical. So, for example, the love of justice will be regarded as a higher form of the general tendency towards equilibrium. From this, one easily comes to identify the order of the universe with the norm of moral value.

But it is, above all, "life" — a word that is so rich and pregnant through being imprecise, and also, for that very reason, thoroughly exhilarating — which seems capable of enlightening us about the true meaning of moral value (life which, moreover, some consider to be coextensive with the universe). Does life not, in fact, appear, to be of its very nature desirable? Is it not, purely and simply, preferable to its contrary? The good action will, in consequence, be the one which promotes the greatest expansion of life, the evil action that which hinders this expansion.

---

[64] Fr. Schleiermacher, at a time closer to our own, provides an example of this religious attitude towards the universe: *Reden über die Religion*, 1799 (Eng. trans.: *On Religion*, New York, 1958). But it is as the origin of religion not of morality — whose source is, in his view, entirely distinct — that he regards the universe. Read, in particular, the second discourse: "On the essence of religion". (Note the author's veneration for Spinoza).

In an evolutionist conception of the world, life will be regarded as a more advanced state of the material world, and humanity as a more advanced state of life. Man stands at the highest point of the universe's evolutionary process: from him it derives its meaning. In his progress, the entire universe progresses. This progress, this ascending evolution of the universe, is not only, in the eyes of many nowadays, the supreme law of reality, the fundamental impetus (as is, in Aristotle, the movement of the first heaven), but also the supreme norm of values. And this all the more so, because evolution seems to affect subjects at the very core of their being, so that nothing can escape its sweep. Consequently, the criterion of moral goodness will be the harmony of an action with the advancement of life and of the world: any action which fosters this advancement is good, any action which hinders it is evil.

The expression: evolutionary ethics, is ambiguous. At times, it means: an ethics in which moral value has evolution as its foundation; at other times, and more frequently, an ethics in which the origin and development of moral ideas and attitudes are explained and interpreted in accordance with evolutionist principles.

92. – The Stoics, in antiquity, provide an example of a type of cosmic ethics. Their maxim was similar to that of the Epicureans: to live in accordance with nature, but by nature they understood that of the universe and not, as did the latter, the individual's own nature. The wise and perfect man, of whom the traditional model is "Hercules", lives not only in accord with himself, by preserving complete consistency of thought and action, but also in accord with the universe, by conforming voluntarily and joyously to the laws which govern it; in this way, he is guided by the fates, to which he freely submits, in place of allowing himself to be pulled and dragged by them against his will. Now, these laws, these fates, are the expression of the supreme Reason, of the guiding and ruling Logos, which is, at one and the same time, Justice, Necessity, Providence. To act in accordance with nature is, then, to be in harmony with this supreme Justice and Reason; it is to make oneself like to Zeus ...

It should be noted that this Logos is entirely immanent in the world. Nature itself is divine (just as it was, more or less, to all the ancient philosophers, even when they acknowledged a certain divine transcendence, as did Aristotle). It is obvious, then, that there is a link between the naturalistic and cosmic ethics of the Stoics, and their pantheism.

There is in Stoicism the double paradox of an elevated moral doctrine grafted on to a materialist concept of the universe (the Logos is a refined form of fire, all that exists is corporeal), as well as of a vigorous affirmation of the individual's power of self-direction in a world which is ruled by determinism. (It is Stoicism which has developed the notion of a universal determinism and has also introduced the concept of freewill — *autexousia*, which literally means mastery of oneself). This latter paradox has occurred more than once in history; in Marxism for example. Lenin speaks somewhere of the "absurd fable" of freewill; but this does not prevent him from insisting vehemently on the importance to the revolution of individual initiative.

As a general rule: whenever philosophers are inclined towards pantheism, they also tend to seek the norm of value in a conformity with the law of the universe, or in a teleological relation with the good of the universe. The British idealists, F. H. Bradley, *Ethical Studies*, 1876, and B. Bosanquet, *The Principle of Individuality and Value*, 1912, are modern examples of this.

St Thomas, too, points at times to the common good of the universe as the goal of the activity of individuals. But what he is in fact speaking about is the transcendent common Good, namely God[65].

93. – The moderns and contemporary writers in general no longer consider nature to be, in the proper sense of the word, sacred. (At least, not on the speculative level; their practical and affective attitude may, at times, be otherwise; cf. n. 91). Evolution is occasionally — particularly among certain philosophers — understood in a more or less pantheistic sense but most, and especially the savants, have a purely positive and even positivist attitude towards it. — But even though nature is no longer considered to be divine, it takes the place of God, where some are concerned. It is for them a type of profane Infinite; to it they look for the norm of action. It is then that evolutionist moralities make their appearance, evolution being the guise which the nature of the universe assumes in contemporary thought.

---

[65] St Thomas, *Summa Theol.*, I, 60, 5; I-II, 109, 3; II-II, 26, 3.

Herbert Spencer is generally regarded as the outstanding representative of evolutionary ethics (*The Data of Ethics*, 1879) [66]. In fact, however, what he treats of in that work is rather the genesis and development of moral consciousness. He does not concern himself with determining the essence and norm of value; with the Utilitarians, he accepts as obvious the equation of morality with altruism.

There are three factors which, according to Spencer, account for the present stage of mankind's moral consciousness.

1. Natural selection, based on the struggle for life and the survival of the fittest.

2. The utility of altruism for the individual. Egoism and altruism are both necessary; the former is indeed the more fundamental, but unless it develops into altruism, it leads to the ruin of the individual and of the species.

3. There is, finally, the psychological law, already met with in Stuart Mill (n. 84), according to which a person's interest tends to be transferred from the end to the means.

The consequence of all this is:

1. That those whose altruistic sense is more developed have a better chance of survival.

2. That the good of others, which was originally sought for one's own sake (ego-altruism), comes to be directly intended (altruism).

3. That humanity, by a natural evolution, is tending towards a state where each will spontaneously seek the good of others, that is, towards a state of perfect morality, where obligation will no longer have any function. It is to this ideal that ethics looks in order to derive its moral rules, for it is only there that perfectly moral activity is possible, *The Data* ..., p. 275.

Also to be noted are: S. Alexander, *Morals and Progress*, 1884; J. M. Baldwin, *Social and Ethical Interpretation*, 1897.

A very clear example of a cosmic ethics, in the full sense of the word, is that proposed by Fr Teilhard de Chardin, particylarly in *Le Milieu Divin*. But it there receives a Christian and indeed, to use his own term, a "Christic" interpretation, by which it is profoundly transformed. — Moreover, the problem with which he was concerned is not the one we are here investigating; hence, one will not look to him to provide an answer to a question he did not pose.

---

[66] The first part, published separately, of the *Principles of Ethics*.

94. – A good example of vitalistic ethics is provided by J. M. Guyau, *Esquisse d'une morale sans obligation ni sanction*, Paris, 1885. For this refined and afflicted thinker, influenced both by Schelling and Spencer and who, in the shipwreck of his Christian faith and his metaphysical certitudes, continued to aspire towards an ideal, the source of morality is to be found in the tendency of all that lives towards a life that is as intensive and as extensive as possible [67]. From this flows the necessity of living for others: life cannot be confined to the individual and even requires of him at times that he sacrifice himself: "the sacrifice of life can become expression of life" [68].

The ethics of Guyau can be called affective, in that it lays greater stress on the subject's interior elan than on the value of the object. It is for this reason that he substitutes for obligation, which is objective, the enthusiastic love of life: the joy of acting, the taste for battle, the "fusion of sensibilities", are for him the "equivalents of duty". But this love of life is the same as life that is conscious of itself. So, in the final analysis, it is from life that the content and norm of moral value are derived.

95. – In a sense, as we have seen (n. 26), Fr. Nietzsche should be regarded as one who rejects and seeks to overthrow all that is morally valuable. In another sense, this opponent of morality is a moralist who is proposing a morality of his own fashioning, a new "table of values". This morality can be called vitalistic and evolutionary in that it exalts the "will to power" (that is, life asserting itself triumphantly), and in that it assigns to humanity the task of preparing for the advent of the Superman (Uebermensch) — even if this latter need not necessarily be understood as belonging to a superior "species". The Masters (Herren), whose morality Nietzsche champions, are precisely the individuals among whom life asserts itself fully: they alone are in possession of the superior values, they alone are worthy of consideration; the others are but a miserable herd, contemptible and stinking. Here again, in consequence, it is life which is the supreme value.

---

[67] *Op. cit.*, pp. 242-243.
[68] *Ib.*, p. 250.

96. – With H. Bergson (*Les deux sources de la morale et de la religion*, 1932) we enter an entirely different atmosphere. He distinguishes two types of morality: the closed morality (to which corresponds the *static religion*) and the *open morality* (to which corresponds the *dynamic religion*). The first is of a social character and, where it is concerned, Bergson admits that the sociological interpretation of morality is substantially correct; in particular, that obligation is explicable in terms of social pressure. But society is itself a biological reality: in it, the "vital impetus", described in *Evolution créatrice*, reaches its goal and, with its drive exhausted, can only circle round on itself so as to preserve the same form. The closed morality, completely orientated as it is towards the conservation of society, is the expression of that stagnation. The open morality, on the contrary, is of a *mystic* nature. Here, there is no longer obligation and pressure, but a call from above, a call which proceeds not from an impersonal ideal, but from certain exceptional personalities: heroes and saints. Does this mean that in such a morality there is no longer anything biological? No: this morality reflects, on the contrary, a renewal of the "vital impetus" which, regaining its force, commences anew and leaves behind the forms into which it had originally hardened.

The passage from the first to the second type of morality is strikingly evident in the Sermon on the Mount: "You have heard that it was said. But I tell you".

For Bergson, then, obligation is nothing other than social pressure. The open morality, the true morality, knows no obligation, because its law is that of love. But he allows that, in daily life, the two moralities are almost always mingled in varying proportions.

This theory, obviously, differs considerably from the other vitalistic and evolutionary doctrines. The supreme value on which the entire moral order is founded is no longer life in the biological sense, but rather spiritual love, to which creative evolution has led and from which it derives its meaning, just as does creation itself. This love in its turn has its source in the creative Love, in a personal God (totally different, in Bergson's view, from the conceptual God of the philosophers) to whom mystical experience, particularly that of the great Christian mystics, claims to have attained (and without whom this experience is unintelligible). In this way, his line of thought blends with and confirms the conclusions of *Evolution créatrice*. For the God-love to whom the mystics attain is identical with the source and centre from which evolution gushes forth, and which was treated of in that work; in communicating itself to man, the final product of the "vital impetus", it reactivates, so to speak, this latter.

97. – We do not propose to discuss each of these theories under the particular forms which they take. Specifically, we shall refrain from examining whether or not the general theory of evolution is well-founded and how far it may be legitimately extended. This is the concern of the philosphy of nature, of anthropology and, to some extent, of metaphysics.

We shall not, then, refuse to consider the theory on the grounds that its genetic explanation of the spiritual dimension of man rules it out of court at once. Methodologically, we shall accept it as its most radical defenders present it: as universally applicable. The question that has then to be answered is whether, by giving it every possible chance in this way, it is capable of providing the norm and essence of moral value.

98. – Note, first of all, that the words *universe, life, evolution* can be understood in two ways. In one sense, the universe refers to the totality of finite objects, exclusive of the dimension of spiritual subjectivity; life will be understood in the "biological" sense of organic and animal life, in which the non-spiritual psyche is included; by evolution, finally, will be understood the ascending order of organisms, linked in phyla, which grow ever more complex and "centred" in their internal structure, until they issue in the human organism. — In a second sense, the universe will include not only objects, but also subjects in their subjectivity; life, understood metaphysically as spontaneous and immanent activity, will find its highest expression at the intellectual and spiritual level; and this latter activity will be part of the sweep of evolution, of which it will accordingly represent the last phase.

Now, if the words universe, life and evolution are understood in their first sense, it is clear that they cannot provide the norm for human action, that they cannot be the standard in relation to which moral value is defined. Since this is the value which affects the spiritual subject as such (n. 33, 1), it cannot be derived from what, essentially, is of less value than he is. But, by definition, the universe, life and evolution, understood in the sense indicated, are of less value than the subject; they are indeed infinitely inferior to him.

As spiritual, the subject transcends the entire order of finite objects, since these do not possess his spiritual subjectivity, his openness to the Absolute. In virtue of this, he appreciates that the entire order of objects is but a particular value which is simply not commensurate with his capacities and aspirations; much less is it capable of imposing itself on him and being the measure of his worth. The same holds true for life and evolution understood in the sense indicated, that is, as confined to the world of objects.

99. – Let us now take the universe, life and evolution in the second sense. Understood as embracing subjectivity and the life of the spirit, can they give us an understanding of moral value? Here again we shall distinguish two meanings of the question, or rather of the hypothesis which underlies it. (It is with evolution, in particular, that we are here concerned):

1. The spiritual subject is considered as a thing among other things and his activity as a stage in the evolution to which everything is subjected, a stage which is destined to be transcended, just as have the preceding ones. But if this is so, then the subject has disappeared, as has reason, and as, in consequence, has morality. For this is possible only where liberty and what is absolute have a meaning. But, in the hypothesis envisaged, there is no longer anything absolute: my judgments simply express my historical situation at this phase of evolution. Liberty has vanished, for this presupposes genuine spiritual subjectivity, transcendence in relation to the object, openness to what is absolute; it dies, and together with it moral value, if the depths of subjectivity have disappeared, so that the subject's existence is at no more profound level than that of objects.

Indeed, there does not seem to be any place for morality if, as Spencer maintains, altruism is inevitably destined to triumph, simply by the force of natural selection.

2. Alternatively, a certain transcendence of the spiritual subject and of reason is affirmed, even though it is also, and paradoxically, maintained that they are the fruit of evolution.

Does not what the dialectical materialists say amount to just this, when they stress the dialectical aspect of their system? But, in that case, what really counts in enabling us to understand moral value is not the substructure which conditions spiritual activity, but this activity itself. The universe, life that is below the spiritual level, evolution, are of consequence for morality, only in the measure in which they prepare for the advent of what is spiritual, receive this, and so come to be crowned by it.

But once reason and, in consequence, spiritual subjectivity make their appearance, they totally transcend their historical and empirical conditions: it is these conditions which are evaluated by reason in place of being the source of its dignity. It matters not at all that reason (as is urged in the present hypothesis) has emerged from the irrational, through the process of evolution; from the moment that it is genuinely reason (and this is granted in the hypothesis), it becomes capable of reflecting on its obscure origin so as to judge and evaluate this. It is, then, within itself, and not in its origins, that the norm of value lies.

But if this is so, then it is immediately obvious that the hypothesis is destroyed: how could what judges and transcends its conditions in this way have in them its *adequate* source? There is in man a dimension for which evolution cannot account.

100. – Note, finally, a confusion which vitiates evolutionary morality: the identification of what is *later* which what is *better*[69]. Do we not normally speak of what is more evolved as if this were the same as being more perfect? But this equation is unjustified. What comes afterwards is not necessarily on a more elevated level: evolution does not inevitably involve an ascent. If, in fact, there is an ascent, this is not imposed *a priori*: the two notions of *later* and *higher* remain distinct. It is not because man comes after pithecanthrope that he is superior to him. The notion of progress is, moreover, a recent one; it was long accepted that some kind of regressive evolution of humanity has occurred (cf. the myth of the Golden Age). If,

---

[69] Cf. A. Lalande, *Evolution, Révolution, Involution*, "Atti del Congresso Internazionale di Filosofia" (Rome, 1946), vol. I, Rome, 1948, pp. 499-505.

then, we judge that evolution is ascending and progressive, this is because we are endowed with the capacity to evaluate it: in virtue of this capacity we measure the "gradient of time".

In order that moral value can be said to consist in the harmony of a human action with the current of evolution, it has, consequently, first to be shown that this is flowing towards a value which is worthy of acceptance by a spiritual subject. But this means that it is this latter value which provides the true moral norm. The true norm is the one which does not itself require a further norm [70].

This last objection is also clearly valid against the "historicist" type of ethics which equates moral value and conformity with the "trend of history". For it is not *a priori* evident that history is always moving towards the realization of higher values. And, even granted that it is, these values are not more elevated because they are achieved at a later stage, but for an intrinsic reason. History does not judge: it is subject to judgment.

It is clear that Bergsonian ethics is, to a great extent, not open to these criticisms, even though his approach can still be charged with a certain empiricism. All that Bergson recognizes as valuable, even in the metaphysical sphere, is experience. Undoubtedly, spirirtual experience, where he is concerned, is supra-rational rather than irrational; nevertheless — if one may here make use of the terminology of the Scholastics — it seems clear that this experience involves the intelligence "virtually" rather than "formally", somewhat similar to the way in which the divine perfection includes "mixed" perfections. As well, the fundamental fact remains that Bergson, because of his distrust of concepts and of reason, has completely bypassed the specifically moral level, which lies between the infra-moral level of social pressure and the supra-moral level of spiritual aspiration.

A simple question helps to pin-point the weakness of Bergsonian ethics. If genuine morality is defined in function of the

---

[70] See the criticisms of evolutionary ethics by Thomas H. Huxley — whose approach to ethics is, moreover, very different from our own — in *Evolution and Ethics*, 1894. He makes a sharp distinction between the physical and the moral orders. "The cosmic process has no sort of relation to moral ends", p. 84. — See also R. Le Senne, *Traité de morale générale*, pp. 403-404.

values revealed in the appeal of the hero or the saint, is there an *obligation* to respond to that appeal? If there is not, morality loses one of its essential characteristics and becomes some kind of an aesthetics concerned with human living. If there is an obligation, this is obviously not the same as social pressure, which would, all too often, lead us in the opposite direction. Now, there is no evidence that Bergson acknowledged any other type of obligation beyond that which he borrowed from the sociological school. In any event, even if he admits another and superior type of obligation, it finds no place in his theory and so he leaves us in uncertainty.

101. – From the doctrines just examined, we can retain, as the positive fruit of our investigation of them, the following points:

1. It is true that moral value involves a relation to "something" which transcends and yet includes within itself, each individual and the entire human race. But this "something" cannot be identified with the universe, nor with the order of life or of evolution.

2. It is true that being is not neutral, indifferent, isotropic in the manner of Newtonian space. There is in it a movement and an orientation; it is hierarchically structured and possessed of "degrees of perfection": all of this is independent of our own way of regarding it, of our subjective preferences. With this order — an order which is not the same as the order of evolution, or the cosmic order, nor is it entirely expressed in them — a human action has to be in harmony, if it is to be morally valuable.

3. Finally, it is true that the natural and the moral orders should be crowned by a higher unity; but this unity is not to be understood in a *univocal* sense, as if the moral order were but a compartment of the natural or cosmic order. It is a unity in an *analogous* sense.

III. THEORIES WHICH EXPLAIN MORAL VALUE IN TERMS OF
    OUR SPIRITUAL ACTIVITY.

102. – It is clear from the preceding discussion that a person's moral worth cannot be defined in terms of any "mundane" reality or value. It cannot be defined even in terms of the person's "happiness", as long as only the empirical and contingent dimension of his being is taken into account, and his spiritual "openness" to what transcends all that is empirical is neglected. Consequently, we are now led to seek the essence of our moral value in the harmony of our actions with the inner "law", the immanent and, if necessary, the ultimate conditions of this spiritual openness. Now the activity of which we are capable because of this spiritual dimension of our being, has to possess a twofold quality before it can be labelled moral or immoral: 1. It has to be free, that is, to be an activity which proceeds from the person as such (n. 13). 2. It has to be animated, not by blind caprice, but by the light of his reason (n. 16). Liberty and reason: these are the two signposts which indicate to us the following stages of our investigation.

A. *Libertarian Ethics.*

103. – There can be a moral value or anti-value in what a person does (and consequently, in the person himself), only to the extent that he acts freely. Indeed, the most commonly accepted view is that all genuinely free actions are always moral or immoral, in some degree. Duns Scotus, if we take what he says literally, goes even further. "It is because an action is free that it is called moral" (n. 33)[71].

It is, then, the moral value of our free actions which determines whether we have used our liberty well or badly. But to say this immediately prompts the question of how our freedom, which essentially means that we are capable of auto-determination, of being "causes of ourselves", could be compatible with any determination which is imposed from without? If we acknowledge that our liberty is determined in this way, are we not betraying and attempting to disown it? Is it not in our power as free subjects to reject any and every objective value, simply because we choose to do so? Do we not experience our freedom as a limitless power to say "no" to the various objects which come to our knowledge? The only determinations we can accept is that which comes from within our liberty itself. "A liberty which confines itself to accepting

---

[71] "An action is said to be moral because it is freely willed", *In II Sent.*, d. 40, q. un.

values which are presented to it — and it makes no difference whether these are presented by God or by nature — is a slave; docile, eager and ingenious, yes, but still a slave" [72].

Moreover, if we examine the various moral ideals which have been proposed to mankind down the centuries, we find that none of them compels our allegiance [73]. We retain the power to accept or refuse them all; in the last analysis, it is we ourselves who make these ideals to be "our" ideals, the guiding stars of "our" lives. But what does this mean except that the source of our worth as persons is ultimately to be found in nothing outside our liberty itself?

So liberty, which at first seemed to be no more than the necessary condition for moral activity, now seems to be also the source of our moral value; for, as has just been considered, we have the power to weigh in the balance, and to find wanting, all values, all norms with which we are faced. As the source of our moral value, liberty may be considered to be the arbiter of good and evil; or the degree of auto-determination with which we act may be regarded as the measure of the moral value of our actions, so that this will be present to the degree to which these express us as persons. They will do this to the extent to which we are fully responsible for them.

In an ethics which makes the fundamental values in a person's life to be dependent on his free choice, the role of reason will be limited to ensuring that particular choices are in line with the radical choice. According to Aristotle also, we need to use our reason in order to ensure that we shall make a judicious choice of the means which will most effectively lead us to the desired end. But, for him, this ultimate goal is one to which we tend by our very nature, which is itself penetrated by reason; it is not, as it is in the present context, a goal on which we decide arbitrarily.

104. – Now all this seems to be very much in harmony with the moral judgments which people commonly make, and with the teaching of various religions. How frequently do people make excuses for their evil actions, on the grounds

---

[72] H. Duméry, *Philosophy de la religion*, t. I, Paris, 1957, p. 287. — We do not at all attribute to Duméry the ideas here presented, but this sentence contributes to an understanding of the mentality which has given rise to them.

[73] See R. Polin, *La création des valeurs*, Paris, 1944.

that "they were overcome by passion", that "that's the way they are built", that "they could not resist", that "something, or someone, drove them to it" etc. But when they act well, they do not, in general, speak in this manner (with the exception of those genuinely religious people, who attribute all that is of good in themselves to God). They then have an awareness of really being themselves, of acting in accordance with their true selves etc. — Moreover, do not moralists describe moral development as a progressive liberation? The same note is struck in various religions. Think, for example, of the *moksha* of the Hindus (liberation from our existence as individuals, liberation from sorrow, from illusion); think, also, of the rational liberty described by Spinoza in the fifth part of his *Ethics*, which treats of human liberty (liberation from our passions, from the inadequacies of our present knowledge). Reflect, above all, on the liberty of the Spirit of which St Paul writes and which is a recurrent theme in Christian writers down the centuries, St Augustine and St Bernard for example: liberation from sin, from the "law" of the flesh, from a law which is purely exterior; this liberation is the fruit of the Holy Spirit's action upon us, of the inpouring to our hearts of His love. ... So, to act well, to act reasonably, to do what our heavenly Father wishes us to do, is to be guided by a genuinely interior principle; it is to be without constraint; it is to be really free.

But, if to act morally is to be really free, can we not also say that to act freely is to act morally; that the good person is the one whose actions are the authentic expression of himself, so that he is determined by nothing that is exterior to his own 'I': neither by laws, nor by objective values, nor by a nature which would map out in advance the "paths of freedom"?

Spinoza concluded his *Ethics* with this proposition: "Beatitude is not the recompense for virtue; it is the same as virtue". Man does not become happy because he acts well: he acts well because he is happy. But since to be really happy involves being really free, should we not here say, in the same spirit as Spinoza: "Liberty is not the fruit of morally good activity, but is identical with it"?

We seem, then, to be led by two different paths to the same conclusion, namely, that liberty which, at first sight, seemed to be no more than the condition of morally good activity, or its fruit, is really identical with it.

105. – Consequently, it is in no way surprising that a number of philosophers have looked to liberty to provide the essence and norm of moral value.

In antiquity, the Cynics, following Antisthenes (444-365 B.C.), held that virtue consisted in the faithfulness of the individual to his own essence, and in his independence of everything that was exterior to him. This is a frankly ascetical ethics, even though its tenets are not always these of which future moralists and ascetics would approve [74].

The Stoics — of whom the Cynics were, in some measure, the precursors — also attributed a very particular moral value to mastery of oneself (*enkrateia*); but, in their view, this mastery is that of our reason (which is part of the universal, n. 92, Logos) over our feelings and passions. This stress on reason marks an important difference between Stoical self-mastery and the Libertarian self-asertion which will be outlined in n. 107.

Recall also, in this present context, what has been said in n. 61 about the Cyrenaics whose hedonism, at bottom, was perhaps a morality of independence.

106. – Amongst many od the moderns — and notably amongst a number of Anglo-Saxon writers — the purpose of ethics is to help us to affirm ourselves fully and to achieve complete self-realization. Now, if the emphasis is placed on the individuality of this "self" which is to be realized, that is, on what distinguishes this self from other selves, the way is cleared for an ethics of liberty. For it is by the way that a person uses his liberty that he distinguishes himself from others and that he comes to "stand out" from them as an individual. On the natural distinction that exists between us all, we superimpose new and farreaching distinctions by the choices that are our own.

An extreme, and indeed pathological, example of this type of approach to morality, under the form of an anarchical

---

[74] Diog. Laert., *Lives of the Philosophers*, bk. VI, c. 1. — Ritter-Preller, *Hist. phil. graec.*, n. 277.

individualism, is presented by Max Stirner (Johann Caspar Schmidt), who was at first an extreme Hegelian, in his book *Der Einzige und sein Eigentum* (*The Unique and what belongs to Him*), 1845. He is not so much concerned with proposing a systematic theory as with asserting vehemently the absolute rights which are his, as one who is different from all others and "unique". "I am not just one among the many who call themselves 'I': I am unique" [75].

107. – But the most explicit affirmation of liberty as the source of our moral value, is to be found in some contemporary Existentialists and, in particular, in Jean Paul Sartre (*L'Etre et le Néant*, Paris, 1943; *L'Existentialisme est un Humanisme*, Paris, 1945; *Critique de la raison dialectique*: I: Théorie des ensembles pratiques, Paris, 1960).

According to Sartre, "what we call freedom is therefore impossible to distinguish from the being of the human reality" (*L'Etre* ..., p. 61), that is, from the being of man. This freedom is itself identical with consciousness and existence. But what Sartre has in mind, when he speaks of "existence" is not what the Scholastics had in mind, nor is it what people normally mean when they use the word. For him, it is opposed to the inert way of existing which is proper to what he calls the "en-soi" (the "in-itself"), that is, the being below the level of the human which is simply what it is, but does not become; 'it is, but only in a brutish fashion". The existence of which Sartre speaks is had only at the level of consciousness and freedom; it is the emergence of what he calls the "pour-soi" (the "for-itself"), from the massive opaqueness of being. This "absolute happening" introduces "nothingness" into being; for this freedom which is the being of man, is his nothingness (his emptiness) of being, which constrains him to make himself, instead of simply existing in the inert and petrified way in which the "en-soi" exists. — Sartre considers that the notion of "potency" has been once and for all eliminated; everything, then, is "actual". It follows from this that it is consciousness and freedom alone which can account for experiences such as those of limitation, absence, expectation, in which what is negative is involved.

But if everything is actual, liberty and the exercise of liberty have to be identical. Liberty is in no way distinct from the act of choice; it is in no sense the attribute of a nature, for there are no

---

[75] *Der Einzige* ..., 2nd ed., Leipzig, 1882, p. 373.

natures, least of all a human nature. Liberty and, in consequence, the being of man, is a radical choice, that is, pure contingence, an "absurd" choice. This choice is not absurd in the sense that man has no reasons for choosing, but in the sense that all his reasons, all his values, are consequent upon this radical choice which is himself. They depend on him; they are reasons and values only because of his choice. Hence the emergence of consciousness, of this radical choice which is man, is not subject to them and so is "absurd". (Particular choices, on the other hand, are judged in relation to, and in function of, this radical choice). A further elaboration helps to bring out more clearly the "absurdity" of the human condition. In all that man values and chooses, he is seeking to achieve a goal which it is impossible for him to achieve and which, moreover, is contradictory in itself. This is the synthesis in himself of the "en-soi" and the "pour-soi", i.e., a synthesis in which the transparency and lucidity of the "pour-soi" would be joined with the solidity and opaqueness of the "en-soi". Such a synthesis is what is meant by "God", and man seeks to become God in ways which are described at length in *L'Etre et le Néant*. But the effort is in vain; man is a useless passion.

The liberty of which Sartre speaks is not the "noumenal", outside-of-space-and-time, liberty so beloved by Kant; it does not determine once and for all, in the intelligible world, the course of man's temporal life. Its exercice is spread out over the span of man's life and what has been chosen can always be later rejected. It is also, at least in *L'Etre et le Néant*, presented as an absolute liberty. Through it, man chooses himself; in doing so, he chooses his "situations, the conditions in which he lives (or rather, the way in which he concretely experiences and "lives" those conditions), his character and, naturally, his values. Sartre stresses all this to the point of paradox but, in fact, what he is saying is less paradoxical than it appears. The essential point that he is making is that we never experience things and events simply as they are; that they never come to us in their "nudity", but "dressed" and altered because of the response which we make to them. Our attitudes and dispositions affect our experience of them. The same accident will be experienced by one person as absurd, unjust, revolting and by another as a cross, as a trial which has come from the hands of a loving Father. ...

The radical choice is expressed by means of particular choices; even though these are made in function of and in dependence on the radical choice, there is still room for a certain flexibility. By choosing in this way, man gradually creates his own essence. Hence the Sartrean dictum: "in man, existence precedes essence".

Since the synthesis "en-soi-pour-soi" is illusory, it is liberty which is the sole source, and the true point of reference, of value.

Even though Sartre has not published the book on ethics which he signalled at the end of *L'Etre et le Néant*, it seems that,in his view, moral value consists, above all, in acting lucidly and authentically. Man has to strive to become more and more conscious of the radical liberty to which "he is condemned", to assume completely the burden which this places on him, and to avoid seeking to escape from what he is. He has to turn away from the "conniving" reflection which is a betrayal, and an evasion, of liberty, and results in an artificial and insincere "I", so as to attain to that "purifying" reflection through which liberty is chosen as liberty, and is acknowledged as the fundamental value which is not to be subjected to any value that is objective or absolute. This attitude Sartre also calls the "renunciation of the spirit of seriousness", that is, of the belief that there are ways of acting which are absolutely valuable. — But, on the other hand — and this introduces a universal outlook which does not seem to fit very well into the framework of Sartre's thought — man should try to help others achieve freedom. What this will primarily call for, will be opposition to capitalist and colonialist oppression. He develops this theme in the *Critique de la raison dialectique*. Here, too, he maintains that there can, in the present age, be no philosophy that is not Marxist; he himself openly espouses materialism, even though his version of it is not that of the Marxists [76].

Simone de Beauvoir's thought in *Pour une morale de l'ambiguité*, Paris, 1947, is very similar to that of Sartre; but her approach manifests a more noticeable humanity.

R. Polin's work *La création des valeurs*, 1944, is also worth noting. He expressly states that the source of all values lies in man's power of "transcendence", that is, in his capacity to say "no" to all that is "given" through juxtaposing the real and the ideal. This power of transcendence is nothing other than liberty. Consequently, there are no values which have a claim on our liberty, on the grounds that

---

[76] In this work, Sartre lays stress on the necessities by which man is oppressed, in a way which contrasts with the paradoxes of *L'Etre et le Néant*. The nature and the import of Sartrean materialism are, moreover, still discussed: see W. Desan, *The Marxism of Jean Paul Sartre*, Garden City, N.Y., 1964. — On the ethics of Sartre, consult Fr. Jeanson, *Le problème moral et la pensée de Sartre* (with a preface by Sartre), Paris, 1947.

they are truer. Truth does not enter into the question of values, for knowledge is immanence not transcendence; there are no judgments of value. Our moral consciousness, our appreciation of values, is not a cognitive function, for knowledge implies immanence, not transcendence. We do not *know* value: we *create* it. Concerning what we value, we cannot say simply that it *is*. Rather we should say: *it is of value* (or *of worth*); and it is of value or of worth because we ourselves have made it so. We have not, then, to ask ourselves: "what should we do?" as if there were a moral norm which was independent of our liberty. What we have to do is to choose our values and live completely in accordance with them. This is the attitude which Polin calls "cynical"; but he does not intend this in the pejorative sense in which it is normally used. What he has in mind is the fidelity of the individual to his own essence, which had been advocated by Antisthenes and his followers (n. 105).

108. – Finally, another philosopher whom we shall briefly mention is Bergson. (In him, it is not a question of a systematically elaborated doctrine, but of a tendency which does not quite come to the surface). From the notion of liberty which he expounds in the *Essai sur les données immédiates de la conscience*, it could be concluded — and perhaps some readers of Bergson do come to this conclusion — that the morally good action is the one in which the subject determines himself, so that his action comes from the profound depths of the "I", and that the evil action is the one in which he yields to the automatism of the superficial and shallow "I". "Free" and "good" would thus be identified. But, let us hasten to add, the liberty which Bergson has in mind is not an empty liberty; it is not a liberty from which our rule of conduct would have to be derived afresh at each, constantly changing, instant. It is a liberty which has been "filled out" and enriched, in the sense that the person's past is operative in the present, so that he does not derive the rules for his conduct from a liberty which faces each new moral situation as if no others had preceded it. Since, then, the two notions of liberty are different, the ethical systems which are based on them cannot but differ.

109. – Before we begin to evaluate these various viewpoints, it is important to make clear the different meanings of the word "liberty". It has at least three fundamental senses and unless these are distinguished, confusion is inevitable [77]. 1. The power to do what one wishes ("freedom from constraint"): this is the liberty of which the prisoner and the slave are deprived. Civic, political, economic etc., liberty are all instances of it. In its higher and perfected form, it coincides with beatitude; it is what Maritain calls the "liberty of exultation" and St Bernard "freedom from misery". As Maritain notes, it is in this type of liberty that people are most interested; to preserve or to recover it, they go to war and lay down their lives. — 2. The liberty of auto-determination by the exercise of which, as we have already noted (n. 13), the spiritual subject stands revealed as such. He now not only does what he wishes to do, but his doing of it has its source in the unique "I" which he is; it is not an activity that flows necessarily from his (spiritual) nature. This type of liberty is that inner "freedom from necessity" which is called freewill. — 3. The liberty of the sage and the saint, of which Spinoza and St Paul, respectively, write: the domination of reason, or the Spirit, over everything in man that is exterior and inferior. In its highest form, it is, as St Bernard expresses it, "freedom from sin", and its achievement is the crown of our moral striving.

The confusion between these different senses has, perhaps, helped to provide a soil in which Libertarian ethics can take better root (n. 104). But, as we have already pointed out, it is essential that they be distinguished. In the present context, it is not with the third type of liberty that we are concerned. To see in it the source of our moral value, would be to identify this with reasonableness. While this is a possible solution to our problem, it is not here relevant; it awaits discussion at the next stage of our investigation (n. 102). Neither are we now concerned with the first kind of liberty, since to explain moral value along such lines would be to fall back into Eudaemonism (n. 83). It is the liberty of autodetermination which is relevant in the present context. Does it provide the source of, and the point of reference for, our moral value?

---

[77] On the different meanings of the word: liberty, and the various ways of posing the problem, see the monumental work of Mortimer J. Adler, *The Idea of Freedom*, 2 vols., New York, 1958-1961.

110. – Here, as always, our first criterion will be moral experience. Our question, accordingly, is: does the identification of moral value with the freedom of our choice harmonize with this experience, or clash it?

If we reflect on this experience we find that morally valuable courses of action present themselves for our choice. We undoubtedly have the power to accept or reject these values, for we are free; but we have not the power to change a moral anti-value into a value, to make what is good to be evil and what is evil to be good. Now this incapacity — and it is a central feature of our moral experience, in the absence of which there would be no point at all in using the term — is sufficient to exclude the identification of our moral value with the freedom of our choice. For if this theory wishes to maintain that we are aware that the source of the moral value of our actions lies in their freedom, then what we choose to call our moral experience is no more than a form of words, an empty verbalism; moral value has vanished into thin air, because what we can freely make to be a moral value, we can likewise make to be an anti-value, and *vice-versa*. We need never again concern ourselves with moral failures, with agonising moral dilemmas, be they our own or those of others [78]. On the other hand, if the theory wishes to maintain that we are not aware that the moral value of what we do is identical with the freedom of our choice, it can, in consequence, maintain that it does not dissipate moral value and moral experience; for we experience that we are subject to moral value and under its "authority". But is this "experience" anything more than an illusion which a moments genuine reflection suffices to dispel? How odd that we can have experience of this value, only as long as we refrain from reflecting on it! How strange that it has to be protected from the light!

What about Polin's slant, namely that values are simply values and that they in no way belong to being? In his view, the two orders of value and being are quite separate, and, like East and West, "never the twain shall meet". This answer is of no help. At the very heart of

---

[78] R. Mehl, *De l'autorité des valeurs*, Paris, 1957, pp. 66-67, observes shrewdly that anguish, on the contrary, supposes a goal which imposes itself on our liberty and which we can fail to attain.

our knowledge and our loving is our acknowledgment and acceptance of being. This acknowledgment permeates all our judgments,
not excluding our judgments of values. Consequently, if value *is not*,
if it is not in some sense independent of my subjectivity, and in this
very sense objective, it is no value at all. As a consequence, moral
scepticism is inevitable; my attitude comes to be that it does not
really matter what I do, or what I omit. In order to avoid this
sceptical attitude, I would have to be capable of never questioning
myself on why I act in this particular way and avoid acting in some
other way. I would have to be capable of forging ahead on the path
of life with a naive confidence in myself, and in the values to which I
had, oblivious of reality, decided to commit myself.

But this naivety could not always be my cloak (or perhaps, my
blinkers?) Critical reflection on oneself, on one's attitudes and
decisions, is part and parcel of human living. Sooner or later I shall
be brought face to face with the question: why do I act in these
particular ways and avoid acting in other ways? Why have I
committed myself to these, rather than to other, values? In the light
of questions such as these, I can avoid ethical scepticism and
indifference, only if I come to realize that there is an order of value
which is independent of me, an order that I can refuse to live by, but
which does not thereby bend to my will: the moral order.

111. – As well, Libertarian ethics, as proposed by Existentialists such as Sartre, is based on a notion of liberty which
is quite untenable, for this power which we have as human
beings, is rooted in our reason[79]. We can exercise it only in the
light which comes to us through our prior understanding of,
and appreciation of, the values to which we are committing
ourselves. Without this light which enables us to distinguish
between values and anti-values, our exercise of liberty would
not be a human activity, but would be in irrational, haphazard
process whose analogue would be the "swerve" of the atoms,
which Epicurus describes, or the indetermination which contemporary physics recognizes to be part of the structure of
matter (if we understand this indetermination as being in the
thing itself, and not only as relative to our knowledge). If this
really were what human liberty consisted in, then it would be
quite valueless in our lives, and would be attributable not to

---

[79] "It is in reason that the source of all liberty is to be found", St Thomas,
De Ver., 24, 2.

the perfection of a being who has a spiritual dimension, but to the imperfection of a being to whom, or rather, to which, there is no dimension beyond the material. How could this haphazard, completely contingent, liberty be the source of values and, in consequence, of our value as persons?

Liberty understood as the power to reject, to say "no", does not make sense. This rejection and negation presupposes and involves the affirmation and acknowledgment not only of the value that is rejected, but also of a value towards which we are tending, so that what is "given" is judged to be insufficient in relation to it and is, in consequence, rejected. It is this value, in relation to which we appreciate the insufficiency of what we reject, that makes liberty to be the vital factor, which it is, in our lives.

Perhaps it will be said that by rejecting what is "given", we are simply asserting our freedom? But what is it that we affirm by this assertion of our freedom? If our freedom is no more than a power of negation, then all we are asserting is a "not", a negative value. The power of auto-affirmation (which for Descartes represented a motive able to balance all other motives) that our liberty gives us, has point and importance only because this liberty is a liberty for the Absolute of value, to which alone it will completely surrender. ... Liberty is so far from being the source from which values spring, that its own value and importance comes from the capacity which it gives us to commit ourselves to, and to realize in our lives, what we acknowledge to be worthy of ourselves as human beings. But this is possible only bzcause there is already an order of values, in relation to which we are indeed "condemned" to taking up a position, either of acceptance or rejection, but which is not pliant to our likes and preferences.

A determined objector may still not be satisfied! Do we not express ourselves as persons through our free actions? Consequently, does not the point and importance of our liberty spring from the value and dignity which we ourselves have as persons? Yes; but why have we a value and dignity as human persons? Only because of our openness, in virtue of being spiritual and reason-endowed subjects, to the Absolute, to the Universal. Consequently, it is from this Absolute and Universal that the point and importance of our liberty, as well as of our self-expression through the exercise of this liberty, spring. As we shall soon see at more length, it is because of its relationship to the Absolute that our reason plays a vital role in our lives (and in its turn, conditions the role which our liberty plays).

A point which is worth reflecting on is that Sartre has attributed to us a power which Descartes considered to be reserved to God, namely, the power to create truths and values at will. Now, even though Descartes' theory is not sustainable, there is at least this much to be said for it, that God's liberty is identical with His essence. Consequently, this liberty really does contain within itself the plenitude of all that is good; it really coincides with its norm and with the ultimate foundation of all values (n. 157). But human liberty is far from being one with the plenitude of being and of goodness; it is a liberty which, in itself, is simply a capacity, a "thirstiness". It does not coincide with its norm, and it possesses the importance which it has, only because it enables us to choose what is genuinely worthwhile and to manifest these choices through our style of living.

112. – A final point. Once our moral value is identified with the freedom of our actions, it does not seem possible to maintain any distinction between those which are morally good and those which are morally evil. This consequence involves the theory in yet another clash with moral experience. For if an action is good because it is free, there can be only two types of action: those which are good (and the extent to which they are good will depend on the extent to which they are free), and those which are non-moral or morally indifferent (since actions which are not free, are outside the moral zone). Immoral actions will thus be happily eliminated. ... But, alas!, this vanishing trick has been performed only on paper and at the writing-desk; it is only if we allow ourselves to be blinded by specious theory, and dazzled by the fascination of words, that we shall rest content with this "amelioration" of the human condition.

But could it not be maintained that man has not the right to surrender his liberty, and that he would be acting immorally if he freely submitted to determinism of any kind? But why would he then be acting immorally? Surely, if moral value is identical with freedom of choice, this value will be present no matter what he chooses, no matter in what direction he exercises his liberty. If a person freely surrenders his liberty (which he would do, in Sartre's view, if he accepted absolute values and an absolute moral law, so that he became infected by the "spirit of seriousness"), would not this surrender still be morally good, since it is freely made?

But the Libertarian position will still be doggedly defended! The reason for this persistence lies in a certain ambiguity in the use of the term liberty. In place of simply identifying liberty with the free act, with the exercise of liberty, as Existentialism in its pure form does, these defenders of the theory have in mind liberty as an idea, a value which is not identical with the free act, but must be realized by means of it. Then moral value is not identified with the exercise of liberty, but rather with libertu considered as what ought-to-be-done. In other words, these defenders of Libertarian ethics are really appealing to the nature of liberty, to its inner law, and in doing this they are abandoning Existentialism in Sartre's sense. Once there is a dimension to liberty beyond that of its actual exercise, there is also a human nature of which liberty is an attribute.

It is instructive to note that Sartre cannot avoid speaking about the "nature of liberty" and of its "essence". Polin, too, finds a norm by which to guide our actions in what he styles "the laws that govern our consciousness of values", that is, in the structure which is present in the "power of transcendence". Our actions will be authentic or absurd according as they harmonize, or clash with, these laws and that structure.

113. – It is obvious, then, that the person who speaks about the attainment of liberty, mastery of oneself etc., as the goal of human action, is only using an empty form of words unless he has in mind the mastery of the higher self, of the "I who is worthwhile" (Le Senne), who is radically open to others and to the Absolute and Universal, over the lower self, the "Private: Keep Out: Beware of the Dog" self, who has closed and barred himself to others. Through self-mastery in this sense, an individual grows as a person; he grows in that dimension of his being where he is affected by his own free decisions. But he does not thereby impoverish his originality as an individual; on the contrary, he enriches and perfects it.

On the other hand, the ideal of self-mastery where the relationship between "self" and an absolute Value (from which a person derives *his* absolute value) is not recognized, and where a person deludes himself that he possesses an absolute value simply because he is different from others and has a will of his own, leads inevitably to the unprincipled living of the moral sceptic and nihilist.

Note that some of the points which have occurred in the doctrines just criticised are valid, and worth retaining. Moral theory should ever bear in mind the value and dignity of every human person. It should not fall into the error of considering that the person is but a means to the realization of objective values, an instrument at their service; it should also be mindful that moral value can never be forced on a person, for this value is inseparable from the freedom of a person's choice (n. 32, 1). It is true that there is nothing really new in all this, but modern man is more sensitive on these points, and we should take account of this.

It is possible to go even further. There is room in the moral order, no less than in the aesthetic order, for approaches and discoveries which manifest the originality of individuals. It is not we who make kindness and generosity to be morally good, but it is we who, by the many different ways in which we are kind and generous ("nameless, unremembered acts of kindness and of love"), manifest new and varied facets of these virtues (n. 192). — The Saints and, in particular, the founders of religious orders and of schools of spirituality, are particularly noteworthy creators of value. — In short, no matter what, or how many, specific moral principles a person has to guide him, he will in his concrete actions contribute a value which is his own, and which is different from that which is enshrined in the principles. The exercise of our liberty, and the discovery of values, go hand in hand. Just as a person discovers his true thoughts only by means of his words, and of the stimulus which the feedback of this expression brings him, so, likewise, his appreciation and discovery of what a particular virtue requires of him personally, results from the stimulus which the feedback of his actions brings him.

B. *Rational Ethics.*

114. – Liberty cannot be the key to the meaning of moral value, since it is itself measured by the order of value with which it is confronted. Moreover, the source and root of our liberty lies in our reason. It seems clear, then, that it is reason which provides the norm for the good use of our liberty, and that the essence of moral value lies in rational action.

As well, has not this insistence on the central role of reason been one of the most constant affirmations of philosophers all down the centuries? Have not moralists from the earliest times been, for the most part, united in their definition of the moral life as a life lived "in accordance with reason"? Even in Aristotelian eudaemonism, what characterizes the virtuous action is its conformity with the rule of reason (nn. 64, 73). In going in this direction, we are following a royal road.

However, in addition to the fact that this happy agreement among philosophers is not, in itself a proof, it is advisable, and indeed essential, to see where this thronged roadway ends. The necessity for this caution is forced on us by the fact that all who speak of the role of reason in morality, have by no means the same thing in mind.

The most usual meaning which reason has for the Scholastics is: discursive intellect. Reason in this sense distinguishes man, not only from the animals, but also from beings whose intelligence is intuitive. — We arrive at a further and more profound meaning, if we take account of the relational or "relating" aspect of our intellects, that is, our intellects as capable of grasping relationships, of passing from the effect to the cause, from what is conditioned to the condition. This restlessness and liveness of our minds can be satisfied and come to rest, only in the unconditioned Condition, the Ultimate, the Absolute from which each and every relationship that we grasp draws its meaning, and on which it is grounded. For what is relative, precisely because it is relative (to something beyond it), can be thought of only in relation to what is absolute (and so has nothing beyond it). If we are to affirm and acknowledge something as relative, our affirmation has itself to be "situated" on a higher and different plane than the object which is affirmed. Consequently, because our reason has this "relating" aspect, it also has a relationship with, or capacity for, what is absolute (absolute in the sense of being the point of reference for, and condition of, the affirmation of anything as relative). — In this sense, we can speak even of God's reason. God is Reason in that He knows all other beings in their relationship of complete dependence on Himself, as interconnected with, and in varying degrees dependent on, one another, as internally structured, each type of being in its own way; and in that He makes them to be — makes them in knowing them and knows them in making them — by the very same act through which He relates and orientates them to Himself.

Accordingly, reason can now be defined as that capacity which enables us to relate the objects about which we judge, to what is absolute (at least in the sense of being their ultimate, and normally implicit, point of reference); consequently, it can be said to be illumined in its activity by the light which emanates from what is absolute, that is, it judges in accordance with norms which are absolute, necessary and universal (and so are the enemies of subjectivism and arbitrariness).

It is this absolute, which is obscurely present to the human spirit, that endows our affirmations with their solidity, their full objectivity, their harmony with what is. For every judgment which lays claim to be true and whose object is asserted as independent of the mind which asserts (as not being a concoction of that mind), involves what is absolute and holds good only through it.

Among the various beings of which we have experience, it is man alone who is capable of judging in accordance with what is absolute and of attaining to a universal standpoint. This is not to say that he always maintains himself at this level. Far from it; and even his very efforts to do so, are very frequently half-hearted and wavering. All too often, what motivates his choices is caprice, the "fascinatio nugacitatis" of which Scripture (Wisdom 4,12) speaks, the pleasure and excitement that can be snatched from the passing moment, a point of view which is both partial (narrow) and far from impartial (biased). But, even then, he does not abandon all pretence of being human and, in consequence, reasonable, in his actions. He seeks a rational justification for what he is set on doing; but since he is striving to give an air of rationality to what is irrational, he will have to make use of different, and even opposed and contradictory, maxims, in accordance with the particular line of conduct which happens to suit him and which he wishes to justify. ... True morality begins only when a person seeks to respond to the challenge to his egoism and self-assertiveness which genuinely universal principles make on him, and when he makes use of norms which he really permits to direct his conduct, in place of manipulating them so as to provide himself with an apparent justification for following courses of action on which he has already decided, and which all too often are beyond all justification.

We are consequently led to distinguish between two aspects of human reason.

a) It can first be considered as grounded in and "in touch with" what is, as "imbedded in being", so that its own requirements will also be the requirements of being. Reason in this sense we shall also call "open reason". In a rational ethics in which reason has this meaning, the judgment, or dictate, of reason which provides the immediate rule for moral action will be the expression of a requirement of reality (an ontological requirement), since reason is the spokesman for reality. Reason (*Logos*) proclaims (*legei*) the law of reality and transmits to us, by interpreting them, its requirements. Consequently, the conformity of our actions with reason only mediates and expresses their conformity with an objective rule, into whose nature we still have to inquire. But whatever be the precise nature of this requirement, the absolute in relation to which our reason judges is here an absolute in the real order, or that is founded on this order.

b) But this absolute can also be understood in a more formal sense, that is, as the "form", or inner law, in accordance with which we make reasonable judgments; for once these are true, they are absolutely so; they express the truth for everyone and not just for the person who happens to make them. In line with this interpretation of reason, the absolute will not now mean what it meant in a) but becomes the same as the universality, the "valid for everyone" quality, that characterizes our judgments when these are reasonable. Where our practical reason is concerned, that is, our reason as capable of judging about what should, or should not, be done, this "true for all" quality which inheres in it, will express what is "true-in-action-for-all"; the universality of our reasonable judgments will express what is binding on all, that is, what is lawful and unlawful. Hence the moral person will be the reasonable person, in the sense that he is acting in accordance with judgments which are universal and obeying laws which are binding on all. In a word, the moral person is the one who acts in conformity with the universality which is the "form" of the law.

As we have already noted, universality is, in fact, one of the characteristics of moral value (n. 33, 5). Now, in order to avoid every suspicion of making our worth as persons depend on what is empirical (i.e., of defining moral value in terms of our own advantage and convenience, our material prosperity etc.), which would be to ignore our real dignity, it could well be argued that the norm and essence of moral value should be sought in this direction. In any event, this was the path which Immanuel Kant trod. Shall we arrive at our destination by following in his footsteps?

I. *Kant's Formal Ethics.*

Grundlegung zur Metaphysik der Sitten, 1785 (GMS): *Formation of the Metaphysics of Morals.*
Kritik der Praktischen Vernunft, 1788 (KpV): *Critique of Practical Reason.*
These are here cited according to the Royal Academy of Prussia (Reimer) edition, tomes IV and V respectively.

115. – Kant, in virtue of his education, doubtless, had a vivid appreciation of the unparalled excellence of moral value. "Nothing in the world — indeed nothing even beyond the world — can possibly be conceived which could be called good without qualification except a good will", GMS, p. 393. Now, a good will is one which not only acts in conformity with the law (gesetzmässig), but out of respect for the law. Only at this level is true morality present. The majesty of the moral law, the absolute character of obligation, or of the "categorical imperative", have inspired Kant to write some admirable pages. (See, for example, his celebrated words on duty: "Duty! Thou sublime and mighty name" etc.", KpV, p. 86).

Since the moral law is absolute, it cannot have an empirical foundation any more than, as he taught in the *Critique of Pure Reason*, the necessary principles of our knowledge can be founded upon experience. For this reason, Kant rejects every form of eudaemonism. We do indeed desire happiness, but what is desirable depends on factors which cannot be known *a priori* (for example, the empirical nature of man) and consequently lack necessity. (Note that, for Kant, ethics has as its subject every reasonable being and is not merely concerned, as it is in Aristotle, with man. Consequently, it has to prescind from "anthropology"; only in applied ethics, does man enter the scene). — Moreover, even if it were possible — which is it not! — to form a clear idea of happiness, and of the conditions required for it, and even if, in addition, this idea were valid for every reasonable being, all that would result from it would be an hypothetical imperative ("if you wish to be happy, act like this"), or rather, an assertoric imperative ("since, in fact, you wish to be happy, act like this"); it could never give rise to an imperative which would be categorical (n. 42). Hence Kant makes a sharp distinction between "Gute" (the moral good), and "Wohl" (the eudaemonist good), for example, in KpV, pp. 59 ff.

Together with eudaeminism, Kant rejects Christian Wolff's notion of ethics; this may be called an "ontological" ethics, in that the concept of the perfection of our being is central to it. But, in Kant's view, an ethics of this kind means that there is a nature whose law is to be imposed on reason. Since man's nature is contingent, the law to which it gives rise will likewise be contingent, so that reason will be submitted to an external law — this submission he calls heteronomy — which would be a violation of its dignity, GMS, p. 443.

Kant also excludes a "theological" ethics. By this he means an ethics which bases duty on the will of God. His point here is that the divine will can be regarded as holy and perfect, only by making use of the notion of moral value. Consequently, this matter cannot be explained in terms of that will (*ib.*; cf. nn. 58 and 163-164). If the person to whom God's will is revealed, does not already have an appreciation that there is a moral order and that he is bound to carry out his duties, God's command could influence him only by playing upon his desires, that is, by means of promises and threats. Since motivations of this kind are only empirical — they are inextricably bound up with our experience of pleasure, pain etc. — they would deal a deathblow to all true morality.

116. – It is, then, absolutely unthinkable that the moral law could be imposed on the will by anything, or anyone, external to it; in consequence, the source of this law has to be within the will itself. Now, in Kant's view, the will is not, as it is in St Thomas, a rational appetite; it is the same as the practical reason, or better, it is the practical dimension of reason. Consequently, the moral law is nothing other than the command of the practical reason prescribing for itself what it should, and should not, choose. This "autonomy of reason" is one of Kant's famous themes and it is central to his moral philosophy.

"Reason must regard itself as the author of its principles, independently of foreign influences; consequently, as practical reason or as the will of a rational being, it must regard itself as free", GMS, p. 448. It may be recalled that the *Critique of Pure Reason* had left the question of freedom an open one: it cannot be demonstrated that we are free, but neither can the contrary be demonstrated. (This is the third antinomy of the pure reason). This agnostic conclusion still remains, for the certainty of freedom that we have, because of the fact that the autonomous reason is the source of obligation, is an entirely practical certainty. We do not understand any better than before how this freedom is possible nor what its nature is. The only difference is that we now see that we can act only under the idea of reason "as the author of its principles", that is, under the idea of freedom. "Now I say that every being which cannot act otherwise than under the idea of freedom is thereby really free in a practical respect", GMS, p. 448.

But what is commanded by this reason which is the autonomous source of the obligation to which we are subject? The *categorical imperative* cannot, as such, have any material content, for this could only be derived from experience and so would be empirical. Consequently, its only content can be its "form" (its inner and permanent structure), which is to call for obedience to the law because it is the law, out of reverence for the law. ... But it is of the essence of the law to be *universal*; it does not distinguish between person and person, but is impartial towards all; it does not concern itself with the preferences and convenience of individuals. What we are left with, then, when we have abstracted from its material content, is simply this universality of the law. Hence it is clear that the categorical imperative can have no content other than, and beyond, this *form of universality*. What this imperative enjoins on us is to act only according to that maxim — the subjective principle in accordance with which the will determines itself — which we can at the same time will to become a universal law. "Handle nur nach derjenigen Maxime, durch die du zugleich wollen kannst, dass sie ein allgemeines Gesetz werde", GMS, p. 421.

Only that will which determines itself in this way out of pure respect for the law can be called unqualifiedly good. But we can never know with certainty if this has really been the motive for our actions. Indeed, it could well be that not even one genuinely moral action has ever been performed. But this does not detract in the slightest from our certainty that we are under the authority of the moral law.

Note that it is *respect*, and not *love*, for the moral law that Kant constantly urges upon us. Love, in his view of it, is linked with pleasure; it is a sentiment from which we derive satisfaction. Respect, on the contrary, restrains and curbs our feelings; it does not give us the thrill which love gives us! Kant describes it as an attitude which results from the penetration of our reason into our feelings and is entirely singular.

117. – It might well seem to the reader of Kant that the inevitable result of his approach to the moral law will be that this will always have to remain in its formal purity, so that, in consequence, it can never be applied to concrete actions. But this is not so. Just as the "categories" of the understanding (discussed in the first *Critique*), are applied to sense data by means of the "schematism" of the transcendental imagination, so also (although in a different way), the moral law is applied to concrete actions by means of the maxims on which we act. Now, to apply the form of universality to these maxims, is to attempt to make universal norms of them. But if we try to do this, it becomes immediately obvious that not all maxims are capable of being universalized in this way; in many instances, the result would be contradiction or disorder. For example, if everyone is allowed, when he finds it convenient, to make a promise which he has no intention of keeping, no one will trust in promises and no advantage would then be gained by making promises of this kind: the universalization of this maxim would deal it the deathblow of contradiction. At other times, while there would, strictly speaking, be no contradiction involved in the universalization of a maxim, it would be quite impossible to will this sincerely. There is no contradiction in the notion of a world in which everyone is an egoist, but it is not possible for me to will that egoism become a universal law, for I myself want to be helped by others in time of need. Hence the formulation of the categorical imperative which has been already noted and which Kant also formulates in this way: "Act as though the maxim of your action were by your will to become a universal law of nature" GMS, p. 421. By "nature" he mean "the existence of things so far as it is determined by universal laws".

"*Morality* is thus the relation of actions to the autonomy of the will, that is, to possible universal lawgiving by maxims of the will", GMS, p. 439. In other words, we act morally when, and because, we act on maxims which are capable of being genuinely universalized.

As a moral being, capable of obeying the law out of respect for the law, man possesses an incomparable dignity which renders him an end in himself, one who should never be treated as a mere means to an end. From this there follows another and less abstract formulation of the categorical imperative: "Act so that you treat humanity, whether in your own person or in that of another, always as an end and never as a means only", GMS, p. 429. On first reading this, one might be tempted to think that Kant is here grounding the moral value of our actions on their relationship with human nature, in much the same way as do many Scholastic philosophers. Does he not speak of the "foundation" (Grund) of the categorical imperative? But lest we be misled by reading into Kant what is not there, recall that, as we have already seen, the dignity of human nature, or better of rational nature, is explained in function of the law. "Now, morality is the condition under which alone a rational being can be an end in itself... Autonomy is thus the basis of the dignity of both human nature and every rational nature", GMS, pp. 435-436. Consequently, respect for persons is in reality respect for the law, KpV, p. 78. It is, of course, true that since our actions take place in the empirical order, they affect only empirical, phenomenal human nature and not human nature as it exists in the intelligible, noumenal order and, as such, is deserving of respect. But since this latter is presented and exhibited to us in empirical human nature, we show our respect for it by acting towards empirical humanity, both in ourselves and in others, *as if* this were an end in itself [80].

This line of thought results in a third formulation of the categorical imperative, which is "the idea of the will of every rational being as a will giving universal law", GMS, p. 432. In other words, since humanity, in myself and in others, is never a mere means, it is not simply *under* the law, but gives itself the law, a law which it knows to be valid for every reasonable being. It is possible then to judge of the moral value of actions by considering whether they are in harmony with this idea of a will which legislates for everyone. Hence, the establishment of what Kant calls a "realm of ends", is the ideal at which every reasonable being should aim, that is, the establishment of a society of reasonable beings each of whom would be recognized by all the others as an end in himself. In such a realm, the maxims for which the categorical imperative gives the blueprint (or perhaps better, provides the framework), would be translated into a living reality, if only they were universally obeyed. ...

118. – From the categorical imperative Kant concludes (in KpV) to the three *postulates of practical reason*, which have to be affirmed because of their connection with the moral law; if they were not affirmed, then our affirmation of this law would become incoherent. These postulates, which do not themselves form part of the law, are as follows:

1) Freedom, without which it would be impossible to carry out our duties. (One of the classical problems which commentators on Kant discuss is whether the freedom which

---

[80] On this topic, see Fr. Marty, *La typique du jugement pratique pur. La morale kantienne et son application aux cas particuliers*, "Arch. de Phil.", 1955, pp. 56-57. — On the ethics of Kant, one could profitably read, in addition obviously to the classical work of V. Delbos, *La philosophie pratique de Kant*, Paris, 1905 (summarized at the beginning of the same author's translation of the *Foundations of the Metaphysics of Morals*, Paris, 1907), H. J. Paton, *The Categorical Imperative*, London, 1947 (an explanation of the *Foundations*), and L. H. Beck, *A Commentary on Kant's Critique of Practical Reason*, Chicago, 1960. Nor should the small, but extremely enlightening, book of J. Lacroix, *Kant et le kantisme*, Paris, 1966, be forgotten.

Kant has in mind here, is the same as the freedom which is involved in the autonomous legislation of the moral law. If, in fact, it were, it would not then be a "postulate", but a "fact" of reason. Should we not, rather, here interpret freedom in the way that the movement of Kant's thought invites us to interpret it, namely, as the capacity to fulfil the moral law, without being submerged in the world of space and time, the phenomenal world?).

2) The immortality of the soul. The moral law commands us to strive for holiness or moral perfection. But since this cannot be attained, there has to be the possibility of advancing indefinitely on the path towards it. This possibility, in its turn, presupposes, and calls for, the absence of any fullstop to our existence.

3) The existence of God. Even though it is true that we act morally only when we act out of respect for the law, it is also true that we cannot but propose to ourselves as the *object* (but not as the *motive!*), of our activity, the attainment of the "soveign good", that is, the establishment of a harmony between the degree of our moral perfection and our happiness. Now since "virtue" cannot be derived from the analysis of "happiness", nor "happiness" from the analysis of "virtue", their union can only be synthetic. Consequently, in order to secure this synthesis, it is necessary that a supreme Cause of the world, who is at the same time supremely moral, should exist.

These postulates do not add in the slightest to the speculative dimension of our knowledge, but they do procure for us a practical certainty which Kant calls "moral faith".

119. – There is much in the moral philosophy of Kant that deserves praise: his fine description of the moral law and of duty, his high esteem for "good will" and for the human person, the very definite distinction which he makes between what is morally good, and what is good because it is useful or pleasant, his rejection of eudaemonism and of ethical empiricism (a utilitarian etc., approach to ethics). It is true that long before the time of Kant, St Anselm (11th century) had established an analogous distinction between *rectitudo* (uprightness) and *commoditas* (expediency [81]; but it must also be confessed

---

[81] *De concordia praescientiae Dei cum libero arbitrio*, c. 11; Pl. t. 158, col. 556.

that the subsequent great influence of Aristotelian ethics had blurred that distinction somewhat, and had given to morality a more eudaemonist flavour. Hence, there is undoubtedly a very salutary aspect to Kant's reaction.

Neither was Kant in error in refusing to accept that the moral law is imposed on the human will by some source which is completely external to it (pure heteronomy). There can be no moral law apart from some recognition of, some assent, and indeed consent, to this law, on the part of the persons who are subject to it (n. 41).

But what judgment is to be passed on Kant's view of what morality essentially consists in?

120. – In the following discussion a number of themes which occur in Kant's moral teaching will not be examined, since they are not strictly relevant to our present inquiry. Consequently, we shall not concern ourselves with the question of the limits within which the human will can, and should be regarded as the autonomous source of the moral law. (Later, we shall take up this question, when we come to treat of the ultimate foundation of the moral order, and of obligation, in chapters four and five). Neither shall we be concerned with the rigorism with which Kant has so often been charged. But it is worth noting that he was not at all opposed to the attractive presentation of virtue and moral goodness. This can help to make virtuous living easier by counteracting the dazzling allurements of vice, but it cannot enter into the moral motivation, which can never be anything other than pure respect for the law. (In n. 124 we shall see what Kant's error on this point was). Finally, we shall not be dealing with the question of the extent to which "the proper study of (ethics) is man", namely, the question of the importance for ethics of that knowledge of man, and of his nature, which Kant calls "anthropology"; nor with the associated question of the role of the affections and emotions in moral living.

We here concentrate on that aspect of Kant's ethics which has been called his "formalism". Our question, accordingly, is: does the universality of the law, which is its pure form, its inner and abiding structure, provide the norm and essence of moral value?

121. – In our discussion of "extrinsic morality" (nn. 56-57), we observed that there can be moral value in obeying a law only if this law is itself good and just; and that it is only in relation to the good which is to be achieved through our obedience, that the law has this quality. If we leave aside this good, and exclude all consideration of it, the law becomes no more than a limitation on our freedom, so that there can, in consequence, be no positive value in obeying it [82].

It is quite true that the possible universalization of the maxims on which we are acting often provides, as in the examples given by Kant, a criterion for distinguishing between good and evil actions. But note that its application calls for a certain delicacy and finesse. If it is too rigidly applied and fails to take into account the concrete and particular conditions in which an action is to be performed, it excludes the possibility of special and exceptional moral vocations. If it is too loosely applied, it runs the risk of justifying anything and everything, for each person will then readily believe that *he* is the exception, since the circumstances are never absolutely the same. — But whatever about this, let us now suppose that the criterion has been accepted. Now clearly, it is not a self-evident criterion; it needs some justification, and this can be had only by answering the question: why *should* we act only on maxims that can be universalized?

Is the answer to be because what is universal is opposed to, and is the denial of, what is individual? But why should we react against what is individual? Two reasons could be suggested for this. Firstly, because what is individual is considered to be simply evil, as in some pantheist-inspired doctrines (cf. n. 74); but what foundation is there for pessimism of this kind? Secondly, because even though the value of what is individual is readily acknowledged, it is also maintained that this value has to be subordinated to one that is higher. But then, it is in function of this latter value that morality will have to be defined. The flight from what is individual can have no

---

[82] Our aim here is not at all to revise Utilitarianism, but simply, by using positive law as an example, to help the reader appreciate that the moral law, without which no other law would have any binding force, has itself to be related to some good — but a good of another order.

more than a negative value, apart from its role of enabling us to accept, and say "yes" to, a value which is higher.

Or is the answer to be: because a maxim which can be universalized without contradiction and disorder, is by that very fact stamped as in accordance with reason and rational nature? Since these are identical in all men, and indeed in all rational beings, it follows that, all other things being equal, what is in harmony with reason and rational nature in one subject, will be in harmony with reason and rational nature in all subjects. — But, in that case, what really gives an action its moral value is this harmony with reason and rational nature. Note also that reason cannot here be simply identified with the pure "form" of universality. It has to be taken to mean a certain perfection which, since it is found in all human, and indeed in all rational, beings, is being considered in its "absolute nature" (cf. n. 7 end), and which is the source of guidance for the individual, as well as being characterized by the "form of universality". Not to understand reason in this sense here, would be to become involved in the futile process of chasing one's tail: we would be reduced to saying that there is a moral value in acting on maxims which can be universalized, because we are thereby acting reasonably, and that there is a moral value in acting reasonably, because we are thereby acting on maxims that can be universalized.

Or is the answer to be: because to have a norm for action which is common to all, helps to bring about a unity in human society and because, to highlight another aspect of the same answer, it is only maxims which can without contradiction be willed as universal laws, that can help to achieve and preserve the "realm of ends", the republic of fre beings? — But then, it is clear that moral value is being explained, in the final analysis, in relation to this goal or ideal. The true norm of moral action is the achievement and preservation of a society that is worthy of human, or rather, spiritual, beings.

No matter what angle one takes on the "possible-universalization-of-the-maxims-we-act-upon" criterion, it is clear that there is either no moral value in acting upon it, or that if there is, this arises only in relation to, and in dependence on, some further value (the value that lies in acting in accordance with reason, with rational nature, or in achieving and preserving the republic of free beings etc.). Consequently, it is impossible that the essence of our value should depend on whether or not we act only on maxims which we can universalize without contradiction; rather will it depend on the relationship we come to have, as a result of our free actions, with the value on which the value of acting on these maxims is itself dependent, and towards which we are increasingly oriented in obeying all laws which are worthy of the name.

This is not to deny that a certain *general* value can be found in universality as such (n. 24). But singularity and what is exceptional has also its value, and unless some fresh factor is introduced, why should the former be preferred? In fact, one finds easily enough (for example, in religious communities!) two types of people who serve to illustrate these two different values. There are those who feel at ease and have a sense of security only when they "do as the others do", only when they are faithfully observing the approved usages and customs, and are perfectly incorporated into the community or group. There are also, on the contrary, those for whom it seems to be a matter of life and death to distinguish themselves from "the others" by something which is peculiarly their own, be it the reflected glory of their family and relations, some privilege which is theirs, an occupation that is out of the ordinary, or simply the great freedom of conduct which they allow themselves, with very often no other motivation than that of asserting themselves as individuals. In these and similar ways, people of this second type strive to preserve that singularity which means so much to them... but is there a negative value in what they do *simply* because they are being singular, or a positive value in what people of the first type do, *simply* because they are in line with others ...?

With regard to the reason given by Kant, in one of his examples, of the immorality of acting on maxims that could not be willed as universal laws (namely, that if we were allowed to make false promises, then all trust between man and man would perish, and with it the very possibility of making such promises), it is certainly true that a person could not without contradiction will that the maxim on which he is acting when he makes a false promise, become a universal law. But the contradiction here involved is, of itself, no more than a fault in the *logical* order; it becomes a *moral* fault only if we presuppose that there is a moral value in avoiding this inconsistency, and an obligation to do so here and now. If, then, I make a false promise, even though at the same time, I do not want others to follow my example, because I hold that so to act would be *immoral*, I myself am acting immorally, not because I am doing what

I do not want others to do, but simply because I am doing what I judge to be evil. The moral anti-value of telling lies it presupposed and does not result from the impossibility of universalizing my maxim without contradiction.

122. – Could it be said that the value towards which we are orientated by our obedience to the Kantian universal laws, is nothing other than the attainment of a good will? But, in Kant's view, what is a good will? It is a will which obeys that law out of respect for the law. Hence we would be reduced to saying that the value towards which we are orientated by our obedience to these laws, is the attainment of "respect for the law"; or that a good will is a will that wishes to be good (for the value towards which our morally valuable obedience would orientate us, would be the attainment of a good will). But this does not throw any light at all on what a good will is, nor on the value towards which our obedience to the Kantian law orientates us as free subjects.

It can, of course, be maintained that a good will is a will that wishes to be good, but only in the sense that what, in the final analysis, measures the goodness of a person's will, is his intention, even when he is invincibly ignorant of what he should do in order to respond to the claims which the objective moral order is making on him (nn. 245-247). But his intention has to be directed to some object other than the intention itself; unless it is, then it is no more than an empty husk. As St Thomas notes: "What is first willed cannot be the willing itself" [83]. Something other than the act of willing, has to be willed. Hence, in order to intend to have a good will, I have to give some content and body to the word "good". I cannot do this simply by drawing on an analogous notion of goodness, formed for example, from the notion of the pleasant or useful good; a good will is one which is morally good. What this means I cannot understand, much less set about achieving it, if I do not have within me the notion of some ideal or value to which I should commit myself, of some type of human being that I ought to strive to become. I may not, indeed, be able to express very clearly, even to myself, what this ideal is; but, for the reasons already given, it is clear that it cannot be accounted for in terms of the universality of the laws which I obey.

---

[83] St Thomas, *Cont. Gent.*, III, 26.

123. – It is impossible to define what a good will is, apart from the notion of some hierarchy and ascending gradation in the real order, with which a good will, precisely as such, intends to be in harmony (n. 101, 2). The stress which he placed on the universality of the law and on the role of obligation in moral living, represents Kant's partially valid insight on this point. "Universality" can be regarded as his attempt to allow its righful place in morality to the "openness" of a being to whom there is a spiritual dimension and who, as such, is not encased within his nature as an individual, or even within his nature as a member of the human species, but is capable of reaching out to all that is, through knowledge and love; and is himself "a universe", not merely part of "*the* universe". Consequently, a person's will is good — we shall have more to say on this point soon — when he decides in accordance with this "openness" which defines his status as spiritual and rational, that is, when he "stands out", determines himself and reveals himself in a way which is rational, and does not limit himself to the boundaries which his desire for self-preservation, self-gratification and self-aggrandizement would impose on him. Kant's emphasis on the role of obligation helps, in its turn, to bring to light the duality that is intrinsic to every finite spiritual being (a duality, be it noted, which is not reducible to, or identical with, the duality that is in us because we are not purely spiritual beings, but sensitive-spiritual beings): the opposition between our subjective finitude (our finitude as existing subjects) and our objective infinity (the limitless range that opens out to our knowledge and our love). "Limited by nature, infinite by desire...". To experience obligation is to experience the supremacy of this openness over our natural preoccupation with, and concentration on, ourselves; and as a consequence, the supremacy of the Being to whom as spiritual subjects, we are radically open (cf, Chapter Four).

Kant has shown very well that our moral value could not be derived from any value which is empirical, so that it has, in consequence, to be grounded on what transcends this entire order. But this foundation could not be provided by the

---

[84] *Ib.*, II, 89.

universality of the law, since this universality is something abstract, nor can it be accounted for by something formal, as it would have to be if man's dignity were identified with his capacity to legislate laws whose "form" would be their power to bind every rational being. (In that hypothesis, to act in accordance with our dignity as human beings, that is, to act morally, would be the same as acting in accordance with this universal form). It is only in the order of reality, to which we are open as spiritual subjects, that the source of our moral value can lie.

124. – Another weakness of Kant's ethics is worth reflecting on here, even thogh it is only indirectly connected with our investigation. It is his exclusion of everything that is not done out of pure respect for the law, and in particular of what is done out of love. Kant can see nothing more in love than an emotional attraction from which we derive pleasure. He fails to distinguish between this emotional level of love, and the spiritual, or sensitivo-spiritual, level which is directed towards, and concentrated on, the *person* of the one loved. Love at the first level is infra-rational and infra-moral, but at the spiritual level, where the one who loves not only appreciates the other for what he is, but seeks to help him become his true self more fully, it is of its very nature morally good[84], as is sensitivo-spiritual love also, under certain conditions (for example, in marriage). The affective and bodily element of a human being's love comes to have a moral value, not only because of his intention of obeying the law and doing what he should do, but because of this spiritual element of which it is the expression, and by which it is animated. A mother's caresses for her child have a moral value not only because she is obliged by the moral law to show him signs of affection, but because this affection, if it is what it should be, is the expression in a bodily and affective way of the spiritual love which she has for her child as a human being, as a unique person. (This spiritual element is lacking when the child is loved in a selfish, sensual way, as if he were but a small animal, a pet).

---

[85] As long, at least, as the person loved remains capable of responding to moral value and has not definitively closed himself to it. Once that has happened, he can no longer be the object of an authentically spiritual love.

As we have seen (n. 120), Kant is quite willing to allow us to take advantage of the help which our natural likes and preferences can give us, in our struggle to lead moral lives. But this does not make the relationship between the moral value of our actions, and our feelings, to be any the less extrinsic — just as in his anthropology (his view of what man is), the relationship between soul and body is extrinsic, and as in his metaphysics the relationship between what can be understood and what can be experienced (between the noumenon and the phenomenon), remains extrinsic (the intelligible world lies "beyond" the world of experience, so that the noumenon cannot be understood "in" the phenomenon).

125. – It is perhaps this "extrinsicism" which accounts for Kant's approach to ethics. Just as, in his theory, our knowledge of the intelligible world is a purely negative knowledge — that there is such a world he does not deny, but he insists that we cannot know it — in which there is no element of immediacy (this is present only in our knowledge of what we can experience, our knowledge of what belongs to the spatio-temporal order), so likewise our knowledge of the "moral world", our knowledge of what we are required to *do*, remains negative. It is when we are *not* making an exception for ourselves, and *not* doing ourselves what we would not wish others to do, that we are acting morally. It is also in consequence of this extrinsicism that the application of the moral law to our concrete actions, results in the exclusion of an element — the affective and bodily element — of these actions, from the moral order.

One of the gravest defects in Kantian ethics is his equation of love with emotional satisfaction. This attitude can be partially accounted for by his justifiable abhorrence of the confusion into which people can so frequently fall on this point. — It is, however, true that spiritual love (love of another as a person), includes and requires respect for the one loved, and that this respect helps to purify and spiritualize love, that is, helps to deepen the lover's appreciation of the other as a person. But it is no less true that there is in respect something which heralds the approach of love, something that tends towards love. There is evidence of this in the very way in which Kant speaks, with restrained emotion, of the beauty of moral value (GMS, p. 393), and of duty (KpV, p. 86), and of the contentment (Zufriedenheit) which they bring to our will (GMS, p. 396).

Note in conclusion that Kant's ethical teaching has been understood in more than one way (as has indeed the teaching of Aristotle and the other great moralists), and that there are those who wish to interpret in a less strict sense what he has written about the need to act only on those maxims which we can will to become universal laws. From our point of view, which is not that of the historian, the possibility of other and divergent interpretations is only of secondary importance. What is essential for us is that we have advanced in our understanding of the essence of moral value. Even should we have done this by tilting at wind-mills, we have been far from beating the air, as far as our main aim is concerned!

II. *Theories in which reason has the "open" sense.*

126. – If the source of the moral value of our actions lies — as the whole movement of our investigation has brought home to us — in their reasonableness, and if, on the other hand — as our evaluation of Kant has revealed — reason in the sense of prescribing courses of action which could be willed as universal laws, cannot of itself provide this source, we have now to see if reason in the other sense, namely, as expressing the requirements of reality, will yield more fruitful results (n. 114). Note, though, that even in this sense, reason can still be understood in two ways.

It can be regarded as simply manifesting *moral* requirements, which are already "given" as moral by the very nature of the situation in which we happen to find ourselves. Now, obviously, if we regard reason in this light, the real source of our moral value and the true norm of morality will be identified with these requirements, so that the role of reason will be no more than that of an intermediary. To take this view will not mean relapsing into empiricism (hedonism, utilitarianism etc.), for these requirements are reasonable ones which we can appreciate as such only by our reasonable judgments. (These requirements can be variously regarded as flowing from our human nature, rational nature as such, the order that is intrinsic and essential to reality, etc.). But, apart from these judgments, this order cannot be grasped, nor can our nature be appreciated as the reasonable nature that it is, etc. Neither has the rightness of our reasonable judgments, in this view of reason, to be verified by comparing them with some exterior norm, because judgments which are made in accordance with the requirements of reason are by that very fact faithful expressions of the requirements of reality. It is of the very nature of these judgments to acknowledge and "welcome" what is [86]. — In this interpretation of reason, our actions will be morally good because, and to the extent that, they harmonize with the requirements of reality; if there is a clash, the extent of it will be the measure of the moral evil of what we do.

But reason can also be regarded as not simply manifesting and transmitting objective requirements, which already possess a moral character, but as itself conferring this character on these requirements. In this interpretation, our reasonable judgments will be not merely declarative but constitutive, so that a requirement of reality acquires a moral character only because it is also a requirement of reason. Note that this view does not have to face the difficulties that result from understanding reason in the kantian sense, since the reason that is now in question is a reason which is open to what is Absolute, open to the Ideal, as we shall soon explain (nn. 135-136 and the third chapter).

Accordingly, we have now two aims in mind. Firstly, to verify directly (and not, as heretofore, simply by excluding other hypotheses), whether moral value, as our phenomenological reflection has revealed it, has as its true, immediate and essential norm the judgment of reason. Secondly, presupposing that this first aim has been accomplished, to discover in what precise sense reason is the norm of morality, how it exercises its normative function, and whether its role in morality is merely declarative or is constitutive. In pursuing this second aim, we shall likewise be careful not to become involved in irrelevant controversies that would distract our attention from the "one thing necessary".

There is another way in which the present stage of our inquiry is linked with the stages that have gone before. When we there rejected erroneous or insufficient notions of the moral norm, we

---

[86] St Thomas, *De Ver.*, 1, 9.

noted that these notions were to a great extent tacitly appealing to another norm, whose nature we were not then concerned to determine: reason, rational nature, the order of reality ... (Thus, nn. 69, 73, 84, 85, 90, 101). The required clarification of this tacitly assumed norm will be an important fruit of our present investigation.

127. – The general view of Thomistic philosophers seems to be that the role of reason is *constitutive*. It is in acting in accordance with the judgments of "right reason" that we act morally. But what, for them, is "right reason"? It is our practical reason (reason as concerned with how we should decide, and put our decisions into effect), as animated by the knowledge of God's law, or by that habitual knowledge, which St Thomas calls "synderesis" (n. 240), of the general principles of the moral law, and perfected by the virtue of prudence (nn. 192, 272). It is as impossible to err concerning these general practical principles — we are still giving the Thomistic viewpoint — as it is to err concerning the basic principles of speculative thought, such as the principles of non-contradiction and that the whole is greater than the part. It is these practical principles which express the basic natural goals of human action, since in the sphere of decision the well-spring of our activity is the goal at which we are aiming. Now, a human being, by his very nature, has an inclination towards these natural goals and, again by his very nature, appreciates that his good lies in obtaining them (n. 21). Consequently, his reason is always where these goals and these principles are concerned.

Right reason should not be confused with the moral conscience of each individual, which may be either correct or erroneous and about which we shall speak later (nn. 242-246). Conscience is a subjective guide to moral action; it makes clear what is morally good for the individual subject to do, in the concrete situation in which he finds himself here and now (with, for example, his limited knowledge of the objective norm and his blindness to some of the factors involved in the situation), even though this may not, in itself, be worthy of a human being. Right reason is, however, an *objective* guide to moral action; it brings to light the course of action which, when everything is weighed in the balance, is worthy of a human being.

As examples of writers who hold this view of the role of reason in morality we note the following in particular: L. Lehu, *Philosophia Moralis et Socialis*, Rome, 1914, t. 1, pp. 145 ff. The same author's *La*

Raison Règle de la Moralité d'après Saint Thomas, Paris, 1930. C. Boyer, *Cursus Philosophiae*, Paris, 1936, t. 11, pp. 465 ff. S. Schiffini, *Disputationes Philosophiae Moralis*, Turin, 1891, t. 1, pp. 99-102.

This also seems to have been the view of St Thomas who sees in human reason the "proximate and homogeneous rule" of human actions[87]. Reason is called the proximate rule because there is no intermediary between these judgments and the immediate source of his human actions (his will), which is directly dependent on his reason for light and guidance[88]. Reason is called the homogeneous rule because, in common with the will which it guides, it is a created and spiritual capacity and is, in this way, distinguished both from the divine Reason and from what is infra-rational.

In making reason the "proximate" rule of morality, the authors of whom we speak are far from denying that our judgments have to be based on an objective foundation, whether this be human nature, the order that is intrinsic to reality, or our orientation to our ultimate end. All that they wish to maintain is that what makes this foundation to be morally significant is its, at least possible, relationship with a judgment of reason.

These authors also maintain that human reason is, in its turn, "measured" and regulated by the divine Reason from which its moral binding power is derived. It is, then, the divine Reason which is the supreme norm of morality, a norm which is communicated to us through the different natures of the various finite beings. For human nature (or the essential order of reality etc.), can serve as the basis for moral judgments only because it derives its meaning and purpose from the divine Reason which, in making it to be, makes it to be dependent on and orientated towards its source, so that it is an object and creation of that Reason by whose decrees it is regulated and "measured"[89]. Considered independently of, and apart from, their relationship with the divine Reason, human nature and the essential order of reality have of themselves no moral

---

[87] St Thomas, *Summa Theol.*, I-II, 71, 6.

[88] St Thomas, *De Malo*, 6 (art. unic.).

[89] "Human nature, considered prior to and independently of the eternal law, can in no sense be called the foundation of morality", L. Lehu, *op. cit.*, p. 119.

significance. Consequently, the principle that "the true norm is the one which does not itself require a further norm", of which we have made such frequent use, does not find the Achilles heel in this theory that it found in others. For here, it is not human nature as such which grounds and measures the rightness of our reasonable judgments, but this nature as the product and achievement of the divine Reason to whose decrees it is subject. Hence, the norm and essence of moral value remain entirely interior to the rational order.

128. – Many Scholastics, however, and they form perhaps the greatest number, allow reason no more than a declarative role in morality: the moral norm, in their view, is already given to us as moral in the objective requirements of reality. Their preoccupation seems to be to ensure that there will be a solid foundation for the judgments of our practical reason, and thereby ward off the danger of arbitrariness in these judgments. In addition, some of the more recent of them seem to be fearful that, if they allow reason more than a manifestative role, they will end up as Kantians, idealists (in a philosophical sense!) or subjectivists. If reason is granted a constitutive role in the moral order, has not the "Copernican revolution" been effected in ethics? — Perhaps this fear springs, at times, from a forgetfulness of what it is that distinguishes moral good from other types of good, and a spiritual subject from the other beings of our experience. In wishing to escape from the net of idealism, they run the risk of becoming prisoners of an Aristotelian naturalism and of not taking sufficiently into account man's interiority and subjectivity.

But even though these authors agree in denying to reason anything more than a declarative role, they disagree concerning these "already moral" requirements, which reason reveals.

Some of the more metaphysically-minded of them identify these requirements with the order or hierarchy that is intrinsic to reality, or with the system of relationships that exists between one perfection and another. M. Liberatore[90], and among non-Scholastics, Malebranche, who treats of the problem in ac-

---

[90] M. Liberatore, *Institutiones philosophicae*, vol. 3, Rome, 1878, p. 50.

cordance with his "ontologism" [91], and A. Rosmini [92], write in this vein.

Others prefer to consider the question in a teleological perspective. What distinguishes between the good and bad activity of any being whatever, is whether or not this being is fulfilling its proper function (or at least the function for which it is being used). So, for example, a radiator is working well when it fills the room with a pleasant heat. To do this is the function of a radiator. Likewise, a human being is functioning well as a human being — that is, he is acting morally, in an authentically human manner — when and because he conducts himself in a way that harmonizes with his radical orientation to his "ultimate end". To attain this end is the finality which is his as a human being. If, then, an action helps him to advance on the path that leads to his final end, it is morally good; if it blocks this road, it is morally bad. This is, more or less, the view of J. Gredt and J. Mausbach [93].

---

[91] "The Reason which enlightens man is the Word or the Wisdom of God himself. ... In contemplating that divine substance. ... I can also discover God's will to some extent: for His will is always in accordance with the Order, and this is not entirely unknown to me ... In contemplating the intelligible substance of the Word, who alone makes me and all intelligent beings to be reasonable, I see clearly the relations of perfection, which are the unalterable Order which God consults when He acts, an Order which ought also regulate the esteem and love of all intelligent beings", Malebrance, *Traité de Morale*, Ie, p., Ch. 1. — On Malebranche's moral teaching, see Leonardo Verga, *La Filosofia Morale di Malebranche*, Milan, 1964.

[92] After having formulated the "first moral law" as: "Follow in your activity the light of reason", Rosmini explains it as follows: "Will, or rather, love being wherever you recognize it, in whatever order it presents itself to your intelligence". For "it is not reason which really constitutes the supreme moral law but the idea of being, of whose light this power makes use, and advances securely by means of it, but goes astray through departing from it", *Principi della scienza morale*, in "Opere edite ed inedite", vol. XII, pp. 7, 68, 8. — On Rosminian ethics, see M. F. Sciacca, *La filosofia morale di Antonio Rosmini*, 2nd ed., Rome, 1955.

[93] The position od these authors is, in fact, nuanced. J. Gredt (*Elementa philosophiae aristotelico-thomisticae*, 6th ed., Frib. in Br., 1932, t. II) affirms that "the supreme rule of the morality of a human action is man's last end", p. 349. This end is God; however, the supreme rule is not God considered in His essence, but God as regulative Reason, directing man to his end. The proximate moral rule is the dictate of (human) reason, which partakes of the eternal law, p. 350. — For J. Mausbach (*Katholische Moraltheologie*, 8th ed., Bd II, Münster

129. – There are, finally, other authors (and they are the most numerous), who say that it is *human nature* or *rational nature as such*, which provides the norm and essence of moral value. Since what is morally good is the genuinely human good (the good which makes a human being to be humanly good), and since what makes a being to be good of its kind has to be in harmony with its nature, they conclude that what makes an action to be morally good is its harmony with human nature. The particular champions of this are the Suarezians who are led into the fray by Suarez himself: "Objective moral goodness (by this he means the goodness which the object chosen confers on the act by which it is chosen, n. 224), consists in the direct harmony of the object with rational nature as such" [94].

He then goes on: "Objective moral goodness, of which we are here speaking, cannot simply consist in the perfection of the object that is chosen, for whatever is morally good is so in relation to the person to whom it presents itself as an object to be loved or sought after; this means that it has to be in harmony with his nature. ... Note carefully that this harmony has to be with rational nature as rational and as capable of being guided by right reason (cum natura rationali ut rationalis est et recta ratione gubernari potest); since moral goodness is the supreme value for man, it has to consist in a relationship with what is highest and most perfect in him, that is, with his rational nature as rational". But, he adds, "the harmony with rational nature is not with the judgment (dictamen) of reason, but with this nature considered in itself (secundum se); the role of our reason is simply to enable us to discover what is in accordance with our rational nature and to apply this knowledge to our concrete actions (ratio autem solum est applicans et proponens quid conveniat

---

Westf., 1954), the absolute value of the moral act can only be derived from its relation to the Supreme Good, to the total goal (Gesamtziel) of creation: "The moral good is the highest in kind and degree; it surpasses in value all created things and deserves an unqualified esteem. Consequently, the moral deeds and dispositions of human beings are, as such, finite and limited, so that it is only in relation to the supreme good, the total goal of creation that they have an unqualified value", p. 67. The ultimate norm of morality is the essence and holiness of God, p. 71. But the proximate norm consists in the order of essences grasped by reason, p. 74, an order in which human nature occupies a central place, pp. 75 seq.

[94] Suarez, *De bonitate et malitia objectiva actuum humanorum*, disp. II, sect. 2, n. 10; ed. Vivès, t. IV, p. 294 b.

naturae), and our judgment is right only when what we judge to be in conformity with our nature, really is so" [95].

Even though his phraseology is somewhat different, the influence of Suarez is clear in what V. Frins writes: "The objective rule and foundation of morality is human nature both as possessed of an intrinsic and innate dignity, and as related essentially and accidentally to various beings; in other words, this is what we have to reflect on (intueri) in order to judge whether a proposed course of action is really and truly of a human being (ut de vera et simpliciter dicta convenientia obiectorum et actionum pro nobis iudicet)" [96]. — V. Cathrein [97] and Ed. Elter [98], write in a similar vein.

Some Thomists also adopt this position. Among them is R. Jolivet who places great emphasis on the relationship between our actions and the achievement of our last end. But it is not this relationship that *immediately* establishes the objective moral value of what we do; rather is it the harmony of our actions with our rational nature. It is this harmony or the lack of it, which provides the criterion for distinguishing between actions which lead us towards, or away from, our last end. In applying this criterion, we have to be mindful of the various tendencies of our rational nature and to keep a proper balance between them; we have also to be mindful of the general and particular relationships we have with God and with other creatures [99]. (The distinction between the essence and the norm of moral value is evident in this text, n. 47, 1).

Obviously, the human nature of which there is question here is not this nature considered in the abstract but "adequately", that is, in conjunction with the various relationships by which it is affected. "We call an action morally good", writes Schiffini, "because it harmonizes with each of these relationships, not as considered in isolation from one another but where due regard is had for their relative importance (cum debita proportione quam ex se habent ad invicem); an action which clashes in any way with this order of relationships will, on the contrary, be evil (si fiat quidpiam huic ordini contrarium)" [100].

---

[95] *Ib.*, nn. 11, 12; p. 295 a.
[96] *De actibus humanis*, t. II, p. 58.
[97] *Philosophia moralis*, 14th ed., Frib. in Br., 1927, pp. 80-81.
[98] *Compendium philosophiae moralis*, Thesis I.
[99] *Morale*, 2nd ed., Lyons, 1945, p. 183.
[100] *Op. cit.*, n. 57; p. 94.

Clearly, the above-mentioned writers do not at all deny that reason is the moral norm, in the sense that we have to use it in order to discover what is, or what is not, in accordance with our rational nature. But, they insist, this is the limit of its role; it is not our judgments which give this harmony its moral character, except in the sense that as our reason is an element in our rational nature, it will, accordingly, form part of the object on which our judgments have to be based, if they are to guide us aright. (Cf. the words of Suarez which we have quoted above). — Schiffini [101] takes issue with Suarez on this last point and so he cannot really be considered to hold the Suarezian viewpoint, even though he does so verbally (n. 134).

130. – Our task now is to attempt to shed light on this debate.

That the judgments of right reason provide the proximate norm of morality, as St Thomas holds, seems to be undeniable; moreover, provided that the term is not made more precise, the truth of this is not, ordinalily, challenged or denied. For what is moral value but the value which makes a human act to be humanly good, that is, good as a human act? Now, it is quite evident that a free, human act can be called humanly good, only to the extent that it is in harmony with the source from which its humanness flows. As St Thomas notes, it is always the source and well-spring that provides the required rule and measure of goodness [102]. So, for example, what measures the artistic value of a painting is not the faithfulness with which it reproduces reality (a photograph would do this much better), nor the rich ornamentation of the frame, the durability of the materials used etc., but its correspondance with the artistic intention of the painter, with the idea, or rather the value, which he wished to express and which takes clear shape in his own mind only by being embodied on canvas. It is that intention, that value, which is the well-spring of his artistic creation.

Now, the well-spring of the humanness of a human action is human reason. What is essential to such activity is that it be

---

[101] *Ib.*, n. 61; pp. 101-102.
[102] St Thomas, *Summa Theol.*, I-II, 90, 1.

voluntary and free; and the root of our freedom lies in our reason (n. 111). Our will is a *will*, that is, it is distinct from our natural and animal appetite, only in virtue of its rational character; and its free exercise is inseparable from the exercise of our intelligence which, since it presents to us the object that we choose, plays its part in making our choice to be this particular one rather than some other. (In more technical terms, as expressed by St Thomas, our free acts are "informed" by the activity of our intelligence [103]. Indeed, since it is the movement by means of which we strive to put into effect an idea that has not yet become a reality, or (which comes to the same thing), that movement from "interiority to exteriority" which is impossible without an understanding of what it is we wish to effect — "inclinatio consequens rem intellectam" as St Thomas writes [104] — a free decision can be animated or "informed" only by what our intelligence, or rather our reason, contributes. This last qualification is made because we are moved to choose a particular object only if it appears to us to be good and it can so appear only because of its, at least apparent, harmony with our inclinations, that is, only in virtue of its relation to ourselves. But, as we have already seen, what characterizes "reason" is precisely this "relating" capacity. Since, then, reason is the source of the humanness of our acts, it is also the measure and rule of this humanness; in other words, it is the measure and rule of their moral value.

All that has been said in the present number will be strengthened and supplemented by what remains to be said in nos. 134-136 and 139.

131. – Our task is, however, still far from finished! For if it is true, as Thomistic psychology, for example, teaches, that the free, voluntary decision always and necessarily corresponds to the final judgment of our practical reason, every human act, to the extent that it is human and free, is in conformity with reason. Hence, we have now to clarify what was said in the previous number: the moral norm is not provided by any

---

[103] *Ib.*, I-II, 13, 1.
[104] *Ib.*, I, 87, 4.

judgment whatever of our practical reason, but only by the judgments of what we shall call our "right" practical reason.

To say this immediately prompts the question: what is "right reason"? [105]. We have already noted the definition of the Thomists: "our practical rzason as animated and 'informed' by the knowledge of God's law, or, by the knowledge of the general principles of the moral law" (n. 127). This definition leaves little to be desired, if all we are concerned with is to evaluate the correctness of some particular moral judgment. But how can I be sure that my reason will be "right" in obeying the divine law, or that what the Thomists call the moral, or natural, law really is moral? What guarantee have I on this score? For the moment, let us leave aside the question of the divine law and concentrate on the natural, moral law. The principles of this law, it will be said, are known to us through the inclinations and tendencies that are natural to us as human beings. But since these inclinations are, of themselves, no more than a matter-of-fact, how can they confer rights on me and create duties for others? What assurance have I that in obeying them I shall be acting in the way that right reason requires of me? I can, it is true, simply choose to believe, in a spirit of ingenuous and irrational confidence, that I am so acting; but, if I do, how can I then maintain that I am acting in a way that is worthy of a human, rational being? The alternative is that I receive this assurance through a — perhaps very confused — judgment, by means of which I recognize that these natural inclinations blend and harmonize with the inclinations and requirements of reason. In other words, I come to appreciate that these natural tendencies are moral tendencies, only because I judge that they are in accordance with right reason. Consequently, since these inclinations presuppose the rightness of reason, they cannot be used to define it.

The situation is in no way improved by defining right reason (as the virtue of prudence is defined, n. 272) in relation to "right appetite". For our will is right when we love what is good and we love what is good only when we are true to what right reason demands of us. ...

---

[105] See the *Essai*, nn. 127, 128; pp. 306-309.

The rightness of our reason cannot be defined or known in relation to any rule that is exterior: this rule is within our reason itself. Right reason is reason that is faithful to its own essence and to what we shall call its own "Ideal"; reason that is *rationally* exercised, in accordance with its own law, and is not subordinated to a law that is foreign to it (for example, the law that guides sense activity), so that through this subordination it becomes unfaithful to its own essence, untrue to its own "Ideal". Consequently, because of the relationship between reason and liberty, an ethics to which right reason is central, is likewise centred on liberty.

A person who exercises all his ingenuity to discover and make effective use of the means which enable him to satisfy his pride, his lust, his desire to dominate others, or who engineers the "perfect murder", is certainly using his reason, and often in a far from common degree, but he is not exercising it reasonably, since the goals which he is pursuing do not reflect the requirements of reason; and what is not fully rational is not moral, that is, it is not morally good. "When in our exercise of reason, we fall away from the standards of reason, we are not (really) exercising it, just as we do not (really) make a syllogism in making one that is false; hence, the rule that is to guide our human actions is not any judgment whatever, but the judgment of right reason" [106].

The moral act has, then, to be rational not simply in the sense that otherwise some effect which we happen to desire will not be achieved, for example, the success of a business enterprise; the rationality which is moral is not simply the same as the rationality that is required in order to achieve "results". After all, would it not be preferable to a sick person to be restored to health by a quack, and even absurd, remedy than to be allowed to die by a doctor who insists on treating him "according to the book", in the manner of Molière's doctors. But where it is a question of the moral value or anti-value of an action, this line of thought is not applicable; rationality has here a value in itself. An irrational act is immoral, no matter what may result from it on the economic and eudaemonist plane.

Accordingly, what measures the moral value of our free actions is their harmony with the judgments of right reason, that is, their harmony with our practical reason when this is

---

[106] St Thomas, *In II Sent.*, d. 24, q. 2, a. 3.

functioning in accordance with its own finality. This seems to be an initial conclusion to our present investigation, which is incontestable. Another conclusion, which immediately follows, is that the object of our choice also receives its moral qualification from its relationship with the judgments of right reason. But what, it may be asked, is meant by speaking of the moral value of the object of choice? That there will be a positive or negative value in this object, according as we can, or cannot, choose it while still remaining faithful to the norm of our free decisions. This obviously means that the object is either in harmony, or disharmony, with this norm and, in consequence, with the judgments of right reason.

Even though the conformity with reason is in the object that we choose prior to being in our choice, it is to the latter that the term "moral value" is primarily applicable; the heart of morality lies in our freedom and it is only in an analogous sense that moral value can be attributed to the object which is chosen. It is only because this can affect, for better or worse, the will which chooses it, that it can be spoken of as morally good or evil. There is a parallel here with truth: ontological truth, or the intelligibility that is intrinsic to being, is the ground of the truth that is in our minds (logical truth), but, nonetheless, it is to this latter that the term "truth" is primarily applicable.

132. – On the other hand, it is undeniable that rational nature as such, and the order that is intrinsic to being, are involved in the moral norm and are, in some way, its basis. That this is so becomes obvious, with regard to rational nature, from a consideration of the very notion of moral value, and with regard to rational nature and the order of being taken together, from a more searching examination into what is involved in this harmony with reason of which we have spoken.

If we turn first to the consideration of the notion of moral value, we find (n. 33, 1) that this is immediatelt revealed as the value by which a human act is affected as human and, in consequence, by which the person is affected as a person. But, at every level of being and in every species, the value of the individual, his success, his perfection as a representative of this type and as a member of this species, consists in the correspondance of his activity, of the habits he has acquired, of the aptitudes he possesses, with the requirements that stem from the animating principle which makes him to be a representative of this type of being, a member of this species, that is, with the requirements of his specific nature. Consequently, the moral value of a human being's free actions cannot but be measured by their conformity with the requirements that stem from the animating principle through which he is human, that is, with the requirements of his specific nature as man, his *rational nature*.

This line of thought is similar to that which we have just used in n. 130. This should be in no way surprising. Since reason penetrates our human nature, whatever is reasonable will necessarily be in accordance with our nature. "Man's reason is natural to him; consequently, whatever is contrary to his reason will also be contrary to his nature" [107].

There is, however, a certain difference between the two lines of approach. In n. 130, what we were concerned with was the internal structure of the free, human, act; we are considering this act as proceeding from the human will, which has reason for its immanent rule. Our point of view was psychological or phenomenological. Here, however, our point of view is objective, ontological: the human act is considered as an activity which has its source in a nature whose requirements it has to satisfy so as to be "what it should be".

But note well that the harmony which is involved in the moral value of our actions is a harmony with rational nature *as such*, that is, with this nature inasmuch as it is *not only a nature*. A harmony with this nature considered simply as a nature could be the foundation of no more than a natural value; but, as we have seen, moral value is of a different order. It is present, properly speaking, only at the level of free activity, of which a person is capable because he is not only possessed of a nature, by which his place in the ascending scale of beings is fixed, but because he is also "in a certain sense everything" (n. 13). Consequently, the relationship which is involved in the moral value of our actions is with our rational nature as transcending its finitude, in other words, as not merely a nature [108].

---

[107] St Thomas, *De Malo*, 14, 2 ad 8um. — Cf. *In II Eth.*, bk 2; ed. Pirotta, n. 257.

[108] What is characteristic of a being whose nature is intellectual or spiritual is his capacity to transcend finitude. The adjective: rational can be understood in two senses. In the broad sense, it means the same as intellectual (n. 114). In the restricted sense, it refers to the way in which human beings are "intellectual".

"Reason is, at one and the same time, both reason and possessed of a definite nature. As reason, it is capable of being a cause in a way that is additional to that in which an effect is caused by some natural agent. It is in this way that reason is the source of virtuous activity" [109].

133. – While it is true that the judgment of reason provides the immediate rule for moral guidance, this judgment has itself to be grounded on, and to be the expression of, what is objective. If it is not, it can only be an arbitrary guide. There is an order, an ascending scale (n. 101, 2) in reality, and a complex of essential relationships, both of which bear the impress of the creative Reason and which, far from depending on our reason, impose themselves on it. No matter what the degree of "rightness" or "openness" of our reason, it would be quite incapable, in the absence of an objective order, of guiding us to choose one course of action and to shun another.

But, obviously, if it is to provide the basis for moral judgments, the objective order has to include rational nature. Firstly, because this nature is evidently part of the real order. Secondly, and more particularly, because we cannot be as detached and non-involved in our moral judgments as we can be in our speculative judgments, since what we are judging about are actions which are to be performed or avoided; and these cannot be considered in isolation from the person and, in consequence, from the nature of the person, who makes these judgments and acts upon them. Hence this nature forms part of the objective order; it is included in this order, but only as "structured" through its relationships with the other factors which constitute the objective ground of our moral judgments. Or, perhaps better, insofar as the subject is at the centre of a moral judgment, it is he who, in a sense, is at the centre of the objective order: what is of vital and abiding importance is *his* attitude towards it. — But, what else is the objective order with, at the centre, the spiritual subject whose nature is rational, but this nature "adequately considered", that is, considered in conjunction with the different relationships by which it is affected, since these are co-extensive with the objective

109 St Thomas, *In III Sent.*, d. 33, q. 1, a. 2, qa 1 ad 2um.

order. Precisely because this nature "is in a certain sense every-thing", an adequate consideration of it cannot be separated from the consideration of the Universal which is its "horizon". The realm of reason and rational nature is inseparable from the realm of reality. — This line of reasoning, also, leads us to the conclusion that our rational nature is the basis of our moral judgments.

134. – We are now at the point where we can acknowl-edge that the Thomists are right in making right reason the proximate rule for moral living and that the Suarezians have not erred in insisting that the basis of this rule is our rational nature. Does this mean that both are saying the same thing in different words? Or, if there is more than a verbal difference between them, what is its focal point?

As we have seen, the point at issue centres on the role of reason in morality. Is this role purely *declarative*, as Suarez holds (n. 129), so that the only result of our exercise of reason is that we come to know what the requirements of the objective order are, or has reason a *constitutive* role?

Note carefully what we are not inquiring about: we are not putting the question of whether prior to, and indepen-dently of, our judgments there is an order which provides the ground for our moral judgments: that question has already been settled. What we are asking is whether this order can be defined as moral and accepted as such by our practical reason, without the relationship between it and the judgments of this reason entering into the definition.

Note firstly, as Schiffini [110], points out in disagreeing with Suarez, that our reasonable judgments cannot be isolated from our rational nature; to this they are related as its perfection, since whatever exists, exists in order that it may act in the way that is appropriate to it. We cannot conceive of our nature as rational unless we consider it as oriented towards enabling us to judge reasonably. Consequently, the harmony of an action with rational nature, adequately considered, cannot but in-volve, as the source from which it derives its ultimate meaning, a harmony with the rational judgments of which this nature

[110] *Op. cit.*, n. 61; pp. 101-102.

makes us capable. Hence, it cannot be said that the harmony with rational nature is constituted independently of all reference to these judgments. It is, then, false, and indeed contradictory, to maintain that the sole function of right reason is to make known and to apply the moral rule [111].

In other words, and more briefly: since the activity of our reason is a completion and perfection of our rational nature, the harmony with this nature is completed and perfected by the harmony with that activity. But this means that when we judge reasonably, we do not find the harmony with our nature already completely constituted. Hence, our judgments have their part to play in constituting it.

135. – But we cannot rest content with establishing this. For not only does the harmony with our judgments complete the harmony with our nature, but it confers on this its moral character.

Firstly, let us examine this notion of "harmony with our rational nature". If one wishes to speak of a harmony which is entirely constituted prior to any relationship with a reasonable judgment, so that the only purpose of this is to acknowledge the harmony and make possible a free choice concerning it, this harmony is no more than a "natural" one. An action which is simply in accordance, in this sense, with my nature, is so because it helps to satisfy my natural, human tendencies and appetites, or because, by means of it, I can achieve a higher degree of completion of my nature than I now possess (sense of achievement, of having filled in, to some extent, the emptiness and void that is in me), or because this particular line of action strikes a responsive chord in me. ... But all this can be the ground only of what is *naturally* good, not of what is *morally* good. The fact that our natural appetites are receiving the satisfaction which we crave and that the poverty within our nature is giving way to a richness, the joy that we feel in responding to what appeals to our nature, the fact that a particular action expresses what we are — all this still leaves us within the "physical" or, if one prefers, the ontological zone; and if the role of our reason is limited simply to manifesting

---

[111] *Ib.*

and acknowledging this type of harmony, the moral order has vanished into thin air.

It is only if this natural harmony takes on an absolute character that we enter the moral sphere. For what distinguishes moral value from other values, is its absoluteness (nn. 33, 3; 41). Now, it is only by using our reason that we can grasp that the note of absoluteness is involved in this natural harmony, and we grasp this through recognizing that the natural harmony is itself in harmony with our reason, *as open to what is absolute*; and we recognize this second harmony in the very act of judging, by which and in which we affirm that our reason has a relationship with, and a capacity for, what is absolute (n. 114).

Consequently, without reference to an, at least possible, judgment, there can be no morally valuable actions, no moral order. The harmony of our actions with our nature becomes moral only by being revealed to be in harmony with reason.

When we make the reasonable judgment: "it is morally evil to tell lies", what we are expressing is not simply a relationship which is "written into" the objective situation, nor the conclusion of an objective reflection on the facts (as we are when we say: "telling lies, since it destroys trust, is harmful to society", or "telling lies is harmful to the liar, since it causes him to lose his credit and his reputation"). Over and above this, we are expressing a relationship (in this example, it is a negative one), between "telling lies" and our *reason itself*: we have recognized that, in telling lies, we are acting in a way which does not harmonize with the requirements of reason, but clashes with the law that is intrinsic to it, the law of openness to what transcends one's own particular and restricted preoccupations, one's self-centredness.

What has been said about the harmony of our actions with our rational nature is also applicable where their harmony with the order of reality is concerned. (As we have seen, in n. 133, the realm of rational nature is inseparable from the realm of reality; the realm which opens out to us because of our rational nature is the realm of reality). Here, also, if we abstract from the harmony of our actions with the judgments of our practical reason, all we are left with is a purely ontological harmony — our actions are, in fact, in accordance with reality — which, as such, is not moral. It is true that these judgments are themselves expressions of reality and that this is, accordingly, the norm to which they have to conform; but the normative function of reality can be grasped only by means of the judgments which reveal to us its absoluteness (that it cannot be relative to or conditioned by anything else). In isolation from these judgments, the order of being remains simply a "given", matter-of-fact order.

It is also true that our rational nature, in virtue of its eminent dignity, might appear to possess an absolute value quite independently of all reference to our practical judgments. But, again, how does this dignity come to be revealed except through the exercise of our reason and, primarily, of our practical reason? We judge to be "worthy", in the true sense of the word (worthy of our human dignity), only what we can reasonably approve of, only what measures up to the requirements of our reason and reflects them.

A final point. Does not human nature possess an objective finality quite apart from our recognition that we are reasonably required to act in accordance with it? Doubtless it does; but if this finality is regarded as immanent in the dynamism of our nature, the goal towards which it is directed can be, in consequence, no more than a natural good. Alternatively, this finality may be regarded as constituted by the divine Reason from which it originates; but, in that case, this finality can be the ground of moral value, *as far as we are concerned*, only if we recognize that this Reason is the absolute Value and the source of values. Now, in default of the intuition to which the Ontologists lay claim, the value of the divine Reason can be known by us only through the activity of our own reason, by which we come to appreciate the *supreme reasonableness* of our conformity with the Norm from which our finite reason derives its normative power. (In other words, I understand that to respect and foster this finality is morally good only because I know that I am doing what God wishes me to do; and I know that it is morally good to obey God only through judging that I could never reasonably disobey Him who is the source of my reason). Cf. nn. 136 and 163.

There is, however, a sense — and we have already touched on it in n. 134 — in which it can be said that it is precisely from their harmony with our rational nature that our actions derive their moral value. What this sense is becomes clear if the close relationship between this nature and our rational judgments is kept in mind. For, as we have already noted, we cannot conceive of our nature as rational unless we consider it as oriented towards enabling us to judge reasonably. Now, it is quite clear that the activity towards which we tend because we have judged in this way cannot but be morally good. Hence, the sense in which our rational nature is here spoken of is that of the completion and expression which it receives from our rational judgments. Perhaps there is a certain initial appreciation of this point in Suarez, when he underlines that the harmony of which he is speaking, is with "rational nature as rational and as capable of being guided by right reason" (n. 129). But whatever about Suarez, it is clear that if the moral harmony is with the completion which our nature receives from our rational judgments, that is, the judgments made in accordance with right reason, then this harmony is, in the first place, with reason. It is because what I choose is reasonable that it is in harmony with the completion of my nature which comes from my rational judgments.

Hence, there is a certain reciprocity and complementarity between the harmony of our actions with our nature and their harmony with our reason. What we choose is in accordance with our rational nature only if it is in accordance with our reason, but we cannot judge that it is reasonable unless we likewise judge that it harmonizes with our nature. It is, however, our recognition that this natural harmony is in accordance with our reason which, at one and the same time, perfects (completes) it and transforms it into a moral harmony. If what is being spoken of is the harmony which makes an action to have a moral value, then it is because the morally good action is in accordance with reason that it is in accordance with our rational nature, and not *vice-versa*. The purely natural harmony can, accordingly, be called the necessary material substructure of the harmony with reason.

What has just been said, and the emphasis we have placed on the role of our reasonable judgments in morality, should not be interpreted as if our human nature "adequately considered" (the objective order on which these judgments are grounded), were of itself outside the rational order and received all its intelligibility from the judgments which we make! The very opposite is true, as we have pointed out (n. 133), for this natural order, on which our judgments have to be based under penalty of being arbitrary, is already a rational order, since its origin is the creative, divine Reason whose impress it bears. All that we wish to insist on is that this order is grasped as moral, only through reflecting on it and coming to appreciate its relationship with the right judgments of reason which are themselves related, by their very structure, with what is absolute and, in the final analysis, with the divine Reason (as we are now going to consider in more detail).

136. – But could it not still be maintained that our rational nature, in virtue of its intrinsic dignity, is capable of conferring an absolute value on the actions which are in harmony with it, so that independently of its relationship with our judgments, this harmony is moral?

We have, in fact, already dealt with the objection. The dignity that we possess as human beings is not a datum which is immediately obvious; we have to use our reason and to reflect in order to appreciate it (n. 135). — But let us now probe a little further and ask ourselves what is the source of that eminent, and in a certain fashion, absolute, value of our rational nature.

It certainly is not in that nature considered purely in itself, as one *particular nature* among other particular natures (of animals, of plants etc.), that this source is to be found. Why should the value of our will, which is endowed with an openness to what is universal, depend on its relationship with, and attitude towards, this particular good? It is quite true we necessarily will to be, and to be more fully, but as long as that necessity remains on the plane of the dynamism which is common to every nature, it does not yet possess any moral character.

Our rational nature derives its eminent and absolute value from that openness towards what is Absolute which belongs to it as rational. Absolute of truth and of value: under the first aspect it is the Ideal and "horizon" of our speculative intelligence and under the second aspect it is the Ideal and horizon of our practical reason and our liberty [112]. As such, it communicates its own dignity to our rational nature and, in so doing, it elevates the harmony of our actions with our rational nature to the moral level. Note well, then, that man's pre-eminent dignity does not primarily spring from his capacity to know the world or, as Marx requires of him, to transform it: it resides above all in his ability to acknowledge, and to respond to, what is of value. It is only by acting in this way that he conducts himself as "homo sapiens". In other words — a point which Kant has emphasized — the moral value of our actions can be said to spring from their conformity with our human nature only if we presuppose that this nature is made to act morally; and this amounts to saying that to appeal to human

---

[112] *Essai*, n. 130; pp. 312-315.

nature cannot really answer the question which is here being asked; all it does is to indicate a factor — and an important one — which is involved in the answer.

Consequently, the harmony of our actions with our rational nature takes on an absolute value (so that it is capable of providing the objective basis of our practical judgments), only because it involves a harmony (of our actions and of the objects we choose) with the Ideal of value towards which that nature, as rational, is open and oriented, towards which, one could say, it *exists*.

Now — and this is the crucial point — the harmony of our actions with the Ideal is the same as their harmony with the judgments which are true to this Ideal, that is, the judgments of right reason, and it is known through this latter harmony, in the very act of judging.

Note that the practical Ideal is not presented to us in an intuition or in some other objective fashion. It is not possible, then, to make a direct comparison between the Ideal and the object we are choosing or the action we propose to perform, so as to discover if these are in harmony, or at variance, with it. In and by the activity of our reason and will, we direct ourselves towards (and "take our bearing from") this Ideal, not, however, as the known object of that activity but as its horizon, or better, its ultimate point of reference. In judging and coming to his decision about some particular course of action, the human subject, in the measure in which he has attained to an enlightened sincerity, has an awareness of his *"existence-towards"* something or rather, as we shall see, someone, from whom his value and dignity as a human being springs. (Cf. *A Man for all Seasons*, the play based on the life of Sir Thomas More: "When a man takes an oath, he's holding his own self in his hands. Like water... and if he opens his fingers *then* — he needn't hope to find himself again"). If, then, the harmony between the Ideal and what we are doing (as well as what we are choosing), needs to be grasped, this can be done only through grasping the harmony of the latter with the openness of our reason to its own Ideal, in other words, the harmony of our actions (and the object of these actions) with the judgments in which our reason is faithful to its own law, its own finality.

Consequently, what directly and immediately confers an absolute character on the harmony of our actions with our rational nature, is their harmony with right reason. Hence, it is this also which makes the former harmony to be moral.

In other words and more briefly: the value which lies in acting in accordance with our rational nature is moral, only if that nature is already regarded as the immediate source of moral value; and it is such only in the sense that it makes us capable of judging and deciding in accordance with the finality of our reason (in accordance with "right" reason), and provides the ground on which these judgments and decisions have to be based. The moral value of our actions is, in consequence, directly and immediately derived from their conformity with the judgments of right reason.

It is not, then, correct to say: it is because our nature is a rational nature that it is good to act in accordance with our reason; on the contrary: it is because we cannot reasonably disregard the requirements of that nature that it is *morally* good to respect them. However, since reason is an element of our nature, to act in accordance with reason is not only morally but also naturally good; it is *good-for-us*.

137. – We can now bring this long investigation to a conclusion. It has become clear in what the moral value of our actions essentially consists, namely, in the harmony of our actions and their objects with right reason, with the judgments which are faithful to reason itself and which are open towards its Ideal. This harmony involves a harmony with our rational nature as such, but it is the harmony with reason which gives to this latter its moral character.

The relationship with the Absolute and the Ideal makes clear and precise the sense in which the rational action can be said to be the moral action. To act in accordance with right reason, to perform genuinely rational actions, is by no means the same as simply ensuring that these will preserve a structural consistency or will continue to manifest a distinctive "style": the most that is involved in these is the logic of human living or an aesthetic approach to life; what they do not involve is the morality of human living and a moral approach to life. Neither, as we have seen, is acting in accordance with right reason simply the same as acting in accordance with Kantian universal norms (nor, for that matter, with the principles of the Thomistic natural moral law). The moral action is the rational action in the sense of being the action in which we live *our openness to what is Absolute*. In the next chapter, we shall turn to the task of throwing further light on what this means.

We have not discussed the opinion which identifies moral value with acting in a way that leads us towards our final end (n. 128). Let us now briefly do so. "Final end" could be understood in the sense of our final *subjective* end, which is nothing other than beatitude; if it is so understood, our evaluation of Eudaemonism indicates to us the evaluation which has to be made of this present opinion (nn. 71-73). Final end could also be understood in the sense of our final *objective* end, which is to glorify Him who has made us; but while it is undeniably true that to glorify God is what is of most consequence in a human life, how do *we* come to know and appreciate that this is so? Is it through judging that to live our lives in this spirit is in conformity with the Ideal of our practical reason? Hence, it is not the relationship of our actions with the glory of God that answers our questions about the norm and essence of moral value, but their relationship with our right judgments. (As we have already noted, in n. 133, we cannot properly appreciate the moral order unless we keep in mind that we ourselves, as reasonable beings, are, in one sense, at its centre). The relationship of our actions with His glory is the heart of the matter as far as God himself is concerned; but we who are not God, can appreciate this only by starting from ourselves and exercising our reason. Moreover, it is not only by acting morally that we give glory to God; consequently this, our final objective end, could not, on this score also, provide the answer to our questions. (If God is glorified in ways other than that of morally good activity, then the value of that activity cannot essentially depend on its relationship with God's glory). Another possible sense in which final end could be understood is that of the connatural development which man achieves through his activity; but this is only another way of expressing the view that the moral value of our actions springs from their conformity with our human nature.

There is, however, a sense in which the relationship of our actions with our "final end" does define their moral value; what this sense is we shall see in n. 141.

CHAPTER THREE

DEDUCTIVE APPROACH TO THE SAME PROBLEM, FOLLOWED BY SOME CLARIFICATION OF WHAT IS MEANT BY THE IDEAL OF OUR PRACTICAL REASON

I. DEDUCTIVE APPROACH TO THE MORAL ORDER.

138. – Our inquiry, up to this point, has been conducted along phenomenological and dialectical lines. As a result of it, we now appreciate that the only interpretation of moral value which is entirely faithful to the data which prompted our investigation, is that which identifies the essence of this value with acting in accordance with the judgments of right reason.

In the entire course of this inquiry, we have never had any doubt that we are already involved in the moral order, that obligation is a feature of this order and that we are subject to the authority of our conscience in our decisions. But, even though there is ample evidence for our certainty on these points (n. 46), this lack of doubt might, nonetheless, be regarded as naive and even arbitrary by a sceptical and hard-headed questioner. Such a critic might pose the question of whether, in submitting to the authority of our conscience, we were not submitting to an illusion, a noble one it is true, but an illusion for all that.

But the possibility of even raising this question is excluded, once the moral value of our actions is shown to lie in their harmony with the judgments which are true to the finality of our reason. Since such judgments are characterized by their absoluteness, nothing can be more solidly certain — at least in the order of natural knowledge — than what we approve of because we recognize it to be in conformity with the requirements of our reason. Consequently, the progress of our investigation has led us from a "faith" in (or rather from an uncritical and far less reflective certainty about), the moral order and moral value, to a certainty which has grown from our reflection on the data and our prolonged attempts to understand them. By bringing to light what the moral value of our actions essentially consists in, we have by the same stroke arrived at a far deeper certainty about this value and the moral order. We have left behind the phenomenological order, in the sense that we have advanced from description of the data which call for explanation, towards a fuller understanding of them.

We could, however, have set about our task in a way directly opposite to the one we have actually taken, namely, the way of reflecting on the very structure of our practical reason, so that, in consequence, we are led to an understanding of moral value and a critical certainty concerning the moral order. This is the approach which we are now going to take.

But note at once that we cannot arrive at this understanding of moral value, if we try to deduce it simply through a logical analysis of the structure of our practical reason, considered in isolation from our moral experience (as we would be doing if, for example, we simply considered the practical activity of our reason which is involved in building houses, constructing bridges etc.). Hence, it is by no means our intention to begin our journey from a non-moral starting point, in the fond expectation of arriving at a moral terminus; what we wish to do is to show how moral value is necessarily involved in the activity of our practical reason and, as such, is at the very heart of the claims which our conscience makes on us. (Not only is there a necessary connection between our practical reason and moral value, but the full "practicality" of this reason is revealed only through it and by it, cf. n. 1).

139. – Our reason, as we have said, is characterized by the absoluteness of its judgments. No matter what judgment we make, no matter how particular and contingent its object, an element of necessity and universality is involved. Even in affirmations of what is relative, this absolute character is present.

This applies not merely to our speculative reason (or better, to the speculative function of our reason), but also to our practical and evaluative reason (or better, to the practical and evaluative function of our reason). In these latter judgments, too, something absolute is present. An important distinction has, however, to be introduced now.

Observe, firstly, that all our judgments are made in relation to certain norms. In our speculative judgments, these norms will be, on the one hand, the basic principles of speculative knowledge (the principles of identity, non-contradiction, sufficient reason etc.), and on the other hand — if we are judging whether something is or is not a fact — the appropriate experience. — In our practical and evaluative judgments, the norm will be the harmony of a particular action with our own natural tendencies and aspirations (n. 21). This harmony can, however, be considered under several aspects.

1. Simply as a harmony with the empirical dimension of our being, that is, a harmony with ourselves insofar as we are but one kind of material being among all the other kinds of material beings that are in the world. In this context, what will be judged good will be what helps to preserve and promote our health, what satisfies our desire to see, to touch, to taste etc., what calms us at times of anxiety and disquiet, what relaxes us when we become over-tense, what contributes to our mental balance etc. Such a good, as is obvious, is of itself, no more than a natural good; it is good simply in relation to the material, empirical dimension of our being. Nothing more absolute is involved in our acknowledgment of what is good in this sense, than is involved in our acknowledgment that something is a fact, or appears to us in a particular light, or that some particular physical law is operative in the universe. It is absolutely true that, to a person with a sweet tooth, a present of a box of chocolates would be very acceptable. But, while the affirmation is absolute, the value which is affirmed is relative. Value judgments of this kind are made in relation to tendencies and aspirations which are not ours as reason-endowed beings (whether we recognize them to be such or whethetr, as more often happens, we do not).

2. There can also be a harmony between our actions, and ourselves as reason-endowed beings. Where such a harmony exists, our value judgments are made in relation to the inclinations which are in us because we possess the gift of reason. We are not now judging the value of what we choose, in relation to any other finality than that of our reason. But, here also, we

have to make a distinction, for our reason, in its turn, can be considered either as a capacity which has definite, fixed limitations (as an element of our human nature it shares in the limitations and finitude of that nature, cf. n. 132, end), or as a capacity which enables us to transcend — but not to escape from — the finitude to which we are naturally subject, a capacity, in other words, through which we are radically open towards what is Absolute.

As an element of our human nature, there is in our reason a tendency towards what is good-for-it, towards what will satisfy it. (A similar tendency is operative in the nature of every finite being). What will be judged good in this context, will be what brings us *satisfaction on the rational level*, for example, the joy that follows on an intellectual discovery and the acquisition of fresh knowledge, aesthetic pleasure, the contentment we experience in exercising our talents and abilities, the sense of victory and exultation that is consequent upon successful achievement. ... These are no mean values and, in their more elevated forms, they border on those which are moral and are, indeed, coloured by them; but despite their nearness to the moral sphere, they still remain outside it. They belong, of themselves, to the realm of the pleasurable, or perhaps better, to use St Anselm's term, the advantageous; it is because they help to satisfy our natural desires whose horizon (since our nature is spiritual), is beatitude, that they are good).

Values of this kind can be classified with those which, as we have already outlined in n. 24, 2, lie between economic and eudaemonist values, on the one hand, and moral value on the other. They can be called intermediate or mixed values, because in them a quasi-moral element mingles with a natural element.

It is because of its relation with the Absolute towards which it opens us, and whose impress it stamps on our judgments, that our reason enables us to transcend the finitude to which we are naturally subject. When, then, in our value judgments we judge in a *genuinely reasonable* way — when our judgments are true to the finality of our reason and are, in consequence, *right* — we relate what we are judging about, in the very exercise of our judgment, not now to the goals of our other tendencies, nor even simply to the goals towards which we tend because our reason is an element of our human nature, but to the goal, or rather, the Ideal, of our reason in its open dimension — the practical Ideal, the horizon of our will insofar as it is a rational power, *a Value which is absolutely valuable*. The Ideal is valuable simply because it is the Ideal, because of its own intrinsic perfection, and not in relation to some other goal. If its value were relative in this way, it would not be the Ideal of our practical reason in its open dimension, nor of our will as a rational power, but of a reason and will at the service of a tendency towards goals other than their own, so that, in consequence, they would not be functioning in accordance with their own proper finality.

Consequently, what is in harmony with our value judgments when these are made in accordance with our openness towards what is Absolute, will be absolute in a unique sense. In our acknowledgment of such values, something absolute is involved, not merely in the sense in which it is involved in any and every affirmation, but in the sense that *what is affirmed* — the value in question — involves, by its very structure, what is absolute; in other words, the value that is acknowledged, is acknowledged as being in harmony with the Absolute to which our reason is open. To deepen one's appreciation of this point, reflect on the two judgment: "this food is good", and: "loyalty is good". I make the latter judgment not simply because I find loyalty emotionally satisfying or pleasurable, or because it brings me a measure of the rational satisfaction for which I crave, but because I have a rational appreciation that it is desirable for its own sake, that I *ought* to be faithful to my friends and dependants. My loyal action is my response not simply to a natural and subjective requirement (the benefits that loyalty will bring me), but to a requirement which is objective, in that it has its source in my reason, a requirement which cannot be reduced to a relative status. When our judgments are "right", we cannot but acknowledge that our reason is superior to our other tendencies, and that its true dignity lies in being open to what is Absolute, rather than in being a capacity which, as an element of our human nature, has definite, fixed limitations. We cannot, then, fail to acknowledge that the source of all its value springs from this Absolute, so that, in consequence

— always on condition that our judgments are right — we cannot but judge that the values which are in harmony with these judgments, prevail unconditionally over all others.

Now, these values constitute the order of moral value. To say that a particular action is morally good (or evil), is the same as saying that it is in harmony (or disharmony) with a Value which is absolutely valuable, so that, in consequence, it has to be approved of (or condemned) by every reasonable subject who judges reasonably. Hence, precisely because I choose to act in this way, I am deserving of the respect and appreciation (or condemnation etc.) of all such subjects; and there is no power in heaven or on earth which can make their judgment to be otherwise. ...

140. – We now wish, in conclusion, to reply to some difficulties, and to forestall some possible confusion.

To say that moral value is the properly human value, the value which lies in acting in accordance with our rational nature as such, is not the same as reducing it to a relative status, as if it were a value only in relation to and in dependence on that nature, whose dignity it reflected. On the contrary, as we have seen (n. 136), it is because it is a nature which is open to the Absolute that our nature has such an eminent dignity and has a right to be respected.

We would, obviously, be involved in a vicious circle, if we claimed that we were *defining* moral value in relation to our human nature, since this could fulfil the role assigned to it in the definition, only in virtue of its openness to the Absolute of value. (In other words, it would first have to be regarded as a "moral nature", so that moral value could then be defined in relation to it). But we are not attempting to do this. To make the point here which has already been made, it is not a question of *explaining* moral value in terms of what is *non-moral*, or of *reducing* it to something more basic and primary. As with every other form of good, the moral good is a primary datum which, just as it cannot be reduced to what is non-moral, cannot, either, be deduced by means of a conceptual analysis [1]. What

---

[1] "Our conclusion is that the moral good cannot be defined other than by this tautology: the moral good is what conscience recognizes to be good", Th.

we *are* attempting to do, is to clarify the notion of moral value, by correctly interpreting the data within ourselves which call for understanding (the data of moral consciousness); further, we are attempting to unravel the connections between this and other values, as well as to discover its ultimate foundation.

Note, also, that the absolute of Value to which we relate (in the very act of judging), the actions that we are evaluating, is not the same as moral value inasmuch as this connotes "blood, sweat, tears and toil": it is *the Ideal of our practical reason*, whose likeness is deepened in us and towards which we approach, to the extent to which we make the effort to do what is of moral value. Through the activity of our reason, we appreciate this Ideal as what is perfect in the rational order (we appreciate that it represents perfection in this order). But keep well in mind that it is not from the subject whom it brings to perfection that this Ideal derives its value; on the contrary, it is the subject who derives all his value from his relation to the perfection of the Ideal, the end towards which he is radically orientated. Cf. n. 141.

The Ideal of practical reason holds, accordingly, in our analysis of ethics, the same place as happiness holds in Aristotelian ethics; this latter, for the Philospher, is more excellent than virtue and is deserving not only of praise (as is virtue), but of honour (as are the gods)[2]. But note that the Ideal is in alignment with our moral activity, whereas happiness, simply as happiness, is not.

141. – It is in this sense (and in this sense only), of "end", that one can equate the moral value of our actions and their harmony with our "last end". We have shown that this equation cannot be made when our "last end" is understood in the sense of "beatitude" (nn. 71-73 and 137). But the sense in which we speak of "end" here, is not the eudaemonist sense of the good which satisfies our natural desires. What we are now speaking of is the Ideal to which we have to conform ourselves in the decisions of which our rational nature makes us capable,

---

de Régnon, *Etudes de théologie positive sur la Sainte Trinité*, Paris, 1892-1898, t. III, 2e p., p. 336. — In place of: conscience, we would prefer to say: practical reason.

[2] *Nicom. Eth.*, I, 12, 1101 b 10 - 1102 a 4.

if we are to be "what we should be" and merit the approval of all reasonable beings.

Note carefully that we can speak of "end", as well as of "perfection", in two senses [3]. In one sense, it refers to the good whose possession brings completion to the subject, enables him to realize all his potentialities, satisfies his natural tendencies etc. Considered in this way, the end is the same as the good which is "desirable", because it can perfect the one who desires it (n. 17); as such, it is the object of our "need" (amor concupiscentiae in the language of the Scholastics), or of our "friendships of utility", both of which are the manifestation on the personal and spiritual level of that drive towards completion which is present in all finite beings, that is, they are an expression of the movement from what is potential to what is actual, which is to be found at every level of finite being [4]. — Likewise, "perfection" can be understood in relation to, and as centred on, the subject as "perfectible", as *his* perfection, and thereby sharing in his unique value.

In this context, the true end, the end for which the subject acts, is the subject himself. But let us not label this as egoistic: what is here in question is a natural structure, which is not in our power to alter and so cannot be in any way the measure of our moral worth. What does measure this worth are the free decisions by which we channel and direct this natural desire for completion and for the perfect realization of our potentialities (nn. 73 and 286).

But "end" can also refer to the good towards which the subject freely orientates himself and on which he centres his life, not so as to fill the void that is in him, but because if what this good is — because of *its* perfection and intrinsic lovableness, because of the value which it already has and to which the subject's positive attitude cannot add, any more than his negative attitude can take from it. Considered in this way, the end is the same as the good defined as "perfect"; it is the object of our "love of friendship" — a love of "appreciation" and self-giving — which is the expression on the personal and

---

[3] *Essai*, n. 31, pp. 71-73 (on the end); n. 47, pp. 88-89 (on perfection).

[4] St Thomas, *Summa Theol.*, I-II, 27, 3. Cf. *Essai*, nn. 31 and 133; pp. 71-73 and 319-320.

spiritual level of the relationship that exists between one being and another insofar as each is actual and does not still stand in need of completion[5]. — In this fresh perspective, what is "perfect" is revealed as communicating its value to the "perfectible" subject, who has his meaning only in relation to it and exists only for it, in the same way as what is potential exists only by and for what is actual. It is in this sense that the Ideal of our practical reason can be referred to as our last *end*: it is supremely lovable simply because of what it is, and independently of what it brings to us.

II. FURTHER CLARIFICATION OF WHAT IS MEANT BY THE IDEAL OF PRACTICAL REASON.

142. – Some readers may feel that all the Ideal requires of us is that we act on maxims that could be willed as universal laws, so that the position here defended is really not very different from that of Kant. Hence the need for some further clarification which will bring to light the positive character of the Ideal and show more clearly what fidelity to it demands of us. But note well that we are not yet concerned with the question of the ultimate foundation of the Ideal; our aim here is simply to deepen our understanding of its nature.

143. – The point has already been made that the Ideal of our practical reason is what is perfect in the order of rationality, the perfect realization of rational (or spiritual) activity. Hence, in order to arrive at a deeper understanding of its nature, we have first to consider what exactly this activity consists in; once we have done that, we shall be in a position to have a better understanding of what its perfection is[6].

Now, it is clear (particularly to anyone who is familiar with Thomistic principles), that it is only a person (spiritual subject) who is capable of "receiving" other beings, and, in particular, other persons, without subordinating them to himself. He can receive them into himself through appreciating

---

[5] St Thomas, *ib.*
[6] On what follows, see the *Essai*, nn. 132-136; pp. 318-327.

them for what they are; he is capable of responding to their perfection with the perfection which is now his; he is not limited to treating them as means to his own further development and completion. In other words, a person is capable of welcoming others in a way that is not an instance of that movement from what is potential to what is actual, which exists in all finite beings, but is an expression of the relationship that exists between one being and another to the extent to which each is actual and has not yet to realize its potentialities. Again, the person's mode of existence "in himself" is not simply at the level of that identity with itself, that physical presence to itself, which is common to every being on the face of the earth, but is at the level of knowledge, appreciation, and possession of himself; his existence "in himself" involves the mode of existence which is proper to a being who exists "for himself", that is, a being to whom there is an "immaterial" dimension, so that in consequence, he possesses himself in a way that is not possible to a being who lacks this further "non-physical" dimension. — In order to appreciate better the point which has to be made in the next paragraph, keep in mind that all activity which occurs at the "natural" (non-cognitional) level of being, necessarily involves a transition from what is potential to what is actual. What was only possible becomes actual, a perfection which was lacking is acquired through activity.... But nothing of this kind is necessarily involved in cognitional and, above all, in intellectual activity. Thought, in its pure essence, is simply a plenitude, a perfection; even though it is true that *our* thinking involves a process, this is not because we are *thinking*, but because we are *human* thinkers. The thinking subject does not, as such, receive any addition to his natural being from the object which he knows, nor is this object physically affected by the fact that it is known. Knowledge, of itself, does not involve the transition from emptiness to fullness, from poverty to riches; what is essential to it is the relationship between the perfection which the subject has as "knower" and the perfection which the object has as "known".

Now, at that level of existence of which we have been speaking, a dynamism is operative which is not operative at lower levels, namely, the dynamism of *rational* appetite. The

fundamental activity of this appetite is love, under its two
forms of desire and friendship. (It is this latter which is love in
the truest sense of the word). Desire, as we have seen, is the
expression of the drive towards completion that exists in all
finite beings, while friendship is the expression, on this same
personal level, of the harmony and rapport that exists between
one being and another insofar as each is perfect and complete
of its kind (nn. 17; 141). In other words, desire is the form
which the natural dynamism, that is common to all finite
beings, assumes at the spiritual level of finite being: desire is
the prolongation of this dynamism on the spiritual level: the
same pattern is still operative. Love of friend for friend, on the
contrary, is spiritual, rational, through and through. By such a
love the spiritual subject is revealed, not now as a being who is
intent on receiving what he lacks, but as a being who out of
the fullness that is his, is open and welcoming, who is in a
certain sense infinite.

But just as it is characteristic of a person to receive other
persons into himself by his knowledge of them, by "allowing
them to be what they are", as Heidegger writes, without
pretending that they are other than they are (which would be
to receive them in a distorted way), and without transforming
them in his own mind into the persons he would like them to
be, so also is it characteristic of him to be one with other
persons through welcoming them into himself by an authentic
and self-forgetful love; and his love will be of this kind — will
be genuine and disinterested — only if he wills that they
should exist as themselves and for themselves, so that he is not
at all concerned to use them for the attainment of his own
ends, or to impose on them his personal ideals.

Those whom I love as my friends, or with whom I have person-
to-person relationship, have to be similar to me in nature, that is,
they have to be human, or rather, spiritual; as St Thomas expresses it,
likeness is the cause of love[7]. But note that it is to the person of the
other that my love is directed, not to the likeness to me that he has.
This likeness is certainly required, but it is not this which moves us
to be friendly towards one another. We act in this way because each
appreciates the value and dignity of the other — even though we

---

[7] St Thomas, *ib.*

could not have this appreciation if we were not both "alike", through being situated at the same level of being (possessed of the same nature).

144. – The perfection, or perfect realization, of rational activity which we have called the Ideal of our practical reason, has already revealed itself to us as worthy to be loved simply because of what it is, just as what is morally valuable, of which the Ideal is the summit, is to be loved (n. 141). Now, at this further stage of our investigation, it becomes clear that what this perfection consists in, or that what is perfect in the rational order, is love (in which justice as preparatory to love and as the condition of its growth and permanence, is included).

To act justly towards another is to acknowledge in practice that he is on the same level of existence as you yourself, that you enjoy no privilege in regard to what is his (nn. 195-198). Between you and him there is, accordingly, a relationship of the type that exists between one being and another insofar as each is actual, as opposed to a relationship of the type which necessarily involves a movement from what is potential to what is actual; you are not treating him as a mere means to the attainment of your ends, nor are you making use of him to obtain what you lack. But to be a friend to another requires more than this of you: a friend is not content simply to refrain from interfering in the will-to-be-and-to-be-more-fully of the one he loves: he positively accepts this and co-operates with it, so that the other may become the person he is capable of becoming. Love seeks to do more than not place barriers in the way of the other's development as a person: it is willing to help knock down the barriers that stand in the way of that development.

But when we say that the perfection of rational activity consists in love, this should not be interpreted to mean that others, as such, occupy a privileged position in the moral order; simply as others, there is no reason why they should be so regarded (n. 81)[8]. The love of which we are here speaking in no way excludes the subject himself; on the contrary, it is concerned with him in a very special way. For it is only reason-

---

[8] According to Scheler, love for the other as other, and consequently as "not-I", involves "resentment" towards myself, *L'homme du ressentiment*, pp. 124-127.

able that a person should make a special effort to appreciate,
and to guide on the right path, the one whom he has a unique
opportunity of influencing for good and for whom he has a
unique responsibility.

But note that just as the presence to himself which a
person enjoys when he is thinking, inquiring, judging, differs
immensely from the merely physical presence to itself that a
being which simply exists "in itself" possesses, and differs
greatly also from the presence to himself which the person
possesses when he is not thinking etc., but merely ex-
periencing and "vegetating" (even though both these types of
presence are required as its foundation), so also the moral
love which a person has for himself differs immensely from
the tendency towards completion which is at the heart of
every finite being, and also from that spontaneous love of
himself which is but the manifestation at the level of spiritual
activity of this ubiquitous drive towards completion (even
though this moral love, in its turn, is grafted onto both of
these tendencies). What effects this difference where both our
presence to ourselves and our love of ourselves is concerned,
is a relation with what is Absolute; in both instances, this
plays a mediatory role — as the Absolute of truth on the one
hand and as the Absolute of value on the other — not
however as an object which we intuit and contemplate, but as
the ultimate point, the horizon, towards which we are
tending, and in relation to which this higher form, not only
of presence, but also of love, becomes possible (n. 136). To
love ourselves morally is to love ourselves in the way that our
reason requires of us; and what this requires of us is that we
appreciate and rejoice in, not only the value that we possess as
human beings, but also the value that lies in that very
appreciation and joy. This is not to say that our spontaneous
and "unmediated" love of ourselves ought to be uprooted —
an impossible task anyway. This love is natural and infra-
moral and, hence, there is nothing at all blameworthy about
it: considered ontologically, it is good. But it needs to be
animated, channelled and transfigured by our reason; to be
subordinated more and more to a love that is spiritual and
authentically human, but of which it nonetheless remains the
ever-present condition and groundwork.

Even though other people are not entitled to any privileges simply because they are "not-I", it is, however, true that where they are concerned, we can distinguish more easily between the spiritual love of friendship and a purely natural, spontaneous love of ourselves. It is easier to love in them the value to which the love of friendship is a response. But just as our natural love of ourselves conditions our love for others (to love others as ourselves has meaning only on the supposition that we love ourselves), so also does our love for others help to spiritualize, humanize and purify that natural love. Purified in this way, our natural love will, in its turn, impart a new purity and unselfishness to our love for others, so that these two loves will always affect one another by their reciprocal action and reaction [9].

145. – What has been written should help to make clearer what is meant by the Ideal and, in consequence, should deepen our understanding and appreciation of moral value. But does it now follow that, in company with a good number of our contemporaries (n. 75, end), we have to identify this value with what fosters intersubjective relationships and to acknowledge that its norm lies in the communion of person with person, the dialogue of mind with mind? [10]. Now, it is very obvious that such a position is not subject to the criticisms which have been made of altruism, utilitarianism, sociological ethics etc. (nn. 81-90), since the goal at which it is aiming is entirely in accord with the dignity of the spiritual subject. Nonetheless, the value of this goal is derived from that of the persons who are aiming at it, so that, in consequence, it cannot answer the question: on what does their value as person depend? The gift of what one is can have moral value only because one is a spiritual subject; a dog, too, gives itself,

---

[9] E. Weil makes clear, although in a somewhat different perspective and in perhaps too absolute a fashion, the role of the other in rectifying one's love of self: (Kant did not appreciate that one's duty to oneself) "can be grasped and made real only by the mediation of one's duty towards others: my duty towards myself, in view of my own happiness, is to do my duty towards all men, for it is only through contact with them that the question of duty towards myself can present itself; only in this contact is the primary separation between the arbitrary and the universal effected", *La philosophie morale*, p. 115.

[10] "The moral good is to be found in the relation between one will and another", L. Lavelle, *Traité des valeurs*, II, p. 29.

insofar as it can, but all it has to give is a canine existence ... the communion of persons is of such value precisely because it is *persons* who are united and not a host of termites ... What radically defines a person is not his relationship with some finite and contingent "Thou", but his openness to what is Absolute and Universal, from which he derives his wonderful dignity [11].

Moreover, what are person-to-person relationships but the way in which oneness between those who share the same spiritual nature is achieved, so that, in consequence, this nature is completed, perfected and unified as a specific or generic nature common to many individual subjects. (These subjects may belong to the same species, as do human beings, or to different species so that they form only a generic community, as do the angels in St Thomas' opinion). Humanity will fully exist as humanity only when each human being is fully accepted and acknowledged by all. ... Since, then, there is moral value in fostering a union of this kind only because of the dignity possessed by beings whose nature is spiritual, this value is ultimately dependent on the Value from which their dignity flows.

Even though moral value cannot be identified with what fosters intersubjective relationships, our attempts to bring about such relationships are morally valuable, for to encourage union among those who all exist for the same Ideal cannot but be in conformity with that Ideal. One could say that this Ideal lies *in the direction* in which the person orientates himself when his attitude towards others is open and when he welcomes them with a love that is spiritual and, in consequence, worthy of a human being. Just as beatitude is the horizon of desire, so is the Ideal the horizon of love.

146. – Let us summarize briefly. Since the Ideal of our practical reason is the perfection, the perfect realization, of activity that is on the spiritual or rational level, the highest expression of this Ideal in our lives and the surest indication that we are responding positively to it, are to be found in the activity that manifests, in the highest degree, our spiritual and

---

[11] *Essai*, nn. 94 and 135; pp. 224-226 and 323-325.

rational character. Now, this character is never better revealed than in that openness to others, which authentic love requires. Consequently, it is through love of this kind, the love of friendship and charity, the disinterested and self-forgetful gift of ourselves, that we best express the Ideal in our lives; by remaining open to others in genuine love we have the surest guarantee that the Ideal will ever continue to be the horizon of our activity.

147. – It should now be rather obvious how much our analysis differs from that of Kant. For him, reason is the "autonomous" source of values; it has no norm or measure other than itself. What has here been proposed, on the contray, is that we recognize ("athematically") that our practical value judgments are measured and regulated by an Ideal, an absolute Value, which is not presented as the object of these judgments — we do not have an intuition of it — but to which they are related, implicitly and in virtue of their own finality, in the very act of going beyond, or transcending, values that are relative (cf. n. 139). This is the Value to which, by the very structure of our reasonable judgments, we relate the possible objects of choice which confront us.

It is only if "reason" is understood in the all-embracing sense, in which the divine Reason is also included, that its total autonomy in the moral order can be maintained. In that sense, it would indeed be true that reason could receive its law from reason itself, so that it would be pointless to search for the source of the moral law outside the sphere of reason (just as it is entirely true that being, understood in the all-embracing sense in which the divine Being is included, can have no source other than itself).

Moreover, according to Kant, to judge reasonably about what we should do, is to judge that we can, without contradiction, will that the maxim on which we act become a universal law; conformity with the "form" of the law, which is its universality, is the norm of reasonable judgments. According to our analysis, to judge reasonably about our actions is to relate them to a standard or norm which discloses their moral value positively and intrinsically and which, in consequence, from this point of view at least, is not a purely formal norm; it does tell us what kind of positive actions we have to perform if we are to live morally; it has a content which is morally valuable. (Kant's "universalizing" approach, as we have seen, n. 121, is devoid of "value-content", whereas in our analysis the love of friendship is at the very heart of rational activity and marks its highest point: the reasonable person is "a man for others", while the unreasonable person is the one who refuses to be open and welcoming). The Ideal of practical reason cannot be interpreted in a merely negative way, as if all that were required of us in order to live in accordance with it were to restrain and keep in check our egoistic and pleasure-loving tendencies. In reality, what living in accordance with the Ideal above all requires of us is something positive, namely, that we be faithful to the radical openness, whose horizon is the Ideal, which we possess as spiritual subjects, and which we best express in our lives by a love for others that is thorough and unfeigned. Love is no less positive than is reality and, in consequence, the attitude which responding to the Ideal requires of us is a positive one. It is, however, true that there cannot but be a negative aspect to our love for others. Saying "yes" to the absolute value that we acknowledge in them, will inevitably involve a "no" to the unruly elements that, some-what like the poor, we have always within ourselves. (But note that a negative aspect is involved not only in our present context, but whenever we speak of what is "spiritual", for example, when we are seeking to understand our intellect and will, which are "non-material" capacities).

148. – But does it not seem that in making the value of human beings, of existing persons, to be dependent on an ideal Value, we are leaving ourselves open to the charge of idealism? We have been insisting that this Value is not founded on the value of the human person but that, on the contrary, the human person derives his dignity from this Value and that it is only in virtue of his relationship with it that he is worthy of love. Consequently, we seem to be suggesting that there is an ideal world of Values, which is somehow superior to the human person, and that his reason, while it is firmly planted in one world, mediates to him this ideal world to which it is open.

We frankly admit that there is a certain resemblance between our position and what Plato has written about the idea of the Good. Indeed, was it not precisely in order to throw light on the true nature of morality that the theory of the ideas was first introduced? But if every affirmation of a primacy — no matter in what sense — of the ideal and intelligible order, over what is empirical and contingent, is to be labelled "idealist", then every philosophy which seeks to rise to a higher than empirical level, has to be so labelled. But this is not what is ordinarily meant by the term. A philosopher can be called an idealist in the proper sense of the word, only if he stops short at the affirmation of the primacy of the ideal order, in place of going on to acknowledge that this cannot be regarded as a world apart, self-contained and self-sufficient, but requires a real foundation — a foundation that transcends what is empirical and contingent.

149. – Moreover, it simply is not possible to stop short at the point we have reached and not go on to seek the foundation for the Ideal in the real order. Our affirmation of an order of truths, essences, laws etc., does not clash with and cancel out our radical affirmation of what exists and which alone *is* in the full sense; for truth would be reduced to nothingness and would be, in consequence, not truth, if it were not grounded and established on what exists. In the same way, our affirmation of the Value should not clash with and cancel out the immediate evidence which we have of the eminent dignity of the human person. In consequence, we are faced with an antinomy — or apparently so, at least. On the one hand, "person" represents the highest possible form of existence; personal beings are at the summit of being [12]. On the other hand, persons seem to derive their dignity from their relationship with an impersonal Ideal. Hence the need for a further investigation, so that by discovering the real or ontological foundation of the Ideal, we may resolve the antinomy. This will be our aim in the following book.

---

[12] "Person signifies what is most perfect in the entire universe", St Thomas, *Summa Theol.*, I, 29, 3.

BOOK TWO

THE FOUNDATION WHICH THE
MORAL ORDER HAS IN THE REAL ORDER

CHAPTER FOUR

THE ULTIMATE FOUNDATION AND
SUPREME NORM OF MORAL VALUE

150. – The course of our inquiry has led ut to situate the moral norm in the judgments in which our reason is faithful to itself, that is, faithful to its openness to the Ideal, and this result, while it has solved some problems, has raised a fresh one. How can the Ideal be the source and measure of the value of persons, since the undeniable evidence of the eminent dignity which is theirs seems to indicate that it is they, and not some impersonal Ideal, who are the ground of values? The Ideal cannot be left without a foundation in the real order; to situate it in a world of ideals and values which is outside and above what exists is to contradict and to deny the primacy of our radical affirmation. This is our affirmation of what exists and it is basic to all our thinking and willing: without what e-xists, outside of what *exists*, ideas and values *are* nothing so that, in consequence, they mean nothing and are worth nothing.

Serious though it be, this difficulty should not, however, discourage us but rather stimulate us to resume our onward march!

It is indeed not too difficult to foresee how our problem can be resolved, namely, by the existence of a Being who would at one and the same time possess the plenitude of being and an absolute value, or rather, who would *be* the plenitude of being and also the supreme Value. But there will not be lacking those who will pounce on this solution as contradictory and meaningless, on the grounds that what is characteristic of values is that they transcend what exists, so that an opposition between what is valuable and what exists is inevitable (cf. n. 22). Hence, to speak about an existing supreme Value is to speak in terms of square circles. ...

Now, clearly, this objection is very much imbedded in the metaphysical theory of its proponents. But even if we suppose that is has been refuted in the metaphysical arena, and that the existence of the supreme Value — that is, to speak un-equivocally, of God — has been arrived at by some process of reasoning, the difficulties that here confront us are still not eliminated. Questions such as the following have still to be faced. What relationship has moral value with God? In what sense is it dependent on Him and grounded on Him? — We have already, it is true, excluded the theory that the moral order is an arbitrary creation of God (n. 58). But in doing that, do we not run the risk, as Descartes feared, of having to regard this order as an Absolute which is independent of God and, in some way, even superior to Him? — On the other hand, if the conclusions arrived at in the previous book are valid, does it not seem that our reason and our rational nature provide us with a perfectly sufficient explanation of moral value, so that there is now no need at all to appeal to God in order to understand it. Undoubtedly, it will still be possible, once the existence of God is known, to acknowledge that He is the cause of the moral order; but He will be the cause here in exactly the same sense in which He is the cause of the geometrical order whose subject-matter (extended bodies) He causes to exist, but whose internal structure does not call for the slightest reference to Him and which can be perfectly understood without involving Him in the explanation.

The question discussed in this and the following chapter is connected with a very serious problem of our own times, namely, the problem of the relationship between religion and morality and, more particularly, the problem of whether or not it is possible for an atheist to lead an authentic moral life. The Fathers of the Church and the Scholastics, in their time, had already posed an analogous ques-tion concerning the "virtue of the pagans". Our own question was the object of lively controversies in the 17th and 18th centuries [1], but

---

[1] For more information, consult C. Fabro, *Introduzione all'ateismo moderno*, Rome, 1964, especially pp. 168-205 and 247-269. On the meaning which moral

has become a more burning problem of recent times, both because atheism is at present very much in evidence in the world, and because professed atheists often manifest sterling human qualities and show forth in their lives an unquestionable moral worth.

151. – To raply to the objections which reject the identity of what *is* and what is *good*, which insist on an opposition between what is *valuable* and what *exists*, and which regard the very notion of a supreme Value in the order of existence as contradictory, is a task for a metaphysical inquiry. Our contribution here, in our ethical investigation, is to face the question of the relationship between moral value and God and to throw light on the sense in which it is grounded on Him.

There are four types of solution to this problem.

Firstly, the Kantian solution which has been outlined in n. 116: the absolute autonomy of reason. Moral value has no other foundation than the dignity of rational nature which, in the final analysis, is derived from the law (of which the autonomous reason is the source), and explained in function of it (cf. n. 117). In this perspective, God cannot be the source of moral value but, inasmuch as His will is essentially holy and always fully in conformity with the law, He is the head of the moral order, of the "realm of ends": He is purely and simply an end, whereas the other members of this realm are at one and the same time end *and* means, in the sense that they may use one another as means, but not *merely* as means.

Deists also, in general, maintain that the moral order is quite independent of God and is in no way based on Him. If a relationship between religion and ethics is admitted, this relationship is envisaged as merely subjective: it will be allowed, for example, that the idea of a supreme spectator who judges our actions can exercise a beneficial influence on our conduct [2]. As well, the attitude of these authors towards morality is most often eudaemonist or utilitarian.

---

notions have for the atheist, see G. E. Moore, *Ethics*, p. 95. According to this author, who says that he himself is an atheist (p. 94), the existence of the "moral atheist" shows that "should be done" is not identical with "is commanded by God" (p. 95).

[2] Cf. the question posed by Shaftesbury at the beginning of his *Inquiry*: "What honesty or Virtue is, considered by itself; and in what manner it is

Another solution is that of certain Scholastics such as G. Vazquez[3], Cardinal Mercier etc., who agree that God is the ultimate source and foundation of the moral universe, but also insist that we have first to establish His existence in some other way in order to be in a position to deduce this truth. The moral order, as such, is sufficiently explained in terms of human nature, reason etc.: consequently, it is not possible to construct an argument for the existence of God from the structure or nature of this order. — More radically and in a manner which clearly reveals his rationalism, Christian Wolff goes so far as to declare that even without God there could still be a moral order[4].

A third type of solution is favoured by a considerable number of contemporary Scholastics. These authors agree with Vazquez and Mercier that the immediate foundation of the moral order lies in rational nature or reason and that this order can, in consequence, be known even when God's existence is unknown; but they consider, at the same time, that there will be a definite lacuna in our understanding of this order and that we shall be unable to give a satisfatory explanation of it, simply as a moral order, unless we are led to acknowledge that God is its basis. In their view, the truth that God is the ultimate foundation of the moral order is not arrived at simply by a synthetic and deductive process, which presumes that His existence has already been elsewhere established, but by an analytic and inductive process. In other words, they maintain that it is possible to be led from the fact that there is a moral order to the knowledge of God as the necessary and supreme condition of its possibility and intelligibility: there is a path to the existence of God that starts from our moral conscience (n. 159).

There is, finally, the opinion which insists that without a prior and explicit knowledge of God, we can have no authentic

---

influenced by religion: How far religion necessarily implies virtue; and whether it be a true saying, That it is impossible for an Atheist to be virtuous, or share any real degree of honesty or Merit", *Characteristics of Men, Manners, Opinions, Times*, Basle, 1790, vol. II, p. 2.

[3] *In Iam IIae*, disp. 97, c. 3; Lyons, 1620, t. I, pp. 454-455.

[4] *Philosophia practica universalis*, p. I, c. 2, nn. 245-248; Verona, 1779, pp. 95-97.

awareness of moral value and, even less, of moral obligation. The authors who hold this view are not, however, allying themselves with Pufendorf, for they do not claim that the moral order is founded on an arbitrary decree of God. The kernel of their argument is as follows: we cannot appreciate the rightness of a particular activity unless we also know what goal it is meant to achieve (its finality); consequently, the rightness of specifically human activity cannot be appreciated without a knowledge of the ultimate end which man is meant to attain; this end is nothing other than God. Consequently, as long as a person is ignorant of His existence, it is impossible for him to appreciate the rightness (or wrongness) of his free actions, that is, he can have no authentic experience of moral value, much less of moral obligation. — The attitude which is most representative of this tendency is that of Cardinal Billot: "The simple notion of moral good and evil essentially presupposes the knowledge of God's existence" [5]. — For these authors, as for thos of the second group, but for a diametrically opposed reason, it is impossible to construct an argument that will lead from the moral order to God: even to attempt to do so would be to beg the question.

It is worth adding that those who acknowledge that God is the foundation of moral value are not always in agreement on the problem of the precise way — in accordance with our human way of regarding God and speaking about Him — in which He plays this role. Some writers consider that this foundation is to be found in the divine essence, exemplary cause of all that is, and measure of all rightness [6]. Others point out that order, finality and due relationships are crucial in morality and that in all these, the activity of reason is essential; in consequence, these writers stress the importance of the divine reason [7]. — Note, however, that what these latter have in mind is the "supreme rule" rather than the "foundation" of morality: hence the opposition between them and the former writers should not be forced; what is involved is rather a difference in point of view.

---

[5] *De Deo uno et trino*, 7th ed., Rome, 1926, p. 49.
[6] For example, V. Cathrein, *Philosophia moralis*, 14th ed., p. 86.
[7] For example, L. Lehu, *Philosophia moralis et socialis*, I, pp. 104-105.

152. – Since moral value and the entire moral order are related, by means of our reasonable judgments, to what we have called the Ideal of practical reason, the heart of our problem here is to discover if this Ideal, in its turn, is founded on God and if so, in what way.

Now, if one supposes the existence of God to be elsewhere established, the problem is resolved easily enough, at least for those who admit, in line with traditional metaphysics, that the true and the good are "transcendental" attributes of being and are founded on it. For it follows immediately that what is primary and ultimate in the order of being is also primary and ultimate in the order of truth and the order of value. The absolute Being is also the absolute Good, the source and foundation of all that is good. The only objection to this can come from those who, while they are willing to acknowledge the existence of a supreme Being, insist at the same time that there is a metaphysical divorce between being and value. But such a position is untenable for, as we have already pointed out, all our thoughts and aspirations are but variations on a theme whose leit-motiv is, ever and always, being. It is not, however, our task here to enter into a discussion of questions which stem from a particular theory concerning the relationship between being and goodness, questions, in other words, of general metaphysics.

153. – We believe, however, that it is possible to arrive at the same conclusion without presupposing the existence of God but, on the contrary, establishing this as the fruit of the approach here proposed.

Let us reflect more closely on the Ideal of practical reason. What is its source? A basic distinction becomes readily apparent. Either this Ideal is simply a concept, in the strictest sense, no more than the fruit and result of our intellectual activity, and as such, stamped with no priority in relation to this activity; or, on the contrary, it enjoys a certain priority (the exact nature of which remains to be determined).

Now, if the first member of the disjunction were the correct one, moral judgments would simply not be possible. Since the condition of their possibility is the Ideal, in relationship to which our judgments of what is morally valuable

are "right", it follows that if this Ideal is itself entirely the
product of reason, this latter — and we are speaking, obviously, of human reason — has, no rule other than itself;
consequently, since it is now no longer measured in its activity
by the Ideal, it sinks back into itself, remains encased within its
own subjectivity and has no broader horizons than the world
of experience, which it is now no longer capable of
transcending. The consequence of this subjectivism and relativism is that moral value, such as our phenomenological
reflection has revealed it to be, disappears into thin air; moral
judgments would no longer be possible. In other words, to
deny any priority to the Ideal in relation to our judgments, is
to make the human person his own norm and so administer —
or attempt to administer — the "coup de grace" to morality.

Let us now turn to the second hypothesis in which a
certain priority is granted to the Ideal. Two possible ways of
conceiving this are open: firstly, the priority in question could
be that of an objective Idea, a Value which, from the height of
an intelligible world, dominates and conditions all that exists;
alternatively, this priority could be that of an existing being
which is superior to the Ideal, inasmuch as it provides the
ground in the real order of what, of itself and by definition, is
in the ideal order. Now the first interpretation is excluded, if it
is true, as we hold it to be, that outside of what exists there is
nothing, and consequently, no value. Ideas and values cannot
possess any priority in relation to what exists taken in its
entirety, since it is on this that they are grounded. There is no
possibility of going beyond or transcending the order of being,
the order whose very "heart" is existence. (To the extent that
something exists, to that extent is it a being). — Consequently,
the Ideal has to have a foundation in the order of being; there
has to be some existing being in which, or in whom, it takes
concrete shape. But what, or who, is this being?

An immediate reply that comes to mind is: it is nothing
other than the human person (or human nature), of whom the
Ideal would represent the idealization. But this reply is unacceptable. Firstly, because the value of the person and of his
nature springs entirely from his openness to the Ideal (nn. 136;
145): hence this value cannot be the *foundation* of the Ideal.
Secondly, because this idealization — if it is to be anything

more than the impoverishing reduction of the real to its abstract components — is possible only in relation to the Ideal, in whose perfection the person who is idealized already participates [8]. — For the same reason, union between all the members of the human community (which, as we have seen in n. 145, has been *a priori* proposed by some writers as the goal and horizon of our thinking and willing), cannot be the foundation in the real order of the Ideal. As has been pointed out, the value which this union has is immediately dependent on the value of the persons who are to be united, and mediately on the Ideal of which it is supposed, in this hypothesis, to be the foundation.

The only solution that now remains open (unless we are to be naively content to dismiss morality as a subjective illusion), is that the Ideal which makes moral judgments to be possible is founded on an existing, or better a Superexisting, being who is prior in himself, and in all respects, to every value as well as to every being; who, in consequence, cannot himself be endowed merely with a limited value, nor simply be situated at a particular level of being, but is *the* Being, the absolute and unconditioned Good. But the being in whom this "superexisting" identity of Being and of Value is found, is the Being that we call God.

It is not possible to evade this conclusion by maintaining that the Ideal is a *regulative Idea*, in the Kantian sense: an Idea which expresses and, as it were, projects to an ideal limit, the elan through which the person transcends all values without allowing any to dominate him, so that he himself arranges them in ascending order. For the same disjunction which we made at the beginning of n. 153 is applicable now also. Either this Idea is in no sense prior in relation to this elan, so that once again the Ideal is simply immanent in the

---

[8] The idealization is possible only in virtue of the attraction of an already existing Ideal, just as the activity by which the subject seeks his complete fulfilment supposes, in the last analysis, the attraction of a goal that is already real. If the goal or the Ideal have no more than an "intentional" existence, in the elan of the subject's willing or desiring, they undoubtedly form part of the structure of that elan and consequently explain it in terms of formal causality; but since they in no way account for the dynamism of the elan, they fail, in consequence, to explain it in terms of final causality. The very notion of value is ultimately explicable only by the attraction of an existing value.

human person (or rational being), and the moral order vanishes in everything but name; or else this Idea has some priority, and then the questions of what this priority consists in and what makes it possible, have to be faced.

154. – Let us now see in what way and under what aspect God can be said to be the ultimate foundation of the moral order.

As *the* Being and *the* Good, beyond whom and without whom there cannot be anything, or any value, God, of his very Essence (which is in no way distinct from his Existence), is the source and exemplar of all perfections that have been, or could be, created. But He is not the source and exemplar of spiritual perfections, such as those which are displayed in activity which is distinctively human, in the same way as He is of non-spiritual perfections, such as those of the rose or the lion, or even of man insofar as he is an animal. As a spiritual or rational being, man, in his activity, reaches, or at least aims at, what is absolute, so that in consequence he can be said to have a resemblance to the Absolute which no other being in this world of ours possesses. He shares in a perfection which, even though the way in which it is found in God far, far surpasses the way it is found in man, is nonetheless present in Him as to what we intend to signify by it and is not merely virtually present. Man possesses a participated infinity in that, by virtue of his intelligence, there is nothing which is outside or beyond his range[9]. It is for this reason that "only a being whose nature is rational is immediately oriented to God, for other creatures do not attain to what is universal but only to what is particular... while the being whose nature is rational, on the contrary, through knowing the notion of universal good and evil is immediately oriented to the universal fount of being"[10]. (We prefer to say "absolute" rather than "universal"). It is for this reason also that only such a being is capable of being loved by God as friend loves friend[11]. Similarity is a requirement for

---

[9] "The fact that a substance is intellectual means that all being comes within its range", St Thomas, *Cont. Gent.*, II, 98; "Every being whose nature is rational possesses either an actual or a potential infinity", Id., *Comp. Theol.*, 103.

[10] St Thomas, *Summa Theol.*, II-II, 2, 3.

[11] *Ib.*, I, 20, 2 ad 3um.

love, as we have seen (n. 143), and no other creature resembles God in the way that a rational creature does.

155. – We have, however, to go further than this, for while God is the exemplar of all spiritual perfections, He is the exemplar of moral value and moral perfection in a special way. The reason for this is to be found in the very special relationship between this value and liberty.

Moral value is the value which we increase or diminish in through the choices we make; in choosing, we fashion and mould ourselves and we decide what the ultimate meaning of our lives is to be. Now, this power of auto-determination stamps the spiritual subject with a very particular resemblance to the absolute Being, so much so that several Fathers of the Church, St. Bernard for example, and, among philosophers, Descartes, have regarded liberty as that endowment of our human nature by which we chiefly resemble God [12].

To say that God freely wills Himself and, even more, to say that He freely exists, are jarring and misleading expressions, if "liberty" is understood in the sense which the word commonly has, since it is then implied that He could choose not to exist, or not to love Himself; consequently, it is much better to avoid them. Nonetheless, it is true that His activity does not spring from a source, be it the divine nature or the divine will, which is in the slightest way really distinct from His existence: where God is concerned, nature, will, existence and activity coincide perfectly. When, then, in our actions we are, in the final analysis, determined by no source other than ourselves as spiritual subjects (n. 13), we in some measure participate

---

[12] "For (the will), in its very origin, possesses a twofold good: one is general, simply from its creation ... while the other is special: it is the freedom of choice which it has and because of which it is, in a special way, made in the likeness of Him who created it", St Bernard, *Tractatus de Gratia et Libero Arbitrio*, c. 6, n. 19; PL. t. 182, col. 1021 B. "This is perhaps the reason why only the free will cannot suffer any decrease or diminution: because in it, a certain substantive image of the eternal and unchangeable divinity is revealed in a very special way", *ib.*, c. 9, n. 28; col. 1016 B. — And Descartes writes: "I experience that nothing within me is as powerful as my will, so that I cannot conceive of anything superior to it; indeed, it is this which principally reveals to me that I am made in the image and likeness of God", *Méditation quatrième*, Adam-Tan, t. IX, p. 45 (Latin: t. VII, p. 57). The same idea is expressed in the Pastoral Constitution *Gaudium et Spes* of the Second Vatican Council, n. 17.

in that identity of activity and existence which is God's; and we do so in virtue of our immediate relationship with and orientation towards Him, in virtue, that is, of the resemblance to God that is ours as human beings. Our free activity can be said to be the reflection in us of the divine aseity.

It is clear, then, that God is the exemplar of moral value from the objective point of view, inasmuch as He is the source and archetype of the rational order to which we ought to conform, and of the rational good to which we should cleave. More than that, He is also the exemplar of this value inasmuch as the unconditioned character, the absolute independence, of His existence and of His willing is at one and the same time the source and transcendent exemplar of the free conformity and responsible commitment, which are at the very heart of moral living [13].

156. – We can express the truth we have just been discussing in a more simple and more synthetic fashion, by saying that moral value, since it is the value *par excellence* of the person, has God, considered precisely as the supremely personal being, as its foundation. That God is a personal being can be established by reflecting along these lines (in which use is made of some metaphysical concepts); if a person is essentially a spiritual subject, who is nothing other than an existing spiritual or intellectual nature (cf. n. 13) [14], then who has a better title to be called a person than God, since He is the plenitude of existence which is derived from no source other than Himself [15], and since this existence is identical with the plenitude of thought and willing that is His, as well as with His absolute consciousness and possession of Himself, in which are involved a consciousness and possession of Being that are no less absolute? He is, then, the supremely personal being and the very pinnacle of the generosity of which only a person is

---

[13] "It is not because they could have sinned that the angels are to be praised for their goodness, but because it is, in a certain sense, from themselves that their incapacity to sin is derived; in this they are, to some extent, like God, who is Himself the source of all that He has", St Anselm, *Cur Deus homo*, III, c. 10; PL. t. 158, col. 409 C.

[14] St Thomas, *Summa Theol.*, I, 29, 3.

[15] "The subsistent perfection of subsistence", L. Billot, *op. cit.*, p. 464.

capable. (The fact that our human reason cannot, of itself, know the way in which God is personal is not all surprising, if one considers the depths that are present in any person simply because he is a person, depths which defy all our efforts to plumb them by seeking to objectify them). — Another way of approaching this present question — if we make use here of what has been established in nn. 152, 153 — is to start from the fact that the human person is capable of growing or diminishing in his stature as a person. Now, if he does this because of the response he makes to the Ideal, the foundation in the real order of this Ideal cannot be less than a person [16]. Consequently, it is simultaneously established that God (who is this foundation) is personal, and that it is as such that He provides the ultimate ground of moral value.

157. — All that now remains to be done in this present chapter is to inquire what precise role the divine essence, the divine reason and the divine will play in founding the moral order.

But note carefully, as we have already pointed out, that these three concepts mutually involve one another; they cannot be understood in isolation since the aspects under which they refer to God are not really distinct in Him. With this in mind we can now say:

The divine essence or existence — for between these there is not even a rational distinction — should be called the ultimate foundation of moral value and the moral order.

---

[16] "It would be paradoxical to acknowledge that the individual is a person precisely because he has ascended to the level of the universal, but to refuse to allow that this universal, because of which he is a person, is itself personal", L. Lavelle, *De l'acte*, Paris, 1938, p. 142. — Similarly, Ed. Le Roy: "God reveals Himself in spiritual experience as the efficacious principle of our growth as persons", *Le problème de Dieu*, "Bulletin de la société française de philosophie", Jan. 4 1930, p. 26. — Strictly speaking, this argument is valid only if it granted that personality is, as the Scholastics say, a "simple perfection", unconditionally superior to its negation: otherwise, all one would prove is that personality should be present in God either formally or virtually (that is, as a transcendent perfection which would not itself be personality). And, in fact, many regard personality as a limitation, antithetic of what is absolute (Brunschvicg, for example). Nevertheless, the supreme value of personality as such clearly seems to be a datum of an "axiological" consciousness that has not been falsified, just as is the primacy of what exists over what is possible or purely ideal.

The divine reason is the archetype, the supreme analogue, in the rational order, the exemplar of every judgment of reason that is "right"; it is also in consequence, the supreme norm of morality.

Finally, the divine will, which cannot but be "right" since it is identified with its norm, is the exemplar or archetype of every will that is morally good.

Since no real distinction between these three is possible, the divine will should not, in any sense, be regarded as subordinated to an ideal and impersonal value: the value which it "has to love" is that of the divine being itself, which includes that will, which *is* that will. Further, this rightness which God's will cannot but have, is not for Him something which is "given" and which He finds Himself possessing: God does not find anything, God does not "find that He possesses": He *is*, with all the force, with all the spontaneity and independence and uncondionality of that plenitude of existence which is His. Since His will is identical with that plenitude, God's holiness is the transcendent exemplar of all moral value; it is a holiness which stands in the same relationship to our constantly renewed efforts to make moral progress, as does the plenitude of existence to all that changes and develops; all the positive value that lies in our efforts is present in a surpassing degree in his Holiness [17].

---

[17] Moral value immediately presents itself to us under the appearance of conflict, of effort, of the choice of good as opposed to evil. The morally good person, who merits our praise, is he "who could have transgressed and has not transgressed; who could do evil things and has not done them" (Eccli., 31, 10). A will that of its nature adheres to what is good appears to us to be outside the sphere of morality. As D. Parodi writes: there would be a contradiction involved in maintaining that God, without struggling, without conquering, without meriting, is already morally perfect; for goodness of this kind would no longer be moral (*En quête d'une philosophie*, Paris, 1935, p. 145). It is for this reason that the Stoics regarded the wise man as superior to the gods. He is the son of his own actions. ...

The source of all this is anthropomorphic imagination, from which likewise springs the criticism of the divine immobility, in the name of life which changes and develops. The possibility of transgressing cannot of itself be regarded as a perfection; it is no more than the sign that our action really comes from ourselves. But that spontaneity is only a shadow of the spontaneity possessed by the Being who is the plenitude of existence — a spontaneity which is the well-spring of the former. Cf. the text of St Anselm cited in note 13.

CHAPTER FIVE

FOUNDATION OF MORAL OBLIGATION

158. – It does not, at first sight, seem that the question of the ultimate foundation of moral obligation should involve us in any fresh problems; is it not sufficient to say that it has the same foundation as moral value? Our phenomenological analysis has revealed to us that the objective, unconditioned necessity of obligation is a property of this value or, more exactly, it is a property of this value in the sense that our vocation as human beings requires us to do what is good, but not *all* that is good (nn. 34-44). To act in accordance with right judgments is not simply a question of "moral stylishment"; it is a duty, a demand from which we may not slip away, at which we may not cock our noses.

However, when we reflect a little more, the question of the foundation of obligation takes on a certain complexity. There are several reasons for this. Firstly, every action whose moral goodness we appreciate, does not thereby become obligatory on us; hence what suffices to account for this appreciation (the conformity of the action with reason and with rational nature), does not necessarily account for the binding power of obligation. This adds something to the moral value of an action and this extra "something", interpreted in terms of our human experience, is conceptualized as a command that has been issued by some authority. As well — and this point is of particular importance — a person's awareness that he has a particular obligation or duty is very often closely linked with his religious attitudes and beliefs: for the great majority of people, the moral code which they try to follow is associated with divine sanctions (the code is the same as the "commandments of God"): morality forms, along with beliefs and rites, one of the three essential elements that are found in varying degrees in all religions.

In consequence of this line of thought, it may well be argued that obligation requires a foundation which is distinct from that of moral value; more precisely, that it requires God not only as its ontological and mediate foundation, but as its immediate foundation in the noetic order. In other words, without God not only would obligation lack the ultimate foundation which it requires but, in addition, without the knowledge of God, without the God who has come to exist *for us* as the source and author of the "law", *we* would not be subject to any obligation. In still other terms, obligation exercises its binding power on a person only because he knows (with certainty) that God is its ultimate source.

Is this line of thought and the conclusions to which it leads, valid? This is the problem to which we have now to turn our attention. But first, let us see the different solutions that have been offered[1].

159. – These views can be classified fairly simply. There are two widely supported and opposing theories, the first of which derives obligation immediately from the norm and essence of moral value (and, in consequence, does not require that obligation be mediated to us by our knowledge that God is its source), while the other insists that this mediation is necessary.

In addition to Kant (nn. 115, 116) and those whose approach to the question of God's role in the moral order is deistic or rationalistic (n. 151), with none of whom we have now to concern ourselves, a good number of Scholastics, among whom Gabriel Vazquez is usually singled out, belong to this first group. Note that this author considers the common opinion to be that sin has an intrinsic malice, independently of all "law"; this is his own view also, and in his defence of it he criticises at length, and finally rejects, the distinction which some writers had sought to establish between "sin" and "fault"; in their view, what would be a "sin" if God had not given a command on the matter, becomes a "fault" because He has, in fact, so commanded. But, they insist, God could not but command us to avoid what is sinful, in that it is contrary to

---

[1] For a discussion of the problem, and for the various views of contemporary Scholastics, see Cl. Desjardins, *Dieu et l'obligation morale*, Montreal, 1963.

our rational nature; on this point their theory diverges from that of Pufendorf (n. 54)[2].

The authors who compose this first group are not, however, all of one mind. Some of them, such as Cardinal Mercier, in line with their theory concerning the foundation of moral value (n. 151), deny all possibility of concluding to the existence of God from our experience of moral obligation (which, they maintain, is sufficiently explained in terms of "reason" and "rational nature" etc.). Others, on the contrary, argue that a thorough explanation of this experience — which is accepted unquestiongly as a starting-point — involves the acknowledgment of God as its source. For these authors, what is referred to as the "deontological" proof of God's existence is valid; that is, they accept that there is a path that leads from the experience of obligation and duty to the existence of God. They do not all, however, indicate the same path: some of them reduce it to one of the "five ways" of St Thomas (their preference is for the fourth), while others prefer to work out an original proof.

As the reader may already know, it is in the context of the famous passage in St Thomas concerning the very first free action of a person's life that Thomists primarily discuss the problem of the relationship between a person's knowledge of God's existence and his capacity to experience a genuine obligation. In this passage St Thomas is dealing with a strictly theological question, namely, the question of the eternal fate of a person who dies in the state of original sin, but has also committed a venial sin. The answer he

---

[2] "I have always favoured the common opinion that not every sin is such because it has been forbidden by law, or been in some way or other prohibited, but rather because, of its very nature, it is an evil for man ... But some more recent writers, impressed by the force of the argument (that is, the argument proposed by Vazquez), have maintained that every sin, which is said to be such because of the natural law, is first an evil of its very nature, since it is contrary to rational nature, and is on this account a sin but not a fault; it is a fault only on account of the positive precept of God who forbids us to act in this way. It is not, however, in God's power to regard this sin as if it were not a fault. ... This opinion is very much open to criticism", etc., G. Vazquez, *op. cit.*, disp. 97, c. 3, nn. 6, 8, 9; pp. 454-455. Vazquez adds that "all (sins) are indeed contrary to the law of God and are prohibited" (n. 10; p. 455); it is for this reason that a violation of the natural law is in a true sense an offence against God (disp. 96, c. 2, n. 6; p. 453).

makes is that it would be impossible for anyone to die in that state, because once a person reaches the age of reason, he cannot avoid making a fundamental option: he has then to decide whether he will begin to live for or against God; and in so deciding he gives a meaning (but not irrevocably) to his life. If this option is morally good it will involve, or will infallibly lead to, an act of charity, so that original sin will be wiped out; if, on the other hand, the option is evil, the person will sin mortally, because he has given a wrong orientation to his life in the first act in which it was in his power to do so[3].

But, inquire the Thomists, what happens when the person making this option is a "young savage" who has grown up in a wild and remote region? How can such a person turn to a God of whom he has never heard? Bañez replies that conscience is God's spokesman to that person, so that it is possible for him to follow a path that leads to the knowledge of God and which starts with his conscience. It may well be that a person is invincibly ignorant of God's existence, but this does not at all mean that he is free of the obligations which the natural law imposes and through which God makes His will known. Once he has come to the use of reason, these obligations will begin to press upon him and, with these as a starting-point, he can come sooner or later to the knowledge of the God who is his supreme judge. To claim that a person cannot know that he is morally obliged until he first knows that God is the source of this obligation is much the same as saying that in order to know that there is an eclipse of the moon, we have first to know that the earth has come between the moon and the sun![4]. — This view which, in

---

[3] *Summa Theol.*, I-II, 89, 6.

[4] "Even though he has no explicit knowledge of God's existence and even though his ignorance is invincible, it does not follow from this that he is not obliged by the natural law of God. The reason for this is that this law is made known to him by *synderesis*, through which God imposes obligation on him. As a result of his experience of obligation, a person will afterwards be able to reason to the existence of God as his supreme judge. The process will be as follows: I experience that I am naturally obliged, that I am bound to do this and avoid that; therefore I have a superior who obliges and governs me. The conclusion is obvious: otherwise, I would be the supreme judge of good and evil, nor could I sin, since I would be in control of the law, which no one superior to me has made so as to subject me to himself...". Bañez goes on to point out that there is no rule of logic which maintains that a person will be invincibly ignorant of a particular conclusion, once he is invincibly ignorant of the premise. His illustration of this is: the earth comes between the sun and the moon so that, in consequence, an eclipse of the moon occurs. But even though a countryman is entirely ignorant of the premise, it does not follow that he is ignorant of the

essentials, has already been taught by Cajetan, has been re-echoed by John of St Thomas and a large number of Thomists. In recent times, J. Maritain has provided a penetracing interpretation of the theory[5].

Another subdivision of the authors in this first group results from the three different ways in which God is regarded as the ultimate foundation of obligation. Some identify this foundation with the divine essence[6], others with the divine reason (this is the view of the majority of Thomists, whose theory of law places great emphasis on the role that reason plays: nn. 176, 177[7], while still other authors identify it with the divine will (the majority of Suarezians[8], whose general theory of law lays much greater stress on the will, fit into this category: n. 177)[9].

160. – Among the authors in the second and opposing group, a certain number of recent Scholastics can be noted, such as V. Cathrein, I. González-Moral, O. Lottin etc. Many of them are Suarezians and, in consequence, place the root of obligation in the will of the supreme legislator[10]. But Thomists are also to be found in their ranks; of these Cardinal Billot provides a particularly striking example: "The knowledge that he is obliged, clearly supposes in a person the prior knowledge of the one who has the power to impose this obligation, par-

---

conclusion: this is known to him through his experience. Similarly in the present context: a person knows through his experience that he is bound by the natural dictate of synderesis, even though he is not immediately aware it is God the legislator who has imposed this obligation and introduced it into the minds of men, *In IIam IIae*, q. 10, a. 1; cf. Cajetan, *In IIam IIae*, q. 10, a. 4; John of Saint-Thomas, *In Iam*, q. 2, disp. 3, a. 1, n. 19.

[5] *La dialectique immanente du premier acte de liberté*, in *Raison et raisons*, Paris, 1947, pp. 131-165 (Eng. trans.: *The Range of Reason*, London, 1953, pp. 66-85).

[6] For example, Ed. Elter, *op. cit.*, p. 75.

[7] For example, L. Lehu, *op. cit.*, pp. 250-256.

[8] For example, P. Descoqs, *Praelectiones theologiae naturalis*, t. I, Paris, 1932, p. 482.

[9] This opposition should not be exaggerated. The difference, at times, springs more from the way the question is posed. So, Ed. Elter, while holding that the divine essence is the foundation of obligation, nevertheless regards the divine intellect as its "first formal principle".

[10] For example, V. Cathrein, *op. cit.*, p. 156: "The obligation of the natural law ... is immediately derived from the will of God".

ticularly when what is in question is that absolute, imprescriptible, inescapable obligation against which nothing in the world can prevail, and with which the moral law is acknowledged to be endowed. Now, the only one who could impose such an obligation on us is God. Consequently, before a person knows of God's existence, it is absolutely impossible for him to know that there is a moral law, or to be morally bound; if such a person apparently chances to have a conscience, this is really no more than the vain and empty product of his imagination" [11]. Even further, as we already noted (n. 151), Billot insists that a person is incapable of distinguishing between good and evil (that is, of knowing the moral order), unless he knows explicitly that God exists; other authors who share his views on obligation, but who are perhaps less logical than he, find a sufficient basis for this distinction in the harmony or disharmony of a person's actions with his rational nature etc.

The position of some writers in this second group seems to be motivated by a desire to steer clear of anything which might appear to smack of Kantianism, and also by their fear that, if they admit that a person can be morally obliged even though he is ignorant of God's existence, they would in consequence be strengthening the hand of those who maintain that God has no part at all to play in the moral order.

161. – No more than was Vazquez, we are not at all enamoured of this second line of approach to our present problem. In our view, moral obligation does not require a foundation different to that of moral value.

That this is so emerges from an analysis of the nature of obligation. What this analysis reveals is that what creates an obligation for a person to perform or shun a particular action, is his appreciation of its relationship with a Value which, as our phenomenological analysis has brought to light, he cannot but acknowledge, implicitly it is true, to be supremely worthy of his respect and love, and on which his value as a person is dependent (nn. 39-42). This Value we have called the Ideal of our practical reason (n. 139). In other words: the necessity which moral obligation imposes on us is at one and the same

---

[11] *Op. cit.*, p. 50.

time conditioned ("you ought to act in this way, if you wish to be faithful to the Ideal"), and unconditioned or categorical ("you ought to remain faithful to the Ideal").

Now a necessity of this kind is imposed on us whenever it comes home to us that the teleology, the structure, the objective meaning of a particular action are intrinsically linked — either positively or negatively — with our radical openness to the Ideal, and with the reverence and love that we owe to the Value (and which we express in the concrete by our reverence and love for other human subjects). An action whose intrinsic meaning and finality involve a practical rejection and refusal of this Value — an act of egoism or pride, which centres the subject on himself, an act of debauchery which violates the dignity that he and others possess as spiritual subjects and turns topsyturvy the internal order that characterizes them etc. — and which, in consequence, a person could not genuinely will and perform, while still remaining "open" and faithful to the Ideal, is linked intrinsically and negatively with this Ideal; it shares in an inverse fashion in the necessity which the Value imposes on us, so that it *ought*, in consequence, to be avoided. An action, on the contrary, whose omission would signify a refusal of or a contempt for the Ideal, so that the subject would be in practice choosing to "close" himself — for example, to help one's neighbour when one is in a position to do so and his need is urgent — such an action is linked intrinsically and positively with the Ideal; it shares positively in the necessity which this imposes on us so that, in consequence, it ought to be performed.

But this intrinsic link between an action and the Ideal is precisely what grounds the moral value of the action in question. Hence it is clear that the necessity which obligation imposes on us has its origin in the same source as the moral value of the obligatory action.

Does it follow from this that the area of what is obligatory coincides perfectly with the area of what is morally valuable? No; a positive, intrinsic connection with the Ideal does not suffice to make an action obligatory. This connection has to be of such a kind that the subject cannot at one and the same time aim at the Ideal (that is, be guided by a judgment of right reason), and refuse to perform the action in question. In other words, the connection has to be reciprocal. An action is purely and simply good when it involves fidelity to the Ideal; it is obligatory when fidelity to the Ideal involves it. An action is evil when it excludes fidelity to the Ideal and fidelity to the Ideal excludes it, (here, the exclusion is always reciprocal). — But are there actions which in their singular and concrete reality neither involve nor exclude fidelity to the Ideal? This is a question which has to be discussed later (nn. 236-239).

162. – The same concluion results from a reflexion on the first principle of our practical reason. This principle, it is commonly agreed, particular among the Scholastics, can be formulated in this way: "Good is to be done and evil avoided" (n. 44). Whar the principle of non-contradiction is to our speculative reason, this principle is to our practical reason. Further, quite apart from the agreement to which we have referred, what other principle can be more basic than this? All possible rivals will be found to presuppose it. Take, for example, the principle: "What contributes to the progress of humanity, what is in accord with the trend of history, of evolution etc., is to be done; the opposite of these is to be avoided". But if the proponent of this principle is asked: "why"?, the only reply open to him is "because what contributes to the progress of humanity etc., is *good* and what stands in the way of this progress is *evil*". Hence, it is clear that in accepting the above-mentioned principle we are not simply following a venerable tradition, nor are we using an argument from authority: we accept this principle as the basic one because of the internal evidence in its favour.

Now if this principle is primary, then the connection between its subject ("good") and its predicate ("to be done") has to be immediate, just as has the connection between "evil" and "to be avoided". If the connection were mediate, there would be need of a middle term, so that what was claimed to be the first principle would, in fact, be a conclusion. If we suppose that this middle term is "x", then the following line of reasoning results: "x" (for example, what God commands) is to be done; but the good is "x"; consequently, the conclusion that the good is to be done, follows. But then the first practical principle will no longer be what we have admitted it to be and what, indeed, it has to be.

It is, in consequence, somewhat inconsistent to admit, on the one hand, that the principle in question is "primary", but to insist, on the other hand, that moral obligation cannot affect us unless it is mediated by the knowledge that God is its source. For if this mediation were required, the first principle should be formulated: "God's commands are to be obeyed".

The conclusion that emerges from this line of reflection is that the necessity that is imposed on us to do what is good etc., is derived from the nature of the good, just as the necessity to avoid what is contradictory stems from the nature of reality. This is not to say that this former necessity can be arrived at logically, by a mere analysis of the notion "good", so that the principle would be, in the strict sense, analytic. (If it were, then whatever is good would be: "to be done"). What "good", as such, means is not "to be done" but "desirable", "agreeable"; and what moral good, as such, means is "agreeable to, or in harmony with, reason". Hence, even though this necessity cannot be derived from a logical analysis of moral good or value, it has the same source as this latter, so that, within the limits indicated above (n. 161), obligation is a characteristic of moral value: this proximate source and immediate foundation is nothing other than the harmony of an action (and of the object on which it centres), with the Ideal, for it is our appreciation of this harmony which makes a rational demand on us, in the sense explained in nn. 44 and 161.

163. – The above line of thought may be criticised by some on the grounds that the predicate "to be done" has been interpreted in too strong a sense. The true sense, it will be maintained, is not that of strict obligation but simply of an invitation from our reason. It is only when we know that God is its ultimate source that this invitation becomes an obligation in the strict sense.

But if the first principle does not bind us morally, then nothing or nobody can ever do so; in particular, it will be impossible to deduce the fact that we are subject to moral obligation, simply by starting from the knowledge that God is commanding us. Note that the impossibility we are speaking about is concerned with the very fact that we are subject to obligation at all, so that we are bound to do good and avoid evil; we readily admit that God can and does create particular obligations for human beings (by His positive laws, by the particular tasks to which He calls them and the special paths He marks out for them etc.).

The reason for this impossibility is that the knowledge that God is commanding us can oblige us morally, only if we already appreciate that we are obliged to obey when He commands. Suppose that we lack this appreciation: then this knowledge is no more than speculative — we acknowledge the fact that He is commanding — and makes no demands on our liberty, no more than would the orders of someone to whose authority we are not subject. Hence it is clear that our obligation to obey *when* He commands cannot arise simply from our knowledge *that* He is commanding. From this knowledge alone the conclusion can never be drawn that there is an unconditioned necessity to good; our appreciation of this necessity has to be prior to, and more basic than, this additional knowledge. Since, however, this affirmation may appear somewhat shocking to some people — they may feel that the knowledge that the God of incomparable dignity is commanding, is of itself sufficient to impose an absolute necessity on a human being — it will be worthwhile investigation at more length the validity of the view we have expressed.

A preliminary point that has to be made is that God can be considered either under a purely "ontological" and non-moral aspect (as the supreme Being, the Creator, the Omnipotent, on whom everything, even our liberty, is dependent, and who alone can provide unending rest for our troubled hearts etc.), or under a moral aspect, as the supreme Value, the pinnacle of Holiness etc. Now, as long as we confine ourselves to the first aspect, all we can say is that God can move our will as He pleases, can reward or punish us, can be found (can allow Himself to be found) by us or can be lost, can reveal or "hide" himself etc. But in all this, as we have seen (n. 39), there is nothing of a moral character, nothing which can be said to be morally significant, unless it is first supposed that God's rewards and punishments are deserved, that to refuse to strive for true and lasting contentment is morally evil and forbidden etc. Still, it may be maintained, is it not fitting and entirely in harmony with reason that the created being should submit to his Creator, that the one who participates in being should conform his will to the One from whose plenitude he has received, or rather, is receiving? — To this line of argument our reply is that the immediate source of this obligation, as far as we human beings are concerned, is this *harmony* with reason (which, if it is to fulfil that function, has to be understood as a harmony with the Ideal of reason, n. 135).

Another line of argument might be that "God is supremely *worthy* of our obedience; He has an absolute *right* to our submission" etc. But to say this presupposes that there is an order of rights and duties, so that the argument is involved in a vicious circle. For while it is true, as we shall see (n. 203), that a right is of its nature prior in relation to the correlative duty, it is also true that we come to appreciate the existence of a right only by coming to understand that we are obliged not to violate it, or that we are allowed to make use of it (which is only another way of saying that there is no obligation on us to abstain from using it). ... Hence, to say that God *has rights* where we are concerned, presupposes that we are *obliged* to obey Him. Consequently, it is not possible to prove that we are obliged to obey God by starting from the notion of His rights over us, and so it is also impossible to conclude to the fact that we are subject to moral obligation from the notion of "the divine rights".

We now turn to consider God under a moral aspect, that is, as the supreme Value in relation to whom the uprightness of our free decisions is "measured". But — in addition to the fact that, as we shall soon have occasion to indicate, I would be incapable of understanding what is meant by "moral uprightness" if the basic demand that I do good and avoid evil has never actually been made upon me — in this perspective, the immediate source of obligation, as far as a human being is concerned, would not be God's *existence*, but His *value* (known through the Ideal of reason). To be morally bound, we have to grasp that the action in question is linked with the absolute Value (in the sense explained in n. 161); this certainly means that this Value has to be appreciated as actually valuable, as the Ideal of value for our practical reason, but not necessarily as actually existing.

It is quite true that, as we have pointed out already (n. 150), what is isolated and divorced from what exists cannot be valuable, since outside the order of being there is nothing. But it does not follow from this that to appreciate a value is the same as knowing that it has taken concrete shape in the real order; on the contrary, the order of values seems, at first sight, to be in opposition to the order of reality. Our affirmations of truth are also grounded on what is; nonetheless, everything that can be affirmed as true does not exist (think, for example, of mathematical truths concerning the "realities" of mathematics). Consequently, it is possible for me to have an understanding of moral value and of the Ideal, which is sufficient to make me subject to the claims of moral obligation, even though I do not yet know clearly that the ground of this Ideal is God.

Another line of objection that may be raised is the following: we deduce that we are morally obliged from our knowledge that God is our last end, the "centre" towards which a spiritual being "gravitates" with all the weight of his "natural" love; further, since we can acquire this knowledge by reflecting on the structure and dynamism of our knowing and our loving, it cannot be said that this end is simply imposed on us by God. He is not only the Creator who has made me for Himself etc.; He is the one towards whom I exist, apart from whom I have no meaning. But if the necessity by which I tend towards God is simply a factual necessity, if God is no more for me than the one apart from whom I cannot find final rest and contentment, my relationship with Him does not create any moral obligation for me; I have not yet entered into that sphere (n. 42). If no more than a factual necessity is involved, to reject my final end would indeed be stupid and would cause me pain, but I could not yet be said to be acting immorally. I can be said to violate an obligation only if I know that God is the final end towards whom I *ought* to tend, so that my refusal to do so would be purely and simply detestable. But, once again, what emerges from this, except that the immediate source of obligation lies in the supreme Value? The point at which this necessity "touches" us is when we are faced with the choice of performing (avoiding) a particular action, or of being unfaithful to this Value. It is only as absolute Value, as the Ideal of practical reason, that God is for us the immediate source of obligation [12].

---

[12] J. Maritain rightly observes that obligation is immediately grounded on the good considered as "value" rather than as "end", *Neuf leçons...*, pp. 83-84.

A final difficulty may still be urged: independently of the claims which moral obligation makes on me, I possess no norm for the right use of liberty, and if there is nothing in relation to which this may be "measured", I am in the position of having to create my own values, by simply deciding what is good and what is evil. Now, since I am created by God and dependent on Him, I could not be the arbiter of good and evil; and what enables me to appreciate this is my knowledge that there is a God on whom I depend in my inmost being. It is because I know of His existence that I also understand that my liberty is not its own norm, but that it is in Him that this is to be found.

The problem that this line of approach faces is that of giving a meaning to the phrase "right use of liberty", which will be independent of, and prior to, a person's actual experience of a genuine obligation. (For on the terms of the suggested explanation, it is through the understanding of a "right use of liberty", which our knowledge of God gives us, that we become subject to moral obligation) Undoubtedly, it can be maintained that a person's will is right when it does not deviate from its goal, but this rectitude is moral only if the end in question is stamped with a moral character; hence, the ambiguity which we have just noted, when dealing with another version of this present objection, again emerges. In order to be the source of obligation as far as we human beings are concerned, this end has itself to be endowed with an obligatory character or, if one prefers, it has to be "objectively necessary" (in the sense that we could not reject it without also diminishing in stature as rational, human beings). Moreover, it is not necessary to introduce the notion of final end (God) at all, in order to appreciate what a "right use of liberty" immediately means. A person's will is said to be "right" when he decides "as he should", when he chooses what he ought to choose, when he is faithful to the Value. Hence an appreciation of moral value and obligation is a presupposition for understanding what is meant by a will that is "right". Without this appreciation and actual experience, it is impossible to have a genuine understanding of a "right use of liberty" and of the norm for this. Hence, the experience of obligation to which the proposed course of reasoning wishes to conclude is the presupposition which makes the process possible. This latter can indeed help us to interpret our experience of obligation and our initial appreciation of it, but cannot substitute for their absence.

Note carefully that it would not be sufficient to admit on the one hand, that the person who does not know of God's existence could have an appreciation of obligation in the abstract but to insist, on the other hand, that it is only his knowledge of the relation of obligation to God that effectively exposes him to its demands and transfers what was in the abstract and speculative realm into the concrete and practical. For the very notion of obligation can mean nothing to a person unless he has actually been subject to the radical, fundamental necessity of doing good and avoiding evil, just as the notion of being can mean nothing to him apart from his actual experience of existing beings, nor the notions of love or desire apart from his experience of the radical, fundamental appetite that is his as a human being. Ideed, what does "to be obliged to do this particular action" mean, except that if I do not perform it, I will be rejecting the Value which gives point and purpose to my existence so that I will lose my *raison d'être* etc. But all this would have no meaning for me and would not enable me to appreciate that I am now morally obliged, nor even to envisage a situation in which I could be obliged, if I did not at the same time understand that I *ought not* to reject the Value and so lose what gives point to my existence etc. In other words, the definition of what obligation consists in presupposes that we have the appreciation of it which is the fruit of being actually subject to it; it is an irreducible datum (n. 42).

In brief, then, either God is known under a non-moral aspect, so that His commands could not create any moral obligation for us; or else He is known under a moral aspect, under an aspect which grounds His right to our obedience, so that our appreciation of obligation is logically presupposed. Either way, it is evident that God, or the commands of God, could not be for us the immediate source of moral obligation as such (of the basic obligation to do good); consequently, knowledge of Him is not required in order that we be subject to an authentic obligation.

164. – In addition, the view that we are criticising would lead to the quite extraordinary conclusion that a good part (and perhaps the greater part) of the human race is outside the moral order!

The reason for this is that there are many people nowadays who are either ignorant of God's existence, or at least doubtful concerning it; if the above-mentioned view were true one would have to say that, as far as they are concerned, there is no moral law from which obligation in the strict sense flows. Note well that if the authors of whom we are writing are to be consistent, they cannot allow that *any knowledge whatever* of God is sufficient to subject us to moral obligation. God has to be *explicitly* known as the source and ground of the moral order and, in consequence, not only as the supreme Being and Creator, but also and especially as the One whose moral perfection is supreme. (Obviously, it is only the person whose religious development is at a somewhat advanced state who will possess this knowledge). To admit that an implicit knowledge of God is sufficient would be for these authors the equivalent of a *volte-face*; what makes their theory to be distinct and original would have disappeared (for we also admit, as we shall make clear, that this implicit knowledge is required).

When this question of the explicit knowledge of God is raised, the line of approach which the defenders of the theory ordinarily take is to deny the possibility of a blameless ignorance of God (except in rare and exceptional instances). But this reply, in addition to the fact that it is unrealistic in the extreme and is blind to the realities of the human condition, is clearly contradictory. How can a person be culpable when he is not subject to obligation? Also, what will be the source of a person's obligation to inquire about the existence of God if he is at present ignorant of it, or to control the passions and desires which, if yielded to, could blind him to the truth about God?

Hence, it seems to us that the theory we are here opposing leads logically to one of the following conclusions:

1. It is admitted that not only rare individuals but countless multitudes can commit what the theologians call "philosophical sin", that is, can act in ways which are morally evil since they are contrary to reason, but which would not involve "theological sin", or, in other words, would not be an

"offence against God". But this theory, which found several proponents in the 17th century, is in very little favour with theologians of the present-day; the most that will be granted, and that only by some of them, is that such an hypothesis is not intrinsically contradictory and might be verified in very exceptional circumstances. In addition, the advocates of the view we are here opposing themselves acknowledge, with V. Cathrein, that "philosophical sin is not, at least generally speaking, possible" [13], so that it could occur only in extremely rare circumstances. But this admission seems to stamp them as inconsistent [14].

2. Alternatively, if the possibility of philosphical sin is rejected, one is led to opt for the solution — it can be called an "heroic" one — of Cardinal Billot. This solution steers clear of all contradictions and is willing to admit, as we have already indicated, that a considerable portion of the human race, even though in other respects (for example, culturally) very developed, is morally "infantile". The condition of these morally under-developed adults is, accordingly, in no way different from that of children who have not yet come to the use of reason [15]. But despite steering clear of the rocks of contradiction, this theory has had a stormy voyage. It is difficult in the extreme to concede that so many adults, who are otherwise normal, and capable of assuming business responsibilities etc., are in reality no more than moral infants.

Many authors distinguish between an *imperfect* obligation for which the knowledge of God would not be required and a *perfect* obligation which would require it. This distinction can be under-

---

[13] *Op. cit.*, p. 200.

[14] We shall say nothing about the proposition condemned by Alexander VIII: "A philosophic or moral sin is a human action which clashes with rational nature and right reason; a theological and mortal sin is a free transgression of the divine law. A philosophic sin, no matter how grave, is not an offence, nor a mortal sin which disrupts friendship with God, nor is it deserving of everlasting punishment, when the person who commits it does not know of God's existence or does not actually think of Him — even though it is a serious sin" (Denzinger-Schönmetzer, *Enchiridion symbolorum*, 32nd ed., n. 2291; in the older editions, n. 1290); our reason for this is that the theologians are not agreed on its exact interpretation.

[15] *La Providence de Dieu et le nombre infini d'hommes en dehors de la voie normale du salut*, "Etudes", Aug. 20 1920, pp. 385-404; Dec. 5 1920, pp. 515-535; May 5 1921, pp. 257-279; Nov. 20 1921, pp. 385-407; Sept. 5 1922, pp. 513-535.

stood in a number of senses and it is essential to make these clear:
1. In the sense that a perfect sanction (nn. 297, 298) either is or is not
attached to obligation. 2. In the sense that obligation is more, or less,
pressing. 3. ... that obligation is more, or less, serious. 4. ... that
obligation is acknowledged to be a rational requirement or is accepted irrationally. 5. ... that obligation is adequately or inadequately
explained. 6. ... that obligation imposes a *de jure* or merely a *de facto*
necessity. 7. ... that obligation is absolute or conditional. 8. ... that
obligation creates a demand that is absolute or simply relative.
9. ... that obligation extends to the entire moral order or merely to a
sector of it. 10. ... that to violate obligation is objectively an
"infinite" evil (in that God is thereby "offended") or simply "finite"
(in that the requirements of reason, of the real order etc., have been
rejected).

According to our analysis, the obligation which is imposed on
the atheist is imperfect only in senses 2, 3 and 5. The point involved
in the 10th distinction will shortly be discussed (n. 169).

165. – But while we refuse to acknowledge that God is
for us the immediate ground of obligation, we do not at all
deny that He is its ultimate foundation in the order of being
and the ultimate ground of its intelligibiliy. In saying this we
do not merely wish to make the trite observation that since
God is the source of everything, He has to be the source of
obligation, or that since it is He who creates the beings who
are subject to obligation, it is from Him that this originates.
The point we wish to stress is that the very nature, the
intelligible structure, of obligation is such that it requires God
as its foundation in a way what is peculiar to itself. Hence, a
legitimate query concerning obligation is left unanswered if the
relationship between it and God is not grasped; there will be a
real danger that the person who desires to unify his knowledge
may decide, despite the protestations of his conscience, to
regard the demands which obligation makes on him as without
foundation. (For what are referred to as speculative and
practical reason are but one and the same reason, or rather, are
but two functions of the same reason).

Since, as we have seen (nn. 161-163), an obligation to act
in a particular way is immediately derived from the link
between the action to be performed or shunned, and the Ideal
of our practical reason, its ultimate ontological foundation will
be the same as the foundation of this Ideal. Now, if the Ideal is

to be anything other than "a figment of the mind", it has to be grounded on a Superexisting Being who transcends all other beings (nn. 152-153), and whose existence is marked by the same absolute necessity with which the Value is endowed, or rather, whose underived, necessary existence is the ground of this latter necessity. In other words, the Ideal can have no foundation other than God. He is, in consequence, the ultimate foundation of obligation just as He is (and because He is) the ultimate foundation of the Value.

The same conclusion can be arrived at in a way that is more appropriate to our present context, by starting from the absoluteness of obligation.

Since the order of being enjoys a priority in relation to what is only a property and attribute of this order (to be good, to be true), everything that presents itself as necessary and absolute in any line of perfection whatever, has to be grounded on what is necessary and absolute in the order of being. Now, in obligation, what we are faced with is an absolute necessity in the order of value (n. 139). Consequently, in virtue of this necessity, which is peculiar to it, obligation has to be grounded on what is necessary and absolute in the order of existence, that is, it has to be grounded on a being whose existence is absolutely necessary. But the only being whose existence is necessary in this way is God. Consequently, moral obligation, in virtue of a title which is all its own, requires God as its foundation. The necessity by which it is characterized springs from the necessity of the divine existence, of which it is the expression in the order of value, just as the no less absolute necessity of truth expresses, in its own order, this same divine necessity.

This point calls for some clarification.

The plenitude of existence which is God, excludes the very shadow of non-existence and, in consequence, removes from Him all contingency, all possibility of not existing. He i-s, in virtue of a necessity which is both absolute and intrinsic, which is in no way different from Himself and consequently, cannot be said to condition Him in any sense; this necessity transcends, and at the same time grounds, every other necessity, whether it be *de jure* or *de facto*, natural, logical or moral.

Consider, for example, logical necessity. We come to know that God exists by relying on and making use of rational principles; in virtue of these, we are led to the conclusion that our affirmation of the world about us and of ourselves, is not fully coherent etc., if we do not go on to acknowledge the existence of God. Nonetheless, as soon as we affirm His existence (provided it really is God whom we affirm), we appreciate that He is not just one being among many other beings, but the fount of all being; that He cannot, strictly speaking, be included *under* the notion of being, as if He were but a "type" of being, and that He cannot be said to be subjected to these rational principles as is the human mind, which is led to Him by their means, since He is their source and supreme condition; and that, in consequence, while this notion and these principles are undoubtedly valid where He is concerned, they apply to Him in a way that is *utterly different* from the way they apply to all other beings. So, even though the necessity with which the divine existence is endowed is grasped by means of principles which are rationally necessary, this necessity is not itself dependent on these principles, any more than it is dependent on some "law of being": on the contrary, the necessity which the principles and the laws of being possess is derived from the necessity of the divine existence and expresses this for us. It is because God *is* absolutely, necessarily, immutably that whatever is true is so, absolutely, necessarily, immutably.

Now, what we have just been saying applies also in the order of value. We come to appreciate that there is a duty, an "objective necessity", to love, respect and obey God, by means of moral principles. If we refuse Him this respect, submission and love, our will cannot be fully "right", faithful to itself and to the Ideal of practical reason. But, at the same time, we recognize that God is not just one being who is good among many other beings who are also good; that he cannot, strictly speaking, be included *under* the notion of value, and that He does not derive His dignity from the Ideal: quite the contrary, it is He who is the ground of this Ideal and of the entire order of value. In virtue of His plenitude of existence, He *is* the absolute Value, unconditioned and transcendent, from whom is excluded the least shadow of non-value and in whom is found, in a surpassing degree, whatever is valuable in any other value. In consequence of this, He is necessarily *to be loved*; and even though we are led to appreciate this necessity because of the necessity which the Ideal imposes on us (the necessity to act rationally), we also recognize that God as necessarily-to-be-loved is of His nature prior and that the necessity with which the Ideal is endowed is only an expression of this prior necessity (which, indeed, is nothing other than the necessity of the divine existence under the aspect of value). But since this necessity, as we have already pointed out, transcends every other necessity, whether it be *de jure* or *de facto*, logical or moral, God's love for Himself should not be simply considered as physically or logically necessary (because of the identity that exists in God between the one who loves and the one who is loved, the perfect lovableness of the perfectly-known beloved and the impossibility for the One of not adhering totally to Himself etc.): He is supremely *deserving* of the love He has for Himself. God is, in Himself and for Himself, not only *necessarily loved* but *necessarily to be loved*: He is supremely worthy of love and in His love for Himself there is a fittingness that is infinite. It is from this existing-for-Himself as necessarily to be loved that, in our analysis, the order of value and of duty originates; in this is to be found the supreme archetype of all obligation (but which cannot itself, evidently, be called an obligation).

166. – Up to this we have been considering God under the aspect of absolute Being and supreme Reason. But an adequate understanding of obligation does not seem possible unless we also consider Him under the aspect of Will. The reason for this is not, as Descartes considered, because the order of essences and values is of itself contingent, so that there is need for a creative decision to settle matters one way rather than another (n. 54); neither is it, as some people think, because obligation is tacked on to moral value in an extrinsic and more or less arbitrary fashion, but because of the *existential* character of obligation.

This character is manifest both in *what* is obligatory and in the way in which the moral *subject* is obliged.

Firstly, consider what is obligatory (the object of the obligation). From this point of view, obligation is a requirement that something ought-to-be (the course of action whose obligatory character I appreciate, should not remain merely possible: it should become actual). But this demand does not spring from the action in question simply as possible in itself, that is, abstractly considered; it is in relation to the existing subject that the demand arises. Hence this "ought-to-be" character of the action crystallizes into "what ought-to-be *done*". Take,for instance, the demand that "justice should be done". Now, since there would be no injustice involved if the persons who are to act justly had never been called into existence, this demand arises only because beings who are subject to it already exist. — Likewise, even though there is an obligation on human beings to strive to develop the potentialities of their rational, human nature, there is no transcendent law, nothing which is written into the structure of reality, that makes it essential that beings with a rational, human nature should exist. It is only because such beings already exist that this demand arises.

Consider, secondly, the person who is subject to obligation. Not only is it necessary that he exist in order that he be obliged — we are not at all concerned here to stress this banal truth — but, in addition, the various obligations to which he becomes subject always have an intrinsically personal and, in consequence, profoundly existential, character (n. 33). The person who is obliged is not simply *an* existing person, but *this* uniquely existing person. The course of action which is obligatory is not simply "to be done", but "to be done by me, a task for me alone". The demand is made on me as the unique person that I am; here and now, I am called upon to do something which without me will never come to be, to make a response which will never be made, if I do not make it. Others can make a response that will have a higher or an equivalent value, but no one will ever again be able to make *this* response. No one can now take my place or deputize for me; the most that Providence can provide is an understudy. ... The reason for this is that what is morally valuable and obligatory calls for a response which only the free subject, in virtue of his free decisions, can give. Despite the universal dimension which is also involved in it (cf. n. 33, 5), what I am called upon to respond to, when I am morally obliged, is always a strictly personal vocation.

Because of its existential character, obligation is not fully intelligible unless its relation with the ultimate source of all that exists is taken into account. Now, this source is nothing other than God, as free Will. Consequently, the role of the divine will has to be considered, if we are not to leave out of account a factor that is essential to a full understanding of the nature and structure of obligation.

167. – In causing beings to exist, this will "moves" them towards the completion which is not yet theirs. The natural tendency which they have to conserve and develop themselves by means of their activity is, according to St Thomas, an "impression" stamped on them by the divine command (a command which proceeds from the divine reason no less than from the divine will) [16]. But when it is a being with a spiritual nature, a person, who is in question, the achievement of this completion also becomes an imperative of his reason; further, it will be impossible to achieve it, unless he is thoroughly faithful to the Value. Consequently the natural inclination of the spiritual subject is revealed, from the objective point of view, as a demand which is made on him by the Value (and, implicitly, by God), so that while he is called upon, in an objective manner, to do what is good, to respond to the claims which the rational order makes on him, he is, at the same time, subjectively moved to give this response: what is morally good is at the same time a natural good, good for him [17]. Now, this

---

[16] "By such a pronouncement a human authority imparts a kind of inward principle of activity to its subjects; so also God impresses on the whole of nature the principles of the proper activities of things", *Summa Theol.*, I-II, 93, 5 (Trans. by T. Gilby, London, 1966; vol. 28, p. 67, of an English translation of the *Summa Theol.*).

[17] "Reason can intimate or make known something in two ways. One way is absolute: this kind of intimation is expressed in the indicative mood, as when, for example, one person says to another: this is what you should do. At times, however, reason intimates something to a person by moving him to do it; this kind of intimation is expressed in the imperative mood, as when it is said to a person: do this", *ib.*, 17, 1.

(In this text, St Thomas does not speak of being moved through a natural tendency, but as we have seen — cf. the preceding note — this latter is regarded by him as the impression of a divine command). Cf. also J. Maritain's distinction between "norm-pilot" and "norm-precept", *Neuf leçons...*, pp. 130-140.

subjective attraction, without which the objective demand would be ineffective and, indeed, could not even be made upon us, is the "impression" in our spiritual nature, and the expression in our minds, of the divine Will which, in causing us to exist, requires of us that we achieve the completion of our being by being faithful in our activity to what He has made us to be. — The significance and importance of this point will emerge more clearly at a later stage of our investigation (nn. 190 and 286-287).

168. – What has been said in this present chapter should help to make clear the falsity of Kant's theory of the will's autonomy, insofar as he maintains that our own will is the source of obligation. We are, however, far from denying that the will, or practical reason, of a rational being (to use the term Kant prefers) enjoys no autonomy at all: pure heteronomy is unthinkable, for no obligation can impose itself on us unless we recognize it in our practical judgments (even in spite of our desire not to do so, and even when we shirk fulfilling it and do our utmost to repudiate it). Note that the knowledge that is in question here is not merely speculative: in order that we be morally obliged, our knowledge of a proposed course of action has to be evaluative: we have to recognize that to act in this way is "good" and is the only reasonable course open to us. In this sense, every person is a law to himself[18]. But this autonomy is no more than relative; an absolute autonomy has simply no meaning. The presupposition that makes us capable of freely assuming and of becoming subject to particular obligations is that we are already under a fundamental obligation. The person who makes a vow or a promise does not create the obligation of "fidelity to one's promises": all he does is to make that obligation actually binding on himself. He enters into a sphere of value and of duty where he is faced with a requirement that is not pliable to his will, the requirement, namely, that "a person who makes a promise ought to keep it". It is not he who constitutes this sphere, that is, it is not he who decides that fidelity to promises is morally valuable. — But, it may be urged, cannot the distinction which Kant makes be-

---

[18] St Paul, *Rom.*, 2, 14.

tween the noumenal and the empirical "I", be used in the
present context, so as to give a satisfactory meaning to his
theory of the will's moral autonomy? Is not what he says
acceptable if we keep in mind that it is the noumenal "I" who
imposes the obligation on the empirical "I", so that the one
who obliges is not simply the same as the one who is obliged?
(The impossibility and the meaninglessness of a complete
identity between these two is, accordingly, granted). But since
obligation is possible only where there is liberty and since, in
Kant's theory, it is only the noumenal I who is free, the
distinction which has been urged is of no service. It is the
noumenal "I" who both imposes obligation and is subject to it;
and that identity, for the reasons already given, has no
meaning.

The only sense in which what Kant writes can be given an
acceptable meaning, has already been pointed out in n. 147:
that is, the source of obligation is rightly said to be reason
understood in that all-embracing sense in which the divine
Reason is also included; in other words, it is true that obligation has no source that is exterior to the entire order of reason,
so that it is ultimately grounded in what is at the summit of
that order, the absolute Reason. Since, however, we are not the
absolute Reason, but only participate in it, the autonomy which
we undoubtedly possess is a participated and dependent autonomy that is shot with heteronomy. The judgments which
intimate to us that we should do what is good are, it is true,
our own, but the power of reason, in virtue of which we are
capable of making these judgments, is not from ourselves, any
more than our existence is from ourselves: it is the impression
on us of the supreme source of the entire rational order.

169. – Another conclusion that follows is that *philosophical sin is not possible*. To reject knowingly what the Ideal of
practical reason requires of us is nothing other than to offend
God whom, in practice, this Ideal represents for our reason.

What has just been said needs, however, to be rightly
understood. It is not sufficient to say: since moral value has its
source in God, to reject it is to reject God; or again: since our
reason and nature come to us from God, to say "no" to what
they require of us is to say "no" to God. In order that a person

can be said to "offend God", the value he rejects (or the reason or nature to whose requirements he says "no"), has to possess some characteristic which makes it to be *for him* the representative of God. But how is this possible when a person has no explicit knowledge of God's existence? The person who, in times past, defaced the statue of the emperor was indeed considered guilty of high treason, but only because he knew that it was the statue of the emperor.

To say "no" to God is possible if the value which is rejected is characterized by what belongs to God alone (even though the person who rejects this value does not explicitly grasp its relationship with God, since he is not yet aware that He exists); better still, if this characteristic is precisely what founds the right of the supreme Being to our unconditioned obedience. Now, as is clear from what has been said already, this hypothesis is, in fact, verified. The Ideal of practical reason, the Absolute of value which is the centre and pivot of all that is morally valuable, is the aspect under which God is presented to us in our practical judgments (not, we repeat once again, as one whom we know explicitly, but as the ultimate in relation to which we make our practical judgments and decisions).

Hence, it can be maintained that a person who acknowledges an Ideal of value, even though he does not explicitly recognize the existence of God, and perhaps even denies His existence, should not be reckoned an atheist in the full sense of the word. Consequently, certain authors who apparently take the view opposite to the one here proposed do not, in fact, do so, since they are thinking in terms of implicit knowledge of God, whereas what those we have criticised have in mind is explicit knowledge [19].

If the Ideal of reason is capable of representing God to us in our practical value judgments and decisions, this is because human reason is not enclosed within itself, but is radically open to and tending towards what is Transcendent. This "tending towards" affects all our thinking and all our loving: we are ever led beyond our present knowledge and our present

---

[19] For example, P. Claeys-Boúúaert, *Tous les athées sont-ils coupables?* "Nouv. rev. théol.", 1924, pp. 172 seq.

capacity to love, towards the ultimate goal of knowledge and love: the Transcendent. Hence, our reason, in a sense, plays the role which some philosophers have attributed to an innate idea of God. We have not, in fact, an innate idea of God, any more than we have of any other being, but this "tending towards" what is Transcendent is woven into the very "texture" of our reason in such a way that it fulfils the function which an innate idea would have to fulfil (if it existed). Consequently, it cannot be maintained that a person who goes counter to the rational requirements that are made on him is only offending against an immanent order. This immanence (of reason or of rational nature) is essentially "open" to what is Transcendent; it is an immanence whose very meaning lies in being directed towards this Transcendent, from which it "takes its bearings".

Hence, even though I can, through ignorance, act in a way that is contrary to God's will and still not offend Him, I cannot knowingly reject what the moral Ideal requires of me without offending Him (despite my insistence that I do not know of His existence).

170. – A third and final conclusion that emerges is that the opinion we have here defended does not serve to strengthen the secularized approach to morality, that is, an approach which would exclude God completely from the moral order[20]. Far from minimizing the role of God in our moral life, we have simply aimed at making clear what His real role is

---

[20] Moveover, one could reply *ad hominem* that a secularized morality is better than no morality at all. From the opinion which we are criticising, an atheist could logically conclude that obligation is non-existent for him, so that, in consequence, "everything is permitted", as Sartre has said in making use of the words of one of Dostoievski's characters. Through drawing the practical consequences of this very convenient principle, an atheist would make himself more and more incapable of receiving light. This blindness would not, strictly speaking, be a sanction — since, by hypothesis, he would not have committed a fault — but a natural consequence, the effect of some type of negative connaturality, of an anti-connaturality (to what is spiritual) which has developed in a spirit "grown carnal". — On the contrary, in our perspective, the atheist exists in a moral regime; he can hear, and does in fact hear, the call of duty; if he responds to it faithfully, he is disposing himself excellently for the acquisition of the spiritual finesse which will perhaps eventually enable him to penetrate the screen of his prejudices and to welcome the truth in all its splendour.

and at establishing the stage at which the moral order becomes unintelligible, if His role as ultimate foundation is not recognized. As a result of this analysis, it seems to us that the divine transcendence shines out all the more brightly.

We need to be on our guard against equating God with human legislators whose commands can undoubtedly introduce certain ways of acting into the sphere of good and evil, but presuppose that this sphere already exists. Now, despite what it may try to maintain, it is to this way of regarding God that the theory we have contested (in nn. 161-163) remains tied. But the reality is very different; the relation between the moral order and God is far more profound. He gives us His law by making us capable of the activity which constitutes the moral sphere, that is, rational activity which, even though it is in us, is not from us, and so cannot be purely and simply autonomous; when our exercise of reason is genuinely rational, it makes known to us the law of the supreme Legislator who is its source.

It is, however, true that we spontaneously tend to interpret this radical dependence on God (of which we can catch confused glimpses in our moral judgments and decisions), in terms of positive legislation. Moral precepts are associated with the law which has been given by God to men in determined circumstances, as is evidenced in the religious traditions of the great majority of peoples (n. 36).

Nonetheless, it would be a big mistake to conclude forthwith that all "revelation" of the moral law can be simply dismissed as a myth. Such a summary and wholesale dismissal is the mark, not of an open, but of a closed mind. Could not what has been written in the previous paragraph be equally well regarded as witnessing to mankind's expectancy of an authentic "revelation", which would "verify" the myth (in much the same way as a sketch stands waiting for the hand that will fill it in with bold and colourful strokes?) Is there not need of an unbiased inquiry in order to decide between the two interpretations? — We shall not be straying away from the ethical investigation we are embarked upon, if we here note that such a "revelation" would seem to be extremely helpful and desirable for mankind. Quite apart from the strict necessity — given that man has been called by God to a share in God's

own life, that is, has been called to a divine, not human, destiny
— for such a revelation, where truths of this divine and
"super-man's-nature" order are concerned (truths which it
would be impossible for man to discover), it also ensures that
"in the present condition of the human race truths concerning
God which are not of themselves beyond the reach of human
reason, can be readily known by all men, with a firm certainty
and without any admixture of error"[21]. In consequence of such
a revelation, God will be clearly known as the foundation and
source of the moral order and it will be manifest that the moral
law comes from Him. Now, this is of the highest importance
— and that for two reasons. Firstly, because it is extremely
desirable that man should not be left in ignorance concerning a
truth of such moment and which concerns him so intimately.
Secondly, and more particularly, because if we do not appreciate that God is the true and ultimate foundation of the
practical Ideal, there is a real danger of our deciding that this
Ideal is without foundation, or, which comes to much the same
thing, that it has no foundation other than man (n. 46). The
history of "secularized" ethics demonstrates that, unfortunately, these conclusions have all too often been arrived at. It is
worth noting in this context that while it is possible for a
person to lead a moral life before he knows of God's existence,
it is very difficult for him to continue to do so when, after he
has come to a knowledge of the *true* God, he explicitly denies
His existence. This is true not only of individuals but also of
entire cultures. An age and a country that are dechristianized
are in an entirely different condition from an age and a country
that have not yet become Christian. A philosophy into which a
rejection (or perversion) of Christianity has been woven cannot
be likened to a philosophy which is still ignorant of the Light
of the world.

---

[21] The Dogmatic Constitution *Dei Filius* of the First Vatican Council, ch. 2,
in Denzinger-Schönmetzer, *Enchiridion* ..., n. 3005 (in the older editions, n. 1786).
Cf. St Thomas, *Cont. Gent.*, I, 4.

CHAPTER SIX

A SYNTHETIC AND DEDUCTIVE APPROACH

171. – Our method up to this point has been analytic and inductive; we have started from our moral experience and by probing into this and seeking to understand it, we have been led to recognize that our moral consciousness is the echo and "impression" in our minds of the divine reason and will. But, just as after we had discovered, as a result of our analysis, that the judgments of right reason provide the moral norm, we then showed that another and deductive approach was possible, so now also we can acquire a deeper understanding of the moral datum — value and obligation — by taking a synthetic and deductive approach. It is obvious, since all our knowledge of God is arrived at by an inductive or *a posteriori* process, that this fresh approach will not contribute anything substantially new to what we have already learned, but will simply enable us to view it from another angle, so that we shall come to have a deeper understanding of the results at which we have already arrived. Hence, there is no question at all of now withdrawing what has already been said (n. 163), and of striving to deduce that there is a moral order by starting from a non-moral notion of God: the deductive process that is involved here is interior to the moral sphere, on which it seeks to throw light from within.

The stages in this deductive process are as follows:

1) As is shown in natural theology, it is because of their relationship with Himself that God loves all other beings and wills them to be, in the sense that as He is supremely Independent, He cannot be related in His activity to any End other than and beyond Himself; and, likewise, in the sense that He wills the existence of other beings and loves them, in the measure in which they share in His perfection. The absolute Truth loves other beings only to the extent to which they are really lovable; and they are lovable only because they share in

His infinite lovableness, just as they exist only because they share in His being. In loving His creatures, God loves Himself in them.

It does not follow from this that God does not love other beings for what they are, but only on account of something which is extrinsic to their true being and additional to it. It is only because they share in His being, and in consequence, resemble Him that they exist at all; it is from Him that they derive the individual existence, be this shallow or be it profound, which is theirs. Note also that in loving us because of our relationship with Him, "through" what He Himself is, God loves us more truly and more fully than we love ourselves (just as in knowing us in that supreme archetype of our existence which He himself is, He has a knowledge of us that is far more profound than the knowledge we have of ourselves, since the human self as knower never completely coincides with the self who is known). In consequence, we are more secure "between God's hands" and under His guidance than we ever could be "between our own hands" and under our own guidance.

Note, too, that God's love for us is not a response to the appeal of some value which already exists in us. In human love, a response of this kind is normally present. But God's love for us is not consequent on our value: we have a value because of that love. He does not love us because we are already good, but so that we may become good. — Nonetheless, endowed as we are with the goodness which His prior love has conferred on us, we are genuinely lovable in His eyes.

We should be particularly careful to avoid speaking, as people sometimes do, of a *divine egoism*. Egoism is present only when a person puts his own particular good before the universal good and strives to place himself at the centre, even though he is not the centre. But God is the centre; He is the personal Being in whom the plenitude of all that is good is to be found. He is not just one particular being among a host of other particular beings. His "individual existence", if one can use this expression concerning Him, is radically different from ours. He does not lack our perfections; it is we who lack His. Since He is the plenitude of being, He is not in opposition with any other being, He excludes no other being; all that He excludes is what is not.

2)   Consequently, the love with which God loves other beings and wills them to be, is derived from the love with which He loves Himself and wills His own existence; or rather, it is that same love as extended to other beings, to the extent to

which they participate — and so that they may participate — in His being and His value. God has not two loves; but the extent to which He loves us is indeed limited by our capacity to receive, by our poverty in being and in goodness.

3) This will and this love are the expression, on the plane of activity, of the unblemished unity of the absolute Being, His perfect "cohesion", or better His total identity, with Himself: God is God "through and through"; everything in Him is God, etc. Better still: this will and this love are the same as His divine unity, because there is in Him no real distinction between His existence and His activity. — It is of this supreme unity that our self-possession and lucid self-mastery are the reflection and the participation.

172. – 4) The activity by which God makes His creatures to exist is the same as that by which He wills them to be, since the divine will, which is identical with the divine plenitude of being, is a creative will, whereas we are limited to aiming at a particular result and using various means to achieve it (n. 14, 2). His creative activity is, in consequence, the same as that by which He loves Himself and wills His own existence — by which He *is*. Because of this, all created existence, considered as what is effected by this activity, shares in the dynamism that is intrinsic to it: all that is created is theocentrically oriented. The creature "exists towards" God. — Note that it is not because of something which is extrinsic to the true being of the creature that it is spoken of as "existing towards" God. In making His creatures to exist, God communicates to them what is most profound and intimate in them: their individual existence[1]. Just as the moral law, according to St Thomas, is the impression on us of the divine reason (nn. 167, 178)[2], so also, in that it moves us to act in particular ways, this law can be called an impression of the divine will on us.

5) In man, God's reasonable creature, who possesses an openness to the Absolute which is not found in other creatures, this existing-towards — God is interiorized; it becomes the

---

[1] "Existence is what is more intimate to each being and what is more profound in all beings, St Thomas, *Summa Theol.*, I, 8, 1.

[2] *Ib.*, I-II, 91, 2.

existing-towards-God of an "I". Implicit in man's knowing and loving is an appreciation of this "existing-towards", in that in his heart of hearts he cannot but approve of the Value and cannot but acknowledge that it deserves to be preferred before all else. In other words, our moral consciousness, immediately expresses for us our theocentric orientation, our being-towards-Being, even though the horizon of this orientation still remains anonymous, known simply as the Ideal of reason[3].

6) Our reason reveals to us the resemblance to, the reflection and incarnation of, this Ideal which is found in beings whose nature is rational; this, in the concrete, means human beings: we ourselves and the "others" who are in the world with us. Because of our openness to the Absolute, our "kinship" with it, we ourselves and all human persons are rightly called *images of God*. Hence, to be "existing-towards-God", "oriented to the Value", means that we are called upon to live in a way that befits an image of God, to express in our concrete existence, in our daily-to-be-renewed decisions, the likeness to God which we bear simply because we are human beings.

In this sense, if all creation can be called a theophany (for "ever since God created the world, his everlasting power and deity — however invisible — have been there for the mind to see in the things He has made"[4], the good person, the person who is faithful to the practical Ideal is, in a very real sense, a higher and more striking theophany.

Simply as a rational being, man is the image of God but, as the Christian faith reaches, he becomes this in a way that is incomparably more expressed and more expressive, through the grace which makes him a sharer in the divine nature[5]. This divine likeness in the full sense is, at the same time and inseparably, both a natural likeness and

---

[3] It is in this sense that we interpret certain authors who speak of a quasi-immediate knowledge of God through obligation and moral value, somewhat in the way in which a thing is perceived and recognized through the phenomena which manifest it. See, for example, J. H. Newman, *Grammar of Assent*, London, 1903 (reprinted), pp. 101-121; Schiffini, *Disputationes metaphysicae specialis*, Turin, 1894, pp. 56-58 and 61-63; M. Scheler, *Repentir et renaissance*, in *Le sens de la souffrance*, p. 75.

[4] *Rom.*, I, 19 (Jerusalem Bible translation).

[5] *2 Peter*, 1, 4.

one which is the effect of God's grace. Hence, if we are faithful to the moral demands that are made on us, we express in our living this image of God, while by our infidelity to the practical Ideal we, on the contrary, obscure and disfigure this likeness. Once, then, the likeness which is the effect of grace is disfigured, we inevitably become less capable of expressing in our lives even the natural likeness to God which we bear. This damage can be undone and the full splendour of the divine likeness can be restored only by Christ, who is the true likeness of the God we cannot see[6].

7) Consequently, in our morally good decisions we share in a special way in the activity of the divine will by which, in loving Himself, God also orientates all other beings towards Himself. We do this both in *what* we will and in the *way* in which we will it: the objective task which is ours as spiritual subjects — to respond to the demands which the rational order makes on us — associates us, in a singular fashion, with the activity of the divine will which is guided by and, indeed, is one with the divine reason; the subjective way in which we ought to respond to these demands, that is, by the exercise of our liberty, by orientating ourselves to the Ideal, in place of simply being passively orientated, involves, in its turn, a very special sharing in the activity of this will.

173. − 8) Now, to say that spiritual beings "exist towards God" so as to manifest His likeness in their concrete existence, is the same as saying that they exist "for the glory of God". For the (extrinsic) glory of God is nothing other than the revelation of His infinite perfection by means of the subjectively finite perfections of creatures and, in particular, of spiritual creatures (who are, in a certain sense, objectively infinite, that is, in the range of their intellects and wills).

Theologians customarily distinguish between the *objective* glory of God, which consists in the fact that the creature is sharing in the divine perfection, and the glory which God receives from the submission, praise, adoration etc., of reasonable creatures (formal glory). But, in fact, what is this latter kind of glory but a higher form of objective glory? To say that the rational creature can know and love God in a way that infra-rational creatures are incapable of, is only to say that he can share in and manifest the divine perfection in a higher degree.

---

[6] *Col.*, 1, 15.

From the philosophical point of view, we can distinguish three, or even four, meanings in the classical formula: "the world has been created for the glory of God" [7].

1. A negative sense: the world is not a means whereby God receives what He lacks; the beings He creates cannot be useful or advantageous to Him; creation is an act of pure generosity on God's part. Even on the human level, the person who is moved by the desire for glory and fame is living on a higher spiritual plane than is the person whose aim is material prosperity and wealth. There is in the first person, the beginning, at least, of a purification of selfish desires which indicates to us how we can form some elementary notion of the untained generosity of the divine creative action [8].

2. A pragmatic sense, which is twofold: to strive that God should be glorified both in ourselves and in other beings is our obligation; this is our task as rational beings, and it is by accomplishing it that we shall attain that completion of our being which is called "beatitude".

3. There is, finally, a metaphysical sense: "to be created for the glory of God" means that our existence has its origin in the love which God has for His own infinite perfection and in which, by creating us, He invites us to share. This point can also be expressed by saying that creatures are born of that infinite joy which God finds in Himself, or rather, which He *is*. There is nothing more generous, more exuberant than joy and admiration; and God's creation is the "exterior" expression of the joy which is His, and of that "internal glory" which consists in the perfect transparency to God of His own absolute Value. — But what we are here trying to express in words, is beyond all words.

9) Even though the end for which all creatures, and particularly all spiritual creatures, have been made is the glory of God, this should not be understood as if the perfection and, in particular, the moral value of His creatures, are simply the *means* by which God procures His glory. Far from it: the glory of God, of its very nature, is identical with the good and the perfection of His creatures. "The glory of God is the living person" [9]: what glorifies God is that man should be fully alive, that he should develop, open out, and achieve that plenitude of

---

[7] See *Existence et Liberté*, pp. 228-234. For a theological discussion, cf. Z. Alszeghy-M. Flick, *Gloria Dei*, "Gregorianum", 1955, pp. 361-390.

[8] Cf. Ps. 50 (Vulg. 49), vv. 8-15.

[9] St. Irenaeus, *Adversus haereses*, IV, 20,7; PG. t. 7, col. 1037.

being which is possible for him; in a very particular way, the moral growth of His rational creatures glorifies Him. The glory of God is, then, nothing other that theocentric dimension which is necessarily involved in the perfection and beatitude of finite spiritual subjects.

174. – It follows that to respond genuinely and authentically to the requirements which moral living imposes on us — without deliberately seeking to turn what is of moral value to our own advantage, without becoming pharisaically self-righteous because of our good actions and regarding ourselves as not like the rest of men etc. — is to glorify God in action and *in truth*.

Another consequence is that although religion is nor simply identical with morality, as Kant wished it to be in *Religion within the Limits of Reason Alone*, it is not authentic if it is divorced from morality. "Religion that is pure and undefiled before God and the Father is this: to visit orphans and widows in their affliction, and to keep oneself unstained from the world" [10]. The true God is a *holy* God: to His holiness a moral perfection which far surpasses that of any other being is integral.

A final conclusion is that the person who does not acknowledge the Absolute of value, the practical Ideal (even though he affirms or concedes that there is a supreme Being), is at bottom more of an atheist than the person who acknowledges this Absolute, but fails to appreciate the necessity of grounding it on a Being who is personal and is the plenitude of value.

---

[10] *James*, 1, 27 (RSV).

PART TWO

THE MORAL ORDER

BOOK THREE

THE OBJECTIVE MORAL ORDER

175. – What is called the objective moral order is nothing other than the sumtotal of the ways of acting which are in harmony with reason (considered as perfectly right and perfectly enlightened), that is, the sumtotal of objective moral values, or rather (n. 24, 3), of the forms of objective moral value. If we consider these insofar as they involve obligation, the objective moral order is revealed to be a complex of laws, or better, it is revealed as one fundamental moral law which crystallizes, in accordance with the areas of behaviour to which it becomes applicable, into particular laws. But note that the entire objective moral order cannot be expressed in the form of laws, since all the forms of moral value do not entail a strict and universal obligation.

To describe the objective moral order, it would be necessary to describe all the forms of objective moral value — which is what, in effect, is done in a study of the various virtues, where an effort is made to describe what is involved in putting each of them into practice. In such a study, the phenomenological method can very profitably be made use of; it can be of great help in making clear the purpose and meaning of each virtue. Vl. Jankélévitch's work *Traité des Vertus* (Paris, 1949), exemplifies the use that can be made of this method. — Nonetheless, chiefly for reasons of a practical order, we shall confine ourselves to describing the moral law. Even where this is concerned, we shall not be dealing with the particular laws into which it crystallizes — this is a task for special ethics — but with its general character and with the broad and more universal principles which are contained in it, as well as with the method by which it is possible to arrive at particular and specific determinations of it. We shall pay special attention to the notion of *right*, since this marks out an important area of the objective moral order.

As an introduction to our study of the moral law, it will be useful to try to clarify the general notion of law, of which we have already made frequent use. This clarification will also have the advantage of throwing retrospective light on the stages of our investigation which have already been completed.

CHAPTER SEVEN

THE NOTION OF LAW

176. – St Thomas, in the opening question of his treatment of laws, has this general definition of law: "a rule or measure of activity by which someone is moved to act or held back from acting"[1]. He derives the word "law" from *ligare* ("to bind"), since a law "obliges" us to act. Nowadays, this etymology has been abandoned; the derivation is thought to be rather from *legere* ("to gather together, to select, to read out"), but even this is not certain. But whatever about the derivation of the word, the proposed definition is rather loose, since it is applicable to every practical rule, such as the rules that govern artistic and technical activity, the rules of games, and even to the advice which one person gives another. It can also be applied to physical laws, if a small grammatical change is made (that is, by substituting "something" for "someone").

But, at the end of the same question, St Thomas proposes another definition which has become classical: "an ordinance of reason for the common good promulgated by him who has the care of the community"[2]. We shall now explain this definition briefly.

1) A law is an ordinance of reason. St Thomas notes that it is by our reason that we grasp the connection between our decisions and the end at which we are aiming. Now, it is only because of this end that we are moved to act at all, and since it is to the source that we must always look to find the appropriate measure and rule of anything, it is clear that where law is concerned, these are to be found only in reason[3].

---

[1] *Summa Theol.*, I-II, 90, 1.

[2] *Ib.*, I-II, 90, 4 end. — On the origin of this definition, see O. Lottin, *Psychologie et morale aux XIIe et XIIIe siècles*, II, Ie. p., pp. 11-47; the same author's *La valeur des formules de saint Thomas d'Aquin concernant la loi naturelle*, "Mélanges Joseph Maréchal", II, pp. 345-377.

[3] *Ib.*, I-II, 90, 1.

Obviously, the reason of which he is speaking is right reason: if a law did not proceed from a judgment of right reason, it would have no obligatory force; it would be lawlessness, rather than law[4].

2) The ordinance of which St Thomas is speaking should be understood in an active sense, that is, *as the establishment of an order* (between the subjects of the law and the ends that are to be achieved, by means of the actions that have been commanded). So, for example, the law of military service "orders" the citizens in relation to the defence of their country. As active, this ordinance has its source in the will of the person who issues it, for it is only because the ruler wills that his subjects obey his rational ordinance that this effectively binds them. While the command has to be rational, its necessary presupposition is that the ruler wills it to be obeyed[5]. It is in view of the end which is intended (by the person's will) that the means are determined upon (by his exercise of reason); nevertheless, the decision that these means be used has the character of a law only because it is regulated by reason[6]. — But, precisely because it proceeds from the legislator as the effect of a reasoned decision, this ordinance, whose active power in relation to others is derived from him, can be called passive in relation to the legislator himself: in this context, the active aspect of the ordinance will be the regulative activity of the legislator's reason. Clearly, then, a law is an intermediary between the legislator and those who are subject to him.

3) Such an ordinance is made in view of the common good, and it is this which distinguishes a law from a particular command which is imposed on an individual. A law, of its very

---

[4] "The reason gets its motive force from the will... For it is because a person wills an end that his reason effectively governs arrangements to brings it about. To have the quality of law in what is so commanded, the will must be ruled by some reason, and the maxim, *the prince's will has the force of law*, has to be understood with that proviso, otherwise his will would make for lawlessness rather than law", *ib.*, ad 3um. (Trans.: T. Gilby, *op. cit.*, p. 9). — St Thomas is here replying to an objection drawn from Roman Law. The maxim: "The prince's will has the force of law" seems to attribute the law to the legislator's will rather than to his reason.

[5] *Ib.*, I-II, 17, 1.

[6] *Ib.*, I-II, 90, 1 ad 3um. (Cf. note 4).

nature, is universal and is addressed to the community [7]. As we have seen, it was on this aspect that Kant placed particular emphasis (n. 116). St Thomas' treatment of the point is as follows. Laws, he notes, are meant to affect our decisions. Now, in the field of decision, which is the proper domain of our practical reason, the well-spring is the last end towards which we tend (which is happiness). In addition, since the part is subordinate to the whole, a law has to be concerned with the relationship between the actions of individuals and well-being of all. Now, a particular notion is primarily applicable to that in which it is most verified [8]. Consequently, since a law is primarily called a law because of its relationship with the common good (the well-being of all), it follows that any other particular order which is given to a person can be called a law only in the measure in which it is related to the common good [9].

4) The source of this ordinance has to be the person who has charge of the community. The task of planning for the end to be achieved always belongs to the person who is primarily responsible for seeing that this end is achieved [10]. Moreover, someone who is not in authority, since he lacks the power to impose sanctions, is incapable of effectively leading others to cooperate as they ought, in the attainment of the common good [11]. Note that the community which is here spoken of is a "perfect" or complete community, such as the "republic", the state, the Church, as distinct from an "imperfect" or incomplete community, such as the family [12].

5) Finally, this ordinance has to be promulgated. A rule and measure are ineffective unless applied to what they are intended to regulate and measure; hence, if a law is to be

---

[7] *Ib.*, I-II, 90, 2.

[8] Cf. *ib.*, I, 2, 3: "the fourth way".

[9] *Ib.*, I-II, 90, 2.

[10] *Ib.*, I-II, 90, 3.

[11] "A private person can persuade, yet he cannot effectively bring another to virtue, for if his advice is not taken he lacks the force, such as a law should possess, to compel good conduct ... This coercive strength resides in the people, or public figure who personifies them; such authority can inflict penalties ... and to it, therefore, the making of law is reserved", *ib.*, ad 2um. (Trans.: T. Gilby, *op. cit.*, p. 15).

[12] *Ib.*, ad 3um.

effectively binding on those subject to it (and this is what is characteristic of a law), it has to be applied to them: and it is applied to them by the knowledge of it which they acquire in virtue of its promulgation [13].

The effects of the law, St Thomas writes, are "to command, to forbid, to permit. to punish" [14] and, in consequence, to help make people good [15]. The "goodness" that is here spoken of should be understood in relation to the well-being of the community in question; what the laws of the state are aimed at is the formation of good citizens [16]. But this is really a mediate effect; the immediate and proper effect of a law is the obligation which it creates for those subject to it [17].

177. – What is called the "voluntarism" of Suarez is often opposed to the Thomistic notion of law. Suarez' definition is: "a just, stable and sufficiently promulgated precept which is binding on all" [18]. As is obvious, this definition is similar enough to that of St Thomas with, however, the added condition of stability. But when Suarez faces the question of whether, strictly speaking, the source of the law is the legislator's intelligence or will, the reply which he gives is sinuous. He first shows that a law is the product both of intellect and will, so that even if, strictly speaking, its source is in one only, it still depends intrinsically on the other [20]. But the final conclusion to which he comes is that the more intelligible and defensible view is the one which regards a law, as it originates in the legislator, as a just and upright act of his will, by means of which he decides to oblige those subject to him to act in this or that particular way [21]. Quite clearly, in Suarez' view, the decision of the legislator is far from being arbitrary and irrational. His decision has to be "just and upright", that is, regulated by reason; a law which is not in conformity with reason is no law [22].

---

13 *Ib.*, I-II, 90, 4.
14 *Ib.*, I-II, 92, 2.
15 *Ib.*, I-II, 92, 1.
16 *Ib.*, ad 3um.
17 Suarez, *De legibus*, I, c. 14.
18 *Ib.*, c. 12.
19 *Ib.*, c. 5.
20 *Ib.*, n. 22.
21 *Ib.*, n. 24.
22 *Ib.*, c. 9, n. 7.

We should be careful not to exaggerate the difference
between the Thomistic and Suarezian notions of law. Thomists
also acknowledge the important role of the legislator's will in
establishing a law — a role which is twofold. On the one hand,
underlying the rational activity which results in the formulation of the law, is the legislator's intention of the end to be
achieved (the common good); on the other hand, the legislator
has often to decide which of two (or more) possible ordinances
he is going to choose. It will by no means always happen that,
by the "very nature of things" or of the situation, there will be
only one rational decision open to him, at least in detail and
with compelling reasons in its favour. Where the majority of
positive laws are concerned, more than one possible line of
action will, in fact, present itself. There will not always be such
objectively strong reasons that the adoption of one particular
ordinance, in preference to some other, becomes a matter of
imperious necessity — and this not only because of the impossibility of having an exhaustive knowledge of the concrete
situation, but also because one and the same situation will have
various facets, and will be open to different interpretations, so
that it will be permissible for the legislator to concentrate on
achieving some particular values at the expense of others. So,
for example, the adoption of one plan of economic development, of one programme of studies etc., implies an option
between various possibilities, interests, values, even where
there is no question at all of an objective hierarchy (not even
when all the circumstances are taken into account). To make a
law, then, is not simply a matter of formulating what is
required in order to meet the needs of the situation.

But, despite all this, it remains true that the Thomistic and
Suarezian notions represent two different and typical ways of
regarding law. According to St Thomas, the legislator's intelligence animates and channels the movement of his will
towards the end which he intends (and towards the achievement of which, his will moves those subject to him). According to Suarez, it is, on the contrary, the legislator's will which
singles out from the different possible ordinances that he
grasps intellectually, the one which he prefers. In the former
approach, greater emphasis is placed on the objective requirements of the situation while, in the latter, the emphasis

is on the legislator's preference with regard to these requirements. These two approaches are, however, complementary
rather than opposing; if either is adopted to the exclusion of
the other, serious difficulties will result.

178. – A distinction which has traditionally been made
by the Scholastics is that between the eternal law and temporal
laws. The first, the archetype of every law, had already been
defined by St Augustine as "the divine reason or will commanding that the natural order be preserved and forbidding
that it be disturbed"[23]. In giving this definition, St Augustine
reveals his debt to Cicero; this latter, who was in his turn much
influenced by the Stoics, writes that the true and primary law,
the law which commands and forbids in a way that no other
law can, is the unerring reason of mighty Jupiter[24]. — St
Thomas' view is that the eternal law is the plan in accordance
with which all things are guided, a plan which is in the mind of
God, who is the supreme source of the universe[25]. Or again: it
is the same as the divine wisdom considered as directing all the
activity of creatures[26].

That God so governs all things and directs them to their
goal is clear from natural theology. As well, as our own
investigation has shown (nn. 157, 165), the entire moral order
has its source in the divine reason. This should not, however,
be taken to mean that God has merely thought out an objective
order of values, to which it is our task to conform, but that He
is in no way concerned about how we fulfil this task. For it is
in our free response that moral value primarily and essentially
consists (n. 33, 1). Hence, what God plans (or, perhaps,
"programmes") and wills, is not only the objective order of
values which is proposed for our acceptance and love, but this
very acceptance and love. Consequently, it is clear that God, as
the source of the moral order, is also the author of a plan
which can well be called the "eternal law".

---

[23] *Contra Faustum Manichaeum*, c. 22, n. 27; PL. 42, col. 418.
[24] *De legibus*, II, c. 4.
[25] *Summa Theol.*, I-II, 91, 1.
[26] *Ib.*, I-II, 93, 1.

The Scholastics have, however, disagreed among themselves about whether "law" is here the right word. The chief
reason for this disagreement has been centred on the need for
laws to be promulgated. As we have seen, they have included
this in their definitions; in consequence, they are faced with the
problem of how there could be an eternal law, when those who
are subject to it and to whom it has to be promulgated, are not
themselves eternal. St Thomas' reply is that the promulgation
is eternal where God is concerned, but not where His creatures
are concerned; this reply, however, scarcely removes the
difficulty [27].

179. – Temporal laws are, in their turn, divided into
what is called "natural law" and "positive laws".

The natural law is nothing other than the practical
judgments of right reason which, as such, invest with a moral
significance (introduce into the moral order) the tendencies of
our rational nature towards its true goals. It is described by St
Thomas as a sharing by human beings in the eternal law, since
the light of our practical reason is an "impression" on us of the
divine light [28]. By the very fact that we are capable of moral
judgments, this law is promulgated to us. As is only to be
expected, the diversity of opinions concerning the norm of
morality and the essence of moral value is here re-echoed. One
school of thought will primarily regard the natural law as the
expression of the requirements of our rational nature, while the
opposing school will regard it as the expression of the
requirements of reason [29].

The role of positive laws, whose source is the reason and
will (provided that these are "right" and true to themselves) of

---

[27] *Ib.*, I-II, 91, 1 ad 2um.

[28] "... implying that the light of natural reason, by which we discern what is
good and what evil, is nothing but the impression of divine light on us.
Accordingly, it is clear that natural law is nothing other than the sharing in the
eternal law by intelligent creatures", *ib.*, I-II, 91, 2 (apropos of the words in Ps.
4, according to the Vulgate: "There be many who say: Who will show us any
good? The light of thy countenance, O Lord, is signed upon us"). Translation:
T. Gilby, *op. cit.*, p. 23.

[29] On the natural law in St Thomas, read in addition, *ib.*, I-II, 94, a
question which is entirely dedicated to this topic.

the legislator, is to determine what the natural law leaves indeterminate, or to make possible the achievement of goals which could not be achieved in virtue of the natural law alone. Here, also, the Scholastics have distinguished between positive divine law, which is subdivided in its turn into the divine law of the old Covenant (the Mosaic law) and that of the new Covenant (the Evangelical law or the "law of grace"), laws revealed by God and whose treatment is part of theology, — and positive human laws which can, for their part, be either ecclesiastical or civil [30].

Positive divine law and ecclesiastical laws provide particularly apt examples of laws which have been made in view of a goal for whose attainment the guidance provided by the natural law would not suffice.

180. – We have just given, in brief outline, the Scholastic, and more particularly the Thomistic, conception of law [31]. Obviously enough, it is perfectly verified only in positive human laws, which have provided the data of which it is the fruit. The Thomistic definition (and this is still more true of that of Suarez) has a distinctly juridical flavour; indeed, given the sources used by St Thomas, this could not be otherwise.

Consequently, it is only with difficulty and by straining the meaning of the words used, that this definition can be applied to the natural, and to the eternal, law. We have already noted the difficulty where the "promulgation" of the eternal law is concerned; and the relationship with the common good also gives rise to difficulties. To consider this relationship as

---

[30] On human law, see *ib.*, I-II, 91, 3 and 95-97.

[31] Among other conceptions of law, we note, in particular, the celebrated definition of Montesquieu: "Laws ... are the necessary relationships which derive from the nature of things", *Esprit des Lois*, Ie p., ch. 1, beginning. This definition is too broad, since it refers equally well to physical and to moral laws; also, it can only with difficulty be applied, in any proper sense, to positive laws concerning which one cannot, in general, say that they are necessary. Another definition, which he gives a little further on, has more in common with the notion of the natural law we have here presented: "Law, in general, is human reason as governing all the peoples of the earth; and the political and civil laws of each nation should be nothing other than particular instances of the application of that human reason", *ib.*, ch. 3.

essential to the natural law (and to the eternal law) leaves one open to serious objections. One reason for this is that the difference between a particular command and a law that is binding on all, is quite accidental as far as the moral conscience of the person who is obliged, is concerned. Whether my duty is or is not yours, whether its source is a stable law or a specific command, does not increase or diminish my obligation: where my moral interiority is concerned, I am as obliged in one situation as in another. (On the other hand, if one turns from the subjective point of view of a person's conscience, to the objective point of view of the philosopher, the consideration of the universal character of the moral law becomes very fruitful and rewarding. The question of whether there is a natural moral law will then involve the further questions of whether all human beings are subject to the claims of morality and obligation, and of the extent to which these claims are the same on all. In the following chapter we shall take up this topic).

Secondly, even though the citizen *as such* and, consequently, as subject to human positive law, can rightly be regarded as part of the state, and his individual good as subordinate to its good, the same is not true of the subject of the natural law, who is each human being as human, as one who shares in a common humanity but is yet unique — each human being as a person. Now, the person, as such, cannot be considered as simply part of the community: because he is openness to the Universal, he has a corresponding value. In consequence, his good cannot be purely and simply subordinated to the good of the state. He is an *end in himself* and should never — as Kant well insisted (n. 116) — be regarded merely, nor indeed principally, as a means. — For these reasons, the relationship with the common good does not seem to be essential to the notion of natural law. What this directly requires of me is to observe the rational order, and to live by the values of this order; it does not directly speak to me of the need to aim at the common good [32].

---

[32] On the relation of the person to the common good, see J. Maritain, *La personne et le bien commun*, Paris, 1947 (*The Person and the Common Good*, London, 1957); J. H. Wright, *The Order of the Universe in the Theology of St Thomas Aquinas*, Rome, 1957. — On the controversy to which Maritain's views have given rise in

One could, however, if one wished, understand this relationship with the common good as a relationship with God who is man's last end and the good of everything that is in the universe (the common good of the universe). It is this relationship which, in fact, is the well-spring of the natural law. As St Thomas notes, man's practical reason can establish nothing firmly except through grasping its relationship with his last end, which is the common good; what is, however, established in this way has the quality of law [33]. Now, it is quite true that God deserves to be loved on account of His infinite perfection — simply because He is God — and not solely or principally because He is "the good of the universe"; but it is also true that it is only as the source of every perfection, of every participated goodness, that we naturally know God. — In addition, even when my moral act remains hidden in the depths of my conscience, I am not the only one whom it concerns. I have a confused appreciation that my act cannot be disengaged from a universe of values, that it concerns the universal Value: the Value which includes and grounds all particular values, even the value of the universe itself. — Finally, as we have already noted (n. 33, 5), moral value and moral obligation are characterized by their universality. No matter how specific and singular the command, it derives its obligatory force from the most universal law of all: "Good is to be done..." [34].

All this is true. Nevertheless, the classic definition of law can be applied to the natural, and to the eternal, law only in an analogous fashion. The natural law — and still more the eternal law — is the source from which every positive law derives its force: it can be called the transcendental, the ultimate and necessary, condition of these latter. Since our distinct knowledge commences with the knowledge of what is exterior to us, the law with which we are initially most familiar,

---

America cf. Ch. De Koninck, *De la Primauté du Bien Commun contre les Personnalistes*, Quebec, 1943, with the reply of I. Eschmann, *In Defence of Jacques Maritain*, "The Modern Schoolman", 1945, pp. 183-208 and the response of De Koninck, *In Defence of St Thomas*, "Laval théologique et philosophique", 1945, pp. 9-109.

[33] St Thomas, *Summa Theol.*, I-II, 90, 2 ad 3um. Cf. *Cont. Gent.*, II, 17.
[34] Cf. *Summa Theol.*, I-II, 90, 2 ad Ium.

and of which we have the clearest notion, is positive law. It is by reflecting on this that we arrive at an understanding of the natural and the divine law. But the paths by which we are led to this understanding are not identical. We come to know, or rather to ackonwledge, the natural law as a structure that is operative within us: reflection that is nourished by a growing moral experience enables us to make explicit what was formerly implicit in our moral decisions. The eternal law, on the other hand, is, by definition, outside of us. By starting from the natural law we can conclude to the eternal law, and once we do, we appreciate that both can be called laws only in a very analogous sense. Our knowledge of the eternal law helps, in its turn, towards a better understanding of the natural law, just as our knowledge of this latter helps towards a greater apprecia- tion of positive laws, by throwing light on their meaning and function.

Consequently, there is little point in making determined efforts to show how the general notion of law is verified in the natural or the eternal law. Our understanding of the nature of law as such will be better and more profound if we start from the natural law (which we come to know through the demands which obligation makes on us); on the other hand, to start from the abstract notion of law would prevent us from arriving at a true and deep appreciation of the natural law [35].

181. – After these reflections on the natural law, which can be called the "animating principle" of the objective moral order (at least within the limits in which we are treating of it), we have now to turn to an examination of the structure of this order. To fill in the details of this structure by determining what is to be done and what is to be avoided, is the task of special ethics. Our task, here, is to seek an answer to a prior question, namely, the question of the possibility of special ethics. Is there a firm and stable structure in the moral world and if so, how great is its extent? In other words: are there in the objective moral order rules which are fixed and are binding on all? Or should we not rather say that no norm, no principle,

---

[35] Cf. O. Lottin, "Mélanges Joseph Maréchal", *art. cit.*, especially pp. 366 seq.

which will not admit of exceptions, can enable human beings to deal with the concrete and singular problems which they face? If this is so, a completely original solution will have to be worked out on each occasion.

Note well that the necessity imposed on us to do good and avoid evil, to act in accordance with right reason, to be faithful to the Ideal etc., does not immediately entitle us to decide, in an absolute fashion, that some actions are, of their nature, good or evil, in conformity or at variance with right reason, compatible or incompatible with fidelity to the Ideal etc. It might well be that this harmony or disharmony is entirely conditioned by the concrete circumstances, so that, in each successive situation, a person would be called upon to seek a fresh solution, simply by exercising his practical reason (strengthened of course by the virtue of prudence). Hence, granted that every human being should act in the way which is most in accordance with the spiritual dimension of his being, should it not then, perhaps, simply be left to the prudent judgment of each one to decide whether, and to what extent, a particular action fulfils this requirement? What place can there be for abstract and general norms, which a person will inevitably find to be inadequate as he attempts to deal with concrete problems that each unique situation will present?

This is the question we are going to consider in the following chapter.

CHAPTER EIGHT

THE POSSIBILITY OF UNIVERSALLY BINDING AND UNCHANGEABLE MORAL RULES?

182. – To assert that there are unchangeable and universally binding moral laws is, nowadays, to run into serious difficulties.

One reason for this is the patent fact that the concrete situations in which moral subjects find themselves are so different that it does not seem possible to point to any norm which would always be applicable. The difficulty of having such a norm becomes even more pronounced if account is taken, not only of the external circumstances in which an action is performed but also, and particularly, of the interior dispositions of different people. What is good for one person will not necessarily be good for another. Did not Aristotle, and St Thomas in his wake, rightly teach that the notion of good is analogous, by which they meant that what is good in the concrete for a particular subject can be determined only in relation to that subject?[1].

In addition, we find that, as a matter of fact, moral rules are not interpreted by everyone in the same way. This diversity provides sceptics, positivists and "sociologists" with a warhorse on which they charge into the fray. (n. 6). "Different times mean different morals" they cry. "What is good and right in one region is wrong and evil in another". Many actions which the conscience of modern man finds repugnant were formerly considered, among other peoples and in other epochs, as licit and even as praiseworthy (and can also, for that matter, find defenders even at the present day). Examples of this are the murder of one's parents and of prisoners of war, the abandonment of infants, human sacrifices, ritual prostitu-

---

[1] Aristotle, *Nicom. Eth.*, I, 6, 1096 b 26-31; St Thomas, *Summa Theol.*, I-II, 64, 2.

tions, so frequent in the ancient Oriental cults, acts of theft, encouraged at Sparta as an exercise in aggressiveness and craftiness etc. Even today, among peoples who are held to be civilized, how many there are who do not seem to appreciate that there is any disorder in certain actions which others judge to be clearly immoral: dishonesty which is practiced at the expense of the state or of large business organizations, evasion of taxes and other fraudulent procedures, the practice of contraception, abortion, the elimination of deformed infants etc.! — It is in consequence of all this that, as we have seen (nn. 52. 78), the sociological school of ethics maintains that it lies with each particular society, distinct as it is from all others, to determine what is to be considered good and what is to be considered evil. If what they say is true, it can obviously no longer be claimed that moral rules are stable and universal.

The Existentialists, for their part — and we have particularly in mind here Sartre and his followers — cannot acknowledge a natural moral law that is binding on all human beings (not at least if they remain faithful to their own theory), for the very simple reason that they do not acknowledge a "human nature" (n. 107). Where man is concerned, they insist, "existence precedes essence": it is by his free choices that man makes himself to be this rather than that; he is free to determine what his values are to be and what they are not to be. — Even though man has the task of striving to make himself ever more free, this does not at all mean that it is possible to point to "the paths of liberty" on which all are to walk.

Note also that certain Protestant theologians (notably in Germany) under the influence of Sören Kierkegaard, reject, on other grounds, moral norms that are universal and objective, or at least allow them no more than a conditional value. Human beings are involved in a succession of concrete, singular situations, none of which is reducible to any that has gone before, none of which can ever be repeated in the future, and in each of which a new and personal call from God rings out. Since morality, at least in its higher and more refined regions, is the concern of the person as such, who is always unique, it cannot be genuinely elaborated in terms of human nature, in terms of what is universal. — This, in very brief outline, is the view that is referred to as "situation ethics", which is very much in vogue nowadays, and which aims at substituting for the classical consideration of man as man ("homo ut sic"), the consideration of man as this-man-here, at this actual moment ("homo ut hic").

Kierkegaard's theory, expressed in *Fear and Trembling*, concerning the "suspension of ethics", is wellknown. Man's relationship with God, he emphasizes, is an existential, not an objective, one; it is the relationship of a being who exists in the human way to the Being whose existence is absolute, the relationship of the human subject to the absolute Subject. Now, the subject is always "unique". Hence, Kierkegaard concludes, man's relationship with God, which is in the religious sphere, transcends the ethical sphere, which is objective and regulated by universal norms. (Curiously enough, this sphere seems to be summed up, in Kierkegaard's eyes, in the state of marriage). God can, in consequence, ask man to do what ethics forbids, as the example of Abraham, who was commanded by God to immolate his son Isaac, makes clear. (This example provides the theme for *Fear and Trembling*). — It has, indeed, to be admitted that there are some incidents in Scripture (the despoliation of the Egyptians by the Hebrews, the marriage of Osee) which, if we accept them literally, seem, at least at first sight, to indicate that God has suspended the moral law.

In the context of our present reflections, it is worth noting that Lutheran theology, in the measure in which it holds that human nature has been totally corrupted by original sin, so that human reason is now entirely incapable of grasping moral and religious truths, cannot but reject the notion of natural law. It is only Revelation which gives man the knowledge of moral truths. (In practice, this Revelation will gradually come to be identified with the here-and-now testimony of the individual's conscience "in the situation").

Note, too, that long before the Reformation, the Nominalists claimed that the order of values was entirely derived from the free will of God (n. 54); if this were true, it would mean that moral laws are radically contingent. This contingency was also admitted by Scotus, but only where secondary precepts of the moral law are concerned, that is, precepts which do not deal with our "duties towards God" (all the commandments of the Decalogue, with the exception of the first three)[2].

---

[2] On Scotus see Et. Gilson, *Jean Duns Scot*, Paris, 1952, pp. 603-624, especially pp. 615 seq. "Contrary to what St Thomas had taught, Duns Scotus maintains that in several instances God has granted dispensations from certain

183. – That the moral law, as regards its material content, is subject to a cartain measure of diversity and change, is quite undeniable and is not, in fact, denied — even by the most traditional authors. An illustration of such a change is provided by the changed attitude towards lending money at interest. Up to the beginning of the last century, Catholic moralists considered this practice to be fundamentally illicit. It was tolerated, in certain instances, on the grounds that the person who had given the loan was forfeiting a profit he might otherwise have made, that he was running a certain risk for which he deserved to be compensated etc. In other words, there might be extrinsic titles, which would justify the payment of interest. Nowadays, scarcely anyone would dream of condemning this practice, provided the interest charged is not exorbitant. Inversely, older authors allowed slavery in the strict sense, or at least did not condemn it as absolutely illegitimate [3]: some theologians of the sixteenth and seventeenth centuries have written treatises in its defense. Bossuet maintained its legitimacy against the Protestant minister Pierre Jurieu, and Scholastic manuals of more recent times have continued to defend it, albeit in a more circumspect fashion [4]; the pastoral Constitution *Gaudium et Spes* of the Second Vatican Council, on the contrary, condemns

---

commandments of the Decalogue; consequently, he concludes, these commandments cannot strictly pertain to the natural law. The two Doctors are accordingly in agreement that even God could never grant a dispensation from the natural law, but while Thomas Aquinas concludes from this that, in spite of appearances, God has never granted such a dispensation, Duns Scotus comes to the conclusion that certain commandments of the Decalogue do not pertain to the natural law, since God has on occasion granted dispensations from them", pp. 612-613.

[3] For example, St Thomas, *Summa Theol.*, I-II, 94, 5 ad 3um; II-II, 57, 3 ad 2um.

[4] For example, Schiffini, *Disputationes philosophiae moralis*, t. II, p. 302: "Complete servitude is not a violation of natural rights, provided the essential duties that men have towards one another are observed". Similarly, V. Cathrein, *Philosophia moralis*, 14th ed., p. 374: "Any servitude in the strict sense is less in harmony with human dignity and is open to various dangers; nevertheless, of itself, it does not, strictly speaking, involve a violation of natural rights, as long as it deprives no one of his inalienable and essential rights". But what is being discussed is serfdom rather than slavery: this latter, since it denies all rights to the slave, is "a violation of natural rights", p. 375. St Thomas does not make this distinction.

slavery unequivocally, on the grounds that it is a violation of
human dignity, just as are prostitution, the selling of women
and children, degrading conditions of work etc.[5].

But our problem here is whether all moral rules are of this
type, or whether there are some which remain unchanged in
spite of changing times and circumstances; as well, we have to
see whether there is a universally binding and permanent moral
structure, which underlies the evident variety and changes to
which we have referred.

A further and separate question that arises, is whether
these universal rules (supposing that there are such) are really
known universally, and if so, in what depth. These two
questions — are there universal rules and if so, are they
universally known — are not always sufficiently distinguished
by the Scholastic authors when they discuss the problem of the
universality of the moral law. Perhaps this is the result of their
definition of law in general, for which the model is positive
law, and in which the need for promulgation is included
(n. 176). A consequence of this approach is that the natural law
cannot be called universal unless it is universally known, at
least as regards its more general precepts.

The distinction on which we are here insisting has,
however, been made clearly enough by St Thomas, when he
discusses the question of whether the natural law is the same for
all, both as regards its claims on them and their knowledge of
it[6]. In dealing with this question, he acknowledges that there
will not necessarily be an identity between the universality of
this law as it is "in itself" (the judgments of right practical
reason, which express the ways of acting that are authentically
human and, in consequence, binding on all), and its universality
in the consciousness of mankind (the knowledge they have of it,
and their capacity to make these judgments, n. 188).

184. – The first question to which we turn — that of the
universality of the moral law in itself — presents two different

---

[5] Pastoral Constitution *Gaudium et Spes*, n. 27.

[6] *Summa Theol.*, I-II, 94, 4. On the question treated in this chapter, it will be
helpful to read: *La nature, fondement de la moralité*, "Supplément de la Vie Spirituelle", n. 81, May 1967.

facets, according as we are inquiring about the basic principle of morality, or about the concrete forms into which this principle crystallizes (the more, or less, proximate conclusions which can result from it).

As regards the first principle: "Good is to be done and evil avoided", there is scarcely any need to prove its universality and unchangebleness. It is obviously such, in the measure to which man (the being on whom it is binding) is always and everywhere a moral being. What, in fact, on the supposition that man is a moral being, would be the meaning of a change in this principle, or of an exception to it? If, where some human beings are concerned, good is not to be done, this signifies either of two things: that for them there is no moral good or moral evil (that these words have no meaning for them), so that, in consequence, and contrary to our present supposition, such people would not be moral beings; or, alternatively, that even though they appreciate that moral good is "good", they do not appreciate that it is to be done, and similarly as regards moral evil: but, as we have seen (nn. 161, 162), this is impossible. "To be done" is, under certain conditions, an essential property of moral good, while "to be avoided" is always and unconditionally an essential property of moral evil. — On the other hand, if the principle in question could change, this would be for one of two reasons: firstly, because it could be abolished, so that, in consequence, and again contrary to our present supposition, man would cease to be a moral being; secondly — and this would be the height of absurdity, — because it could be inverted, so that evil (while still remaining evil) would become "to be done", and good (while still remaining good) would become "to be avoided".

But, the impatient reader will ask, is the supposition a valid one? Is man always and everywhere a moral being? One could well doubt it. Admittedly, ethnology makes clear that the categories of good and evil are operative among all peoples and in all human groups (nn. 27-28). But, on the other hand, one can meet human beings — and not only in psychiatric hospitals — who seem to be quite insensitive towards moral good and moral evil; they are so lacking in any understanding of morality that the words "good" and "evil" seem to convey nothing to them.

But to admit all this does not take from the fact that reason is an essential attribute of a human being, even though particular human beings, such as small infants and the insane, are unable to exercise it (as are all human beings when they are sound asleep!) Now, as we have seen (n. 139), morality is essentially linked with the exercise of reason. Hence, man is always, of himself and radically, a moral being, so that, in consequence, the basic principle of morality is, of itself, universally binding and unchangeable.

The diversity of moral standards and moral judgments, no matter how wide it may be, presents no difficulty here, since it concerns, not the principle itself, but its application (n. 6), that is, it concerns the more detailed clarification of what is good and evil, and not the fundamental obligation to choose the one and reject the other. — On the other hand, the difficulty which is based on the existence of people who are apparently deaf to all the claims of morality, retains its force. For among such people, there are not only individuals who are clearly insane, but also some, at least, who are intelligent, capable in other spheres, cultured, even refined — but quite blind where good and evil are concerned. How could this be, if the acknowledgement of moral values is essentially linked with the exercise of reason (n. 139)?

But, in fact, the existence of such people proves nothing except that a human being, in certain circumstances — often enough he will be in a pathological condition as a result of psychic or social pressures etc. — can be prevented from grasping, concretely and effectively, what is required of him in order that he live a life that is in accordance with reason and is worthy of a human being. It does not at all prove that others are wrong when they say that *they* have the appreciation which he lacks! Once we understand that our vocation as reasonable beings is to live in accordance with the Ideal of reason, and that it is this which gives meaning and direction to our lives, the existence of people who lack this understanding should no more weaken our certainty on these points, than the existence of people who are incapable of distinguishing between the *ninth Symphony* and the clash of saucepans, should weaken our admiration for Beethoven.

Note, moreover, that what these unfortunates who are morally blind and deaf, lack, is not precisely the knowledge of the principle:

"Good is to be done and evil avoided" (as if they possessed the notion of "moral good", but failed to appreciate that it is "to be done"); what they lack is, rather, the very notion of moral good and moral evil, the power to appreciate moral value. Very frequently, this lack has its ultimate origin in an emotional deficiency or mal-adjustment. As we have already indicated (n. 21), our knowledge and appreciation of values come to us through our inclinations and appetites; as well, our moral judgments have as their normal accom-paniment a certain affective "aura" (feelings of admiration, aversion, desire, regret, joy, sadness, self-respect, loathing etc), which is, at one and the same time, the echo of these judgments, and the atmosphere without which they cannot survive. Now, just as a person's intellect cannot function properly when his imagination is diseased or troubled, so also his practical reason and will cannot play the part they are meant to play in his life, when he is emotionally parched and maladjusted. The dependence of our thinking and willing on our senses, our emotions, our imaginations, is, indeed, extrinsic, but that does not make it any the less real and profound. (But beware of confusing what is a required condition of our exercise of the capacity to reason and to choose, with this capacity itself).

Finally, is there not, frequently enough, even among the most perverted, a remnant of misguided morality? Have not thieves and bandits their code of honour ("the law of the underworld"); does not their common avocation move them to defend and help one another? Rudimentary and aberrant though they may be, the moral categories are operative, and it will be possible, at least at times, to rectify them.

185. – The crucial question, then, that we are here faced with, is concerned with the particular forms which the basic principle takes. Are we, or are we not, entitled to say: this kind of conduct is always morally evil and, in consequence, ab-solutely excluded; this other type of conduct, in certain circumstances, will always be obligatory? In other words: is it possible to conclude from the first principle to norms which share in its universality; or have we to say that the principle is immediately applicable in every particular situation, so that a unique solution will result each time? To express the problem in the terms we have already used (n. 181): is there a structure in the ethical world, in the objective moral order?

A morally good action, as we have seen (nn. 130-137), has as its material component a harmony with human nature and the objective order; but what makes this component to be moral, in the strict sense, is its harmony with right reason.

Now, if there is a structure in the ethical world, it will have to arise from the material component of moral value, since it is only this which is capable, in virtue of its different facets, of grounding a plurality of relationships with right reason. Reason, as such, is simply openness to what is Absolute, so that it is impossible for it to give rise to a multiple ethical structure. Human nature, on the contrary, is composite; it is structured by relationships that are internal and external to it, and is inserted in different ways into different spheres of reality etc.

Consequently, if there is a human nature, a reason-endowed nature, which always and everywhere and in all individual human beings is the same, which gives rise to requirements which are fundamentally the same in all, and which is structured by the same typical relationships, both internal and external — then such a nature will provide the basis in all individual human beings for the same structure of harmonious and discordant relations with right reason, so that there will necessarily be ab objective moral order which is the same for all. Whatever is in accordance with these requirements and these internal and external relationships, will also be in accordance with right reason and will be, of itself, "good" (permissible, and even, in certain circumstances, obligatory); what is opposed to them, will also be opposed to right reason, and will be, of itself, always and everywhere "evil" and forbidden. Hence there will be norms which are valid for all human beings, norms which are universal.

But what has just been said reveals the vital importance of the question: is there a human nature? We have already indicated, in our references to Existentialism, that there is much debate and controversy on the point nowadays. Now, even though a detailed and formal study of the matter is the task of philosophical anthropology, its importance for ethics is such that it will be worthwhile considering it here, even in an abbreviated fashion. — If, then, in company with many of our contemporaries (and Aristotle, also, at times), we understand nature in a univocal sense — in the sense in which we speak of the nature of a stone or of an animal —, as something which is simply given and is beyond all modification, by whose laws the individual is simply governed, without having any capacity to transcend them, it has to be said, as Aristotle has already said concerning the human intellect, that man has not a nature. He is transcendence. He is the capacity to go beyond, to raise questions about data. He is "everything". Nevertheless, at the same time, he is "what he is". He is indeed all things, but not in any way whatever: he is so only in the human way. He is finite and corporeal. His liberty is always exercised "in a situation". This does not mean that his liberty is simply faced with limitations and obstacles which he is called upon to reject and to surmount. On the contrary, these limitations are the conditions which make possible the exercise of his liberty, the conditions which are essentially linked with his existence as a human subject. *Man* cannot choose to exist as an intellect and will that are divorced from what is corporeal, any more than he can choose to be a corporeal being that is bereft of the power to reason and choose. Neither beast nor angel. To claim that he is not limited in these ways, to affect to be what he is not, would be to disown his nature, to be untrue to his reason.

Even further: this nature, whose openness "on to" being is conditioned by its openness "on to" the world, is not for man an instrument, a thing which is exterior to him — which he could use as he (reasonably) decided, and which would receive from him alone its ultimate meaning — as are the other natures that come within our experience. Human nature and the human subject are one and the same existing being (n. 13). That pre-eminent dignity, in virtue of which the subject is aware that his value far surpasses that of the entire world of objects, comes to him from this nature, in which he acknowledges the image of his Ideal (n. 172, 6). Consequently, he is not morally free where this nature is concerned. He is obliged to satisfy the essential requirements that flow from it, to respect the hierarchy or order that is internal to it, not to subordinate reason to desire, the spirit to the flesh. But this does not mean that he is to aim at an "angelism" which would be disdainful of the realities of our human situation and would, as such, be deserving of suspicion. Human nature is essentially corporeal, and man's body shares in the dignity which is his as a person or spiritual subject. Hence, even though it is possible to say that for the human subject his body is a primordial possession, it should also be kept in mind that this relationship cannot simply be expressed in terms of *having*: it is a relationship in the order of *being*. "My body is myself"; and we have to be grateful to contemporary phenomenology, and notably to Merleau-Ponty, for having brought to light the importance of this notion of the body as one with the human subject. In consequence, the requirements that flow from human nature, even in its corporeal dimension, will, up to a certain point, be the requirements of reason.

Hence there is an obligation on the human person to respect the movement towards a continued and ever deepening existence which is essential to his nature: the conservation of his life, of his physical integrity, of his liberty insofar as it is the condition for genuinely human activity, the effort to attain a certain level of cultural development and, in general, the conditions of life in default of which human existence degenerates — all these will constitute inevitable and universal obligations, even though on certain points, such as the last-mentioned obligation, the manner in which they are applicable can vary considerably.

In brief, there is a certain obligation to strive after the values which we have called infra-moral, insofar as these values correspond to certain human tendencies; and the more human these tendencies are, the greater will be the obligation.

But a human being is not an isolated individual: his life is inextricably linked with the lives of others who are, no less than he, endowed with a rational nature, so that they too "exist towards" the same Ideal of reason, and have the same radical capacity for the Absolute. No less nor no more than I myself, they are persons. Consequently, they are to be respected and loved; through them the Ideal requires this of me, and requires it always and everywhere. Always and everywhere hatred, in the strict sense, will be morally evil: it is repugnant to reason that we should wish absolute and definitive misery to one who is still capable — even should he be at present the most miserable of men — of reflecting the Ideal of reason by choosing to guide his life in accordance with reason; it is repugnant that we should regard as non-existing, one who is our companion in the vocation which we have as human beings to be faithful to the Ideal. — Similarly, to be just towards others is a requirement of reason: what grounds have we for claiming that, all other things being equal, we ourselves should be preferred to others, since our reason reveals to us they have the same absolute value as we have, and bear the same likeness to reason's Ideal (nn. 144 and 195-198)? On the contrary, is it not characteristic of a being whose nature is reasonable, to will, in opening himself to others, that they be what they are, and develop freely into what they are capable of becoming?

Note again, here, that if our love for others is to be authentic, it has to include (even though it goes beyond) justice, and has to respect in those whom we love the same requirements that we are reasonably required to respect in ourselves. That love is deceitful, which degrades or subverts the one "loved", and seeks to find expression in actions whose objective significance is that the other is being used as a mere means. Because of the unity in man of spiritual subject and organism, even his animal activities have a teleology which rises above the purely biological and animal level, and already share in some degree in the teleology which is his as a spiritual subject. (This is particularly true where the generative function is concerned, in that the life towards which it is aimed is a *h-uman* life — and also in that its exercise is, of its very nature, expressive of a love that is generous and self-giving). — On the other hand, our love for others cannot be authentic, unless we respect in ourselves the rational nature that is common to them and to us, unless we respect ourselves out of respect and love for those whom we say we love. — These considerations help to make clear how great is the influence of our relationship with others on the significance and value of our apparently most private decisions. The area of ethics which is concerned with the individual cannot neglect this relationship, even though the influence that this exercises does not adequately account for all that is involved in individual ethics. (One cannot, for example, explain the obligation to be temperate, simply and solely in terms of the concern we should have to respect in ourselves the nature which is common to others also).

Finally, and above all, man has a radical relationship — still more radical than the preceding one, since it is linked with his condition as a creature and not solely as a human creature — with God, as the one who is the source of his existence, his last End, his living and personal Ideal. This total dependence (together with the infinite distance between the human and the divine natures), is clearly an absolutely universal and unchangeable state for mankind. One could, in theory, conceive of a conscious being who would be isolated from the network of relationships in which human lives are lived; but one could not conceive of a created and finite being who would not be radically related to God. In consequence, there arises for man an imprescriptible necessity which admits of no exceptions, of loving, reverencing and obeying God. It is at this point that morality (the list of our "duties towards God") involves religion, just as here also religion involves morality, inasmuch as this love, reverence and obedience will inevitably call for the accomplishment of all our other duties (n. 174). — But, for anyone who accepts the existence of a creative God, there is no difficulty about acknowledging that His creatures have duties towards Him; it is not in this area that the heart of our problem lies[7].

It is clear, then, that in virtue of its internal structure, as well as of its relations with the other subjects to whom it is common and of its radical dependence on God, human nature

---

[7] However, if one is to believe certain contemporaries such as Sartre, Jeanson etc., even if God existed, man would still have to revolt against Him as soon as he was created: only on this condition could man assert himself. Cf. the famous declaration of Jaurès to the Chamber of Deputies, Feb. 12 1895: "... if the idea of God were to take a palpable form, if God himself were to stand visibly before the multitudes, the first duty of man would be to refuse Him obedience (applause), and to treat Him as an equal with whom one enters into discussion, but not as the master to whom one submits" (cited by Lecanuet, *La vie de l'Eglise sous Léon XIII*, Paris, 1930, p. 416, n.). — We do not have to take account of these declamations. If God does not exist, this means that His existence is not possible, so that, in consequence, hypotheses such as those imagined by the above-mentioned can have no meaning for them. The problem posed by the need to reconcile human dignity with the acknowledgment of a God who is Creator, "Supreme Lord" and Saviour — a problem which is at the source of the mentality which postulates atheism — requires for its resolution a deeper metaphysical appreciation of how, through our creation, we come to share in existence, as well as the abandonment of the anthropomorphic notions which represent God as a Master who is purely exterior, a liberty which is foreign to ours, so that to submit to Him unconditionally would be, in effect, an "alienation" of ourselves. But the study of this problem lies outside the field of our investigation.

provides the general framework which makes special ethics possible. This framework can be expressed in the traditional terms of the catechism as: duties towards oneself, towards others, towards God. Personal morality, social morality (person-to-person, familial, social in the strict sense, with its sub-divisions: professional, political etc. morality), religious morality. ... Inasmuch as the rules which are operative in these various "moralities" spring directly from the essential relationships of which we have spoken, they are universally and permanently applicable.

Note that each of these three groups of duties involves the other two. In one sense, all our duties, as Eric Weil writes, are duties towards ourselves, since in acting unjustly or irreligiously, we ourselves become degraded. But, in another sense, all our duties are duties towards others, since even the most secret of our actions is not without some social resonance; since, by self-respect, I respect in myself the others whose nature I share; since, finally, there can be no authentic love for others unless fidelity to the Ideal is at its heart and, in consequence, openness, at least implicitly, towards God. As He is the foundation of the entire moral order, all our duties can, then, be said to be duties towards Him.

But, despite the way in which these three groups of duties involve one another, there are equally good reasons for maintaining the distinction between them. To regard my love for others and my service of God as simply required by the respect I should have for my own dignity, is to make others and God gravitate around my person; if this were literally my outlook, it would be the most monstrous of perversions and, in any event, even if it were no more than an implicit and unformulated attitude, it would bring about an inevitable moral decline. On the other hand, to regard all my duties as no more than means of loving and serving others, is to expose myself to two dangers. Firstly, I can easily come to underestimate the importance of personal morality, for example, of exercising temperance, of preserving and deepening that interior harmony and equilibrium by which desire is subjected to reason etc., since these requirements would not possess the same degree of urgency if their sole source lay in the love and respect that I owe to others; secondly, I can be led to regard God as no more than the means by which harmony and co-operation in society can be attained, the means by which the greatest happiness of the greatest number will result etc. Finally, simply to identify all our duties with duties towards God, is to risk developing into an inhuman zealot. It is only the intuitive vision of how all other beings share in *the* Being, which can enable us to appreciate concretely that man's good and God's good are not two but one, and that in loving others "purely in God", we love them in themselves and for themselves, love them as they really are lovable (n. 171, 1). But in default of this vision, simply to equate the love of others with the love of God, the service of others with the service of God, would be to fail to appreciate their unique value, the lovableness that is intrinsic to them, and to treat them as no more than a means of, or an occasion for, the service of God etc. The second commandment is, indeed, like to the first, but, for us, it remains distinct.

186. – Some secondary considerations which will help us to have a better appreciation of the need for universal and unchangeable rules, can be included here.

1) As Plato has long since noted[8], it is possible to introduce unity into diversity only by means of "universals", which are intermediate between pure diversity and pure unity. This applies in the practical order no less than in the theoretical. Just as a person's thinking becomes disordered, vague and inconsistent, when it is divorced from the solid rules for coherent thought, so also does his moral living disintegrate, when it is not held together by absolute principles. The people whom we esteem, and in whom we have confidence, are those who have their principles and hold by them; we respect them, even if their steadfastness is, at times, accompanied by inflexibility[9].

2) In our moral choices we are not directly confronted with the Absolute, but express our fidelity towards it by fidelity to absolute and universal moral rules. It is by so acting that a person learns to put moral uprightness, devotedness to the Ideal (which is implicitly devotedness to God), before every material and personal advantage. In consequence, there are no grounds for setting up an opposition between humanism, on the one hand, and on the other, formalism (in

---

[8] *Philebus*, 16. D.

[9] To those such as A. Bayet, in *Le suicide et la loi morale*, who wish to substitute for "simple morality", with clearly defined laws, a "nuanced morality", moulded by the singularity of the situations that arise, R. Le Sene objects with good reason: "If one enunciates the nuanced morality in a system of imperatives, before it is applied in the given conditions, each of them will result, in these conditions, in a morality that is severe, categorical and simple; if one does not attempt to make explicit its requirements, everything is then left to the good pleasure of individuals, so that nuanced morality becomes the equivalent of the dissolution of morality", *Traité de morale générale*, p. 485.

the sense of submission to universal moral rules). The dignity of man, about which humanism is so concerned, is never more manifest than when he sacrifices himself, at the empirical level of his being (his pleasure, his convenience etc.), for the Ideal.

3) Finally, because our nature is a social one, we have need of the help of others in order to rise to an appreciation of moral values, in order to learn how to live in a way that befits a human being. Now, without universal norms, it is impossible for us to be helped in this way. Moreover, a person cannot judge himself and bring himself under control, unless he is objective, that is, unless he regards himself from a standpoint that is universal. To know myself objectively, to know myself as I really am, is to know myself as I can, in principle at least, be known by all. Such a knowledge can, besides, be expressed in words, which are, of their very nature, intended for communication with others. Hence, our moral judgments cannot but possess a certain universality; they cannot be purely individual and subjective. — Note, however, that this line of thought proves no more than that moral rules possess a certain universality; it would not, of itself, suffice to establish their absolute universality, that is, the universality that our argument in n. 185 shows them to have.

187. — But, if moral rules are universal and unchangeable, what is the source of the evident variety of moral standards to which history and ethnology testify?

It has two sources, one of which is objective and the other subjective; at times, both these sources exercise their influence simultaneously, and at others, only one or other of them does so.

The objective source is to be found in the diversity of circumstances which, without changing the law itself, modifies its content, so that, in consequence, the ways in which the law is applicable in the concrete will change. Now, this modification can be rather far-reaching, so that, at a superficial glance, the law may have become unrecognizable. Where questions of right are concerned (of which we shall speak later on) these modifications are particularly evident. — Note at once, however, that among the circumstances which result in a modification of the content of the law, must be reckoned the attitudes and judgments which are prevalent in a particular society.

Some concrete examples of these modifications will help to make the point clearer. Nowadays, we have an attitude to the rights of an author concerning his writings, which was unknown in the middle ages, when everyone could reproduce and circulate manuscripts as he pleased. Similarly, in a regime where there is a strict social hierarchy (the "orders" that were formerly in France, the "castes" in India etc.), certain usages, certain practices, will be considered as just which, in a democratic society, would be regarded as violations of justice (such as the privileges with some enjoyed under the *ancien régime*). As well, some forms of behaviour, some situations — which are of themselves at variance with the requirements of a human nature at a mature stage of its development and grown more conscious of its dignity — could represent — when that same nature is still at a rudimentary stage — the less evil solution, for that period, of certain practical problems. (Slavery, in times long past, would seem to be an example of this; without it, very probably mankind would never have been able to achieve the first great collective advances, which were necessary in the public interest). — In the midst of all these changes, the law, strictly speaking, remains unchanged. It is always true that we should not take what belongs to others: the only difference is that, nowadays, in virtue of social and economic changes (notably the invention of printing, which makes possible the multiplication, diffusion and sale of writings on a grand scale) we include under "what belongs to others", the authorship-of-this-particular-book, with all the rights and advantages that flow from this. It is always true that we should give to each his due, and should work for the common good; but what is due to each, and the nature of the common good, will be conceived of differently in a democratic society, and in a feudal or hierarchic one. It always was, and it ever will be, true that man's dignity demands that his liberty be respected, and that men should strive to ensure that the liberty of all is, in fact, so respected; but, for a long time, this ideal seemed to be but a chimera which was impossible of attainment, and which, even today, is far from having been completely realized.

Another example is concerned with our duty to respect our neighbour's life. It may be objected that this duty no longer exists in time of war, so that here we have an instance of a change in a moral rule, which is more than a modification of its material content. But, as is shown in special ethics, what is here prohibited is "murder", the taking of one man's life by another who is acting on his own authority. Now, in a war, if this is just — under what conditions a war can, nowadays, still be just, is quite another and separate question — a soldier is not killing on his own authority. But, on the other hand, even if a soldier is engaged in the most just of all possible wars, in which injustice and cruelty without precedent are being opposed, hatred, in the proper sense of the word, always remains purely and simply evil, and he is not allowed, in any circumstances, nor for any reason, to foster and encourage it.

In a general way, we can say then: natural moral laws — or rather: the particular forms which the natural moral law takes — are always applicable, if all the requisite conditions and qualifications are included. If the natural law calls for, in this particular situation, this particular conduct, it will be always true that the same conduct will be required each time that the same situaton and the same circumstances recur. ... (Whether or not the same circumstances could recur, does not affect the truth of what has just been said).

188. – The subjective source of the variety of moral standards is to be found both in the imperfection of people's knowledge of the moral law, and in the erroneous views which they form concerning it.

On these points, the Scholastics have had a lot to say. After St Thomas had distinguished between the "first common principles" which flow immediately from the axiom "Good is to be done", and which express the basic requirements of our rational nature (n. 190), and those which flow from this axiom less immediately, he concludes in this way (treating simultaneously of the questions of the unchangeableness and of the universal knowledge of the moral law):

"It has, then, to be said that where the first common principles are concerned, the natural law is the same for all, both as regards its objective validity (*secundum rectitudinem*), and as regards the knowledge which they have of it (*secundum notitiam*; cf. n. 183)". But, he goes on, where certain particular rules, which are conclusions from the common principles, are concerned, this law is the same for all in the great majority of instances (*ut in pluribus*), both as regards its objective validity, and the knowledge which they have of it; in a small number of instances, however (*ut in paucioribus*), it is not the same either as regards its objective validity, as a result of some unusual hindrances, or even as regards the knowledge had of it, either because a person's reason has been affected for the worse by his indulgence of his passions, or by the evil habits he has contracted (or even by the evil customs that are prevalent), or in consequence of some defect in his natural disposition [10]. — When St Thomas writes that the conclusions of the natural law are not the same for all as regards their objective validity in a small number of instances, that is, that the judgments of right reason are not in these instances identical with the natural law, what he says is true only if these conclusions are considered "inadequately", without reference to the concrete conditions in which they are to be applied. It is, indeed, in this sense that they are considered in St Thomas' text. The classic example is that of the person who has deposited a dagger or a revolver with another. When the owner comes to claim his property, it should, in principle, be restored to him. But what if he is then clearly insane or badly upset, and is intent on committing suicide, or has announced his intention of killing his rival? Does not reason then demand that the dagger or revolver be not restored to him? The moral law seems here to be inapplicable, but this is simply because its current formulation is incomplete. It should be expressed: "a person ought to restore what is deposired with him, unless to do so would be the equivalent of becomung an accomplice to a crime, on account of the direct link between restoring the property and a criminal action". But, normally, there is no need to add in that qualifying clause, and so, it is not added in.

From what we have already read of St Thomas' discussion of the natural law, it is in no way surprising that he goes on to say that the common principles cannot be absolutely blotted out from the human heart, where it is a question of a person's habitual knowledge; in a particular and concrete action, however, a person may be unable to apply a common principle because of the influence of lust or some other passion [11]. In other words, a person cannot be invincibly ignorant of these principles. — The secondary principles of the natural law, can, however, be blotted out from the human heart, either in consequence of the erroneous opinions which men allow themselves to adopt, or of degrading customs, or of corrupt habits [12].

---

[10] *Summa Theol.*, I-II, 94, 4.
[11] *Ib.*, I-II, 94, 6.
[12] *Ib.*

189. – Today, perhaps, we would speak in a more nuanced way. We are now in a far better position to understand the extent to which human passions, an evil upbringing, the influence of the environment etc., can disturb and falsify a person's appreciation of moral (and other) values. To consider that what is evidently immoral to us, is so for everyone, is to set foot on the highroad of intolerance.

Nevertheless, we can say that the basic principles of the natural law are so closely connected with the fundamental requirements of human nature, that they cannot, in general, be unknown by human beings who have the use of their reason.

Concerning this point, note firstly that they are not, in general, unknown. The objections which sceptics and positivists raise prove nothing, not only where the first principle is concerned (n. 184), but even as regards the general forms which the moral law takes. It is only where the more specific forms of this law are concerned that these objections are relevant. At this further level there is, indeed, much divergence and inevitably so; many and diverse conditions have here to be taken into account, and the more factors that are involved, the more difficult does it become to know what is the moral course of action. In consequence, it will be all the more easy for a person to come to a wrong decision, that is, a decision that is at variance with the moral law. In order to account for this, it is not even necessary to stress, in company with St Thomas, the influence of evil customs, or of a corrupt milieu; it can be quite sufficiently accounted for by the congenital weakness of the human mind, which so often is incapable of making that sustained effort to think and to reflect, without which it cannot avoid falling into error.

But, it will be objected, among certain peoples it is considered licit to kill strangers. Does this not lead to the conclusion that there is not a universal condemnation of homicide? By no means. Among no people is it permitted to kill another human being simply because one wishes to do so, that is, to take human life arbitrarily. Why then can it be considered lawful in some regions to kill strangers? Either because a stranger is not regarded as human, or because it is taken for granted that he is an enemy, or an impious person who does not honour the gods of the tribe and is, as such, deserving of death etc. The exception that they make where strangers are concerned results from a false minor premiss: but it leaves intact the principle concerning the respect due to human life.

190. – It will be relatively easy to appreciate why the moral law is known universally (in the sense in which we have explained this), if we now reflect on the way in which a human being attains moral knowledge.

Note first of all that, as we have seen, our reason has a very special relation with our human nature. Precisely because it is *human* reason, so that it is one with this nature (n. 155), it is already dynamically structured and disposed to approve of whatever helps to achieve the goals to which this nature tends, and to condemn what hinders this achievement. As this dynamically-structured reason is gradually fertilized by a person's growing experience of life, it will be enriched by a knowledge, in the proper sense, of the principles of authentic human living (moral principles). It was because of their appreciation of this process that the older authors spoke at times as if they considered the moral law to be innate in us. It is not, no more than are the principles of our theoretical reasoning: human knowledge is not innate. Nonetheless, it is not sufficient to say that the foundation of the moral law is innate in us, meaning by this simply that reason and human nature are our native endowments. Why is this? Because our nature is not an object which our reason considers dispassionately, as if it were no more than another field of investigation. There are in this nature essential inclinations which, prior to all exercise of our reason, already orientate this to judge some forms of behaviour to be good and others to be evil: for reason is an element of our nature. Such inclinations are those which spontaneously lead a human being to seek his own welfare and the welfare of those near and dear to him, as well as those other, and more peculiarly human, inclinations towards living in community, seeking after the truth etc.[13].

---

[13] "Now since being good has the meaning of being and end, while being an evil has the contrary meaning, it follows that reason of its nature apprehends the things towards which man has a natural tendency as good objectives, and therefore to be actively pursued, whereas it apprehends their contraries as bad, and therefore to be shunned.

Let us continue. The order in which commands of the law of nature are ranged corresponds to that of our natural tendencies. Here there are three stages. There is in man, first, a tendency towards the good of the nature he has in common with all substances; each has an appetite to preserve its own natural

But, note well that these inclinations, even when they are concerned with what man has in common with the animals (such as the power of procreation) are, from the outset, human activities, and that it is as such that they orientate our practical and value judgments. For even the physical dimension of our being is profoundly affected by regulative influence of our reason. It is not a question here, obviously, of a conscious and premeditated influence, because what we are here speaking about are the conditions which make moral judgments possible. Reason, however, directs our human activities in two ways, one of which is explicit — by means of universal concepts and the consequent judgments — but which we are not here speaking about, and the other of which can be called "natural" or "vital", where the function of reason is rather that of an animating principle, which directs from within the energies and tendencies of the human subject. A quite remarkable illustration (which is outside the moral domain), of the regulative influence of reason in this second sense, is to be

---

being. Natural law here plays a corresponding part, and is engaged at this stage to maintain and defend the elementary requirements of human life.

Secondly, there is in man a bent towards things which accord with his nature considered more specifically, that is, in terms of what he has in common with other animals; correspondingly, those matters are said to be of natural law which nature teaches all animals, for instance, the coupling of male and female, the bringing up of the young, and so forth.

Thirdly, there is in man an appetite for the good of his nature as rational, and this is proper to him, for instance, that he should know truths about God and about living in society. Correspondingly, whatever this involves is a matter of natural law, for instance, that a man should shun ignorance, not offend others with whom he ought to live in civility, and other such related requirements", *ib.*, I-II, 94, 2. (Translation by Gilby, *op. cit.*, pp. 81, 83). It is clear that, in man, the inclinations of the first and second stages are incorporated into, and remodelled by, those of the third stage. In his animal inclinations, man is never purely animal. His generative function, for example, transcends the merely biological level: since the existence towards which it is orientated is that of a human person, it possesses a dignity that is absent where the other animals are concerned (n. 185). The apparent naturalism of this article of the *Summa* needs to be properly understood.

A somewhat different division is proposed by Vl. Soloviev. He considers that morality is based on three primordial sentiments: shame, pity and piety. — These three sentiments are concerned with our relation with ourselves (the consciousness of our superiority to the animal world), with our equals, with superior beings and with God (cf. n. 185), *La justification du bien*, 1897-1898, French trans., Paris, 1939.

found in the way in which language comes to be and to evolve. Language undoubtedly involves rational activity: only the rational animal "speaks" in the proper sense of the word; the other animals do no more than cry, groan, howl etc. Now, even among peoples who are called primitive, the structure of their language is such that its premeditated creation would have demanded a considerable effort of thought and reasoning, quite beyond that of which such peoples are capable. Moreover, it is a fact that languages are spoken long before their grammar has been elaborated: in Greek, for instance, the parts of speech where not classified until after the time of Aristotle. What this fact testifies to is that language involves an activity which is essentially rational, but which develops in a "natural" fashion, in that the function of reason is to be the animating principle of this development (in accordance with what it in fact is, since the natural determinant which makes man to be a human, or rational, animal is reason). — It is with this type of rational activity that, as we have already seen (n. 139), spiritual but infra-moral values are linked.

As a result, when a human being does something, or when something happens, which is in accordance or at variance with the tendencies that have been humanized from within in this way, he experiences some delight or some distress, which are not purely on th emotional level, and which are the first stirrings of his moral "sensitivity". He has a confused understanding of a value which he is as yet incapable of singling out from other values and of appreciating explicitly [14].

But if our reason can be interwoven with our natural human tendencies in this way, this is because it is not pure reason but *human reason*, that is, a reason which is in man as an element of his nature. As such, in virtue of its intimate connection with the above-mentioned tendencies, our reason is from the very beginning (and prior to all explicit and scientific consideration), orientated towards definite value judgments and practical decisions [15].

---

[14] Cf. the parallel doctrine concerning the "cogitative power" in St Thomas. (See the helpful study of G. P. Klubertanz, *The Discursive Power*, St Louis, 1952).

[15] See J. Maritain, *Neuf leçons*..., pp. 45-57. — Concerning moral knowledge, consult J. E. Naus, *The Nature of the Practical Intellect according to St Thomas Aquinas*, pp. 46-68 and Y. Simon, *Critique de la connaissance morale*, Paris, 1934.

At a later stage, through reflecting on the values which he has already confusedly appreciated, a person will come to an explicit understanding of them; this understanding he will formulate in judgments and, by the interaction of these, he will acquire a rational and well-grounded appreciation of moral value. Before, he "felt" that some actions were "to be performed" or "to be avoided"; now, he "knows" why this is so. These judgments, in their turn, react upon his feelings and emotions, so that he will come, in consequence, to have a new appreciation of values, one that is richer and more refined. In its turn, this further appreciation will influence his feelings ... — Note, however, that our natural inclinations, insofar as they are rooted in our feelings and emotions, can become perverted. (This also happens among animals; it is not only at the human level that one finds "unnatural mothers"). This is because these inclinations are subject to influences other than that of reason: the influence of external conditions, of one's milieu, of one's organism, which is itself, as a part of the universe, affected by the interaction of cosmic forces etc. In mankind's present condition, our reason is far from being unchallenged in its regulative and directive role.

From all that has been said, it is clear in what sense, and to what extent, it can be said that human beings naturally possess the various virtues in a seminal or embryonic stage, so that under the influence of reason the seed comes to flower and the embryo grows strong[16].

191. — Another and very important conclusion that follows is that there neither is nor can be any dispensation, in the proper sense of the word, from the natural law. This is so because what necessarily stems from a particular nature cannot change, unless that nature itself changes. But that a being should change its nature or essence does not, strictly speaking, mean anything.

A possible objection to this is that in virtue of his nature, man is essentially required to draw closer to God and to obey His commands: hence, while God could not order him to disobey or hate Himself, He could, at times, decree that man's obedience and love be expressed by actions which, if we

---

[16] St Thomas, *Summa Theol.*, I-II, 63, 1; *Virt. in comm.*, 9.

consider only the normal laws, do not seem to be proper channels for such an expression and are, indeed, forbidden by these laws (n. 161). Would not the absolutely exceptional character of certain circumstances, for which the law does not seem to cater, entitle us to conclude that God was, in fact, granting us a dispensation, or exception, of this kind?

The difficulty is a serious one and the type of situation which prompts it is often tragic. But the difficulties and hardships that may be involved cannot alter the truth that when an action is such that its objective meaning and intrinsic teleology are essentially opposed to the dignity of human nature, it is radically incapable of expressing the love and reverence that a human being owes to God. For the nature which is outraged by such an action, and whose dignity is implicitly denied, is the seal and image of God in us (n. 172, 6). — Examples of such actions are those by which the harmony or equilibrium that is essential to man is turned topsy-turvy, so that reason is subordinated to the craving for pleasure and the satisfaction of desire (n. 68), as well as those by which others are treated as if they were merely things or instruments (nn. 185; 213).

It should, however, be noted that it is often quite difficult to decide whether or not a particular type of action is instrinsically evil, as it also is — this is a question which has been greatly neglected — to establish what constitutes it as a *moral unit*. It can, at times, remain uncertain whether a particular action is really a complete ethical unit, so that it is morally good or evil as it stands, or whether it is only a stage in a larger structure, an element of a greater ethical unity, so that its morality has to be measured in a broader context. Moral structures of this kind are, moreover, not reducible to the "choice of means in view of the end" type, if "end" is understood in a subjective sense. They are built up in a way that is peculiarly their own, with a teleology that is immanent and objective. There is here an important field of study whose investigation will serve to complete and, if necessary, to correct, the consideraion of individual actions.

Note, in conclusion, that certain actions are said to be good or evil only on the supposition that they are performed in particular conditions and circumstances which, in the normal course of events, are always present, so that there is, in consequence, no need to mention them. Where such actions are concerned, an exceptional divine arrangement could become a circumstance which, without affecting the principle itself, would change its material content; as a result, an action which would otherwise be contrary to right reason, would cease to be so in a given instance. It is in this way that Scholastic theologians have generally explained the morality of Abraham's decision, and of several others which are mentioned in Scripture [17]. — Leaving aside all question of Scriptural exegesis, such "dispensations improperly so called", to use the language of the theologians, can be granted only where the essential requirements of man's rational nature and his orientation to his ultimate End are not being tampered with, that is, only where a relationship or condition that is not absolutely essential is concerned and which is, absolutely speaking, subject to change... In any event, it is clear that such modifications should never be assumed. The story of Abraham represents, at one and the same time, an example of what God could ask of man, and an extreme limit beyond which man would never be entitled to go.

192. — We cannot, in consequence, accept "situation ethics", if this means that the existence of universal moral laws is rejected; since these are grounded on the relationships and requirements that are essential to human nature, no "situation", no matter how singular, can ever exempt human beings from them.

Note, however, that universal rules are not always sufficient to enable us to decide what *exactly* we should do in a given situation. Not that, we repeat, an action whose very structure, objective meaning and immanent teleology are contrary to the right judgments of reason, and the requirements of human nature, can be permitted in any situation whatever. *Such actions ought not to be done: never.* But morality has more than a negative dimension [18]. Ethics should be equally, and indeed more, concerned to indicate the conduct to be followed in order that our actions may have all the "finish" that could be desired. In this respect, universal rules, even when they are indefinitely multiplied, are inadequate for dealing with the singular problems posed by the concrete situation.

---

[17] Cf. *ib.*, I-II, 100, 8 ad 3um.

[18] On this point, E. Weil is wide of the mark (*Philosophie morale*, p. 58): morality "cannot say anything except no". Its positive guidance is borrowed from "concrete morality" — that of society, of tradition — but is not itself the product of reason.

We can be helped to appreciate this point by the well-known teaching of St Thomas on the impossibility of knowing the singular perfectly by means of universal concepts [19]. This does not mean that we cannot *truly* know the singular in virtue of these concepts. When I say: Peter is a man, is white, is a musician, is irascible, is a philosopher etc., I am expressing truths about Peter from which I can draw valid theoretical and practical conclusions. There are no grounds at all for imagining that, in the uniqueness which is Peter's, there is present some mysterious X which could invalidate these conclusions (as if Peter, whom I call a man, had within himself some occult dimension, in virtue of which universal propositions that have "man" for their subject would not be true where he is concerned!). What I have affirmed about Peter is true; what has been excluded by these affirmations, remains excluded. But everything concerning Peter has not been said; there is more that remains to be said, and more than can ever be said. — There is a parallel to all this in the practical order. No "situation" will ever make an action that is evil in itself to become good (even though an action that is good in itself can become evil, because of the circumstances in which it is performed, as we shall discuss at a later stage). But the situation can demand, or suggest, this or that particular *way* of observing the law, about which the law itself is silent. Undoubtedly, by making use of a combination of universal laws, one will often arrive at a fairly clear-cut solution: this is the path that casuistry, justifiably, treads. But if a person is to do just what the situation requires, he has to have something more than the knowledge of these laws: and that something additional is a special habit whose function is to mediate between the generality of the laws and the uniqueness of the situation. This is the role of the habit, or virtue, of prudence, which is not limited to discovering what rules are here and now relevant, but indicates, as well, how these should be interpreted and applied, in order that a person may make the full response that is concretely demanded of him.

The more weight that is given to the way in which a person performs an action (the less content we are simply to consider its objective structure — its "substance"), the more ethics is envisaged as the science which centres on moral value and which aims at promoting more authentic human living (in place of being reduced to the science of what is allowed and forbidden [20], so that it is treated in

---

[19] St Thomas, *Summa Theol.*, I, 14, 11.
[20] I once knew a professor, in other respects extremely estimable and balanced, who defined moral theology as: "the science of sin and, more particularly, of mortal sin".

accordance with categories that are juridical rather than properly moral), then the greater will be the importance which the situation will assume — but without prejudice, we repeat once again, to norms that are objective and universal. The truth of this is evident and is commonly accepted, but it is far removed from "situation ethics", in the sense in which this is ordinarily understood.

It often enough happens that in the very performance of an action — for example, in being of service to someone in need, in helping an injured person etc. — a moral subject becomes aware of a value which had been hidden from him up to that moment: the value that lies in the way in which the action is performed. (Is it not a normal human re-action to feel that the *way* in which something is given is of greater consequence than *what* is given?). The look on the face of a poor woman to whom one has given an alms can be enlightening to the person with eyes to see: the look of a human being who has been humiliated and whose dignity has been disregarded, the look of one who is begging for a touch of human sympathy even more than she is begging for material help, a look which is appreciative of our recognition of her as one who shares in our common humanity. ... It is impossible that at our next meeting with her our act of almsgiving, if it is truly a human gesture, should not be affected by the lesson that has been taught us. In ways such as this, our moral experience is enriched. Values are not given to us ready-made: at the outset, all we can appreciate is their outline. It is by exercising our liberty that we are enabled to discover them in depth for ourselves. Just as a person's thoughts acquire a new precision by means of the words in which he expresses them, and by the impact which their feedback makes on him, so also is his appreciation of values sharpened and deepened by the impact which the feedback of his actions makes on him. By definition, values which are created or discovered in this way cannot serve as norms for the activity by which they are discovered: they are the fruit of this activity and come into view "on the shoulders of the action", as M. Scheler writes concerning the moral value of human acts. It is not that objective rules lose any of their binding power, but simply that there are moral depths and possibilities in the human heart which these rules, of themselves, can never sound[21]. — We shall return to this point later.

---

[21] Cf. St Gregory the Great, *Moralia*, X, c. 15, n. 26; PL. t. 75, col. 935-936: here St Gregory makes the point that while our good works have their source in our minds and hearts, these latter are, in their turn, taught and moulded by our good actions. The love of God moves us to action; but that very activity brings fresh insights into what this love requires of us.

It is clear that moral living involves mankind in a process of discovery. New and unforeseen situations will not change laws that are essential and universal, but they will call for new ways of applying these, from which, in consequence, it will be possible to conclude to universal laws that are more specific and more precise. In this way, an individual, and mankind in general, gradually grows in the knowledge of what it is to lead a moral life and his moral conscience attains a new maturity. (Reflect, for example, on the sharper and more exacting awareness that people nowadays have of the need for social justice; at the present time, we regard as demanded by justice things which, in the last century and even at the beginning of this, were considered to be no more than suggested by charity or equity[22]). Hence, one can speak of a dialectic or interaction between the universal law and the singular situation. The effort which is required in order to apply such laws in specific instances obliges those who are conscientious to discover concrete and specific solutions which, in their turn, will give rise to universal rules that are more nuanced.

193. – A few concluding remarks.

1) The demands which a moral situation creates, far from ever calling for the suspension of a genuinely universal law (because grounded on the true and unchangeable nature of man), will, on the contrary, call for obedience to this law. For this nature is an element, and indeed an essential element, of every "situation". Thought out, "devised", by the divine Reason, made to exist by the divine Will, and having, as a rational nature, a special relationship with and "resemblance" to, that Reason and Will (nn. 154-156), our human nature transmits to us by means of its requirements, the call and invitation of God [23]. It is for this reason that our attempt to do

---

[22] It is also true that, at times, an obligation is perceived only when the possibility of fulfilling it is foreseen. There is truth in the saying of Marx: "The only problems which humanity ever poses are those which it can resolve". This is undoubtedly a partial explanation of why, in former times, the practice of slavery was not called in question: the work of the slaves seemed to be both essential and irreplaceable.

[23] See J. Fuchs, *Lex Naturae*, pp. 57-80 and 116-135 (*Natiral Law*, pp. 59-84 and 123-143). *Morale théologique et morale de situation*, "Nouv. rev. théol.", 1954, pp. 1073-1085. Situation ethics, in the sense in which we speak of it here, has been condemned by the Holy Office, Feb. 2 1956. Concerning this condemnation, see J. Fachs, *Ethique objective et éthique de situation*, "Nouv. rev.

what the situation requires of us (and to respond to God's call) is vitiated from the beginning, if we disregard the universal law which is at the heart of the situation (and of God's command).

2) An exception, a change which affects the material content of the law, a special call from God etc., should never be directly sought after, still less gratuitously supposed. Indeed, the more an action, without being absolutely and intrinsically evil (for then, the question would not even arise), involves a departure from the common norms, the more circumspect we have to be about acknowledging "exceptions" and "special vocations". In general, it can be said that a person has much more assurance of becoming his true self, the unique, original self that he has it in him to become, the less directly he is aiming at this and the more he is simply concentrating on being faithful to the Ideal[24].

3) A cogent and rigorous proof that a particular type of action is in conflict with the moral law can, undoubtedly, be very difficult at times. Even when a person is in no doubt at all that a particular form of behaviour is immoral, it will often be very difficult, or even impossible, for him (or for anyone else), to show convincingly how and why this behaviour is so

théol.", 1956, pp. 798-818 and F. X. Hürth, *Annotationes in instructionem SS.C.S.O.*, "Periodica", 1956, pp. 140-204.

In *Morality and Situation Ethics*, Chicago, 1966, by Dietrich and Alice von Hildebrand, there is to be found a very judicious criticism of situation ethics.

[24] Religious guides urge us to prefer, as a general rule, the common observance to our individual devotions. "Don't let yourself grow slack over community exercises, and hurry on to your own", *The Imitation of Christ*, Knox-Oakley translation, London, 1959, Bk. I, ch. 19, p. 41.

On the pursuit of originality, these lines of André Gide — for once well inspired — can be read with profit. "A great artist has but one care: to become as human as possible; even better: to become banal. And, strange though it may appear, it is in this way that he becomes most personal. The person, on the contrary, who is determined to make himself different from other human beings will only succeed in becoming particular, bizarre, defective", *De l'influence en littérature*, a conference given in Brussels, March 29 1900. (The passage is reproduced in *Incidences*, p. 38).

What Maritain writes is also worth noting: "For St Thomas is only accidentally an innovator; his one desire is the truth: whereas innovations are made nowadays for the sake of novelty as such and truth has becomes a mere accident", *Le Docteur Angélique*, Paris, 1930, pp. 107-108 (Eng. trans.: *St Thomas Aquinas*, J. F. Scanlan, London, 1931, pp. 108-109). — A parallelism exists between the speculative search for what is new, the artistic search for originality at all costs, and the ethical search for exceptions.

much opposed to right reason that it remains irrational in all circumstances. Reasons that are serious and deserving of attention can be advanced, but not always reasons that are compelling and decisive. Certain points in sexual morality provide a good example of this.

In situations of this kind, the attitude that should above all be avoided is the one which regards as doubtful, and as in practice not binding, all ethical norms for which fully conclusive arguments have not yet been provided. On the contrary, if a person is sincerely striving to lead a moral life and to act in accordance with right reason, he will follow, until he becomes better informed, the norms which are commonly and readily accepted as binding in conscience, and which are generally approved of by people who are level-headed and reasonable (those who are "prudent" and whose authority is given so much weight in Aristotelian ethics, n. 268). It is only to be expected that, in such circumstances, there are good reasons for these rules.

Obviously, this does not prohibit — rather does it demand — a hard-headed examination of these rules, an examination that will be critical in the proper sense of the word, in that it will aim at distinguishing the elements that are genuinely grounded on reason, from those which are the legacy of irrational customs, belief and taboos. This examination has, however, not only to be critical but prudent, since it is all too easy to reject as irrational commands and prohibitions whose *raison d'être* lies hidden from us, so that in consequence of our misapprehension, very grave consequences result.

Clearly, then, experience of life, as well as the exercise of reason, is necessary in order to arrive at ethical norms that are more precise and specific: it is on the concrete, changing, social and historical data that we have to exercise our reason. This blend of reason and experience has been, in fact, the method of Aristotle and of all the outstanding moralists. It is this which explains how the various moral systems, greatly though they differ as regards principles, are, much more often than not, in agreement where practical conclusions are concerned and, in general, endorse the norms which are already commonly accepted in a particular society (n. 6). Here, no more than elsewhere, man does not simply decide that things are going to be this way rather than that: in virtue of his rational nature, he is a moral being who finds himself in an ethical world which is not of his own creation, but whose meaning he learns gradually to unravel, while at the same time he strives to bring his life more into harmony with his increased understanding.

Among the norms of the natural law, those which are concerned with what are called "natural rights" occupy special place. It is for this reason that we are now going to devote the following chapter to the study of this important sector of the objective moral order. As an introduction to this discussion of natural rights, we shall first treat of rights in general. But note that this investigation will unfold entirely within an ethical perspective: there is no question here of developing a "philosophy of law", that is, a philosphy of human rights in relation to the laws which are their source. Moreover, it is impossible to have a rounded off notion of rights without a serious study of the nature of society and of the social being of man — a study whose proper place is special ethics. We shall here speak of it only to the extent that it is strictly necessary for our present purpose.

CHAPTER NINE
RIGHTS AND DUTIES

1. RIGHTS IN GENERAL.

194. – The word "right", together with its equivalents in the modern languages of the West (diritto, derecho, direito, Recht, droit), evokes the idea of rectitude, of conformity to the rule ("rule" and "direct" have the same Latin root), to what ought to be and, as we shall go on to speak of, to the *just* order. — This last adjective is linguistically linked to the Latin word for right, namely, *ius*. The etymology of this word remains uncertain. Apart from fanciful hypotheses (such as that which tries to derive "ius" from "uis", force, by an anagram!), the following have been proposed at various times: *iussum*, what has been commanded (Forcellini); *iustum*, what is just (St Thomas[1], following Isidore of Seville); an Indo-European root *Yug*, which is also that of *iungere* (to join) and *yoga* (Jhering's theory). Others, and they are in the majority, decline to give any etymology (for example, A. Ernout and A. Meillet[2]). It seems, in the view of these two authors, that the word *ius*, whose primitive form was *ious*, originally meant: "a religious formula which has the force of law".

The Latin word *ius*, the English word "right" and its equivalents in other modern languages, have had and still have varied meanings. Of these, three in particular stand out:

1) *Objective* rights: the "just" order, which is the object of the virtue of "justice"[3] (nn. 195-196), that is, the establishment and preservation of a certain equality in the relationships between man and man (between individual human beings, or between one society and another). It is this sense of right that

---

[1] *Summa Theol.*, II - II, 57, 1. — This etymology is unsustainable: it is rather *justum* which is derived from *jus*.

[2] *Dictionnaire étymologique de la langue latine*, Paris, 1951, under the word *jus*.

[3] "Right is the object of justice", St Thomas, *ib.*

St Thomas has in mind when he writes that the word *ius* was first used in order to designate what is just [4].

2) *Preceptive* or prescriptive rights, which are also at times referred to, particularly by contemporary writers, as *objective* rights (to the detriment of clarity). Rights in this sense are the equivalent of the sumtotal of norms, rules and laws which define the objectively just order, and prescribe what is required in order to observe it. This present meaning of the word is extended to include the science which studies the just order and seeks to establish "what is just" [5], notably by interpreting the rules and laws. It is in this sense that one speaks of Civil Law, Canon Law, a student of Law, a degree in Law etc. (In English, though not for example in French, the word "law" rather than "right" is used in the present context. This may be a little confusing, but if it is kept in mind that civil and canon law are the immediate source of our civil and canonical rights, the usage will not be misleading).

3) *Subjective* rights: the *moral* capacity or power to possess, to do, or to demand something (whether this is a *thing*, in the proper sense of the word, such as a house, a field, a sum of money etc., or an *action* to be performed by some other person, such as a service to be rendered etc.), which it is *just*, in harmony with the just order, that I possess, do, demand or at least which I am entitled to possess, do, or demand without being hindered by others. The words "capacity" or "power" are here used because a right, no less than physical powers (sight, hearing, intelligence etc.), remains even when it is not exercised. We do not lose our power to see, hear and think when we sleep. Similarly, if some external circumstance outside my control or some personal whim of my own results in my not voting, I do not thereby lose my right to vote (unless the law of the land so decrees); I keep this right when I have voted, just as I had it before I placed my voting paper in the ballot-box. But this capacity is *moral*, which means not only that it is not physical but, in addition, that the effects which it produces are in the moral order. If I have the right to vote, others are bound to respect this right and act immorally if they

---

[4] *Ib.*, ad Ium.
[5] *Ib.*, ad 2um.

seek to prevent me from registering my vote. For my own part, because I have this right, my exercise of it is in accordance with right reason and is, in consequence, morally good, provided I have complied with the other conditions which are requisite for such activity.

Clearly then my subjective right has as its correlative the duty that is imposed on others not to hinder my exercise of it (nn. 199, 201). This point is essential for a full understanding of the notion of right, since this means more than mere "lawfulness" or "uprightness". It is morally permissible to do everything that is not evil and this, of itself, involves nothing more than a relationship with right reason. But we could not, strictly speaking, say that we have a right to perform actions of this kind, unless all that we intended to express was that the Supreme Legislator did not require us to abstain from these actions. — The reason for this is that rights, in common with justice (which we shall discuss in the next number) involve not only a relationship with right reason, but also a relationship with others (n. 197). It is only as "facing towards" others and in reference to them that we have rights. Even when a right seems to refer directly to a material object (as in the right of ownership), what it is, in reality, concerned with is the actions of other people, who are forbidden to take this object from me, to hinder me from treating it as my own etc. This last point helps to make clear why *subjective* rights are here treated of as an element of the *objective* moral order. On the one hand, these rights define for an individual subject the sector of the practical objective field in which he can exercise his liberty without violating the virtue of justice (whatever about other virtues); on the other hand, they impose a duty, a specific requirement of the moral law, on other people.

This third meaning of the word "right" is the one that people are most familiar with nowadays. They very readily appeal to their rights to act in this or that particular way; much is heard of the rights of man and of the citizen, the rights of peoples etc. The spirit of the age is one which is much more inclined to assert subjective rights than it is to strive to promote what is objectively right, that is, to work for the establishment of the just order.

Note, however, that this third meaning is more recent than the first two. It is not, for instance, found among the various senses of the word which St Thomas gives for the word *ius*. (In fact, William of Ockham was the first to interpret the word in this way). In consequence, certain Thomists reject this meaning[6]. As well, there have been vigorous discussions concerning it among contemporary jurists[7]. — Nevertheless, it seems to us that this sense of "right" should not be disregarded, since it has its own valid meaning. For what is a subjective right but the just order (what is objectively right) considered in relation to the aims and interests of the subject, that is, as capable of promoting these? Undoubtedly, in order to be a genuine right, a subjective right has to be in conformity with the just order: if I really have a right to an inheritance, it is objectively just that I should receive it; but this just order is here related to the subject in that it defines the sphere within which he is entitled to be free from interference, and the field in which he may exercise his liberty.

195. – As is clear from what has been said, the notion of right (*ius*), in whatever sense it is understood, is closely linked with that of justice. According to St Thomas, this virtue aims at establishing order in human relationships: it is concerned with equality, as its very name indicates: do we not commonly speak of things which harmonize and are adapted to one another as "adjusted"? Now, obviously, equality implies a relationship between *two*; *another* is essentially involved in it. ... The other virtues, on the contrary, perfect the subject not precisely in his

---

[6] For example, L. Lachance, *Le concept de droit selon Aristote et Saint Thomas*, Paris, 1933; *Le droit et les droits de l'homme*, Paris, 1960.

[7] Among those who are opposed to the concept, we note the following: L. Duguit, H. Kelsen, M. Villey. Consult on the topic: "Archives de philosophie du Droit", t. IX: *Le droit subjectif en question*, Paris, 1964; particularly to be noted is the study of M. Villey, *La genèse du droit subjectif chez Guillaume d'Occam*, pp. 97-127. — Note that the authors are not agreed on the exact definition of subjective right and M. Villey, among others, understands it in a somewhat more restricted sense than it is here understood. — The main objection to this concept is its individualistic, egocentric character which, it is alleged, represents an attack on the primacy of the common good and of impartial justice. There is, however, a legitimate way of putting the subject in the centre, without at the same time making his point of view the ultimate one, on the contrary, acknowledging that, in another perspective, this centre is subordinate. It may very well be that this way of considering the matter is of no interest to the jurists, and that they find this notion of no help: of this, they themselves are the judges. For the philosopher, however, it is of interest.

It is worth noting that the expression "subjective right" did not make its appearance until the 19th century. The definition of right as a moral power or faculty seems to be that of Grotius.

relationship with others, but in "his relationship with himself", that is, in what concerns himself[8].

But what is to be understood by this "equality"? To answer this question it will be useful to turn from the definition of St Thomas, which we have just noted, to another one which is derived from Roman law, and which he gives in the following question: "the abiding and constant resolve to give to each what is his by right"[9]. At first sight, this definition does not seem to throw any fresh light on the notion of justice, since the closely linked notion of right is contained in it. But note that if we omit the words "by right", the formula is still meaningful and valid. The following definition (which St Thomas in effect gives a little further on) then results: justice is the virtue which inclines us to give to each his due, to give him what is "his"[10].

196. – But this prompts the question of what exactly "his" means? — Note, firstly, that it is used both as a possessive adjective or pronoun, and that it is also linked with the reflexive: "himself", where "self" is an inheritance from a form which originally, as it still is in modern Russian, could be used to refer to each of the three persons (the connection is more apparent in Latin: *se – suum*). Let us now consider, in turn, these two aspects of the word and, firstly, the possessive aspect.

Having is often opposed to *being*; but, in fact, it is rather its complement. It involves a certain unity between what is possessed and the one who possesses, but it is a unity in which the distinction between the two is preserved, a unity which implies subordination, finality, completion. What is possessed is related to the one who possesses as the part is related to the whole, the limb to the living being, the instrument to the agent who makes use of it (with whom it forms one dynamic totality) etc. In this sense, one can say that every existing being "possesses" the principles of being that are intrinsic to it, as

---

[8] St Thomas, *Summa Theol.*, II - II, 57, 1. — On the equality implied in the notion of justice, see Aristotle, *Nicom. Eth.*, V, 3, 1131 a 10 - b 24.
[9] *Ib.*, 58, 1.
[10] *Ib.*, 58, 11.

well as the accident qualities which are proper to it: these "belong" to it, because they are linked with its being in a more profound manner than are the effects which are merely worked upon it from without. In the same way, everything without which a thing could not exist, and could not be what it is, can be said to be "due" to it, so that St Thomas feels justified in writing that a certain "debt of justice" is involved in the creation of the world: if God chooses to create man, He owes it to Himself to give him a rational soul and a body composed of the "four elements" [11].

In all these usages, however, and in others of the same kind (as when one speaks of the "domain" of animals), the words "having", "belonging to" etc., should be understood in an extremely analogical sense. Strictly speaking, they are applicable only where persons are concerned, since it is they alone who are capable of disposing of themselves and their goods in virtue of their free will [12]. Someone genuinely *possesses* only what he is capable of making use of so as to attain goals which he himself has chosen. It is here that it becomes necessary to introduce the other aspect of the word "his": its link with the reflexive: "himself". What someone can call "his" is an extension and complement of the "self" to whom it belongs, and it is only a person who has a "self", since only he is capable of *reflection*. What is "his", in the proper sense of the word, is not simply what forms a unity with him, in virtue of an objective relationship of the type described above: it is also necessary that this unity, this relationship, be grasped — or be capable of being grasped-*reflectively*; it is necessary that the bond between what is posessed and the one who possesses be interiorly appreciated by this latter, as one who is master of his decisions. In other words, it is necessary that what is possessed be related to its possessor as one who possesses himself and is capable of disposing of himself, as one who is "for himself", who is a "*self*". If a person can possess things, the reason for this is that he first of all possesses himself, in virtue of his presence to himself and his power of liberty. The root and condition of possibility of all possession, in the true sense, is this prior

---

[11] *Cont. Gent.*, II, 29.
[12] St Thomas, *Summa Theol.*, II - II, 25, 3.

possession of oneself, which distinguishes a human being from all other beings on the face of the earth. Ar a level even deeper than our possession of our bodies (which, for G. Marcel, are our primordial possession), we are, as spiritual subjects, "masters of ourselves", inasmuch as our objective infinity (the infinite range of our intellect and will) enables us to transcend our subjective finitude (our finitude as particular, contingent beings): we govern and determine ourselves (which could not be said of God). — What the goods are which share in this way in the "self", and under what conditions and titles they do so, is the task of special ethics to investigate [13].

To be willing to give to each what is his, is accordingly, nothing else, at bottom, than to be willing that each should be himself. Now, as has been shown (n. 143), what is characteristic of a spiritual or rational subject is his capacity to receive others into himself, to open himself to them, while allowing them to be what they are. In the noetic order, this "allowing-them-to-be" takes the form of *truth*, by which we recognize and affirm things for what they are. In the practical order, the form which this takes is that of *justice*. While our sense appetite aims at obtaining what will be of advantage to ourselves, our rational appetite enables us to impose restraints on ourselves for the advantage and well-being of others; it is in this self-imposed restraint that the rationality of this appetite is manifested in the highest degree.

But note that if we simply consider the relationships between individuals, apart from the strictly social bond, the determination of what "belongs" to each of them, of what is "his", will remain extremely vague. It is only in virtue of a social organization, at least embryonic, that the firm outlines of "mine" and "thine" will begin to appear; customs and laws will, in general, make clear what belongs and does not belong to each person.

---

[13] Obviously, this does not at all mean that the subject is entitled to dispose of himself in whatever way he fancies. For the (finite) subject, in his turn, is one who, at the deepest level of his being, faces towards Another and exists for Another: towards God and for God. This does not at all mean that, where God is concerned, he is but a thing or an instrument. A person is never a mere means in the hands of God: above all, he is never a means which God could use in order to gain some advantage!

197. – From what has been said, it is clear that the rectitude of human acts is "measured" by the virtue of justice in a way that is peculiarly its own. Where the other virtues are concerned, this rectitude is measured in relation to the moral agent (in relation to his nature, his dispositions etc.). Where justice is concerned, this relationship with the agent has, obviously, to be present — since moral value lies in the harmony of his action with the judgments of reason — but there is here present, in addition, a relationship with others. It is, in consequence, possible to consider the object of this virtue in accordance with this second relationship, without taking into account the relationship with the agent (without considering, for example, the way in which an action has been performed). The aspect of the object which is isolated in this way is "what is just", an "objective right"[14]. — This is the "just mean" where the virtue of justice is concerned; as St Thomas[15] notes, the "just mean" of the other virtues is determined by a reasonable judgment, in accordance with the circumstances in which the agent is, but when it is a question of justice this mean is determined by "what is just", by an "objective right" (cf. n. 268).

Since the other person enters — as one who is a subject no less than the agent himself — into the objective structure of an act of justice, it is no longer sufficient to consider the relation of this to the agent himself: account has also to be taken of its relation to the other person, and to the community. Now, this relation is not one that is dependent on the circumstances in which the agent has acted. If Peter, a millionaire, has defrauded Paul of a hundred pounds, the fact that he is a millionaire does not mean that he is obliged to give Paul a hundred and fifty! It is true that if Paul were not well-off and had stolen from the millionaire, his lack of money could excuse him from the obligation of restitution. But, even here, the obligation is no more than suspended; if his financial situation improves, he will, in principle, be bound to pay back the money he has stolen. Similarly, the subjective intention of the agent is, of itself, quite irrelevant. If, by my action, I have

[14] St Thomas, *Summa Theol.*, II - II, 57, 1.
[15] *Ib.*, I - II, 64, 2.

injured my neighbour and deprived him, without an objectively valid reason, of what belongs to him, it matters not at all that my motive has been good, or that I was unaware of the damage I did to him. Subjectively, I may be entirely blameless; but this does not make the situation I have created to be any the less objectively unjust; from the moment I become aware of what I have done, I have the duty to repair the damage.

198. – At this stage, it should also be clear what, in the moral order, is the role of justice and of rights, namely, both to maintain the distinction that exists between each human being (so that they can, in consequence, affirm and develop themselves as individuals) and at the same time, to link them to one another in such a way that they constitute a social body. Undoubdtedly, it is not justice which forms an intimate bond between human beings: this is the fruit of the reciprocal welcome and gift that is called love. Justice is not love and the unity which results from it remains exterior; but the conditions which it creates are those which are required in order that a genuine spirit of love, or at least of civic friendship, be possible in a community. For all love that is authentic presupposes a "recognition" of the other as a person, a "respect" that is mutual (n. 144). It does not consist in such a fusion of individual lives that the distinction between persons ceases: this distinction, on the contrary, is acknowledged (I will that you become the unique person you are capable of becoming), but is also transcended; and it is this which, by uniting the "I" and the "you" into a "we", both maintains the distinction and perfects it.

199. – Three types of justice have, since the time of Aristotle, been distinguished:

1) *Commutative* justice, which aims at the establishment and preservation of a just order between private persons [16]. The equality which is implied by the word "commutative" can be called *arithmetical*. Person A is bound to give to person B the equivalent of what he has received from him (as, for example, in a business deal, or where there is question of resti-

---

[16] *Ib.*, II - II, 61, 1.

tution, of the payment of a debt etc.). As is evident, in order to decide what is required by this equality, various factors have to be taken into account; if, for instance, it is a question of a loan at interest, the time factor is important.

It should be noted here that commutative justice likewise regulates the relationships between a society (the state, for example) and private persons, or between one society and another, when these are playing a role which is not really that of a society, but of a private person. Hence the state, no less than a private individual, is bound, in virtue of commutative justice, to pay its debts; similarly, commutative justice is violated when someone illicitly appropriates what belongs to the state. Many good-living people have, nowadays, a strangely deformed conscience on this point.

2) *Distributive* justice, which aims at the establishment and preservation of a just order in the relationships between the community *as such* and its members. Its role is to ensure that the goods which the community possesses are distributed in proportion to the merits and rights etc., of each [17]: hence the name "distributive". The equality that is here involved is not, then, a strict equality, but one that is *proportional*. So, for example, the top-ranking officers in an army, who are of greater importance where the safety of the country is concerned and shoulder a weightier responsibility, have a right to a salary which is higher than that of the ordinary soldiers. The principle that is here operative is: to each in accordance with the degree to which he promotes the good of the community. In consequence, it is clear how unjust is an order, or rather a disorder, in which the goods which have been won for the community by the resources, the "savoir-faire", the co-operation of all, are of profit, for the most part, only to a select few, in place of being of advantage to all, in accordance with the contribution of each.

3) In addition to these two forms of *particular* justice — so called because they regulate the relationships between "particular persons" — the Scholastics have distinguished a third form which they call *general* justice and which regulates the relationships between *private persons and the community as*

----

[17] *Ib.*

352   RIGHTS AND DUTIES

such. According to St Thomas, it is called *general* because it orientates all virtuous actions towards the good of the community[18]; he compares it with charity which orientates all virtuous actions towards the supreme Good which is God. This type of justice is also called *legal* because, as St Thomas again notes, by means of it a person acts in conformity with the law, which orientates all his virtuous actions towards the good of the community[19]. If they have this virtue, ruler and subject will respond, each in his own way, to the demands that the good of the community makes on them.

Note that general justice plays a part in determining what is required of us in commutative justice. The object of this latter form of justice can be fully defined only in the context of life in community, where the demands of the common good have to be taken into account (cf. n. 196). Hence, even though commutative justice cannot be reduced to general justice, it is nevertheless true that this latter rounds it off, both from the point of view of giving it a fuller definition and conferring on it a greater urgency.

4) Finally, much is spoken and written, nowadays, about *social justice*, even though there is no general agreement about what this means. Some writers regard it as a synthesis of distributive and legal justice, or even of the three forms of justice we have mentioned; others speak of it as *natural legal justice* (the justice which is demanded by the requirements of the common good, independently of all positive laws); others again consider that its role is to orientate our actions in a special way towards the achievement of the common good; yet others hold that it is the form of justice which establishes and preserves a just order in the relationships between various social groups and classes; finally, there are those who maintain that social justice aims at regulating the economic order in accordance with the requirements of right reason and, in particular, at guiding the activities of a society and its members in such a way that all are enabled to live at the level of material prosperity which befits human beings. (The criteria of what this will involve will, clearly, vary in accordance with the age

---

18 *Ib.*, II - II, 58, 6.
19 *Ib.*, 58, 5.

and the particular society in which they live). But even the definitions we have given are not exhaustive! We shall not here choose between them and shall not even attempt to decide if there are good grounds for considering social justice to be a particular form of justice; such problems fall within the province of social ethics and, in consequence, of special ethics.

200. – An objective right (in the primary sense of: "what is just") will, in every instance, manifest itself under the form of a mutual but dissymetric relation between two or more persons, in which is included their relation to some particular thing (which can be called the *material* of the right). So, for instance, when one person lends money to another, the amount which is lent and borrowed is the material of the right that is involved; when a person buys something, the material or object of the right that is thereby created, is both what is bought and sold, and the price to be paid.

Where one of the persons involved is concerned, this juridical relation will take the form of a *subjective right*: the one to whom the thing in question is "due", because it is "his" in virtue of some particular title, and is required for his completion etc., will be the *subject* of the right. If John sells a field to James, he has the right to receive the price of the field from the latter. If James has paid this price, he has the right to take possession of the field. Where the other person involved is concerned, the same relation takes the form of a *duty*. As it is here understood, a duty differs from a moral obligation in that it is always "other-directed". Between obligation and duty there can be said to exist the same nuance that exists between what is simply lawful and a subjective right: in both instances, the difference is due to the relational aspect, the "other-directed" aspect, social in a broad sense, which characterizes the juridical order (n. 194, 3). The person who has the duty ought to ensure that the person who has the right receives what is "due" to him, the "thing" to which he has a right. (This, at the very least, will mean that the former will have to refrain from taking what belongs to the other). James ought to pay the price of the field to John, while the latter ought not to hinder the former from taking possession of what he has bought. Hence, the general rule emerges that whenever one person has a right to something (for example, to his liberty, to his physical integrity etc.), others have the duty to respect this right.

The dissymetry which is inherent in a juridical relation also affects the correlative relation which the persons involved have to the "thing" that is in question. For James, the price of the field is "to be given", while for John, it is "to be received", whereas where the field is concerned, the relation is *vice-versa*. — As is obvious, the structure of a contract such as that of buying and selling is somewhat complicated: what is really involved in it are two complementary juridical relations.

Every relation rests on some *foundation*. Where it is a question of a subjective right, its remote foundation can be said to be the capacity of the spiritual subject or person to possess other things and make them "his own" (n. 196). Hence, the more something is, of its very nature, required for a person's completion, the more will this foundation or title approximate to a right in the strict sense [20]. But in order that a right be completely valid, some contingent fact (action, situation etc.), is normally required; in virtue of this, a specific and definite relation is established between *this* person and *that* object. He may, in consequence, licitly and validly consider it as his own, even if he does not yet actually possess it. Examples of such a contingent fact are: buying, selling, inheritance, performance of work to which there is attached a salary etc.

Recall, here, once again, that a right in the strict sense has meaning only in the context of life in community. No matter how useful or necessary certain things may be for me, I cannot claim that I have a right to them as long as my relations with others are not taken into account; all I can say is that I am allowed to use them, since to do so is in conformity with reason (nn. 194, 196).

---

[20] Authors often speak in this connection of a "moral title". We prefer to avoid this expression, in the measure in which it may tend to suggest that it could be morally licit to dispose of something to which one has no right, simply on the grounds that to do so would be extremely convenient. The case of extreme necessity, where, according to St Thomas, one is permitted to take from others what one stands in need of (*Summa Theol.*, II - II, 66, 7) creates no difficulty, since the person in need has a genuine right (natural, clearly): "as a result of this necessity, what a person takes to sustain his life becomes his own", *ib.*, ad 2um. For the moment and to a degree that is strictly in accordance with a person's need, the goods of the earth again become common property: their radical finality (the good of all) causes, at one point, a crack in the framework of private property, which is indeed no more than the means that is normally best adapted to the attainment of this end. — See G. Couvreur, *Les pauvres ont-ils des droits?* Rome, 1961.

The foundation of the duty which is the correlative in the other person to my subjective right, is, clearly, both his rational nature, which makes of him a moral subject, and more particularly, this right which I possess.

201. – The *object* of a right can be of many different kinds and so, likewise, can the link between it and the subject. Several types of right can, accordingly, be distinguished: the right of jurisdiction and the right of ownership; the right "in an object" and the right "to an object", personal rights and real rights etc.

The right of jurisdiction, which is possessed by superiors, rulers, and all those who hold some authority, has for its object the actions of their subordinates, in relation either to the good of the subordinates themselves or the good of the community. The right of ownership, on the contrary, has for its object both actions and things (see n. 194, 3, however) but in their relation to the good of the person himself: the right which Peter has to his house, his field, his car etc., is related, directly and immediately, to his personal completion, to the accomplishment of his aims and projects etc. This should not be understood in an individualistic sense: on the one hand, the requirements of the common good limit and channel the right of ownership and its exercise; on the other hand, personal fulfilment that is genuine is possible only within the community. (Where there is despotism or tyranny, these two rights — of jurisdiction and ownership — are not distinguished).

A right "in the object" presupposes that a specific object already exists and that the subject has reasons (has a legitimate "title") in virtue of which he is entitled to consider this object as "his". I have a right "in" this car which I have chosen and paid for, but which I have not yet collected. A right "to the object" presupposes that this *is due* to the subject and that it will be his — but that it is not yet so. Consequently, a right of this kind can exist even though the object in question does not yet exist, or is not a specific object. An example of this is the right I acquire when I subscribe for a copy of a book which has not yet appeared. The one who is directly bound by this right is the person (or persons) from whom the subject is entitled to demand what is due to him.

The distinction between personal rights and real rights rests on the diversity of titles that are possible. Rights of the first kind are grounded on some quality or character that is inherent in the person of the subject. (So, for example, the right of inheritance from his father which a son has, is grounded on his sonship). Rights of the second kind are grounded on the possession of something by the subject, or on a particular office which he exercises.

(So, for example, where groups of people who own farms, factories etc., have each formed their own special organization, all the owners in each group will have the right to participate in the meetings, congresses, elections etc., which the organization holds). Such a right is, obviuosly, indirect.

Innate and acquired rights can also be distinguished, as can those which are alienable and inalienable: these terms do not require any explanation, at least not in the context of the investigation in which we are engaged. As regards rights which are called perfect or imperfect (according as the power of coercion is or not attached to them), see nn. 204-206.

202. – From what has been said, it is clear that a subjective right in one person always has a duty as its correlative in another person or persons. The right of ownership which Peter has, creates a duty for others of not appropriating what belongs to him, of not using it without his permission etc.

But is this connection of duties with rights reciprocal? Does every duty involve a correlative right? It seems that the answer has to be "no". The duties which arise simply out of charity, contrary to what many people imagine, are no less pressing than other duties: nevertheless, they cannot be said to create, in this particular poor woman for instance, a strict right to receive help. — It is true that the notion of social justice (n. 199, 4) tends to blur the distinction between justice and charity, so that nowadays we consider certain things to be due in justice, which, not so long ago, appeared to be, at the most, equitable (for example, a family wage). Perhaps too, it could be maintained that even though this particular poor person has not, strictly speaking, a right to receive help from this particular benefactor, "the poor", those who are "economically weak", have a genuine right to be assisted by the "economically strong". It is not, in consequence, so certain that the point we have made about duties in charity is absolutely conclusive. Nevertheless, it does seem that when the domain of justice has been extended as widely as possible, right reason — whose perfection lies in the love of friendship (n. 143) — still requires us to go beyond the duties which we have in justice: a rational demand is made on our generosity.

Another example, and perhaps a clearer one, is provided by what are referred to as "duties towards oneself" (n. 185).

Without doubt, these duties have also a certain social dimension (n. 75): since it is of concern to the society in which we live that we should not render ourselves useless, or less efficient, members, it has, in consequence, the right to take measures which will help us to lead healthy and hygienic etc., lives; it can legitimately forbid excessive indulgence in alcohol, regulate the taking of drugs etc. All the same, it is evident that what is involved in duties of this type cannot be entirely accounted for by these considerations (n. 85). — Can it, perhaps, be said that these duties are correlative to the "rights" which God has, where we, His creatures and images, are concerned (n. 172, 6)? The expression "the rights of God" is somewhat jarring, since it seems to introduce God into the network of rights and duties, whereas He is, on the contrary, their condition and foundation. But, in any event, even if we do speak of God's rights, these arre absolutely transcendent and of another order (as is God Himself); they are on another and different plane from the duties to which they are said to be correlative, and they inhere in a Subject who is not the one on, whom the duties in question are imposed. Note that nothing is gained by objecting that the duties of which we are here speaking are really duties "in relation to ourselves" and not, strictly speaking, "towards ourselves" (in the same way as we are commonly said to have duties *concerning* the animals, but not *towards* them). Since man is a moral subject, since he reflects both in his nature and in his person, the Ideal of reason, since he has a likeness to God which the animals have not, he has the duty not simply to "use himself" reasonably, but to love himself rightly, by respecting the dignity that is his as a person [21]. — Likewise, it is to others as persons that our love and charity has to radiate; they are not to be regarded as if they were merely the material which provides us with an opportunity of exercising our charity and making moral progress (n. 247).

---

[21] J. Maritain (*Neuf leçons...*, pp. 143-154) presents the matter in a somewhat different way and considers that we have duties in the strict sense *towards* the animals; further, that we have such duties, in a certain fashion, where all natural beings are concerned, since they too bear the stamp of God. But, he insists, such non-personal beings possess no rights of any kind.

In all these instances, the person towards whom one has an obligation — whether this be the subject himself or other people — is not to be regarded as "passive" where this duty is concerned: he, so to speak, arouses it, in virtue of the value that is his as one who participates in the Ideal of reason. (This value does not, however, constitute a *right* in the strict sense).

Duties of this kind, to which there is, strictly speaking, no corresponding right, can be called non-juridical. They do not enter into the field of objective rights; they are not part of the just order. Hence, by definition, duties that are juridical always presuppose a correlative right in another person or persons.

203. – But which is prior — right or duty? To answer this question, we have to make some distinctions.

If we consider the relation between a particular duty towards a definite person and the corresponding right that he has, it is the latter which is primary so that the duty is determined by it. Because Peter owns this car, Paul, Andrew etc., have the duty of not using it without his permission.

If, on the contrary — while still remaining on the plane of relations between human beings — we now speak of right and duty *in general*, the question becomes more complex. It seems, at first sight anyway, that duty is here primary. The reason for this is twofold. On the one hand, independently of all relation to others, the individual subject has the obligation of acting in accordance with right reason, and this obligation gives him the right to demand what is necessary in order to fulfil it. But, since this fundamental obligation is not a "duty" in the full and juridical sense of the word (n. 200), this line of reasoning is beside the point. Moreover, does not the spiritual subject possess a dignity which is more fundamental, and is at a more profound level, than his obligation to act in accordance with reason, and which immediately demands that it be respected? Does it not constitute a radical and innate "right"? Can we not even say that where duties which are non-juridical, such as those of charity, are concerned, this dignity stands in exactly the same relation to rights in the strict sense, as these duties stand in relation to those which are juridical? The parity is not, however, complete, for duties in charity are true duties, whereas one cannot speak of a right to be loved; this would be to detract from the generosity and gratuitousness that are proper to love. Note also that human dignity, in its turn, is not in the final analysis intelligible, apart from the relations to the Absolute that is constitutive of a being who is spiritual, and from which moral obligation is derived. (Indeed, at bottom, obligation is nothing other than an aspect of this relation). Inasmuch then as man *truly* participates in the Value, he possesses a dignity which is the ground of all his rights; inasmuch as he simply *participates* in the Value, towards which his entire being is radically related, he is bound by a fundamental obligation which is the well-spring of all his duties. Rather then than seek to establish whether, on the plane of relations between human beings, duties are anterior to rights or rights to duties, it is much better to acknowledge that both arise simultaneously from our human condition as sharers in the Value. But if one wishes to be very exact, one could also maintain here that right is prior to duty, inasmuch as "being" expresses what is more fundamental than "participated being".

If we now go outside the plane of relations between human beings in order to consider the divine Subject, whose "rights" with regard to all beings are absolute and supreme, or rather who is Himself the source and pre-eminent exemplar of all rights, then the primacy of right over duty is very evident. But, once again, we have to remind ourselves of the dangers of anthropomorphism, and of appearing to speak of God and man as if they were two subjects who both owe obedience to a higher rule. God is not part of any order, be it logical, moral, juridical etc.: He is the ground and condition of them all.

204. – Three principal properties of a right are normally distinguished:

1) *Inviolability*: It can undoubtedly happen that a person will be forcibly prevented from exercising a right: but this does not mean that the moral power which is his is diminished in any way. Trampled on and flouted though it may be, it still remains a *right*. Force neither creates nor yet destroys it, for it is of a quite different order.

But note that in consequence of an action which was unjust in itself, a situation can change so much that the foundation of the right which has been violated may be profoundly altered and may even cease to exist. So, for example, when the legitimate authority in a state has been unjustly overthrown, it ceases to be legitimate as soon as it becomes clear that those who have usurped authority are the only ones who are, in fact, capable of effectively procuring the common good (since it is to ensure the attainment of this that power and authority are required [22]).

2) *Limitation*. This means that not only is there a circumscribed area beyond which a particular right does not extend — to have a right to *a* does not involve having a right to *b* — but that, in addition, it can be limited in various ways even within this area: either by the equal or superior rights of others (a person's right to build, for example, is limited, in a town or city, by the right his neighbours have that their view should not be excessively curtailed; the right of a religious community to ring their bell is limited by the right which the nearby residents have not to be awakened in the early morning etc.); or by the requirements of the common good (as when people are compelled to sell their houses or property because of the advantage to the community that will thereby result — construction of new roads, of hydroelectric dams, of airports etc.); or finally, by the law of the land which settles, with a view to the common good, the extent and conditions of the rights which it concedes or recognizes (for example, what is required in order that a will etc., be valid).

Hence, contrary to what is sometimes said, there can be no real *collision* of rights. Such clashes are never more than apparent (even though the suffering and pain that they can cause is very far from apparent). What seems to be a right of one of the parties would, in fact, be a genuine right if the circumstances were different; but since the circumstances are what they are, it is now*suspended* (even though it has not ceased to exist) because of the presence of a superior right.

3) *Coerciveness*. Force may be used in order to safeguard a right. In other words, the person who has a (subjective) right is entitled to use physical force so as to defend or obtain that to which he has the right, that is, to maintain or restore the just order.

---

[22] This principle received a famous application in France when Leo XIII, in 1892, by the Encyclical "Notre consolation", recommended to the Catholics to accept a form of government whose origin many had contested. The Concordat concluded by Pius VII, at an earlier period, was also inspired by the same doctrine.

Given the actual human condition, it is obvious that if rights could not be exacted in this way (so that complete reliance had to be placed on the efficacy of moral motives to persuade or dissuade) then their position would be altogether too weak and vulnerable: little or no respect would be had for them. Human beings, as they actually are, do not respect what they know can be violated with impunity. Moreover, as we have seen (nn. 194, 195), the just order is the object of the virtue of justice; now, the purpose of this virtue is not only that we should will the establishment of the just order, but that we should effectively work to bring it about. But, in order to do this, we may have to resort to coercion, which can, in consequence, be called an instrument of justice. The will of the person who does what is just, as a result of the pressures that have been brought to bear on him, does not automatically become just; nevertheless, a just order has been established and this is, at one and the same time, a victory for reason and a condition which is favourable to virtuous living.

205. – But is the power of coercion of the *essence* of a right? We have here touched on a disputed question.

Kant says "yes" to it. The power to use force against someone who violates my right is, he maintains, linked with the right, in virtue of the principle of contradiction (that is, it would be contradictory to say that I have a right, but lack the power to use coercion to defend it) [23]. For, to have a right to something is nothing other than to have the right to make use of the force which is required to obtain it [24]. Consequently, right and the power of coercion are synonymous [25].

---

[23] *Metaphysik der Sitten*, Einleitung in die Rechtslehre, D; ed. Reimer, t. VI, p. 231.

[24] "To say: the creditor has the right to demand from his debtor the payment of the debt, does not mean: he can persuade him that this way of acting is a rational requirement, but rather: the pressure exerted on someone in order to achieve this goal can harmonize perfectly, in accordance with a general and exterior law, with everybody's liberty, and consequently with that of the debtor", *ib.*, E; p. 232. In other and simpler terms: this constraint is *just*, since, according to Kant, the first and most general principle of justice is: "that action is just, in accordance with whose maxim the liberty of each one can harmonize with the liberty of all, in accordance with a universal law", *ib.*, C; p. 230. See further on, n. 211.

[25] *Ib.*, E; p. 232.

This opinion is likewise that of numerous jurists and philosphers of law, who have been, in varying degrees, influenced by Kant: examples are Jhering, Jellinek etc. As is only to be expected, they do not present their views in a uniform manner. As well, the majority of them differ from Kant (n. 211) in that the only rights they recognize are positive rights (n. 210). Moreover, many of them are concerned with the historical origin of rights rather than with their essence: in their view, rights are primarily the channelling of force in accordance with reason; only to a much lesser degree are they the requirements of reason, for which the use of force is a bulwark and support. (It should be clear at this stage that this entire question is closely linked with one that we shall soon discuss, namely, the question of the relations between what is moral and what is juridical, nn. 218-219).

206. – It does not, however, seem that the power of coercion is of the essence of a right: it is no more than a property of this, from which it is, up to a certain point, even separable. Note at once that there are two different ways in which the power of coercion can be regarded. Firstly, it can be considered as the moral power to use force so as to safeguard rights. Secondly, as the physical power to use force effectively in a given situation. Now, it is all too obvious that coercion in this second sense is in no way essential to a right. If it were, there would be an end to all rights! The strong, the aggressive, those against whom all attempts at coercion would be unavailing or impossible, would by that very fact be justified in their conduct: their use of force and violence would endow them with rights! Oppression and tyranny would be legitimized by the power with which they are imposed, by the terror they are capable of inspiring. Achab would not then have unjustly despoiled Naboth, since the latter had no means of redress against his ruler. The thief would not be bound to make restitution as long as he was able to escape the clutches of his victim. ... To regard the actual and effective power of coercion as essential to a right is, in fact, to cease to regard this as a moral power and to reduce it to the level of might, of being able to take effective means to secure what one wants; or, at least, to make it totally dependent on might so that it becomes no more than a reflection and manifestation of this.

But, even in the first sense, the power of coercion is not essential to a right. This power is itself a *right*: the right to employ force; and this right is, in its turn, founded on the right which the use of force is meant to safeguard. It is because Peter has a right to his car that he has a right to resort to force, should the occasion arise, in order to regain possession of it. Since the moral power to use force presupposes that a person already has a right, this power cannot, in consequence, be of the essence of a right.

Indeed, it cannot even be said that this power always accompanies a right. There are some rights where there can be no question of coercion, either because there is no possibility of exercising it, or because the use of force would cause a harm greater than that which it aims at preventing or undoing. I have the right not to be condemned rashly, not even when the condemnatory judgment is purely internal: a rash judgment is not only an offence against charity, but also against justice. But, despite this, how can there ever be question of compelling another to retract interiorly the rash judgments which he has made? Someone has stolen an object of small value from me, or has said something that is slightly calumnious about me: am I going to move heaven and earth in order to force him to make restitution or to retract? Rights of this kind, to which the power of coercion is not attached, can be called imperfect, in the sense that they lack that additional perfection, that energy which the power to coerce confers. This does not make them to be, of themselves, any the less genuine rights; people who violate them act unjustly; they have the duty to make reparation, insofar as they are able, for the injustice they have done.

What does, however, remain true is that the tendency to employ force to safeguard rights, flows from the need to ensure that these are respected; if, at times, the moral power to use coercion is not present, the reasons for this are accidental: they are extrinsic to the right itself.

207. – As is clear from what has already been said, the power of coercion, even where it would be possible to exercise it, is subject to the condition that it should not result in greater harm than would the violation of the right in question.

Those who hold public authority have the power and the right to compel those subject to them to fulfil their duties towards the society in question. Furthermore, this right ought to be exercised; if it is not, then the laws will be speedily flouted, with consequent great harm to public order and the common good. It is obviously presupposed that these laws are not unjust, nor evidently obsolete as a result of changed circumstances.

Rights in which commutative justice is involved are, in general, safeguarded by the power of coercion. This should not, however, be exercised by private individuals, who are prone to overestimate what is due to themselves and too easily swept along by the flood of their passions, or by their desire for gain; to exercise this power is the prerogative of those who hold public authority. This does not rule out the possibility of exception, when the need for action is pressing and recourse to those in authority is impossible. I have the right to chase after the thief who has snatched my suitcase and, if I am fortunate enough to overtake him, to use physical force in order to regain possession of my case. (Obviously, the means I use and the extent to which I go, should be in proportion to the importance of what I want to achieve).

Rights in which distributive justice is involved are not, in general, safeguarded in the same way. The reason for this should be clear. If every private individual had the moral power to use force in order to exact his rights from those in authority, legal anarchy would be enthroned, since here also each individual would be ever so much more prone to overestimate rather than to underestimate his rights, and to judge that his share of the cake is not as large as it should be.

Nowadays however it can well be maintained that strikes constitute, in this sphere, a type of coercion, and all the more because, quite often, strikers are motivated less by the need to wrest a living wage from their employers (as they were in the last century and earlier in this, and indeed as they still are in certain regions) than by the desire of a more equitable division of the fruits of their work. We leave to special ethics the task of deciding whether and to what extent workers have a natural right to go on strike, particularly where those who are employed by the State are concerned.

Note, in conclusion, that even though might does not create right, both individuals and groups need to be on their guard lest their awareness of "having right on their side" become a pretext for not bestirring themselves or for shirking their responsibilities. If my cause is a just one, I am blameworthy if I do not take the necessary steps to safeguard it, or if, without good reason, I shift the responsibility for this on to others.

II. THE RELATION BETWEEN NATURAL RIGHTS AND THE MORAL ORDER.

208. – A number of different senses in which we may speak of rights has already been indicated (nn. 194; 201). But by far the most important distinction is that between *natural* and *positive* rights.

This distinction was clearly made by Aristotle who, in his turn, was prolonging and deepening the reflections of Socrates and Plato on the notion of justice. He writes that what is just in the context of society (where alone there can be rights in the strict sense) can be either naturally so (*phusikon*), or can be the result of convention (*nomikon*), that is, it can be legally just (cf. n. 52). What has everywhere the same binding force, a force which is not at all dependent on whether or not public opinion acknowledges it, is naturally just. What is legally just, on the contrary, is what originally did not have any binding force, but which now possesses it in virtue of a decision that we are to act in this way rather than that [26]. — Consequently, what is legally or conventionally just has to be laid down or "posited" by a law, an agreement, a decree, a custom etc.: hence the expression "positive rights". What is naturally just, on the contrary, is so prior to all human laws and agreements, because it stems from the objective requirements of man's nature, which are the ground of the judgments of right reason. What is naturally just is what man by his nature is inclined towards, writes St Thomas [27]. — In the *Summa Theologica* he, too, treats of the distinction between natural and positive rights [28]. As is obvious, it is a distinction which presupposes that between natural and positive law (n. 179). It is only because there is a natural law which binds all human beings that each individual human being can have natural rights, just as it is only in virtue of positive laws that there can be positive rights.

209. – In addition to this twofold distinction, the Scholastics have also made a tripartite one from which certain

---

[26] *Nicom. Eth.*, V, 7, 1134 b 18 seq.
[27] St Thomas, *In V Eth.*, bk. 12; ed. Pirotta, n. 1019.
[28] II - II, 57, 2.

difficulties result. They introduce a third type of right which is intermediate between natural and positive rights and which has its source in what they call the "law of the nations" (cf. n. 194, 2). Such rights are, then, those which "the nations" acknowledge.

The origin of this fresh notion of rights goes back to the Roman jurists. In the *Digest* of Justinian, when the question of the definition of a right is being discussed, a fragment from Ulpian is introduced. In this we are told that the rights of private individuals are of three kinds, since they result from laws that are natural, or in force among "the nations", or operative in organized societies. By laws that are natural he means those which nature has taught to all animals. As such, they are not for the human race alone, but are also for all the other animals on the face of the earth, the fish in the sea and even the birds of the air. It is these laws which give rise to that union of the sexes which we human beings call marriage, and also to the begetting of offspring and their rearing. That animals other than ourselves, and even the wild beasts, exercise these rights is all too plain. — The rights which "the nations" acknowledge are those which result from "the law of the nations". The difference between them and natural rights is easy to grasp: these latter are common to all animals, while the former come into play only in the relationships that human beings have with one another[29]. Examples of spheres where these rights are operative are numerous: the worship of God, obedience to parents and loyalty to the place of one's origin, warfare, the creation of separate nations, the establishment of kingdoms, private owner-ship, the boundaries between landed property etc. In a word, these rights are operative in all that concerns man's social life.

This doctrine is to be found in St Thomas also. In his view, natural right and the rights which the nations acknowledge are two subdivisions of natural rights understood in a broad sense, that is, this latter term is taken to include both the rights which are exclusive to man (the rights which the nations acknowledge), and the rights which are common to men and animals (natural rights in the strict sense)[30]. But the obvious question is: what meaning can this have? The animals have no rights; it is only a rational being who can possess them (n. 196). Hence Ulpian's interpretation is indefensible. It is, of course, true that rights and duties are involved not only in the activities which are specifically human (of which the animals are not capable), but also in those which are generically human (of which

---

[29] *Digest*, tit. I: "De Justitia et Jure", 1.
[30] *Summa Theol.*, II - II, 57, 3; *In V Eth.*, ib.

the animals, also, are capable); but this division is purely material and of no particular significance.

It seems preferable, accordingly, to abandon any attempt at defining natural rights in this way. A much more acceptable definition is that given by Gaius and which is contained in Justinian's *Institutes*. Here natural rights are regarded as those which are uniformly acknowledged among all peoples; they have been established by a divine providence and will always remain firm and unchangeable [31]. This definition of natural rights is, in fact, very similar to the one which Gaius gives, in another place, of the rights acknowledged by "the nations". What each people has decided on for itself, he writes, are called civil rights, that is, the rights which are particular to their region. But rights which natural reason has established among all peoples and which are uniformly honoured among them, are the rights which the nations acknowledge, that is, the rights which are operative among all nations [32].

Does this entitle us to conclude that there is no difference between natural rights and the rights which "the nations" acknowledge? Far from it; the latter are not co-extensive with the former, since they refer only to the natural rights which the conscience of mankind (or human reason) has at all times and in all places (morally, not literally, speaking) acknowledged and has sanctioned by laws or customs. Hence, while their content is derived from natural rights, the way in which they bind (that is, in virtue of positive laws and customs) stamps them as positive rights. They are the acknowledgment which natural rights receive in positive rights (understood in a broad sense, that is, rights which result not only from positive laws in the strict sense) and, in consequence, are identical with what is common to the various legal codes of mankind. There are, in fact, St Thomas notes, two ways in which a command can derive from the natural law: either as a conclusion from premises, or as a specific determination of what is of more general application. Both these processes are operative in human positive law; but whereas conclusions which are drawn from the natural law have, in virtue of their derivation, an obligatory force that is independent of human legislation, the specific determinations have, as such, no force independently of this [33] (immediately, that is, since ultimately it is the natural law which enjoins us to obey a positive law which is not evidently unjust, and since, moreover, it is the requirements of this former law that make these determinations, as *determinations in general*, to be just:

---

[31] *Institutes*, tit. 2, end.
[32] *Digest*, tit. I, n. 9.
[33] St Thomas, *Summa Theol.*, I - II, 95, 2.

what is imposed on us merely by human authority is *this* determination precisely as *this*). — Now, St Thomas goes on to say, rights which are derived from the natural law as conclusions from premises are to be classed as rights which the nations acknowledge: for example, rights which require justice in buying and selling and in other contracts of this kind where, if justice is lacking, men cannot live in community. Since man, by his nature, is a social animal, these rights are derived from the natural law. Rights, on the contrary, which are derived from the natural law as specific determinations of this law, are to be classed as civil or positive rights, that is, rights which each organized society or state decides on for itself [34].

Not all rights, however, which are legitimate conclusions from the natural law, are to be classed as rights which the nations acknowledge, but only those which are sufficiently close to the basic principles to be recognized and sanctioned by all peoples. It is for this reason (to turn to St Thomas again) that these rights are, in a certain sense, natural to man; he is endowed with reason and they are derived from the natural law as are conclusions which are not remote from their premises [35]. Inasmuch however as they are the product of human reason and are expressed by means of laws and customs, they can be classed as positive rights. But the distinction between positive rights in this sense, and those which are *merely* positive, in that they are specific determinations of what the natural law requires, should always be kept in mind [36].

The later Scholastics (inspired, apparently, by Suarez) have a different approach. In their view, all rights which are necessary conclusions from the natural law are *natural rights*: what is required in this way is a strictly natural right; to violate such a right will always be intrinsically evil. By the rights which the nations acknowledge they understand those rights which, without being strictly natural,

---

[34] *Ib.*, 95, 4.

[35] *Ib.*, ad Ium.

[36] On this point, see the excellent pages of Schiffini, *Disp. phil. mor.*, I, pp. 380-405, whose solution seems to us to be the most satisfactory one. J. Maritain understands the matter somewhat differently: "The Law of Nations, or the common law of civilization, deals, like natural law, with the rights and duties which follow from the first principle in a *necessary* manner, but this time *supposing* certain conditions of fact, as for instance the state of civil society or the relationships between peoples. It also, therefore, is universal, at least in so far as these conditions of fact are universal data of civilized life", *The Rights of Man and Natural Law*, London, 1944, pp. 39-40. The question remains: why did St Thomas not follow in the *Secunda Secundae* the line he had taken in the *Prima Secundae*? Perhaps because, in his explicit treatment of the question of rights, he believed he ought to accept the Roman jurists as authorities.

are of such advantage and convenience for mankind that they have been universally (morally speaking) recognized and sanctioned in the common customs. To violate such rights is not of itself intrinsically evil. They are, in fact, positive and human; in consequence, there is no reason why they should not be modified if circumstances call for this [37].

Non-scholastic jurists of the modern era understand the rights which the nations acknowledge in another and very different sense, that is, as the rights which result from what is nowadays referred to as international law. This is the law which regulates the relations between nation and nation, or between members of one nation and those of another [38]. As is obvious, this interpretation differs greatly from the interpretations of the Scholastics. On the one hand, as is clear from the preceding discussion, the law of the nations, in their understanding of it, is by no means reducible to international law and, on the other hand, this latter includes elements of purely positive law (treaties and pacts between nations from which purely positive rights result).

210. – As we have seen, it was commonly held in antiquity, in the middle ages and even in the 17th and 18th centuries, that there are natural rights which are independent of those that are positive and which no human lawgiver can ever take away.

But at no time were there lacking those — and they have multiplied for the past two hundred years, so that at times they

---

[37] Suarez, *De legibus*. bk. II, in particular cc. 17-20.

[38] Some examples of their approach: Rachel: "The law of the nations is constituted by pacts between the nations", *De Jure Naturae et Gentium*, Kiel, 1676; p. 233. — Wolff: "By the law of the nations we understand the science of the laws by which the nations or peoples regulate their relations with one another, as well as of the obligations to which these laws give rise", *Jus Gentium*, Frankfurt and Leipzig, 1764, Proleg., n. 1. — Vattel, *Le Droit des Gens*, London, 1758, prologue, n. 3. (the same definition). — Heineccius: "The law of the nations results from the application of natural rights to the social life of man, and to the dealings of societies and entire nations with one another", *Elementa Juris Naturae et Gentium*, Genoa, 1744, bk. 1, c. 1, par. XXXI; p. 44. — Burlamaqui: "The law of nations ... is nothing other than the application of natural rights to peoples, to states or to their leaders, in the relations they have with one another and in the decisions affecting their mutual interest which they have to take", *Principes de droit naturel*, Paris, 1791, p. 224. — As is clear from the foregoing, the law of the nations understood in this sense is, at times, as in Rachel, linked with positive law, and at other times, as in Burlamaqui, with natural law.

drown the voices of those who oppose them — who denied the truth of this opinion and acknowledged rights other than those which are positive, whether these are the result of a decision of legitimate authority, or are enshrined in the "customs" of the people. Such views were expressed in antiquity by the Sophists, in virtue of the opposition they set up between "nature" and the "law" (n. 52), the Sceptics, such as Carneades (ib.) etc. Similar views have again been expressed in more modern times by the proponents of Moral Positivism, such as Hobbes (n. 53), who derive, not only natural rights, but the entire moral order from human laws. We have already discussed and evaluated these views, but there are still other and more specious ones. Chief among these is the historical school of jurisprudence ("historische Rechtsschule") of Savigny and Stahl, which derives all true rights from the "spirit of the people" ("Volksgeist"), a spirit that primarily manifests itself in the spontaneous customs of each nation; the Sociological school of Durkheim, according to which rights, in common with other "moral facts", are a creation of the collective conscience (n. 78); similarly, Marxism, which considers rights (as in general it considers morality, religion, art) to be but an "ideology", which is both conditioned by the prevailing economico-social structure and expresses it in function of the historical situation (n. 79). — There are, finally, a number of jurists who either because their mentality is positivist and agnostic, or in consequence of their professional training, refuse to recognize that there are any true rights beyond those which are *positive*, so that at times they reduce the entire science of jurisprudence to the "exegesis" of the written code.

A partial explanation of why so many intelligent people have such a deep-rooted aversion for the doctrine of natural rights is that they are reacting against the exaggerations of some of its advocates in the modern era and, in particular, in the "Age of Enlightenment" (Aufklärung). The tendency in this age was to consider human nature in abstraction from the concrete conditions in which it was immersed (the family, the community, the nation, historical developments) and with this abstraction as a starting point, the attempr was made to deduce an ideal set of laws which could be regarded as valid for the entire human race. Or perhaps, in the style of Rousseau, a "state of nature" in which men were said to have lived before they formed societies was pictured; their natural rights thus became the rights which they possessed in this state. "Ideologies" of this kind were to inspire the legislators of the French Revolution as well as those who drew up the Napoleonic Code. — It was in direct opposition to this individualistic and anti-historical rationalism that the historical school of jurisprudence reacted, just as elsewhere and in other spheres (for example, concerning the theory of knowledge), the Traditionalist school reacted.

The chief proponents of this historical approach to rights were, as we have said, Friedrich von Savigny (*Vom Beruf unserer Zeit zur Gesetzgebung und Rechtswissenschaft*, 1814) and Friedrich Julius Stahl (*Philosophie des Rechts*, 1830-1837), who gave a philosophic expression, more or less inspired by Schelling, to this theory. These two authors place great emphasis on the social and historical character of man. The society of which they speak, and in relation to which rights have to be understood, is not society in general but always a particular and definite society, with its own particular spirit which develops in the course of history and finds expression in popular and spontaneous customs. In their view, it is custom which is the sole source of rights; all positive rights which are conceded have to be in accordance with it. The common conscience of the people is the well-spring of rights.

This school of thought does not deny that there are certain requirements in human nature which are prior to the possession of rights, but these requirements, they insist, are ethical not juridical. We possess no rights prior to, and independently of, custom. But note that these writers acknowledge a moral order which is distinct from the juridical; in this they differ from the Sociologists, with whom they have much else in common. (The Sociological school has, moreover, some points of contact with the Traditionalist school, through Comte; it has, with Saint-Simon as intermediary, partially received the heritage of this school — less, to be sure, of its religious heritage — to whose affinity with the historical school of jurisprudence we have already alluded). In addition, these authors, since their inspiration was Christian, recognized God as the ultimate source of justice and rights. It is divine Providence which directs the historical growth of the Volksgeist.

While the historical school exalted custom to the point of regarding it as the sole source of all rights, other jurists of the same epoch (Jhering, Jellinek), who were no less anxious to combat anarchical individualism, but in its rationalist dimension, did so by means of an approach which was more or less Hobbsian in its inspiration: the juridical order is a rational order, but to constitute it is the task of the State. The speculative elaboration of this doctrine was provided by Hegel in his *Grundlinien der Philosophie des Rechts*,

1821. For him, the State is "the reality of the moral Idea" [39] — and is, as such, possessed of an authority that is absolute. Rights, in consequence, correspond to a stage in the evolution of the Idea which is alienated in Nature and is becoming itself again in the Spirit.

That Hegel's thought had a great influence on that of Marx is a commonplace. But, where the latter is concerned, the dialectical development of the Idea is replaced by the dialectical development (which is conceived of in a materialistic fashion) of man, in the concrete circumstances of history; here he is, at first, alienated from himself, through being deprived of the fruits of his work, in consequence of capitalist exploitation and the establishment and maintenance of social classes; but, gradually and progressively, he overcomes this alienation until finally, although there will always be room for further progress, he becomes fully human in the society of the future, where all classes will have disappeared and there will be only human beings. Man's rights correspond to particular stages in that evolution and will, in consequence, vary; what they are at a particular period will be determined by the stage at which the movement towards the final goal has then arrived.

There are not lacking, however, some jurists who, in recent times, have expressly acknowledged that there are natural rights. Indeed, since the beginning of the present century, new defenders of this far from new notion have arisen — even outside Scholastic and Neo-Scholastic circles. Examples of these are: in Italy, Giorgio Del Vecchio; in France, Louis Le Fur, François Gény, Georges Renard, Paul Ripert, Michel Villey etc. It is, however, true that all these authors do not understand natural rights in the sense in which they are here understood. Some of them consider that such rights represent rather an ideal, a norm which, in itself, is devoid of any genuinely juridical character, but with which civil law should be in conformity. (This aim is gradually being realized).

It is worth noting that, quite often, those who reject the *term* "natural rights" (because they imagine that it implies a completed system of legislation which is independent of the passage of time and the upheavals of history, or because they understand it in function of the theory of the "state of nature" proposed by Rousseau and the Enlightenment), do not in fact reject what the term refers to; at least in a certain measure, they

---

[39] *Grundlinien* ..., n. 257; ed. Lasson, VI, p. 191.

recognize that there are natural rights, although they may speak of them as objective rights, universal norms of justice etc.[40].

211. – The question of the existence of natural rights is inseparable from the question of the relation between such rights and those which are positive. This further question, in its turn, cannot be answered without discussing the problem of how natural rights are related to the moral order.

For the Scholastics and for the majority of philosophers up to the 18th century, the question of natural rights was simply treated as a part of moral philosophy, namely, as the area of ethics which considered the relation of human beings with one another and with the society of which they are members. Even today, it is by no means impossible to find treatises on "natural rights" which, in fact, simply deal with moral philosophy. In other words, the term "natural rights" is used in a sense where it has no special juridical significance; by "justice" is understood "moral goodness" [41].

Grotius, however, had already clearly distinguished between the two notions in the 17th century; morality, he maintained, is concerned with the activities of individuals, whereas what justice is concerned with are social relations. In making distinction, he prepared the way for the separation that was more sharply urged by Thomasius, who regarded the moral and juridical orders as two divisions of practical philosophy. The discussion of rights can no longer be included as a chapter in the treatment of morality, for it is now co-ordinate with this latter.

---

[40] On this renewal of support for the theory of natural rights, consult H. Rommen, *Die ewige Wiederkehr des Naturrechts*, Munich, 1936 (French trans.: *L'éternel retour du droit naturel*, Paris, 1945). See also the excellent article of M. Villey: *Abrégé du droit naturel classique*, "Archives de philosophie du droit", no. 6, 1961, pp. 25-72. (By "classique" is understood the concept of natural rights proposed by Aristotle and St Thomas). — A recent symptom of this renaissance was provided in the 13th International Congress of Philosophy (Mexico, 1963), where an entire Symposium was dedicated to a discussion of the notion of natural rights. — See also "Supplément de la Vie Spirituelle", May, 1967; in particular: Ch. Robert, *Un renflouage du droit naturel*, pp. 187-207, and J. M. Aubert, *Le droit naturel, ses avatars historiques et son avenir*, pp. 282-323. — But what is being discussed is rather the "natural law".

[41] Cf. the title of the French translation of J. Fuchs' book *Lex Naturae: "Le Droit Naturel"*.

Nevertheless, it is Kant who is generally considered to have made the separation definite and clear-cut. This he did by insisting that the function of rights is to regulate our exterior activity and to protect the *external* liberty of each individual, whereas the moral law aims at guiding our internal activity and, in particular, at ensuring that the *intention* for which we act is what it ought to be. But even though he insisted on this distinction, he also acknowledged a certain subordination of the juridical to the moral order.

Here, as always, we need to be on our guard against over-simplified interpretations. Kant has no hesitation at all about admitting that there are natural rights, based on laws which regulate the exterior relations of one person with another, and which oblige in conscience independently of all positive legislation. In addition, he by no means claims that the moral law is concerned only with our internal activities; it aims at regulating all the activities, external as well as internal, of a reasonable being. But, he insists, juridical duties are *purely external*: once a person does materially what the law here requires of him, he has fulfilled a duty of this kind (Legalität). No demand is made on him, in order to discharge his juridical duties, that he observe the law out of respect for the law. But, as we have seen (n. 115), without this motivation there can be no genuinely moral activity (Moralität).

The reason for this difference is that what the juridical order, as such, is concerned with, are the practical external relations between one person and another, or, more precisely, between one person's liberty and another's (Willkür); and where these relations are concerned all that has to be taken into consideration is the form of universality. To ask oneself whether one's action respects the rights of others, is the same as asking whether one's exercise of freewill in performing this particular action, respects the liberty of others *in accordance with a universal law*; that is, if everyone were to act on the maxim on which I am now acting, would each one's exercise of freewill blend with that of others, or would there be a clash? The juridical order is, in consequence, revealed as "the totality of the conditions under which the liberty (Willkür) of one person can be at the same time in harmony with the liberty (Willkür) of another, in accordance with a universal law of liberty (Freiheit)" [42].

Note that the liberty (Freiheit) he has in mind when he speaks of the universal law of liberty, is not the liberty which consists in the

---

[42] *Metaphysik der Sitten*, Einleitung in die Rechtslehre, B; p. 230.

power to come to a rational decision without being swept along by feelings and likes: it simply refers to that independence of action which we enjoy, when others are exercising their freewill in accordance with a universal law of liberty[43]: this independence is nothing other than *external liberty*, which is man's only *innate right*. Now, this type of liberty can be assured without our intending to achieve it. Consequently, it is possible to fulfil the requirements of the juridical order, even though our inner attitude is not one of respect for the rights of others. The motivation that is peculiar to this order is not that of respect for the law, but is what Kant calls a "pathological" motivation, that is, it is closely linked with our passions (pathos) — in the old sense of the word — and, in particular, with the repugnance that the fear of punishment stirs up in us[44].

This does not mean, however, that all links between the moral and juridical orders have been broken. The former endorses the precepts of the latter (for example, that agreements are to be honoured), and instructs us to observe them even in the absence of coercion. Of itself "to keep a promise is not a virtuous duty (as doing good to others is) but a juridical one, which a person can be forced to observe. All the same, it is an act of virtue to keep your promise, even when no one can force you to do so"[45]. In this way, the moral order impresses its stamp on the requirements of the juridical order. Just as, according to the *Critique of Pure Reason*, phenomena which are presented to our external senses under the form of space, are likewise presented to our internal senses under the form of time — for our perception of space takes place in time — but not *vice versa*, so also all juridical obligations become moral obligations, even though all moral obligations are not juridical. Nonetheless, juridical obligations, as such, are not moral, any more than moral obligations, as such, are juridical (just as space, even though it is perceived in time, is not a part of time)[46].

Juridical duties which are endorsed and stamped in this way by the moral law within us become "indirectly ethical"[47]. Consequently, the difference between the two orders is not so much concerned with *what* each of them imposes on us, as with the *way* in which it does so. (But keep in mind that there are duties, such as those we have towards ourselves, which are non-juridical, so that not every moral obligation is a juridical one[48]).

---

[43] *Ib.*, p. 237.
[44] *Ib.*, Einleitung, III; p. 219.
[45] *Ib.*, p. 220.
[46] *Ib.*, Einl., I; p. 214.
[47] *Ib.*, Einl., III; p. 221.
[48] *Ib.*, p. 220.

212. – There are, then, three questions to which we have now to seek an answer: 1. Are there natural rights? 2. If there are, what is the relation between them and positive rights? 3. What is the relation between the moral and the juridical orders?

Even though the first question is, and has been, the subject of much controversy, there can be no real problem about the answer, once the existence of a natural, moral law is granted (n. 185). The same line of thought which led us to the conclusion that there is such a law, also leads us to the conclusion that there are such rights. Prior to all positive laws, certain relations between human beings are objectively in conformity with the judgments of right reason; other relations clash with these judgments. In consequence, there arises the obligation to foster relations of the first kind and shun those of the second. But what does this mean except that, prior to all positive laws, there is a just and unjust order which imposes itself categorically on human liberty? Now, a just and unjust order is precisely what is meant by the term "objective rights" (n. 194). Consequently, such rights exist prior to all positive laws. But a right which exists prior to all positive laws is, by definition, a *natural right*. Hence, there are natural rights.

213. – This question is, however, of such importance that it deserves to be pursued a little further.

Since the human person is capable of acknowledging and loving the absolute Value, he shares in some degree in the excellence of this Value and in the absolute and ultimate character which it possesses (n. 136). It is for this reason that he is not to be regarded as if he were but "a thing", a mere means; neither is he to be considered as totally related to and "existing-towards" anything other than this Absolute of value (n. 180).

Consequently, any attempt to treat a human being as if he were no more than a thing, to use him as a mere means or as an instrument, is contrary to right reason and is, as such, objectively evil and unjust. Now, an attempt of this kind is made whenever a person's liberty is violated, that is, whenever another or others try to ensure that an action which he performs will not really be *his*, but will proceed from a source that is exterior to his subjectivity, exterior to the unique "I" that he is: when they attempt to rob him of that inner liberty which is his as a human being. The dignity of the human person is likewise outraged whenever others treat what belongs to him, and is in a certain sense an extension and completion of his self (n. 196), as if it existed simply for their advantage and convenience. So to act is to deny in practice that the human person has an absolute value and is never to be treated as a mere means.

Indeed, such is the excellence of the human person that not only is he never to be treated as a mere means, but he also is the centre on which all the things on the face of the earth converge. Hence, if I were the only person in the world, everything else in it would be oriented towards and centred on me. But since there are in my universe subjects other than myself, other personal "centres", things cease to be oriented towards me alone; they are not the instruments which I alone use in order to develop and fulfil myself, for there are other personal centres besides me. Consequently, to act as if everything on the earth were centred on me alone would be to set my face against truth, against reason, against *justice*.

In other and more simple terms: there is a rational demand on each human being to acknowledge every other human being as one who is a person, a subject, no less than he himself is. This demand is the first principle of justice; it highlights the radical *equality* which is implied, as we have seen (n. 195), in the very notion of this virtue. Indeed, what else is this practical recognition of others as human beings, but the rendering to each of what belongs to him, of what is "his"? Just as to deny that a person has a quality which he actually possesses, is the theoretical non-recognition which bears the name of *falsity*, so also to take from him what completes him physically or morally (and, before all else, to attempt to force or bend the freedom of his will), is the practical non-recognition which bears the name of *injustice*.

Our further investigation has, then, reinforced the conclusion at which we had already arrived: prior to all positive laws, there is a rational demand for a just order, that is, a demand that objective natural rights be respected. Rational demands of this kind constitute natural preceptive rights.

From what has just been said, it would be illegitimate to conclude that nobody has the right to impose limitations on the way in which others exercise their freewill: such a principle would both sweep all authority aside and make human society impossible. What is, however, true is that nobody may impose limitations on the liberty of others, insofar as he himself is only one individual, insofar as he merely enjoys a liberty which is similar to theirs. He is entitled to impose limitations only in the measure in which he represents, in one way or in another, the rational order, to which every human being ought to conform his exercise of freewill. It is for this reason that the commands of legitimate authority — at all the levels at which it is exercised — are considered, until proof to the contrary emerges, to be in harmony with this order (which, moreover, enjoins us, in view of the common good, to obey such commands even when their rational character is not evident to us).

In addition, even a private individual has the right to prevent another from abusing his liberty, whenever this abuse constitutes an injustice either where the individual himself or somebody else is concerned (that is, whenever they are thereby deprived of what belongs to them) or when *their* legitimate exercise of liberty is impeded. Since, as a human being, I enjoy the same liberty as other human beings, there is nothing which obliges me to allow them to exercise their liberty to the detriment of mine. Indeed, I would be judging irrationally if I considered that I was obliged so to act [49]. Consequently, it is permissible not only, as men of common sense have always recognized, to limit the liberty of the thief or the assassin, but also to take steps to prevent the abuse of alcohol or excessive indulgence in drugs, because of the dangers to society which result from drunkenness and drug-addition. Society is also entitled to take precautions lest any of its members should destroy his physical or psychic health, so that he becomes unable to co-operate in the effort of all to achieve the common good. But in these and other analogous instances, it is less a question of limiting a person's liberty than of strengthening and supporting him against his own weakness by providing him with the resources that he stands in need of, if he is not to become the slave of his passions and instincts.

---

[49] The evangelical counsel not to resist those who act unjustly towards us is concerned with the voluntary renunciation of the exercise of a right: consequently, the right is presupposed by the counsel and, while the spirit of this latter is universally valid, this is not true of its effective practice. Or rather, let us say, its absolute universalization — the universal reign of a love that is humble and meek — would remove every occasion for observing it according to the letter, since violence and injustice would no longer exist. Until then, its practice, when this is possible without compromising the common good, will have a prophetic value.

On the other hand, however, a human being ought to remain master of his own actions, so that by their means he gives to his life a direction for which he himself is responsible. No one ought to seek to relieve him of this responsibility. Now, since human beings are what they are, this involves both the possibility and the danger of choices that are irrational. Consequently, we have not to aim at preventing all evil. (Indeed, in any event, how could we do so?) Each human being has the right, not indeed to choose what is evil, not indeed to "be in the wrong", as it is sometimes expressed with more temper than accuracy, but to retain the power of deciding for himself the direction that his life is to take; and in the present human condition, this power is inevitably linked with the possibility that he will err or choose what is evil[50].

A final point remains to be noted. When a person comes to be in an unjust relationship with regard to others, that is, a relationship through which the equality that should exist between him and them has been upset, then he has not only, objectively, done what is immoral but has also brought about an objective situation, an enduring "state of affairs", which is objectively at variance with the requirements of the rational order. The subjective malice which was involved in his performance of the unjust action remains as long as, and insofar as, this state of affairs is not rectified when it could be (for example, through the restitution of what he is unjustly retaining) or, at least, insofar as he is not even resolved to rectify it when he becomes capable of doing so. — Even when he has in all innocence upset the equality which justice calls for (through ignorance, inadvertence, unjust coercion on the part of others etc.), all that has just been said is applicable, once he comes to know of the situation which has resulted from his action, and is in a position to restore the balance that has been upset.

214. – It has to be stressed, however, that as long as we consider only the relations between one individual and another, the notion of rights (in common with that of justice) remains extremely vague and jejune (n. 196). In order to arrive at a

---

[50] Cf. the *Declaration on religious freedom* of the Second Vatican Council, in particular nn. 2 and 3.

fuller and richer notion of natural rights, we have to take into account the social nature of human beings. Life in society is, on two scores, natural to them. On the one hand, since each human being is in individual in whom the human possibilities are only partially realized, he is incomplete in isolation from others: it is only through them and with them that he can be fully human. The help which he receives from others and, in his turn, gives to them, is not confined to the economic sphere; it is also given and received, in large measure, on the cultural and person-to-person level: we cannot live unless we are sustained and nourished by the presence, the interest, the affection of others. — On the other hand, since each human being is a person, a spiritual subject, he is essentially capable of genuine communication with other human beings, other spiritual subjects. Life together with others (the *Mitsein*) not only provides a human being with resources that he himself lacks and with a remedy for the inner poverty that results from his finitude, but also offers him constant opportunities of enriching others — in virtue of the depths that his infinity creates in him — through the welcome he offers to their uniqueness and the gift he makes of his own. Recall too, as we have already considered (nn. 143-144), that the Ideal of our practical reason requires us to live in such a way that we play our part in helping to create a human community which is knit together by mutual respect and love.

Where social relationships of the first kind are concerned, the guiding principle is one's own advantage and what Aristotle called *useful friendship*: where relationships of the second kind are concerned, the guiding principle is friendship in the true sense of the word. These two types of friendship can, however, be intertwined, and the first often leads to the second: two people who were originally only business acquaintances can gradually come to know one another as persons and to respect and love one another as such. (But this happy sequence is by no means inevitable, as the history of colonisation makes abundantly clear).

Since, then, whatever is necessary in order that fellowship and unity among human beings should flourish, expresses a requirement of human nature, it is, in consequence, a requirement of right reason: it is a natural right. Not only has man

— as an individual — the right to preserve his physical integrity, to have the inner sanctuary of his liberty regarded as inviolate, not to be deprived without just reason of what is an external support and completion of his self etc., but also — as a social being — he has the right not to be excluded from the fellowship of other human beings. A state of affairs in which a section of the nation finds itself, in practice, isolated from and rejected by the remainder of the national community, is an unjust state of affairs, and is a violation of their natural rights. — It is the task of special ethics to establish in greater detail what is necessary in order that this fellowship and unity among human beings may be fostered.

Implicit in this radical right to fellowship and unity with others is the entire juridical order. For if a human community which is knit together by mutual respect and love is to be established (and this is the goal of man's life in society), it is first of all necessary that each person be acknowledged as the distinct individual that he is (n. 198). Now, it is juridical order, the complex of rights and duties, which expresses and sanctions these distinctions on the level of possessions and external activities. This order is, then, the essential basis for the establishment of that friendship and openness among human beings which will give concrete expression to each one's fidelity to the Ideal of practical reason (nn. 143, 144).

This consideration of the social nature of man also helps towards a better appreciation of the coercive character of rights. Since human beings are what they are, the absence of this power would unleash the selfishness and covetousness of many individuals, so that the peace and order which are necessary if human beings are to live together, would soon be destroyed. But note that the necessity for this bulwark against human greed does not spring from human nature absolutely considered, but from this nature as it in fact is, historically and concretely (n. 7) [51].

215. – Note, in conclusion, that anyone who considers that there is a true obligation to respect the positive rights of others cannot, without contradiction, refuse to admit that they have natural rights. For the positive laws which require us to

---

[51] Cf. J. Fuchs, *Natural Law*, pp. 95-99.

respect the positive rights of others impose an obligation on us, only if we are already obliged to obey the commands of the legitimate authority to which we are subject. But since this obligation is not from the positive laws themselves, it has to be from a law that is prior to them, that is, from the natural moral law. Consequently, it is on the obligation to respect the natural rights of others that the obligation to respect their positive rights is based. (The criticism that we made of Moral Positivism earlier in our investigation, nn. 56-57, is equally applicable where juridical positivism is concerned) [52].

In particular, if society in general has not a natural right to punish in an appropriate manner — which has to be determined — those who violate public order or the rights of individuals, no particular society could justly use force against the unruly and recalcitrant, punish the guilty, or, in consequence, establish sanctions.

It is, however, the existence of international law which brings out in particularly sharp relief the reality of natural rights,. In order to appreciate the truth of this, suppose for a moment that international law were purely positive. We would then have to say that it is either imposed by some international authority or that it results from pacts, from bilateral or multilateral agreements among states. But even though there are nowadays some limited instances of an international authority (the United Nations, the Executive of the Common Market), the concept of international law was acknowledged and put into practice in the modern epoch, long before these institutions made their appearance. This law can, then, result only from pacts and agreements. But, obviously, the obligation to observe these cannot itself be the result of a further pact. If it is maintained that each state imposes this obligation on itself, then it could just as easily grant itself a dispensation. The consequence of this possibility would be to deprive international law of all its force.

---

[52] This point has been expressly affirmed by Kant: "Accordingly, it is possible to envisage external legislation which would contain merely positive laws; but this would presuppose some natural law on which the authority of the legislator was based, that is, his power to bind others simply in virtue of his decision", *Metaphysik der Sitten*, Einl., IV; p. 225.

Moreover, the existence of natural rights is implicitly accepted whenever some types of activity are condemned as "crimes against humanity", even though there is no law or pact which condemns them. From this point of view the Nuremberg trials, no matter what reservations one may have concerning them, can be regarded as an unintended testimony to the existence of natural rights.

216. – We now come to our second question: what is the relation between natural and positive rights?

We have already partially answered this question for, as we have seen, natural rights are the condition of the possibility of those which are positive.

Furthermore, positive rights will either express or make more specific the natural rights on which they are grounded, and from which they draw all their force.

Particular positive laws (which establish particular positive rights) are aimed either at declaring and confirming rights, together with their correlative duties, that already exist (by sanctioning these in an appropriate manner), or else at defining the way in which the general duties to which natural rights give rise — duties towards others, towards society, the duties of society towards its members etc., — should be understood and fulfilled in a given society, with its own particular structure, with the heritage of customs and traditions that are peculiar to it, at this stage of its historical development etc. Clearly, this second aim involves determining the rights which each person may claim, in these specific conditions, as well as the way in which natural rights themselves (such as, for example, the right of ownership) may be exercised so that the common good is not damaged but, rather, advanced.

Note that natural rights can be understood in two senses. Either the nature which is considered is the "absolute nature" (n. 7) of man, or even, if one so prefers, the nature of man as it is to be found in every human community throughout man's historical existence: in this context, only very general natural rights can be established. If, on the other hand, we consider human nature and human communities as they actually exist in a variety of different concrete circumstances (at this stage of man's historical development, in this region of the world), a network of relations will result which will constitute, for a particular community in particular circumstances, a system of rights and duties that it would be contrary to the dictates of right reason to violate: such a system will, in consequence, be a system of objective natural rights and duties.

Those whose task it is to draw up the positive legislation for this particular community have to discover, to express and to sanction by their laws this rational order, which is grounded on the concrete and historical situation in which the members now exist. They have, however, to do more than this. Quite often, the most painstaking examination of this concrete situation will still leave room for legitimate freedom of decision; hence, it is the further task of the legislators to make some specific decisions with regard to this area that still remains undetermined. They may, in such situations, be in two minds concerning the choice of certain values or goals, choices which, in their turn, will govern subsequent decisions of detail. In a planned economy, for example, there may well be hesitations of this kind. Is priority to be given to the manufacture of tractors, of household equipment or of computers? Should the aim be a more affluent or a more cultured society? To concentrate on supplying immediate and urgent needs or on laying the foundations for a more prosperous future? No matter how desirous a people and their legislators may be to sacrifice no values, some options are inevitable. — A point that is worth noting in the present context is that because a decision corresponds less than others — which are equally possible here and now — to the requirements of the rational order, it does not thereby become unjust. Once it does not clash with these requirements, this is sufficient. If it were not, there would have to be an end to all positive legislation, for it is almost always possible for those subject to this legislation to devise a better arrangement (or at least one that they consider better) than that which has been decreed by law.

217. – If the relation between positive and natural rights is properly appreciated, it becomes clear that there can never be a genuine clash between them. Whenever an opposition arises, the positive right is abrogated or, at least, suspended. A human law which imposed what the natural moral law condemns (for example, the killing of innocent people, abortion etc.) loses all claim to our obedience; we have no duty and nobody has any right in virtue of such a law.

The truth of this may not, however, be immediately evident. Someone may wish to maintain that the state has a natural right to our obedience even when its commands are opposed to what is indeed a conclusion drawn from the basic principles of the natural law, but which is less fundamental than the principle of "obedience to the state so that the common good may be safeguarded". It is well worth sacrificing some conclusions that have only been derived from basic moral principles, in order to secure the public welfare. Let the well-being of the people be the supreme law!

But the public welfare cannot be secured if the purpose of human society, the goal at which it is essentially aimed (which is to make it possible for the members to lead lives that are fully human), is not respected. Now, a person is not leading a genuinely human life, a life that is worthy of a human being, if he says "no" to the demands which the natural moral law and, in consequence, his nature as a man, make on him. Consequently, once a right that has been granted by a positive law conflicts with a natural right, it comes to be at variance with its own *raison d'être*; since it has become a contradictio,n of and an obstacle to the purpose it is meant to serve, it no longer makes a rational demand on us, so that it is only in an equivocal sense that it can now be called a *right*.

The situation is entirely different when the law of the land, in order to avoid greater injury to the common good, tolerates or recognizes, without imposing them, practices which are contrary to the natural moral law, and to the natural rights of human beings (for example, civil divorce). This kind of tolerance or recognition is not in itself contrary to the moral law, nor a violation of human rights; while we ought never to do what is evil, we are not always obliged to strive to prevent it, particularly if such attempts would only result in worse disorders. Neither is the state to be faulted when its law recognizes as valid the juridical effects that flow from a situation that is in itself unjust, and safeguards these effects against those who would challenge them by resorting to force. It is not the state itself which creates the unjust situation; and if the protection which it affords, where the juridical consequences are concerned, is an inducement to some people to act unjustly, this is but a lateral, indirect effect which, for sufficiently serious reasons, may be tolerated (n. 230) [53].

218. – The third and final question that remains to be discussed is that of the relation betwen the juridical and the moral order.

---

[53] Cf. J. Fuchs, *Natural Law*, pp. 101-103.

From what has been said already, it should be clear that they are not adequately distinct. Since, if we are to act justly, we have to acknowledge and respect objective rights (nn. 194-195), the juridical order forms part of the moral, inasmuch as it defines what is required in order that a certain type of action be objectively, materially, good. Note that when we speak of the juridical order here, we include positive rights as well as those which are natural; it is too often forgotten that human laws normally oblige in conscience [54]. Hence, while the juridical order furnishes the moral order with part of its content, the latter, in its turn, stamps juridical obligations as moral.

Nevertheless, the juridical order is not purely and simply identical with the moral order. (This is as true of the natural juridical order as it is of the positive juridical order). On the one hand, the moral order extends more widely: there are many obligations which are non-juridical, many duties to which there is, strictly speaking, no corresponding right (nn. 194, 202). The juridical order does not extend beyond the sphere of the virtue of justice, whose "just mean" is not measured in relation to the agent himself, but in relation to a "state of affairs", in relation to what belongs to another (n. 197). On the other hand, even within the sphere of justice, of social relations between individuals, the juridical order is concerned *rather* with the objective, the material, aspect of an action or situation. Whether a person pays his debts, fulfils his civic obligations etc., out of a love of justice, or of a fear of legal proceedings, or because he has an evil ulterior motive, is of no importance — as Kant well saw (n. 211) — from the juridical point of view: once he hands over the money, he owes nothing more to his creditor; nothing further than this can be required of him. Similarly, if John intends, in a spirit of revenge, to destroy what belongs to James, but mistakenly destroys what belongs to himself, he has, without doubt, acted immorally because of the intention which inspired his action, but he has no juridical obligations of any kind towards James. The moral order, on the other hand, as has already emerged to some extent and will soon do so more clearly (nn. 227-229), is equally, and even *chiefly*, concerned with the intention of the moral agent and the goal at which he is aiming.

---

[54] St Thomas, *Summa Theol.*, I - II, 96, 4.

Hence, even where the content of the juridical and moral orders coincides, the viewpoint from which they each consider it remains different, What is of moral consequence is the relation between what the person has done and his liberty, the effect his action has had on his attitude towards the Ideal of practical reason. What is of juridical consequence is the relation between this same action and the human community, the social order etc.

In the discussion we are at present engaged upon, the words "rather" and "chiefly" should be carefully noted. It would be just as inexact to claim that the moral order is not concerned with what we do, with the material dimension of our actions, but only with our intention (nn. 224-229), as it would be to maintain that the juridical order is not at all concerned with our inner dispositions. For — quite apart from "imperfect" rights, such as the right we have that others should not *interiorly* judge us to have acted immorally when they have not good grounds for this — a person will often have even a positive right (when charged, for example, with a criminal offence), that his intention be taken into consideration.

It is, however, true that the juridical and ethical orders each consider a person's inner dispositions from different viewpoints. What a juridical investigation is concerned to discover is whether the accused has deliberately, and with clear knowledge of what he was doing, violated the law; the fact that his motives were idealistic and that he believed he would bring about a greater good through his violation of the law of the land, has not here the capital importance that it has from the ethical point of view. To probe and sound the secrets of the human heart is the prerogative of God.

In this context, it is worth reflecting on the problem with which a judge is faced when he is morally certain that the accused, even though guilty in the eyes of the law, is innocent in the forum of conscience, because he was sincerely convinced that the importance of the values and goals at which he was aiming, justified his violation of the law. (Such a situation is by no means impossible, and can occur even quite frequently, when a country is going through a period of inner turbulence and unrest). A military tribunal would undoubtedly have no hesitation in condemning to death a soldier who had deserted in time of war, even if it were satisfied that he had deserted because he considered the war to be unjust. But what are we to think about such a sentence? It could not be justified by the requirements of the common good, for these requirements cannot authorize us to do what is unjust; and is it not unjust to punish someone who is innocent of all moral fault? Can we then distinguish

between the justice which the juridical order requires and the justice
which the moral order requires, and maintain that the court is
juridically, even though not morally, entitled to condemn the soldier?
But does not a right which clashes with the moral law thereby cease
to be a right (n. 217)? These reflections help to make clear how
delicate and complex is the question of the interaction between the
moral order and the juridical, both on the natural and the positive
levels. It is worth noting that contemporary legislation, insofar as it
acknowledges that there can be conscientious objectors, has lessened
the gap that exists between a juridical and a moral appraisal.

It is sometimes said that human beings should not attempt to
take God's place as they do, it is maintained, when they hold trials
and juridical investigations; He alone can know the secret places of
the human heart. But if this principle were pushed to its extreme
conclusions, the consequences would disrupt human society and
make human living impossible. The solution to the difficulty is,
rather, that the juridical order should be brought into a growing
conformity with the moral order, even though the two can never be
completely identified.

219. – It is clear, then, that while what is juridical is
inseparable from what is moral, each continues to preserve its
own distinctive character; each has a dimension or sphere of
human activity as its own special preserve. Morality, even
though it does not neglect the "without" of human actions, is
more concerned with their "within": it concentrates on the
freedom of these actions, on the source from which they
proceed (the spiritual subject as such, the unique "I") and, in
consequence, attaches great importance to a person's intention,
the goal at which he is aiming (n. 228). The juridical order, on
the other hand, is more concerned with the "without" of
human actions: it is on our actions as inscribed in the universe,
in society, in history, and on the objective situations to which
they give rise, that this order primarily concentrates.

As a result of this discussion, it should be clear how the
position here defended differs from that of Kant. In our
analysis, the link between what is juridical and what is moral is
intrinsic. The just order, which is the object of the virtue of
justice, forms part of the moral order, just as does every moral
object, every object, that is, which can be chosen rationally. In
Kant's analysis, on the contrary, this link, as we have seen
(n. 211), remains extrinsic. Without doubt, this difference has

its origin in the two different ways in which the relations between the internal intention and the external action, between the intelligible world and the world of experience, between the noumenon and the phenomenon, are conceived.

Note also that a moral action as such, possesses, in its turn, a juridical or quasi-juridical aspect, once man's relations with God are taken into account; even if we remain on the human level, this aspect is also present in virtue of the fact that our actions, no matter how private they may seem to be, always have some repercussion on others and, in consequence, have an inevitably social dimension (n. 75). This is eminently true in the supernatural order, in virtue of the new union that exists between all mankind through Christ and in Christ. — In consequence of this, the sacrament of Penance, for example, has a juridical aspect; this, in its turn, has inevitably affected moral theology and has helped to develop in the Church that care for validity, legality etc., for which She is so often attacked but which, in reality, is no more than an expression of the social and relational character of all human activity.

220. – There is one other very important question that should be discussed before we conclude, namely: are natural rights unchangeable?

The reply that we made to a similar question concerning the natural law is applicable here also (nn. 187-190). There are certain very general rights which mankind cannot renounce without at the same time refusing to live rationally and thereby attacking the foundations of human society. Examples of the duties which are correlative to rights of this kind are: the duty not to injure others, to keep one's promises, to observe pacts and agreements, to obey the legitimate commands of legitimate authority and, in general, to respect the human dignity of every human being, and to play one's part in ensuring that life in society becomes more and not less possible.

Historical and social conditions will, however, frequently suggest or require diverse applications of these general principles. In the measure in which these applications result as necessary conclusions from the principles considered in conjunction with the requirements of the "situation", they still express natural rights (n. 216). In consequence, one and the same natural right could require in certain circumstances what it would forbid in others. In this way slavery, in antiquity, could be reconciled with human rights, in the measure in which the conditions of the period did not genuinely permit of any other practical solution. (Mankind would perhaps never have settled into the rhythm of work if external pressure had not first been exerted, or at least, it would have been content to do only what was needed in order to satisfy the most immediate needs). Nowadays, since these conditions no longer exist, slavery, even in modified and concealed forms, is certainly a violation of human rights. — If we keep the foregoing in mind, we shall have a better appreciation of the attitudes towards slavery that formerly existed (cf. n. 183).

It is in this sense that we are entitled to speak of variations and developments where natural rights are concerned, or even, as it is sometimes expressed, of natural rights whose content varies. On the other hand, as we saw when discussing the natural law (n. 187), one is equally entitled to say that not only the most general natural rights, but also the most specific applications of these rights, allow of no change, inasmuch as the propositions: "in the set of circumstances a, b, c, d etc., ... respect for human rights will call for x type of activity", is an unchanging truth. ... Nevertheless, it is a truth which becomes clear only progressively, through man's historical developments; man does not possess a code of rights to which the passage of time and the upheavals of history are immaterial. His appreciation of what respect for human rights involves is a discovery which he gradually makes, in the measure in which he faces up to the problem of finding new solutions for the new circumstances in which his life has to be lived. Indeed, inasmuch as these solutions depend in part on the changes which man effects in the real order (for example, through the social and economic structures which he introduces), he can be said not only to discover the code of human rights, but to play his part in fashioning it.

From what has been said, it should not be concluded that all these variations in natural rights are of equal value. Certain circumstances, and the applications of natural rights that are in consequence called for, are more in harmony with man's dignity and the requirements of right reason than are other circumstances and other applications. So, for example, circumstances in which all possible justification for slavery have disappeared are certainly preferable to those in which it could be a lesser evil. Similarly, on the day in which all possibility of a just war, no matter what the circumstances, will have vanished for good (in consequence, for example of an international organization that will be far more effective and united than those we have known up to this), humanity will certainly have made a notable advance where natural rights are concerned. — Hence, it is clear what nuances and distinctions have to be introduced into the common teaching of the Scholastics that neither slavery nor war is absolutely opposed to human dignity and human rights. The criticism that has to be made of this teaching is not, strictly speaking, that it is false, but that it is incomplete: it concentrates on the abstract essence of natural rights and has a static and minimal attitude towards them, in place of envisaging them as dynamic requirements which become manifest to the extent that the state of development at which humanity has arrived allows them to be perceived and to be satisfied.

Finally, we have here also to make a distinction, similar to that which we have made in our discussion of the natural law (nn. 187-188), between the *objective* development of natural rights, which is consequent upon the emergence of new objective conditions and circumstances, and their *subjective* development, which is the result of a more exact knowledge of requirements that were already objectively present, but which had hitherto not been perceived or had been insufficiently appreciated.

BOOK FOUR
THE SUBJECTIVE MORAL ORDER

221. – From the *objective* moral order, that is, from what presents itself to the moral subject as "to be done", we now turn to the *subjective* moral order (to the action or the complex of actions through which the human subject takes up a position in relation to this objective order), in which moral value in the strict sense is immediately to be found (n. 33, 1). We have already described the psychological structure of these actions (nn. 13-16); what we now wish to discover is how they come to possess a moral value; how this value becomes "incarnate" in them.

The first stage in this investigation is to determine what factors condition the moral character of a human act and make it to be a particular type of moral action. In dealing with this question, we have to remember that, as we have already seen (n. 13), there is a distinction between volition in the strict sense (the actual activity of our will) which alone can be qualified as simply good or evil, and the actions which we perform in virtue of this activity (actions which are commanded by our will and are under its control). Actions of this type can be, as is volition itself, spiritual and internal (as when, for example, the diligent student concentrates his attention on what he is studying, or when the gangster plans the details of the perfect crime), but ordinarily they involve some exercise of our powers of execution, some exterior actions and movements; it is for this reason that they are fairly generally referred to as "external", so that the title "internal" is, in consequence, reserved for volition in the strict sense. Additional support for this way of speaking can be found even where activity that is spiritual and internal is concerned: intellectual activity, as such, is in some way exterior to the act of decision, in that it is less directly concerned with the core and centre of the person (n. 24, 2).

We should also keep in mind, in dealing with the present question, that the complete human act (internal intention and external performance) always has a definite and determined object, in virtue of which it is structured as this type of action, and which can, in general, be defined as the creation of a new state of affairs, a new arrangement of physical or social reality: for example, the transfer of a certain sum of money from my wallet to another person's — or vice versa. But this object is presented to the subject and is attained by him, only in the context of certain *circumstances* which complete it as a moral object: the person to whom I give the money in question either is or is not poor; the money is my own or has simply been entrusted to my keeping etc. — Above all, by means of the object he chooses, the person is aiming at a certain *end* (n. 14, 3); it is from this that a human act receives its profound orientation: I can give away my money in order to honour God, to bring relief to my neighbour, to feel pleased with my generosity, to put an end to persistent requests, to be regarded as charitable by others etc. Our problem then is to discover which of these elements or factors determine the moral chsaracter, the moral value, of an action, and how they do so.

On the reply we make to that question will depend the reply to another, even though less important, question: is the domain of morality coextensive with that of human actions, or is there room in this latter domain for a morally neutral region: that of *indifferent* human acts?

After that, we shall again turn our attention to the subjective conditions under which a human action is performed, by inquiring how the moral law, or, if one wishes, objective moral value, is concretely brought to bear upon it, penetrates it, is interiorized in it, and in this way, through becoming its immanent rule, affects both its value as a human act and the value as a person of the one who performs it. In other words, our area of investigation will be that which is concerned with *moral conscience*. Two questions in particular will engage our attention: the problems that arise when a person's conscience is mistaken concerning the objective value of the action he is contemplating, as well as those that arise when his conscience is hesitant and a prey to doubts. In situations such as these, how is the morality of the decisions he takes to be measured? How is he to act when he is in error, and when he is in doubt?

Finally, we shall turn from the consideration of the moral *act* to the consideration of moral *activity* and the moral *life*, of which the individual, isolated act is no more than a passing moment. This will be the proper place to speak of the *virtue*, whose precise role is to make the moral subject's response to the demands of reason more personal and more enduring. Nevertheless, this study — whose importance in Aristotelico-Thomistic ethics is so great — will not here be undertaken at any great length, since such an investigation will yield much more fruit in a theological (dogmatic as well as moral) context.

CHAPTER TEN

THE FACTORS ON WHICH THE MORAL VALUE OF HUMAN ACTIONS DEPENDS

222. – A human action, as we have just noted, has more than one aspect and each of these has now to be considered at somewhat greater length. Firstly, the action is centred on some particular object, which can be called its practical theme and is the goal at which it is aimed by its very structure. A concrete example, that of reading, will help to make this clear. The person who reads has to read some written text, and what his action is immediately aimed at, of its very nature, is the understanding of this text, that is, the formation in the mind of the reader of images and concepts which will correspond, as far as possible, to those which the author had in mind when he was writing and which he wished to communicate. It can also happen that what the action is immediately aimed at is, in its turn, essentially directed towards the achievement of a certain effect: a watch is made in order that it may indicate the time, a refrigerator in order to freeze and preserve food etc. Now this effect — the goal of the work that has been produced — can be such that the moral problems to which it gives rise can create controversy concerning the morality of producing its cause: an instance of this is the manufacture of thermo-nuclear weapons. — It is clear that the notion of "object" in a moral context is rather elastic: it does not simply refer to an already — existing exterior reality (the book that is to be read) but to a certain result that is to be produced, a new state of affairs that is to be brought about; in a certain, even though less exact sense, the "external" dimension of the person's act is the object in relation to its "internal" dimension. — Since the relation between the person's act and the object has some analogy with the relation between the animating principle of a being, and the material element of the same being, the object is also referred to as the material element of the act (or, more exactly, as the matter on which or in connection with which the person acts). It would, however, be more advisable to use this term only when we wish to refer to an already-existing exterior reality.

But there are other aspects to a human action beyond that of being centred on some object from which it receives its typical structure: it occurs in a concrete situation, spatial and temporal, in a context of antecedents and consequents, as well as of concomitant occurrences etc., which ring it round with a circle of adjoining factors, with "circumstances" (*circum-stare*, "to stand all around"). To illustrate this, it will be helpful to return to our example of the person who is reading. This book is a definite book: if it is a novel, it is this particular novel; the reader is not man in general, but a particular person: if he is an adolescent, then he is this particular adolescent, living in a particular milieu, with this education, this temperament, this character etc. He reads at a definite time, in a definite place: perhaps while he is at school and during the class-period. It may well be that those to whose authority he is subject, his parents for example, have forbidden him to read that particular book. Finally, the person is motivated by the desire to achieve some subjective end which lies beyond the immediate and specific purpose of his reading: the adolescent we are envisaging may read in order to satisfy his curiosity, for the emotional thrill which it gives him, or perhaps out of snobbery, in order not to lose face with his companions etc. — These and still other circumstances are expressed in capsule form in the tag: who, what, where, by what means, why, how, when?

Now, it becomes immediately obvious that the circumstances in which a human action is performed are divided into two categories. One category is *objective*, and the circumstances in it are such that together with the object in the strict sense, they form a constellation whose varied elements are objectively linked together (even though, it is true, this comes to be only through the subject's action). The adolescent in our example reads his novel during the class-period of his own free will: nonetheless, the fact that he is reading this particular book, in this particular place, at this particular time, is an objective state of affairs which it is possible for others to know of, without it being in the least necessary for them to know the thoughts and intentions of the reader. Other circumstances, on the contrary, are *subjective*, and are linked with the object only by means of the subject, since no one but him is in a position to know of this link. This is the case, for example, where the intensity and duration of the "internal" act are concerned. (That his reading is stirring up ardent desires in the young person and that he is dwelling at length on these desires are circumstances which directly affect the "internal" act; only through it do they affect the "external" act and the object). But by far the most important subjective circumstance is *the goal which the agent is aiming at* (the "why" of his action) and which, in our example, we have put in the last place. The reading of the book, and the added prestige which the adolescent hopes to gain as a result, do not already form an objective and observable union, for the simple reason that this successful outcome has not been here and now achieved, and will perhaps never be achieved: the end (this outcome) is present only on the level of *intention*, on the level of thought and desire. The link, so far, between the action and the desired end is merely subjective [1].

Now that we have cleared the ground, our problem is to discover how, and in what measure, these various factors influence the concrete morality of a human action. For it is all too obvious that the object, the end and the other circumstances can all be related in different ways with the moral norm.

The point that is of capital importance in this present investigation is to discover whether the morality of our actions is principally a function of the object or the end. What is

---

[1] With regard to the intensity and duration (of the "internal" act), this should be noted: even though both can be directly willed, there is a difference between intensity and duration *as willed*, and the *actual* intensity and duration of an act of will. Simply because someone desires to love God as much as St Teresa, it does not follow that his love will, in reality, be as great as hers. What illusions there can be in this area! Cf. St Thomas, *Summa Theol.*, I-II, 19, 8: "Is a person's will actually as good or as evil as he intends it to be?" Compare this with Hartmann's distinction between *Intentionswert* and *Wertintention*, 2nd ed., pp. 347-349.

Moreover, in order to have a genuine intention of willing something intensely, it would seem to be necessary to have a precise notion of what this means. But when I speak of "loving God as St Teresa loves Him", my understanding of what it is I desire is extremely faulty. And it cannot but remain so, as long as I do not have within me the intensity of love which I desire.

involved in the reply we make to that question is not so much the truth or falsity of the widely propagated dictum that "the end justifies the means"; what is involved is rather one's basic approach to morality (as we shall soon see more clearly, nn. 224, 228, 270). Nor is the importance of the question merely speculative. If the role of the object is regarded as primary then, for example in moral education, very great stress will be placed on correcting young people for what they do, with the attendant danger of encouraging formalism; if, on the contrary, the role of the end is regarded as primary, then the chief stress will be placed on interior dispositions, with the attendant danger that the importance of actions may at times be underrated.

Our present inquiry also touches on two points which are relevant to the usage and administration of the sacrament of Penance. Firstly, are good and evil actions (and, in consequence, the corresponding habits, nn. 272, 274) specifically different in virtue of their different objects, or, on the contrary, should we say that all virtuous actions (and habits) are specifically the same, just as are all vicious actions (and habits)? Secondly, is it possible, and if so, under what conditions, that one and the same action should belong to two different moral species?

223. − 1) That the object plays a role in making an action to be *this* specific moral action rather than some other, is *implicitly* denied by all those who recognize only one type of morally good action (or only one virtue) and only one type of morally evil action (or only one vice). This is so because, as we shall presently show, objects differ specifically, so that if the object plays a role in making an action to be this specific moral action, there cannot but be specifically different moral actions and, consequently, moral habits (virtues and vices which are specifically different).

In this context, the obvious example is the doctrine of the Stoics and, in particular, that of Zeno and Cleanthes, for whom there is only one virtue. For Zeno this is wisdom (*phronēsis*), while fro Cleanthes it is the "tension" (*tonos*) of the will. The Stoic paradox of the equality of all failures to observe the moral law, and of the absence of any intermediate stage between perfect virtue and vice, is wellknown.

Descartes too — who in certain (but only in certain!) respects has such great affinity with the Stoics — seems to have acknowledged only one virtue which, he writes, consists in the resolution and vigour with which a person does what he believes to be good[2], just as he acknowledged only one science, which uses only one method (the method of mathematics). However, here as in other places, we have to be on our guard against forcing the meaning of what an author writes, and of attributing to him a reply to a question which he did not expressly pose.

The *logical* conclusion that follows from the theory of those who maintain that there is only one virtue is that it is simply and solely because of its relation (positive or negative) with the Ideal of practical reason that a human action is morally good or evil. This, in turn, amounts to saying that it is only the end which is of moral significance in human actions, insofar as the Ideal can be called an end (n. 141). For once the role of the object is excluded, there is nothing else which can determine and measure the rectitude, that is, the moral value, of a person's will.

The "tension" of Cleanthes and the "resolution and vigour" of Descartes have to be understood either as indicating the way in which a person's will adheres to what is good (from which, in consequence, their moral significance is derived) or else, as merely physical or natural qualities which, as such, are outside the moral sphere (n. 24, 2).

2) Much the same can be said concerning any moral theory in which an exclusive stress is laid on the intention, since it is to the end that the intention is directed.

Abelard passes for a representative of this school of thought. In fact, in his *Scito teipsum*, he insists so much on the role of the intention and on the fact that it is a good or evil will which makes a person to be good or evil, that he seems to attribute no importance, from the point of view of morality, to the object and to the exterior dimension of a human action. The intention, he writes, is good and right (or evil and wrong) in itself; the execution (the external dimension of the human action) is called good, not because of any value that inheres in it, but simply because it results from a good intention, that is, the source of its goodness is extrinsic to it[3]. Once the intention

---

[2] *Lettre à Christine de Suède*, Nov 20 1647; ed. Adam-Tannery, t. V, p. 83.
[3] *Op. cit.*, c. 11; PL. t. 178, col. 652.

is right, then all the "works" of which it is the source will be good [4]. Nevertheless, adds Abelard, it is not sufficient that a person's intention should appear to him to be right: it has to be right in itself and in the eyes of God [5]. — We should not then seek to class Abelard among those for whom the end justifies the means: to do so would be to interpret what he says in the context of a problem which is different from the one with which he himself was concerned. His primary purpose was to rebut the crude objectivism which would take into consideration only what a person actually did, that is, only the external dimension of his action.

There are better grounds for regarding Kant's ethical theory as one in which an exclusive stress is laid on the intention. As Kant's writings show (nn. 115, 116), the entire moral value of a human action is made to consist in the inner attitude of the person's will whereby he obeys the law purely out of respect for the law. But we have also seen how Kant was at pains to rebuild an objective moral order around this inner attitude. The entire moral value of the action comes from the intention but, nevertheless, there are objects which we cannot choose and still retain a right intention.

3) The Scholastics generally hold that the object, the end and the various circumstances all play a part in determining the *moral value* of human actions, that is, in making these actions to be good or evil. As regards their *specific* moral quality (is a particular action theft, or intemperance etc.?), this primarily comes, they maintain, from the object, even though the other factors also play a part in determining it. — On the question of the respective roles of these various elements, there are divergent views, which are often, perhaps, more verbal than real.

According to certain of them — Schiffini and Lehu for example — the circumstances can add a supplementary moral quality to an action, so that at times one and the same action will belong to several different moral species (but not to contrary species: an action can never be at one and the same time morally good and evil!) [6]. Others,

[4] *Ib.*, c. 12; col. 653.
[5] *Ib.*
[6] Schiffini, *Disp. phil. mor.*, I, pp. 121-122. — Lehu, *Phil. mor. et soc.*, pp. 136-138.

such as Frins and Cathrein, in the wake of Suarez, admit that the same action can belong to different moral species where evil actions are concerned (we can commit several simultaneous sins), but not where good actions are concerned (we cannot exercise several virtues simultaneously). The reason for this is that more is required of us in order that we act well than is required in order that we be guilty of acting badly, for the former means that a certain perfection has been achieved, whereas the letter means that we have fallen away from the perfection that is required of us [7]. All that the circumstances can add to the virtuous action is an accidental goodness; they cannot add a moral quality that is specifically different.

Likewise, in the view of Lehu and of Thomists in general, the end *intrinsically* determines the moral value of an action [8], whereas Frins and Cathrein consider that the deyermination which results from it is extrinsic [9].

Finally, Lehu and the great majority of Thomists maintain that the external dimension of a human action really and intrinsically, even though analogously, shares in the morality of the inner dimension [10]. Frins and Cathrein, on the contrary, insist that this external dimension can be called moral only in an extrinsic sense. Since it is a good or evil will that makes a person to be good or evil, we can attribute moral value or anti-value to the external dimension of his action only in a manner of speaking [11].

224. – Before we begin to discuss the problems we are here faced with, it is necessary to emphasize a truth that is too often misunderstood: the unity of a human act. The internal and the external dimensions should by no means be regarded as if they were complete actions in themselves and merely linked together from without; if they were, they would remain a union-of-two and would not form a unity. Just as body and soul are not two completed realities but two "overlapping" elements, so also the two dimensions of which we are here speaking are but two elements of the one human action. The

---

[7] V. Frins, *De act. hum.*, t. I, pp. 47-53, t. II, pp. 24-25; V. Cathrein, *Phil. mor.*, 14th ed., pp. 106, 115 seq. — Suarez, *De bonitate et malitia objectiva actuum humanorum*, d. IV, sect. 3, nn. 12-13, ed. Vivès, t. IV, pp. 332b-333, and d. V, sect. 2, n. 19, p. 342.

[8] Lehu, *op. cit.*, p. 141.

[9] V. Frins, *op. cit.*, t. II, pp. 277 seq.; V. Cathrein, *op. cit.*, p. 122.

[10] *Op. cit.*, pp. 154-156.

[11] V. Frins, *op. cit.*, p. 256; V. Cathrein, *op. cit.*, n. 165.

relation between the person's inner decision and the activity by which he puts this into execution is a very special one; the decision is both the driving force and the animating principle of the execution, that is, the inner dimension of the action plays a role that is intermediate between one of initiating the outer dimension, and vivifying or "informing" it. We have then to be on our guard against picturing this latter dimension as if it were an activity of our bodies, which our minds directed from the outside, in much the same way as a workman handles the instruments of his trade (turns the lathe, guides the electric saw etc.). There is but one human action, whose source is the inner decision of the person's will, and which is made manifest through his external activity and movements[12]. But attention can be focussed on one aspect rather than on the other: on the action as it originates in the person's mind and will, or as it is externally expressed and brought to completion in the cosmic, historical and social milieu. We shall, then, now consider each of these aspects in turn.

In doing this we shall be following the example of St Thomas who, in the *Prima Secundae* of his *Summa Theologica* treats successively of the goodness and malice of human acts in general (q. 18), of the goodness and malice of the inner decision (q. 19), and finally of the goodness and malice of the external execution (q. 20).

An additional preliminary point is that there is widespread agreement, particularly in Scholastic circles, concerning this general principle: to every specific relation (whether of agreement or opposition) with the moral norm, there corresponds a specific type of moral value or anti-value, that is, a particular mode of moral goodness or malice. Since the moral value of an action is measured by its conformity with, or opposition to, the ethical norm (which, in our analysis, is the judgment of right reason), it follows that the differences which intrinsically affect the relation of an action with this norm will also intrinsically affect its moral value, or, more precisely, the manner in which this value becomes "incarnate" in it; in consequence, there will be moral categories that are specifically different.

---

[12] *Essai*, nn. 156-158; pp. 382-389.

225. – After making these preliminary points, we now go on to consider a human action as it is inscribed in the world, in history, in society; in other words, we consider it from the objective and juridical point of view (nn. 217-218). So viewed, an action is this specific action rather than some other, primarily and essentially because of its *object*; consequently, it is as such that it has first to be measured against the rule of reason and to be appraised morally. Suppose, for example, that a man takes money to which he is not entitled, simply in order to be able to afford a drinking spree, and that he is caught red-handed. He is a man who had never stolen before and had resolved to do so now, only with regret and as a last resort; but he is a notorious tippler. Despite this reputation, no one would now dream of charging him with the crime of drunkenness; what he would be accused of would be attempted theft.

Nevetheless, an important distinction has here to be introduced between object in the *physical* order and an object in the *moral* order. From the former point of view, the simple transference of a sum of money from my hand into the hand of another is already a specific action; its "physical" nature is not altered by the condition of the persons in question (rich, poor, etc.), nor by the source of the money. From the moral point of view, on the contrary, the action just described is still not specific, for it does not, of itself, involve any special relation of agreement with, or opposition to, right reason. In order that such a relation should appear, some further clarifications are essential: the money is my own; the person to whom I give it is poor or in some need, and he has no claim whatever to it (not even that of extreme necessity). Because of these circumstances, the action acquires the completion which it lacked from the moral point of view, so that it is now revealed as an act of generosity.

From what has been said, it is clear that, from the moral standpoint, there is ordinarily present in the object an element which, from the purely physical standpoint, is a mere circumstance. In other words, what would be but an accidental accompaniment where the object as considered in the physical order is concerned, is often, on the contrary, an essential constituent where the object as considered in the moral order is concerned[13]. Or, as St Thomas also expresses it, moral factors are accidental to the physical reality of an action[14]. — Circumstances can, then, combine with the object and, so to speak, share in its status, so that through the completion which they bring, an action comes to possess its primary and essential moral qualification.

226. – But it can also happen that even where a definite and specific type of moral action is concerned, some additional circumstance or circumstances can introduce a new relation of agreement with, or opposition to, the judgments of right reason. To nourish hatred for another human being, to kill him (on one's own authority): such actions are certainly immoral. But to hate one's father, or to murder him, involves a fresh opposition to the moral law: a son has a relationship with his father which he has with no other human being; in consequence of this, fresh demands are made on him where his father is concerned, so that even if he were permitted (which he never could be) to hate all other human beings, the duty of loving his father would still remain. — Here, once again, circumstances coalesce with the object.

In this context, St Thomas distinguishes two types of situation[15] which we can illustrate in the following way. Suppose that the thief to whom we have previously referred had stolen chalices etc., from a church. Now, this circumstance can be called an objective circumstance: it affects the morality of the action in question, because of the change it has made in the object of the action. The theft is now no longer merely a theft: ir is a sacrilegious theft. This added moral quality is related to the moral quality which the action has simply because of its object, if the circumstance in question is left out of consideration — it is then simply an act of theft — in the same way as what is specific is related to what is generic: sacrilegious theft is a species of the generic crime of theft. — But, on the other hand, the person in our example steals in order to go on the spree. Clearly, this circumstance also has an influence on the overall morality of his action. The person's inner disposition is such that he has offended against the virtue of temperance. Intemperance, however, is not a

---

[13] St Thomas, *Summa Theol.*, I-II, 18,10.
[14] *Ib.*, 1, 3 ad 3um.
[15] *Ib.*, 18, 10; *De Malo*, II, 6.

species of the generic offence of theft. Consequently, there are now in the person's action two specific moral qualities which do not dovetail, as did the two qualities in our first illustration: his action belongs to two *disparate* moral categories. In such a situation, St Thomas even seems to regard the end which is intended as the object of an added human act: two human acts would thus be involved — one an act of theft which has been completed, and the other a bout of indulgence in alcohol which has not yet got under way! (But see n. 228).

The situation would, of course, be altered if what the thief primarily intended were to profane the consecrated vessels. If this were the case, then the sacrilegious theft should be subsumed under the category of sacrilege rather than that of theft. Here, clearly, the person's intention plays a role in determining the primary moral quality of the action in question. This quality will, then, in the example we have chosen, be the result of the intersection of two genera (theft and sacrilege), just as man himself, who is both "rational animal" and "incarnate spirit", is at the intersection of two genera.

There do not, then, seem to be any grounds for denying that one and the same "physical" action can belong to two moral species, both where goodness and malice are concerned[16]. St Thomas keeps the necessary balance when he notes that even though the multiplicity of circumstances in which an action is performed does not make it to belong to several moral species, there is, nevertheless, no reason why one and the same moral action should not belong to several moral species, even disparate ones[17].

At other times, and more frequently, no new specific relation to right reason results from the circumstances, but merely a strengthening or weakening of the conformity or opposition between the action and its norm and, in consequence, of its moral value or anti-value. All things being otherwise equal, it is more serious to steal a thousand pounds than it is to steal a hundred: the requirements of practical reason, as applied to the sphere of justice, are flouted to a greater extent.

At still other times, and these would seem to be by far the most frequent, the circumstances provide no basis for any rela-

---

[16] St Thomas, *Summa Theol.*, I-II, 18, 7 ad Iun.

[17] *Ib.*, 10 ad 3um. Cf. *De Malo, ib.*, ad 3um. In this latter text, St Thomas, because of the nature of the problem he is discussing, treats expressly only of sins, but the reason he advances — namely, that the moral reality of the action is related to its physical reality, as a quality is related to a substance — is equally valid where virtuous actions are concerned.

tion whatever to right reason. They neither ground nor modify the agreement with, or the opposition to, right reason which the action possesses in virtue of its object, its end, or the other circumstances; in consequence, they have no moral significance. It matters not a whit from the moral point of view what type of weapon the assassin uses to kill his victim.

227. – If we now go on to consider the inner origin of a human action, that is, if we consider its internal dimension (the dimension that is of more consequence where morality is concerned, nn. 218-219), it becomes clear that the sense in which its object is then to be understood has changed, and has indeed been considerably enlarged. In relation to the pure subjectivity of the action's inner dimension, everything else — not only the object of the external dimension with its cortege of objective circumstances, but this external dimension itself — constitutes a kind of global object. For it is this ensemble which has been presented to the person's will and has been, either directly or indirectly, chosen by him. But this global object also, and indeed especially, includes the *end*, for it is this which a person aims at before all else and for its own sake. In relation to the internal act of his will, or better, to the human action considered in its subjective well-springs, the end is an objective factor which, in consequence, plays a part in making the action to be this specific action: indeed, it is the end which, more than anything else, fulfils this role. Its function in relation to the inner dimension of the action is, then, similar to that which the object in the strict sense exercises with regard to the external dimension [18].

Consequently, in the context in which we are at present speaking, we can say that the moral value of the internal dimension of a human action is entirely derived from its object [19]. It follows from this that if a person chooses what is good, no circumstance can ever make his decision to be evil [20]. For, in order that a circumstance of the inner decision should affect the morality of this, it would have to be known

---

[18] St Thomas, *Summa Theol.*, I-II, 18, 6.
[19] *Ib.*, 19, 2.
[20] *Ib.*, ad 2um.

and willed, and if it were, it would then be part of the global object [21].

Now, as we already know (n. 224), the inner dimension of an action is the animating principle ("form") of the exterior dimension, which it raises to the moral level. Hence, because of this relation between the two dimensions, the exterior has likewise a specific moral value in virtue of the end at which the person is aiming. This means that there is, in fact, a certain ambiguity in the relation of the end to the external component of a human action. If this latter is considered as animated ("informed") by the interior component, that is, if we wish to speak about a human action in its concrete unity, then the external component has a specific moral value because of the end at which the person is aiming. But if we wish to speak simply about the exterior aspect of an action, or better, if what we are speaking about is a human act as it has been "written into" history and the world, then the end at which the person aims should rather be called a circumstance [22].

228. – From the preceding discussion it is clear that the specific moral value of a human action is derived from two sources: from the object in the strict sense, and from the end which the agent intends. But what is the relation of these two sources to one another? Which of them is the principal determinant of the nature and moral value of the action?

When dealing with this question, St Thomas makes a distinction (which corresponds to the one which has already been made in n. 226) between two types of situation.

---

[21] The circumstances of duration and intensity form an exception; these have an influence on the moral value of an action even though they are not directly willed (cf. note 1 above). They cannot, however, make an action, which is good in virtue of its object, to be evil. — With regard to the circumstance of time ("when?"), St Thomas observes that where it refers to the act of willing, it cannot of itself make this to be evil, "except on the contingency that by willing this good at that time, a person might be stopped from willing another good to which he is bound", ib. (Trans.: T. Gilby, op. cit., vol. 18, p. 33). — But, even then, this omission can be blameworthy or formally evil, only in the measure in which it is, in some fashion, known and accepted, so that the circumstance in question is transferred into the field of the object.

[22] See Cajetan, In Iam IIae, 18, 4.

The first type: the object is internally oriented towards the end which the agent intends; from this latter, it derives its meaning. In other words, the end which the agent intends is in alignment with the end towards which the object and the external dimension of the action are directed[23]. Such is the situation, for example, whenever all that a thief is aiming at is financial gain; or whenever the person who pays his debts, simply intends to satisfy the just claims of his creditors. — In this type of situation, writes St Thomas, the specific value which results from the end intended is more general than that which results from the object; in consequence, the latter value determines the former, in the same way as what is specific determines what is generic. For it is the person's will (whose proper object is the end) which is in control of all his powers of execution, whose proper objects, in their turn, are those at which particular actions are aimed[24]. To the objective hierarchy of what is universal (the end) and what is particular, there corresponds the subjective hierarchy of mover and moved. ... Consequently, when a person is aiming at nothing other than what the exterior dimension of his action is, of its very structure, aimed at, the entire moral value of this action is derived from the object. The thief who steals in order to enrich himself is simply a thief.

The second type of situation: the object is not now, of itself, oriented towards the end which the agent intends. (The thief who steals so as to be able to go on the spree is an illustration of such a situation, as is also the person who keeps his word, not simply from a love of fidelity, but because he wishes to be trusted more by another person, whom he will then be in a position to help more effectively). — When this happens, the two specific values, in place of blending, are independent, so that the action belongs to two moral species which remain in

---

[23] *Essai*, n. 26; pp. 62-63.

[24] "The specific difference arising from the end intended is wider than and is narrowed down by the specific difference arising from what of its nature is a subordinate objective. The will, which has our final end as its proper objective, is the universal motive-power for all our psychological powers, whereas their proper objectives are the objectives of particular acts", St Thomas, *ib.*, 18, 7 (Trans.: T. Gilby, *ib.*, p. 31).

some way disparate [25]. — But then the question arises: are these two species of equal importance, or is one more important? If so, which is it?

Thomistic authors in general, give priority, even here, to the object: it is on this, its immediate source, that the morality of an action essentially depends [26].

This view is at odds with what has emerged from our present investigation. If the inner decision, whose morality primarily depends on the end which the person intends, is the animating principle ("form") of the complete human act, must it not be the end which most profoundly colours the morality of this latter? Indeed, this is the conclusion to which St Thomas himself comes, when he writes that if what we are speaking about is a human act as such, then the end is primary, but that if we consider the same act objectively, that is, as it is revealed externally, the object of the external deed becomes primary. It is for this reason, he goes on, that Aristotle says that the person who steals so as to be in a position to commit adultery is, strictly speaking, more an adulterer than a thief [27].

In order to reconcile the two views, it might be maintained that where the person's *act* is concerned the *object* is of greater significance, as the authors to whom we have just

---

[25] "When the external act's objective is not of its nature ordained to the will's end, then the specific difference arising from the objective is not an essential determinant of that arising from the end, nor conversely. In such a case, neither species falls under the other: instead you find a moral act coming under two disparate species", *ib*. (Trans. *ib*., p. 29). — Note the difference between this doctrine and that of the *De Malo*, II, 6 ad 2um, where the circumstances — and consequently the end — were regarded as the object of an annexed act (above, n. 226). If, as Dom Lottin believes, the *De Malo* is anterior to the *Prima Secundae*, one could maintain that St Thomas had come, in the meantime, to a better appreciation of the unity of a human action. But perhaps we have here simply an indication of the difficulty that one encounters in applying the categories of unity and plurality to psychological and moral realities.

[26] L. Lehu, *op. cit.*, p. 141, writes in this vein: "The morality of an action has its immediate source in the object and its remote source in the end".

[27] *Summa Theol.*, I-II, 18, 6. — In fact, what Aristotle wrote was: "such a person (who commits adultery for the sake of gain) is, without doubt, unjust, but he is not intemperate" (*Nicom. Eth.*, V, 1130a 24). But even though verbally St Thomas misrepresents Aristotle, the thought of the latter is accurately presented: St Thomas is guilty of no more than a lapse of memory: in his commentary, he gives a correct interpretation: *In V Eth.*, bk. 3; ed. Pirotta, n. 916.

referred insist, but that the morality of the *person* depends more on the end at which he aims: the text of Aristotle seems to affirm just this and nothing more. But the opposition between the two views cannot be dissolved in this way, since it is only in virtue of his free actions that a person becomes morally good or evil (n. 33, 1).

The key to the desired reconciliation is to be found in the distinction we have already used. If we consider a human action as it originates in the mind and will of a human being, its morality depends more on the end which he intends, and which has moved him to act; further, it is the end for which he acts that expresses him more fully and affects him more profoundly as a moral subject. It is the goals for which a person acts that most reveal his inmost dispositions, his moral habits, his character, his fundamental attitude towards values and the Value. Because of what a person is, and has made of himself, certain goals come to have an increasing attraction for him and certain others come to have less appeal. — It is clear, then, that the role of the end is less to make an action to be this specific action than it is to determine its positive or negative value and, in consequence, the value or antivalue of the person who performs it. This is eminently true when the end in question is the ultimate end in a person's life, that is, the fundamental value whose choice conditions the attraction which all particular ends and values will have for him. In the final analysis, there are only two possible attitudes which a human being can take towards the Ideal: to be open towards it, or to be closed [28]. It is on this radical choice, whose effect is operative to a greater or lesser extent in each particular choice [29], that a human being's moral value essentially depends. — The role of the object is rather to affect the way in which an action is moral or immoral, that is, to make it be a particular type of action which is in conformity with or opposed to right reason [30].

---

[28] See the *Essai*, nn. 119, 120, 129; pp. 287-292, 309-312.

[29] *Ib.*, n. 131; pp. 315-317. — On the notion of fundamental choice, see H. Reiners, *Grundintention und sittliches Tun*, Freiburg-im-Br., 1966, especially pp. 15-46.

[30] Cf. S. Pinckaers, *Le rôle de la fin dans l'action humaine selon saint Thomas*, "Rev. des sc. phil. et théol.", 1961, pp. 393-421.

The subject's inner disposition, of which his action is the fruit, is his response to the appeal of the end. It is not necessary that this disposition be distinctly and expressly accepted in order that it exercise its influence: moral and religious writers have long since pointed out (well before the advent of depth psychology) the importance of a person's basic attitudes, of his radical and secret options which, at least as long as they are not revoked, exercise a very considerable influence on his particular choices [31]. The young man in the Gospel did not respond to the invitation of Christ because, on the scale of values which effectively governed his preferences, his "many possessions" stood higher than a "perfect life". To say "yes" to the call of Christ, he would have had to adopt a different table of values.

It is worth recalling, in this context, that in the Thomistic analysis of a human act (n. 15), it is the *initial stage* of the will's activity (the root of all further stages of the act) which is, properly speaking, aimed at the *end*, and that the further and crucial stage of *choice* is concerned rather with the *means* to this end.

In addition to the fundamental options which each of us makes personally, the society, the milieu etc., in which we live has also committed itself to certain values, has chosen them for us, so that independently of our own options, the field open to our liberty is already to some degree structured for us. Think, for example, of the excessive value that the modern Western world places on sex. Very often, it is only a person of exceptional quality who is capable of breaking free of the shackles which prior options of this kind impose, so that the correct solution of certain moral problems can become, in practice, impossible to achieve. — It might seem to some that this last point is not relevant to our investigation: is not the fundamental uprightness of the individual person independent of choices which are made without consulting him and are exterior to him? But the question that has to be faced is whether, and up to what point, it is possible for an individual to continue to be a man of genuinely good will, to be open and responsive to the Value, when the society in which he lives seeks to promote values that are not true, nor worthy of a human being.

229. – But the eminent role which the end plays in determining the moral value of an action is not an exclusive one: the object and, in consequence, the means, have also to be taken into consideration. Even though a person's will is pri-

---

[31] D. von Hildebrand calls these dispositions "superactual attitudes", *Christian Ethics*, pp. 241-243.

marily aimed at the end he wishes to achieve, he also chooses, as we have seen, the means to this end (the object and the attendant circumstances). Many non-professional thieves would prefer to acquire the money of which they have need by honest means, but in fact they decide to perform an action that it is in their power to avoid. Consequently, if the means chosen are, of their very nature, contrary to right reason, the person who freely makes use of them becomes unfaithful to reason and to its Ideal, no matter how legitimate and praiseworthy the end at which he is aiming. This latter is, indeed, the animating principle (the "form") of the global object which he wills, but it is not identical with this object.

We can go even further than this. If a person seeks to achieve a morally good end by making use of means which are immoral and which he recognizes as such, then it is no longer *t-his end as morally good* which he is seeking. The end itself has not changed, true, but his attitude towards it has. For if a person is to aim at a morally good end as morally good — an essential condition which he has to fulfil in order to act well (nn. 238-239) — his will has to remain open to the Value, and this openness becomes impossible once he freely and knowingly makes use of evil means. The person whose love for another moves him to violate the virtue of justice, or of chastity, cannot claim that his love is deep and genuine; in closing himself to the Value from which the value of the other is derived, he has here and now made himself incapable of bestowing the love for which the human dignity of the other calls.

There are correspondingly stronger grounds for maintaining (but the truth of this is not contested by anyone) that when the end which a person seeks is evil, an action which would otherwise be licit, and even praiseworthy, is thereby vitiated: so, for example, to give alms to a beggar in order to induce him to blaspheme, is evil because of the end sought. "To do the right deed for the wrong reason". In situations of this kind, the principle (cf. n. 223, 3) that in order to act well a person has to fulfil all the required conditions, but does wrong when he fails to meet any one of them, is particularly applicable. Good is a perfection to which all the required conditions contribute; evil is a privation which results from the lack of even one necessary element.

On the other hand (and the truth of this is likewise not contested) an action whose object would, of itself, be indifferent (morally neutral) takes on a positive moral value if the end to which it is directed is in accordance with reason (n. 238).

230. – We should be careful not to confuse the use of an intrinsically perverse means with the use of a means which, of itself, is morally praiseworthy or indifferent, but which, in addition to the morally desirable or tolerable effect at which it is aimed, also produces an effect which it would be immoral to seek. A person is entitled to make use of a means of this kind, when he has reasons for doing so which are proportionate both to the good he aims at achieving and the evil he foresees will result. There are, however, two conditions which have to be fulfilled: the first is that the evil effect should not be in any way intended; the second is that it should not flow more immediately from the means used than does the good effect. (If it did, then it would be a causal link between the means and this latter effect, so that the person would be willing what is evil in order that good might result). So, for example, in the time of war, a military leader is morally justified in ordering a bridge to be blown up when this is urgently required in order to halt the advance of the enemy, even though such a decision may entail the death of some loitering non-combatants. Similarly, a person is entitled to take a medicine or to undergo an operation which, while they have the effect of saving his life or restoring him to health, also involve, and even necessarily involve, consequences which he has not the right to choose and to seek: so, for example, a pregnant woman is entitled to have her cancerous womb removed, even though this will inevitably lead to the death of the fetus. There is nothing immoral about this operation, since her restoration to health does not result from the effect which she is forbidden to seek (the death of the fetus) and the surgery is essential if she is not to die.

Why is a person entitled to act in ways such as those we have indicated? If we reflect, the reasons become clear. In the hypothesis envisaged, the significance of the means employed is not defined in terms of the prohibited effect; if it were, then the means would be intrinsically perverse and this the hypothesis excludes. In addition, this effect is not a means whereby the desired result is obtained. Consequently, there is no reason whatever why a person cannot aim at this result as a morally good end which he intends as such (n. 238), while at the same time choosing to achieve it by the means in question; in other words, he can choose this means without acting immorally. There is nothing in the object, as it presents itself to him, which clashes with his openness to the Value.

Obviously, as we have already indicated, a person requires a proportionate reason for permitting the evil effect to occur. Carelessness in this respect would witness to a culpable disregard for the objective order, to an egoism that pays but little attention to others and their rights; in a word, to an insufficient openness to the Value. This carelessness and indifference are, all too often, evident in time of war, when the proportion of which we have spoken is rarely respected, it has, however, to be confessed that to determine this proportion is not at all easy. — But, on the other hand, if a person were entitled to permit an evil effect under no circumstances whatever, human life and, in particular, all progress would become impossible. The advances and discoveries that man has made inevitably involve undesirable side-effects, dangers to life and even actual loss of life. Are motor-cars to be banned because of the accidents that occur, or because the smoke and fumes which they emit increase the risk of cancer for city-dwellers? Are supersonic aircraft to be grounded because the noise they cause can be harmful to those who have heart trouble? To fetter mankind's progress and development is very far from being in accordance with right reason [32].

231. – A brief summary of our findings:

1. It is from the various elements of an action which give rise to special relations of conformity with or opposition to right reason, that the moral value of this action is derived. Now, since the object, strictly so called, the end at which the agent is aiming, and, in certain situations, the other circumstances, can all give rise to a relation of this kind, the moral value of an action is derived from those various elements.

2. The subject's moral value depends chiefly on whatever it is that makes the inner dimension of his action (his intention) to be of this kind rather than some other, since it is this which reveals and expresses his inmost dispositions. But

---

[32] For a different interpretation of the principle, see P. Knauer, *La détermination du bien et du mal moral par le principe du double effet*, "Nouvelle revue théologique", 1965, pp. 356-376. According to this author, "an evil effect will be indirect or direct depending on the presence or absence of a proportionate reason", p. 365. Now, "a proportionate reason will be present, if one genuinely aspires to the maximum realization of the value (sought for in the action) at the level of its total reality", p. 370. Consequently, "one will permit an evil, if this si the only way of not directly contradicting the maximum realization of the value which is opposed to it", p. 371. The arguments adduced by the author do not, in our view, make it necessary to abandon the current presentation of the principle.

since what plays this role is the end at which he is aiming, it is also on this that his moral value chiefly depends.

3. If a person's choice of a particular means is incompatible with his intention to achieve a morally good end, then this latter cannot justify his choice. But it is impossible for a person to fix his will genuinely on a morally good end, once he chooses to achieve it by means which he knows to be immoral. Consequently, no matter how praiseworthy the end, it cannot justify the choice of means which are of their nature immoral and are known to be such.

232. – Some additional reflections. 1. What effect has the external dimension of an action on the moral value of the internal, or, does the execution of an inner decision affect the morality of this latter in any way? [33].

The distinction which St Thomas makes between the two sources on which the morality of the external dimension of an action depends, helps to throw light on this question: one of these sources is the end which the agent is aiming at, and the other is the object together with the objective circumstances.

The morality which is derived from the first source results entirely from the person's own will. For it is he alone who establishes the link between the end in question and the external dimension of his action; as we have seen (n. 222), it is in this respect that the end the person intends is distinguished from the other circumstances which, apart from the intensity and duration (of the action's internal dimension), coalesce with the object. From this point of view, then, it is only insofar as the person's execution of his decision results in a modification of his own inner attitude and, in consequence, of the moral value or anti-value of this attitude, that the external dimension affects the morality of the internal. This can happen in three ways. A person may have to make a fresh resolve in order to execute the decision he has already taken, but which he has not yet put into effect; so, for example, a person who makes a good resolution in the morning will have to renew this when the occasion for living up to it presents itself in the late afternoon.

---

[33] St Thomas, *Summa Theol.*, I-II, 20, 4. See also *II Sent.*, d. 40, 1, 3; *De Malo*, II, 2 ad 8um.

Secondly, the execution may call for a protracted effort, so that the inner resolve has to be maintained in a way that would otherwise not have been required. (Two students set out for the University each of whom is determined to listen attentively to the lecture he is going to attend; one discovers on arrival that his professor is indisposed, and uses the unexpected free time to go and visit some friends, whereas the other listens with admirable attention to a demanding lecture). A third possibility is that the pleasure or pain that flows from the execution results in a greater or lesser degree of personal involvement; a person may start by looking at some spectacle, a scene in a street etc., out of the corner of his eye and with no more than a passing curiosity, but after a while he allows himself to be completely fascinated and absorbed; he is carried away by curiosity and desire, as was Alypius in the wellknown incident related by St Augustine [34]. Note that it is not only the pleasure which he experiences that can cause a person to commit himself more fully to what he is doing: the difficulties he has to surmount often have the same effect, in that they stimulate what the Scholastics would call his "irascible appetite", and what we would nowadays call his aggressive instincts and his desire to triumph. Mountaineers provide a good example of this.

The morality which is derived from the second source (the object and the objective circumstances) does not, on the contrary, result from the person's own will. Quite independently of the subject's choice, a structure of conformity with, or opposition to, the judgments of right reason is already involved here. All that is left to his choice is whether or not he will accept this objective value [35]. — Further, the moral value of the person's decision depends, from this point of view, on whether he puts it into effect, since the external dimension is the goal and completion of the internal. The completion of every tendency, notes St Thomas, lies in arriving at its goal; hence a person cannot be said to have a resolute will, if he is not ready, when the occasion offers, to put his decision into effect [36].

---

[34] *Confessions*, IV, 8; PL. t. 32, col. 726.

[35] St Thomas, *Summa Theol.*, I-II, 20, 1.

[36] "Every bent and motion is completed by reaching its term and attaining its goal. Hence an act of will is not complete, unless given the opportunity it will

In other words, a genuine decision tends, in virtue of the dynamism that is inherent in it, to manifest itself in the appropriate "external" action; the most certain sign that a person is sincere and that his decision is authentic will always be his effective execution of what he has decided on or promised. Even more than this: if a person's inner resolve is genuine, he will at once — unless he is prevented, or has good reasons for delaying — commence to put decision into effect, so that the perfection of what is internal will lie in the performance of what is external. Hence the proverb: "hell is paved with good intentions", that is, with intentions that have remained sterile. A decision which a person is content to conceal within himself, and which he does not make manifest when the occasion for doing so arises, is thereby stamped as shallow and irresolute.

Note the difference between situations of this kind and those which we considered previously. In the first type of situation, the execution of the decision is the occasion of the person's will becoming better or worse. In the second type, the execution reveals that the person's will is, in fact, better or worse (than it would be if he did not carry out his decision).

233. – II. The distinction between a human act as a physical and as a moral reality.

A question which the Scholastics discussed, and which is worth nothing briefly here, is: what does the moral reality of a human act consist in, and what does this reality add to the physical or natural reality of the act? The answers which they have given to this problem can be reduced to three principal ones [37].

---

finish the deed", *ib.*, 20, 4. (Trans.: T. Gilby, *op. cit.*, vol. 18, p. 97). – Whenever a person makes a genuine decision, its execution presents itself to him, at the "intentional" level, as the necessary consequence of his "project", on condition that this latter is not abandoned, that the means of executing it are not lacking and that no obstacle presents itself. See the analysis of volition in n. 14, 2 and in the *Essai*, n. 14, pp. 39-42. — If, however, it is impossible for a person to execute his decision, the consequent lack of completion that affects his act of will is purely involuntary and detracts in no way from the value of this latter, St Thomas, *ib.*

[37] For a fuller exposition, consult V. Frins, *De actibus humanis*, II, pp. 9-53 and I. González Moral, *Philosophia moralis*, Santander, 1945, pp. 87-88.

The first view is that what endows a human act with a moral character is the freedom with which it is performed. This is said to have been the view of Scotus, who writes that the actions which we perform are called moral because of their freedom [38].

But if this is taken as a definition, and as a reply to the question here posed, it is inadmissible. Liberty is the condition of morality, but it is not equivalent to morality. Every free action is undoubtedly a moral action, in the sense that it is either morally good or evil (see n. 238); nevertheless, mastery of oneself, the power to decide for oneself, are not synonymous with the attitude one takes up with regard to the Value. Morality is an added quality of a free act (*good* as a act, or *evil*).

A second opinion is that of Suarez. Nothing is added to the physical reality of a human act by its moral reality, except that where the latter is concerned, what is of consequence is that the act proceeds from the free will of a person who has adverted to what he is doing. This dependence on the person's reason and free will does not effect any physical or intrinsic change in the human act: its external dimension is called moral because of its dependence on the internal dimension, while this latter is, in its turn, called moral, not only because it emanates from the person's will, but also because his reason is guiding him, so that he is in full control of himself [29]. But note that while the source of the moral act is extrinsic to the act itself, it is not extrinsic to the subject: his act springs from powers and capacities which lie within him [40]. Note also that the distinction between the physical and the moral reality of the act is not a purely rational distinction and is not simply the creation of our intellects: there is a real basis for it [41].

A third and final opinion is that of the Thomists and, in particular, of Billuart. In his view, morality adds to the natural reality of a human act a transcendental relation to the moral norm, or, more precisely, to the object as governed by this

---

[38] *Opus Oxoniense*, II, d. 40, quaest. unica, n. 3; ed. Wadding, Lyons, 1639, t. VI, 2 p., p. 1028.

[39] *De bonitate et malitia objectiva actuum humanorum*, disp., I, sect. 2, nn. 15, 16; ed. Vivès, t. IV, p. 284 a.

[40] *Ib.*, n. 19; p. 285 a.

[41] *Ib.*

norm; in other words, what lifts a human act to the moral plane is a relation, either positive or negative, with the moral norm: without this relation a human act would not be a moral reality [42].

This last opinion seems to have most to recommend it. It is by means of the light which his intelligence throws on the object that a person makes *this*, rather than some other decision. Now, the object of a moral decision, which is what we are here concerned with, is revealed as either in conformity with, or in opposition to, the moral norm. Hence the person is aware of this conformity or opposition as he makes his choice, so that, in consequence, this latter cannot but be intrinsically affected: by means of the object which he chooses, the person's will is inevitably related, in a way that is either positive or negative, to the moral norm: this is the transcendental relation of which Billuart speaks, without which a human act would not be a moral reality.

234. – III. Moral Evil.

Another question which the Scholastics discussed and disagreed about is that of the true nature of moral evil. Does it consist in a mere privation, as does evil in a general sense, or is there a positive element in it? When it is a question of "sins of omission", all that is involved, by definition, is a lack of what should be present (a person *has not done* what he ought to have done); but is more than this involved when a person *has done* what he ought not to have ("sins of commission")? Note, in order to have a better appreciation of the point at issue, that what we are here speaking about is moral evil in the strict sense, that is, the *malice* that affects the will of the person who knowingly and willingly chooses what he should not choose. In its concrete reality, as is all too obvious, the blameworthy action — a lie, an act of murder — is "something"; it has occurred and it has affected the real order. But what is involved in the evil choice precisely *as evil*?

---

[42] "Morality in general consists formally in a real transcendental relation (or tendency) to the object as subjected to the moral rule", *De actibus humanis*, diss. IV, art. I (*Cursus theologicus*, t. II, Brescia, 1837, p. 77a).

1) It is evident that moral evil as such involves a privation of some kind, since this is of the essence of evil as such (as the study of metaphysics reveals). Where *moral* evil is concerned, what is lacking is the "uprightness" of which St Anselm speaks, that is, the conformity of an action to right reason and to the practical Ideal. It is not, however, the question of the privation which is involved in moral evil that gives rise to controversy, but the further question of the *subject* of this privation. Is it in the person's action, or in his will, or in the person himself, that this lack of uprightness is to be found? — The answer, it would seem is: in the person's action. Is it not here that moral value is primarily present (n. 33, 1)? The difficulty that can be made about this reply is that it is not at all obvious how an action which is intrinsically evil, such as an act of hatred of God, could be said to lack a perfection (moral, obviously) which it ought to have [43]. An action of this kind is not susceptible of any (moral) perfection at all. — To this difficulty, the reply which is made is that it is not as considered in its particularity (as an act of hatred) that this action lacks a perfection, but considered simply as a human act [44]. To every such act there is an element that is common: the dynamism whereby the person seeks the fulfilment which is not yet his; but in doing what is intrinsically evil, the person deprives himself of the guidance of reason in his attempt to achieve this goal.

2) In addition to this negative element, Thomists generally maintain that there is also a positive element involved in moral malice: the person accepts and turns towards a goal which he ought to reject (for example, the satisfaction of his desire for revenge). In virtue of this second element, moral evil is not only the privation of moral good, but also its contrary. Even further: it is in this positive element, they maintain, that the essence of moral malice as such consists; the privation of

---

[43] This is the view of: Vazquez, *In Iam IIae*, disp. 95, cap. 6, 7, 8; Lyons, 1620, t. I, pp. 444-447; Suarez, *De bonitate et malitia*..., disp. VII, sect. 5, especially nn. 3 and 13; ed. Vivès, t. IV, pp. 397, 390b-391a.

[44] Billuart, *De peccatis*, diss. I, art. III, III (*Cursus theol.*, t. II, pp. 165-166). — Lehu, *Philosophia moralis*, p. 93. — According to Frins, what is involved is not a privation in the strict sense but a "moral and legal" privation, *De act. hum.*, t. II, pp. 366-374.

uprightness is simply the consequence of this. At times, authors of this school go so far as to write that the term *evil* is *equivocally* applied to the evil of which metaphysics treats (which is a pure privation) and to moral evil[45].

Other writers, on the contrary, do not see the need to place moral evil in a special category and consider that the term "privation" is no less adequate here than it is where other types of evil are concerned[46].

235. – We shall now attempt to throw some light on the preceding points:

1) A morally evil act is not such on account of some defect in the *nature* of the subject (in the way that defective vision is the consequence of a disease in his eyes), or on account of some hindrance that is external to him (in the way that a fall is due to stumbling over some obstacle): the evil that is in the act has come from the act itself; it is in this that the moral malice, the anti-value, is primarily and immediately to be found (n. 33, 1).

2) Where natural (non-free) agents are concerned (and also even where free agents, insofar as their activity is fixed and determined, are concerned) their activity is always what it should be, in the sense that it is always in harmony with what can be called its "rule", that is, with the nature of the particular agent, taken in conjunction with the block of circumstances in which this nature is now situated and by which it is concretely affected. Consequently, it can easily happen that, because of these circumstances, this activity does not correspond to the requirements of the agent's nature considered "in itself"; but it is not possible for an agent of this type to contradict these requirements, in the sense of deciding to oppose them. In other words, the natural elan of the agent towards what is good for it can be obstructed and disorientated, but the reason for this

---

[45] Cajetan, *In Iam IIae*, q. 18, a. 5, n. 2; q. 71, a. 6, nn. 3 seq. — Billuart (*op. cit.*, art. III; pp. 157-165) presents the two opinions and discusses them at length. There is also a good exposition in Deman, art. *Péché* in the *Dict. de Théol. Cath.*, col. 149-153. Frins is in agreement with the Thomists on this point, *op. cit.*, t. II, pp. 405-418.

[46] For example, Suarez, *op. cit.*, disp. VII, sect. 3; pp. 379-384. — In an earlier period, Scotus, *Ox.*, II, d. 37, q. 1, n. 6; Wadding, t. VI, 2 a p., p. 981.

remains exterior to the agent. — The moral agent, on the contrary, in virtue of his liberty, is capable of acting in a way which not only fails to meet the requirements of reason — the true guide of his free actions — but intentionally contradicts them.

3) The conclusion that follows is that moral evil is not simply a privation; there is involved not only a lack of moral goodness, but an opposition to it that is in some way polar. The vicious person is not simply one who has not yet crossed the threshold of virtue. Hatred is far different from a lack of love.

4) But this positive element is itself grounded on what is negative. In every choice, no matter how evil or unprincipled, that a human being makes, he is seeking some good; this good becomes morally evil only because it is sought in a disordered way. Hatred of others and of God himself is the reverse side of a love of oneself, of a quest for personal preeminence, of an affirmation of one's liberty etc.; this love, this quest, this affirmation are, of themselves, aimed at values that are authentic, but which are not sought within the limits prescribed by reason. The subject loves himself as if it were he who is the supreme Good; he asserts his freedom as if this were not essentially dependent: "he does not remain steadfast in the truth", to use the profound words of the Gospel. From this falsified point of view, God and other human beings cannot but appear to him as menacing rivals. There is, in consequence, at the root of his attitude, a lack, an absence: the absence from his vision of life of a factor which is essential for the practical understanding of his true situation. It is in this sense that ignorance is at the heart of sin: this is what Socrates understood and emphasized; but what Socrates did not appreciate is that this ignorance is voluntary. It is produced by the subject himself, who diverts his attention from the moral norm, or at least refuses to give it the required attention, so as to leave the field of choice open to the influence of inferior motivations.

The line of thought we have been following has now linked up with the classical doctrine of the Thomists that the non-consideration of the moral rule is the negative root of sin [47].

---

[47] On this doctrine read, in addition to the classical texts of St Thomas (*Contra Gent.*, III, 10; *De Malo*, 1, 3), J. Maritain, *De Bergson à Thomas d'Aquin*,

However, if this non-consideration is in itself blameless, as is generally said (on the grounds that a person is not obliged to think of this rule always), it is difficult to see how the disorder by which the subsequent action is inevitably affected, could be blameworthy. If I know that not to keep the rule in mind will result in a violation of it, then I am to blame for this failure in my attention; if, on the other hand, I do not know, then I cannot be blamed for the subsequent violation (nn. 16 and 245-246). We maintain then — and this is completely in accordance with the Thomistic doctrine concerning the reciprocal causality of intelligence and will in the free action — that this non-consideration is already a misuse of liberty; the person freely closes himself to the light so as to be more capable of sinning: "he would not understand that he might do well" [48]. Though closing himself in this way the person lives — for the moment at least — in a world of illusion, in which what is but relative is accepted in practice as if it were absolute. This illusion gives birth in its turn to another, namely, that of a positive and enriching experience of evil. It is indeed through the evil that is in us, or at the very least through the enticements to evil which we experience, that we come to have a knowledge of evil; we find that it strikes a chord in us which virtue does not strike and that it has a sweet taste which virtue lacks. (As St Thomas profoundly remarks [49], we are unlike God in this respect: He knows the negative through the positive and consequently the evil through the good, whereas we know also the negative through the negative which is in ourselves: through our needs and desires, and consequently also the evil through the evil in ourselves). Nevertheless, the more faithful we are to our vocation from the Ideal, the more also do we come to know evil through what is good — as does God and those who share in His holiness in an eminent degree and whom we call saints — and come, in consequence, to recoil from it all the more strongly. Think of the knowledge of

---

Paris, 1947, pp. 283-287 (Eng. trans.: *Bergsonian Philosophy and Thomism*, New York, 1956), *Court traité de l'existence et de l'existant*, Paris, 1947, pp. 148-153 (*Existence and the Existent*, New York, 1948) and, more recently, *Dieu et la permission du mal*, Paris, 1963, pp. 37-60.

[48] Ps. 35, 4 (Vulg.): in the Douai version.

[49] *Cont. Gent.*, I., 71.

evil that a Cure of Ars can attain, a knowledge which is so different and so much more profound than that which a novelist ordinarily has — and which will often be the fruit of his own secret surrenders to evil. ...

We can conclude our present discussion by noting that the positive element which moral evil as such manifests is nothing other, in the final analysis, than the product of a debased reason (a practical reason and will that are untrue to their own "openness"). It has no more substance and solidity than that which it derives from our voluntary blindness.

The preceding discussion enables us to reply to the question which has been posed by certain contemporary thinkers concerning the possibility (where human beings are concerned) of willing what is evil for the sake of evil [50]. What a human being chooses will always be ontological good; nevertheless, he can choose this good in a spirit of deliberate contempt for the moral law and for the Ideal, because he considers that in so doing he is asserting his independence of them and his own self-sufficiency. But even then, the question could be put as to whether a person who acts in this way and in this spirit has not succeeded in deluding himself that he is fulfilling some vague and ill-defined duty which he owes to himself, that is, he may succeed in deluding himself that it would be a betrayal of his own dignity not to act in this way. It is difficult, once an action is genuinely free, to avoid seeking some moral motivation for it (n. 36, end).

There is, however, no escaping the fact that moral evil poses a considerable problem for philosophy. This problem is concerned not only with the possibility of such evil (which is considered in metaphysics and philosophical psychology), but even more with its universality and with the brutish forms in which it is so often mani-

---

[50] So, according to N. Hartmann (*Ethik*, 2nd ed., pp. 343-345), if it is true that man always chooses some good and that moral evil (das Böse) consists in the choice of inferior values, the choice of evil for the sake of evil, "an absolute teleology of non-value", is, of itself, in no way contradictory, even though impossible for man: it is this "teleology" which is expressed by the concept of "Satan". H. Reiner goes further and considers that human beings sometimes choose evil for the sake of evil (*Das Prinzip von Gut und Böse*, pp. 14-15). — On the question, consult J. L. Aranguren, *Etica*, pp. 369-373. Also J. Nabert, *Essai sur le mal*, Paris, 1955, pp. 67-69. On moral evil and on evil in general see, in addition to the authors already mentioned: L. Lavelle, *Le mal et la souffrance*, Paris, 1940 and Et. Borne, *Le problème du mal*, Paris, 1958. For the historical aspect, in particular: A.-D. Sertillanges, *Le problème du mal*, I. *L'histoire*, Paris, 1939; II. *La solution*, Paris, 1951 (posthumous).

fested. How is it that such excesses are possible? How is it that the rational animal is, ordinarily at least, so falteringly rational? Why is it that man, from the evidence of his actions, fails to be man so much more frequently than other beings fail to be what they are? — When faced with these enigmas, philosophy and human reason are made keenly aware of their limitations; the questions to which man's inhumanity give rise constitute an invitation to be on the look out for, and to welcome should it appear, the revelation of a truth about man that philosophy alone cannot unveil.

An ethical investigation which aims at being complete, and which wishes to be completely in contact with the human situation as it concretely and historically exists, cannot leave aside the sinful condition of man, a condition which, in fact, influences profoundly our experience of moral value (n. 31). Nevertheless, to be "sinners" is not essential to human beings as such. Consequently, we are entitled, given the purpose of our present investigation (which is a philosophical not a theological one), to pay no particular attention to man's sinful condition; if we were engaged in that practico-practical study of morality which is the prerogative of the moral theologian, this omission would be capital [51].

---

[51] On the legitimacy of this procedure, see P. Ricoeur, *Philosophie de la volonté*, I, pp. 23-31: "L'abstraction de la Faute".

CHAPTER ELEVEN

THE POSSIBILITY OF ACTIONS THAT ARE MORALLY INDIFFERENT

236. – In discussing the morality of human actions, it is clear that up to this point we have implicity supposed that every such action is a moral action and is affected by a positive or negative value, simply because it is human. But it is not immediately evident that our supposition is correct. Could there not be actions which, while they are genuinely human, that is, quite deliberate, still remain neutral or indifferent from the moral point of view?

Obviously, in posing this question, it is human actions in their concrete individuality, considered in conjunction with all the circumstances in which they are performed and by which they are affected, that we have in mind. If all we consider are human actions in the abstract and if we prescind from their circumstances, so that the only source of their moral value could be their object, then it is abundantly clear that a large number of them are neither good nor evil. To go for a walk, to sit down, to play a game of football or of chess, to open or close the window of one's room etc.: as long as we merely consider these actions in themselves and take into account no more than their objects, how can we discern in them any relation at all, whether of opposition or of agreement, with the judgments of right reason? Everything will depend on the way, the time, the place, the intention etc. The person who relaxes, at the end of his day's work, by solving a crossword puzzle, is acting well — he is then exercising the virtue of *eutrapelia* — but there is a disorder in his action when the attractions of the crossword cause him to neglect the duty that here and now calls for his attention.

But even when actions of this kind are considered in conjunction with their concrete circumstances, the possibility that they may still remain morally neutral does not seem to be excluded. When I go for a walk on a summer's evening, simply because the weather is fine and the soft seabreezes are calling to me, what moral value could there be in what I am doing? A negative value? Surely not: I have no bad intention and I am neglecting no duty to which I should now be attending: I am on my summer holidays. A positive value? This does not seem to be present either. I am simply following my inclinations; I am choosing what gives me pleasure. In coming to my decision I had no thought of "doing what is morally good", of acting in accordance with reason or anything at all of this kind. Hence, it would seem that I have neither ascended nor descended on the scale of moral value (n. 42). But what does this mean except that my action has been, in its concrete reality, morally neutral?

This neutrality can be understood in two ways. Actions of this type can be regarded as outside the moral sphere which, in consequence, will not be co-extensive with that of human actions. Alternatively, this neutrality can be equated with zero on the moral scale, so that the domain of human and of moral actions will remain co-extensive.

237. – It is then in no way astonishing that certain Scholastics have held that it is possible for us to perform human actions which, even when they are considered in conjunction with all the relevant circumstances, still remain morally indifferent. Among these writers St Bonaventure[1], Duns Scotus[2] and Vazquez[3] have been particularly prominent.

According to St Bonaventure, the contrary opinion would make the straight and narrow path to salvation either too broad or too narrow[4]. It would have the first effect if it claimed that an intention which is *habitually* oriented towards God is sufficient to make an action good. It would have the second effect if one insists that an *actual* intention of pleasing God is necessary in order to avoid committing sin. But is there not room for a distinction between the

---

[1] *In II Sent.*, d. 41, a. 1, q. 3; ed. Quaracchi, t. II, pp. 942-946, esp. 943/4. — On the question in the middle ages, see O. Lottin, *Psychologie et morale aux XIIe et XIIIe siècles*, t. II, 1 p., pp. 469-489: "L'indifférence des actes humains chez saint Thomas d'Aquin et ses prédécesseurs".

[2] *Ox.*,II, d. 41, q. unica, ed. Wadding, t. VI, 2 p., pp. 1034-1035; *Reportata parisiensia*, II, f. 41, q. unica, Wadding, t. IX, 1 p., pp. 408b-409a.

[3] *In Iam IIae*, disp. 52, Lyons, 1620; t. I, pp. 256b-264a, esp. 260a-261.

[4] *Op. cit.*, p. 944a.

person's inner decision and his execution of that decision, so that while this latter, which concerns the person's will only indirectly, can be morally indifferent, the former, which directly concerns his will, cannot be? This conclusion Bonaventure finds unacceptable: to decide to study or to seek the truth is an eminently reasonable decision; nevertheless a person often so decides without intending to please God; to maintain that he thereby sins would indeed be a hard saying[5]. There has then to be an intermediate type of deliberate action which is neither good nor evil. Every human action, it is true, is either performed for the love of God or not so performed. But an action of this latter type does not automatically become evil. It is only if it results from an inordinate attachment to one of God's creatures, or from negligence, that it becomes sinful: in the first instance the sin is one of commission, and in the latter, one of omission. But if the failure to act for the love of God springs from the person's human frailty and miserable condition, then his action is morally indifferent. Any action, then, which does not result from an inordinate attachment to some creature and which is not performed for the love of God, but simply in order to satisfy some natural need (as when a person walks as a means of recreating himself, or eats in order to restore his strength) will be of this kind[6]. — As is obvious from what has been written, St Bonaventure does not make any distinction here between the moral value of our actions, and their orientation to God through the supernatural charity which makes them to be deserving of eternal life.

It is the view of Duns Scotus that there are many actions which are not only naturally or physically neutral but also morally so. This is often true even where the inner decision of the will, considered in the concrete, is concerned, and not only where movements of the will which do not fulfil the conditions required for human action — which are not here in question — are concerned[7]. It is quite possible, he insists, for a person to perform a human action which does not satisfy all the requirements of a genuinely moral action, but which nevertheless is not immoral. For example, a person gives an alms without forming any deliberate intention but because he is stirred by the need of the poor person. Now, this action is not immoral; but neither is it purely and simply moral, since it does not fulfil all the necessary requirements[8]. — Unlike St Bonaventure, Duns Scotus' discussion of the problem is in an ethical not a theological context.

---

[5] *Ib.*, p. 944.
[6] *Ib.*, p. 944b.
[7] *Ox.*, loc. cit., p. 1035.
[8] *Rep. par.*, loc. cit.

— There appears, however, to be a certain difference between these two texts. The first speaks of a *moral* action which is *neutral* in the sense that its moral value is zero, while the second refers to a *human* action which is *outside* the moral sphere. This second sense is at variance with the position of Scotus on the question of the relation between the moral and physical reality of a human act (n. 233). But perhaps "moral" is here to be understood in the sense which it so frequently has among the moderns, of "morally good".

But the great majority of authors exclude the possibility that human actions considered in their concrete singularity can be morally indifferent. Such is the view in particular — to mention only its most distinguished proponents — of St Thomas [9] and Francis Suarez [10]. There is, however, a notable difference in their positions; this will be indicated in due course.

238. — There is no escaping the fact that the question of the possibility of morally neutral actions presents a real difficulty to which the solution of St Bonaventure — expressed in a manner which gives evidence of compassion and humanity — might seem, at least at first sight, the most balanced. In any event, it cannot simply be disregarded.

Nevertheless, as has already been indicated (n. 222), every human action, no matter how morally neutral it may be as far as its object is concerned, is always performed in a definite set of circumstances, chief among which is the end at which the person is aiming. Hence, as St Thomas points out, these circumstances, and the end which is sought, are either what they ought to be or they are not: if the former, that is, if the action is performed when it ought, where it ought, as it ought, for a purpose which is in conformity with reason, then it has a positive moral value: if the latter, that is, if the action is performed when it ought not etc., then it has a negative moral value. Consequently, morally neutral actions are ruled out.

But this process of reasoning, whose Aristotelian inspiration is evident, does not really solve the problem. Could not the circumstances in which the action is performed also be morally neutral? And what is the end which, the argument

---

[9] *In II Sent.*, d. 40, a. 5; Summa Theol., I-II, 18, 9; *De Malo*, II, 4,5.
[10] *De bonitate et malitia ...*, disp. IX, sect. 3, n. 10.

seems to presume, will always either be in conformity with or
contrary to right reason? Is it the ultimate end? But it is neither
necessary nor, in general, possible to seek this end expressly in
our every action. Is it a good but intermediate end? But then
the question arises: does a person act well once the end which
he intends is *in fact* in accordance with reason, or is he also
required to intend it *as such*? Suppose that he eats in moderation, simply because he is hungry. Are we to say that his action
has a positive moral value and that he has acted virtuously?
There is no doubt that what he has done is morally good: it is
reasonable to eat when one is need of food, a need to which the
feeling of hunger draws attention. But has he fulfilled all the
conditions required for morally good activity; has *he* acted
well? For this, is it not necessary that he should in some way
intend this objective moral value which the action has; that this
value should in some way enter into his motivation[11]? If all
that motivates him is his natural appetite, the pursuit of
pleasure, or simply the desire to satisfy his hunger, so that he is
in no way influenced by the reasonableness, the moral
goodness, of what he is doing, then his action, always supposing of course that it is human and deliberate, has not
fulfilled all the conditions required for morally good activity; *he*
has not acted well. To maintain that he has would be to
champion the opinion which the "Seraphic Doctor" rightly
judges to be over-indulgent.

Is an action of this kind to be classed as morally indifferent, then? No; in our view it has a negative moral value,
since the person who performs a deliberate action without
paying any attention to the reasonableness what he is doing is
not living up to what his dignity as a human being requires of
him; he is being unfaithful to his vocation from the Ideal. A
dimension is missing from his action as a result of which it is
not reasonable and so not moral. — But in taking this view
have we not now adopted the solution which the same Doctor,
with equal right, judges to be too severe?

Again the answer is no! The moral intention which is
required in order that an action of this kind be morally good is
nothing other than the general resolve to live one's life in

---

[11] Cf. Suarez, *op. cit.*, disp. V, sect. 2, nn. 6-7; pp. 338b-339b.

accordance with reason, a resolve which is always implicitly present, as long as the person remains a person of good will (as long as his basic commitment to the Ideal has not been withdrawn). It can, obviously, often happen that a person who is disposed in this way may act without attending expressly to the reasonableness of what he is doing, to its moral goodness etc.; he may then seem to be simply following his natural inclinations: he decides to take a drink because he is thirsty and there appears to be no more to his action than that. In reality, however, he follows his inclination only in the measure in which he discerns no opposition between so doing and the demands his reason makes on him. He tilts his glass "because he sees nothing wrong in doing so": so he would reply to anyone who took him to task. However unformulated it may remain, this motivation is present and operative: if the action has been decided upon quickly, and without reflection on its reasonableness, this is precisely because it fitted in with the habitual orientation of the person's will towards what is good. (If what were in question were an immoral or a doubtfully moral action, then such a person would experience a sense of uneasiness, of disturbance, of hesitancy — signal warning of moral danger). Hence, in choices of this kind, the person is motivated in a negative manner by the reasonableness and moral goodness of what he is doing: he takes his drink etc., because he sees nothing unreasonable or immoral in so acting; his particular action is really, even if tenuously, linked with his radical resolve to live a virtuous life, a life that will be worthy of a human being, and this link is sufficient to confer a positive moral value on the action.

But what if this radical resolve if lacking? The problem which then arises is more difficult. On the one hand, it cannot be said every action of a person of "bad will" (a person who is radically "closed" to the Ideal) is necessarily evil: such a person is capable of good resolutions, of occasional kindly impulses. These resolutions and impulses can be the dominating influences in entire areas of his moral life, so that, in consequence, these are not affected by the basic disorder of that life. Hence, he too could choose to take a drink etc., without expressly attending to the reasonableness of what he is doing, and still act well. But there is also a very good chance that, where he is concerned, this non-attention to the morality of his action simply betrays a habitual indifference with regard to the Ideal. When this happens his choices will have, in consequence, a negative moral value.

239. – The above approach to the problem, it is suggested, answers the difficulties to which St Bonaventure draws attention and also reconciles the differences between St Thomas and Suarez: the two latter agree that there cannot be, in the concrete, morally neutral actions, but they differ with regard to the conditions which are required in order that choices of the kind we are here considering should be subjectively good.

Suarez observes that a human being can satisfy his natural and bodily needs in either of two ways. He can rest content with regarding these as merely animal needs, or he can go on to appreciate that the satisfaction of these needs is to be governed by the rule of reason. The first attitude does not suffice to make a person's action morally good and does not excuse him from all fault and negligence, since he has always to apply the criterion of reason, if he is to act as befits a human being[12].

St Thomas, on the contrary, seems to consider that a person acts well once the purpose of this activity is in itself (or objectively) in agreement with reason, even though he intends to achieve nothing other than what his activity is of its very nature aimed at achieving: for example, the person who eats simply so as to satisfy his hunger[13].

But what we have been insisting on in our discussion of the problem is that an action which tends of itself towards a goal which is in conformity with reason harmonizes, by that very fact, with the general resolve to live a morally good life. Even though the person has not been expressly motivated by the moral value of what he is doing, nevertheless, this global project has, in fact, regulated his here-and-now decision. Moreover, when he "eats in order to satisfy his hunger", he cannot

---

[12] *Op. cit.*, disp. IX, sect. 3, n. 9; p. 423b. — Cf. V. Frins, *De act. hum.*, t. II, pp. 522, 543.

[13] Cf. Schiffini, *Disp. phil. mor.*, I, n. 78.

but have some, perhaps confused, appreciation that this is a reasonable procedure. Without intending anything more than the satisfaction of this need, he is, nonetheless, in some way aware that he is acting reasonably and that he is being faithful to the Value, in virtue of his general resolve to live as befits a human being.

This, we suggest, is what St Thomas had in mind. He writes that a person who aims deliberately at the attainment of an end cannot but observe or violate some virtue. Hence, the person who uses his bodily health in order to live a virtuous life will act virtuously when, for example, he eats or relaxes with due moderation [14]. To use one's bodily health in order to lead a virtuous life — to put one's body and one's entire existence at the service of virtue: this is precisely what we had in mind when we spoke of the radical resolve to guide one's life in accordance with reason and to be always faithful to the Ideal.

It is obvious that, all other things being equal, an action will have a greater positive or negative value the more explicitly a person attends to, and intends, its conformity with or opposition to reason. Hence the utility of frequently renewing our "good resolutions"; without this constant renewal a multitude of our actions will possess no more than a minimal degree of moral value, so that, for all practical purposes, they may be classed as indifferent. For, as St Thomas notes, actions whose positive or negative moral value is minute can also be called neutral [15]. They are not, it is true, indifferent in the strict sense, but they scarsely rise above or fall below zero on the scale of moral value; their effect on our moral lives is, in practice, negligible.

N.B. The question we have here been discussing should be carefully distinguished from the question discussed by the theologians of whether a person in the state of grace can perform a human act which is neither sinful nor meritorious. (It was in this context, as we have seen, that St Bonaventure discussed our present question; he did not separate the philosophical from the theological problem). The fact

---

[14] *Summa Theol.*, I-II, 18, 9 ad 3um. — A solution very similar to our own is to be found in W. G. Maclagan, *The Theological Frontiers of Ethics*, pp. 98-100.
[15] *Ib.*, 92, 2.

that not all theologians admit that every morally good action which the "just man" performs immediately merits an increase of grace serves to underline the need to keep this distinction in mind.

Another related but separate question is whether the decision to take a course of action that is morally good, but less so than another course which is here and now concretely possible, comes by that very fact to possess a negative moral value. It is a question which can be more profitably studied in the context of moral theology, since the interpretation of the evangelical doctrine of the "counsels" will have an important bearing on the answer given [16].

---

[16] Among those who answer in the affirmative ("perfectiorists") are: Et. Hugueny, art. *Imperfection.* "Dictionnaire de Théol. Cath.", col. 1286-1298; O. Lottin, *Morale fondamentale*, Tournai, 1954, pp. 498-505 (ample bibliography); E. Ranwez, *Morale et perfection*, Tournai, 1959; J. Fuchs, *Theologia moralis generalis*, pp. 57-58. This opinion seems to be the one more favoured nowadays.

Among those who take the opposite view are: T. Richard, *Etudes de théologie morale*, Paris, 1932, pp. 1-176; M. Zalba, *Theologiae moralis summa*, 3rd ed., Madrid, 1959, nn. 994-999.

All these authors are theologians. The philosophers are inclined to take the first view; this is particularly true of Scheler for whom moral evil essentially consists in the preference given to an inferior value. But note the vigorous defence of the second view made by D. von Hildebrand, *Christian Ethics*, pp. 379-392: "Moral rigorism".

The question is touched on in the *Essai*, n. 124; pp. 299-303.

CHAPTER TWELVE

CONSCIENCE

240. – Now that we have studied the structure of a human action insofar as this results from the object (understanding by this not only the object in the strict sense, but also the attendant circumstances, as well as the end at which the agent is aiming, cf. n. 227), we turn to the consideration of the ways in which the subject's knowledge, or the lack of it, affects the morality of his action.

As we already know, a human act is an act which proceeds from the will of a human being under the light which his intelligence casts. More precisely, and inasmuch as it is a moral act, it supposes a certain attention or advertence on the part of the agent to its moral value, a knowledge of its agreement with, or opposition to, right reason. It is this knowledge which constitutes his *moral conscience*, in the proper and precise sense of the word. Hence, conscience differs from that immediate awareness which he has of the reality of his act (his awareness that he is here and now choosing). In its exercise three stages may be distinguished:

Before a person acts, the role which his conscience plays is to enlighten him; it reveals to him the moral quality of the course of action which he could choose, and in consequence commands, permits, forbids etc., this course (antecedent conscience).

While he is acting, his conscience testifies that his action is moral or immoral: conscience at this stage is nothing other than his immediate awareness, not simply of the reality of his action, but of its moral value (concomitant conscience).

After he has acted, his conscience testifies that he has acted morally or immorally: it approves of or condemns what has been done (consequent conscience).

Obviously, then, the role of conscience is confined, properly speaking, to the *application* of the moral law to concrete situations; it should not be confused, as it often is, with a person's habitual knowledge of this law or of its most general principles (nn. 188-190), a knowledge which, where these principles are concerned, St Thomas calls *synderesis*.

This term (synderesis or synteresis), of which the Scholastics have made use from the 12th century onwards, was first discovered by them in St Jerome's *Commentary* on Ezechiel, in the chapter in which he treats of the symbolism of the four animals. Among the interpretations which he recounts is that of certain Greeks, who regarded these animals as symbols of the four parts or powers of the soul. The man naturally stands for *logikon*, The rational part; the lion for *thumikon* or the irascible appetite; the ox for *epithumētikon* or the concupiscent appetite. What of the eagle? This represents, St Jerome says — or at least the Scholastics understood him to say — a fourth power which is separate from, and superior to, the three preceding ones, a power which the Greeks call *sunterēsis* (literally "conservation"): this is the spark of conscience which was not extinguished even in the heart of Cain after he had been expelled from paradise (!); it is thanks to this that when we have succumbed to the attractions of pleasure, or have been overcome by the heat of anger, or even when at times we have rationalized our evil deeds, we are still made aware that we are acting wrongly[1]. The word could be understood to mean: the tendency to preserve one's nature and, in consequence, fidelity with regard to it, fidelity with regard to the requirements of reason — in which, as we have seen, the well-springs of morality lie. In fact, this notion is rather frequently found in the writings of the Stoics, while the word itself, in its Latin form of *conservatio*, is often employed by Cicero, Seneca etc. — But there is no need to go so far afield in order to understand this word, if in fact, as now seems to be established, what St Jerome really wrote was *suneidesis*, that is, "conscience"[2].

---

[1] *Op. cit.*, I, c. 1; PL. t. 25, col. 22.

[2] This is the reading accepted in the critical edition of Fr. Glorie, "Corpus Christianorum", Latin series, t. XXV, Turnhout, 1964, p. 12. None of the manuscripts of St Jerome has *sunteresis*. All have *suneidesis*, or variations of it explicable in terms of the errors of copyists ignorant of Greek. On the topic, see R. Leiber, *Name und Begriff der Synteresis in der mittelalterlichen Scholastik*, "Philosophisches Jahrbuch", 1912, pp. 372-382 and, more recently, J. de Blic, *Syndérèse ou conscience?* "Rev. d'ascét. et de myst.", 1949 ("Mélanges Villers"), pp. 46-57, where 22 manuscripts are examined (additional to the four studied by Leiber). Rabanus Maurus (9th century), who relied on the gloss of St Jerome (*Comm. in Ezechielem*, I, PL. t. 110, col. 508), seems to be the originator of the spelling *sunteresis*. It reappeared in the 12th century in a certain "Master Udo", the first known commentator on Peter Lombard. The Scholastic tradition had no

As is not too surprising, the Scholastics have been far from unanimous in their understanding of "synderesis" and of its relation with a person's conscience. Some of them have identified it with his will, or with a habit of his will: this was the view of St Bonaventure and Henry of Ghent; others, such as St Albert the Great, have identified it with his practical reason[3].

241. – Up to this point in our inquiry, we have considered no hypothesis other than that in which the requirements of right reason are clearly manifest to the subject: no allowance has been made for error, obscurity or ignorance: the disorder which can be present in a human action has been regarded as solely imputable to the bad will of the agent. It is undoubtedly true that every evil choice we make is accompanied by some darkness in our minds, some distortion of the truth: we can choose nothing except what we judge to be worthy, here and now, of being chosen: the free choice which a person makes is always guided by the ultimate practical judgment at which he has arrived[4]. But this darkness and this distortion are voluntary in their origin; they have their source in a depraved appetite which buttresses the evil choice with evil reasons (reasons that are unreasonable): it is the person himself who makes *this* judgment rather than some other to be the one which becomes effectively "practical". This he does by putting a stop to his deliberation and so allowing this judgment and these reasons to dominate his field of consciousness. — But in making his disordered choice, the subject retains his awareness of the right order and of the universal law to which his particular choice is opposed; it is precisely in this opposition *as known and accepted* that the negative moral value of his action is to be found. It is not at all a question of being aware of the law (for example, that stealing is immoral) at one moment, and then deciding at a subsequent moment, but without thinking any more of the law, to take what does not belong to him. No;

---

suspicion that there could be any other spelling and it was under its influence that the word *synderesis* passed into the printed editions. — See O. Lottin, *Psychologie et morale aux XIIᵉ et XIIIᵉ siècles*, t. II,Ib.: "Syndérèse et conscience", pp. 103-108.

[3] On these authors, consult O. Lottin, *ib.*, pp. 103-349.

[4] St Thomas, *De Malo*, q. 6. Cf. *Essai*, nn. 91-92; pp. 210-218.

he acts immorally only because in coming to his decision, through forming the ultimate practical judgment that to steal is better *for him* (better, that is, for that aspect of his being with which he freely identifies himself) he simultaneously knows and interiorly judges that to steal is an evil *in relation to his reason*. So even though he is blind to the truth, this blindness is itself voluntary; it is generated by his own decision.

But it often happens that prior to any decision which a person makes, his initial grasp of the rational order is distorted. In other words, his conscience can be mistaken; it can fail to fulfil its function of promulgating the moral law interiorly and of applying it to concrete situations. Undoubtedly, as we have seen (n. 184), error is impossible where the very general principle that good is to be done and evil is to be avoided — a principle which is without content — is concerned; error is also ruled out, at least in general, when what is in question are the most general forms which this principle assumes (nn. 188-190). But when the problem is to know what is good and what is evil in a definite, determined situation, error is, unfortunately, all too frequent. When this occurs, how is the morality of the subsequent action to be judged? In relation to the law as it is and, in consequence, in relation to the requirements of right reason? In relation to the law as it is known by the subject, which means, in our present hypothesis, in relation to a reason that is in error? The reply may seem extremely obvious to us, but that is because we inherit the fruit of a long process, about which we shall presently speak; but even though the issue has been clarified for us, it has nonetheless to be acknowledged that the problem is real. For if the morality of an action of this type is to be judged in relation to the law as it is, then a person who thinks he is acting morally is, in fact, acting immorally, whereas the person who thinks he is acting immorally is really behaving well; on the other hand, if the morality is to be judged in relation to the law as it is known by the subject, then he acts virtuously when he does what is, in fact, evil, and sins when he does what is, in fact, good! Both answers present us with a paradox. If nowadays we are less concerned about the drawbacks of judging the morality in relation to the law as it is known by the subject, this is perhaps because we have a diminished appreciation of the objective order and of its requirements. The prominence which we give to the moral subject, which we shall soon discuss, is accompanied by the danger that we can more easily forget that the objective order is a reflection of the divine Reason.

Not only can a person's conscience be mistaken but it can also be doubtful. It does not clearly indicate what the person is reasonably required to do. This can happen in two ways: he remains uncertain concerning the law itself — above all when what is in question is a particular moral rule whose connection with the general norms is not evident; alternatively, it is the application of the law to the concrete situation which gives rise to problems and doubts. Is it permissible to attempt this brain operation which may seriously affect the patient's mental balance? There are reasons for and against; several principles have to be taken into consideration. The most typical and most agonising situation of this kind is that in which an (apparent) conflict of duties is involved: such situations provide the stuff out of which tragedy is woven. Think, for example, of Hamlet's dilemma: to kill his step-father, or to leave his true father's death unavenged?

But, if one at least of the duties which give rise to a tragic conflict of this kind is imaginary, there are also real-life situations in which a person may have to make a heartrending choice between two duties that are far from imaginary: his choice may lie between fidelity to his personal ideal (religious, scientific, artistic vocation) and the demand which his obligations to his family, to his country, make on him. ...

How is a person to act when he is faced with problems of this kind? How can he remain faithful to a Value whose requirements he is unable to discern? How can he decide which is the right road to follow when he has lost his sense of direction?

We have then to concern ourselves with two problems in the two sections of this chapter: the problem of the *erroneous conscience*, and the problem of the *doubtful conscience*. — There is no need to consider the question of the ignorant conscience separately, since, from the practical point of view, ignorance is always linked with error. What is not forbidden is permitted: not to know that A is forbidden or that B is obligatory, is to believe, erroneously, that it is licit to do A or to omit B.

I. The Erroneous Conscience.

242. – The problem of the erroneous conscience can, in its turn, be subdivided, since two questions concerning it arise: 1. Does such a conscience oblige, that is, does a person act immorally if he disobeys it?; 2. Does such a conscience excuse him, so that in following it (and to the extent that he does so) he is in no way to be blamed? As the history of the problem clearly reveals, the two questions are not identical; to reply to one is not necessarily to have replied to the other.

Both questions furrowed the brows of the Scholastics. Their extremely "objectivist" mentality made it appear intolerable to many of them that an action which was intrinsically disordered should not also involve a disorder in the will of the person who performed it. But, on the other hand, they saw very well that the person who disobeys his conscience is prepared to act in a way that may be contrary to the will of God, so that in consequence, he offends Him. ... How could this dilemma be overcome? Some endeavoured to escape by taking the road of distinctions. When a person's conscience commands him to omit a course of action that is essentially good (and obligatory), or to follow a course that is essentially evil, he is not obliged to obey it; he has, however, the obligation to correct his error (as if this were an easy accomplishment!). In other situations, a person is obliged to follow his erroneous conscience, but here also he is bound to correct the error [5]. In consequence, these authors do not admit that an erroneous conscience excuses a person, when what is in question is an essentially evil action. If, in following his conscience, he does what is contrary to the law of God, he sins mortally, since to violate this law is a mortal sin [6].

All agree, however, in excluding a true necessity of sinning. This lets one suspect, though they do not say so, that

---

[5] This is the view expressed in the *Summa Theologica*, attributed to Alexander of Hales, L. II, p. 2, inq. 3, Tr. 3, s. 1, q. 3, a. 1; Quaracchi, 1930, t. III, p. 388; by St Bonaventure, *In II Sent.*, d. 39, a. 1, q. 3; Quar., t. II, pp. 906-907. The Seraphic Doctor adds, however, that it is a sin not to follow thre dictate of one's conscience, even when erroneous, for so to act would be to disregard the divine law.

[6] St Bonaventure, *ib.*, p. 907.

the ignorance of which they are speaking is considered by them to be "vincible" [6bis].

It is this which will be made clear by St Thomas. At first sight his position does not seem to differ much from that of his contemporaries [7]. A person is always obliged to follow his conscience, in the sense that it is always evil to disobey its commands. But to obey it is not always good: in other words, an erroneous conscience does not always excuse a person, but only when the person's error is invincible and inculpable. (An error is culpable when it is concerned with what a person is obliged to know, or when it proceeds from some negligence on his part). When a person's error is vincible and culpable, he sins whether he follows his conscience or whether he disobeys it; nevertheless, his situation is not hopeless — he is not entangled in the web of sin — since he has the power to overcome his error through dispelling the ignorance that is voluntary and vincible [8]. — But St Thomas, by a more exact analysis of the moral act (an analysis inspired by Aristotle) gives the principle of a more human solution. What specifies an act from the moral point of view is the object as such ("secundum rationem objecti"), that is: the act to be performed such as it is represented to conscience not only with regard to its nature and circumstances, but also with regard to its relation to reason, and hence with regard to its moral value [8bis]. Consequently, if the act is represented as good, one must conclude that the subject *does well* in performing the act — supposing, of course, that the error is involuntary and innocent. Nevertheless St Thomas does not say this, at least in his theological works

---

[6bis] In fact, the problem of ignorance, of its culpability, and of the conditions under which it can excuse, is treated by these authors, often with great finesse. See, for example, St. Bonaventure, *In II Sent.*, d. 22, a. 1, q. 2, pp. 522- 525 (Utrum ignorantia in aliquo homine possit esse sine culpa) and *ibid.*, q. 3, pp. 526-527 (Utrum ignorantia sit culpae excusatio).

[7] Thus, in the *Commentary on the Sentences*, II, d. 39, 3, 3, while he admits that it is always obligatory to follow an erroneous conscience, the person who does so is not always blameless. But this does not mean that he necessarily sins, for he can always correct his error. Obviously, this supposes that the error is culpable. But what if the error (or the ignorance) is blameless? In this text, such a situation is not envisaged.

[8] *Summa Theol.*, I-II, 19, 6 ad 3um; as well, see aa. 5 and 6.

[8bis] See, for example, *Quodl.* 3, 27; *S. Theol.*, I-II, 19, 5.

(is it due to the fear of shocking?). According to St Thomas, the subject *does not sin* in following a conscience which goes astray invincibly and without his fault. That is all St Thomas says. But, besides the principle set forth above, St Thomas' doctrine on indifferent acts (n. 237) called for a bolder answer[9]. Subsequent writers, such as Suarez, have placed greater stress on it. When a person performs an action whose object is evil in itself but which he, in virtue of an involuntary and invincible error, believes to be good, then his action is genuinely and subjectively good[10].

As this brief history of the question makes clear, moral reflection over the centuries has led to a heightened appreciation of the role of the moral subject.

It remains true that St Thomas seems to think that certain cases of outrageous ignorance, bearing upon what everyone is bound to know (for example; that fornication is a sin) are always vincible and culpable. We would be less certain today.

Obviously, we have not here to concern ourselves with the views of those, such as the Marxists and the Hegelian school in general, who identify the moral value of a person's action wth the effective achievement of results. Such views, as is evident, fail to appreciate the true nature of morality and the importance of conscience.

243. – Before we begin to discuss the problem we are here faced with, we have first to make clear what is meant by ignorance (or error) which is vincible and invincible, culpable and blameless. An error is vincible when the subject, *as he actually is here and now*, could correct it; this supposes that he at least suspects that things are not what he thinks them to be, that he is not in possession of certain relevant data, so that he in some way appreciates his need of further information and his obligation to seek it. ... If this possibility of correcting his error

---

[9] It seems to be insinuated in the commentary *In VII Eth.*, lect. 9 (Pirotta edition, nn. 1437-1438), where St Thomas adds no restriction to the principle laid down by Aristotle. On who follows a reasoning which is false but which he believes is true, really intends to follow right reason, and only "by accident" follows wrong reason. — On the history of this question in the middle ages, see O. Lottin, op. cit., pp. 354-406; "La valeur obligatoire de la conscience".

[10] Suarez, *De bonitate et malitia*..., disp. XII, sect. 4, n. 8; p. 445.

does not exist, either because he does not suspect that his conscience is, in fact, erroneous, or else because he does not appreciate the relevance of his ignorance — which he acknowledges — to the morality of his action(s), his error is invincible.

The preceding distinction is concerned with the effect of error on future actions, on the decisions that still have to be taken. The distinction between culpable and blameless error, on the other hand, is concerned with past actions, with error as the effect of decisions that have already been taken: a person's error is culpable if it results from his evil use of liberty (n. 246). Note that a vincible error is not necessarily culpable: it becomes so only in the measure in which the person perseveres in it. But note also that a culpable error is not always here and now vincible.

Having made these points clear, we are now in a position to decide whether and to what extent an erroneous conscience (i) ought to be obeyed, (ii) excuses a person from blame.

244. – There is an obligation on a person to do something, when to omit it would be immoral (nn. 41; 161). Since this is so, we have now to ask ourselves whether the person who omits to do what his conscience commands, by that very fact violates an obligation; if he disobeys his conscience, does he act immorally despite the objective rectitude of his action?

Now, a person's will becomes evil if he chooses an object which he knows to be evil, that is, to be contrary to the requirements of right reason. This is so because what makes a person's choice to be this choice rather than some other is not the object as it really is, but the object as he knows it and, in consequence, chooses it. What we desire is not what we simply know as a being, but what we know to be good: what determines the morality of our choice is the moral value of the object as we are aware of it when choosing. — This principle, which follows immediately from the nature of a human act, provides the key to the entire problem we are here investigating.

When then a person refuses to obey his invincibly erroneous conscience, he is choosing an object which in his eyes is morally evil. It follows, in virtue of the key principles we have just mentioned, that he is acting immorally, that he is

misusing his liberty. Consequently, we have to conclude that
when a person's conscience is invincibly erroneous, he is
always obliged to follow it.

But what if the error is vincible? When this happens, a person's
conscience is not certain, even though the moment of decision is at
hand. (If it were certain, then his error would be invincible, n. 243).
He suspects that he should seek for further light. ... In this situation,
his primary obligation in conscience is to dispel the ignorance and
overcome the error. But if, even though he is alive to his ignorance,
he neglects to seek further information and then does what he was
bound to avoid, or omits what he was bound to do, he acts immorally (nn. 249-250).

245. – The same key principle enables us to reply readily
to the second question. If a person is not aware of the objective
disorder of his proposed action, then his decision to act in this
particular way could not be tainted by this disorder: he is
excused from all guilt — but always on condition that his error
is involuntary and invincible.

But why is this restriction made? The principle on which
we are relying seems to be always valid: a disorder of which the
person is unaware cannot affect his will in any way, since it is
his knowledge of the object chosen, which determines the
morality of his choice.

It is certainly true, as St Thomas points out, that even
ignorance which is blameworthy because of its voluntariness
diminishes the voluntary character of the subsequent action
and, in consequence, its sinfulness [11]. Even though this ignorance, since it is blameworthy, taints the person's will, nevertheless, it also has the effect of making his disordered choice to
be less sinful than it would be if he acted with clear knowledge.
— But not every type of culpable ignorance has this effect.

246. – There are, in fact, three types of culpable ignorance and a clear distinction has to be made between them. The
first and the worst type is ignorance that is *affected*: the subject
does not want to know whether his proposed action is morally
good or evil, etc., for fear that if he discovered that it were

---

[11] *De Malo*, III, 8 ad 4um.

illicit, he would be deterred from performing it. For example, I suspect that some of the books in my library are not mine at all; it would be quite easy for me to establish whether or not they are, but I take good care not to do so, for if I were to discover that they belong to somebody else, I know that I would not be able to hold on to them in peace of mind ... and I am very attached to these books! This studied ignorance, far from excusing a person, has the effect rather of increasing his guilt; more precisely, it manifests how committed he is to a particular line of action. For, remarks St Thomas, in a sentence that clearly reveals his intellectualism, the person who is willing to deprive himself of knowledge, so that he may not be held back from sinning, betrays the extent of his love for what is evil[12]. — Another but less blameworthy type is that in which a person's ignorance (and consequent error) results from a certain negligence in seeking the information which he lacks. This negligence, in its turn, can be concerned with his knowledge of the law (a doctor who neglects to acquire the requisite knowledge of medical ethics) or with his knowledge of some circumstance which has a bearing on the morality of his action (a doctor who gives a blood transfusion without verifying that the blood of the donor and of the recipient both belong to the same group). All the professional faults which are imputable to laziness, lack of earnestness etc., during the years of study, provide examples of this type of culpable ignorance. — A third and final type is that in which the agent either directly or indirectly chooses something which results in ignorance on his part. The drunkard provides an example of a direct choice: he drinks more than he should, so that, in consequence, he loses the use of his reason. An example of an indirect choice is provided by the person who is negligent about checking the initial surge of his passions: as a result, these grow stronger, so that in the act of choice his reason is partially swamped[13]. — The second and third types of ignorance are blameworthy in varying degrees, but they differ from the first type in that they attenuate the person's guilt for the subsequent action[14].

---

[12] *Ib.*, corp. art.

[13] *Ib.*

[14] *Ib.*

This guilt, moreover, presupposes that in performing his action the person still persists in some way in his direct or indirect decision to remain ignorant of what he ought to know. If this is now no longer his attitude, then an action which he performs as a result of his ignorance, no matter how objectively immoral it may be, cannot be subjectively so. When his ignorance was voluntary, the fact that the subsequent action was objectively good rather rhan evil was immaterial. Through neglecting to inform himself, or, worse, through positively deciding to remain ignorant, he has already incurred guilt; he has manifested his determination to choose what is evil, or, at the very least, his lack of concern to do what is right. The action that he subsequently performs may well be, in itself, quite innocent: but this does not alter the interior disorder. The doctor who, as a result of culpable carelessness, prescribes a medicine which could kill his patient is not freed from guilt by the fact that the latter recovers from the "medicine", just as he would not have been any the more guilty if death had resulted. The present does not make the past to be anything other than what it has been. But, reciprocally, the past, no matter how evil it may have been, cannot now make a person who has been converted and is determined to do what is right, to be in any way guilty.

There is a certain analogy between this last point and what has been written in n. 232, but only an analogy: what was there in question was the effect the *external* dimension of an action has on the internal, whereas what we are speaking about here is the way in which a person's present choice (the *internal* dimension of his action) can be influenced by a prior choice.

Moreover, in considering this entire question of culpable ignorance, it is important to distinguish between *moral* guilt and *juridical* responsibility. Where this latter is concerned, what counts are the consequences: the doctor in our example will, in general, have nothing to fear, if his patient is cured despite the treatment; but if the patient dies as a result of the doctor's ministrations, then the penalties imposed on the latter may well be dire. Note, though, that our moral notions are to a great extent strongly contaminated by juridical notions, and all the more so because Catholic moral theology is largely orientated towards the reception and administration of the sacrament of Penance: in this latter, part of the priest's role is that of judge; he acts as the representative of the society which is the Church, so that a juridical aspect, in the good sense of the word (n. 219, end), will necessarily be involved.

A mistake that we should be on our guard to avoid when discussing the relation between past negligence and present guilt is the Cartesian one of considering time as divided up into independent moments. Our actions are not isolated and detached from one another so that the past has no power to affect the present: on the contrary, there is a unity in our moral lives, so that through all the gradations between fully deliberate actions and habitual dispositions, there is an unbroken link. Mention has already (n. 228) been made of these profound and enduring dispositions, these "superactual attitudes", as D. von Hildebrand refers to them, which dominate and animate entire sectors of our lives for periods of greater or lesser length. It is these above all — as we shall soon see when we turn to the consideration of the role which virtues and good habits play in our lives — which ensure the unity and continuity of a person's moral existence, and result in the solidarity of his past with his present. Just as the external and the internal dimension of a human action are not two but one, so also our past and present actions, linked as they are by these basic dispositions, are united at a more profound level; from this point of view, a disordered action which a person here and now performs as a result of his negligence — never repaired nor repented of — to acquire the information he lacks, is the fruit and, at the same time, the immanent sanction of a prior disorder which still persists.

Note, in conclusion, that even though affected ignorance is a sign of how attached a person is to what is evil, it also reveals a certain desire on his part not to sin with clear knowledge of what he is doing, a desire which testifies to a final vestige of respect for moral value and the moral law. (Cf. La Rochefoucauld's remark that hypocrisy is the homage that vice pays to virtue).

247. – It is clear then that since ignorance which is invincible and blameless excuses a person, his will can be upright and virtuous even when what he is doing is objectively disordered. This conclusion follows not simply from the fact that morally neutal actions are ruled out, but directly from the key principle we are using (n. 244). Since the moral value of the acting subject depends immediately, not on the intrinsic moral value of the object he chooses (or of the external action he performs) but on his knowledge of this value, his will is good whenever the object of his choice presents itself to him as morally good.

There is no parallel between a situation of this kind and one in which a person seeks to achieve a good end by making use of means that are evil. In this latter situation, the immorality of the means is known and accepted, so that a person's will is, in consequence, tainted. In the former situation, on the contrary, the subject does not know (and the hypothesis is that he is not to blame for this ignorance) that there is an objective incompatibility between what he is choosing and his fundamental resolve to do what is right (nn. 230, 238).

One should not, however, conclude from what has been said that the objective value of our actions is of minor consequence and that all that really matters is whether we are acting in accordance with our consciences. To be indifferent to the objective value of an action is already to be unfaithful to what the Ideal requires of us. Implicit in a good will, a will that is faithful to the Ideal, is the resolve to conform to the objective rule which reason provides, and not to rest content with one's present defective appreciation of what this involves: in other words, the genuinely moral person is not satisfied to do what is evil, provided he is in good faith; he is concerned with more than "keeping his conscience clean". The necessity for this attitude springs from the fact that the subject is not himself the ultimate foundation of moral value: he is "measured" and "gauged" morally by the objective order of right reason and, radically, by the divine reason, on which the order of being is grounded, and of which it is the expression. Consequently, it is clear in what sense one can say, in company with M. Scheler and N. Hartmann, that it is not by being preoccupied with his moral value that a person grows in moral stature but rather by concentrating on doing what is right: it is through actions of this kind that his moral growth is most assured: from them it will inevitably result [15]. The person of good will is not the one who is centred on his own moral advancement — this is priggishness and pharisaism — but on responding to the demands which objective values make on him, values that are in harmony with the judgments of right reason (even though, admittedly, he can make this response only in the measure in which he has come to know and appreciate these values for

---

[15] See n. 33, 2.

himself). Unless he is centred on objective values in this way
and is striving to bring his life into ever growing conformity
with them, he is failing to meet the claims which the supreme
norm of a good conscience has on him. Consequently, if he is
negligent about discovering what is objectively required of
him, here and now, in order that he act reasonably, he reveals
how little concerned he is about respecting the objective order
(which is the reflection of the divine reason); he scarcely
troubles himself about this order, and such an attitude is the
beginning of infidelity.

The truth of this point is particularly evident when what is in
question is the good of one's neighbour. A mother, for example,
would be blameworthy if, in looking after her sick child, she were
exclusively preoccupied with *doing her duty, obeying her conscience* etc.,
and not rather with *choosing the most competent doctor, using the most
effective remedies*. ... What right reason requires here of her is that she
be directly and single-mindedly concerned with the restoration of her
child to health. Hence it is possible for a person to be "indifferent"
with regard to success, in a way that is reprehensible; his indifference
can be a caricature of that which the saints and religious writers
praise. This latter is on a higher level; it supposes that a person is
aiming earnestly, whole-heartedly and with all the means at his
disposal, at the goal which his activity, of its very nature, is meant to
achieve, and which God — speaking to him through the duties of his
state in life — *wills him to aim at determinedly*. (In the example we have
used, this is the child's recovery). But not only is the genuinely
indifferent person determined: he also accepts in advance, and says
"amen" to, the possible frustration of his aims: his determination to
succeed is real, yet it does not occupy his entire horizon. But note
that a possible frustration cannot be accepted, unless there is
something which can be frustrated: unless the person is resolved to
strive for success. — In connection with this point, it is useful to
read what St Thomas has written on the question of whether we are
bound to conform our will to the Divine will, where the object
willed is concerned [16].

The answer to the problem touched on earlier in our
investigation (n. 33, 2) is now clear. A person cannot, and
ought not to, aim at obeying his conscience, as if this could be
done in independence of objective moral values; as well, he can

---

[16] *De Ver.*, 23, 8; *Summa Theol.*, I-II, 19, 10.

genuinely aim neither at having a good conscience, nor at responding to the demands which objective values make on him, unless he remains opne to the Ideal of practical reason. To aim exclusively at one's own moral advancement for its own sake is to deteriorate morally. To aim at conforming to the objective moral order, apart from living in openness to the Ideal, will lead to a counterfeit morality; all that one will then attain to, to use Kant's term, will be "legality". True morality commences only when a subject begins to live (no matter how implicitly) this openness, only when his attitude is one of friendliness and self-giving, so that he strives to understand others and to acknowledge them in practice. Neither the subjective nor the objective standpoint is to be neglected; but the proper balance between the two can be maintained, and each of them can develop as it should, only through their common relationship with the Ideal. (Similarly, an authentic grasp of reality is neither purely objective nor purely subjective, but requires that both the subject and the object be simultaneously grasped as included in what unites them from within, but which is also the foundation of the opposition between them).

A possibility which is, unfortunately, all too often verified should be noted in conclusion: actions which a person performs in consequence of ignorance and error that are completely blameless, can, nonetheless, give rise to habits and tendencies which are objectively perverse, so that as a result, his feelings are coarsened, his moral judgment is clouded, his conscience is blunted; there will also be a very real risk that when he finally discovers the disorders in which he has indulged, but to which he has now grown accustomed, he will not only continue to behave as before, but will want to do so and will, as a result, sin subjectively.

II. The Doubtful Conscience.

248. – Strictly speaking, a person never has a *doubtful conscience*, for when he doubts he does not know (he has not *scientia*) and, consequently, he has not that knowledge of the morality of his action which is called his conscience. (He has not *conscientia*). But here we leave aside these linguistic subtleties and use the term "doubtful conscience" to designate the state of mind of a moral subject who lacks certainty concerning the moral value of a proposed action of his. (The doubt can also be concerned with the value of an action which he has already performed, but our problem here is not with this latter kind of doubt). This state of uncertainty can be of two kinds: the person may hesitate between two opposing views without inclining to one view more than another; or he may accept one view, but without complete conviction, so that he still remains fearful of error: the possibility that the other may be the true view is very much present to him. The person who is uncertain in the second sense is more accurately said to have an "opinion", while it is only the person who is uncertain in the first sense who is, properly speaking, "doubtful". But this distinction is of epistemological rather than moral relevance: for the moralist, the person in both states of uncertainty is "doubtful". (The expression "probable conscience" should be avoided: probability refers to an assertion which presents itself to a person as worthy of acceptance as an opinion.

Other states of conscience which can also be distinguished are: "correct", "lax", "scrupulous". A person's conscience is said to be correct when he habitually distinguishes correctly between his good and evil actions [17]; it is said to be lax if it is only with much difficulty that he can appreciate the moral disorder of his actions: he is sensitive only to his gross deviations from the moral law; it is said to be scrupulous if he is hypersensitive to moral evil and brings it to light even where it is non-existent. But while these states of conscience are of great importance in practico-practical considerations (pastoral theology, spiritual direction etc.), they are peripheral to our investigation.

The problem we have now to discuss is, accordingly: what is a person to do when he is unable to know with certainty

---

[17] More precisely, a correct conscience is one which correctly applies the principles to particular situations, insofar as these are known to the person in question. Consequently, such a conscience can be erroneous, when a person's knowledge of the situation is, through no fault of his own, insufficient. One who, through an unavoidable practical error, regards as legitimate an authority which in fact is illegitimate, can have a perfectly correct conscience where his duties towards this authority are concerned.

whether an action which he has occasion to perform, here and now, is licit or not, obligatory or not?

A. *The Judgment of Conscience.*

249. – Note this point carefully first: the judgment which a person makes on the objective morality of the action he proposes to perform (or to omit) is not yet a judgment on the morality of his performance (or omission) of this action. This distinction may appear at first sight to be no more than a somewhat refined point of logic; and, in fact, it is true that when a person's conscience is certain, the two judgments merge to the point of being practically indistinguishable. When a person knows that a particular way of acting is evil, he also knows that it would be evil for him to act in that way. But when he cannot make the first judgment with certainty, the distinction between it and the other judgment becomes manifest, as what follows will make clear.

On the basis of this distinction, there is general agreement (as indeed there should be) that a person ought never to act with a doubtful conscience, *when his doubt concerns the moral value of his performance of an action.* To say: "I do not know whether I am acting morally or immorally, but it can't be helped", is to accept in advance the possibility of a subjective moral disorder, of a voluntary unfaithfulness to the Value; and to accept this possibility is already to be unfaithful. For I am not allowed to call in question my fidelity to the Value, or suspend my allegiance to it (n. 45).

Moreover, to probe into the matter a little more deeply, we *never*, in fact, act with a doubtful conscience (in the sense that has been indicated above). To act without knowing whether I am acting morally or immorally is really to act with the knowledge — more secret but no less certain — that I am acting immorally [18].

---

[18] In this sense, the dictate of conscience concerning the performance of an action can be said to be always absolutely certain. Cf. J. Fuchs, *Theologia moralis fundamentalis*, p. 176. But this jdgment is not always explicit and formal. Conscience extends more widely. (Cf. nn. 16 and 252).

250. – It is clear then that, in order to act well, a person has to be certain that he does well to act, that his performance of this particular action is in conformity with right reason. Obviously, the certainty which is required is not the metaphysical certainty which would exclude all possibility of the truth of its contradictory, but the certainty which is called moral, in virtue of which the contradictory is deprived of all serious probability. (In practice, this certainty scarcely differs from a very high degree of probability). The reason for requiring no higher degree of certainty than this is that what would, in the very great majority of instances, make it impossibile for us to act at all, cannot be required in order to act well. But if we had always to be absolutely certain, before we acted, that we would do well to act, it would, in general, be impossible for us to act [19].

Note carefully that to act with no more than moral certainty that our performance of an action is good is by no means the same as accepting the possibility (of which mention has just been made) of a subjective moral disorder. The possibility of error which has not now been excluded remains speculative and abstract; as such, it is of no account for our practical reason: in relation to the judgment of conscience, it is as if it did not exist. This is why, at the heart of this moral certainty, there is to be found a certainty that is more profound, a certainty that is absolute. For I am absolutely certain that I act well once I have moral certainty on the point. (Concealed in my moral certainty that my performance of this action is morally good is the absolute certainty that I act well in performing it).

Once a person has this certitude, his performance of the action in question will evidently have a positive moral value (unless some other factor, such as a subjectively evil end, intervenes). Since, by hypothesis, he has first evaluated the action in its relation to himself, it has become, in consequence, the object which he chooses, so that it determines the moral value of his choice in the same way as does every object

---

[19] On these various types of certitude and the connected notions, cf. F. Morandini, *Critica*, 5th ed., Rome, 1963, pp. 267-308. The classical division has been criticised by J. Lebacqz, *Certitude et volonté*, (1963), pp. 46-47.

(nn. 225-226). By choosing it, he does not change its moral quality; on the contrary he accepts this, to the degree to which it is known to him.

It should however be noted that it is very difficult for us to be completely certain concerning the subjective morality of our actions, since the depths of our conscience and our real motivations so often escape us. The absolute certainty of which we have spoken is, in consequence, always linked with the qualification: "provided, at least, that I am not deceiving myself (about my intentions, my motivations etc.)". It is for this reason that St Paul could write (and what he has to say is applicable even on the purely ethical level): "I am not aware of anything against myself, but I am not thereby acquitted" [20].

251. – But could not this truth be applied in reverse, where actions performed with an apparently bad conscience are concerned? Is it certain that such actions are always as evil as the subject, at the level of discursive thought, judges them to be? Undoubtedly, what is true where good actions are concerned will not necessarily be true of evil actions, in virtue of the principle that to act well *all* the required conditions have to be fulfilled. An additional factor can reveal as evil an action which at first seemed to be good; no new factor can make what is evil in itself to become good. Nevertheless, the problem raised calls for further reflection.

Let us leave aside the situation where the subject is mistaken about the free character of an action, as often happens with those who are controlled by a particular habit or are scrupulous [21]. We assume then that what is in question is really a human action, and on the basis of that assumption we make the following points.

1. To know that a particular way of acting is good or evil is not the same as simply knowing that it is accepted as such in a certain milieu. This latter knowledge, of itself, provides a person with no more than an extrinsic appreciation of the action in question; he can apply the words "good" and "evil" to certain actions, but he is quite incapable of filling out the content of these words in relation to these actions. In order, then, to be capable of making a moral judgment about his proposed action, a person has to have a real and not merely verbal, grasp of its value and, in consequence, has to have a certain openness, in his judgment, to the Value. ...

---

[20] 1 Cor., 4, 4 (RSV).
[21] *Essai*, n. 112, pp. 269-273. See also *Existence et liberté*, pp. 20-26.

For the same reason, it is not sufficient to have been told that an action displeases God, that He has forbidden it etc.: it is also necessary to fill out these expressions with a content of value, to have a concrete appreciation that to obey God is morally good etc. (cf. n. 163). In a society where religious values and a sense of the sacred are alive in the collective conscience, there is no difficulty about admitting that the abstract and verbal knowledge that an action has been forbidden by God, is accompanied, in general, by a concrete appreciation of its negative value. But in a society where the religious sense has grown weak, will this knowledge involve anything more, very frequently, than the memory of a catechism formula which the person had to learn, a long time ago, in preparation for his first communion, but which has always been to him simply a matter of words? Could it not then happen that such a person would act with the clear but purely notional knowledge that he was disobeying God, so that, in consequence, he would not be guilty of the subjective malice of an offence against God? (The fact that the person is capable of stating a number of propositions concerning God, all of which are purely verbal, or simply notional, does not alter his situation at all). This could well be the position that many people are in, whether they have grown completely indifferent to religion, or are still more or less vaguely "practising". — This is not to say that we should not be concerned for such people. Their present incapacity to appreciate moral value could stem from a "closed" attitude whose origin has been voluntary: habitual carelessness and thoughtlessness, lack of determination, lack of love. Beneath the superficial conscience which does not concretely discern the real value of the action commanded or forbidden by the will of God, nor the value which the traditional moral norms possess, does there perhaps lurk a more profound conscience which has turned away from God, from the norm of moral good, and which is fleeing from the light so that its quietude may not be disturbed (n. 246)? — Our reflections have, accordingly, uncovered three levels of conscience: 1. a superficial level which does not go beyond notional and verbal thinking: "I know that this way of acting (for example, to miss Mass) is a sin", that is, it is considered by the Church and the Christian milieu to be a sin. 2. A more profound zone where the concrete appreciation of moral value occurs: "I do not really see any negative value in this way of acting, even though it is said to be sinful". 3. The most profound and central zone, where the option which governs our appreciation of moral value is made: "and I do not have this appreciation (of a particular value) because in my inmost being as a rational subject, I am closing myself to it".

252. – 2. But now suppose that a person has a concrete appreciation of the negative moral value of a particular way of acting and still proceeds to act in that way. Is it absolutely certain that he has sinned?

It would seem that very often between the thematic judgment that it would be immoral to act in this way, and the decision to perform the action all the same (or the ultimate practical judgment), an athematic judgment slides in: this is an unformulated conviction, hidden in the depths of the person's mind and it can be expressed in some such terms as these: "No! it is not possible that this way of acting could really be immoral! Everybody does it! God could not demand this! There must be a way out, even though I am ignorant of it!" In this situation, also, a person might be quite clear that he had sinned, even though he had not really done so. Where scrupulous people are concerned, there is no problem about admitting that this occurs; at the profound and central level of conscience they judge reasonably, but at the notional and surface level they are muddled.

But again the question becomes complicated. The situations we are speaking about here can be likened to those in which a person's conscience is erroneous, with the difference however that here error is situated, not at the level of clear practical judgments, but at the profound level. (It is also in this respect that these situations are distinguished from those in which scrupulous people are concerned: these latter are not confused at the profound level). — In consequence, we have to re-introduce some distinctions which we have already used (nn. 242-246). Error excuses a person from guilt only if it is invincible and blameless. Are the ignorance and error, which are involved in the situations here envisaged, of this kind? The doubt which, in the depths of the person's mind, undermines the clear judgment of conscience he has already made, and the unformulated judgment which, barely prior to the decision, neutralises the effect of the formulated judgment — are not these culpable in their cause? Do they not proceed from a spirit of insubordination, from pride, from desires that are depraved etc.? — Without doubt, they often do; but can they be said to do so always? The pressure from the milieu in which he lives, the force of prejudice etc., can become so strong that it will not any longer be in the subject's power to break free from them. His responsibility, if it still remains, can, in consequence, be notably diminished.

One could say that a person in a situation of this kind spontaneously applies a type of situation ethics. But note that his judgment — which moreover is erroneous — remains entirely subjective; hence it would be a grave mistake to regard as objective, and as aimed at determining what ought to be done, a judgment which he has made when all objective aspects of the case have been considered. If our analysis has been correct, no normative conclusion can be drawn in consequence. The course which he should follow is laid down by the specific forms which the moral law takes, and which he will interpret and apply to the concrete situation by exercising the virtue of prudence. In his situation, as in every other, this guidance is valid. Consequently, the advice which such a person stands in need of, is not: the moral law commands you to act in this way, but all the same take account of your own situation: perhaps you will be led to do, as more called for in your case, what the law forbids. On the contrary, he should be advised: obey the moral law; do all that it requires of you to the best of your ability. The relevance of the theory we have here proposed is not *prior* to the action, in order to provide guidance, but *subsequent* to it, in order to throw light on its moral quality. It would be illegitimate to propose as a rule for future activity what is valid only as a reflection on activity that is past.

B. *How the Final Judgment of Conscience is to be Formed.*

253. – The distiction that has been made (n. 249) between two moral judgments, two levels of moral knowledge, is not sufficient to resolve the problem posed by the doubtful conscience. If the second judgment is a copy of the first, if a person's doubt concerning the moral value of an action necessarily involves him in doubt concerning the moral value of his performance of it, then our initial problem is still with us. In situations of this kind, one could of course decide to avoid this action ("when in doubt, don't do it"), or, if the doubt is concerned with the obligatory character of the action, to perform it. By so deciding, one will at least be sure of avoiding evil. This solution, since it resolves the doubt in favour of the morally "safer" (Latin: *tutior*) course, is called the "tutiorist" solution.

Now, it may well be preferable, very often, to decide in this way. But is a person really obliged so to decide? If this solution were adopted as a rule of conduct, would it not make life impossible for a person (unless, exasperated by the constraints imposed on him, he sought to break free of them by cocking his nose at "the voice of conscience", and by choosing what he judged to be evil?).

Note, in passing, that in following the morally safer course, a person will not necessarily be doing what is of greater moral value.

Think, for example, of someone strolling near a river, who sees a person falling into the water. If the stroller is a mediocre swimmer, has he the right to enter the water in an attempt to save the other? He is the father of a family; the risk involved is great; the probability of being able to save the drowning person is small. Nothing obliges him to this act of heroism — or of folly. The *safer* course, from every point of view, is to remain on dry land, and to raise the alarm by shouting, running for help. ... And perhaps, in the secret of his heart, this person might wish that he *should not have the right* to risk his life. His inferior self, the "I" who is of less worth and is attached to the empirical existence that he now possesses (his existence in this present world) might desire that the call of duty should defend him against his higher self, the "I" of greater worth, who invites him to make the sacrifice. ...

The grave disadvantages of this first solution suggest that we should seek some other one. What we look to this other solution to provide, is a principle which, while it does not at all remove a person's doubt about the moral value of an *action*, will still enable him to decide in a way that is less uniformly negative concerning the moral value of his *performance* of it.

It was in order to discover and exploit such a principle that, starting from the 16th century, various moral systems have been elaborated. To these systems we now turn our attention.

254. – The medieval Scholastics, in virtue of their "objectivist" mentality, were inclined to favour a type of "morally safer" ("tutiorist") approach. (But in fairness to them, it should be noted that the problem did not present itself to them in the terms in which it is here envisaged). Their attitude can be divined by the way in which they solved specific problems. St Thomas, for example, in dealing with the question of how an ecclesiatic should act when he doubts whether he is entitled to hold several prebends simultaneously, writes that such a person certainly sins if, with his doubt unresolved, he accepts the prebends, since by acting in this way he shows that he is willing to sin. (The fact that he is really entitled to hold the prebends does not alter the situation)[22]. Strictly speaking, St Thomas says nothing more here than is contained in the

---

[22] *Quodl.*, 8, 13. — On the mentality of the medieval authors, see Lottin, *op. cit.*, pp. 407-417: "La solution des doutes de conscience".

commonly held doctrine, which we have treated of already
(n. 249), that it is immoral to act with a doubt about the
morality of the performance of an action. But, from the manner
in which St Thomas expresses himself, it is clear that he does
not envisage the possibility of resolving the doubt concerning
the morality of performing the action, while leaving unresolved the doubt about the morality of the action itself, so
that, in consequence, provided certain conditions are fulfilled, a
person would be quite entitled to act with a doubt of the latter
kind. In other words, the possibility of what would later be
called *reflex principles* did not occur to him [23].

When, at the beginning of the modern epoch, moralists
began to concern themselves of set purpose with the problem
of the doubtful conscience — a study which was rendered all
the more necessary by the numerous new problems that were
arising, in particular from the new social and economic conditions — certain rigorists were to be found who, systematically
this time, defended the morally safer approach to the problems
raised. In order to act well, it was necessary, they maintained,
to be certain (the absolute version of the theory) or, at least, to
have a very high degree of probability (the mitigated version)
that the action in question was licit. — We note, in passing,
that the absolute version has been condemned by the Church [24].

255. – Without going as far as the rigorists, a good
number of other authors required — or require, since this view
has still its supporters — that in order to be entitled to follow
the morally less safe course (to perform an action whose moral
value is doubtful) a person had to know that the positive value
of this course was more probable than its negative value. Hence
the title "probabiliorists" (Latin: *probabilior*, more probable).

---

[23] These principles — whose function is to remove the doubt about the
performance of an action when the morality of the action itself remains uncertain
— are called *reflex*, because they do not result from a direct consideration of the
action's objective morality, but are concerned with the morality of the subject;
this is manifested only by way of reflection.

[24] Denzinger-Schönmetzer, *Enchiridion*, n. 2303 (older editions, n. 1293): the
proposition that a person is not allowed to follow a probable opinion, or one
that is the most probable of various probable opinions, was condemned on Dec.
7, 1690.

Others, less rigid still, were content to require no more than that the two probabilities should be evenly balanced, or, at least, more or less equivalent. These are the "equiprobabilists". Their system has become somewhat complicated by distinctions about whether "liberty" or "law" is "in possession", that is, they have distinguished between situations in which a person's doubt is concerned with the existence of a law, or with its cessation. — This was the solution adopted by St Alphonsus de Liguori, at least in the last period of his life; it has also been adopted by his disciples.

256. – The previous two systems, unlike the morally safer approach, involve a comparison of probabilities. *Probabilism*, on the contrary, resembles this earlier approach, in that it is concerned with the probability, in itself and absolutely, which favours the liceity of an action; but it differs from this approach, in that it maintains that a person is morally entitled to act, once there is a "true and solid" probability that the action in question has a positive moral value, whereas "tutiorists" are either not content with a probability, or else demand a degree of it which is almost equivalent to a certitude. Even if the probability is less than the contrary one, probabilists are not perturbed. The probability which they have in mind can be either intrinsic or extrinsic: an examination of the actual problem, of the principles that are operative, of the concrete circumstances etc., is required in order to establish the intrinsic probability in favour of an action: the authority of those who are "prudent" (this, in practice, means the moralists) will establish its extrinsic probability. — The principle on which probabilists rely is ordinarily formulated as: *a doubtful law does not oblige*, or better, *a doubtful obligation is no obligation*. — This system first seems to have been expressly taught in the 16th century by the Dominican theologian, Bartholomew de Medina; at the present time it has numerous staunch supporters [25].

---

[25] On the history of probabilism, see Th. Deman, art. *Probabilisme*, "Dict. de théol. cath.", col. 418-602 and L. Rodrigo, *Tractatus de conscientia morali*, t. II, Santander, 1956, pp. 120-218. This enormous work (close on 900 pages) is almost exclusively devoted to the theory of probabilism, of which it makes a penetrating and exhaustive study.

With the passage of time, probabilists have been led to introduce certain distinctions. Many authors maintained that the theory is applicable only to doubts about the *law* (when what is in question is the existence or cessation of a law). Where the doubt is concerned with some *fact* (when a person is not sure whether he has performed some particular action, or whether a particular event has occurred — have I paid this debt? — is the man who is lying on the grass margin, sick, dead or asleep?), the theory is applicable only in the measure in which the doubt can be changed into a doubt about the law, as happens, for example, when it is not evident that the legislator intends to urge the obligation once a factual doubt arises[26]. But, they add, a doubt of this kind can be resolved in most instances by making use of the principles which are commonly employed in legal matters. Examples of such principles are: facts are not to be presumed but to be proven; when a doubt arises, the person who has possession is in a stronger position; doubtful issues are to be resolved in the light of what ordinarily happens etc. — The most important distinction which probabilists make is, however, between situations in which all that is involved is the *liceity* of an action, and situations in which its *objective validity* ought to be ensured (for example, where the administation of the Sacraments is concerned), or in which, cost what it may, a certain effect should be striven for, a serious injury to one's neighbour should be avoided etc. In situations of this latter type, they insist, probabilism is not to be employed. It is not permissible to baptize with water that is *probably* natural (unless no other is available and time is pressing). It is not permissible to allow the sale of a medicine which is *probably* free from dangerous side-effects, or to allow passengers to board a plane that is *probably* airworthy. When a person's action can have consequences which he is in no way entitled to permit — situations of this kind chiefly arise when the welfare of other people could be seriously endangered — the morally safer solution imposes itself.

N.B. The lax views in this matter, which have been condemned by the Church[27], have never been formulated as a distinct system: they are really nothing more than an immoderate extension of probabilism. Those who advanced these views claimed that an extremely slight degree of probability was sufficient; as well, they often neglected to make the distinctions of which we have just spoken.

---

[26] But not all probabilists accept this limitation of the principle. L. Rodrigo, *op. cit.*, pp. 443-446, rejects it.

[27] The proposition that a person always acts prudently when he relies on an intrinsic or extrinsic probability, no matter how slender, provided it remains within the bounds of probability, was condemned on March 2, 1679, Denzinger-Schönmetzer, *Enchiridion*, n. 2103 (older editions, n. 1153).

257. – Another system has found supporters in recent times. This is called the *system of compensation or the system of Christian prudence* (Prümmer); according to this theory, a person is entitled to follow the "less safe" course, even when the probability in favour of its positive moral value is less than the contrary probability, whenever he has reasons for so acting which are proportionate to the risk he is running of violating the objective moral order. The more serious the violation which is feared, the greater the probability of its occurrence, the stronger also have these reasons to be. The position here, these authors maintain, is analogous to that which prevails when an effect which is indirectly voluntary follows from a person's free choice (nn. 13; 230). He is entitled to tolerate an evil effect of this kind, if he has proportionately serious reasons for doing so (if, for example, to endeavour to avoid it at any cost would only lead to a still greater evil). Similarly, in this present context, the achievement of a certain good, the fear that greater damage will result, can compensate for the risk of an objective disorder. — Note well that these authors, in company with most moral theologians, consider the problem primarily from the point of view of the confessor. For the latter, it would be imprudent to impose on this penitent, or even to reveal to him, demands which he is psychologically incapable of meeting; the penitent would, in consequence, lose his "good faith", so that what were formerly objective sins would now become subjective sins. Our point of view, here, differs from that of the moral theologian and the confessor: it is that of the moral agent himself.

258. – In all these systems, with the exception of the morally safer one, a reflex principle comes to be inserted between the two judgments of conscience. This principle does not shed any further light on the objective value of the action, but removes the person's doubt concerning the value of his performance of it. The process by which his conscience is thus enlightened can be explicitly formulated in this way: the probability that this action is in conformity with the moral norm is greater than (a), or as great as, approximately as great as (b) the contrary probability; at all events, there is a true and solid probability in its favour (c); or again: this action is probably in conformity with the moral norm and, in addition, there are reasons for performing it which compensate for the possible violation of the objective order (d). Now, it is certainly licit to perform an action of the category a (or b, or c, or d: it is on this point that the systems differ). Consequently, it is certainly licit to perform this action *here and now*.

It is interesting to note that the legitimacy of employing these moral systems, and the reflex principles on which they are based, has been challenged in recent times by certain authors, who advocate a return to the position of the medieval Scholastics and of St Thomas in particular. If the Thomistic teaching on the role of the virtue of prudence were better exploited, this would suffice, they maintain, to resolve the doubts to which concrete problems give rise [28].

259. – Before we offer our own solution, we wish to draw the attention of the reader to several important points:

1. The question that is here being discussed is concerned with only one of the problems which will confront the person who strives to lead a moral life; consequently, it should not be regarded as if it were central and fundamental to the study of ethics. The situation that is envisaged is that of a person who, after having made a serious and sincere effort (within the limits of the means at his disposal) to discover how he is obliged to act, is still in the dark (or, perhaps better, the twilight) when the time for acting arrives. Consequently, he is presupposed to be a man of good will, one whose basic resolve is to lead a life that is worthy of a human being. No system, no reflex principle, can supply for the absence of this fundamental uprightness.

2. Before having recourse to a *remote* and *universal* reflex principle, a person should first consider whether he could not obtain the desired light by making use of *proximate* reflex principles, drawn, not from a reflection on the factors that are involved in every moral act, but from a reflection on some less universal aspect of the act in question. An example of such a principle is: when a person is already obliged to make every effort to attain some definite end, he should then choose the

---

[28] For example, Th. Deman, *art. cit.*, especially col. 612 and 615.

most sure means. Other examples are provided by the principles which are relevant to the solution of factual doubts
(n. 256), or by the principle that positive laws are to be
interpreted in accordance with the mind of the legislator[29]. If
principles such as these suffice, it would be superfluous and
otiose to have recourse to those which are remote.

3. These systems should not be regarded as if they were
substitutes for the virtue of prudence, whose function it is to
guide us in the application of laws to particular situations and
which is of such crucial importance in Aristotelico-Thomistic
ethics (nn. 192, 272). On the contrary, the systems are proposed as instruments which will help us to exercise this virtue
more effectively.

4. It is of particular importance that the present question should not be dissociated from the rest of a person's moral
life. The person whose sole concern is whether he is *bound* to
act in this or that particular way, and who is completely deaf to
the liberating appeal of what is *better*, stands revealed as a
moral light-weight. Attention has also to be paid to the
motives or subjective influences by which the moral agent is
drawn to perform (or to omit) an action, about whose liceity
(or obligatory character) he remains doubtful.

5. Finally, we should avoid setting up an opposition
between "law" and "liberty" as if to be free meant the same as
to be exempt from all rule and control. This fiction had better
remain the exclusive copyright of the Existentialists. Far from
being a restriction on our liberty, the natural moral law expresses the conditions which have to be fulfilled, if our liberty
is to flower and to expand, happily and harmoniously. It is for
this reason that knowledge of the moral law, the knowledge of
what it requires of us here and now in this concrete situation, is
a pearl of great price for a free being; he would impede the
growth of his liberty, if he tried to "protect" himself from this
knowledge.

260. – We shall centre our present discussion around the
theory of probabilism, since it is in relation to this that the

---

[29] On reflex principles, see J. Fuchs, *op. laud.*, pp. 197-200, on whom we are
here dependent.

other systems chiefly define themselves, just as it is in opposition to it that they are proposed.

It has already been noted that the basic principle of probabilism is: "a doubtful law does not oblige", or, as expressed in less juridical terms: "a doubtful obligation is no obligation". This principle, it is sometimes maintained, is to be found in St Thomas. He does, it is true, say that a person cannot be bound by a command unless he has knowledge of it [30]. But, as we have seen, St Thomas never dealt with the problem we are here considering; as well, in the text adduced, "knowledge" is simply opposed to "ignorance": now, it cannot be said purely and simply that a person who is doubtful is in a state of ignorance. (For St Thomas' attitude to the problem of the doubtful conscience, see n. 254).

But whatever about St Thomas' opinion, the principle in question is open to several objections, particularly when it is applied to the natural law. (It is worth noting the rather striking fact that the majority of the examples used by probabilist authors have to do with positive obligations, principally ecclesiastical: fasting, abstinence, attendance at Mass ...). Is it not contrary to right reason to expose ourselves to a violation of the objective order which it requires us to observe?

Undoubtedly, if the moral law depended entirely on an arbitrary decree of God, so that its requirements simply presented us with an occasion for paying homage to the Creator's authority, one could admit that a person had fulfilled his obligations once he had done his best to discover the divine will, and that God demanded nothing more of him. In the measure, on the contrary, in which this law has its foundation in the nature of reality, and to the extent to which a moral value is immanent in the objective structure of an action, the demand that a person should not rashly expose himself to the danger of violating the objective order, becomes, it would seem, all the more pressing. The difficulty, however, with a number of the presentations of probabilism is that they seem to be linked to a purely voluntarist conception of law.

It is quite true, of course, that a doubtful law, precisely because it is doubtful, cannot oblige. If it is not clear that this

---

[30] *De Veritate*, 17, 3.

way of acting is immoral, I am certainly not bound by the possible crystallization of the moral law which would forbid me so to act. Nevertheless, all my decisions should be made in accordance with the virtue of prudence which requires us, with an insistance that is proportionate to the seriousness of the evil that may be involved, to avoid the risk of an objective disorder: and this requirement is not doubtful. Hence, to be too ready to resign oneself to such a disorder is the mark of a will that is badly disposed (n. 247).

261. – On the other hand, to make an absolute rule of: "when in doubt, dont't do it", or: "follow the morally less safe course, only when it is more probable", would be far from prudent. Such a rule would not only be a barrier, at times, to the performance of actions of high moral value (n. 253), but would also be an unwarranted limitation on our freedom of choice. While it is true that an authentic law, expressing as it does requirements that are genuinely rational, fosters our growth in liberty, a pseudo-obligation, which is born of ignorance, can only stunt this growth. In this context, one can undoubtedly speak about the "rights of liberty", rights which need to be safeguarded, not against the law, but against its counterfeit. Finally, the soundness and trustworthiness of our moral judgment, which we are certainly not entitled to forgo, would be endangered, if we were too ready to impose on ourselves duties or prohibitions whose foundation had not been established. Consequently, we would be imprudent and blameworthy, if we were to agree in principle to regard what only resembles a law, as if it really were a law [31].

262. – It is clear then that we have to avoid not only the danger of an objective disorder, but also that of assuming obligations gratuitously. This twofold aim will be achieved, if we act on the principle that we are entitled to perform an action, whose objective value remains doubtful, when we have

---

[31] Obviously, we are not saying that someone who does what he is not strictly obliged to do, is imprudent. But the person whose interior disposition leads him to perform, through fear of evil, actions which should be done out of a free love of the good, is undoubtedly imprudent: his attitude is injurious to his moral development.

reasons for so acting which are proportionate both to the gravity of the disorder which we fear may be involved, and to the risk we are running of bringing this about. The evil of the possible disorder will be compensated for by the good from which these reasons derive their force.

It is, of course, obvious that if the same aberrancy were involved in accepting *the risk of a disorder*, as is involved in directly accepting *the disorder itself*, it would never be possible for us to have the proportionate reasons which we require. But, in fact, the two situations are very different. As we have seen (n. 229), it is obviously contradictory to claim that one can preserve moral uprightness while choosing to perform an action whose objective disorder one clearly acknowledges. But no such contradiction is involved in wanting to preserve this rectitude, and at the same time choosing to perform an action whose objective value is doubtful. For, in this instance, it is as (probably) in harmony with right reason that a person chooses this course of action; he would shun it if it were revealed as opposed to reason. Since then, under the aspect which he envisages the action, no opposition is manifested between its objective structure, and what fidelity to right reason requires, his choice does not close his will to the Ideal of reason. Even supposing that this opposition actually exists, it remains extrinsic to his will, and does not taint it, since he has not chosen the action under this disordered aspect [32].

In brief: unless a subject is completely unconcerned about fulfilling the requirements of the objective order, his acceptance of the danger of violating this order does not merit the same moral judgment, as would his direct acceptance of a violation. It is for this reason that the moral necessity to avoid the danger is less imperious than is the necessity to avoid a violation which is clearly recognized as such [33].

Our reflections up to this point have led us towards the solution which the supporters of the "system of compensation"

---

[32] A person sins by acting in a state of doubt, not only because he exposes himself to the danger of violating the objective order, but much more because, through not distinguishing between the morality of the action and that of its performance, he exposes himself to the danger of *acting immorally*; consequently, he accepts the possibility that he is being unfaithful to the Value; and to accept that possibility is already to be unfaithful.

[33] See what has been said in n. 230 concerning the principle of the "double effect". If it is sometimes permitted, for just motives, to accept the *reality* of an evil effect, with all the more reason will it be permitted — always for proportionate motives — to accept the simple *probability* of an objective disorder.

have proposed. Is this the definitive solution? Has everything been said that needs to be said? No; for a further question which is of great practical consequence immediately presents itself: how will we know whether our reasons are proportionate to the danger of an objective disorder?

263. – Here again the need for a prudent appraisal is obvious. If, whenever he is doubtful, the subject may act only after making a careful examination of the pros and cons, weighing them against one another in order to discover the extent to which the reasons in favour of the morally less safe course genuinely compensate for the danger of an objective disorder, then, most often, he would remain petrified with doubt; decisiveness and promptness would be stifled, so that the moral law, in place of guiding and fostering his liberty, would only paralyse it. A further danger would be that, once again (n. 253), a person would be much inclined to break free of these shackles by deliberately violating the so-called rule.

It is for these reasons that prudence itself dictates this line of conduct: whenever there does not appear to be a *manifest disproportion* (one which "leaps to the eyes") between the good that one hopes to achieve, and the danger of an objective disorder, a person is entitled to perform an action whose objective moral value is in itself doubtful. This norm, obviously, should be understood against the background provided by the conditions enumerated in n. 259.

The disproportion we are here speaking of should be estimated not solely in function of the probability of an objective disorder, but also in function of its gravity.

Note that "probability" in this context does not mean the same as the "probability" that a particular event will occur etc. A view is probable when it is such that a "prudent man" can approve of it, that is, can be of the opinion that it is true; consequently, he holds it only with reserve, since the fear that he might well be wrong remains with him. Now, undoubtedly, I cannot be of the opinion that a particular view is the true one, and at the same time judge that it is "less probable": on this point the "probabiliorists" and the "equiprobabilists" are correct. Nevertheless, I can be inclined towards a particular view, while still being perfectly well aware that another person, who is no less prudent, no less sincere, no less desirous to act morally, could be of a different opinion. The very fact however that both of us have no more than "opinions" is a sufficient indication that our judgments have not a purely rational source. The judgment which is genuinely rational simply expresses: this is true or this is false. Extra-rational, subjective, contingent factors are operative in the formation of an opinion; their influence and their relative character can become clear to the subject if he reflects on himself[34].

What has just been said is relevant when what is in question is intrinsic probability. *Extrinsic* probability is established along the lines of the argument that "if something is, we can validly conclude to its possibility": even though the intrinsic probability of some opinion may not be apparent to *us*, once it has manifested itself to those on whose authority we rely, the opinion becomes, where we are concerned, extrinsically probable; its probability is known to us extrinsically. Consequently, this kind of probability disappears once it becomes clear that the authors — no matter what their authority is — who defend a particular opinion have done so simply because they believed it to be the view of some renowned authority, who did not, in fact, lend his support to it; such probability likewise disappears when their reasons are subsequently revealed to be weak and unconvincing[35].

264. – There is, however, another important clarification which needs to be made. It centres on the fact that all our morally good actions are not good in one uniform manner, just as all our evil actions are not evil in one uniform manner. There are, on the contrary, two categories into which our actions fall. Certain of them are of a more subjective character; their moral value consists principally in the accord between their meaning (their objective orientation and teleology) and the orientation of a will and a reason that are upright: these actions possess a value primarily because they are the expression of an inner rectitude of mind and will. Inversely, the negative value of actions of this category will consist almost entirely in the contrast between their objective orientation and the orientation of a will and reason that are upright: such actions are the expressions of the subject's own moral disorder.

---

[34] See P. Rousselot, *Quaestiones de conscientia* (written around 1912), Paris, 1937, pp. 50 seq., especially 76-77.

[35] There is an example of this in E. Hamel, *L'erreur sur la personne dans la damnification*, "Sciences Ecclésiastiques", 1956, pp. 335-384.

There are other actions, on the contrary, which have an *additional* relationship with some objective good, a relationship which is in no way dependent on our inner rectitude. They have a value not solely because their orientation is in conformity with the orientation of reason (so that in performing them a person's will remains open to the Ideal) but also because they are objectively directed towards the realization or attainment of this good. Such actions are those in which the interests of other people are at stake, as they are when the question of their right in justice to what belongs to them, arises (nn. 197, 268). Other actions which belong to this category are those which are concerned with the good of the subject himself, insofar as the good of which there is question is one which he has not the right to reject (his life, his faith in God etc.).

It becomes immediately obvious that our solution cannot be applied in the same way to the two types of action and that it is only to the first type that what has been said in n. 262 is fully applicable. We can choose to perform *these* actions without ceasing to be men of good will, since their objective orientation appears to us to be probably in conformity with the moral norm. The reason why we have to steer clear of an objective disorder is that if we freely accept it, the goodness of our wills would be vitiated; but in situations of the kind that are here envisaged, we do not accept the disorder that may be involved in our choice: it is as probably in accordance with right reason, and not as necessarily opposed to it, that we choose this course of action. Consequently, where actions of the first type are concerned, it is not contrary to right reason to run the risk of an objective violation, provided we have reasons for so doing.

In practice, these "good reasons" will almost always be present. Obvious examples are: the need, which has already been stressed, to avoid imposing intolerable and crippling restrictions on freedom of choice; the fact that the end at which a person is aiming is morally good and praiseworthy; the harm that can result, particularly where those of delicate conscience are concerned, from the creation of pseudo-obligations. In short, the person who is ordinarily guided by reason in his choices, whose motivations are habitually right, need not, in general, concern himself about the necessity to avoid an objective disorder which is simply probable (provided, of course, that the action in question belongs to the first category).

Our reflections have led us to conclusions which, in the main, are the same as those of the probabilists, even though the path by which we have travelled has been rather different. Nevertheless, we hold back from adopting their conclusions unreservedly. Will the "good reasons" indicated above *always* be sufficient? Would our freedom of choice be intolerably cramped, the danger from imaginary obligations so menacing, if prudence required us to refrain from performing a particular action, when the good we hope to achieve is small and the danger of an objective disorder is serious? Once more, it is clear that the systems and reflex principles should be at the service of the virtue of prudence; they are not intended to replace it. In particular, their role is not to absolve a person from responsibility for the choices he makes.

Where actions belonging to the second category are concerned, particularly those in which we are bound to make every effort to achieve some good result, it is clear that another line of approach is required. A person cannot act in an upright manner, if he is willing to imperil interests — be they those of others or of himself — which he ought to respect, and which the inner rectitude of his will is, of itself, quite incapable of safeguarding. Consequently, in such situations, probabilism is not applicable.

A further and more profound study of this thorny question is the prerogative of moral theology.

Conscience, in fact, seems to be guided fairly spontaneously by the principles of probabilism. How often do those of delicate conscience imagine that they have acted in a state of doubt, and have, in consequence, done evil, when all they have really done is to apply, confusedly, the principles just proposed. (On confused judgments of this kind, cf. n. 252).

265. – The situation in which a person hesitates between two apparent obligations presents no particular difficulty. On the one hand, there can never be a true conflict of duties, no more than there can be a genuine clash of rights (n. 204, 2): one of the duties is either a false creation (to avenge the death of one's father, to defend one's honour by engaging in a duel etc.) or else it loses its force, in the concrete situation, in the face of a duty that is more pressing, more fundamental. On the other hand, since, by hypothesis, it is not possible for the subject to recognize where his authentic duty lies, the situation he is in is reducible to that of a person whose conscience is doubtful. He remains free then to follow whichever of the two courses he prefers, or not to follow either of them.

266. – N.B. There is an important distinction between the judgment by which a person decides whether he is morally justified in performing a certain action, and the judgment by which he decides whether it is expedient that he should so act. I may, for example, judge that I am perfectly entitled to go to a particular film or play, and still judge it preferable, for other reasons. not to do so: because I could spend the time to greater advantage, because I feel drawn to a life of greater prayerfulness or renunciation etc. Consequently, there is no point in saying, as it is sometimes said concerning probabilism, that in practice it is generally more praiseworthy not to make use of this system. No: if probabilism is true, and in the measure in which it is true, use should be made of it, but in accordance with the purpose which it is designed to achieve: the formation of a person's moral judgment concerning the liceity of his performance of a particular action. The formation of the other judgment calls for the exercise of the virtue of prudence, but does not bring the principles of probabilism into play. The moral relevance of this system is precisely to ensure that the more worthy action be performed out of love for what is good rather than out of fear of what is evil.

267. – From all that has been said in the present chapter the capital importance, especially for young people, of a careful formation of conscience, emerges clearly. This formation is achieved in two ways, both of which are indispensable: by way of instruction (moral guidance, enlightenment concerning general principles and specific requirements) and by way of practice. Speculative knowledge is of little avail unless it is accompanied by an assiduous effort to put theory into practice. On the contrary, the person who strives to lead a good life, so that virtue gains an entry into his heart, becomes more and more capable of discerning the most refined requirements of a virtuous and authentically human life: he acquires that connatural knowledge of which St Thomas, in a wellknown text, writes. There are two ways, he notes, in which a person's moral judgment can be right. One way is the result of his correct use of his power of reason, while the other is due to the "connaturality" (the affinity) that exists between him and the object of his judgment. Hence, where chastity is concerned, the person who is well versed in the science of ethics will judge correctly through examining the point in question rationally, whereas the person who has acquired the habit of chastity will judge correctly through the "connaturality" that exists between him and this virtue [26].

---

[36] *Summa Theol.*, II-II, 45, 2.

CHAPTER THIRTEEN

MORAL LIFE AND GROWTH

268. – A person's moral life does not consist in a succession of single and discontinuous actions in which, by means of a constantly renewed effort, he seeks to regulate his natural tendencies in accordance with reason. He needs to create habits which will permanently bring these inclinations under the influence and control of reason, and will ensure his unwavering fidelity to the Value in his decisions. Habits of this kind are called *moral virtues*.

The Scholastics considered a virtue, in a general sense, to be a certain perfection with which some capacity or power is endowed[1]. They defined it as an operative habit by means of which the capacity in question (whose activity is to some extent indetermined) is helped to grow towards its perfection. It is this last characteristic which distinguishes virtues from habits in general, which do not necessarily help towards growth in the appropriate perfection (sickness, vice). In this sense, an *art* (in the old sense, which was closer to that of an artisan's technique) was considered by the Scholastics to be a "virtue"; they also spoke, as did Aristotle before them (n. 64), of "intellectual virtues". Theologians distinguish between *infused* virtues, which are supernaturally conferred by God, and those which are *acquired* by the repetition of virtuous actions. Obviously, it is only with these latter virtues that we are concerned in this philosophical investigation.

In a more restricted and, nowadays, much more usual sense, the term "virtue" applied to those habits which help to channel the activity of a person's will (and of his other capacities insofar as they are under the control of his will) towards its true good, which is also the true good of the rational subject as such. Virtue in this sense is, accordingly, synonymous with *moral virtue*.

---

[1] St Thomas, *Summa Theol.*, I-II, 55, 1; *Virt. in comm.*, 1.

The definition of a virtue given by Aristotle is justly famous: it is, he writes, "a state of character concerned with choice, lying in a mean, i.e., the mean relative to us, this being determined by a rational principle, and by that principle by which the man of practical wisdom would determine it" [2].

In this definition there are five points which need to be noted:

a) A virtue is a state of character concerned with choice: it not only, in common with all habits, inclines a person to *act* in a certain manner but also, since he is capable of self-determination, inclines him to *choose* well.

b) This habit lies "in a mean". This mean is the most characteristic, and certainly the most acclaimed, element in the Aristotelian definition. Virtue steers clear both of excess and defect but is not, however, always equally removed from each extreme: some virtues are nearer to one extreme than they are to the other. Courage is closer to rashness than it is to cowardice. Note also and particularly that the mean is not to be regarded as if it were a neutral point: the virtue which Aristotle has in mind is far removed from a spirit of "prudent pettiness". In point of fact, the mean of neither too much nor too little is rather the objective, material element of a virtue: it is the element which can be empirically verified, measured and described, as in a psychological or sociological investigation. From another point of view and considered in another dimension (which is the genuinely moral and value dimension) a virtue stands at the summit.

c) This mean is "the mean relative to us". What Aristotle wishes to emphasize here is that the objective demands which a virtue makes should be judged in function of the subject; they cannot be defined in an absolute manner and independently of him. Virtue is the good for man, the human good; what it requires is, accordingly, suitable for man. Hence the ideal to be striven for varies between two extremes in such a way that the "just mean" will be the precise point at which what is suitable in relation to this particular subject lies. There is, in consequence, room for a certain flexibility: a diet that would be excessive for a shrimp of a person would be insufficient for a burly athlete.

d) Nevertheless, this mean should be determined by the exercise of reason (or, as some commentators on Aristotle prefer to say, "in accordance with the norm"): we do not arrive at the mean if

---

[2] *Nicom. Eth.*, II, 6, 1106 b 36 (in the trans. of W. D. Ross). — In place of 'by a rational principle", R. Gauthier and Y. Jolif would translate: according to the rule". (*Ethique à Nicomaque. Commentaire*, Louvain-Paris, 1959, pp. 147-148: Justification of this translation).

we are arbitrarily led by our instincts, our passions, our irrational desires and inclinations. Subjectivism is ruled out: what is right in relation to this particular subject can be established only on rational grounds.

e) Finally, the mean has to be determined in the way that the man of practical wisdom would determine it. The "prudent man" plays an important part in Aristotelian ethics and in Scholastic morality in general. The reason for this is that it is not always possible where moral questions are concerned to give a rigorous proof. This deficiency in our powers of reasoning has to be supplied for, through recourse to the counsel of those who are learned in moral matters, those who are experts in this field, who have had much experience and are recognized authorities. In them, also, it is to the voice of reason that we listen, but to reason as concretized and incarnated in some way in their lives, and speaking to us through their reactions and spontaneous judgments (cf. the Thomistic doctrine of connatural knowledge, n. 267).

The Scholastics have adopted Aristotle's definition but have refused to apply it, just as it stands, to the theological virtues: could a person ever have too close a union with God, too great a desire for Him? Could we ever have too much confidence in God, too much love for Him? To the extent that the notion of the just mean is applicable in this context, it is so only in a quite accidental fashion, in relation to something other than the object of these virtues: in this sense, faith, for example, can be said to be a mean between two heresies[3]. — Where the moral virtues are concerned, the Scholastics, St Thomas in particular, distinguished between two different categories. In one category they placed virtues whose mean is determined simply by exercise of reason but not, however, independently of the individual subject ("the mean relative to us" of the Aristotelian definition); in the other category they placed virtues such as justice, where the mean cannot be determined in isolation from the thing to which another has a right: the mean that is here involved is also "objective" (concerned with the object that is due in justice to the other). Justice, St Thomas notes, differs from the other moral virtues in that it is concerned with what is exterior to us: the rectitude which it aims at ensuring is that we respect the rights of others. The other moral virtues, on the contrary, are concerned with our own passions, where what is right and wrong cannot be the same for all since, in this domain, individual differences can be great; consequently what is here required of us, in order that we act

---

[3] St Thomas, *Summa Theol.*, I-II, 64, 4; *Virt.*, 13.

virtuously, has to be defined in relation to ourselves [4]. — In speaking in this way, St Thomas obviously does not intend to advocate moral relativism, since in this "mean relative to us" is included a relation to the unchangeable human nature that is common to all men (n. 185); moreover, as we have seen, there is a certain juridical aspect to all our moral activity (n. 219, end).

269. — When a person has acquired a particular virtue the effect on him is to ensure that his performance of the appropriate actions is prompt, unhesitating, even joyous, and sufficiently regular. As with habits in general, virtue introduces a unity into a human being's existence. It represents a victory over inconstancy and fickleness. Beings which are at a lower level than man possess a natural constancy in their activity. As a spiritual subject who, nonetheless, exists in time, man trascends the determinations to which they are subject but does not possess the uniformity by which their activity is marked. Because of his liberty, there is at work within him a principle of change that is not found in these other beings: this principle serves to dissociate his present from his past, his future from his present. Spiritual, he is not naturally determined as are infra-spiritual beings; temporal, his choices are not irrevocable. But it is within his power to confer on himself, by the creation of virtuous habits, a dynamic disposition that is relatively

---

[4] *Ib.*, 64, 2. — The Scholastics based this doctrine on a text of Aristotle: "justice is a kind of mean, but not in thr same way as the other virtues, but because it relates to an intermediate amount", *Nicom. Eth.*, V, 5, 1133 b 32-33 (in the trans. of W. D. Ross). They understood this "mean" (that is proper to the virtue of justice) to be an objective one, as distinct from the mean relative to ourselves, of which the Philosopher speaks in another place, *ib.*, II, 6, 1106 a 29 seq.

This interpretation is contested by many today (see Gauthier-Jolif, *op. cit.*, pp. 406-408). The meaning of Aristotle's remark, as is clear from the words that immediately follow: "while injustice relates to the extremes", seems to be that justice, as distinct from the other virtues, does not lie between two opposed vices, but has one opposite in which the extremes meet. To oblige the purchaser to pay more than he should, is as unjust as obliging the seller to accept a price lower than the one to which he has a right. One offends as much against distributive justice by granting a particular individual either more than, or less than, his rightful share etc. — Moreover, Aristotle does not at all wish to reduce the role of the other virtues to that of keeping the passions under control, while reserving to justice the role of rectifying exterior relationships.

stable and which, without necessitating him to choose what is
good, will strongly incline him to do so and will help him to
be unswervingly true to the requirements of moral living.
Since such a disposition is the product of reason, the inclinations to which it gives rise are rational ones, so that as a result
of their influence, a person's entire existence comes to be
gradually penetrated by reason and he becomes more spiri-
tualized, more genuinely human.

But even though virtues do not take away a person's
liberty (since they do not necessitate his choice of what is
good), do they not diminish it, and diminish, in consequence,
the moral value and merit of his actions? It is not a sufficient
reply to this difficulty to say that these virtues were acquired
voluntarily and freely. The fact remains, it would seem, that
once they have been acquired, they render a person's actions
less human. Would not the fully virtuous man, such as he is
depicted by Aristotle, be one for whom morally good actions
would no longer pose a problem, one who would react
virtuously in a quasi-automatic fashion, without deliberating
on the matter or debating whether he will or will not so act,
one who could be described as a moral robot? But would such
a person still deserve to be called human?

A first stage in dealing with this problem is to note that
the moral value and merit of an action are not essentially
measured by the inner difficulties and repugnances which a
person experiences in performing it. These repugnances are
rather a sign that the person's existence is still imperfectly
unified, that he is not tending towards what is good "with all
his soul". Now, all other things being equal, a person's action
will have greater moral value, the more unified, and the more
centred on the Value, is the person from whom it proceeds.
The person who is torn by his passions can undoubtedly have a
certain degree of good will, but that will is not yet fully in
command of itself; it is far from having attained the perfection
that is proper to it, since it has not yet succeeded in controlling
and unifying these other tendencies and appetites. It is the will
which expresses the dynamism of the subject, and just as he
cannot concentrate properly, nor think clearly and coherently,
when his mind is distracted ("drawn out of itself") by flitting
images, so also is the activity of his will impaired when it is

drawn hither and thither by tendencies that are as yet unruly and uncontrolled. We have always to be on our guard against the "angelism" which regards mental hygiene and emotional development as of little consequence from the moral point of view; in saying this we do not, of course, wish to deny that God can, if He so pleases, compensate for deficiencies of this kind (cf. n. 276).

Where people who have made considerable progress in virtue are concerned and who are very much aware of the distinction between the inner citadel of their wills and the zones which are more peripheral — a stage which a person has to reach if his attitude to what is on the sense level is to be transformed and illumined — psychic disorder can remain exterior and need not detract from the vigour of their wills: indeed it can stimulate them to make even greater progress in virtue. But where people who have not discerned their true selves (as St Augustine would express it) are concerned, psychic disorder will always have some repercussions on the moral level.

Finally, we should not confuse the difficulty in acting well which springs from the disunity within the person, with the objective difficulty which has its source in the high demands that a particular course of action makes. (It was this latter difficulty that the Scholastics had in mind when they spoke of the moral good as "arduous"). These demands will increase the moral value of a person's action in the measure in which this value is dependent on the value of the object in question; the fact that the person overcome the difficulties involved is also an indication of how strongly his will is tending towards what is good. It is *possible* to have much love for one's neighbour in doing him small services, but it is *necessary* to have much love for him in order to sacrifice one's comfort, one's health, one's life, for his sake.

270. – A second stage in dealing with this problem is to distinguish between the two elements that are present in virtue, one of which can be called material and the other formal. The first element is nothing other than what is often referred to as a "good habit": a happy and stable condition of the "powers" that the will is called upon to govern and by means of which a person is helped to do what is morally good. As a consequence of this disposition, which permeates the organic stratum of his being, a person develops not only an ease in performing certain actions but a tendency to repeat them; this tendency can at times become an imperious need. When the habits in question are the negative ones by which a person's appetites and passions etc., are bridled, all that has been said is obviously no less applicable. An example of such a "good habit" is the temperate man's practice of eating and drinking in a frugal manner: this habit can become a demand, so that the person may feel unwell, if, on occasion, he has to eat more heartily, or if the food is richer than that to which he is accustomed. This disposition however is not, of itself, a virtue; indeed, in certain circumstances, it could even be a barrier to a greater good (for there can be circumstances in which a person needs to be capable of responding to the lowliest values). But, ordinarily, such a habit will help a person in his practice of virtue. Nevertheless, tjhe ease with which a person performs certain actions because he possesses this habit, and even the joy which he feels in so acting, remain outside the moral order. — The second element which is present in a virtue is the uprightness of will, by means of which a person utilises the "good habit" so as to ensure that the exercise of the "power" in question will be in accordance with reason. This habitual uprightness of his will should not be conceived of as an extrinsic factor which places a limit on his freedom: on the contrary, this rectitude ensures that his will becomes more itself, by ensuring its fidelity to its own norm: the person whose will is disposed in this way is greatly helped to determine himself in accordance with motives that are homogeneous with the will itself (rational motives), rather than in accordance with those which are extraneous to it (n. 139). Indeed, the pleasure which is attached to the virtuous action as such springs primarily from the awareness which a person has of this inner liberty, of his fidelity to the Value [5].

---

[5] It would be more strictly in accordance with the mind of St Thomas to say that what the formal element of a virtue refers to is a certain participation, by the power of which the virtue is the habit, in the will's uprightness. For, in his view, the moral virtues, except for justice, do not reside in the will, but in the practical intellect (prudence), or in the "concupiscent" sense appetite (temperance), or finally in the "irascible" sense appetite (courage), to the extent that these powers are controllable by the will. The reason for this is that while the will has no need of a special habit in order that the subject should tend towards his own good, it does not so naturally incline him to respect the interests of

Moreover, for Aristotle and the Scholastics, the notion of habit means much more than a mere disposition, or even a tendency, to perform repeated actions of the same type. The very word helps to make this clear: it is linked with the Latin *se habere* (to be, to be in this or that condition) rather than with *habere* (to have), just as the Greek word for habit (*hexis*) is linked with the word *echein* which, when used with the adverb, has the same meaning as *se habere*. It is clear, then, that they are speaking not so much about something which the subject *has* as about what he *is*, about the way in which his presence to himself (his subjectivity) is structured. A habit affects a person interiorly (in mind and will) and is not merely concerned with fostering the repetition of certain actions. Its role is not confined to introducing a continuity into our free activity; it has a further and more important part to play, namely, to make our actions more fully our own, to make them a truer expression of ourselves both as *human* and as *uniquely* human. The effect of a habit is not to link our actions together from the outside: it permeates them and brings them to their perfection. An action which is performed under the influence of a genuinely spiritual, that is, fully human, habit is better, and is better performed, not only because the person is acting more readily, more joyfully, more effectively etc., but also and principally because he is more perfectly centred on the end on which the moral value of his actions chiefly depends (and in relation to which, as we have seen, each person is called upon to make his fundamental moral option, n. 228). As well, some habits are at a more profound level of our being than others; when these have gained sufficient strength, they "colour" our entire human activity and constitute a horizon which is present to us in all our choices [6]. Since the fundamentally good orienta-

---

others ... Whatever about this point, which could be further discussed, it seems to us that what virtue, understood in its full sense, primarily refers to is the right disposition of a person's will. A twofold formal principle can accordingly be distinguished: one in the will, the other in the power which receives, through the will, the guidance of reason. We prefer not to employ here the words extrinsic and intrinsic, since, in view of the unity of the subject, it is only in a very imperfect fashion that the will can be called extrinsic in relation to the other powers.

[6] Cf. D. von Hildebrand, *Christian Ethics*, pp. 241-243.

tion of a person's will is the well-spring and animating principle of all the virtues, it ensures that he will normally take all his decisions within the ambit of his global project to lead a moral life, and that he will not exceed these bounds without an inner struggle and a certain turmoil (n. 238).

The distinction that has already been made between the two ways of considering a human act reappears here to some extent (nn. 224; 228). If we are more concerned with the objective aspect of human acts, and if our mentality is rather juridical, then we shall pay more attention to the isolated, individual action, and shall not take great account of the intimate dispositions of the moral agent. In this context, a person's moral value will be measured by the conformity of his actions with the law, with the "commandments". If, on the contrary, we are more concerned with the inner and profound springs of human acts, we shall lay much greater stress on these dispositions; "virtues" will have a priority over "actions" in our attitude to ethics.

Both of these attitudes are legitimate and necessary. At an earlier stage of our investigation, we stressed that to acknowledge the primacy of the end, where a person's moral value is concerned, does not at all mean that the importance of the object is diminished. Similarly, at present, in saying that a person's moral value depends primarily on his habits, we in no way wish to maintain that his actions are of small importance, and that he ought to be judged solely in relation to his habitual dispositions. The purpose of a habit is to enable a person to act; it is useless if it does not have this result.

To what extent should the knowledge of habitual dispositions (tendencies, virtues or vices) influence the moral appraisal of a person's action? If, for example, a person who is habitually virtuous acts immorally, is he deserving of more blame, all other things being equal, than an evil-living person would be, on the grounds that his action is at odds with the fundamental orientation of his life, which has thereby been disrupted? Or should it be said, on the contrary, that his fault is less serious, on the grounds that it affects him only peripherally, rather than at the centre of his being?

In our view, a simple reply is not possible. Several situations and several points of view need to be distinguished.

1. From the point of view of an external observer (and of the subject inasmuch as he observes himself), the second interpretation

has a prejudice in its favour. An isolated evil action in a life which is ordinarily virtuous is, in general, no more than a surface wound; very often the person's fault is more apparent than real. His habitual dispositions make it probable that he has not deliberately deviated from the path of virtue and that his fault has not affected him at the core of his being.

2. Two actions, both of which are to all appearances equally superficial, will have a very different moral significance and value if one of them corresponds to the subject's habitual dispositions, whereas the other forms an exception so that it is accidental in relation to these dispositions. The first action, since it stirs up no reaction, no distress, in the subject, and is indeed often scarcely noticed by him and quickly forgotten, both expresses and confirms his evil dispositions, or at least the negligent attitude towards moral value which he has allowed himself to adopt. The particular action forms part of a greater whole from which it derives its full meaning. The superficial and uncharacteristic action, on the contrary — a momentary failure on the part of a person who is ordinarily upright, or, where a person of the opposite calibre is concerned, an ephemeral response to the attraction of the good — has, from the moral point of view, little or no significance unless it inaugurates a process of decline or of growth. It does not really express the subject; it is, in fact, and not only in appearance, peripheral, even though the person himself may be persuaded to the contrary, confusing, as is often done, the surge of his emotions with the depths of his will, or his apparent with his true will. (A person is not always as good or as evil as he believes himself to be, or as he believes that he desires to be, n. 251).

3. To the extent, however, to which a person seriously deliberates, is genuinely in possession of himself and makes a fully resolute decision, preference has to be given to the first interpretation. An uncharacteristic action performed in these circumstances testifies, whether for better or for worse, to a decision that affects him at the centre of his being, to a choice which gives a new direction to his life. The deeper the opposition between the particular action and the prior orientation of the person's life, the more profound, the more radical will be the effect on the person.

It is clear, then, that there are two ways in which he commits himself as a person by his actions: through identifying himself more and more with his habitual dispositions, or, on the contrary, through opposing these by means of a profound choice which alters his existing adhesion to certain values and goals.

271. – But even the material element of a virtue helps a person to grow in the inner liberty of which we have spoken, since he is thereby absolved of the necessity to occupy himself with decisions which are of no real consequence and which could otherwise overwhelm and stifle him. Think for a moment of what a plight we would be in, if we had not acquired the ability to walk, so that we had to pay attention to every step we took, reflect upon it, calculate, and choose! Or, if we had not accustomed ourselves to eating and drinking in moderation, what heroic combats we should face whenever we sat down to a meal! Our decisions would then, it is true, be more deliberate, more fully our own, but most of our life would be spent in making them, so that we would have neither time nor energy to devote ourselves to the pursuit of higher values. Thanks, however, to "good habits" of this kind, a person is enabled to use his liberty to better purpose and to discover values to which he would otherwise be closed. There is a certain parallel between him and the pianist who, once he has acquired the habit of striking the right chord automatically, is then free to concentrate entirely on expression; or between him and the scholar who, since he does not have to occupy himself with matters of organization done by the computer, can dedicate himself to the true work of a thinker: making discoveries, raising problems, exploring new avenues of approach.

It is then by acquiring virtues that we come to adhere more and more to what is good, so that the probability of our choosing what is evil diminishes accordingly. Far from destroying our liberty, this steadfastness perfects it; or rather, by the correct use of our free will we advance gradually on the path that leads to true liberty.

272. – As with our various powers, our actions, and operative habits in general, one virtue is distinguished from another by the object which is proper to it. What marks a particular virtue off from others is the inclination it imparts to the subject to act in accordance with right reason in one particular area of his life.

This at least is the position of the Scholastics. As we have seen (n. 223), certain philosophers recognize only one virtue: Stoics such as Zeno and Cleanthes, Kant etc. Other Stoics, in particular Chrysippus, admit that there is more than one virtue, but insist that they are all strictly connected (n. 273).

From the time of Plato[7] it has been customary to distinguish four *cardinal* virtues: prudence, justice, fortitude and temperance. They are called *cardinal* because it is on them that a person's entire moral life "hinges" (the Latin word *cardo* means "hinge"); another and perhaps better way of expressing their role would be to say that they are the axis around which his moral life revolves. St Thomas treats of them, and of their various subdivisions, right through the *Secunda Secundae*[8]. In his view, the virtue which is of primary importance is prudence, since it is this which ensures that our choices will be habitually upright. It is at one and the same time an intellectual and a moral virtue; it perfects our intellects directly, it is true, but only in order that we may choose well: in other words, it is a perfection of our intellects in their practical function. As well, this virtue can be acquired only on condition that a person is

---

[7] Plato, *Republic*, IV, 427 E; *Laws*, XII, 964 B - 965 D — Aristotle also treats of these virtues (*Nicom. Eth.*, VI, 5 seq.) but without distinguishing them from others as a particularly notable "quaternary".

[8] For each virtue, St Thomas distinguishes *integral, subjective* and *potential* parts. The first are necessary in order that the act of the virtue in question be perfect: where prudence, for example, is concerned, these will be: the memory or knowledge of the past; intelligence, in the sense of understanding the present; docility, or the ability to learn from others; the art of sure inventiveness (*eustochia*), in particular of arriving quickly at the middle term (*solertia*); reasoning, or facility in making correct deductions; "providence", which prescribes what is useful in view of the end aimed at; circumspection, by which account is taken of the circumstances; an awareness of the obstacles (*cautio*), so that they may be avoided. — The second are related to the virtue of which is question, as species to genus: so, again with prudence as the example, there will be the prudence which regulates the conduct of the individual and that which regulates the government of the multitude, which, in its turn, is subdivided into economic (familial), military and political prudence. — The potential parts, finally, are adjoined virtues; they are concerned with certain secondary activities or objects, and do not have all the power of the principal virtue. Examples are: the art of deliberating well (*eubulia*), *synesis* or right judgment concerning what happens in accordance with the common laws, and *gnome* or the spirit of finesse, by which a person judges accurately of the occasions when it is necessary to deviate from the law, *Summa Theol.*, II-II, 48, art. un. — It is true that these distinctions are somewhat artificial in places, for St Thomas, as is his custom (cf. the structure of the human action, n. 15), makes every effort to accept, and to synthesize, the traditional elements derived from different sources (here, for example, Aristotle, Cicero, Andronicus, Macrobius). Nevertheless, to disregard them would be an error: they often result in analyses of a rare finesse.

resolved to guide his life in accordance with reason. (Its acquisition is conditioned by the "rightness" of his desires and appetites) [9].

Another and perhaps preferable division of the virtues is that which is made between *general* and *particular* virtues. Those of the first kind are exercised in every morally good action; those of the second kind guide a person's actions in a determined sector of his moral life. Prudence, strength of character, sincerity, disinterestedness etc., are required in varying degrees in all genuinely virtuous activity. Other virtues, on the contrary, such as "magnificence", by which a person spends freely when there is call for it, *eutrapelia*, by which he makes good and healthy use of his times of relaxation, are exercised only on certain occasions; it is perfectly possible for a person to lead a life of very high moral worth even though he lacks one or other of these virtues. A poor person will never be in a position to display "magnificence". — The cardinal virtues have at times been regarded as general virtues [10].

Moral education consists to a considerable extent in fostering the growth of the virtuous dispositions which are required in all morally good activity. It is also worth noting that what chiefly distinguishes the different types of approach to morality is the emphasis they place on one or other of these dispositions [11].

---

[9] See *ib.*, 47-56; also J. E. Naus, *The Nature of the Practical Intellect* ..., pp. 112-140.

[10] This opinion was known to St Thomas but he rejected it, *In II Eth.*, bk. 8; ed. Pirotta, nn. 337-338. He is more sympathetic towards it in *Virt. card.*, 1 ad Ium, and ad 5um (cf. n. 273).

[11] Thus, Buddhism exalts pity, while Christian morality regards charity (*agapē*) as central. Descartes, even though he seems to reduce all the virtues to uprightness of will (n. 223), manifests a predilection for "generosity", by which a person has the highest esteem for his own dignity and strives to act in accordance with its requirements. Malebranche lays great stress on attention or "strength of mind" and "liberty", by which a person suspends his judgment when the evidence is not sufficient. For the positivists and empiricists, subjective morality often seems to consist essentially in altruistic dispositions and habits: sympathy, benevolence etc. — R. Le Senne, who himself principally exalts "courage", provides in his *Traité de morale générale* (especially pp. 105-304) a description of the chief types of morality, centred around historical figures (religious thinkers and geniuses).

273. – Are the various virtues connected and if so, to what extent? The Stoics — when they do not simply deny that there is any distinction of virtues — insist on their strict connection (n. 272). To violate one virtue is to lose all the others: there is no middle position between perfection and vice. — The Scholastics more often than not treat of this problem from a theological point of view: the infused virtues are linked by the virtue of charity. Where the simply human virtues are concerned, the link is made, St Thomas maintains, by the virtue of prudence: without this virtue a person can possess no other moral virtue; reciprocally, he cannot be prudent unless he possesses the other moral virtues[12]. This does not, however, involve a vicious circle, since a person can perform a good action before he possesses the corresponding virtue; by the repetition of such actions he will acquire this virtue, and his practical reason will come to be endowed with the habit of prudence. — But if, St Thomas continues, the four cardinal virtues are regarded as general virtues, then the connection between them is such that all have to be present in order that a person perform morally good actions[13]. They are also connected, we would wish to add, in the sense that a person cannot excel in one without possessing the others in a high degree. On the contrary, where particular virtues are concerned, a person who possesses one virtue in an outstanding degree will not necessarily and immediately possess the others in any great depth. A person who is suddenly promoted from a position of comparative insignificance to one of honour and power will not all at once acquire the virtue of "magnificence", nor the other virtues which his new state requires. Nevertheless, if he is a genuinely virtuous person, he will be able, when the need arises, to respond in a satisfactory manner and without excessive difficulty to the demands that will be made on him.

Note, finally, that one virtue can be preferred to another from two points of view: 1. In itself, objectively: the preference will then generally depend on the way in which one conceives of the essence and norm of moral value. 2. Subjectively and practically: this will depend on individual dispositions.

[12] *Virt. card.*, 2.
[13] *Ib.*

274. – The habits which are opposed to the various virtues are called vices. Here also we can distinguish a material and a formal element. The first is the inclination that is present in us to exceed the mean (or to fall short of it) in certain spheres, so that in consequence, we tend to repeat disordered actions frequently ("a bad habit"). As a result of this repetition, our disordered inclinations are strengthened, and our activity is canalised in a fixed and irrational direction; often these inclinations will become tyrannical, so that they create what are in effect needs which demand to be satisfied; this tyranny can, in certain instances, become so great that it eclipses the influence of reason and takes from a person's action its human character. — The second element is the lack of uprightness in a person's will. Obviously, this element will be affected by the first. Our psychic and physiological states modify our power to appreciate values and sway our judgment in one direction or another, so that all too often we attempt a rational justification of what is irrational and unjustifiable. Nevertheless, there is not always a strict correspondence between the degree of rectitude in a person's will and the degree of his psychic rectitude; the two elements of a virtue neither grow nor diminish at the same rate, and the changes which can occur, where both are concerned, admit of an infinity of degrees. Consequently, there can be any number of intermediate stages between that perfect virtue which establishes in a person the peaceful reign of right reason, and that complete moral degradation in which he surrenders completely to his perverse instincts. So, for example, according to Aristotle, between the *temperate* person who has achieved control of his passions, and the *intemperate* person who yields completely to them, there is, on the one hand, the *continent* person whose will is good but who has not yet brought his passions fully under control and cannot in consequence do what is virtuous in a virtuous way, and on the other hand, the *incontinent* person who, even though he yields to his passions, is still sensitive to the reproaches of reason [14].

Since virtue is the mean between two extremes, we can offend against each of the virtues both by excess and by defect.

---

[14] *Nicom. Eth.*, VII, 1-10. — Cf. St Thomas, *Summa Theol.*, II-II, 155, 4; 156, 3.

Consequently, there are more vices than virtues. Vices are not, however, linked in the way that virtues are: the very fact that excess and defect are contraries ensures that such a connection does not exist, or at least that it is not universal. Avarice is opposed to prodigality, temerity to timidity etc. Since unity and goodness are but two aspects of the same reality, the world of evil cannot be a unified world[15].

275 – A person's moral progress essentially consists in living in such a way that he comes to have an ever deepening love for what is of moral value; he advances by bringing his entire activity into an ever closer conformity with the rule of reason, so that in his choices he comes to express more and more perfectly the "openness" which is his as a spiritual subject, in accordance with the individual, social, historical etc., situation in which he finds himself. — In this context, one could say (developing th wellknown saying of Pindar[16]) that a person is called upon to strive to become, through his free choices and his free activity, what he already is in virtue of his vocation as a spiritual, rational being and in virtue of his own particular ideal (which is nothing other than the Ideal of reason, but as "adapted" to the subject's situation and condition).

There is no question at all here of a "spiritualization" which would ignore or despise man's body and his sense activity. A human being's life is not, and cannot be, that of an

---

[15] Unless one prefers to follow N. Hartmann's interpretation of Aristotle (*Ethik*, 2nd ed., pp. 517 seq.), that the "mean" of a virtue results from the synthesis of two partial virtues, ordinarily unnamed, whose "extremes", in which vice consists, would be their degenerate forms. So, for example authentic courage would include both daring and prudence (in the usual sense of the word), whose degenerate forms would be, respectively, rashness and cowardice. However, Hartmann refuses to apply his theory to the higher moral values: these cannot be the result of a synthesis; a synthesis where they are concerned (for example, of justice and love) becomes an unrealizable demand and necessarily results in conflict. Accordingly, where Hartmann is concerned, the moral universe is not unified.

[16] "Become what you have learned yourself to be", *Pyth.*, 2, 72. The saying is often attributed to Nietzsche; he has in fact used it and made it famous, but he did not coin it. Moreover, what Pindar was speaking of was formation of oneself through knowledge (*mathon*) rather than through moral action.

angel; consequently, he ought not to strive to become what he is not and can never be. The spiritualization which man is called upon to achieve consists in an ordered and harmonious balance between what is corporeal and what is spiritual, so that the former gives expression to the latter, and is at its service.

In addition, even though moral growth involves striving to respond to ever higher and worthier values, it would be disastrous to attempt to force on a person (oneself or someone else) values for which he is not yet prepared. When this is attempted, there is a danger that a vacuum will be created in his life, and that this will soon be filled by the love of values which are lower and less worthy. It is for this reason that the judgments passed on certain intermediate values (honour and fame, for example) need to be discreet; otherwise a person may come to be deprived of what had, up to that moment, elevated his moral living above the level of mediocrity. What is required is that he should already have some real appreciation of the new value to which one wishes to "convert" him; this value should not be just a word to him, or known in a merely abstract manner. Otherwise the very most that will result will be artificial, forced, unauthentic virtues.

On the other hand, too great an attachment to a particular value often makes a person deaf to the appeal of a value that is higher. There is need here to exercise the virtue of prudence so that we shall know when the time is ripe for advancing beyond the lower value; this will be when the conditions which make it possible for a person to have a genuine appreciation of the higher value have been realized [17].

276. – Among the factors which are operative in our moral life and growth the passions occupy a special position.

Philosophers are divided concerning their importance and values. The Stoics, for example, dismissed them as a sickness of the soul: they are irrational impulses, the fruit of a judgment that is erroneous and misguided. The "sage", the perfect man, has in consequence to be completely dispassionate. He may at times appear to be moved by his passions and his actions may

---

[17] See the *Essai*, n. 149; pp. 366-370.

give that impression; but all this remains exterior to his inner self, his soul, which remains unaffected. He will indeed help those who suffer, but in so doing he will not experience the least feeling of pity[18]. Kant also left the passions, and the entire affective life, outside the sphere of morality. Our morally good actions are those which we perform simply out of regard for the law. He does however admit that one sentiment is integral to the moral order: respect (for the law); but what he has in mind here is a sentiment which is like no other and whose origin is not to be found in this (empirical) world, this world of space and time: it is the restraint and curb which reason imposes on our feelings (n. 116). — Others, on the contrary, exalt the passions as the voice of nature, the voice of God: Fourier, for example, and many of the romanticists (George Sand ...).

It is important to note that the word "passions", as it is used nowadays, has not exactly the same meaning that it had for the ancient philosophers and for the Scholastics: in their understanding of the word, what the moderns call the "emotions" would also be included. For the ancients, and also for Descartes, joy, sadness etc., are passions: nowadys we do not speak of such emotions in this way.

Our passions are of themselves neither moral nor immoral since, whether we like it or not, they are part and parcel of our human nature. They are, however, of moral significance to the extent to which they are subject to rational control. In this respect, they are similar to the external dimension of our actions, but with this difference that they are by their very nature much more closely linked with the inner decision of our will: between this and the external dimension, they can be said to mediate. If then this latter dimension deserves to be qualified as good or evil to the extent that it is voluntary, there is all the more reason to qualify our passions in this way. The manner in which they can be voluntary is twofold: either because a person freely arouses them (or at least is responsible for bringing them into play), or because he neglects to resist

---

[18] In place of the passions, the Stoics attributed to the sage certain rational sentiments (*eupatheias*): joy in place of pleasure; circumspection in place of fear; an upright will in place of desire. Sadness alone had no analogue in the sage.

them [19]. — It should, however, be stressed that a person's passions escape from the control of his will more easily than does the external dimension of his actions, so that he has greater difficulty in bringing them under rational control. It is easier to refrain from striking someone than it is to master one's interior anger. Note also that "passion" can exert its influence both before a person decides (so that it moves him to decide in one way rather than another) and after he has decided (so that it is the effect of his decision). In the first instance, passion diminishes a person's power to choose freely and, in consequence, the moral character of his action (n. 16), since it interferes with the exercise of his reason [20]. When this happens, passion does not, strictly speaking, any longer mediate between the person's inner decision and the external dimension of his action; it is, on the contrary, the person's will which performs the role of mediation (between his passions and what is external). — Passion can exert its influence, after the person has decided, in one of two ways. His decision may be of such a kind that it "overflows" on to his feelings, which express in their own way what takes place within his mind and will. (A resolute, energetic decision will normally produce an ardour to surmount obstacles, an impatience with all contradiction, a certain feeling of boldness etc.). Alternatively, a person may deliberately excite his emotions which he then makes use of in order the better to attain some goal. (So, for example, a person who is by nature meek and timid, but who has to take someone to task, or to put forward some claim, will deliberately work himself up into a state of anger so that he may present a bold front). When a person's decision simply overflows on to his feelings, he identifies himself with them only in an indirect and non-thematic fashion, for example, by continuing to keep his attention on what is exciting his emotions, even though he is not aiming at this disturbance, or merely in the sense that the activity of his will crowns the activity of his lower forms of appetite: one could say that the quasi-physical energy of his will overflows on to his feelings in virtue of the unity that he

---

[19] St Thomas, *Summa Theol.*, I-II, 24, 1. — On the passions, read A. Ponceau, *Initiation philosophique*, 4th ed., t. II, pp. 19-32. On the moral life in general, *ib.*, pp. 196-248.

[20] St Thomas, *ib.*, I-II, 24, 3 ad Ium.

is. It is clear that in these circumstances passion does not add anything to the morality of a person's action: it is simply a sign of the intensity with which he is acting and, in consequence, of the heightened moral value or anti-value of his action. When a person voluntarily excites his emotions, these become involved in the structure of his volitional act, that is, they come to be part of the object which he is choosing so that they influence the morality of his action accordingly (nn. 227; 232). The significance of this is that the more an action is aimed at orientating the *entire person* towards a good or an evil end — and the more this aim is achieved — the more will it be morally good or morally evil. It is better, St Thomas insists, that a person should not only will what is good, but should execute his good decisions. Similarly, it is better that he should give himself to what is good, not only on the level of his will, but also on the level of his feelings and emotions, in accordance with what is written in Psalm 83: "my heart and my flesh sing for joy to the living God". ("Heart" is here to be understood as rational appetite and "flesh" as sense appetite) [21].

Finally, keep in mind that for the Scholastics the will too has its affectivity (n. 16, end). This, as such, is of moral significance, since it can be inclined towards values that are true or false, even without any free and deliberate act on the person's part. In consequence, the feelings and emotions which always accompany our volitional affectivity and elan (and which they re-echo at a lower level), share in the moral character of this latter. It is for this reason that it is far from being a matter of indifference whether a person is spontaneously drawn towards what is noble, pure, fine and generous, or, on the contrary, towards what is low, cheap, shoddy etc., even when there is as yet no question of merit or fault. It is not only that dispositions of this kind are a help or a hindrance to a person's uprightness of will and to his achievement of what is good and worthwhile: *in themselves*, such dispositions constitute a positive or negative reply to the call which the person receives from the Value [22].

---

[21] *Ib.*, corp. art.

[22] Cf. D. von Hildebrand, *Christian Ethics*, pp. 191-243: Value Response; also a much earlier article of the same author, *Die Idee der sittlichen Handlung*, "Jahrbuch für Philosophie und phänomenologische Forschung", III (1916), pp. 126-252. especially pp. 162 seq.

Consequently, on this ground alone, they deserve to be cultivated or opposed. Indeed, the moral education of young children and adolescents, consists, to a great extent, in fostering in them an affectivity that is healthy, refined and generous (n. 81, end). — Once again, it becomes clear that the moral ideal to which man is called to respond is far from being that of a purely spiritual and disembodied being.

The various points that we have here discussed need to be complemented in two ways: by the contribution to them that moral theology makes, and by the appreciation of them which the reader has as the fruit of his own personal experience.

PART THREE
HAPPINESS AND MORALITY

BOOK FIVE

HAPPINESS AND MORALITY

CHAPTER FOURTEEN

THE DESIRE FOR HAPPINESS AND ITS ROLE IN THE MORAL LIFE

277. – Our reflections on moral value, on the good which deserves and indeed demands to be chosen for its own sake, have carried us to the present stage of our investigation. When we were dealing with the question of the essence of this value, we insisted on the necessity to advance beyond considerations of self-interest, utility, eudaeminism (nn. 71-74), since it was only in this way that we could arrive at the accurate understanding which we sought.

Moral value is not, however, man's only value and while his attempts to lead a good life impress upon him that the meaning and justification of his existence lie in fidelity to the Ideal of reason, he is also aware that there is in him an irresistible drive to seek happiness — a drive which is at the very heart of even his most disinterested actions. The desire to attain happiness, no less than the demand that he live morally, presents him with an ultimate; both are on the horizon of the project which, as a human being, he is called upon to achieve. Both of them possess, as we have already indicated (nn. 14, 3; 60; 66; 73), a certain *final* character. But even though they have this in common, the way in which both are ultimate is quite different: one is an ultimate which *cannot* be refused, while the other *may not* be refused. — But these reflections inevitably prompt the question: what is the relation between these two goals? How do these two orientations of our human existence blend and harmonize? Because of the method we have followed, we have had to abstract from the question of this relationship, but this methodological abstraction cannot be definitive. Between the *physical* necessity that is imposed on us to aspire to happiness, and the *moral* necessity to be faithful to the Value, there cannot but be some connection.

A consideration of the relation between moral value and all other human values is integral to the complete study of ethics: all too frequently, however, this question is very inadequately dealt with in special ethics. The relation between moral and aesthetic values, for example, calls for careful examination. Does a work of art have to aim at "edification" in order to be classed as "moral", or is it already moral once it is genuinely beautiful? Will a more refined aesthetic taste also involve a more delicate moral conscience, or at least, can it foster the formation of such a conscience? (Recall the aesthetic ethics of a John Ruskin). Similarly where the "vital" values are concerned: what, for example, is the relation between hygiene and morality? Is there a moral value in physical culture, athletic exercise, the cultivation of bodily cleanliness? (To this last, our age — which has an obscure appreciation that cleanliness is a form of respect for human dignity — attributes much more importance than did, for example, the 17th century).

Likewise, too, with regard to cultural, scientific, technical progress and man's increasing mastery of nature: are such values purely and simply *indifferent* from the ethical standpoint — technical progress, for example, is capable of being indifferently utilised for good or for evil, for peace or for war, as a help towards more authentic human living or to make the pursuit of pleasure easier — or should we acknowledge that they already possess a *semi-moral* character, since, of themselves, they are in alignment with our normal development as reasonable beings? The second reply seems to be the correct one and deserves a lengthy treatment: this, however, is not the place for it. It is clear that such a study would be extremely useful, not only in order to determine with more accuracy the various categories of duties — as is attempted in special ethics — but also in order the better to weave our moral activity into the totality of our human lives.

278. – Happiness, or, to retain its traditional title, "beatitude", has been defined by Boethius as that perfect state which results from the possession of all that is good[1]. A better and

---

[1] Boethius, *The Consolation of Philosophy*, III, 2: happiness is that good which, once it is obtained, makes the desire of anything else impossible. It is the greatest of all goods and contains within itself whatever is good; if anything

more precise definition would be: the perfect completion of a human subject, or, in more general terms, of a spiritual subject[2], or, with St Thomas, the perfect good of a being with an intellectual nature[3]. Such a being is totally happy when his nature is so completely fulfilled that there is nothing left for him to desire — not, at least, in a way that involves disquiet and creates frustration.

Note that what we are speaking about is the fulfilment of a human being's *nature*: it is only by means of this fulfilment that the subject attains happiness. The perfection which this signifies does not consist simply in moral uprightness; neither is it sufficient for happiness that a person wishes to be happy, or decides that he is and that there is now nothing more for him to desire! It is necessary that his *natural* appetite be genuinely satisfied. On the other hand, it is not sufficient that the subject has actually been "perfected" (objectively): it is necessary that he be conscious of this, that he delight in his perfection. This delight should not, however, be conceived of as if it were an additional element: it is integral to the completion of a being whose nature is spiritual. Such a being's existence is not confined to the level of the "in-itself", but rises to the level of the "for-itself". Consequently, the completion of the subject's being also, and essentially, involves his completion as one who is "for-himself"; it is precisely in completion of this kind that happiness consists.

Happiness can, however, be understood in two senses. It can be considered simply in the abstract — as we have just done — without determining its nature in the concrete. But it can also be considered in the concrete: the question can be raised of what precisely will bring perfect fulfilment to a being whose nature is rational; what is the good which he needs to

---

were lacking to it, it could not be the greatest good, since there would be something external to it which could be desired. It is clear, then, that beatitude is a state whose perfection consists in the possession of all that is good. — Prior to Boethius, Cicero had defined beatitude as that state in which all troubles have finally disappeared and a person enjoys the harmonious abundance of all that is good, *Tusc.*, V, 10.

[2] "Felicity is to persons, what perfection is to other beings", Leibniz, *Discours de Métaphysique*, n. 36; ed. Gerhardt, t. IV, p. 462.

[3] *Summa Theol.*, I, 26, 1.

possess in order that this fulfilment may be his etc. In our present investigation, it is with the first sense that we are concerned. What is the relation between our desire for happiness, happiness that will be unalloyed — a desire which no one can sincerely reject, even though the way in which it can actually be satisfied may not be at all clear to him — and our vocation as moral beings? This is the problem to which we now turn.

279. – The solutions offered, as one might expect, have been diverse. Some of them have already been considered and rejected (nn. 71-74), namely, those which either reduce moral value to happiness, or at least define it in relation to this latter (Eudaemonism, Utilitarianism etc.).

The solution of the Stoics is at the opposite extreme: man's sole good, they assert, is virtue. It alone suffices to make a person happy. The wise man would be happy even inside the bull of Phalaris! If we are to believe them the virtuous man has no need to supplement virtue with pleasure: in virtue alone he finds all that he requires for happiness [4]. Consequently, a happy life is nothing other than a virtuous one [5]; the moral good is to be regarded as the sole good [6]. Obviously, then, moral evil will, inversely, be regarded as the sole evil [7]. Apart from virtue and vice, there is nothing which can be classified as good or evil; everything else is indifferent [8].

For both of these schools of thought, the questions of the relation between the love of virtue, and the desire for happiness, has either no meaning, or else allows of only one obvious answer.

Most thinkers, however, consider that the question poses a real problem; they are agreed that there is a definite connec-

---

[4] Cicero, *De finibus bonorum et malorum*, I, 61.

[5] Id., *Tusc.*, V, 48.

[6] Id., *De finibus*, III, 28. (This is the: "only what is beautiful is good", of the Stoics).

[7] *Ib.*, III, 29.

[8] Nevertheless, among the things which are indifferent, the Stoics distinguished between what was suitable (*kathekonta*) and what was preferable (*proēgmena*). But that distiction is concerned only with the material of our choices and is of no ethical significance, since the entire moral value — which, for the Stoics, is the only value — consists solely in the intention of the will.

tion between a person's moral goodness and his achievement of happiness, but they disagree about the nature of that connection.

For some of them, the connection in question is *extrinsic*. The tendency towards happiness has, of itself, nothing to do with morality. Nevertheless, our practical reason necessarily proposes to us, as an object to be attained, a final harmony between virtue and happiness; in consequence, there arises the practical postulate of the existence of God as the "moral" author of the natural order, who, as such, is capable of ensuring that the desired harmony be achieved. Kant, as we know (n. 118), wrote in thsi vein. — Prior to Kant, and in a much more radical fashion, the Nominalists had attributed the connection between morality and happiness solely to the arbitrary decision of God; indeed, for that matter, He could, absolutely speaking, save the unrepentant sinner and damn the guiltless!

Note, apropos of Kant, that he attributes the tendency towards happiness solely to our faculty of desire (Begehrungsvermögen), which is a *sense* faculty.

For other philosophers, on the contrary, the link between moral goodness and happiness is *intrinsic*. A being whose nature is rational cannot achieve complete fulfilment unless he lives in accordance with reason. Moral goodness is, without doubt, insufficient to make a person completely happy but, nevertheless, it is not simply the necessary condition for happiness: the virtuous person has already achieved a certain degree of this complete fulfilment (cf. n. 71). This is the view of most of the Scholastics — the Nominalists excepted — and, among non-Scholastics, of a good number of philosophers (often under Christian inspiration) such as Leibniz.

Christianity teaches us that in the historical order of human existence there has always been only one authentic happiness possible for man: a *supernatural* happiness whose achievement absolutely surpasses human strength and energy. But, on the other hand, the activity of human beings in this historical order, above all of those who are in God's friendship, is never purely human, purely natural; factors of another order always mingle with this activity, even though the extent to which they do so cannot be discerned. In this way, the proportion between man's moral activity as it occurs in the *concrete*, and the happiness for which he is destined, is to some degree restored.

280. – Before we propose our own solution, we shall first investigate in what sense one can speak of a natural tendency, not only towards happiness in some general sense, but towards "beatitude", complete and unalloyed happiness. Note though, that strictly speaking, this is a question for philosophical psychology rather than ethics; in addition, it would doubtless have been more logical to have treated of it when we were discussing human action (n. 14, 4). But because of the practical advantage of treating the question here, we have omitted to do so at the earlier stage.

Is it true that a human being, prior to every free decision and in every free decision, necessarily seeks complete and unalloyed happiness? Is there in him — as a being with a certain nature, who, in consequence, is subject in his activity to the laws of that nature, no less than are other beings to the laws of *their* nature — a determinism (anterior to and interior to his liberty) which inevitably orientates the activity of his will towards this satisfaction of his desires? The traditional affirmation that there is, seems to be in conflict with the fact that we but rarely propose happiness to ourselves as the express, *thematic* goal for our endeavours. What we desire is this or that particular good: this situation, this car, this woman, wealth, peace, the realization of a cultural, moral or religious ideal etc.; we scarcely ever say: I wish to be (completely) happy.

But, if we probe into the matter a little more deeply, it becomes clear that it is precisely because we desire happiness in all our choices that we do not experience the need to propose it to ourselves as an express, thematic goal. We do not *choose* to be happy — as Aristotle has pointed out — but we cannot prevent ourselves from *desiring* it [9]. Human experience provides ample evidence — and each one can verify this experience within himself — that even though human beings do not constantly speak about "the land of heart's desire", they nonetheless seek it, tenaciously, persistently, despite disillusion-

---

[9] *Nicom. Eth.*, I, 12, 1101 b 10 seq.

ments, in the teeth of contradictions. One can, one often should, renounce this or that particular form of happiness: but one never renounces — except in words — happiness itself. There is not one of our decisions which, albeit obscurely, is not influenced by this desire — despite the denials which may be present at the superficial level of our consciousness. We have it in our power not to dwell on this desire but, if we are asked, we can never *sincerely* reply: I do not desire to be happy, or: it is a matter of indifference to me whether or not I attain happiness. Choices of this kind, which a person attempts to make, cannot but remain empty. — In fact, without this constant and profound desire, the cultural development of humanity and, very particularly, the technical progress that has been made in the past few centuries, would be rendered inexplicable. Human beings — and it is in no way cynical to acknowledge this — will not impose burdens on themselves unless, in one way or another, they find it is to their advantage to do so.

281. — What experience testifies to so forcefully can be rationally justified by means of a metaphysical analysis of human activity, in which the conditions of the possibility of such activity come to be revealed.

Firstly, contrary to what many contemporary authors [9bis] maintain (Simone de Beauvoir, for example, in *Pyrrhus et Cinéas*), it has to be pointed out that, for each of us, there is some ultimate subjective goal which we are implicitly aiming at in all our choices, and which, in the last analysis, occupies this position in our lives because of the "attraction" which it has for us. If there were not such a goal in our lives, then either there would be an unending regression in the goals at which we ail (we would desire A in order to obtain B, we would desire B in order to obtain C, and so on indefinitely), or else there would be several independent goals, at each of which a particular series of choices would terminate definitively. But neither of these hypotheses is tenable.

[9bis] Cf. the earlier statement of Hobbes: "Felicity is a continual progress of the desire, from one object to another, the attaining of the former being but the way of the latter", *Leviathan*, p. I, ch. XI, English Works of Thomas Hobbes, ed. Molesworth, vol. 3, p. 83.

An unending regression is impossible: if one goal is chosen as a means to achieving another, so that nothing is desired simply for its own sake, then there is no reason for choosing anything at all. Hence, a series of choices would not even commence. (Note, in passing, that the end, since it grounds the value of the means, cannot simply be willed prior to the choice of these latter: interior to this choice is the intention of the end, from which indeed, as from an abiding root, the former derives its vigour). The second hypothesis — a plurality of ultimate goals — is likewise impossible. Every tendency is unified, and distinguished from all others, by the goal toward which it is directed. If the human will is a unity, there can be but one goal to its "movement", that is, to its radical inclination, Otherwise, it would not be the same will when it is set on seeking pleasure, as it is when it is resolved to sacrifice pleasure to the demands of morality. But, in fact, it is one and the same will which is capable both of subordinating pleasure to moral goodness, and moral goodness to pleasure. — But, perhaps, it may be maintained that the human will could be equally attracted to two ultimate goals, which have however a common aspect, so that the unity of the will is, in consequence, unimpaired? Beware! In order that the unity of the will may be genuinely preserved, this aspect has to be common to the diverse "ultimate goals" *precisely as ultimate*. Even further, this aspect has to be *at the root* of what makes them to be ultimate. If it is not, it cannot serve the purpose it is meant to serve; it can endow the goals in question with no more than an exterior unity, so that the human will remains a bundle of independent tendencies which are linked together from without, as a result of the attraction which this common aspect has exercised. Hence, it is clear that the true ultimate end, the true goal of the will's radical inclination, the goal which makes it to be a unified tendency and distinguishes it from all others, is this common aspect, as grounding, for the subject in question, the value of the proposed "ultimate ends". But this contradicts the hypothesis, according to which each of these ends is desired for its own sake.

Consequently, there has to be in each person's life an ultimate goal, which he desires for its own sake, and on account of which he desires everything else.

282. – This ultimate goal is precisely what we have in mind when we speak about "beatitude", or complete and unalloyed happiness. For, by definition, an ultimate goal allows of no further tendency, no further movement in the same direction. Consequently, the goal which is absolutely final for the human will excludes all desire of something more, of something which has not yet been attained. If it did not, it would be for us only an anticipation of, a foretaste of, some greater good towards which we were still tending, and in relation to which the lesser good seemed desirable. As is only too obvious, such a goal would not be ultimate. But what excludes all desire of something more, will completely satisfy us: it will bring us that complete happiness which is termed beatitude. This reflexive analysis of human action makes clear, then, that in our voluntary activity a fundamental aspiration towards happiness, as our ultimate subjective end, is ever operative. (This end is subjective in the twofold sense that it is the end which the subject desires, n. 48, 3, and that it will bring him that satisfaction for which he naturally craves. Our ultimate objective end, however, as natural theology helps to make clear, is God himself, or, if it is a question of the end which we are called upon to achieve, the glory of God, n. 173).

283. – The same conclusion can be arrived at by reflecting on the dynamism which is inherent in a spiritual being. Where such a being is concerned, the activity of his will is the expression on the spiritual level, on the level of interiority, of his total dynamism as a subject. (Hence, a human being's decisions express mote than the dynamism of his spirit). This point is fairly generally acknowledged even by non-Scholastic philosophers, who have no difficulty in admitting that it is this "synthetic", total character of the will which distinguishes it from all particular inclinations.

Now, all that exists, aspires to be fully: every being tends by its nature towards its completion, towards the maximum development of which it is capable. A human being, inasmuch as he too has a nature — a nature which extends even to the spiritual dimension of his being — is no exception. Hence his will, expressing as it does this basic dynamism, is naturally drawn towards what completes his human nature and results in its maximum development. This clearly involves a luminous consciousness of himself, for such a consciousness is essential to human perfection. But this perfection, this completion of one's nature which is consciously possessed, is nothing other than perfect happiness (n. 278).

From the preceding reflections the conclusion follows that *the human will, or rather a human being through his will, tends naturally towards perfect happiness as his ultimate subjective goal.*

The ultimate explanation of this tendency is to be found in the generosity of God, who has created all that is "so that it might be", so that it might grow and come to completion, but who has nonetheless subordinated the completion of irrational beings to that of rational beings, in such a way that it is only through these latter that the former can attain their destined perfection. For it is man who, by his understanding of the world and his transforming action upon it, endows this with a new value, confers upon it a new mode of being and so guides it to its destined end.

284. – We are now in a position to turn to the problem we are concerned with in this chapter: is there a link between a person's happiness and his response to moral value, between his desire for the former and his love of the latter; and, if there is, is this merely extrinsic?

Inasmuch as perfect happiness is nothing other than the completion of an intellectual being's nature, a life in conformity with reason is necessarily included in it. For this completion involves the maximum development of a person's intellect (which is not possible without knowledge of the truth and, in consequence, of the true good, of the true order of values, of the demands which reason makes on him), as well as of his will (which, in its turn, is not possible without love for the known good and the firm resolve to cleave to it). But, as we have seen (nn. 135-137), it is in this conformity with reason, a conformity which is the fruit of a disinterested welcome and acceptance, that moral value essentially consists.

It is clear, then, that happiness which is authentic includes moral goodness. But note carefully that the goodness that is in question here does not involve the efforts, the conflicts, the repugnances, the "blood, sweat, tears and toil", which are normally part and parcel of our moral striving (n. 140): the moral goodness which is an integral part of happiness represents the achievement of an ideal. The person who attains complete happiness will necessarily be morally good in a *pre-eminent* degree. It is in this sense, and in this sense only, that we can say, in company with Aristotle, that happiness surpasses virtue.

A point that should be noted carefully is that a person's will cannot attain its maximum development, unless he loves what is morally good — the objective moral value — for its own sake. It is by making this response that he manifests himself as rational and spiritual, as open to others in a relation of welcome and generosity (n. 143).

That the link between a person's happiness and his moral value cannot be regarded as merely extrinsic is now evident.

The conclusion we have just arrived at could also be arrived at by a somewhat different process of reasoning. In order that he may attain that completion of his nature which will bring him happiness, a rational being has to act, to the highest degree of which he is capable, in accordance with his rational or spiritual nature, that is, in accordance with his openness to all other beings, to all other persons and, in the final analysis, to the Ideal of reason (nn. 143-145). Now, it is precisely this openness which is, from the point of view of the subject, the necessary condition for morally good activity, and its source. He acknowledges what is of moral value and increases in moral stature, only in the measure in which, in his practical judgments and decisions, he opens himself to the Absolute, the Universal, through opening himself to others. Consequently, authentic happiness cannot but include moral goodness, since what this essentially and radically consists in is openness towards, and acceptance of, the Ideal of reason, out of love for this Ideal. (But the moral goodness that is in question here is not, obviously, conditioned by the possibility that a person will choose what is evil — as it inevitably is in our experience).

But does not what we have just said prompt the question of why we have refused to define moral value in terms of happiness (nn. 71-73)? The reason for this refusal was that unless the essence of moral value is first understood, it is not possible to form a true notion of happiness (the completion of a rational being's nature), since one does not understand what reason is, and what type of activity it demands of us [10].

---

[10] Man can find beatitude only in transcending it, through loving what is good for its own sake. Hence the internal contradiction involved in egoism. If

285. – The next stage of our present investigation is to consider how, in the unity of a human action, the necessary desire for happiness blends with the response to moral value. (As we already know, there is no question of reducing either the desire to the response, nor the response to the desire).

The desire for happiness — in the abstract sense in which it is here understood — is an undetermined desire, precisely because it is present in all our desires. In all that we choose, its influence is operative, for it is inseparable from the dynamic structure of our *nature* as rational beings; it is the expression, on the level of interiority, of the tendency towards their development and perfection that is present in all beings.

The response to moral value, the decision to be faithful to it, can then be said, initially at least, to channel this general desire in one definite direction. The virtuous person desires no happiness that is not in accordance with reason, that is not in conformity with the moral norm. He would not be content with *any kind* of happiness; the happiness he is intent on has to be worthy of being desired. This does not at all mean that he identifies happiness and moral goodness: despite the insistence of the Stoics, a virtuous life does not, of itself, suffice to satisfy the desires of the good person. But he would reject any happiness which could be obtained only at the cost of unfaithfulness to the Ideal. Indeed, in living a virtuous life, a life in which he responds to the demands which his reason and his rational nature make on him, he perfects that nature, and so comes to possess some foretaste of the complete happiness

---

the egoist desires to be genuinely happy, he ought to choose what is morally valuable. But, as long as he remains a prisoner of his egoism, he can choose it only by subordinating it to himself; and so to choose it is not to choose it at all. The truth in action for man is that, in place of loving what is morally valuable simply for his own sake, he should, on the contrary, move himself for its sake.

The dawning consciousness of moral value is a crucial stage in a person's development, for it is then that the conversion from egoism to a disinterested love of the good begins to be effected. But it is then also that the possibility of a more refined perversion emerges: a perversion which consists in choosing to be virtuous simply for one's own advantage or ornamentation. (An example of this is the religious person who completely subordinates the love of God to the pursuit of his own perfection). This kind of egoism is of much greater consequence than the spontaneous and innocent egoism which precedes the revelation of moral value.

which he has not yet attained. In the very sacrifice of joy, joy is still to be found.

It is clear, then, that a person's response to moral value determines and channels his desire for happiness. Since such a relation is analogous to that which exists between "matter" and "form", a person's desire for happiness can, in consequence, be said to be *quasi-materially* related to his fidelity to moral value.

286. – But the question cannot be allowed to rest here: there is need of further clarification. To be faithful to moral value is, as we have said, to choose the happiness that is in accordance with that faithfulness: it is to choose *true* happiness, and in that choice a person already finds joy. But note that in this very decision to be faithful, two aspects can be distinguished, and two directions in which the will's activity is tending can be recognized: the *love* of moral value *for its own sake*, that is, on account of its harmony with the Ideal of practical reason, and the *desire* of this value, inasmuch as it fosters the subject's perfection and gives him a foretaste of the authentic happiness he has not yet attained. Under the first aspect, the person chooses what is morally valuable because of what this value is *in itself*; he does not subordinate it to himself, but on the contrary, subordinates himself to it; his decision presents itself to him as in harmony with his rational nature precisely in its *rational* dimension, as in harmony with himself as a *spiritual* being, capable of receiving *others* into himself, not so as to achieve his perfection through nourishing himself on them, but so as to allow them to be and to promote their well-being. Under the second aspect, the person chooses what is morally valuable because of the perfection which this will bring *to him*, because it will satisfy his natural appetite: his decision presents itself to him as in harmony with his rational nature precisely in its *natural* dimension. One and the same decision, then, possesses two distinct aspects, two orientations, according as one envisages it as proceeding from a person's rational nature, precisely as a *nature*, or, on the other hand, precisely as *rational*. This further avenue of approach has again made it clear that the first aspect can be said to stand in a "material" relation to the second.

From all that has been said, it is quite clear that the desire for happiness is a presupposition — after the fashion of a "material" principle — in every moral decision.

Since the moral subject, considered in the "open", or spiritual, dimension of his being, has the dignity of a *person*, his fidelity to moral value can be said to express him as a person, whereas his desire for happiness, of itself, simply expresses the natural dimension of his being.

287. – We should however be careful not to regard a person's resolve to do what is moral, as no more than an epiphenomenon, an imaginary and ineffectual commitment, as if all that really moved him to act in this way were his desire for happiness, so that his choice of what is good is made solely in view of this latter[11]. This is a pessimistic interpretation of human activity, and it reflects a view of man which is no less improverished, no less degrading than that which regards moral activity as a simple "superstructure", which can be explained and understood only in terms of the solid reality of the economic, biological etc., "infrastructure"; or that which regards it as an unconscious camouflage of the "libido"... On the contrary, since the resolve to do what is good channels the desire for happiness, it is the latter which is vivified by the former, from which it comes to possess its significance, just as in Husserl's phenomenology the noetic (or cognitive) intention vivifies the psychic *hyle* (the subjective sense data) to constitute the cognitive act.

On the other hand, we have to keep in mind that just as a formal principle of being requires its correlative material principle, in order both to be and to be operative, so also the desire for happiness has an essential role to play in moving us to choose what is good. It provides us with a motivation — what Kant would call *Triebfeder* — in the absence of which we would not be moved to act at all. I can choose nothing unless I appreciate it as *my good*. But it depends on me, on my love of the Value, whether this good will lie for me in a life of egoism

---

[11] La Rochefoucauld, for example, writes: "As rivers are swallowed up by the sea, so are virtues by self-interest", *Réflexions morales*, n. 208. — See on this question, *Essai*, n. 145; pp. 350-354.

or of generosity, in a life dominated by impulses and instincts or by the requirements of reason etc. It is I who freely decide, in virtue of a radical option, that I shall live at this or that level and find my good in so living; it is I who choose whether I shall be this or that kind of person.

Note, finally, that although the desire for hapiness is, of itself, neither moral nor immoral, since it is a desire that is natural and necessary, we cannot reasonably disavow and reject it. For, as we have seen (n. 172, 6), our rational nature bears the image of the Ideal of reason, so that, in consequence, we cannot reasonably disapprove of the essential tendencies of that nature. — When what is in question is *authentic happiness as such*, to desire it obviously possesses a positive moral value; it is a happiness to which fidelity to reason is integral, and to desire what involves this fidelity cannot but be moral.

288. – As a result of our analysis, it should be clear that there are not two disparate and opposing finalities in the one moral act. Far from being opposed, the person's choice of what is good and his desire for happiness really involve one another. By the very fact that his choice of what is good helps him to attain happiness, and provides him with some foretaste of it, this choice is desirable; it is a genuine means of obtaining happiness, even though it should not be made simply because it leads to this goal. The desire for happiness, in its turn, as we have seen, cannot but be consonant with the Ideal of reason — since happiness is nothing other than the completion of a rational being's nature — even though this is neither the only, nor the strongest, reason which moves us to desire it.

Notwithstanding all this, it remains true that a certain duality still persists. But this is nothing other than the consequence of that deficiency which is intrinsic to a being who is not *the* Being, and for whom, in consequence, a complete identity between the love of what is good and the pursuit of *his* good, is rendered impossible.

CHAPTER FIFTEEN

THE FINAL HARMONY BETWEEN A PERSON'S MORAL VALUE AND HIS HAPPINESS, OR THE PROBLEM OF SANCTIONS

289. – Included in authentic beatitude is a life that is in accordance with reason: this beatitude lies, in consequence, in the direction of moral value, or if one prefers, moral value indicates the direction in which beatitude should be sought. As well, a person comes to have a foretaste of beatitude by acting morally. Nevertheless, this mutual involvement does not seem to define their relationship completely. It is the common persuasion of mankind that happiness is also, and indeed primarily, the fruit of virtuous activity, while actions that are contrary to the moral norm are generally regarded as, in the last analysis, injurious to the one who performs them. This persuasion, which manifests itself even at the level of spontaneous reactions and judgments (cf. n. 28), finds a reflective expression in religious tenets, under very different forms, it is true. So, for example, in Indian thoughr, *karma* (actions which, once a person has performed them, come to be endowed with some kind of independent existence over which he has no more power) fructifies to his advantage or disadvantage, so that the quality of his reincarnation is determined in an inevitable manner. — Some religions consider that a person will reap the fruit of his actions in this present life (primitive Judaism, for example), while others look beyond the grave; but all religions concur in acknowledging a link between what a person does and what he receives. It is for this reason that religious people are prone to suspect that unhappiness is the result of sinfulness ("Who sinned, this man or his parents, that he was born blind?", was the query of the disciples concerning the man who was born blind, *John*, 9.2); for the same reason, the sufferings of the innocent (*Ps.* 73, Vulg. 72) have always been a problem, and often a scandal, to the religious mind.

The presence of this persuasion, not only in the Judaic and Christian tradition, but also in religions of purely human origin, seems to testify to man's spontaneous appreciation of a certain harmony between upright living and happiness, of *a priori* demand that those who do "what is good" should be happy. If this were not part of the "due order", if there were not a value in this final equation between a person's moral goodness and his happiness, why should the task of establishing it be regarded as the sovereign prerogative of God? Where this order is conceived of as a supreme law, to which the divinity itself is required to conform, men's expectation of a final harmony becomes all the stronger.

It is undoubtedly true that the ordinary person does not always make a precise distinction between the way in which happiness and misery, respectively, result from good or evil actions, and the way in which something results simply as a natural consequence. Man easily reifies moral realities and thinks about them in non-moral terms. But the more he comes to appreciate these realities for what they are, the more he understands that the link between good actions and happiness, evil actions and unhappiness is not a physical one, or is at least not merely physical: it is the *moral* link which is called *merit*. Happiness is not simply the *natural* effect of virtue, as health is of temperance: it is the *recompense* of virtue. Misery is not simply the *natural* effect of sin, as cirrhosis of the liver is of alcoholism: it is the *chastisement* of sin. Happiness as recompense, and misery as chastisement *sanction* the observance or violation of the moral law.

Now, all this gives rise to several philosophic problems. Firstly, since moral value and happiness belong to two distinct and incommensurable orders, there does not seem to be any reason why the former should require the latter. Such a requirement does a wrong to moral value: this may not be sufficient for the subject, but it is sufficient where reason is concerned: it is self-sufficient, since to love and choose it in view of something else, is to destroy it. As well, to consider the question from another angle, how could suffering, which directly affects a person's nature by thwarting its tendencies, compensate for the faults which are the fruit of liberty? The person's nature, as such, is innocent: why chastise it? — Secondly, supposing that a requirement of this kind exists, the question arises of how, and on what conditions, it can be satisfied. For, as we have said, and as experience makes rather clear, this cannot be done by way of mere physical causality. — Finally, if there is a rational and necessary link between value and happiness, why is this so little in evidence in the world around us?

290. – Before tackling the problem, the notions of merit and sanction need to be clarified: these notions are inseparable from the problem, but their sociological origin creates the danger that its essentially ethical and metaphysical dimension may be overlooked.

According to what has just been said, we may define merit as follows: a property of a human action, in virtue of which a certain *requital* is due to it, that is, a certain *natural* good or evil, according as the action has been *morally* good or evil. (In this latter instance, one should rather speak of demerit). — But this *moral* notion emerges in consciousness only by means of an empirical notion, which is tied to the relationships between the members of a society. The person who does what is of advantage to another, or to society, deserves well of them; he deserves badly of them, when he injures them[1]. When someone has done a service for me, or for the community, or the state etc., he has, in the common estimation, a certain right to be rewarded. This right is, however, imperfect, unless the reward has already been promised. Where no promise has been made, the reward is due, not in justice, but only in fairness. If, for example, before I have had a chance to make a promise of any kind, someone returns me the wallet which I had left lying on a bench in a public park, he has no strict right to receive anything, except to be compensated for any expenses he may have incurred. And nevertheless, it is fitting that, in one way or another, I reward him.

Merit in the strict sense the theologians call "condign"; merit, where no more than equity is involved, they call "congruent". In justice, as we have seen (n. 195), a certain equality is involved: where this equality does not exist from the very nature of a relationship — either because there is no proportion between the benefit and the

---

[1] St Thomas, *Summa Theol.*, I-II, 21, 3 and 4.

reward, or because the conditions for a strictly juridical relationship are lacking etc. — it is established by means of a promise; in virtue of this, one's benefactor is now worthy to be rewarded.

Let us analyse this: "it is fitting"[2]. Since, by hypothesis, no promise has been made, there is no question of keeping faith. Neither is it a question of a spontaneous reaction of contentment, such as occurs in those moments of euphoria in which one feels one's heart to be overflowing with generosity. No: I understand that it is fitting for me to give to this other person, because there is a quality in his action which, objectively and of itself, quite apart from my subjective reaction, calls for a reward. (In fact, it may well be that I am not particularly pleased to recover the object I have lost: there can be providential states of forgetfulness which dispense us from irksome tasks ...; and we all have experience of those fussy but well-intentioned people whose solicitude we would so willingly forgo, but towards whom we nonetheless feel ourselves obliged ...). Can it be maintained that, in rewarding my benefactor, I am but encouraging him to continue to do good, as well as stimulating others to imitate him? But how then explain the fact that the less he seems to need this encouragement, the more I appreciate that I am bound to recompense him — even if others were to know nothing of it? Or is it that the stimulus to do good requires, in order to be fully efficacious, that there be a consciousness of an unconditional link between an action and the appropriate sanction? But, in that case, there would be question of no more than a myth of some kind, which a mature

---

[2] In order to elucidate the notion of merit, the Scholastics generally take as their starting-point "condign" social merit. We believe that it is preferable to start from "congruent" merit. For, even when a promise has been made, it does not constitute the essence of merit, but simply increases the force of the demand which is present. The proof of this is that when a right is founded on a promise alone, there is no question of merit. The person who draws the winning ticket in a lottery has the right to the first prize, but no one could say that he has *merited* it. On the contrary, even in the absence of a promise, merit is already present in the fitness which, as we have indicated, is involved in "congruent" merit.

Things would be otherwise if we were speaking from a theological point of view. Only a loving initiative on God's part, expressed in a promise, could make our good actions deserving of eternal life. But we are here considering the philosophic notion of merit.

mind would be capable of appreciating for what it really is. The fact of the matter is that what we are here presented with, in our moral experience, is an irreducible datum. The utilitarian and sociological motivations of which we have just spoken are undoubtedly of importance and can at times appear to be the most apparent. But not to go beyond them would be to miss the essential point. What stands revealed in the bestowal of a reward on one's benefactor is not only an action that helps to promote the common good, or even the moral progress of humanity, but, above all, an action that is just[3]. But to speak of justice is to speak of equality. The bestowal of a reward aims, then, at a certain equality. Of what kind is this equality?

An objective equality, between the benefit and the reward, would annul the benefit, make it impossible to bestow a free gift, reduce the human relationship to the level of the commercial. As well, to envisage the reward as an objective compensation, as a sort of payment, would be, in most instances, to wrong the benefactor. The equality we are here trying to define is concerned with the equation between the (objective) moral value that has been manifested, "incarnated", in the benefit and a certain "natural" good of the benefactor, a certain amount of happiness that is to be his. Moral value on one side, eudae-monist value on the other. So true is this that we do not, in general, say of someone who has rendered us a service through acting unjustly — through being false to the duties he was charged with or whose intention has been perverse — that he *deserves* our thanks. A two-faced individual whose own deeds were shameful, but who provided the police with useful information, out of love of gain or to rid himself of a rival, has a right, if one wishes, to draw his pay, but does not strictly *merit* anything. Consequently, even where its sociological aspect is most evident, merit is intelligible only by means of moral value. It is not only because he has *conferred a benefit* on me that my benefactor merits my thanks, but because, in so doing, he has *acted well*. The moral notion of merit cannot originate from the analysis of human relationships, because it is presupposed by the judgments which enable us to formulate these. Or better perhaps: formed by starting from the notions

---

[3] St Thomas, *Summa Theol.*, II-II, 80, art. un.; 106,1.

of interpersonal and social merit, the moral notion reacts on these and controls their use.

It is clear, then, that in addition to all pragmatic, sociological and juridical considerations, there is present in the notion of merit the appreciation of a proportion, that *ought to exist*, between moral value and happiness. Note that what is involved is something quite different from a mere bundle of general ideas. The notion which I grasp is not simply that of a proportion between happiness and value: I appreciate that this proportion *ought to exist*. The notions of happiness and of value are not just externally linked: in judging that the person who does good merits a recompense, I appreciate that they are linked from within.

This "ought to exist" is transformed for me into an "ought to be achieved", by the benefit received, by my reaction of gratitude and by my promise, if I happen to have made it. The harmony between virtue and happiness, whose universal achievement is not my task, I am now called upon to bring about in a precise and delimited way. But the appeal which stems from the benefit borrows its force from a more profound appeal, that stems from moral value. It is this, as manifested in the benefit conferred, which grounds the rational demand that it be rewarded with happiness.

At this level of reflection, the notion of merit appears to be totally independent of that of benefit. Stripped of its interpersonal and social character, it shares in the impersonal character of reason. The virtuous man merits a recompense simply because he has been faithful to the norm of goodness. In consequence of this, one is led to conceive of an order in which the proportion between moral value and happiness would be perfectly and universally realized.

All that is as yet in question is an ideal order. But the world of ideas does not subsist in itself. Since it is God who is the ultimate foundation of the order of essences and values, whatever is done in accordance with or contrary to that order is, in reality, done in accordance with or contrary to the divine will (n. 169). While it is true that God receives no advantage from our actions, nor is He injured by them, the fact remains that in choosing what is good, a human being identifies his will with the eternal will, by which God, in loving and willing that absolute Value which is Himself, loves and wills the entire order of values. And this love of God for Himself is but an aspect of that infinite act, by which, transcending the opposition between the static and the dynamic, He *is*. To choose the good is, then, so to speak, to go in the same direction as the being of God, to be one in an analogical way, through the activity of one's Will, with the act by which God is. For what is it to do good to another, if not, radically, to go in the same direction as his dynamism? One being is a good for another, only by that accord. And when the beings in question are persons, this accord is called love. If then, the good act does not do good to God, it nonetheless has the same source as all love that is true; it possesses the same meaning as this love. — Inversely, his evil action opposes the sinner to the direction of being, and consequently, in some fashion, to the very being of God; an opposition which, where the being thus set in opposition is a passible and corruptible one, finds its normal exteriorization in suffering and death.

Accordingly, philosophical reflection that takes on a religious dimension, rediscovers, in its own way — a very analogous way — the link between merit and the conferring of a benefit, and, in consequence, the other-orientated aspect that was present in our initial (sociological) definition of merit, but which we had afterwards eliminated. Here, as in other contexts, the mediation of philosophy is indispensable, in order to pass securely from the empirical, scientific or sociological plane to the religious.

291. – Sanction is the correlative of merit (or of demerit — and indeed, in ordinary language, particularly of this latter). It can be defined as: a certain "natural" good or evil (a certain positive or negative eudaemonist value), which is dependent, as on its necessary condition, on the observance or violation of the law.

It presents three aspects: *preventive, retributive* and *medicinal*.

Sanction is *preventive* in that its anticipation (by means of promises or threats) provides the agent with a subjective motive for doing good, and so, by linking the moral and the eudaemonist orders (n. 302), makes the law to be efficacious. It is for this reason that a human law remains imperfect, as long as it lacks a sanction.

Sanction is *retributive* in that, once an action is performed, its merit or demerit is, in fact, sanctioned by the appropriate reward or chastisement.

Finally, sanction is *medicinal* in that his punishment helps the culprit to reform, and also in that the reward received encourages the person who has acted well, and invites him, when the opportunity offers, to act even better.

Now, in the world in which we live, where the possibility of a conversion always remains open, and where the assessment of responsibility is so difficult and so uncertain, this medicinal aspect, where punishment is concerned, takes on great importance. Consequently, as civil law advances, it tends increasingly to treat this aspect as primary: prisons become more and more centres of reeducation. Nevertheless, strictly speaking, this aspect is not essential to the notion of sanction. — Neither is the preventive aspect. If there were not already, in the moral disorder itself, something which justifies the chastisement, this would be unjustly inflicted and, likewise, unjustly decreed. For, either one really has the intention of imposing the sanction, if the need should arise, and so one is prepared to act unjustly, or else one has not this intention, and so, one lies[4]. (As well, in this latter instance, experience will quickly cause the deterrent to become ineffectual).

The essential aspect of sanction is, in consequence, the retributive aspect. Through moral reflection, as has been noted (n. 290), sanction is revealed as the establishment of a certain proportion or harmony between the natural, the eudaemonist, good of the agent and the moral value which he has manifested in his action.

But the problem still remains: what is the foundation of the demand that a harmony between two such heterogeneous orders be achieved?

---

[4] Perhaps the objection will be raised that positive law prescribes punishments for activities which are of themselves indifferent. The common good can require, in certain situations, that compensation be made for damage that has been involuntarily caused, or for which one has not been morally responsible, and the subject concerned can have no reasonable grounds for complaint. What is then in question is not, strictly speaking, a *punishment*. — But, where there has been a deliberate violation of the law, the situation is different. By the very fact that an activity is prohibited, it ceases to be indifferent: it becomes "axiologically" negative and deserves to be punished, in the way which the law determines.

292. – The difficulty is such that some have considered it can be resolved only by abandoning the notion of sanction. This is the attitude of J. M. Guyau who, moreover, rejects the notion of obligation (n. 94); it is the attitude of the Stoics, who regard virtue as its own reward (which is but another way of suppressing the problem, n. 279). Or, if the notion of sanction is still accepted, it is regarded as purely interior: the joy of a good conscience, the satisfaction that results from doing one's duty or, contrariwise, shame, remorse etc.

Others, however, recognize a sanction which is not simply the consciousness of a value that has been acquired or lost; but they regard it as a natural consequence of the good or evil action. Accordingly, they allow that there is a biological sanction (health or sickness, well-being or malaise); a social sanction (esteem or contempt) etc. To these *immanent* sanctions, due solely to the play of physical laws and, in consequence, entirely contained within the natural or physical sphere, they add the sanction of positive law. In this view, obviously, the notions of merit and sanction tend to be confused with that of causality. It is right that one who has injured society should be rejected and punished by it, just as it is right and completely in order that one who touches a high-tension electric cable should be electrocuted. What remains is the notion of a certain rationality, a certain order, where there is no special need for God.

All these sanctions are, obviously, sanctions which take effect in this present life. — The ethics of Aristotle provides a rather good example of this approach.

The notion of *karma* has some similarity with the idea of a natural fruitfulness of actions, whose effects will, however, be experienced only in a future life.

Kant does not deny the existence of sanctions; he recognizes that happiness is not analytically linked to moral value; he affirms that the will necessarily proposes to itself as an object (but not as an end) the achievement of the "highest good", the harmony of moral value with happiness, and that it is necessary to believe, by "moral faith", that this achievement is possible; this possibility "postulates" the existence of God, as the moral author of the natural order (n. 118). — But he

absolutely excludes from the moral motivation all consideration
of recompense or chastisement (n. 115); and if he allows us to
link the notion of happiness to that of virtue, this is only so as
to counterbalance the seductiveness of vice.

The Scholastics, in general, hold that, even without the
help of divine revelation, it is clear that the moral law possesses
genuine sanctions. These remain imperfect in this life: they
require to be perfected in a life to come, so that the doctrine of
the immortality of the soul is, in consequence, guaranteed.
These perfect sanctions consist in the attainment or loss of
beatitude, which, in the actual order, is a supernatural beatitude
(n. 304). — This view is also held by a certain number of
philosophers, such as Leibniz, whose thinking has been
influenced to a greater or lesser extent by Christianity.

Two tendencies can here be distinguished. Sanctions are
rather regarded by some as if they were attached to the law by
the will of the legislator; in treating of merit, they underline the
role of the promise in creating a strict right. Others, on the
contrary, pay greater attention to the intrinsic link between
sanctions and moral activity, so much so indeed that they seem,
at times, to regard the former as no more than the natural fruit
of the latter.

We have now to turn our attention to the problem itself.

293. — It is often alleged, in order to demonstrate the
necessity for sanctions, that without them the law would
remain a dead letter. This argument is not without weight (cf.
n. 302), but the conclusion should not be drawn from it that, in
that case, fidelity to the moral Ideal is no longer justified. The
final harmony of virtue and happiness is not required in order
that a person should "have reason" for acting well. He already
has a reason for so acting, a reason that is fully sufficient in
itself, a reason that lies in the intrinsic value of this activity. Is
not this in harmony with the order of reason? But what is in
harmony with reason has no need of a further "reason", in
order to become worthy of being chosen. "Reasons" are
required in order that an action should be reasonable, but the
action which of itself is in accordance with reason is reasonable
of its very nature; there is no point in seeking further justification for it.

There is need, then, to be careful about speaking of punishments and rewards, and of their effectiveness in inclining the will towards what is good, as if it would be absurd, in the event of our deriving no advantage as a result, to sacrifice our well-being and even our lives for the sake of the moral Ideal. This manner of speaking many people nowadays justifiably abhor (even though a certain hypocrisy can, at times, be mingled with their abhorrence). "The noble good is (worthy to be) chosen for its own sake"[5] (cf. nn. 71-73).

On the other hand, to regard the recompense as no more than an incentive, is to make of happiness a mere means to virtue, of the natural and physical a mere instrument of morality; it is to forget the subject himself, whose total good is achieved in accordance with the two dimensions of the free act: that of an elan towards happiness and of a devotion to the Value.

294. – After discarding this extrinsic justification as insufficient, we now return to that spontaneous evidence of moral consciousness from which we started (nn. 289-290), evidence which prompts us to say, when we are presented with the sufferings of the good and the prosperity of the guilty: "this is unjust, this ought not to be..." Our aim is to examine philosophically this spontaneous insight, in order that the truth contained in it may clearly emerge. To this end, we shall make use of three considerations: the first is drawn from the common foundation of the natural and moral orders; the second, from the nature of moral value; the third, from what an authentically human happiness requires.

1. The first consideration is a rather metaphysical one. Distinct though they are, the natural and the moral orders are not absolutely heterogeneous. They are both included in the higher unity of being; they have their common foundation in the divine essence and reason; God equally, although not in the same way, wills that the laws proper to each be observed. — In a spiritual being, the desire for beatitude and the devotion to moral value are not radically opposed: both express and continue in the creature that elan, by which the Creator, in causing him to exist and in promoting his growth in being, at

---

5 St Thomas, *Summa Theol.*, I, 5, 6.

the same time "converts" him to Himself (nn. 171-172). In virtue of this creative impetus, creatures adhere to the being which is theirs and tend towards *the* Being, with one and the same elan; they seek to be unified internally and to unite themselves to the One; they pursue their own good and they direct themselves towards *the* Good. The willing-of-himself of the creature, which finds expression in the quest for happiness, and the love of God, involved in moral dedication, are the two forms under which the creature shares in the divine Willing-of-himself. — To this common origin of the moral and natural orders, there should correspond, where their final goal is concerned, a convergence and a harmony; it is this harmony which the meritorious aspect of a person's good actions both entitles him to anticipate and to claim as his due. And so, just as the relations of causality, which knot all existing beings and make of them one universe, express, on the level of their full-blown multiplicity, their common rootedness in being, the common foundation of their existence in underived existence, so does merit, which binds the physical and the moral orders, express, on the very level of their distinction, their common foundation in the Absolute.

Moreover, as we have seen (nn. 284-285), to act morally, to act in accordance with reason, is to travel in the direction of the perfect flowering of our rational nature, in the direction, consequently, of beatitude. Virtue and happiness harmonize in their common harmony with our natural in-clination. Their convergence, then, is in no way surprising. On the contrary, the wonder is rather that this harmony should ever be lacking.

What accounts for this lack? Firstly, the fact that our nature is not purely rational, so that, in consequence, it is orientated towards more than the rational good. As a result, the rectitude of a person's will in relation to its goal does not automatically ensure the rectitude of his other activities in relation to their particular goals. This latter depends on conditions which have nothing in common with his moral attitude. Moral uprightness is no safeguard against toothache! The state of one's body, in this present life, is not only determined from within, by one's soul, but also, and in a very large measure, from without.

Moreover, independently of bodily suffering and other crosses of this kind, the mixed character of our nature suffices to explain why the subject does not at once reap the fruit of his moral rectitude. The screen — the internal screen — of matter is a barrier to his full enjoyment of the value he possesses, the value he is. The practical necessities of life perpetually tear him away from himself; they impel him towards what is external, and present him unceasingly with new tasks, which leave him no time to rest in the contemplation of his perfection. As well, even if it were possible, such contemplation could well be fatal for him: the virtue which is transformed into an object that one rejoices in as one's own possession, is thereby corrupted.

A final and more profound reason is that the human spirit, finite as it is, does not contain within itself its adequate object, and attains only gradually to its full natural growth. Hence, while an upright will is undoubtedly a *natural* good and the source of an extremely pure and refined joy, it is not sufficient to satisfy the natural desire of the human spirit, nor, as a consequence, to ensure complete happiness.

But, just as a rational demand is made on us to strive unceasingly to bring our natural inclinations under the control of reason — to adapt these inclinations to the requirements of reason — there is also, it seems, a rational demand that the relationship of our nature to its goal should finally be the same as the relationship of our liberty to its Ideal, that is, that our nature should be fulfilled in the measure in which we freely adhere, through our choice of what is morally valuable, to the Ideal.

It is clear from all this that the divorce between the moral and the physical orders is only temporary. It has a purpose, for because of it a person's love of the good is purified. To live virtuously would present no difficulties, if this always paid off (cf. the prologue of *Job*). — From the philosophical point of view, this divorce preserves the characteristic traits of moral value. A constant coincidence of the moral and the advantageous could well lead one to believe in their formal identity.

295. – 2. As we have already noted (nn. 22: 41; 45), moral value presents us with a demand that we acknowledge and approve of it. What is morally valuable is lovable, and demands to be loved for its own sake. Now, in the measure in which the subject, through acting in accordance with the moral order, becomes a bearer of value, he shares in this characteristic. There emanates from him an invitation, directed towards all reasonable beings, that he be respected and loved. But to love is to will, and to promote, the good of the one loved. Of itself, moral value renders its subject worthy of being helped by all others to achieve happiness. Through his nature, this value, become incarnate in him, claims the homage of all. In loving the virtuous person, in "doing good" to him, we manifest our esteem and our love for virtue. His happiness is no longer simply the goal of his subjective appetite; it has become for all the objective requirement which is called *merit*.

Without doubt, in the present order, where the true moral worth of others ordinarily escapes us, where our ability to advance their happiness is so limited, the appeal which moral value makes in them can be only falteringly answered. Moreover, it is not only the moral value of others which regulates the order of our love for them: other factors, which can be more accurately measured, intervene: kinship, need etc.[6]. Nonetheless, we conceive of an ideal order where the love each person meets with would be supremely efficacious, as well as being in exact proportion to his moral value: and this we recognize to be a requirement of practical reason, since a requirement that stems from moral value by that very fact stems from reason. — Now, we know that the ideal order, just as the order of existing beings, has for its foundation the absolute Being. In reality, through this requirement of moral value and of reason, it is God himself who makes a demand in us and of us (nn. 165; 172). It is God, supreme love and supreme wisdom, who knows and loves human beings in accordance with their true value; and since His love is, of its very nature, efficacious, man — and any other rational creature — will not fail to achieve fulfilment in proportion to his moral quality. But if, unfaithful to the Ideal, he comes to be an evil person and remains one definitively, through an irrevocable choice, he will share in the odious character of evil, so that his lot can only be universal aversion.

---

[6] *Ib.*, II-II, 26, 7; *Car.*, 9 ad 12um.

Merit can, then, from this point of view, be defined as that claim to esteem and love which moral value communicates to its subject, and which, of its nature, is addressed to all persons, but which only God is capable of fully satisfying.

Under this aspect, man's fulfilment is revealed as a homage that is paid to moral value, through the nature of the spiritual subject in whom this value has become incarnate. This fulfilment, in consequence, expresses the subordination of his nature to his moral value, and in this, the present argument links up with the preceding one.

296. – 3. The happiness towards which man naturally tends cannot consist in any satisfaction whatever of his tendencies and desires. Since the nature which this happiness has to satisfy is that of a person, it has to have a personal character. Now, the activity that is characteristic of a person is free activity, by which he becomes, at a certain level, the *cause of himself*, the one who makes or breaks himself as a person. In consequence, true happiness cannot simply be conferred upon him; it has *also* to be, in a certain fashion, his own achievement; it has to depend on himself as subject, that is, on his liberty.

In effect, if happiness in the full sense (beatitude) were but the fruit of his natural qualities (ability, cleverness, talent etc.), if it resulted from his activity by way of physical causality (in the way in which a person's industry makes him rich), then it would be, not *his* achievement, but the achievement of his nature in him; it would not be attributable to the spiritual subject precisely as such, to the subject as transcending his nature. The attainment of happiness, in order to be genuinely human, in order to correspond genuinely to the condition of the spiritual subject, needs to depend not on his human activity considered under its physical aspect, but on that activity as it proceeds from the "I", that is, as free and, in consequence, moral. But to attain beatitude as a result of activity that is free and moral, is to attain it by way of *merit*. — If beatitude is obtained in this way, and only in this way, the conclusion follows that it will elude those who have not deserved it by leading a good life. The attainment or non-attainment of beatitude is, then, nothing other than the sanction of the moral law.

In order the better to appreciate what has been said, it should be remembered that the free activity on which beatitude is dependent cannot be an activity which is aimed at beatitude in general, since this latter is necessarily willed, nor even an activity whose object presents itself as immediately leading to beatitude, since such an object would also be necessarily willed. The free activity that is in question here has, then, to be directed towards an object which, without presenting itself as immediately leading to beatitude, is, however, intrinsically linked with it.

This link cannot, however, simply be of the means-to-end type, as if the free activity in question consisted in the judicious choice of the means which will effectively ensure happiness. For, at this level — which is that of the Aristotelian *proairesis*[7] — the true moving principle is still the elan of a person's nature; liberty is exercised only in a superficial fashion, so that the subject is not genuinely committed. Liberty in depth comes to be exercised, only when the other, or the "vertical", dimension of the human act is envisaged: the taking up of a position before the ultimate End or the Ideal. It is in this attitude, essentially involved in all moral activity, that the subjective condition for the attainment of beatitude is to be found; it is in opting for the good, in a choice where *he himself*, in the profound depths of his being, is committed and expressed, that the subject makes his happiness to be genuinely *his*. — Moreover, as has been shown, the link between moral activity and beatitude is neither extrinsic nor arbitrary, since both happiness and moral value are, each in its own way, the perfection of man as man and present themselves to him as ultimates (n. 276).

It may appear paradoxical that a beatitude which is simply merited, but whose effective attainment depends on a liberty other than our own, can be said to be more ours than a beatitude that is acquired as the fruit of our own energy. The purely moral link of merit does not, it seems, provide the same security, does not have the same solidity, the same closeness as is present in the physical identity between the subject and the activity he exercises. But what we are here concerned with is not the way in which beatitude is, so to speak, physically achieved, but rather with what it is in the subject himself which rationally justifies its attainment. And since beatitude, in order to fulfil the person, has to have a personal character, it must be attained by him through the activity in which he is committed as a person: through activity that is free and moral. — In

---

[7] *Nicom. Eth.*, III, 4, 1111 b 26-30. — Cf. *Essai*, n. 117; pp. 282-285.

addition, as Aristotle has noted: "what we are capable of achieving through our friends, we are, in a way, capable of achieving personally"[8]. The union which love establishes between subjects is more intimate, in a way, than the physical union between the will and the activities which it commands, just as, according to the Scholastics, the union of subject and object in knowledge is closer than that between matter and form. Consequently, a happiness whose attainment depends immediately on a love that is infinitely powerful and faithful, is more assured, more our own, than a happiness obtained by the exercise of natural powers, whose link with liberty remains, in the final analysis, exterior (in comparison with spiritual interiority). — All the more so, since God's closeness to us is of an entirely singular character. He is more interior to us than we are to ourselves; He is at the very well-spring of our being, at the heart of our subjectivity, at the source from which our free actions spring. The good that we do was His achievement before being ours; not in a more or less faithful likeness, but in our original exemplar and the well-spring of our being. To look to Him for our happiness is not to look to someone outside ourselves: it is to look to one in whom we exist spiritually, not as one of whom we are a more or less faithful likeness, but as one without whom we could not be; it is to look to Him whose presence conditions all interiority. — Reciprocally, to insist that our happiness has to be, in some sense, our own achievement, does not imply the least trace of Pelagianism, since it is God himself who enables us, and that not only in an initial and general fashion, to satisfy the required conditions, and who, in crowning our merits, is crowning the gifts He has himself bestowed. Far from substituting for our exercise of liberty, His grace makes us more free, and enables us to become what, at the most profound level of our being as persons, we already are.

The fate of the infants who die after being baptized does not provide an objection to what has been said. What we are here speaking about are the human beings whose development has been *normal*, so that they have become capable of performing human actions. No matter how frequently it may occur, the situation of

---

[8] *Nicom. Eth.*, II, 3, 1112 b 27-28.

these infants remains *abnormal*. — Does this mean that their beatitude is incomplete? In the measure in which this has not been achieved by any personal act, it is simply less human. But this is in no way scandalous. A soul that enjoys the beatific vision is undoubtedly in a far superior state to that of *homo viator*; this state is, however, less human, for a soul is not a human being and, according to the Scholastics, is not, in the strict sense, a person.

In addition, is it not required that the personal character of human beatitude should also be present in the way in which it is bestowed? A happiness which came to us in an impersonal and automatic fashion, in response to our own efforts, could not fully satisfy us. The response which our liberty requires is the gift which another Liberty bestows. Consequently, to depend on the goodwill of the Other, far from compromising the personal aspect of beatitude, is, on the contrary, an element of this. — In this way, there is reintroduced, in an unforeseen manner, the factor which our analysis seemed at first sight to have discarded: the notion of a *promise*. It is not an impersonal law which links happiness and moral value; it is nothing other than the act, supremely personal, in which God, in making human beings to exist, causes them to share in a twofold way in that will by which He loves himself, in willing that they love themselves and also love Him (albeit under the temporary anonymity of moral value). — This line of thought has, then, led us back to the first consideration.

The limitations of the present argument should be noted. Firstly, since it does not take moral value as its starting-point, it could not reveal this to one who did not already possess the notion. The moral character of the activity which conditions the achievement of beatitude is defined only from the outside. — Secondly, what the argument proves is that without some moral activity there can be no beatitude, not that every moral action merits a sanction.

297. – It is clear that sanctions are a rational requirement, so that the expectation of a harmony between a person's moral value and his happiness is entirely rational. But what is the actual situation? What do we see around us? Does experience reveal that this harmony has been achieved?

In a certain measure, yes. A virtuous life brings many advantages: peace of heart, health (often at least), a good reputation, the confidence of others, the very sweet joys of family life etc. It preserves a person from much misery. Vice, on the contrary, is the source of troubles, of interior conflicts, of physical and psychical illnesses; it forments discord, hatred, results in disgrace and ignominy etc. All this is even more evident if we pass from the individual to the social level, where the effects of both virtue and vice have more time and space in which to reveal themselves. The civic virtues: obedience, probity, a sense of duty, justice, devotion to the common good, are singularly favourable to the peace, concord, prosperity and happiness of all.

All this is true, often at least, and perhaps more often than not. Nevertheless, things by no means always turn out this way. And even where sanctions are apparent, they always remain imperfect. One has but to open one's eyes: how many good people are unhappy, reduced to miserable straits, tortured by illness, victims of persecution etc.! How many unscrupulous men have flourished! Similarly in the social sphere: upright and peace-loving peoples have at times been ravaged, deported, exterminated; others have grown and have prospered for long centuries, by means of violence and treachery.

In addition, there are sufferings, at times more excruciating, which stem from virtue itself, from the requirements of a conscience that is delicate and easily perturbed, or, at all events, dissatisfied at falling so far short of its ideal.

There is no escaping the fact that the harmony between moral value and happiness remains very imperfect in this present life. Where reason is concerned, this is a type of scandal.

298. – Clearly, this scandal cannot be removed by having recourse to the immortality which A. Comte calls "subjective" ("objective" would be more accurate), that is, the "imperishable" remembrance which the "just, whose memory is held in benediction", leave behind them. For, on the one hand, the just are no longer there to enjoy this: where they are concerned, this recompense is reduced to the joy of thinking, during their lives, that if they do good, they will — perhaps — be remembered for this: on any reckoning, this remains a rather jejune reward. On the other hand, there are numerous good, excellent, and even heroic actions of which others can have no knowledge and cannot, in consequence, keep in mind. (For example, the action of a shipwrecked person who gives his lifebelt to another... and both are drowned). To be immortal in the dimension of my being-for-others is of no account, if I am not first immortal in the dimension of my being-for-myself.

The scandal is removed only if the harmony between moral value and happiness, which reason requires, but which is not realized in this present life, is attained in another form of existence after death. This implies the continued existence of the subject. Now, it is precisely this that rational psychology demonstrates, in showing that the human soul, since it possesses existence in its own right (and not simply in virtue of being the "form" of the body), is not automatically swept away with the dissolution of the organism, and, being simple in its essence, has within it no principle of disintegration: in other words, that it is, of itself, immortal. The requirements of reason in its practical function fuse, then, with the conclusions of reason in its speculative function. Human hope is well founded.

It is true that to speak of the human soul, spiritual and immortal, is nowadays considered, in certain quarters, to be in rather bad taste. But is not the justified reaction to Platonic-Cartesian dualism going to an excess which is even worse than that from which it seeks to preserve us? If caution is not observed, it runs the risk of leading to a more or less concealed materialism, whose symptoms have already been experienced to some extent even in theology and morality. It is an excellent thing to strike at "angelism", or the tendency to regard man as a disembodied spirit — we have not hesitated to do so in the course of our investigation — but not at the cost of downgrading the authentically spiritual dimension of his being. Man is not pure reason, but he is more than his living and sentient body, and he has within him what is immune from the inexorable law of corruption to which his organism is subject.

We have not here to determine the moment at which the harmony in question is realized. Will this be immediately after death or later, at the end of a period of preparation? Reason cannot solve this problem; it is to theology that we have to look for an answer. It would appear, however, to be perfectly plausible, from the philosophical point of view, that the soul, which has become, in virtue of its "separation", entirely transparent to itself, (entirely "for itself" and capable, in consequence, of a fuller commitment), should no longer be able to alter the radical choice that has been made.

Neither shall we enter into a discussion of the recent theory which holds that the definitive choice occurs at the instant of death, at the moment in which the subject enters into a mode of existence different from his temporal existence. This hypothesis can be of interest to the theologian, but not to the moralist. The function of ethics is to regulate the actions of man during his existence in time. As well, it is necessary, at all costs, to avoid whatever could tend to conceal the seriousness of the challenge to which we are here and now subjected, or the profound effect that the options we make have on ourselves as persons — options which are expressed and articulated, during our life-span, in the diverse but reversible choices which we make.

299. – Obviously, the rational demand of which we are speaking could not be satisfied by an immortality in which the personal "I" is suppressed, through the absorption of the individual in the All. Such an absorption would render impossible the establishment of a proportion between the beatitude and the moral value of each individual subject [9].

But, following another line of thought, one could ask whether, in place of an immortality that is definitively acquired after death, it would not be at least as reasonable to admit a "reincarnation", whose quality would exactly correspond to the moral quality of the person's former life. This doctrine is present in many religions: it is to be found among the ancient druids and it is fundamental to Indian thought (even though only after Vedic times) [10]. A number of philosophers have professed it: among the ancients, Plato (the myth of Er the Pamphylian, in the 10th book of the *Republic*), Plotinus etc.; among the moderns, Renouvier in particular (as the more

---

[9] At the time of the Averroist debate, around 1270, there were some who maintained: St Peter is saved and consequently I shall be saved, since we both have the same intellectual soul. See St Thomas, *De unitate intellectus*.

[10] There is no mention of reincarnation in the *Veda*. It seems to be taught in the *Brahmana* (commentaries on the *Veda* dealing with sacrifices). It is clearly contained in the *Upanishads* (philosophic and theosophic treatises, often of a very elevated nature). As is wellknown, the chronology of the sacred Indian writings is extremely uncertain.

plausible hypothesis). It has been championed in recent times by many spiritists and above all by the theosophists (Annie Besant) and the anthroposophists (Rudolf Steiner).

If one is to believe the proponents of this opinion, there is no other way of explaining, in a satisfactory manner, the inequality of human conditions and the wretchedness, apparently unmerited, of so many here below.

On purely philosophical grounds, this doctrine is open to the following objections:

1. An individual human soul is the form of an individual body, *of this body here*, to which it is strictly adapted. It cannot, in consequence, be the form of another body. That *this* soul should lose its intrinsic relation to *this* body and acquire a different one, is unthinkable: its individuality would change and it would no longer be *this* soul. (This would be all the more true, if the "body" in which its "rebirth" occurs is not a human body!).

2. One could, it is true, reply: by the sole fact that this soul receives a new body, it communicates to this its own individuation, which it has never lost, and makes the new body to be *its* body — the same as the one which it had in its former life. Is it not in this way, moreover, that many contemporary theologians, following Billot, understand the resurrection of the body? But the obvious questions which this line of thought prompts is: how is it that we retain no memory of our former existences, even of that which has immediately preceded our present one? The few facts that are adduced to show that we do have such a memory are almost all susceptible of a psychological explanation; there is none, at all events, which provides undeniable evidence of the presence of these memories.

It will be said that, if the soul forgets in this way, this is because it is now clothed in a new body. But this reply wishes to have its cake and eat it. Either this body is *another* body, and then the *same* soul cannot be its form. Alternatively, it is the *same* body; but this supposes that the soul has appropriated it, and then how strange it is that this body, which has been appropriated in this way — "made its own" — by the soul, prevents the soul from making use of the experience and knowledge which had been previously acquired. These experiences are now of no use; as far as this soul is concerned, they are as if they had never been. How strange it also is that the person, even when most profoundly recollected, can know nothing of his former state. And if, as certain proponents of the theory of reincarnation maintain, the soul retains from its past life tendencies which manifest themselves in the course of the present one, this forgetfulness becomes all the stranger. Why does it not also retain memories which would, at least after intense reflection, emerge clearly in consciousness?

3. Moreover, the hypothesis of reincarnation serves no purpose. If one life is too short to determine the *definitive* destiny of man, many life times will be likewise insufficient, since the disproportion between the finite and the infinite will always remain. If the cycle of rebirths is endless, beatitude becomes impossible [11]. If a person has to keep on being reborn until he is fit to attain happiness, the lot of both good and evil will finally be the same: the consequence of this would be to diminish greatly the significance and challenge of human life. One would then be presented with this paradox — or this scandal: a person who with full deliberation and total commitment turns away from what is good could still be certain of enjoying the same happiness as the good-living person...

4. Finally, sanctions take on a moral significance, only if the reason for them is known: it is only under this condition that the order of justice is manifested, so that good living is encouraged and evil living becomes, even at the level of "nature", an object of horror. But, in the hypothesis of reincarnation, a person is completely ignorant of the good or evil he may have done prior to his present life; it is impossible for him to repent of a fault of which his conscience does not accuse him.

300. – If we reflect on the reasons produced in support of the theory of reincarnation, their lack of weight becomes evident. The inequality of human conditions is sufficiently explained, on the one hand, by the differences which cannot but exist between finite beings

---

[11] Speaking of this hypothesis, St Augustine commented, in *Epist.*, 166, c. 9; PL. t. 33, col. 732: they maintain that through the incomprehensible cycle of rebirths, and after innumerable years, human beings have still to return to the burdens and pains to which corruptible flesh is heir: "I cannot imagine any more horrible prospect". — Note that it is with *moksha*, or liberation from the cycle of rebirths, that Indian thought is preoccupied.

and, on the other, by the effects produced both on human beings themselves and on the universe in which they live, by each one's exercise of liberty: for the divine "discretion" allows creatures, both to be what they are, and to act in accordance with what they are [12]. As regards the problem of evil, reason, left to itself, throws, it is true, little enough light; but it does throw some. The difficulty is not so much to explain the possibility of evil: this — in common with the inequality of which we have just spoken — has its sufficient reason in our creaturely finitude, in the fact that a universe in the process of becoming cannot be perfect all at once, and by the interaction of free beings. To develop this topic is the task of natural theology. The real difficulty — just as where moral evil is concerned, n. 235 — comes from the frightening proportions which evil assumes *in the actual order*. Faced with these, philosophy has to acknowledge its limitations. But the hypothesis of reincarnation would pose more problems than it would solve.

It should also be noted that this doctrine often entails consequences that are pernicious, both morally and socially. Not only does it abolish, or at least greatly reduce, the difference between good and evil, since even the most depraved person can believe that he too will infallibly attain beatitude, but, viewed from another angle, it tends to breed a sense of desperation, when a person feels himself burdened by the weight of unknown faults, whose effects he is completely powerless to avoid. (It is in this sense that the theory of reincarnation is most frequently presented). From the social point of view, once the inequalities that exist are attributed to *personal* faults, one is less inclined to pity and to help the poor, the oppressed, the unhappy; often, even the effort to improve their condition will be discouraged, for this would be to oppose the supreme Law.

But there is no denying that, to those who admit no beatitude other than that obtainable by man's own efforts, at the termination of his natural development, the arguments in favour of reincarnation may take on added weight. In this hypothesis, it would indeed be difficult to believe that a good-living but incultured person, whose intellectual horizons have scarcely gone beyond the practical necessities of daily living, whose mind has never grappled with the "great problems", should find himself, immediately after his death, in possession of the Truth! Is it not more reasonable to suppose a series

---

[12] Cf. St Thomas, *Cont. Gent.*, II, 44: "That the distinction between beings does not result from the diversity of their merits or demerits", and 45: "What is the first cause of the distinction between beings?" (This distinction, he replies, has its source in God, who gives to each creature the perfection of which it is capable).

of intercalary lives, by means of which this person will gradually arrive at his full spiritual maturity? It is for this reason that certain authors, even Catholics, while they reject the theory of reincarnation, do not consider themselves entitled to regard it as absolutely impossible [13]. — Be that as it may, the difficulty vanishes, once our beatitude is not simply the fruit of our own efforts, but, much more, the fruit of the grace of Christ-in-us. The Catholic doctrine of Purgatory sheds much light on this question, particularly if Purgatory is not conceived of, as it all too often is, in a purely juridical fashion (as the payment of a "debt"), but as a passive and progressive purification which prepares the soul to know and to appreciate the ultimate reality — a purification that bears some resemblance to the "nights" which the mystics experience.

301. – The importance for moral reflection of the problem of death is clear from what has preceded. In a eudaemonist perspective, the truth of this is evident: not only does the certainty of death exclude perfect happiness, but also, as Pascal has said so well, "all our actions and thoughts must take a very different direction, depending on whether or not there are eternal joys to be hoped for, so that it is possible to advance with sense and judgment only by taking our bearings from what ought to be our ultimate goal" [14]. But the problem of death is no less relevant to the analysis that we have made here. For, if death is the end of everything, then the effort to lead a moral life, justified though it is in itself by its harmony with right reason, cannot but appear to be futile. The values which have become incarnate in a person will perish at his death! Hence the contradiction, and how tragic it is, between the transcendence, where values are concerned, of a life lived in accordance with reason, which partakes of the absolute of Value, and the precariousness of this same life, where existence is concerned. (And it is, perhaps, simply of this that those to whom reference has been made in n. 293 wish to remind us). — We very readily grant, however, that in this matter, the light which unaided philosophic reflection can cast is very limited; the conclusions to which it can come, through its own

---

[13] For example, J. Leclerq, *Les grandes lignes de la philosophie morale*, Louvain, 1947, p. 320.

[14] Pascal, *Pensées*, ed. Brunschvicg, n. 542.

resources, are possessed more completely, and with greater assurance, through the light which Revelation brings[15].

302. – Two remarks in conclusion.

The first is concerned with the duration of the final sanction. This, where a life has been good, is happiness, which, as we have just noted, would not be perfect if it had to come to an end[16]. It is not true, no matter what the Stoics say, that duration is here of no importance, that "one instant of happiness is worth an eternity". As regards the sanction of a guilty life, it would definitely seem that this should involve the definitive loss of beatitude, for the reason indicated in n. 299, 4. Can the hypothesis of annihilation be excluded on philosophical grounds? At any rate, philosophy has little enough to say in this area: a wise pragmatism is here in place. The important thing is not to know exactly what is the lot of those who have made shipwreck of their lives and to what extent it is tolerable, but rather to act in such a way that the question becomes, for ourselves and for others, an unreal one.

---

[15] On the problem of death, see, for example, J. L. Aranguren, *Etica*, pp. 403-416; M. F. Sciacca, *Morte e immortalità*, Milan, 1959; K. Rahner, *Zur Theologie des Todes*, Freiburg – im – B., 1958 (Eng. trans.: *On the Theology of Death*, C. Henkey, London, 1961). R. Troisfontaines, *Je ne meurs pas...*, Paris, 1960 (*I do not die*, New York, 1963): *J'entre dans la vie*, Paris, 1963; G. Martelet, *Victoire sur la mort*, Paris, 1962. — For a different approach, see Vl. Jankélévitch, *La mort*, Paris, 1966, who concludes both to the "absurdity of survival" and the "absurdity of annihilation": something that is eternal remains: this is the "core" of the person: "to have been, to have lived, to have loved". Nonetheless, this remains quite deceptive...

[16] "Since beatitude is the perfect and sufficient good, it has to quiet man's desire and exclude every evil. Now man naturally desires to retain the good which he has and to have the assurance that he will do so; otherwise he cannot avoid being upset by the fear of losing it, or by sorrow at the certainty of this loss. In order then to be thoroughly happy, man needs to believe that he will never lose the good he possesses. If this belief is justified, it follows that he will never lose beatitude; but if it is unjustified, then to be mistaken in this way is itself an evil... But one who is subject to what is evil cannot, in consequence, be genuinely happy", St Thomas, *Summa Theol.*, II-II, 5, 4. — Cf. St Augustine, *De Trinitate*, XIII, 8: A person who loses the beatitude he possessed is either unwilling that this should happen, willing or indifferent. If he is unwilling, he is frustrated: he is unhappy. If he is willing, what he possessed was not beatitude, since he is content to lose it. Finally, if he is indifferent, what he possessed was, once again, not beatitude, since it could not win his love.

The second remark is concerned precisely with this pragmatism: it deals with the role of sanctions and, more exactly, with their anticipation, in conferring on the moral law a force and a practical efficacy that it would otherwise lack. As we have already noted (n. 293), this consideration is not the primary one, but it has its importance. It is all too clear that, if there were no link between virtue and happiness, temptation would be too strong for the great mass of mankind, and even the best would be subjected to discouragement.

One might perhaps object that this efficacy of sanctions is far from evident, since so many people — even among believers — are not influenced by them. If the reply is made that this motive is operative only where those who are determined to live in accordance with reason are concerned, then it appears to be superfluous: one who possesses this determination finds, in the moral value of his actions, sufficient reason for living virtuously.

The truth of the matter is that the thought of sanctions furnishes an efficacious motive to the person who is resolved to act rationally *in the line of eudaemonism*. Now, this consideration is licit and praiseworthy (n. 287), provided that it is not exclusive, with the consequence that moral value is reduced to the utilitarian level. It is a consideration which harmonizes with the natural dynamism of the will, or rather of the spiritual subject. Since beatitude is at the *horizon* of all our activity (nn. 139; 280), we neither can, nor should, renounce happiness. It is, in consequence, licit and praiseworthy to present to the will motives which incline it, as a *natural* dynamism, in the direction in which it is drawn, as a *rational* power, by moral value. Undoubtedly, the good action is already, in virtue of its harmony with reason and with rational nature, a perfection of this latter (nn. 132; 135); it is for this reason, as we have seen, that the moral value of an action already provides us with a subjective motive for performing it: it is desirable to us (n. 286). But this motivation is very frequently rendered ineffective or neutralized by the weight of our lower tendencies, whose demands are not always in harmony with those of reason. So, even though the good action is, as such, a perfection of our nature, it does not generally present itself to us under that aspect. The preventive role of sanction (n. 291) is precisely to complement the subjective motivation in this respect, by revealing that this action is linked to beatitude and is, in consequence, purely and simply desirable, just as is this latter.

Nonetheless, in the measure in which the subject progresses morally, in that same measure the desire of happiness and, in consequence, the thought of sanctions, are more and more penetrated by the love of moral value, so that the principal reason for seeking happiness comes to be the desire of being thereby totally dedicated to the Ideal.

CHAPTER SIXTEEN

WHAT IS TRUE HAPPINESS?

303. – Where is happiness to be found, what is it that will bring us the total satisfaction for which we crave, or, in a word, what is the *supreme good* for a human being: this, as we know, was one of the themes which constantly recurred in the moral discussions of the philosophers of antiquity. To this question Varro, St Augustine tells us [1], recorded no fewer than 288 possible solutions! Whether or not all of these have been seriously defended need not concern us here, all the more so as the great majority of them have already been eliminated at this stage of our investigation, namely, all the views which identify happiness with pleasure or, in general, with the good things which this earthly life of ours has to offer. An additional and decisive reason is that this life is transient and that a "complete happiness" which will come to an end, is far from being complete, and does not deserve to be called "happiness" in the sense in which it is here understood (n. 302) [2]. — One of the great weaknesses of Aristotelian ethics is that it proposes no happiness to man beyond that which can be attained within the limits of his existence on this earth (n. 64), even though, as is readily acknowledged, this happiness necessarily remains imperfect. This impasse, with which Aristotle and other great thinkers were faced, can be overcome only if the human soul is immortal, so that true happiness, which is impossible in this life, can then be obtained after death [3].

But even though the truth of this is clear, as a result of our investigations in the previous chapter, the question we are here faced with still remains unanswered. How are we to

---

[1] *Civ. Dei*, XIX, 1; PL. t, 41, col. 621-623.

[2] For the principal opinions concerning beatitude and for a discussion of them, see St Thomas, *Cont. Gent.*, III, 27-36 and *Summa Theol.*, I-II, 2.

[3] *Cont. Gent.*, III, 48.

conceive of this happiness which awaits us *after our death*? Several hypotheses are possible.

The first is that the "separated" human spirit finds its full joy in the lucid contemplation of its own essence (now no longer concealed by a corporeal screen), in a full and perfect presence to itself and possession of itself. Is it not precisely this total transparence, this perfect consciousness of ourselves, that we are constantly striving to achieve by means of the progressive acquisition of knowledge? Indeed, what, in the last analysis, is the chief purpose of man's work but to transform and humanize the world, so that he may rediscover himself in it, and so come to possess himself at an ever deepening level [4]? — A point worth noting is that this hypothesis does not exclude moral sanctions. What the "separated" human spirit takes possession of is not simply the rational, spiritual nature which makes possible a human being's endeavours, and which remains no matter what options he makes: what is taken possession of is the *spirit itself*, as affected by the choices which have been freely made, as conformed or not to the Ideal, as matured or stunted.

Some of the philosophers of antiquity, notably among the Stoics, have identified happiness with the knowledge of the universe and its secrets, the contemplation of the order that is in the world [5]. Others, in particular certain Arabian philosophers, have maintained that it is knowledge of and association with "separated substances" (pure spirits) which will satisfy all our desires; they proposed this view either because they attributed to one of these (and not immediately to God) the creation of the human soul, or else because they believed,

---

[4] L. Lavelle's way of expressing himself *seems* at times to be open to this interpretation.

[5] Seneca, for example, writes: "Now the soul of my brother — freed as it were from the prison in which it had long been contained and at length in command of itself — is exultant and rejoices in its contemplation of the nature of things" *Consolat. ad Polyb.*, 9, 3. "Some day the secrets of nature will be revealed to you; the mist will disperse and you will be bathed in a bright light", *Ep.*, 102, 28. — But, in Seneca's view, this beatitude is not eternal: in common with the other Stoics, he accepts the cyclic theory or, as Nietzsche expresses it, the theory of the "eternal return". The soul will enjoy its happiness only until the conflagration, which will mark the end of the present cycle, occurs: it will then be merged with the great Totality.

as did Averroes, that there was a separated Intellect, which is one in all men, by which and in which they know the truth[6]. These theories are long since out of fashion but, nevertheless, once we reflect on the matter, it seems to be quite reasonable to equate human happiness with the presence and companionship of other persons and, in the first place, of *human* persons. What human beings find their greatest delight in, is other human beings[7]. Indeed, it would be by no means impossible to give contemporary humanism an eschatological development, so that complete human happiness would be identified with perfect and eternal communion with all other human beings, that is, with the companionship which each human being would have, once the human race had definitively achieved the complete unity for which it is destined[8]. Moreover, is it not true that what chiefly seems to console many dying people, even those who are good Christians, is the hope that soon they will be reunited with "their own"?

For Christian thinkers and, outside of Christianity, for most of those who admit the existence of a supreme reality, an

---

[6] This is the view of Ibn-Badja (Avempace), Ibn-Roshd (Averroes); cf. *Cont. Gent.*, III, 41-44. — According to St Thomas, however, these authors were speaking rather of a beatitude to be obtained *in this life*, through union with the separated intelligences.

[7] "Nothing is so pleasant to man as man", Aristotle, *Eud. Eth.*, VII, 2, 1237 a 28-29 (Trans. of J. Solomon, Oxford, 1949, ed. W. D. Ross).

[8] The doctrine of the immortality of the soul is not always, in fact, linked with the affirmation of God. Even though the religion of Israel was strictly monotheistic, it was almost completely ignorant, until late in its development, of any sanctions other than those, individual or collective, of the present life: immortality was either not conceived of, or at any event had no moral significance. Inversely, there are doctrines in which immortality is asserted but which do not acknowledge God. C. Renouvier goes so far as to see an opposition between the thesis of immortality and monotheism. He himself, in the later period of his philosophy, tends towards a type of polytheism (which he judges to be more "democratic"!), where the divine persons and the divinized human persons differ only in degree (*Traité de psychologie rationnelle*, Paris, 1912., t. II, pp. 300-315). — In Indian thought, the system (darçana) *Sankhya* teaches that the individual soul (purusha) is immortal and indeed eternal; it tends, by means of successive reincarnations, towards that definitive liberation from material nature (prakriti) which is achieved through returning to its pure essence: nevertheless, the system also teaches atheism. See R. Grousset, *Les philosophies indiennes*, Paris, t. I, pp. 96-139; more briefly, E. Gathier, *La pensée hindoue*, Paris, 1960, pp. 87-91.

Absolute, happiness essentially consists in a union with this reality, this Absolute. The nature of this union is not, however, envisaged in the same way by all. In Monistic and Pantheistic systems, what is envisaged is a fusion between the individual and the Universal, such that the former ceases to be a distinct person. The doctrine of *advaita* (non-duality) of the Vedantic philosopher Shankara is along these lines — although where he is concerned, the individual does not cease to be a distinct person for the simple reason that he never was such: what disappears is the illusion that one is a distinct person[9]. Spinoza too writes in this vein; but note that his thought, on this point, is not altogether clear and that his interpreters are not in agreement; in addition, it has to be borne in mind that, in his view, complete happiness is to be possessed in this life, in which we feel and experience that we are eternal[10]. — Thinkers who acknowledge a personal and transcendent God maintain that the attainment of happiness, far from resulting in the disappearance of the distinct human personality, will result in its perfection and completion. The union with God will occur not on the level of being — by the identification of the human with the divine being — but on the level of spiritual activity, that is, of knowledge and love.

304. – The Christian faith teaches us that true happiness, the only happiness for which man has ever, in fact, been destined, is a supernatural and gratuitous happiness, which exceeds both the possibilities of achievement that are open to him, and the rewards to which he may lay claim, simply as man. This happiness consists in an immediate spiritual union

---

[9] On Shankara, see G. Dandoy, *L'ontologie du Vedânta*, Paris, 1932; O. Lacombe, *L'absolu selon le Vedânta*, Paris, 1938; Johanns, *La pensée religieuse de l'Inde*, Louvain, 1952; E. Gathier, *op. cit.*, pp. 51-59.

[10] "We feel and experience that we are eternal", *Ethics*, Va p., prop. 33, schol. — On Spinoza's doctrine of "salvation", see, for example, A. Rivaud, *Histoire de la philosophie*, t. III, Paris, 1950, pp. 309-313. "The language of Spinoza is — perhaps deliberately — ambiguous. He appears to speak of a future life, such as Christianity proclaims, or else of an immersion in the divine, which, without adding one instant to our limited duration, instantly reveals to us its vanity. He has been careful not to make his meaning more precise, in order to speak both to those who are still swayed by the dogmas of their religion and those whom wisdom has definitively emancipated", *ib.*, p. 311.

with God, a union of intuitive knowledge ("beatific vision") and pure love. A question which the Scholastics debated was whether the activity of our intellect would hold the primacy in this union, as St Thomas [11] taught, or whether this role would fall to our will, as Scotus [12] maintained, or whether, as Suarez [13] proposed, neither would hold the primacy over the other.

It is important to remember that, up to the middle of the 17th century, the only happiness Scholastic writers had in mind when they spoke of "true happiness", was supernatural. When St Thomas, for example, spoke of "imperfect happiness", what he meant was the happiness which the "philosophers" discuss: the happiness which is possible *within the limits of this present life*. In later times, as a result of further reflection, through which the theological question of man's final destiny came to be viewed in a fresh light, another notion of "true happiness" was introduced, namely, a happiness that would be proportioned to the purely *natural* requirements, and possible achievements, of man (considered, however, as endowed with an immortal soul): a happiness that would be possessed *after death*, and whose principal element would still consist in a union of knowledge and love with God. The question has been raised — particularly in our own day — whether a happiness of this kind — which has never been man's actual destiny — would have sufficed to satisfy his *natural* desire. St Thomas does not seem to think so [14]. This however is rather a theological than a philosophical question, and so we turn from it to the problem that directly concerns us.

305. – It seems clear that no more than four hypotheses can be formulated concerning the nature of true happiness, and of the good whose possession will satisfy man's natural desire.

---

[11] St Thomas, *Summa Theol.*, I-II, 3, 4.

[12] *In IV Sent.*, d. 49, q. 4; Wadding, t. X, pp. 381-383.

[13] *De ultimo fine*, disp. VII, sect. 1, n. 32; Vivès, t. IV, pp. 79 seq. — A. Marc, *Dialectique de l'Agir*, pp. 197-201, provides a less rigid interpretation of St Thomas and Scotus.

[14] *Cont. Gent.*, III, 50: "That the natural knowledge of God possessed by separated substances does not satisfy their natural desire"; *ib.*, c. 51; I, 12, 1 etc. Between the two world wars, there was much writing on this question. See the *Bulletin Thomiste*, 1932, pp. 651-675, and 1935, pp. 573-590, for lists of works concerning the interpretation of St Thomas.

This happiness is to be found in a spiritual possession of the world (through knowledge, aesthetic contemplation etc.), or in the subject's spiritual possession of, and delight in, *himself*, or in his association and friendship with *other finite subjects* (whether these be human or not), or finally in some kind of spiritual union of knowledge and love with the infinite Subject, that is, with God. We shall now examine each of these four hypotheses in turn.

306. – The consideration of the first hypothesis need not detain us for long. It is abundantly clear that a human being cannot find complete happiness and abiding satisfaction in what is beneath him. To seek to do so would be to degrade himself. But even if he possessed the entire world, what he possessed would still be beneath his dignity as a spiritual subject, a single one of whose thoughts is of greater value than the entire universe. The physical world, considered in itself, could not satisfy the desire of a being who, by his nature, is open to what is universal and absolute, a desire which transcends the entire order of infra-spiritual *objects* (n. 98) and can be satisfied through nothing less than the knowledge and love of *persons*.

Further, where knowledge and aesthetic contemplation are concerned, it is not the objects known and contemplated which, *of themselves*, enrich our minds and delight our wills: they have this effect only in the measure in which, in virtue of our own mental activity, their intelligilibility and beauty become manifest, that is, only in the measure in which the subject himself lays hold of the truth and beauty which they contain. Consequently, it is clear that the essential and active element in knowledge and contemplation is the human spirit; sense knowledge and, all the more so, the object of this knowledge, should rather be said, notes St Thomas, to present the material which the person's spiritual activity renders intelligible [15].

---

[15] "Sense knowledge cannot be said to be the total and perfect cause of intellectual knowledge; it rather provides the material for the cause of this latter", *Summa Theol.*, I, 84, 6. For St Thomas, the immediate cause of the intellectual act, that which "activates" the intelligence, is not what is sensible as such; rather is it the latent meaning of what is sensible, as made manifest by the intellectual spontaneity of the "agent intellect". The formal element of the cause (that to which the causality in the true sense is to be attributed), is consequently the activity of the intellect.

What is the beauty of a painting, or of a sunset, without the eye and the spirit which contemplate them? The joy which knowledge brings does not come, strictly speaking, from the objects known, but from the knowledge of himself which the subject comes to possess by their means. What he loves in them is, ultimately, the luminous being which he bestows on them — their human meaning.

307. — Are we then to say that true happiness lies in the perfect consciousness of oneself, in the complete possession of what one essentially is as a spiritual subject? No; for a human being is by his nature finite; he is but one individual: hence he does not even possess the plenitude of humanity, much less the plenitude of being. He is, then, utterly incapable of satisfying the infinite capacity which is his as a spiritual subject. How could he, who is but *one being*, set at rest a desire which is open to *all being*, a desire which is characterized by its dissatisfaction with what is limited, by its discontent with all that is not the All?

But could it not be maintained that the subject's true happiness lies in knowing and possessing himself insofar as he is the All, since he is "in some sense everything"? — But what does it mean to maintain this? What is the "totality" of which there is question? If it is a potential totality, that is, if what is meant is the pure capacity of the subject, then the suggestion that the possession of himself could bring him true happiness is quite absurd. What is potential derives all its value from what is actual; the joy which flows from the possession of the pure capacity is entirely in relation to that which the realization of this capacity would provide. In other words, the joy which flows from a person's appreciation that he is capable of becoming everything, is but a mere shadow of that which he would experience if he knew that he actually "had become everything", if he appreciated that this capacity had been realized. The totality of which there is question has, in conse-quence, to be actual. But then the true cause of the person's happiness will not be the person himself — since he, in his being, is far from being everything — but whatever it is that unites itself to him and communicates itself to him and so enables him to become "in a certain sense" everything: a real totality, an existing totality, to which the qualification "in a certain sense" is in no way applicable — *the Totality*. This Totality is not the universe, the totality of objects — we have already explained why this is so (n. 306) — but a totality of a superior order from which the subject derives his spiritual dignity — in the sense that he exists as a spirit only in opening himself to it and knows other beings only in relating them to it — and which, in consequence, has itself to possess a spiritual and personal character.

Moreover, it is all too obvious that a human being can find true and lasting joy only through companionship and friendship with others. It is only persons who can make persons happy. "Let each one search his own heart and without any doubt, and with no fear of contradiction, he will find that just as nothing is greater than love, so also nothing is more pleasant. This our very nature teaches us, as does the repeated experience of mankind... Complete happiness is, in consequence, impossible where love is absent. But in order that there be love, it is necessary that there be someone to give it and someone to receive it" [16].

308. — Are we then to say that this Totality, from which the spiritual subject derives his value, is nothing other than the entire community of persons, humanity for example, and that it is also from this that the subject's happiness flows? As we have already pointed out, this perspective is not without its attraction for contemporary thought, which is markedly humanist and tends to rest content with a "horizontal" transcendence, towards the *other*.

But, as we have already shown (nn. 86, 145), the value of the spiritual subject cannot, in the final analysis, be defined in relation to other (finite) persons. Their value, no less than his, is a participated and limited value; the foundation of their dignity and of their being does not lie in themselves. They, no more than the subject himself, cannot set at rest an appetite which is spiritual: and this remains true no matter how numerous and diversified they may be. Since each of these

---

[16] Richard of Saint-Victor, *De Trinitate*, III, 3, in the critical edition of J. Ribailler, Paris, 1958, p. 138. — Richard is speaking of God and aims, by this line of thought, at throwing light on the mystery of the Blessed Trinity; but the principle that he states is equally valid where man is concerned and is, indeed, conclusive only with regard to him.

persons derives his value from what is absolute, the sumtotal of value which is theirs does not cease to be derivative. No matter what their degree of intimacy, no matter how much they live in one another (through knowledge and love), a multitude of subjects who are ontologically distinct will never enable one another to achieve that perfect coincidence of plenitude and transparency, which ever remains the ideal of presence to and possession of oneself.

Moreover, the companionship which is required for happiness is not any companionship whatever. The company of those who are sick and infirm is not, in itself, a cause of joy; one can find joy in it, but for other reasons. The company of thieves, and of those who are morally depraved, is even less attractive. If our enjoyment of the companionship of others is to be free of constraint and reservations, these others have themselves to be happy, and to be worthy of happiness. But it is precisely companionship of this kind which the fact of human liberty renders problematic. Even though you may live morally, there is no guarantee that I shall do so. Consequently, if true happiness consisted entirely or essentially in the companionship of others, it would itself become problematic, as would, in an even greater degree, the proportion between a person's goodness and his happiness: just sanctions would no longer be assured. Even further, a paradoxical situation would then exist in which the person of higher moral quality would, as a result of his goodness, be less happy than others, since *he* would find nobody of the same moral calibre as himself...

Finally — and this is undoubtedly the decisive reason — there can be a profound and satisfying union between human beings, only through their common love for the same Ideal, their common sharing in the same Value, to which they are related at the most profound level of their being and which, accordingly, is capable of uniting them from within.

309. — The only hypothesis that is now left is the fourth one: that which equates human happiness with some kind of spiritual union with God. We are not, however, limited to this indirect proof. The same rational and spiritual requirement, which has caused us to reject the other hypotheses, is no less capable of enabling us to appreciate the correctness of the fourth one.

The complete fulfilment of a being whose nature is spiritual is impossible, unless his intellect and will attain the maximum development of which they are capable. But this, in its turn, is not possible, unless he knows and loves the being in whom the truth for which his intellect is ever striving, as well as the good towards which his will is ever tending, are to be found in the supreme degree, or rather beyond all degree, in an eminent and original manner. This being is the absolute Being – God. Consequently, it is clear that true happiness requires the knowledge and love of God, to the extent to which this is possible for a human being.

We can better appreciate the point just made, if we keep in mind that, since the true and the good are coextensive with being, our intellect and will cannot be perfectly satisfied with anything less than the knowledge of the absolute and total truth, the love of the absolute and total good. That this is so emerges clearly from the analysis of the dynamism of the human spirit. This analysis reveals that there is an infinite drive in the human spirit, at the level both of thought and desire, in virtue of which it moves beyond all that is finite, contingent, dependent and relative — an infinite drive which would be "evil", in the Hegelian sense of the word, which would indeed not even be possible, if no real and authentic infinite corresponded to it. For further elaboration of the point made here, the reader is referred to rational psychology and natural theology. See also n. 153.

In addition, as we have already shown (n. 308), a person can be fulfilled and find complete happiness only in the companionship of other persons; but unless he knows that they, in their turn, are completely happy and deserve to be so, the joy which he finds in them cannot be full. Complete happiness for a human being is, in consequence, to be found in the companionship of a perfect person, or persons, in whom moral goodness and happiness coincide at a common summit, and in whose joy he is joyful.

Our conclusion is, accordingly, that man's true happiness essentially requires that he be spiritually united with God in knowledge and love.

The identity in God of infinite sanctity and infinite joy, each of which is the expression of the infinite will by which He who is the absolute Being wills Himself, that is, of His infinite "purity" — for God is God through and through and there is in Him nothing that is

not God — both makes possible, and provides the assurance, that we
shall one day see realized on the created level the perfect harmony
between moral goodness and happiness.

310. – The consideration of what is required in order
that a spiritual subject may achieve happiness has been central
to the preceding discussion. But man is also an incarnate
subject. Hence it is clear that his happiness would not be *fully
human* unless it permeated his *entire being*, unless the bodily
dimension of his mixed nature also shared in it. Hence the
supreme fitness — to say no more of it — of the resurrection
of the body. — But note that it is impossible for us to
represent to ourselves this resurrection and the state of our
risen bodies, in an apt and accurate manner; it would, in
consequence, be better not to attempt to do so. Such a body is
henceforth outside the realm of death and sickness; subject no
longer to the various biological necessities, to the decay of age
etc., it is existing in conditions to which there is no analogue in
our experience, and which are contrary to the rhythm of life as
it is at present known to us. It is abundantly clear that the
resurrection of the body cannot by any means be due solely to
the play of the forces of nature; although it is not supernatural
in the strictly theological sense of the word.

311. – A few words, in conclusion, concerning a delicate
question. What has been written about the union with God
which is required for complete happiness is applicable, primarily
and without qualification, to *supernatural* happiness. In what,
then, would this happiness have consisted, in a purely natural
order? Knowledge of God and union with Him would have
been possible only in an indirect and mediate fashion —
doubtless though our appreciation that, in virtue of our spiritual
nature, we ourselves and others are made in the likeness of God,
so that our knowledge and love of God would have been the
crowning point of our knowledge and love of human beings.
But this knowledge, even though incomparably more perfect
than our present conceptual knowledge, would have remained
essentially *analogous*; there would still remain in it, as there is in
our present knowledge, an element of negation. To know God
more perfectly would have meant being able to say of Him,
apropos of higher perfections: but that is not the way with Him!

Would this knowledge have been perfectible, or would its degree of perfection have been, on the contrary, fixed once and for all at the moment of death? Certain authors opt for the second hypothesis [17], but there do not seem to be any good reasons for doing so. Unlike the blessed in heaven who, in virtue of their vision of the divine essence, share in a certain manner in God's eternity [18], the "separated" soul, in its natural state, is still involved in successive duration, even if not in time strictly so called. To maintain that its state remains fixed once and for all and, as it were, petrified, is in some way monstrous. The danger that exists of simply transferring to the natural level what is valid on the level of grace is clearly evidenced here. (The inverse process is, of course, no less harmful). — There is, then, nothing to prevent us from maintaining that the knowledge and love of God which would have been possible to achieve by means of His creatures, would also have been susceptible of indefinite development, so that this natural happiness would have been an "expanding happiness" [19]. — But now, an end to this speculation on what has never, in fact, been man's actual destiny.

Since natural happiness is not happiness purely and simply, a human being's natural desire cannot be satisfied by it. Nevertheless, the subject is, of himself, quite incapable of attaining to the immediate and intuitive knowledge of God. Where this knowledge is concerned, there is in him no demand which requires to be satisfied, no right which has to be respected: the intuitive vision of God is natural to God alone. There is, then, in a spiritual being a capacity and a desire which are disproportionate both to what he is capable of achieving and to what he has a right to obtain: this is the paradox which characterizes such a being.

How to ensure that all these facets of the truth blend and harmonize and, in particular, how to show that the natural aspiration for happiness, in the strict sense, in no way detracts

---

[17] See, for example, Cathrein, *Philosophia moralis*, pp. 39-40.

[18] St Thomas, *Summa Theol.*, I, 10, 3.

[19] J. Maritain, *Neuf leçons...*, p. 101. Cf. Leibniz, "a path through pleasures", *Nouveaux Essais sur l'Entendement humain*, III, c. 21; ed. Gerhardt, t. V, p. 180. Cf. also the same author's *Principes de la Nature et de la Grâce*, n. 18; Gerh., t. VI, p. 606.

from the gratuity of this latter, is a problem that, once again, we leave to the theologians. The question is a difficult one and theology alone is competent to deal with it. We shall here content ourselves with two observations [20].

1. The expression "natural desire" is not univocal. If what we are speaking about is the tendency or aspiration which is aimed at the completion and perfection of a nature *in its own order* (as *this nature*), namely, the possession of all that the physical integrity of this nature requires, the ability to exercise the powers and energies of this nature to their fullest extent etc., then the non-satisfaction of this tendency will necessarily be experienced as a frustration. But the situation is different if what we are speaking about is the aspiration of a spiritual being, precisely as spiritual, to go beyond himself and the finiteness that is his as a creature, through union with a Being who is above and beyond every nature. To speak of a frustration, apropos of the non-satisfaction of this tendency, is to employ a word outside the context in which it has meaning.

2. We should bear in mind the different condition of "mere human nature", and of a human nature which has been effectively elevated to the supernatural order and existentially orientated towards happiness in the full and unqualified sense. Where this latter nature, which is the one we are here speaking about, is concerned, the non-attainment of this happiness will inevitably be experienced as a frustration. But if one merely considers what man essentially is (his "absolute nature") and does not distinguish between this and what he is concretely and historically, one will then come to regard as "frustrated" a humanity which, by hypothesis, has not been elevated above its "natural" condition. But, if that hypothesis were, in fact, true, man's natural desire would have to be viewed in a different perspective, and its non-satisfaction would have to be appraised differently.

---

[20] See our *Etre et Agir dans la philosophie de Saint Thomas*, 3rd ed., pp. 342-355. More briefly, the *Essai*, n. 173; pp. 423-426.

CONCLUSION

312. – The sense in which God is man's *last end* should now be clearer. Whether it is a question of choosing what is of moral value (nn. 172; 173) or of obtaining happiness, man essentially exists as one who is orientated towards Him. All man's value springs, ultimately, from loving Him, all his happiness from entering into the joy of his Lord.

It should likewise be more clear that man glorifies God, not only through living in accordance with reason, as befits one who is made in the image of God (ibid.), but also through finding in Him his supreme contentment. For it is a "glory" for God, a sign of His unrivalled excellence, that He alone is capable of satisfying the aspirations of a spiritual being, just as it is the glory of a spiritual being that no one but God can set his desires at rest.

Further light has, in consequence, been cast on the *goal* at which *creation* is aimed. This is not only to enable man, in virtue of a morally good life, to share, in his own way, in the love which God has for Himself, and to glorify Him through the self-giving and the self-abandonment that the accomplishment of the divine will involves: it is also to enable him — through the full development of his nature and the harmonious exercise of his various powers — to share in that appreciation of His own perfection which God possesses, and which we call "beatitude". For God has created all beings, and in the first place persons, *so that they might be* (n. 283) and might be more fully: where persons are concerned, this involves both their moral goodness and their happiness (n. 284). By this union of happiness and moral perfection, the creature imitates, in his own way, that unity of infinite happiness and infinite holiness that is God's: a unity which expresses the identity of the divine will with the sovereign Good and the supreme Value, and grounds for us the possibility and the hope of arriving at a final perfect harmony between our moral goodness and our happiness.

Hence, it is clear that the scope of creation is not simply that man, through living in accordance with reason, should *objectively* reflect the divine perfection, but that *he himself*, as the *unique subject* that he is, should be fulfilled, and should achieve the contentment which he desires. In other words, man is not for God an *object*, an *instrument*, which He could use in order to derive "glory" from him: he is a *subject* who ought to glorify God through the contentment which the satisfaction of his natural desire brings him. — But, on the other hand, neither could the scope of creation simply be man's subjective happiness: if man's happiness had to be ensured at all costs, why should he not have been created in that state, definitively and right from the beginning? The scope of creation is then — in the *normal* order — that man's happiness should be genuinely *his*: his, in this sense, at least, that he has, in one way or another, contributed towards its attainment by what is most personal to him: his exercise of liberty. Perfect happiness is, normally, a *merited* happiness, a *recompense*. It will be achieved by those who, through acting well, through opening themselves to the Value, lead lives that are worthy of their dignity as persons. If, on the other hand, a person refuses to lead such a life, his lot will be in accordance with what he has freely made himself to be. These reflections make clear the limits within which an absolute value has to be accorded to a person: on condition that he respect the dignity which is his, through acting in a way that is worthy of a person. (Note the exquisite courtesy of God and the great reverence with which He treats us. Our dignity as persons lies in our own hands: whether we preserve or lose it, or, more exactly, disfigure it, depends on ourselves...).

313. – Still another conclusion emerges as the fruit of our long investigation. Even though human reason is capable of shedding some light on the supreme questions of life and human destiny, this light, precious though it is, always remains weak and flickering, and does not provide us with the guidance of which we stand in great need. Suppose, for example, that we have attained a rational conviction concerning personal immortality and definitive sanctions. It is clear that our *practical* appreciation of human values will necessarily be very different, according as the happiness for which we are destined is essentially of the same order as our human joys and satisfactions or, on the contrary, exceeds these out of all measure, not only from the point of view of certainty of attainment, of duration or even of intensity, but from the point of view of intrinsic excellence. It is for this reason that the Christian will at times give the impression of despising terrestrial values, the ordinary joys of this world — "terrena despicere" — of regarding them as of no consequence. But, to the extent to which this "contempt" is in harmony with authentic Christianity, what it primarily expresses is the immensity of the good to which the Christian looks forward, "the eternal weight of glory", in comparison with which the joys and hardships of this present world are of such little consequence. Now this comparison would be pointless and empty if these joys and hardships were really "of no consequence". It is, on the contrary, precisely because they are "something", because they do count, because their flavour and their bitterness are of consequence to a being of flesh and blood, that to sacrifice, reject and "despise" them has a value and a meaning[1]. — There are, accordingly, in Christian morality or, at least, in Christian spirituality, elements which human reason, left to itself, could not really justify and which, in consequence, those who have not put on the mind of Christ will be only too ready to account as errors, follies, affective perversions ("insensibility", in the pejorative sense of Aristotle)[2]. It is here that the "stumblingblock of the Cross" stands revealed, a Cross which no concern to promote "dialogue" entitles us to "empty of its force". This does not at all mean that Revelation contradicts the requirements of reason, but simply that it introduces new criteria of value[3].

---

[1] See the excellent observation of J. Maritain, *Le paysan de la Garonne*, Paris, 1966, pp. 71-79 (Eng. trans.: *The Peasant of the Garonne*, M. Cuddihy-E. Hughes, London, 1968, pp. 44-49).

[2] As an example of this incomprehension, read F. Jeanson's judgment of the Christian precept to love one's enemies: "A vicious humility, a generalized contempt, a defeatist refusal of the human reality — of its bodily reality, of its ambiguity: this does not spring from love but from rage", *La foi d'un incroyant*, Paris, 1963, p. 135. Read the entire critique, pp. 130-135.

[3] Is it necessary to add that the Christian faith (and the philosophical affirmation of immortality), far from diminishing, as the Marxists claim, the urgency of the tasks of this present life, confer on these, on the contrary, a new

It is for this reason that philosophical ethics, even though it can arrive at conclusions which are perfectly valid and reliable, still remains imperfect, not only as regards the concrete determination of what is to be done — this is the task of special ethics — but even as regards the fuller significance of these conclusions. It fails to appreciate the entire import of its own assertions (n. 8).

Here, as elsewhere, Revelation not only makes known to us truths which unaided human reason would never have discovered nor even suspected, but also throws a fresh light on rational truths, and reveals their more profound significance.

---

dimension of value? For it is in striving to establish, here below, the reign of justice and charity that man, in the Christian perspective, fashions his eternal destiny. — Not to speak, even though the point is of crucial importance, of the new value which, in this same perspective, the human person — his rights and the entire order of duties which concern him — assumes.

INDEX OF PROPER NAMES

referring to the page numbers
(footnotes in italics)

ANALYTICAL INDEX

referring to the page numbers

TABLE OF CONTENTS

(The numbers in parenthesis refer to paragraphs)

Second Part: THE MORAL ORDER

Third Part: HAPPINESS AND MORALITY

Finito di stampare il 4 ottobre 1991
Tipografia Poliglotta della Pontificia Università Gregoriana
Piazza della Pilotta, 4 – 00187 Roma